Documents in English Economic History

Edited by

B.W. CLAPP, H.E.S. FISHER
and A.R.J. JUŘICA

England from 1000 to 1760

Edited by

H.E.S. FISHER and A.R.J. JUŘICA

LONDON
G. Bell & Sons Ltd
1977

India
Orient Longman Ltd
Calcutta, Bombay, Madras and New Delhi

Canada
Clarke, Irwin & Co. Ltd, Toronto

Australia
Edward Arnold (Australia) Pty Ltd, Port Melbourne, Vic.

New Zealand
Book Reps (New Zealand) Ltd, 46 Lake Road, Northcote, Auckland

East Africa
J. E. Budds, P.O. Box 44536, Nairobi, Kenya

West Africa
Thos. Nelson (Nigeria) Ltd, PMB 1303 Ikeja, Lagos

South and Central Africa
Book Promotions (Pty), Ltd, 311 Sanlam Centre,
Main Road, Wynberg, Cape Province

ISBN 0 7135 1985 1

Printed in Great Britain by
Latimer Trend & Company Ltd, Plymouth

Contents

1 A GENERAL VIEW
1000–1485

1485–1760

2 THE AGRARIAN ECONOMY
1000–1485

3 INDUSTRIAL ACTIVITY
1000–1485

1485–1760

4 INTERNAL TRADE AND TRANSPORT
1000–1485

1485–1760

5 FOREIGN TRADE AND ENTERPRISE
1000–1485

1485–1760

6 FINANCE, PRIVATE AND PUBLIC
1000–1485

1485–1760

8 ECONOMIC POLICY AND THOUGHT
1000–1485

1485–1760

Preface

Preface

It is now sixty years since A. E. Bland, P. A. Brown and R. H. Tawney compiled their well-known documentary account of English economic history from the Norman Conquest to the repeal of the Corn Laws, *English Economic History: Select Documents* (G. Bell & Sons, 1914). Valuable and admirable as it is, it has become apparent that a more modern collection better representing current views of what English economic history is about, as well as bringing the story nearer to the present day, is needed by students and their teachers. To this end a two-volume collection has been prepared. The first volume covers the period from about AD 1000 to 1760 and the second, edited by B. W. Clapp, deals with the period after 1760. With the present volume, for which both editors share a general responsibility, John Juřica has been primarily responsible for the years to 1485 and H. E. S. Fisher for the period 1485 to 1760.

'Every generation needs to write its own history'—and this dictum applies no less to collections of first-hand evidence illustrating that history. Reflecting what was then a major preoccupation of historians, the volume of documents collected by Bland, Brown and Tawney exhibits an institutional approach to English economic history. Policy-making and the regulation of economic activity by such bodies as the manor, towns, gilds and the state loom large in their pages. Economic history has however developed much in the last sixty years, in a manner involving both new investigation and interpretation, often informed by a conscious use of economic theory and stimulated by the economic events of the twentieth century. It is hoped that the pages below dealing with the period to 1760, while maintaining a proper interest in institutional matters, reflect this development of the discipline. For instance, in line with the greater interest that has come to be shown in actual economic processes, more material is now presented which throws light on the character and functioning of the economy and the influence of market forces. It will be recognised though that the sources available for the medieval historian pose special problems in this area of study. Then the broadening of economic pursuits over these centuries to 1760, with the rise of industrial, commercial and financial activities, naturally attract attention. So does an interest in the varied processes of improvement in economic practice and in their consequences, an interest reflecting recent concern with the question of economic growth. The play of demographic factors, the incidence of fluctuations, the role of religion and the rise of economic rationality, these among other recent and current concerns of economic historians also receive discussion. In the main, because of limitations of space, the treatment of social themes has been kept distinctly subordinate to the economic, although an attempt has been made to consider living conditions and the relief of poverty. The documents have been arranged in eight sections, each section running through the whole period to 1760, to bear witness more easily to the basic continuity of this pre-industrial age in England but also better to reveal the real movement and progress that did occur. To reflect the greater weight of teaching in schools and colleges on the early modern relative to the medieval period, rather more space is devoted to the post-1485 period. Following Bland, Brown and Tawney, instead of comments on each document, a short introduction has been provided for each section.

As well as illustrating a more modern approach to English economic history a related aim of this compilation has been to indicate the wide range of primary materials the historian may use. Documents emanating from official and public sources, statutes, charters, records of the exchequer and customs, manorial and town records, judicial records and the like, figure prominently. But considerable recourse has been had to non-official, private materials when practicable. These include chronicles, treatises, travellers' accounts and memoirs, as well as family and household papers, wills, inventories, estate and business records. Literature too is represented in the form of extracts from plays, essays and poems. The growing supply after 1600 of published writings on economic affairs has naturally been much drawn upon. And more unusual sources such as a church memorial and newspaper advertisements have also been used. Although in making our selection a few previously unpublished manuscripts have been included, we have been content to draw largely from the great body of printed primary sources that is now at the disposal of the historian.

Just over a fifth of the documents presented below appeared in the Bland, Brown and Tawney collection. In some cases these documents have been re-edited. The editors are grateful to their publishers and to the literary executors of Bland, Brown and Tawney for their agreement to the incorporation of such previously used material.

Finally, we would like to record our appreciation of the help we have received from many people and institutions. In particular we wish to pay tribute to the assistance rendered by the late John Rogerson in the early stages of our work, and to the advice given by Professor W. E. Minchinton, who also helped in the initiation of the project. Among the many libraries and archives for whose ready co-operation we are grateful, mention must be made of the Public Record Office, the British Museum, the Library of the University of Exeter, the Exeter Cathedral Library, the University of London Institute of Historical Research, the London Society of Antiquaries, Gloucester City Library, and the Plymouth City Record Office. Our thanks go too to Mr. B. W. Clapp, who has throughout been a source of much constructive comment and criticism. For any faults and errors that remain we alone are responsible.

H.E.S.F.
A.R.J.J.

Acknowledgments

A book of this kind could not be put together without many authors, editors, executors and publishers consenting to the reproduction of copyright material. This consent has been readily given and the editors wish to acknowledge their gratitude for the generosity with which their requests have been met. If they have inadvertently included copyright material without making due acknowledgment they offer their sincere apologies.

The following have kindly consented to the reproduction of copyright material:

Bedfordshire Historical Record Society, publishers of *Jacobean Household Inventories*, ed. F. G. Emmison; T. S. Willan, 'A Bedfordshire Wage Assessment of 1684'; *The Minute Book of Bedford Corporation*, ed. G. Parsloe; and *The Williamson Letters, 1748–1765*, ed. F. J. Manning. Bristol Record Society, publishers of *Bristol Charters, 1155–1373*, ed. N. D. Harding; *Bristol Corporation of the Poor. Selected Records, 1696–1834*, ed. E. E. Butcher; *The Trade of Bristol in the Eighteenth Century*, ed. W. E. Minchinton; and *The Overseas Trade of Bristol in the Later Middle Ages*, ed. E. Carus-Wilson. The British Academy, publishers of *Documents Illustrative of the Social and Economic History of the Danelaw*, ed. F. M. Stenton. Buckinghamshire Record Society, publishers of *Early Taxation Returns*, ed. A. C. Chibnall. Burns and Oates Ltd., publishers of St. Thomas Aquinas, *Summa Theologica*. Cambridgeshire and Huntingdonshire Archaeological Society, publishers of 'Rogues, Vagabonds and Sturdy Beggars', ed. E. H. Vigers. Cambridge University Press, publishers of *A Discourse of the Common Weal of this Realm of England*, ed. E. Lamond; *Anglo-Saxon Wills*, ed. D. Whitelock; C. H. Wilson, *Anglo-Dutch Commerce and Finance in the Eighteenth Century*; E. Miller, *The Abbey and Bishopric of Ely*; *Calendar of Plea and Memoranda Rolls, A.D. 1437–1457*, ed. P. E. Jones; G. A. Holmes, *The Estates of the Higher Nobility in the Fourteenth Century*; and R. W. K. Hinton, *The Eastland Trade and the Common Weal in the Seventeenth Century*. The Chetham Society, publishers of *Customs*

Letter-Books of the Port of Liverpool, 1711–1813, ed. R. C. Jarvis; and *The Autobiography of William Stout of Lancaster, 1665–1752*, ed. J. D. Marshall. The Cresset Press, publishers of *The Journeys of Celia Fiennes*, ed. C. Morris. David and Charles Ltd., publishers of L. T. C. Rolt, *Thomas Newcomen. The Prehistory of the Steam Engine*. Derbyshire Archaeological Journal, publishers of R. Meredith, 'The Eyres of Hassop, 1470–1640'. The Devonshire Association, publishers of John Hooker, *Synopsis Chorographical of Devonshire*, ed. W. J. Blake; and O. A. R. Murray, 'Devonshire Wills of the Sixteenth and Seventeenth Centuries'. Essex County Council, publishers of *English History from Essex Sources, 1550–1750*, ed. A. C. Edwards. Eyre and Spottiswoode (Publishers) Ltd., publishers of *English Historical Documents*, Volume I, ed. D. Whitelock; II, eds. D. C. Douglas and G. W. Greenaway; and IV, ed. A. R. Myers. Harvard University Press, publishers of N. S. B. Gras, *The Evolution of the English Corn Market*. Hutchinson Publishing Group Ltd., publishers of Richard Carew, *The Survey of Cornwall*, ed. F. E. Halliday. The Record Society of Lancashire and Cheshire, publishers of *Quarter Sessions Records for the County Palatine of Chester, 1559–1760*. Lincoln Record Society, publishers of *The Letters and Papers of the Banks Family of Revesby Abbey, 1704–1760*, ed. J. W. F. Hill. Longman Group Ltd., publishers of A. Raistrick, *Dynasty of Iron Founders, The Darbys and Coalbrookdale*; and M. J. Kitch, *Capitalism and the Reformation*. Manchester University Press, publishers of A. P. Wadsworth and J. de L. Mann, *The Cotton Trade and Industrial Lancashire, 1600–1780*; Thomas Nelson and Sons Ltd., publishers of *David Hume, Writings on Economics*, ed. E. Rotwein. The Society of Antiquaries of Newcastle upon Tyne, publishers of J. Conway Davies, *The Wool Customs Accounts for Newcastle upon Tyne for the Reign of Edward I*. Norfolk Record Society, publishers of *The Norwich Census of the Poor, 1570*, ed. J. F. Pound. Northamptonshire Record Society, publishers of *Wellingborough Manorial Accounts A.D. 1258–1323*, ed. F. M. Page; and *The Letters of Daniel Eaton to the third Earl of Cardigan, 1725–1732*, eds. J. Wake and D. C. Webster. Oxford University Press, publishers of B. Mandeville, *The Fable of the Bees*, ed. F. B. Kaye; *The Libelle of Englyshe Polycye*, ed. G. Warner; *Shardeloes Papers of the 17th and 18th Centuries*, ed. G. Eland; Jonathan Swift, *Journal to Stella*, ed. H. Williams; *Chronica Jocelini de Brakelonda de rebus gestis Samsonis Abbatis Monasterii Sancti Edmundi*, ed. H. E. Butler; Richard, son of Nigel, *Dialogus de Scaccario*, ed. C. Johnson; E. Hughes, *North Country Life in the Eighteenth Century*.

The North East, 1700–1750; *Regularis Concordia Anglicae Nationis Monachorum Sanctimonia Pliumque*, ed. Dom. T. Symons; *Gesta Stephani*, ed. K. R. Potter; *Vita Edwardi Secundi Monachi Cuiusdam Malmesberiensis*, ed. N. Denholm-Young; Joseph Addison, *The Spectator*, ed. D. F. Bond; L. F. Salzman, *Building in England down to 1540. A Documentary History*; *Building Accounts of King Henry III*, ed. H. M. Colvin; and *Stuart Royal Proclamations, I, Royal Proclamations of King James I, 1603–1625*, eds. J. F. Larkin and P. L. Hughes. Penguin Books Ltd., publishers of William Langland, *Piers the Ploughman*, transl. J. F. Goodridge. The Royal Historical Society, publishers of *The Household Papers of Henry Percy, Ninth Earl of Northumberland, 1564–1632*, ed. G. R. Batho; and 'Devereux Papers with Richard Broughton's Memoranda, (1575–1601)', ed. H. E. Malden. The Selden Society, publishers of *Select Cases concerning the Law Merchant*, ed. H. Hall. Sidgwick and Jackson Ltd., publishers of *Purefoy Letters, 1735–1753*, ed. G. Eland. Southampton City Council, publishers of *The Brokage Book of Southampton 1443–1444*, ed. O. Coleman. Staffordshire Record Society, publishers of *Collections for a History of Staffordshire. The Gnosall Records, 1679 to 1837. Poor Law Administration*, ed. S. A. Cutlack. The Controller of Her Majesty's Stationery Office, publisher of *Calendar of the Patent Rolls, Philip and Mary, III*; and *Household and Farm Inventories in Oxfordshire, 1550–1590*, ed. M. A. Havinden. Sussex Record Society, publishers of *The Book of John Rowe, Steward of the Manors of Lord Bergavenny, 1597–1622*, ed. W. H. Godfrey; and *Rye Shipping Records, 1566–1590*, ed. R. F. Dell. Sydney University Press, publishers of *Accounts of the Cellarers of Battle Abbey 1275–1513*, eds. E. Searle and B. Ross. The University Press of Virginia, publishers of William Harrison, *The Description of England*, ed. G. Edelen. Wiltshire Record Society, publishers of *Surveys of the Manors of Philip, first Earl of Pembroke and Montgomery, 1631–2*, ed. E. Kerridge. Yale University Press, publishers of *Tudor Royal Proclamations*, eds. P. L. Hughes and J. F. Larkin. Yorkshire Archaeological Society, publishers of *York Civic Records, Vol. VIII*, ed. A. Raine.

Editorial Conventions

P.R.O.   Public Record Office
B.M.   British Museum
. . .   A small deletion has been made
*   *   *   A substantial passage has been omitted
[   ]   Editorial additions

The place of publication of books cited is London unless otherwise stated.

Spelling, capitalisation and italicisation have generally been modernised. Proper names have usually been left in their original form, although some medieval names have been anglicised.

Footnotes are by the present editors, except where otherwise specified.

Dates are as given in the original document, except that where two years are cited, i.e. Old and New Style, the year is assumed to have begun on 1 January.

1

A General View
1000–1485

The medieval English economy was overwhelmingly agrarian in character. At the beginning of the period the towns, with the exception of London, were small and were not sharply marked off economically from the countryside (*2*). Society was land-based and hierarchical (*1*). Landholding and hence power was concentrated in the hands of a few lords, who after 1066 held their estates by military tenure from the Crown. By the mid-twelfth century many had granted part of their land to tenants by military service (*4*). By the thirteenth century the feudal system of tenurial relationships had become blurred and the economic interests of tenants in accumulating property were paramount (*9*). The agrarian economy was based on the powers of the greater landholders over dependent peasants. In the later twelfth century there was a general depression in the status of the peasantry, many of whom were unfree (*8*). Their lives were subject to the will of their lord (*6*) and conditions were often harsh. The interests of the lords dominated and directed economic life (*5*) and in the countryside found legal expression in the institution of the manor (*12*). Economic activity was impeded by lawlessness and the lack of an efficient means of checking it (*3, 7*).

From the mid-twelfth to the early fourteenth century the population grew and the economy expanded and diversified. The towns with their specialist non-agrarian trades became more significant but agriculture remained the chief occupation. The later medieval economy lacked unity. The fourteenth century saw a series of demographic and economic crises in which the poor harvest of 1314 and the following years of heavy rainfall played an important part (*10*). The Black Death of 1348–9, in which about a third of the population died, profoundly affected the fabric of social and economic life (*11*). Labour became scarce and a section of the peasantry, epitomised by Chaucer's Franklin (*14*), prospered. Under such pressures manorial institutions ceased to function effectively (*12*). The Peasants' Revolt of 1381 was an attempt by sections of the peasantry to free themselves from antiquated controls which some lords continued to enforce (*13*). While the end of the period saw the decline of some towns (*15*), traders and merchants came to occupy an important position in economic life. The cloth and wool trades, the bases of English mercantile wealth, flourished (*16*).

1485–1760

Throughout this period the English economy and English society retained their pre-industrial character. Agriculture remained the mainstay of employment, income and wealth, with relationship to the land the prime determinant of social position. Contemporary descriptions of Kent (*24*), Devon (*26*), and Westmoreland (*33*), support a view of a mainly rural social order with great inequalities in wealth and status, although an order modified by groups of men in trade, mining and manufacture, and by not insubstantial numbers of townsmen. If continuity was the keynote of this economy and society, nevertheless important changes did occur. The English population perhaps doubled over the period, with increasing numbers most vividly to be seen in urban growth, London proving an impressive sight to foreigners (*17*), while concern over its expansion led to numerous if ineffectual attempts to restrain it (*28*). Some notable changes too took place in the countryside, more often than not productive of discontent, as with the younger sons of gentry made resentful by an extending system of primogeniture (*25*), or a peasantry driven to open revolt by its grievances as in Norfolk in 1549 (*22*). As the role of industry expanded so numbers grew in manufacturing and mining employments, the wage earning class too proving capable on occasion of serious disorder (*40*). The growth of commerce, both domestic and foreign, meant that more of its practitioners, along with those from the burgeoning professions, entered the ranks of landed society (*39*) taking with them their wealth and sometimes their commercial outlook. At the same time the City of London and the rising financial system, public and private, came to exert a greater sway in national life (*38*). This period saw real material progress, although before the eighteenth century only the most acute, such as William Petty (*35*), noticed it. Perhaps the most significant changes were the least tangible, in the intellectual approach to the material world. By the Restoration, with some decline in the influence of organised religion, attitudes were becoming more practical and rational, as reflected in the questing of the newly-founded Royal Society (*32*), or the interest shown in calculation by political arithmeticians such as Gregory King (*36*).

Despite these longer-term tendencies, the economic outlook of most people in these centuries was immediate and limited. An abiding concern was with the weather, variations in which governed well-being, through their effect on the harvests (*23, 29*). Political and other events also disturbed the tenor of economic life, as with Henry VIII's spoliation of monastic properties (*20*), or wars, foreign and civil (*30*), or local disasters such as the Great Fire of London (*31*). Interest in the aggregate tendency and the important event, however, should not let us forget that this economic world was composed of multitudes of individual men and their families striving to make and maintain a living, as Oliver Heywood's account of his father briefly depicts (*34*).

1 Rank in Anglo-Saxon Society, 1002–23

(Geþyncðo, printed in *English Historical Documents*, I, ed. D. Whitelock (1955), p. 432)

1. Once it used to be that people and rights went by dignities, and councillors of the people were then entitled to honour, each according to his rank, whether noble or ceorl, retainer or lord.

2. And if a ceorl prospered, that he possessed fully five hides of land of his own, a bell and a castle-gate, a seat and special office in the king's hall, then was he henceforth entitled to the rights of a thegn.

3. And the thegn who prospered, that he served the king and rode in his household band on his missions, if he himself had a thegn who served him, possessing five hides on which he discharged the king's dues,[1] and who attended his lord in the king's hall, and had thrice gone on his errand to the king—then he[2] was afterwards allowed to represent his lord with his preliminary oath, and legally obtain his [right to pursue a] charge, wherever he needed.

4. And he who had no such distinguished representative, swore in person to obtain his rights, or lost his case.

5. And if a thegn prospered, that he became an earl, then was he afterwards entitled to an earl's rights.

6. And if a trader prospered, that he crossed thrice the open sea at his own expense, he was then afterwards entitled to the rights of a thegn.

7. And if there were a scholar who prospered with his learning so that he took orders and served Christ, he should afterwards be entitled to so much more honour and protection as belonged by rights to that order, if he kept himself [chaste] as he should.

8. And if anyone, anywhere, injured an ecclesiastic or a stranger by

word or deed, then it was the concern of the bishop and the king, that they should atone for it as quickly as they could.

¹ Not merely military service, but all public charges. (DW)
² The intermediate thegn. (DW)

2 An Account of Hereford, 1086

(*Domesday Book*, I, p. 179, printed in *The Victoria County History of the County of Hereford*, I (1908), pp. 309–10)

In the city of Hereford in the time of King Edward there were 103 men dwelling together within and without the wall, and they had the following customs.

If any one of them wished to withdraw from the city he could with the consent of the reeve sell his house to another man who was willing to do the service due therefrom, and the reeve had the third penny of this sale. But if anyone through his poverty could not perform his service, he surrendered his house without payment to the reeve, who saw that the house did not remain empty and that the king did not lack [his] service.

Within the wall of the city each whole burgage rendered 7½d and 4d for the hire of horses and on three days in August reaped at Marden, and [its tenant] was [present] on one day for gathering the hay where the sheriff pleased. He who had a horse proceeded three times a year with the sheriff to the pleas and to the hundred [courts] at Wormelow. When the king was pursuing the chase, from each house according to custom went one man to the beating in the wood.

Other men who had not whole burgages provided guards for the hall when the king was in the city.

When a burgess serving with a horse died, the king had his horse and weapons. From him who had no horse, if he died, the king had either 10s or his land with the houses [thereon]. If anyone, when he came by his death, had not bequeathed his possessions the king had his goods. These customs had they who lived in the city, and others likewise who dwelt without the wall, except only that a whole burgage outside the wall only gave 3½d. The other customs were common [to both]. Whosesoever wife brewed within or without the city gave 10d according to custom.

There were six smiths in the city; each of them rendered one penny from his forge, and each of them made 120 shoes of the king's iron, and to each one of them was given 3d on that account according to custom, and those smiths were quit from every other service.

There were seven moneyers there. One of these was the bishop's moneyer. When the coinage was renewed each of them gave 18s for receiving the dies, and from the day on which they returned, for one month, each of them gave the king 20s, and likewise the bishop had from his moneyer 20s.

When the king came into the city the moneyers coined money as much as he willed for him, that is of the king's silver.

And these seven had their own sac and soc.

Upon the death of any of the king's moneyers the king had 20s for relief.

But if he should die intestate, the king had all his income.

If the sheriff went into Wales with the army these men went with him. So that if anyone commanded to go did not go, he fined 40s to the king.

In the same city Earl Harold had 27 burgesses who had the same customs as the other burgesses.

From the same city the reeve rendered 12l to the king and 6l to Earl Harold, and he had in his farm all the aforesaid customs.

The king, however, had in his demesne the three forfeitures, namely [for] breaking his peace, for house-breaking, and for assault.

Whosoever committed one of these [crimes], fined 100s to the king no matter whose man he might be.

The king now has the city of Hereford in demesne, and the English burgesses dwelling there have their former customs; but the French burgesses are quit for 12d from all their forfeitures, except the three aforesaid.

The city renders to the king 60l by tale of blanchèd money. Among [them] the city and 18 manors which render their farm in Hereford account for 335l 18s, besides the pleas in the hundred and county [courts].

3 The 'Anarchy' of Stephen's Reign, 1143–4

(*Gesta Stephani*, ed. K. R. Potter (Nelson's Medieval Texts, 1955), pp. 101–3, 108–9)

At this time[1] England began to be troubled in many different ways; on the one side to be very hard pressed by the king and his supporters, on the other to be most violently afflicted by the earl of Gloucester;[2] sometimes to endure the furious attacks of one party, sometimes the unbridled rage of the other; but always and everywhere to be in a turmoil and to be reduced to a desert. Some, seeing their country's sweetness changed to a revolting bitterness, chose rather to dwell in foreign lands; some, putting together humble cottages around the churches, in hope of protection, lived in fear and suffering; some, from lack of food (for a terrible famine prevailed all over England), ate the forbidden and un-accustomed flesh of dogs or horses, others, to relieve their hunger, fed unsatisfied on raw and filthy herbs or roots; some in every county, because the affliction of the famine was more than they could bear, wasted away and died in droves, others, sadly undergoing a voluntary exile with all their household, went abroad. You could have seen villages extremely well-known standing lonely and almost empty be-cause the peasants of both sexes and all ages were dead, fields whitening with a magnificent harvest (for autumn was at hand) but their culti-vators taken away by the agency of the devastating famine, and all England wearing a look of sorrow and misfortune, an aspect of wretchedness and oppression.

*   *   *

Geoffrey then,[3] gathering with him in one body all the knights who were bound to him by faith and homage in any part of the kingdom, and with a very strong force of ordinary soldiers and likewise of robbers, who had collected enthusiastically from every quarter, joining him at once as his allies, raged everywhere with fire and sword; he devoted himself with insatiable greed to the plundering of flocks and herds; everything belonging to adherents of the king's party he took away and used up, stripped and destroyed; he spared no age and no occupation but, fevered with a thirst for brutality that could not be slaked, everywhere he very promptly brought to fulfilment against his enemies any act of refined cruelty that occurred to his mind. For he took and pillaged the town of Cambridge, which was subject to the king, breaking into it when the inhabitants were off their guard, and smashed open the churches by burying axes in the doors, and after plundering their ornaments, and the wealth that the townsmen had laid up in them, set fire to them everywhere. He raged with equal savagery against the whole surrounding district, showing no mercy, and in every church that came in his way; the possessions of the monasteries he re-duced to a desert by taking the chattels and ravaging everything; their shrines, or anything deposited for safety in their treasuries, without fear or compassion he savagely carried off; and he not only pillaged the monastery of St. Benedict of Ramsey, taking the monks' valuables and even stripping the altars and the relics of the saints, but actually drove the monks out of the monastery without pity, put in a garrison and turned it into a castle for himself.

[1] 1143.

[2] Robert, the illegitimate son of Henry I and the leading supporter of the cause of the Empress Maud.

[3] The following passage describes the destruction wrought by Geoffrey de Mandeville, earl of Essex.

4 The Subinfeudation of Land, 1166

(*Cartae Baronum*, printed in *The Red Book of the Exchequer*, I, ed. H. Hall, *Rolls Series* (1896), pp. 412–15, and translated in *English Historical Documents*, II, ed. D. C. Douglas and G. W. Greenaway (1953), pp. 906–8)

Return of Roger, archbishop of York

To his dearest lord, Henry, by the grace of God, king of the English, duke of the Normans and of the men of Aquitaine, count of the Angevins, his man Roger, by the same grace, archbishop of York, and legate of the apostolic see, gives greeting. Your dignity has ordered all your liegemen, both clerks and lay, who hold of you in chief in York-shire to send to you, by letters carrying their seals outside, answers to the following questions: how many knights does each possess by the old enfeoffment of the time of the king, your grandfather, that is to say, in the year and on the day in which that king was alive and dead; and how many knights has he of the new enfeoffment, that is to say, en-feoffed after the death of your grandfather of good memory; and how many knights are on the demesne of each? And there is also be to in-cluded in the return the names of all those, both of the old and new enfeoffments, because you wish to know if there are any who have not yet done you allegiance and whose names are not written in your roll, so that they may do you allegiance before the first Sunday in Lent. Wherefore I, being one of those subjected in all things to your orders, have made as thorough an investigation in my holding as the short time permitted, and in this return I am declaring all these things to you as my lord.

Know therefore, in the first place, my lord, that there is no knight's fee on the demesne of the archbishopric of York, since we have sufficient enfeoffed knights to discharge all the service which we owe you, and which our predecessors have performed. We have indeed more knights enfeoffed than are necessary for that service as you may learn from what follows. For our predecessors enfeoffed more knights than they owed to the king, and they did this, not for the necessities of the royal service, but because they wished to provide for their relatives and servants.

Here follow the names of those who were enfeoffed in the time of King Henry.[1]

William, count of Aumale, holds a fee of 3 knights.

Henry of Lassy, 2 knights.

Roger of Montbrai [Mowbray], a quarter of a knight's fee.

Herbert, son of Herbert, 3 knights.

Gilbert, son of Nigel, 2 knights.

Payn 'de Landa', 3 knights.

Mauger, son of Hugh, 1 knight.

Richard, son of Hugh, 1 knight.

William of Bellewe, 1 knight.

Robert Morin, 2 knights.

Gilbert, son of Herbert, 2 knights.

Hugh 'de Muschamp', 2 knights.

Walter of Ancourt, 2 knights.

Robert Mansel, 1 knight.

Robert, son of Wiard, half a knight's fee.

Peter 'de Perintone', half a knight's fee.

Hugh of Vesly, 4 knights.

William Cokerel, 1 knight.

Thomas of Everingham, 2½ knights' fees.

Simon Wahart, 1 knight.

Ralph 'de Nowewica', half a knight's fee.

Robert Poer, half a knight's fee.

Walter of Denton, half a knight's fee.

Robert, son of Hugh, a quarter of a knight's fee.

William of Lubbenham, half a knight's fee.

Alexander of Newby, 4 parts of half a knight's fee.

Herbert of Markington, a quarter of a knight's fee.

Peter 'de Belingee', 1 knight.

Oliver the Angevin, 1 knight.

William 'de Pantone', 1 knight.

Thomas, son of Aubert, a quarter of a knight's fee.

Alice of Molescroft, a quarter of a knight's fee.

Thomas, son of Hervey, 1 knight.

Benedict of Sculcoates, the eighth part of a knight's fee.

Bernard of Cottingham, a quarter of a knight's fee.

Leofred, a thirteenth of a knight's fee.

John of Meaux, an eighth of a knight's fee.

Ivo, a quarter of a knight's fee.

Serlo of Poole, a third of a knight's fee.

After the death of King Henry there were enfeoffed:

Peter the butler, with half a knight's fee.

Peter the chamberlain, with the twentieth part of a knight's fee.

Geoffrey of Burton, with a twelfth of a knight's fee.

Gervase of Bretton, with a third of a knight's fee.

And since, my lord, I claim from some of these men more service than they are now performing, whereas others are keeping back services which are said to be due, not to themselves, but to the table and the demesne of the archbishop, I humbly beg that this my return may not be allowed to do harm to me or to my successors by preventing the Church from recovering or preserving its legal rights. Farewell, my lord.

And besides the aforesaid knights:

Thurstan 'de Lechamtone' [holds] half a knight's fee.

Gilbert 'de Miners', a third of a knight's fee.

Werri 'de Marinis', a third of a knight's fee.

William of Escures, a half of a knight's fee.

William Pallefrei, 1 knight.

William of Bellewe and Richard 'de Crochetone' hold a quarter of a knight's fee.

[1] Henry I, 1100–35.

5 A Lord and the Local Economy, Late Twelfth Century

(*Chronica Jocelini de Brakelonda de rebus gestis Samsonis Abbatis Monasterii Sancti Edmundi*, ed. H. E. Butler (Nelson's Medieval Texts, 1949), pp. 102–5)

The ancient customs of the cellarer, which we have seen in our day, were as follows: the cellarer had a messuage and barns near Scurun's well, where he used in all due state to hold his court for the trial of robbers and the hearing of all pleas and disputes, and there also he used to place his men in frankpledge, to enroll them and re-enter them every year, and to make profit thereby such as the reeve made at the portmanmoot. This messuage, with the adjoining garden now held by the infirmarer, was once the abode of Bederic, who was of old the lord of this town, wherefore it was called Bedericsworth, and his demesne fields are now in the cellarer's demesne. But that part, which is now called 'averland',[1] was the land of his peasants; and the sum of his holding and that of his men was nine hundred acres of land, which are still the fields of this town, service of which, when the town was made free, was divided into two parts, so that the sacrist or the reeve received a free tax,[2] to wit, two pence per acre; while the cellarer had plough and other services, to wit, the ploughing of one rood per acre without food (which custom is still observed), he had also folds, where all the men of the town are bound to keep their sheep, except the steward, who has his own fold (which custom likewise is still observed); and also had 'averpenny',[3] to wit, two pence for every thirty acres, which custom was changed before the death of Abbot Hugh, Gilbert of Elveden being then cellarer. Now the men of the town used at the bidding of the cellarer to go to Lakenheath and perform cartage-service, bringing eels from Southrey; and often they would return empty and thus be put to trouble without any profit to the cellarer; wherefore it was agreed between them that for the future a penny a year should be paid for every thirty acres, and the men should remain at home. But nowadays those lands are divided into so many parts, that it is scarce known who should pay those dues; so that I have seen the cellarer receive as much as twenty-seven pence in one year, but now he is scarce able to get tenpence halfpenny. Also the cellarer used to have power to prevent anyone from digging chalk or clay on the roads outside the town without his licence. He used also to summon the fullers of the town to provide him with cloth for carriage of his salt. If they refused, he would forbid them use of the water and would seize the cloths which he found there; which customs are still observed. Also anyone who bought corn or anything else from the cellarer used to be exempt from toll at the town gate when he went out, wherefore the cellarer sold his goods at a higher price; this practice is still observed. Also the cellarer is wont to take toll of flax at the time of carting, to wit, one truss for each load. Also the cellarer alone ought or used to have a free bull on the fields of this town; now a number of persons have them. Again when anyone assigned burgage land as alms to the convent, and this land was assigned to the cellarer or another official, that land used for the future to be quit of hawgable,[4] more especially when the cellarer was concerned, because of the dignity of his office, seeing that he is second father in the monastery, or else out of respect for the convent, since the condition of those who procure us our food should receive special favour; but the abbot says that this custom is unjust, since the sacrist loses the revenue that is his due. Again the cellarer was wont to warrant the servants of the court that they should be exempt from all scot or tallage; but this is no longer observed, since the burgesses say that the servants should be exempt because they are our servants, and not because they hold burgage land in the town, and themselves or their wives buy or sell publicly in the market. Also the cellarer used to take all the dung for his own purposes in every street, save from before the doors of those that hold averland; for to them alone it is permitted to collect and keep such dung. This custom gradually decayed during the time of Abbot Hugh until Denys and Roger of Hingham were cellarers, who, wishing to restore the ancient custom, took the carts of the burgesses that were laden with dung, and caused them to be unloaded; but since many of the burgesses protested and prevailed, everyone now collects dung on his own holding, and the poor sell theirs when and to whom they will. Again the cellarer is wont to hold this privilege in the market of the town, to wit, that he or his buyers should have the right of first purchase in respect of all food required for the convent, if the abbot be not in residence. The buyers employed by the abbot or the cellarer shall buy first, whichever come first to market, the former in the absence of the latter or the latter in the absence of the former. But if they are both present, precedence shall be given to the abbot's buyers. Again, when pickled herring is sold, the buyers of the abbot shall always buy a hundred herring at a halfpenny less than the others, so too shall the cellarer and his buyers. Again if a load of fish or other food comes into the court or the market, and if that load has not been unloaded from horse or cart, the cellarer or his buyers may buy the load in its entirety and take it with them without toll. But Abbot Samson ordered his buyers to give way to the cellarer and his buyers because, as he said, he preferred that he rather than the convent should go short. Therefore the buyers, in mutual deference to each other, if they found something to be bought which is not sufficient for both, buy it jointly and divide it equally; and so betwixt head and limbs and between father and sons . . .

[1] Land held by the service of beasts of burden (*averia*). (HEB)
[2] *Liberum censum.*
[3] Payment in lieu of service by *averia*. (HEB)
[4] Land tax.

6 Freedom and Freehold Established, 1236–7

(*Bracton's Note Book*, III, ed. F. W. Maitland (1887), p. 224)

The assize comes to recognise if Thomas of Somerby and many others disseised Roger Gladwin of his free tenement in Spittlegate after . . .[1] whereof he complains that they disseised him of 2½ acres and a toft.

And Thomas and the others come and say that the same Roger is a villein and the tenement whereof view is made is villeinage, and thereof they put themselves on a jury. And Roger says that he is a free man and the tenement is free, and that his ancestors were free men and held freely, and thereof he puts himself on a jury.

The jurors say that the aforesaid Roger holds his tenement in the same town by 2s a year and by two works in autumn at his lord's food, and he shall give two hens at Christmas and eat with his lord. And questioned if he or any of his ancestors had given merchet for marrying his daughter, they say, No. Questioned if he had ever been tallaged, they say, No. And the aforesaid Thomas, questioned if others of his fee do other villein services, he says that others do all manner of villein services. And because he does no service save the aforesaid money payment and the services named, nor gives merchet for a daughter, nor is tallaged, therefore it is awarded that he held freely and that he recover his seisin, and Thomas and the others are in mercy.

[1] i.e. after the king's last return from Britanny. (B, B, T)

7 Foreign Merchants Complain of Robberies, 1249

(Matthew Paris, *English History*, II, translated J. A. Giles (1853), pp. 294–5)

As Lent drew near, the king having come to Winchester, there came to him there two merchants of Brabant to make a complaint, who addressed him in the following words, mingled with lamentations and tears: 'Most peaceful and just king, we, being merchants from Brabant, were passing through your territories, which we believed to be peaceful, to prosecute our trade, when we were attacked on our journey, undefended as we were, by some freebooters and robbers, whom we know by their faces, and whom we found at your court, who basely and robberlike took from us two hundred marks by force; and if these men presume to deny the charge, we are prepared, with God for our judge, to discover the truth by the ordeal of single combat against them.' The suspected parties were therefore taken, and, after it was determined that their case should be decided by the report of the people of the country, the oath of the country released them. And what wonder is it? the country was suited to them, for the whole of it was infected with robbery. But as the aforesaid merchants still pressed their charge, and importunately demanded their money at the hands of the king, he began to be disturbed, and, summoning his advisers, said to them, 'What is to be done? My bowels are disturbed at these men's tribulation.' To this his counsellors replied, 'Your majesty, we have heard, and we know, that a similar suspicion is entertained of all the provinces of England. For very frequently are travellers here robbed, wounded, made prisoners, and murdered; and we wonder that your justices in eyre, whose especial duty this is, have not cleansed this country of such a disgrace. We believe, therefore, that the robbers of this country, who abound here beyond measure, have craftily entered into a conspiracy amongst themselves, that no one of them shall, on any account, accuse another; and thus their conspiracy and cunning has escaped the knowledge of you, as well as of your justiciaries and other bailiffs of yours. Henry Mare, your justiciary, was here, with his colleagues, and did no good. Those persons, too, whom he had appointed as inquisitors, were confederates and abettors of robbers. We must, therefore, deal cautiously against such many-shaped traitors, that cunning may be deceived by cunning. For great numbers of traders, especially those from the continent, pass to and fro here, on account of the adjacent port, as also on account of its being the royal city, and for the sake of the market. These men, who have been robbed, also declare, that if the money, for which they are prepared to prove the truth by single combat, is not restored to them, they will forcibly reclaim it by seizing all property belonging to the merchants of your kingdom in their country, to the loss of your said merchants, and to your own disgrace; and the duke of Brabant, whose friendship we desire, will, and not without good cause, treat you with disdain.' . . . After a long and secret consultation held amongst them, they[1] came forth into the middle of the assembly, and, giving loose to their tongues, they disclosed the thefts and other crimes of many persons, of whom a great many belonged to the neighbouring districts, especially to Alton and the liberty of the bishop[2] at Taunton. On this, some of the citizens and many of the inhabitants of the district, who were formerly considered good and liege men who abounded in rich possessions, and some whom the king had deputed, as guardians and bailiffs, to protect that part of the country, and to apprehend or drive away robbers; others who possessed horses and rich clothes, who had houses and families, and rejoiced in the possession of fifty or eighty librates of land, and some even who were superintendents of the king's household, and crossbow-men in his service, were made prisoners, and, being proved guilty, were hung. Some, however, took refuge in the churches, and others suddenly and secretly took to flight, and never again made their appearance. Some persons belonging to the city itself, who were then present, attending as king's yeomen to keep back the people, who were assembled on account of the novelty of this proceeding, and were much crowded together, cunningly mixed with the people, and, suddenly leaving the castle, either kept themselves out of sight, or flew to the nearest churches. When those who were taken were more closely questioned, they confessed that they had committed unheard-of crimes, both robberies and murders, with the connivance and assistance, and by the advice of others. Of those accused and clearly proved guilty, about thirty were taken and hung, and the same number, or more, were imprisoned, awaiting a like punishment. Those who had belonged to the king's household, when about to be hung, said to the officers who had charged them: 'Tell our lord the king that he is our death and the chief cause of it, by having so long withheld the pay which was due to us when we were in need; we were therefore obliged to turn thieves and free booters, or to sell our horses, arms, or clothes, which we could not possibly do without.' At receipt of which message, the king was touched with shame and grief, and gave vent to his sorrow in protracted sighs. Amongst the other detestable thieves who were taken, was one who made an appeal,—this was one William, surnamed Pope, a man abounding in household goods, so much so, that, on examining his house after he was taken, there were found about fifteen casks full of wine in his cellar: this man made an appeal, but, being found guilty, was immediately hung. One man had done the king good service in battle, and had freed the country from six thieves. . . .

[1] Twelve men elected from the citizens of Winchester and the county of Southampton to give the names of any thieves.   [2] The bishop of Winchester.

8 The Manumission of a Serf, 1277

(*Historia et Cartularium Monasterii Sancti Petri Gloucestriae*, II, ed. W. H. Hart, *Rolls Series* (1865), p. 265)

To all the faithful of Christ to whom this present writing shall come, Reynold, by divine permission abbot of St. Peter's Gloucester, eternal greeting in the Lord.

Be it known to you all, that we have manumitted and have given to freedom Henry Bitele, our neif[1] of Berton, desiring and granting, for ourselves and our successors, that the same Henry, with all his progeny,[2] can freely enter and leave our land without any impediment on our part or on that of our bailiffs, and can take his chattels away from our land at his pleasure, so that neither we, nor our successors, nor anyone in our name, can in the future demand anything or claim anything from him, from all his succession or from his chattels by reason of servitude, and we shall be for ever wholly excluded from every kind of right and claim over him, his succession and their goods. Save to us one pair of spurs of annual rent to be paid each year at Easter for all the service belonging to us by reason of such servitude.

In testimony of which thing our seal is affixed to the present writing.

Given at Gloucester in the octave of Trinity, [in] the fifth year of the reign of King Edward.

[1] Bondman.　　[2] *Cum tota sequela sua.*

9 The Tenurial Complexity of an Estate, 1278

(*Rotuli Hundredorum*, II, p. 350)

Township of Thornborough.[1]—The abbot of Biddlesdon holds 6 hides[2] of land and a virgate[3] in Thornborough, to wit, of John de Hastings one hide of land, and John himself holds of Sir John FitzAlan, and Sir John himself holds of the lord the king in chief.

Again, the said abbot holds a half hide of land and a virgate of Alice daughter of Robert de Hastings, and she holds of Sir John FitzAlan, and he holds of the lord the king in chief, and the said abbot renders to the said Alice 30s a year.

Again, the same abbot holds of Hugh of Dunster 2½ hides of land and a virgate, and renders for the said land to the nuns of St. Margaret of Ivinghoe 40s a year, and maintains the chapel of Butlecote for the aforesaid land. And Hugh held of John de Beauchamp a hide and a virgate of land, rendering to John de Beauchamp 4d a year, and John himself holds of Sir John FitzAlan, and he holds of the lord the king in chief. Again, the same Hugh held of Adam de Bernak 1½ hide of land, and Adam himself held of Sir John FitzAlan, and he holds of the lord the king in chief.

Again, the same abbot holds of the gift of Roger Foliot a half hide and a virgate, and Roger himself held of Reynold Nash, and Reynold held of John FitzAlan, and he of the lord the king in chief.

Again, the same abbot holds of the gift of William Nash and his ancestors a hide of land, and they held of John FitzAlan, and he of the lord the king in chief.

And it is to be known that all the aforesaid land used to render foreign service,[4] except the land which the said abbot has of the gift of John de Hastings and Alice daughter of Robert de Hastings, but John

FitzAlan and his heirs will acquit the said abbot towards the lord the king and all other men, to wit, of the ward of Northampton, of scutage, of a reasonable aid to make the king's son a knight and to marry his daughter, for ever, and of all services pertaining to them. Moreover the same abbot holds fifteen acres of land from William Nash of the hide that belonged to the hall once of William Nash by doing service of the lord the king but the same Sir John FitzAlan will acquit the said abbot towards the lord the king.[5]

[1] Bucks.
[2] A hide comprised as much land as one plough could till in a year, i.e. between 80 and 120 acres, depending on conditions of tillage.
[3] Four virgates or yardlands were equivalent to a hide or plough-land.
[4] i.e. service due to the king, a permanent burden upon the land.
[5] Then follows a long list of the tenants of the abbot and other proprietors.

10 The Consequences of Heavy Rainfall, 1315–16

(*Vita Edwardi Secundi Monachi Cuiusdam Malmesberiensis*, ed. N. Denholm-Young (Nelson's Medieval Texts, 1957), pp. 64, 69–70)

By certain other portents the hand of God appears to be raised against us. For in the past year there was such plentiful rain that men could scarcely harvest the corn or bring it safely to the barn. In the present year[1] worse has happened. For the floods of rain have rotted almost all the seed, so that the prophecy of Isaiah might seem now to be fulfilled; for he says that 'ten acres of vineyard shall yield one little measure and thirty bushels of seed shall yield three bushels': and in many places the hay lay so long under water that it could neither be mown nor gathered. Sheep generally died and other animals were killed by a sudden plague. It is greatly to be feared that if the Lord finds us incorrigible after these visitations, he will destroy at once both men and beasts; and I firmly believe that unless the English church had interceded for us, we should have perished long ago.

*   *   *

After the feast of Easter[2] the dearth of corn was much increased. Such a scarcity has not been seen in our time in England, nor heard of for a hundred years. For the measure of wheat was sold in London and the neighbouring places for forty pence, and in other less thickly populated parts of the country thirty pence was a common price. Indeed during this time of scarcity a great famine appeared, and after the famine came a severe pestilence, of which many thousands died in different places. I have even heard it said by some, that in Northumbria dogs and horses and other unclean things were eaten. For there, on account of the frequent raids of the Scots, work is more irksome, as the accursed Scots despoil the people daily of their food. Alas, poor England! You who once helped other lands from your abundance, now poor and needy are forced to beg. Fruitful land is turned into a salt-marsh; the inclemency of the weather destroys the fatness of the land; corn is sown and tares are brought forth. All this comes from the wickedness of the inhabitants. Spare, O Lord, spare thy people! For we are a scorn and a derision to them who are round about us. Yet those who are wise in astrology say that these storms in the heavens have happened naturally; for Saturn, cold and heedless, brings rough weather that is useless to the seed; in the ascendant now for three years he has completed his course, and mild Jupiter duly succeeds him. Under Jupiter these floods of rain will cease, the valleys will grow rich in corn, and the fields be filled with abundance. For the Lord shall give that which is good and our land shall yield her increase. . . .

[1] 1315.   [2] 1316.

11 The Black Death, 1348–9

(*Chronicon Henrici Knighton vel Cnitthon Monachi Leycestrensis*, II, ed. J. R. Lumby, *Rolls Series* (1895), pp. 58–65, translated in *English Historical Documents*, IV, ed. A. R. Myers (1969), pp. 89–91)

In that year and the following year there was a general mortality of men throughout the world. It first began in India, then spread to Tharsis, thence to the Saracens, and at last to the Christians and Jews. . . .

Then the dreadful pestilence penetrated through the coastal regions from Southampton and came to Bristol, and almost the whole strength of the town perished, as if overcome by sudden death; for few there were who kept their beds for more than two or three days, or even half a day. Then this cruel death spread everywhere, following the course of the sun. At Leicester, in the small parish of St. Leonard's there perished more than 380 people, in the parish of Holy Cross 400, in the parish of St. Margaret's, Leicester, 700; and so in every parish a great multitude. Then the bishop of Lincoln sent a message throughout his diocese, and gave general power to all priests, religious as well as secular, to hear confessions and give absolutions to all men with full episcopal authority, excepting only in cases of debt. And in such a case, the debtor was to pay the debt, if he were able to do so while he lived;

or others were to be appointed to do so from his property after his death. Similarly the pope granted plenary remission of all sins to all receiving absolution at the point of death, and granted that this power should last until the following Easter, and that every one might choose his own confessor at will.

In the same year there was a great murrain of sheep everywhere in the realm, so that in one place more than 5,000 sheep died in a single pasture; and they rotted so much that neither beast nor bird would approach them. And there was a great cheapness of all things for fear of death, for very few took any account of riches or of possessions of any kind. A man could have a horse which was formerly worth forty shillings for half a mark,[1] a big fat ox for four shillings, a cow for 12d, a heifer for 6d, a fat wether for 4d, a sheep for 3d, a lamb for 2d, a large pig for 5d, and a stone of wool for 9d. Sheep and oxen strayed through the fields and among the crops, and there was none to drive them off or collect them, but they perished in uncounted numbers throughout all districts for lack of shepherds, because there was such a shortage of servants and labourers. For there was no recollection of such a severe mortality since the time of Vortigern, king of the Romans, in whose day, as Bede testifies, the living did not suffice to bury the dead. In the following autumn no one could get a reaper for less than 8d with food, a mower for less than 12d with food. For this reason many crops perished in the fields for lack of harvesters. But in the year of the plague, as is explained above, there was so great an abundance of all kinds of corn that they were scarcely regarded.

The Scots, hearing of the cruel pestilence in England, imagined that it had come about at the hand of an avenging God, and they adopted it as an oath, according to the common report, under the form, when they wished to swear, 'by the foul death of England'. And thus believing that a terrible vengeance of God had overtaken the English, they gathered in Selkirk forest with the intention of invading the kingdom of England. There the horrible death overtook them, and their ranks were thinned by sudden and terrible mortality, so that in a short time about 5,000 had perished. And as the rest, some strong, some feeble, were preparing to return to their own country, they were surprised by pursuing Englishmen, who killed a very great number of them.

Master Thomas Bradwardine was consecrated by the pope as Archbishop of Canterbury, and when he returned to England he came to London and died within two days. He was famous beyond all other clerks of Christendom, especially in theology and in other liberal sciences. At this time there was so great a scarcity of priests everywhere that many churches were left destitute, lacking divine offices, masses, matins, vespers, and sacraments. A chaplain could scarcely be obtained to serve any church for less than 10*l* or 10 marks, and whereas when there was an abundance of priests before the plague, a chaplain could be obtained for 5 or 4 marks, or even 2 marks with his board, at this time there was scarcely one who would accept a vicarage at 20*l* or 20 marks. Within a short while, however, a great multitude of men, whose wives had died in the plague, flocked to take orders, many of whom were illiterate, and almost laymen, except that they could read a little but without understanding. . . .

Meanwhile the king sent into each shire a message that reapers and other labourers should not take more than they had been wont to do under threat of penalties defined in the statute, and for this purpose he introduced a statute. The workmen were, however, so arrogant and obstinate that they did not heed the king's mandate, but if anyone wanted to have them he had to give them what they asked; so he either had to satisfy the arrogant and greedy wishes of the workers or lose his fruit and crops. When the king was told that they were not observing his order, and had given higher wages to their workmen, he levied heavy fines on abbots, priors, knights of greater and lesser consequence and others, both great and small, throughout the countryside, taking 100*s* from some, 40*s* or 20*s* from others, according to their ability to pay. . . . Then the king caused many labourers to be arrested, and sent them to prison; and many of them escaped and fled to the forests and woods for a time, and those who were captured were severely punished. And most of such labourers swore that they would not take daily wages in excess of those allowed by ancient custom, and so they were set free from prison. . . .

After the pestilence many buildings both great and small in all cities, towns, and boroughs fell into total ruin for lack of inhabitants; similarly many small villages and hamlets became desolate and no houses were left in them, for all those who had dwelt in them were dead, and it seemed likely that many such little villages would never again be inhabited. In the following winter there was such a dearth of servants for all kinds of work that, so men believed, there had scarcely ever been such a shortage before. For the beasts and cattle strayed in all directions without herdsmen, and all things were left without anyone to care for them. Thus all necessities became so dear that what in former days had cost a penny now sold for 4*d* or 5*d*. Moreover, all the magnates of the realm, and lesser lords too, who had tenants, remitted the payment of the rents lest the tenants should go away, because of the scarcity of servants and the dearness of things—some half their rents, some more, some less, some for 2 years, some for 3, some for one, according as they could come to arrangements with them. Similarly, those who had let lands by days' works of a whole year, as is usual with bondmen, had to waive and remit such works, and either pardon them entirely or accept them on easier terms, at a small rent, lest their houses should be irreparably ruined and the land remain uncultivated. And all victuals and all necessities became too dear.

[1] 6s 8d.

12 The Mobility of Labour, 1358

(P.R.O. Court Rolls, Duchy of Lancaster, D.L. 30/129/1957, mm.45d, 46)

Court held at Bradford[1] on Wednesday, 12 December, 32 Edward III

It is ordered as many times before to take William son of Richard Gilleson, Roger son of William Marsh, dwelling with John of Bradley, Thomas son of John of Yate, William son of William Childyoung (in Pontefract), Alice daughter of John of Yate (in Selby), Alice daughter of William Childyoung (in Methley), and William son of William Childyoung, the lord's bondmen and bondwomen of his lordship here . . . who have withdrawn without licence, and to bring them back hither until [they make fine for their chevage[2]].

Arrest bondmen.[3]

*   *   *

Roger son of Roger makes plaint of Alice de Bollyng [in a plea] of trespass, William Walker [being] pledge to prosecute, to wit that she has not made an enclosure which she is bound to make between his holdings and her own holdings in Mickleton, so that for lack of enclosure there divers cattle entered and fed off his corn, to wit his rye and oats and grass, to his damages of 10s. And the aforesaid Alice defends and says that the aforesaid Roger, and not she, is bound to make an enclosure there, and hereon she puts herself upon the country. But the jurors hereupon elected, tried and sworn, say on their oath that the aforesaid Roger is bound to make the aforesaid enclosure between the aforesaid holdings. And therefore it is awarded that the aforesaid Roger be in mercy for his false claim, and that the said Alice go without a day.

Mercy, 4d. Without a day.

It is presented by the parker that William Walker (6d) with 11 beasts, Roger of Manningham (4d) with 3 beasts, John de Gilles (2d), Thomas Staywal (2d) with one beast, Roger Megson (2d) with one beast, Denis Walker (2d), Richard Wright (4d) with 2 beasts and William Cook (2d) with a horse, have fed off the grass of the lord's wood in Bradford bank; therefore they are in mercy.

Mercy, 2s.

Again it is presented that William Notbroun (6d) and Adam Notbroun (6d) with their cattle have broken down the hedge around the lord's wood, and with the said cattle have fed off the grass of the lord's wood; therefore they are in mercy.

Mercy, 12d.

Again it is presented that Richard Milner of Idle (6d), Richard Bailiff (2d) and William Smith of Caleshill (2d) have carried millstones over the lord's soil here without licence; therefore they are in mercy.

Mercy, 10d.

Again it is presented by John of Denholme, John Judson, Adam Dickson, Robert Moor, Thomas of Chellow, Hugh Barn, Robert of Yate, John of Yate, Richard Curtis, John Rous, Roger Johanson and John de Gilles, that William Toms, the lord's bondman dwelling in Morton by York, Roger of Stanbury, the lord's bondman dwelling in Wirkley, and John Bond, dwelling in Sighelesden, and John son of Roger son of William Marsh, dwelling with John of Bradley, the lord's bondmen here, have withdrawn without licence; and hereupon order was made to take them all, so that they be [here] until . . . And the aforesaid William Toms and Roger of Stanbury were taken and were brought before the steward at Pontefract on Saturday next after the feast of the Circumcision of the Lord.

And the aforesaid William Toms there made fine of 26s 8d before the said steward, to wit, in order to have his goods at the steward's will,[4] to be paid at the feasts of St. Peter's Chains[5] and St. Michael[6] next by equal portions. And also the aforesaid William made fine for chevage, to wit a fine of 2s to be paid yearly at the feasts of Whitsunday and St. Martin in Winter[7] by equal portions; and William Cook of Brotherton became his pledge as well for his yearly chevage as for his other fine for his said goods.

Fine, 26s 8d.   Chevage, 2s.

And Roger of Stanbury likewise on the same day was brought before the aforesaid steward at Pontefract and made fine of 20s to have his goods at the steward's will, to be paid at the terms of Easter and Michaelmas next; and also the aforesaid Roger made fine of 12d for his chevage, to be paid yearly at the terms aforesaid; and Thomas Dantrif became his pledge as well for his yearly chevage as for his fine aforesaid.

Fine, 20s.   Chevage, 12d.

And it was granted to the same William and Roger that they may stay outside the lordship here in the places where they were staying before, and that too at the lord's will, for their chevages aforesaid to be paid yearly as is aforesaid.

And order is made to take all the other bondmen named above, because they come not, and to bring them back hither to their nests until . . .

Take bondmen.

---

[1] Yorkshire.
[2] Payment by villeins for permission to live away from a manor.
[3] This and successive similar entries appeared as marginalia in the original document.
[4] i.e. in order to retain his possessions, which at law belonged to the lord, during the steward's pleasure.
[5] 1 August.   [6] 29 September.   [7] 11 November.

13 The Peasants' Revolt, 1381

(P.R.O. Assize Roll, Just. Itin. 1/103, m.10d)

Pleas in the Isle of Ely before the justices appointed in the county of Cambridge to punish and chastise insurgents and their misdeeds, on Thursday next before the feast of St. Margaret the Virgin,[1] 5 Richard II.

*   *   *

Ely.—Adam Clymme was taken as an insurgent traitorously against his allegiance, and because on Saturday next after the feast of Corpus Christi in the 4th year of the reign of King Richard the second after the Conquest, he traitorously with others made insurrection at Ely, feloniously broke and entered the close of Thomas Somenour and there took and carried away divers rolls, estreats of the green wax of the lord the king[2] and the bishop of Ely, and other muniments touching the court of the lord the king, and forthwith caused them to be burned there to the prejudice of the crown of the lord the king.

Further that the same Adam on Sunday and Monday next following caused to be proclaimed there that no man of law or other officer in the execution of duty should escape without beheading.

Further that the same Adam the day and year aforesaid at the time of the insurrection was always wandering armed with arms displayed, bearing a standard, to assemble insurgents, commanding that no man of whatsoever condition he were, free or bond, should obey his lord to do any services or customs, under pain of beheading, otherwise than he should declare to them on behalf of the Great Fellowship. And so he traitorously took upon him royal power. And he came, brought by the sheriff, and was charged before the aforesaid justices touching the premises, in what manner he would acquit himself thereof. And he says that he is not guilty of the premises imputed to him or of any of the premises, and hereof puts himself on the country . . . And forthwith a jury is made thereon for the lord the king by twelve [good and lawful men] . . . who being chosen hereto, tried and sworn, say on their oath that the aforesaid Adam is guilty of all the articles. By the discretion of the justices the same Adam is drawn and hanged . . . And it was found there that the same Adam has in the town aforesaid chattels to the value of 32s, which Ralph of Wick, escheator of the lord the king, seized forthwith and made further execution for the lord the king . . .

[1] 20 July.
[2] Green wax was used for the Exchequer seal under which were issued the estreats delivered to the sheriffs for levying fines and forfeited recognisances.

14 Chaucer's Franklin, c.1387–1400

(*Canterbury Tales*, ed. J. U. Nicolson (1935), pp. 11–12)

> There was a franklin[1] in his company;
> White was his beard as is the white daisy.
> Of sanguine temperament by every sign,
> He loved right well his morning sop in wine.
> Delightful living was the goal he'd won,
> For he was Epicurus' very son,
> That held opinion that a full delight

Was true felicity, perfect and right.
A householder, and that a great, was he;
Saint Julian[2] he was in his own country.
His bread and ale were always right well done;
A man with better cellars there was none.
Baked meat was never wanting in his house,
Of fish and flesh, and that so plenteous
It seemed to snow therein both food and drink
Of every dainty that a man could think.
According to the season of the year
He changed his diet and his means of cheer.
Full many a fattened partridge did he mew,
And many a bream and pike in fish-pond too.
Woe to his cook, except the sauces were
Poignant and sharp, and ready all his gear.
His table, waiting in his hall alway,
Stood ready covered through the livelong day.
At county sessions was he lord and sire,
And often acted as a knight of shire.
A dagger and a trinket-bag of silk
Hung from his girdle, white as morning milk.
He had been sheriff and been auditor;
And nowhere was a worthier vavasor.

[1] The term was originally applied to a free man but by the late 14th century it had come to mean a wealthy free landholder.
[2] The patron saint of hospitality. (JUN)

15 Urban Decline, 1452

(*Archaeologia*, I (1770), pp. 91–4)

To the king our sovereign lord beseech full humbly your humble true liegemen, the mayor, bailiffs, and commonalty of your poor city of Winchester, that whereas they have been charged to bear the fee farm of your said city, which draws yearly to the sum of 112 marks, and bear also to the master of the hospital of Mary Magdalen beside Winchester 60s; also when the 15th penny or tax is granted to your highness it draws to the sum of 51l 10s 4d within the said city, to which, when it is to be levied, some men in the said city are set at 4 marks and some at 5 marks because your said city is desolate of people; also the expense of burgesses of the said city coming to your parliaments draws to 4s a day.

For the which said fee farm so to be paid your bailiffs have little or nothing of certainty to raise it but only of casual payments, and yearly lessen in payment[1] of the said fee farm 40*l* or more. For which causes abovesaid, and also for the great charges and daily costs which your said poor city bears about the enclosing and murage of your said city it is become right desolate in so much as many persons have withdrawn out of the said city for the causes abovesaid, and 997 houses which were wont to be occupied with people stand now void, and because of these withdrawals 17 parish churches stand without offices at this day, the which parishes and houses are more plainly expressed in a schedule hereto annexed. And where it pleased your highness in relieving of your said poor city, the 24th day of May, the 19th year of your reign, to grant unto your mayor and commonalty of the said city then being, in relief of all the charges abovesaid, 40 marks, to be taken yearly to them and to their successors until the end of . . . winters then next following at the feasts of Easter and Michaelmas[2] by even portions of the issues and profits coming of the aulnage and subsidy of woollen cloths within the said city and suburbs and soke of the same, and in all other places within your shire of Southampton by the hands of the collectors, farmers, receivers and other occupiers of the same for the time being, as in your letters patent thereof to them made may appear more plainly, which annuity is now void to them and wholly resumed to you, because of an act made in your parliament, begun at Westminster and finished at Leicester.[3] And so now your said suppliants stand all utterly destitute of all manner of relief of their charges abovesaid to the utterest undoing of your said city for ever, without your high and noble grace be shown to them in this behalf. That it please your said highness graciously to consider the charges abovesaid and, of your most abundant grace, to grant unto the mayor, bailiffs and commonalty of your said city 40 marks, to be had and taken yearly to them and to their successors, from the feast of Michaelmas in the 28th year of your reign for evermore, of the aulnage and subsidy of woollen clothes to be sold within your said city, suburbs and soke of the same, and in other places within your shire of Southampton by the hands of the collectors, farmers, receivers and occupiers of the said aulnage and subsidy for the time being, at the feasts of Easter and Michaelmas by even portions after the tenor and effect of another schedule to this bill annexed, the which schedule begins with these words 'The king to all to whom,' without any fine or fee in any wise to your use to be taken and paid, the said act of resumption or any other statutes, ordinances, provisions, restraints, acts or any manner judgments or assignments in any wise made or to be made notwithstanding, and they are and shall be perpetually your orators.

These are the streets that are fallen down in the city of Winchester within 80 years last past . . .[4] The number of householders that have fallen is 997 and without[5] these have fallen within the same city, since the last parliament held there, 81 households.

These are the parish churches that have fallen down within the said city . . .[6] The desolation of the said poor city is so great and yearly falling,[7] for there is such decay and ruin that without the gracious comfort of the king our sovereign lord, the mayor and the bailiffs must of necessity cease and deliver up the city and the keys into the king's hands.

Memorandum that on the first day of February, the 30th year of the reign of King Henry the sixth after the Conquest this bill was delivered to the lord chancellor of England at Westminster to be executed.

[1] i.e. fall short.   [2] 29 September.   [3] Act of Resumption, May 1450.

[4] Eleven streets are listed where it is claimed nearly all the householders have disappeared.

[5] i.e. beside.   [6] Seventeen churches are listed.   [7] i.e. increasing.

16 Wool and Cloth in England, temp. Edward IV

(*Political Poems and Songs*, II, ed. T. Wright, *Rolls Series* (1861), pp. 282–6)

> *O England, on account of your ships and wool, all realms*
> *ought to salute you*

*   *   *

For there is no realm in no manner degree
But they have need to our English commodity;
And the cause thereof I will to you express,
The which is sooth as the gospel of the mass.

*   *   *

Meat, drink and cloth, to every man's sustenance
They belong all three, without variance.
For whoso lacketh any of these three things,
Be they popes or emperors, or so royal kings,

It may not stand with them in any prosperity;
For whoso lacketh any of these, he suffereth adversity;
Whiles this is sooth by your wits discern
Of all the realms in the world this beareth the lantern.

For of every of these three by God's ordinance,
We have sufficiently unto our sustenance,
And with the surplusage of one of these three things
We might rule and govern all Christian kings.

* * *

For the merchants come our wools for to buy
Or else the cloth that is made hereof surely,
Out of divers lands far beyond the sea,
To have this merchandise into their country.

* * *

Therefore let not our wool be sold for nought,
Neither our cloth, for they must be sought;
And in especial restrain straitly the wool,
That the commons of this land may work at the full.

And if any wool be sold of this land,
Let it be of the worst both to free and bond,
And none other in [no] manner wise,
For many divers causes, as I can devise.

If the wool be coarse, the cloth is mickle the worse,
Yet into little they put out of purse
As much for carding, spinning and weaving,
Fulling, roving, dyeing and shearing;

And yet when such cloth is all ywrought,
To the maker it availeth little or nought,
The price is simple, the cost is never the less,
They that worketh the wool in wit be like an ass.

The costs into little truly at the full
Is as much as it were made of fine wool,
Yet a yard of that one is worth five of that other;
Better can I not say, though it were my brother.

Take heed to my lesson that I have shewed here,
For it is necessary to every clothier,
And the most prevail to them that may be found,
If they will take heed thereto and it understand.

An ordinance would be made for the poor people,
That in these days have but little avail,
That is to say for spinners, carders, weavers also,
For tuckers, dyers and shearmen thereto.

For in these days there is a usance,
That putteth the poor people into great hinderance,
By a strange means that is late in the land
Begun and used as I understand

By merchants and cloth-makers, for God's sake take keep,
The which maketh the poor to mourn and weep;
Little they take for their labour, yet half is merchandise;
Alas! for truth, it is a great pity.

That they take for 6*d*, it is dear enough of 3,
And thus they be defrauded in every country,
The poor have the labour, the rich the winning;
This accordeth nought, it is a heavy parting.

But to avoid fraud, and set egality,
That such workfolk be paid in good money,
From this time forth by sufficient ordinance
That the poor no more be put to such grievance.

For and ye knew the sorrow and heaviness
Of the poor people living in distress,
How they be oppressed in all manner of thing,
In giving them too much weight into the spinning.

For nine pounds, I ween, they shall take twelve,
This is very truth, as I know myself;
Their wages be bated, their weight is increased,
Thus the spinners' and carders' avails be all ceased.

17 An Impression of London, 1497

(Andreas Franciscius, *Itinerarium Britanniae*, printed in *Two Italian Accounts of Tudor England*, trans. and publ. by C. V. Malfatti (Barcelona, 1953), pp. 31–5, 36–7)

London. 17 November 1497

Now I must write somewhat more fully about the town of London, since it is the capital of the whole kingdom. First of all its position is so pleasant and delightful that it would be hard to find one more convenient and attractive. It stands on the banks of the river Thames, the biggest river in the whole island, which divides the town into two parts and forms the border of Kent, the country and district which extends from Dover to London. The town itself stretches from east to west, and is three miles in circumference. However its suburbs are so large that they greatly increase its circuit.

It is defended by handsome walls, especially on the northern side, where they have recently been rebuilt. Within these stands a very strongly defended castle on the banks of the river, where the king of England and his queen sometimes have their residence. There are also other great buildings, and especially a beautiful and convenient bridge over the Thames, of many marble arches, which has on it many shops built of stone and mansions and even a church of considerable size. Nowhere have I seen a finer or more richly built bridge.

Throughout the town are to be seen many workshops of craftsmen in all sorts of mechanical arts, to such an extent that there is hardly a street which is not graced by some shop or the like which can also be observed by everyone at Milan. This makes the town exceedingly prosperous and well-stocked, as well as having the immediate effect of adding to its splendour. The working in wrought silver, tin or white lead is very expert here, and perhaps the finest I have ever seen. There are also very many mansions, which do not, however, seem very large from the outside, but inside they contain a great number of rooms and garrets and are quite considerable. Six inch oak beams are inserted in the walls the same distance apart as their own breadth, and walls built in this way turn out to be made of the same material as the houses I described at Maastrich.

All the streets are so badly paved that they get wet at the slightest quantity of water, and this happens very frequently owing to the large numbers of cattle carrying water, as well as on account of the rain, of which there is a great deal in this island. Then a vast amount of evil-smelling mud is formed, which does not disappear quickly but lasts a long time, in fact nearly the whole year round. The citizens, therefore, in order to remove this mud and filth from their boots, are accustomed to spread fresh rushes on the floors of all houses, on which they clean the soles of their shoes when they come in. This system is widely practised not only by Londoners but also by all the rest of the island's inhabitants, who, it seems, suffer from similar trouble from mud.

There are a great many churches, but the most important of them is St. Paul's Cathedral, which is very magnificent and was built at great expense. Its roof is all made of lead, a practice that can be seen in many other buildings also. Merchants from not only Venice but also Florence and Lucca, and many from Genoa and Pisa, from Spain, Germany, the Rhine valley and other countries meet here to handle business with the utmost keenness, having come from the different parts of the world. But the chief exports from this island are wool and fabrics, considered the best in the world, and white lead, for the island is more freely endowed with these commodities than any other country. By sea and the Thames goods of all kinds can be brought into London and taken from the city to other destinations.

*   *   *

Londoners have such fierce tempers and wicked dispositions that they not only despise the way in which Italians live, but actually pursue them with uncontrolled hatred, and whereas at Bruges foreigners are hospitably received and complimented and treated with consideration by everybody, here the Englishmen use them with the utmost contempt and arrogance, and make them the object of insults. At Bruges we could do as we liked by day as well as by night. But here they look askance at us by day, and at night they sometimes drive us off with kicks and blows of the truncheon. Some of the men are exceptionally tall. All exercise themselves in a marvellous way with great bows made of yew wood, with which they practise continually outside the walls. They also fight with them on foot in such a way as to show that they have been enthusiastically trained in this from their earliest youth.

They dress in the French fashion, except that their suits are more full, and, accordingly, more out of shape. They show no trace of schooling (I am talking of the common people); but they delight in banquets and variety of meat and food, and they excel everyone in preparing them with an excessive abundance. They eat very frequently, at times more than is suitable, and are particularly fond of young swans, rabbits, deer and sea birds. They often eat mutton and beef, which is generally considered to be better here than anywhere else in the world. This is due to the excellence of their pastures. They have all kinds of fish in plenty and great quantities of oysters which come from the sea-shore. The majority, not to say everyone, drink that beverage I have spoken of before, and prepare it in various ways. For wine is very expensive, as the vine does not grow in the island; nor does the olive, and the products of both are imported from France and Spain. In certain places, mainly inland, silver and iron are found. But although there is abundance of these, gold is very scarce and copper scarcer still: they import it from Germany . . .

18 The Sheep and its Wool, Sixteenth and Seventeenth Centuries

(Traditional)

> I thank my God and ever shall,
> It was the sheep that paid for all.

> Traditional saying of woolmen and clothiers

19 A Devon Clothier's Will, 1526

(Printed in O. A. R. Murray, 'Devonshire Wills of the Sixteenth and Seventeenth Centuries' (Devonshire Association Transactions, LIII, 1921), pp. 55-6)

Thomas Leigh of South Molton: 2 June 1526. My soul to Almighty God and our Lady St. Mary and to all the saints of heaven. To be buried in the churchyard of South Molton. To the store[1] of Allhallows there, 12d. To the store of the High Cross, 12d. To the store of our Lady, 12d. To the store of St. George, 12d. To the store of St. Nicholas, 12d. To the store of St. Erasmus, 12d. To the store of St. John, 12d. To the building of the chantry house belonging to the Guild of the Trinity, 6 dozen of cloth, 40s in money, and all my boards and timber that is in my back-side. To the Guild aforesaid a spruce coffer. To Philip Rashlegh, half a pack of cloth, 3 dozen of racks, a pair of shears, 3 spoons of silver of the best sort . . . To his wife, a pair of beads of coral with gauds of silver and gilt. To Richard Honey, half a pack of cloth, a salt of silver, 3 spoons of the best sort, 3 dozen of racks, a pair of looms &c. To John Hogge, half a pack of cloth, 3 dozen of racks, a pair of shears, 2 spoons of silver &c., he performing my covenants to Thomas Smythe, and also the house he dwells in and the moor during my term, bearing yearly to the church 10s. To my daughter

Alice, a pack of cloth, in money 6*l* 13*s* 4*d*, a girdle with gilt harness, a bed performed, half a dozen of spoons, 3 platters, 3 pottingers,[2] 3 saucers, a pan of 8 gallons, a pot of 3 gallons. To Robert Clerk, my murrey[3] gown, and to his wife, my wife's best gown and 10*s* in money. To Sir Richard Maiour, 6*s* 8*d*. To Sir William Blackgreve, 6*s* 8*d*. To Thomas Haach, my great coffer. My horse, and my wood, cloth, yarn and wool not bequeathed to be sold to find an honest priest singing in the chapel of St. George for me and my friends during 12 months and to have for his labour, bread, wine and wax, 6*l*. Residue to my son William whom I make my executor, that he may dispose of it for the health of my soul and all christian souls in deeds of charity with the supervision of Thomas Haach, gentleman, Sir William Blackgreve and Richard Honey, to each of whom 6*s* 8*d*. To my son William during his life, my house that I dwell in, keeping dirige and mass for me and my friends yearly, and after his decease to remain to the store of the High Cross and then the warden of the said store to keep dirige and mass yearly for me and my friends. If my son William die under lawful age, one half of my goods to remain to my children then living and the other half to be done in deeds of charity by the discretion of my supervisors. Witnesses, Sir Richard Maior my curate, Richard Hunt, Henry Nall, John Barbour and other.

[1] Fund.   [2] Dishes.   [3] Dark red.

20 The Spoliation of Glastonbury Abbey, 1539

(*Three Chapters of Letters relating to the Suppression of the Monasteries*, ed. T. Wright (Camden Society, 1843), pp. 257–8)

Letter to Thomas Cromwell

Pleases it your lordship to be advertised, that since our letters last directed unto you from Glastonbury, we have daily found and tried out both money and plate hid and mured up in walls, vaults, and other secret places, as well by the abbot and others of the convent, and also conveyed to divers places in the country. And in case we should here tarry this fortnight, we do suppose daily to increase in plate and other goods by false knaves conveyed. And among other petty briberies, we have found the two treasurers of the church, monks, with the two clerks of the vestry, temporal men, in so arrant and manifest robbery, that we have committed the same to the jail. At our first entry into the treasure-house, and vestry also, we neither found jewels, plate, nor ornaments sufficient to serve a poor parish church, whereof we could

not a little marvel; and thereupon immediately made so diligent enquiry and search, that with vigilant labour we much improved the
same, and have recovered again into our hands both money, plate, and
ornaments of the church. How much plate we know not, for we had no
leisure yet to weigh the same; but we think it of great value, and we
increase it more every day, and shall do, as we suppose, for our time
here being. We assure your lordship that the abbot and the monks
aforesaid had embezzled and stolen as much plate and ornaments as
would have sufficed to have begun a new abbey; what they meant
thereby, we leave it to your judgment. Whether the king's pleasure shall
be to execute his law upon the said four persons, and to minister them
justice, according to their deserts, or to extend his mercy towards them,
and what his majesty's pleasure is, it may please your lordship to
advertise us thereof. The house is great, goodly, and so princely as we
have not seen the like; with 4 parks adjoining, the furthermost of them
but 4 miles distant from the house; a great mere, which is 5 miles compass, being a mile and a half distant from the house, well replenished
with great pike, bream, perch, and roach; 4 fair manor places, belonging
to the late abbot, the furthermost but 3 miles distant, being goodly
mansions; and also one in Dorsetshire, 20 miles distant from the late
monastery. We have despatched the servants, with their half-year's
wages, giving humble thanks to the king's majesty for the same; the
monks also, with the king's benevolence and reward, and have assigned
them pensions. We find them very glad to depart, most humbly thank-
ing the king's majesty of his great goodness most graciously shown unto
them at this time, as well for his grace's reward as for their pensions.
Cattle we intend to sell for ready money; and to let out the pastures and
demesnes now from Michaelmas[1] forth quarterly; until the king's
pleasure be further known, to the intent [that] his grace shall lease no
rent, for the abbot has much pasture ground in his hand. Other news
we know none, but that almighty God have you in his tuition. From
Glastonbury, this 28th day of September.

Yours to command,
Richard Pollard.
Thomas Moyle.
Richard Layton.

[1] 29 September.

21 Description of a Yeoman, 1549

(*Sermons by Hugh Latimer*, ed. G. E. Corrie (Parker Society, 1844), I, p. 101)

My father was a yeoman, and had no lands of his own, only he had a farm of three or four pound by year at the uttermost, and hereupon he tilled so much as kept half a dozen men. He had walk for a hundred sheep; and my mother milked thirty kine. He was able, and did find the king a harness, with himself and his horse, while he came to the place that he should receive the king's wages. I can remember that I buckled his harness when he went unto Blackheath field.[1] He kept me to school, or else I had not been able to have preached before the king's majesty now. He married my sisters with five pound, or twenty nobles apiece; so that he brought them up in godliness and fear of God. He kept hospitality for his poor neighbours, and some alms he gave to the poor. And all this he did of the said farm, where he that now has it pays sixteen pound by year, or more, and is not able to do any thing for his prince, for himself, nor for his children, or give a cup of drink to the poor.

[1] Where the Cornish rebels were defeated in 1497. (GEC)

22 The Demands of the Rebels Led by Kett, 1549

(B. M. Harleian MSS 304, f. 75, printed by F. W. Russell, *Kett's Rebellion in Norfolk* (1859), pp. 48–56)

We pray your grace that where it is enacted for enclosing that it be not hurtful to such as have enclosed saffron grounds, for they be greatly chargeable to them, and that from henceforth no man shall enclose any more.

We certify your grace that whereas the lords of the manors have been charged with certe free rent, the same lords have sought means to charge the freeholders to pay the same rent, contrary to right.

We pray your grace that no lord of no manor shall common upon the commons.

We pray that priests from henceforth shall purchase no lands neither free nor bondy, and the lands that they have in possession may be let to temporal men, as they were in the first year of the reign of King Henry the VII.

We pray that reed ground and meadow ground may be at such price as they were in the first year of King Henry the VII.

We pray that all marshes that are held of the king's majesty by free rent or of any other, may be again at the price that they were in the first year of King Henry VII.

We pray that all bushels within your realm be of one stice, that is to say, to be in measure 8 gallons.

We pray that [priests] or vicars that be [not able] to preach and set forth the word of God to his parishioners may be thereby put from his benefice, and the parishioners there to choose another, or else the patron or lord of the town.

We pray that the payments of castleward rent, and blanch farm and office lands, which have been accustomed to be gathered of the tenements, whereas we suppose the lords ought to pay the same to their bailiffs for their rents gathering, and not the tenants.

We pray that no man under the degree of a knight or esquire keep a dove house, except it has been of an old ancient custom.

We pray that all freeholders and copyholders may take the profits of all commons, and there to common, and the lords not to common nor take profits of the same.

We pray that no feodary within your shires shall be a councillor to any man in his office making, whereby the king may be truly served, so that a man being of good conscience may be yearly chosen to the same office by the commons of the same shire.

We pray your grace to take all liberty of let into your own hands whereby all men may quietly enjoy their commons with all profits.

We pray that copyhold land that is unreasonably rented may go as it did in the first year of King Henry VII, and that at the death of a tenant or at a sale the same lands to be charged with an easy fine as a capon or a reasonable [sum] of money for a remembrance.

We pray that no priest [shall be chaplain] nor no other officer to any man of honour or worship, but only to be resident upon their benefices whereby their parishioners may be instructed with the laws of God.

We pray that all bond men may be made free, for God made all free with his precious blood-shedding.

We pray that rivers may be free and common to all men for fishing and passage.

We pray that no man shall be put by your escheator and feodary to find any office unless he holds of your grace in chief or capite above 10*l* by year.

We pray that the poor mariners or fishermen may have the whole profits of their fishings as porpoises, grampuses, whales or any great fish, so it be not prejudicial to your grace.

We pray that every proprietary parson or vicar having a benefice of 10*l* or more by year shall either by themselves or by some other person teach poor men's children of their parish the book called the catechism and the primer.

We pray that it be not lawful to the lords of any manor to purchase lands freely and to let them out again by copy of court roll to their great advancement and to the undoing of your poor subjects.

We pray that no proprietary parson or vicar, in consideration of avoiding trouble and suit between them and their poor parishioners which they daily do proceed and attempt, shall from henceforth take for the full contentation of all the tenths which now they do receive but 8*d* of the noble in the full discharge of all other tithes.

We pray that no man under the degree of [*blank*] shall keep any conies upon any of their own freehold or copyhold unless he pale them in so that it shall not be to the commons' nuisance.

We pray that no person, of what estate, degree or condition he be, shall from henceforth sell the wardship of any child, but that the same child if he live to his full age shall be at his own choosing concerning his marriage, the king's wards only except.

We pray that no manner of person having a manor of his own shall be no other lord's bailiff but only his own.

We pray that no lord, knight nor gentleman shall have or take in farm any spiritual promotion.

We pray your grace to give licence and authority by your gracious commission under your great seal to such commissioners as your poor commons have chosen, or as many of them as your majesty and your council shall appoint and think meet, for to redress and reform all such good laws, statutes, proclamations, and all other your proceedings, which have been hidden by your justices of your peace, sheriffs, escheators, and other your officers from your poor commons, since the first year of the reign of your noble grandfather King Henry VII.

We pray that those your officers that have offended your grace and your commons, and so proved by the complaint of your poor commons, do give unto these poor men so assembled 4*d* every day so long as they have remained there.

We pray that no lord, knight, esquire nor gentleman do graze nor feed any bullocks or sheep if he may spend forty pounds a year by his lands, but only for the provision of his house.

By me, Robt. Kett.

By me, Thomas Aldryche.   Thomas Cod.

23 A Prayer, 1552

(*Second Prayer Book of Edward VI, 1552*, in *Book of Common Prayer* (1662), Prayers and Thanksgivings)

In the time of dearth and famine

O God, heavenly father, whose gift it is that the rain doth fall, the earth is fruitful, beasts increase, and fishes do multiply: Behold, we beseech thee, the afflictions of thy people; and grant that the scarcity and dearth, which we do now most justly suffer for our iniquity, may through thy goodness be mercifully turned into cheapness and plenty; for the love of Jesus Christ our Lord, to whom with thee and the Holy Ghost be all honour and glory, now and for ever. Amen.

24 Kent and its People, c.1570

(W. Lambarde, *A Perambulation of Kent, containing the Description, History and the Customs of that Shire*, 3rd ed. (1656), pp. 3–10)

The soil is for the most part bountiful, consisting indifferently of arable, pasture, meadow and woodland: howbeit of these, wood occupies the greatest portion even till this day, except it be towards the east, which coast is more champaign than the residue. It has corn and grain, common with other shires of the realm: as wheat, rye, barley, and oats, in good plenty, save only, that in the wealdish, or woody places, where of late days they used much pomage, or cider, for want of barley, now that lack is more commonly supplied with oats. Neither wants Kent such sorts of pulse, as the rest of the realm yields, namely beans, peas, and tares, which some . . . call vetches . . . The pasture and meadow, is not only sufficient in proportion to the quantity of the country itself for breeding, but is comparable in fertility also to any that is near it, in so much that it gains by seeding. In fertile and fruitful woods and trees, this country is most flourishing also, whether you respect the mast of oak, beech and chestnut for cattle: or the fruit of apples, pears, cherries, and plums for men: for besides great store of oak and beech, it has whole woods that bear chestnut, a mast (if I may so call it, and not rather a fruit, whereof even delicate persons disdain not to feed) not commonly seen in other countries. But as for orchards of apples, and gardens of cherries, and those of the most delicious and exquisite kinds that can be, no part of the realm (that I know) has them, either in such quantity and number, or with such art and industry, set and planted . . .

Touching domestic cattle, as horses, mares, oxen, kine and sheep, Kent differs not much from others: only this it challenges as singular, that it brings forth the largest of stature in each kind of them . . . Parks of fallow deer, and games of great conies, it maintains many, the one for pleasure, and the other for profit . . . As for red deer and black conies, it nourishes them not, as having no forests, or great walks of waste ground for the one, and not tarrying the time to raise the gain by the other: for, black conies are kept partly for their skins, which have their season in winter: and Kent by the nearness to London, has so quick market of young rabbits, that it kills this game chiefly in summer.

There is no mineral, or other profit dug out of the belly of the earth here, save only that in certain places they have mines of iron, quarries of paving stone, and pits of fat marl.

Besides divers piers, jetties, and creeks, that be upon the coasts of the Thames and the sea, Kent has also sundry fresh rivers and pleasant streams, especially Darent, Medway, and Stour; of the which, Medway is more navigable than the rest, for which cause, and (for that it crosses the shire almost in the midst) it is the most beneficial also. The sea, and these waters, yield good and wholesome fishes competently, but yet neither so much in quantity, nor such in variety, as some other coasts of the realm do afford . . .

The people of this country, consist chiefly (as in other countries also) of the gentry, and the yeomanry, of which the first be for the most part . . . governors, and the others altogether . . . governed: whose possessions also were at the first distinguished by the names of knight fee, and gavelkind: that former being proper to the warrior, and this latter to the husbandman. But as nothing is more inconstant, than the estate that we have in lands and living . . . even so, long since these tenures have been so indifferently mixed and confounded, in the hands of each sort, that there is not now any note of difference to be gathered by them.

The gentlemen be not here (throughout) of so ancient stocks as elsewhere, especially in the parts nearer to London, from which city (as it were from a certain rich and wealthy seedplot) courtiers, lawyers, and merchants be continually translated, and do become new plants amongst them. Yet be their revenues greater than anywhere else: which thing grows not so much by the quantity of their possession, or by the fertility of their soil, as by the benefit of the situation of the country itself, which has all that good neighbourhood that . . . Cato and other old authors in husbandry require to a well placed grange, that is to say, the sea, the river, a populous city, and a well traded highway, by the commodities whereof the superfluous fruits of the ground be dearly sold, and consequently the land may yield a greater rent.

These gentleman be also (for the most part) acquainted with good letters, and especially trained in the knowledge of the laws. They use to manure some large portion of their own territories, as well for the maintenance of their families, as also for their better increase in wealth. So that they be well employed, both in the public service, and in their own particular, and do use hawking, hunting, and other disports, rather for their recreation, than for an occupation or pastime.

The common people, or yeomanry . . . is nowhere more free, and jolly, than in this shire . . . it is agreed by all men, that there never were any bondmen (or villeins) as the law calls them in Kent. Neither be they here so much bound to the gentry by copyhold, or customary tenures, as the inhabitants of the western countries of the realm be, nor at all endangered by the feeble hold of tenant right (which is but a descent of a tenancy at will) as the common people in the northern parts be: for copyhold tenure is rare in Kent, and tenant right not heard of at all: but in place of these, the custom of gavelkind prevailing everywhere, in manner every man is a freeholder, and has some part of his own to live upon. And in this their estate, they please themselves, and joy exceedingly, in so much, as a man may find sundry yeomen (although otherwise for wealth comparable with many of the gentle sort) that will not yet for all that change their condition, nor desire to be apparelled with the titles of gentry. Neither is this any cause of disdain, or of alienation of the good minds of the one sort from the other: for where else in all this realm, is the common people more willingly governed? To be short, they be most commonly civil, just, and bountiful, so that the estate of the old franklins and yeomen of England, either yet lives in Kent, or else it is quite dead and departed out of the realm for altogether.

As touching the artificers of this shire, they be either such as travail at the sea, or labour in the arts that be handmaidens to husbandry, or else do work in stone, iron, and woodfuel, or be makers of coloured woollen cloths: in which last feat, they excel, as from whom is drawn both sufficient store to furnish the wear of the best sort of our nation at home, and great plenty also to be transported to other foreign countries abroad.

25 The Plight of a Younger Son, c.1600

(William Shakespeare, *As You Like It*, ed. J. Munro, *The London Shakespeare* (1958), I, pp. 598–9)

ACT I, SCENE I. ORCHARD OF OLIVER'S HOUSE

Enter Orlando and Adam

Orlando As I remember, Adam, it was upon this fashion bequeathed me by will but poor a thousand crowns, and, as thou sayst, charged my brother, on his blessing, to breed me well: and there begins my sadness. My brother Jaques he keeps at school, and report speaks goldenly of his profit. For my part, he keeps me rustically at home, or, to speak more properly, stays me here at home unkept: for call you that keeping for a gentleman of my birth, that differs not from the stalling of an ox? His horses are bred better; for, besides that they are fair with their feeding, they are taught their manage, and to that end riders dearly hired: but I, his brother, gain nothing under him but growth; for the which his animals on his dunghills are as much bound to him as I. Besides this nothing that he so plentifully gives me, the something that nature gave me his countenance seems to take from me. He lets me feed with his hinds, bars me the place of a brother, and, as much as in him lies, mines my gentility with my education. This is it, Adam, that grieves me; and the spirit of my father, which I think is within me, begins to mutiny against this servitude. I will no longer endure it, though yet I know no wise remedy how to avoid it.

Enter Oliver

Adam Yonder comes my master, your brother.

Orlando Go apart, Adam, and thou shalt hear how he will shake me up.

Oliver Now, sir! what make you here?

Orlando Nothing. I am not taught to make anything.

Oliver What mar you then, sir?

Orlando Marry, sir, I am helping you to mar that which God made, a poor unworthy brother of yours, with idleness.

Oliver Marry, sir, be better employed, and be naught awhile.

Orlando Shall I keep your hogs and eat husks with them? What prodigal portion have I spent, that I should come to such penury?

Oliver Know you where you are, sir?

Orlando O, sir, very well: here in your orchard.

Oliver Know you before whom, sir?

Orlando Ay, better than him I am before knows me. I know you are my eldest brother; and, in the gentle condition of blood, you should so know me. The courtesy of nations allows you my better, in that you are the firstborn; but the same tradition takes not away my blood, were there twenty brothers betwixt us. I have as much of my father in me as you, albeit, I confess, your coming before me is nearer to his reverence.

Oliver What, boy!

Orlando Come, come, elder brother, you are too young in this.

Oliver Wilt thou lay hands on me, villain?

Orlando I am no villain. I am the youngest son of Sir Rowland de Boys: he was my father, and he is thrice a villain that says such a father begot villains. Wert thou not my brother, I would not take this hand from thy throat till this other had pulled out thy tongue for saying so. Thou hast railed on thyself.

Adam Sweet masters, be patient. For your father's remembrance, be at accord.

Oliver Let me go, I say.

Orlando I will not, till I please: you shall hear me. My father charged you in his will to give me good education. You have trained me like a peasant, obscuring and hiding from me all gentlemanlike qualities. The spirit of my father grows strong in me, and I will no longer endure it. Therefore allow me such exercises as may become a gentleman, or give me the poor allottery my father left me by testament. With that I will go buy my fortunes.

Oliver And what wilt thou do? beg, when that is spent? Well, sir, get you in. I will not long be troubled with you. You shall have some part of your will. I pray you, leave me.

26 The Men of Devon, c.1600

(John Hooker, *Synopsis Chorographical of Devonshire*, ed. W. J. Blake (Devonshire Association Transactions, XLVII, 1915), pp. 339–42)

This country or province . . . is very populous and very well inhabited as no part of the realm more or better. The people are well compact and of good stature and be very strong and apt to all good exercises and well inclined to all honesty and virtue and some to be framed to any action either civil or martial, whereof there has been and yet is a common proverb, let a Devonshire man come but once to the court and he will be a courtier at the first. In matters of knowledge, learning and

C

wisdom they be of a deep judgment; in matters civil and for the common wealth they be wise, pregnant and politic: in matters of martial, they be very valiant and prudent: in all travails and pains they be very laborious: and in all actions either of the body or of the mind they be very excellent.

[The people] be of four sorts and degrees, nobleman and gentleman: the merchant, the yeoman and the labourer. Under the name of the gentlemen I do comprehend all noble men, knights and esquires, and all such who by birth are descended of ancient and noble parents and such as for their virtues and good deserts be by the prince and sovereign advanced to nobility. The gentlemen for the most part are very civil, courteous, gentle, affable and of good virtue, temperate and modest in all their gestures and no more seemly than moderate in their apparel without any sumptuousness, pride or excess, for it is well known that many ancient gentlemen left to their posterity a velvet gown or a silk garment which has continued three or four descents without alteration or new devices. Which ancient and good order so long as they kept they were never in any merchant books entangled, in any statutes nor bound in any recognisance, neither was the lawyer ever busied to draw up books and conveyances, feoffments, bargains, mortgages, sales and selling of lands, fines and recoveries. They were not beholding to any usurer or money monger but disposed and given unto virtue, learning and knowledge: and all good endeavours: some to honest and good studies; and some to feats of wars and chivalry: and some to good hospitality and housekeeping: good to their tenants, friendly to their neighbours and liberal to the poor and needy, and by such means they were beloved and honoured and lived in credit, worship and honour in the commonwealth. Their exercises were hawking, hunting, riding, shooting, hurling and such like as whereby the minds were no more recreated than their bodies were inseamed and hardened to all activities and good exercises. And not given unto pride, luxury and excess, unto gamings, fond plays, wantons, night watchings, riotness, surfeitings, banqueting, incontinences and such other disorders and filthiness as be found in the courts of Bacchus and palaces of Venus and which be the special causes why so many noble houses be overthrown, so many gentlemen consumed and so many men in these days be brought to misery and to beggary: for by the luxury and like means drawn out of Asia the Roman nobility was destroyed, and by the like this country, this now the fertile country, and such like in this land, by using the like looseness shall receive the like confusion, and lose their wonted grace and honour, which heretofore they have ever had . . .

The second degree or sort are the merchants who for the most part do dwell in towns and cities and having attained to some wealth they do become great adventurers and travellers by seas unto all nations and countries: from whence any profit or gain is to be had, and thereby they do attain to great wealth and riches: which for the most part they do employ in purchasing of land and by little and little they do creep and seek to be gentlemen: which breeds an emulation or rather a disdain between them. But if they were so careful to avoid the occasions of offences and displeasures as they be too much addicted to private lucre and desire to climb to higher advancement: the love and goodwill would be more between them than it is but kind of nobility until by virtue and good deserts the same be ennobled and by signal descents be confirmed.

The third degree is the yeomanry of this country which consists of farmers, husbandmen and freeholders which be men of a free nature and of good conditions, and do live of such grounds and land as which they do hold freely and for term of life of others for a rent, or some of their own freehold being at the least of a clear value by the year of 40*s*. Yet they be called *legales homines* because commonly they be returned in all trials or criminal or civil, and upon their oaths be to set down the very truth as near as they can of the matter given unto them in charge which being allowed and sentenced by the judge; all controversies be decided and the law has his end. These albeit they be not so well accounted of nor had in due reputation as they in times past were wont to be, because every man is now of an aspiring mind and not contented with their own estate, do like better of another's . . . Yet after their portions they are not much inferior unto the gentlemen who be their lords: for his fine being once paid he lives as merrily as does his landlord and gives himself for the most part to such virtues, conditions and qualities as does the gentleman, and delights in good housekeeping, fares well, seemly in his apparel, courteous in his behaviour, and friendly to his neighbours, and when time serves is given to the like exercises of hunting, shooting, &c. But according to his calling his chief travails be most in matters of his husbandry wherein he leaves no pains to make his best profit, whether it be by tilling, grassing, buying and selling of cattle, or whatsoever he can find to be for his gain and profit: and by these means he grows to such wealth and ability that his landlord is many times beholding unto him. And now of late they have entered into the trade of usury, buying of cloths and purchasing and merchandises, climbing up daily to the degrees of a gentleman and do bring up their children accordingly.

The fourth degree be the daily labourers, who do serve for wages whether they be artificers, which for the most do dwell in cities and towns, or of such as do serve and do dwell in the country for wages, and these be of two sorts. The one is called the spader, the daily worker or labourer in the tin-works, and there is no labourer to be compared unto him: for his apparel is coarse, his diet slender, his lodging hard, his feeding commonly coarse bread and hard cheese, and his drink is water, and for lack of a cup he drinks it out of his spade or shovel: and he goes so near the weather as no man can live more frugally and nearer than he does. His life most commonly is in pits and caves under the ground of a great depth and in great danger because the earth above his head is in sundry places crossed and posted over with timber, to keep the same from falling.

The other is also a daily labourer at husbandry and other servile works for their daily wages and hires: but he serves at more ease and more delicately. Notwithstanding they be both of a mighty and a strong body, able to endure all labours and pains: and upon the holy days and times of leisure they do give themselves unto such exercises and pastimes as wherewith they do rather inseam their bodies with hardiness and strength, than otherwise, as with shooting, wrestling and hurling, and they so well framed to any kind of service, as they will soon attain to the use and knowledge thereof and as experience teaches that a small training will soon frame them to whatsoever he be employed whether it be to be a soldier or a perfect serving man. And albeit these labourers be of the most inferior in degree yet they be *liberi homines* and of a free condition, not villeins, not bond slaves.

27 The Extravagance of a Gentleman, c.1600

(B.M. Additional MSS 29442, ff. 44-7, printed in L. Stone, *Social Change and Revolution in England, 1540–1640* (1965), p. 155)

. . . Thomas [Reresby], the eldest son and heir, married Mary Monson, daughter of Sir John Monson of South Carleton, com. Lincs, as appears by the deed of settlement upon the marriage dated the 30 March anno 30 Elizabeth, whereby it is covenanted that she should have for portion, 1,200*l* . . .

This Sir Thomas (for he was knighted about the fortieth year of the Queen, when honour was rarely bestowed) entered to the greatest and freest estate both real and personal of any heir of the family to that day, to which he added also considerably in the beginning of his time by several purchases. . . . This addition to the paternal estate had been a great estate had he kept it entire, but he lived to sell more than he bought and left the remainder much encumbered, as hereafter appears. . . . The reasons given for Sir Thomas his great expenses and debts were his following the Court without any other recompense than empty knighthood, though very rare and consequently of great honour in those days; an expensive wife; his accompanying my Lord Zouche sent anno 1593 ambassador into Scotland; an humour to live high at the first, which he did not abate as his fortune decreased; his quarrel with Sir William Wentworth and his giving a box on the ear at Rotherham sessions upon the bench; and his buildings: first he built the tower to the east of Thriburgh Hall, wainscotted the gallery and boarded it, with several other rooms there. He built Estwood Hall at Ashover of freestone and leaded the roof, which cost him above 2,000*l* only to live in that year that [he] was Sheriff of Derbyshire, which office he is reported to have performed at too prodigal a rate in the year 1613. . . . Another great occasion of his expenses was his great charge of children and great attendance, he seldom going to church or from home without a great many followers in blue coats and badges, and beyond the usual number for one of his quality and fortune.

28 Further Attempt to Limit London's Growth, 1602

(*Tudor Royal Proclamations*, III, eds. P. L. Hughes and J. F. Larkin (Yale U.P., 1969), pp. 245–8)

Whereas the queen's most excellent majesty heretofore in her princely wisdom and providence foreseeing the great and manifold inconveniences and mischiefs which did then grow and were like more and more to increase unto the state of the city of London, and the suburbs and confines thereof, by the access and confluence of people to inhabit in the same, not only by reason that such multitudes could hardly be governed by ordinary justice to serve God and obey her majesty without constituting and addition of more officers, and enlarging of authorities and jurisdictions for that purpose, but also could hardly be provided of sustentation of victual, food, and other like necessaries for man's relief upon reasonable prices; and finally for that such great multitudes of people being brought to inhabit in small rooms, whereof a great part being poor and such as must live by begging or by worse means, and being heaped up together and in a sort smothered with many families of children and servants in one house or small tenement, it must needs follow if any plague or other universal sickness should by God's permission enter among those multitudes, that the same would not only spread itself and invade the whole city and confines but would be also dispersed through all other parts of the realm, whereby great mortality should ensue . . .

For remedy whereof, her majesty by her proclamation bearing date the seventh day of July, in the 22nd year of her reign, did charge and command all manner of persons, of what quality soever they were, to desist and forbear from any new buildings of any house or tenement within three miles from any of the gates of the said city of London, to serve for any habitation or lodging for any person, where no former house had been known to have been in the memory of such as were then living; and also to forbear from letting or setting or suffering any more families than one only to be placed or to inhabit from thenceforth in any house that before that time had been inhabited . . .

And whereas afterwards, in the 39th and 40th years of her highness' reign, upon several bills of complaint exhibited by her majesty's Attorney General into the High Court of Star Chamber before her highness' council there against divers persons for divers offences by them committed and done contrary to the tenor of the said proclamation, the said council, gravely weighing and considering the manifold mischiefs that did then happen, and were like daily to increase for want of due execution of the said proclamation, did make and set down very profitable and necessary orders and decrees in that behalf, as by the said orders and decrees remaining of record in her said Court of Star Chamber more fully and at large appears; and whereas the lords and others of her highness' honourable Privy Council, perceiving great delay, negligence, and partiality used in the execution of the said proclamation, orders, and decrees, have also at sundry times written their letters unto such of her highness' officers to whom it did appertain for the putting in due execution of the said proclamation, orders, and decrees:

Her majesty, perceiving that notwithstanding her gracious and princely commandment signified by her said proclamation, and the honourable care of her Privy Council touching the same, yet it falls out, partly by the covetous and insatiable dispositions of some persons that without any respect of the common good and public profit of the realm do only regard their own particular lucre and gain, and partly by the negligence and corruption of others who by reason of their offices and places ought to see the said proclamation, orders, and decrees duly performed, and yet do undutifully neglect the same, that the said mischiefs and inconveniences do daily increase and multiply . . . does, by the advice of her said council, straightly charge and command the Lord

Mayor of the city of London and all other officers having authority within the same, and also all justices of peace, lords and bailiffs of liberties not being within the jurisdiction of the said Lord Mayor of London, faithfully and diligently to execute and perform, and cause to be executed and performed within the city of London, and within all places being within three miles of the city of London or Westminster, these articles following:

1. First, that no new buildings of any new house or tenement be from henceforth erected or attempted to be erected ... except the same be upon the foundation of a former dwelling house, and if any such happen to be begun, that the same be forthwith, by the view of the justices of the peace within that limit, pulled down, and the timber thereof begun to be set up to be sold to the relief of the poor of the parish where the same shall happen to be.

2. That from henceforth there be no dividing of any house or tenement within the precincts aforesaid into several dwellings, but to be kept as one house; nor any more dwelling houses to be built upon any former foundation of a dwelling house than before was upon the same house.

3. And for such tenements as have been divided within these ten years ... the inmates to be avoided presently if they have no estate for life, lives, or years yet enduring; and for such as have such estate or term, then as the same shall end and determine, so the tenement to be reduced to the former estate, and no tenant to be admitted in place of the other.

4. All sheds and shops to be plucked down that have been builded within the places and precincts aforesaid within seven years last past.

5. All houses, tenements, or buildings erected within these seven years last past and not let out, or being void of a tenant, order to be taken that the same shall not be inhabited nor let to any, unless the owner shall be content that the churchwardens and the minister, by allowance of two or more of the justices of the peace of that division, shall dispose of them for some of the poor, or for the good and behalf of the poor of the parish that are destitute of houses, and at and under such rents as they shall allow.

6. All other tenements or buildings not built upon any old foundation of a dwelling house that are not at this present finished, to be plucked down, and the builders or leasers that bind or tie the tenants to build upon their ground, to be bound to appear in the Star Chamber; and to commit the workmen to prison that shall persist after warning given by any justice of the peace or constable.

7. Those houses and tenements, that are already demised or let, diligently to inquire what term they have; and if they have them from year to year, then the tenant to be commanded to avoid and to provide himself elsewhere without the precincts aforesaid before the end of three months; and order to be also taken that the house be not let again, but in such sort as is before expressed.

8. When and as often as any tenant shall avoid, decease, or leave any of the said new erected tenements, or that their terms do expire, then and so often strict order to be taken that the same be not afterwards let or set, but in manner before set down and allowed; and if any person shall demise or take any the tenements aforesaid, or any part of any of them, contrary to the true meaning and intent of this proclamation, every such person to be committed to prison until advertisement shall thereof be given to the lords of her majesty's Privy Council, and not be delivered before he be bound to answer the same in the Star Chamber as contemners of this her majesty's proclamation.

9. And if any shall henceforth offend in new building or in dividing of any tenement contrary to the true intent and meaning of this proclamation, and all workmen continuing the same work after they shall be forbidden thereof by any justice of peace or constable of the place or limit where the same shall happen to be, shall be committed to prison until they shall find sufficient sureties for their appearance in the Star Chamber to answer their contempts there, and for their good behaviour in the mean season.

29 The Vicissitudes of the Weather, 1604–26

(*Diary of Walter Yonge, Esq. Written at Colyton and Axminster, Co. Devon, from 1604 to 1628* (Camden Society, XLI, 1848), *passim*)

Anno Domini 1604 . . . We had such exceeding drought in all parts of England, that all grass in all places, yea the best meadows by the river sides, were all burnt up, in such sort that all men thought it impossible that we should have any grass grow before the spring following. The very roots of the grass were generally withered away and dry; yet, through the great goodness of God, never a better after-spring seen in any man's memory, at the end of June; and most plenty of grass when people did most despair thereof.

The 20th of Jan. 1606–7, by reason of a great tempest, the sea broke in at divers places on the north side of this country, as at Barnstaple, where was much hurt done. At Bridgwater two villages near thereabouts and one market town overflown, and report of 500 persons drowned, besides many sheep, and other cattle. At Bristol it flowed so high that divers packs, which were brought thither against Paul's fair, standing together in a common hall of the city, for such purposes, stood three foot deep in water.

March, 1607. This winter last past has been such an extreme winter for frosts as no man living ever does remember or can speak of the like.

May, 1607. An extreme dearth of corn. Hay was sold this present winter in some places 2s 6d per 32lb. Mr Southcote, of Moeurs Oterry, [Ottery St. Mary] paid so, as he told me, being low within the same time.

Nov. 1608. An extreme dearth of corn happened this year, by reason of extreme frosts (as the like were never seen), the winter going before, which caused much corn to fall away; so that many did sow barley where their wheat was sown before, thinking their wheat would never come to good. This year were very many tempestuous winds.

August, 1609. Extreme wet causes the price of all kinds of corn to be somewhat high, although great plenty—the like seldom seen—in ground, which by reason of much wet weather was much hurt. Scarce any corn saved this year without great hurt. All kind of corn did grow in stook, and much cast away and spoiled. I myself was forced to turn oats some four, some five times, before I could save it.

15 May, 1611. There was such a dry spring this year as never was before seen or heard of. Yet corn proved reasonably good this year.

1616. This year were extreme rains and tempestuous winds from the end of November till after Candlemas,[1] and scarce any one day fair in all that time. Corn proved this year to be very good generally.

August, 1621. This summer was very cold and wet: corn beaten down with much rain, and like to prove very ill. Yet in regard of the last year plenty. It was sold all this last summer, 1621, for 3s 4d the bushel of wheat; barley at 20d; and oats 14d. This year harvest was not ended before Allhallowtide.[2]

April, 1622. Corn is grown very dear: barley is at 3s 8d the bushel;

wheat 6s 8d; by means whereof the poor greatly complain, and for that all wares are grown so dear as they can get no work whereby to relieve themselves.

The 19th of August, 1622, being Monday, about one of the clock in the morning, the wind arose and blew so vehemently for six hours, that it broke down divers strong trees. It quealed[3] all hedges towards the south that they davered[4] as if they had been scorched with lightning. It spoiled standing corn so, as in many places it seemed that all the corn (especially barley and oats) had been threshed or beaten out of the husks. By report there is 200l loss and hurt done to corn in Axmouth only by the said wind.

July, 1626. This year, 1626, fell out to be extreme wet and unseasonable, that for six weeks' space together we had not one day without rain. Much hay was spoilt and rotten on the ground, because men forbore to cut it, doubting to save it. Corn much beaten down, for which and the increase of the plague and the Spanish invasion, noised for England, there was proclaimed a general fast to be observed throughout the whole kingdom, on Wednesday, the second of August; and the day following, being Thursday, the air cleared and fair weather thenceforth.

[1] 2 February.   [2] 1 November.   [3] Curled up.   [4] Withered.

30 A Parish and the Civil War, 1648

(Messing Parish Register, printed in *English History from Essex Sources, 1550–1750*, ed. A. C. Edwards (Essex Record Office, Publications, XVII (1952), p. 84)

During the siege against Colchester, the county of Essex was at great charge in carrying in of provisions and other accommodations for the army under his excellency, the Lord Fairfax; and our town of Messing, from the 4th of June 1648 to the 10th of September next following, was at these charges hereunder named, viz.

	l	s	d
In victuals, as bread, flesh, cheese, butter, eggs, chickens, beer, oats, etc.	28.	4.	5
At the full charge of hay, straw, carriage and ladders	30.	3.	10
4 town arms, 13 weeks and one day at 12d a per day man	18.	8.	0

	l	*s*	*d*
26 spades, shovels and mattocks at 2*s* a piece	2.12.		0
Constables' time, trouble, etc. for 12 weeks, 6*s* a week	7. 4.		0
The sum total of these 13 or 14 weeks' charge is	86.12.		3
Besides the fourth rate . . . gathered about the same time	11. 3.		0
	97.15.		3

The constables gathered in the parish of Messing in 4 rates towards the aforesaid charges the sum of 92*l* 1.3*d*

The charge for the 8 foot soldiers of the trained band for 13 weeks and one day at 12*d* a day	36.16.		0
The charge for 5 auxiliary foot at 12*d* the day for 13 weeks	20.15.		0 [*sic*]
The charge for 2 auxiliary horse and half a troop horse at 2*s* 6*d* a day a man for 14 weeks	31. 6.		6 [*sic*]
For 5 or 6 days' free quarter for 50 and odd of Col. Rainsborough's men in this parish at the breaking up of the leaguer before Colchester, at 12*d* a man	15.10.		0
	104. 7.		6

31 Lady Hobart and Dr Denton on the Fire of London, 1666

(Printed in F. P. Verney and M. M. Verney, *Memoirs of the Verney Family during the Seventeenth Century* (1907), II, pp. 254–5, 256–7)

Lady Hobart

O dear Sir Ralph, I am sorry to be the messenger of so dismal news, for poor London is almost burnt down. It began on Saturday night and has burnt ever since and is at this time more fierce than ever. It did begin in Pudding Lane at a bakers, where a Dutch rogue lay, and burnt to the bridge and all Fish Street and all Crasus Street and Lumber Street and the old Exchange and Cannon Street, and so all that way to the river and Billingsgate side, and now it is come to Cheapside and Baynard's Castle and it is thought Fleet Street will be burnt by tomorrow. There is nothing left in any house there, nor in the Temple, there was never so sad a sight, nor so doleful a cry heard, my heart is not able to express the tenth, nay the thousandth part, of it. There is all the carts within ten miles round, and carts and drays run about night and day, and thousands of men and women carrying burdens. It is the Dutch fire, there was one taken in Westminster setting his outhouse on fire and they have attempted to fire many places and there is abundance taken with grenades and powder. Castle yard was set on fire. I am almost out of my wits. We have packed up all our goods and cannot get a cart for money, they give 5 and 10 pound for carts. I have sent for carts to my Lady Glaskock if I can get them, but I fear I shall lose all I have and must run away. O pray for us, for now the cries makes me I know not what to say. O pity me. I will break open the closet and look to all your things as well as I can. I hope if it comes to us it will be Thursday, but it runs fiercely. O I shall lose all I have. We have sent to see for carts to send to Highgate and cannot get one [for] twenty pounds to go out of town. Viner and Backwell have saved all, and so has all Lombard Street. All Paul's churchyard cloth is saved. Mr Glaskock is come and says we shall have carts tomorrow. God bless us and send us a good meeting.

Dr Denton

Whether this will find you or no I know not because I know not where the carrier does inn, the fire being now come as far as Holborn Bridge or near it. The short account of the fire is that more than the whole city is in ashes, wherein W. Gape and myself have great shares in St. Sythes Lane, and in Salisbury Court in reversion and I and wife in possession. And to render our condition more deplorable, the depopulation is so vast that it cannot afford us a livelihood so that I want the advice of all my friends to advise what I had best do. Our persons, I thank God, and our movables are saved but at a vast charge, 4*l* for every load to Kensington. The friends in Chancery Lane are safe, but the fire was near them behind the Rowles where it got a great check so that we hope it is stopped. I think they are still in town. We had sent away all but my books so that we were fain to lie only on blankets . . . This fire stops all trade and traffic and posts, the sad consequences of which may easily be guessed at . . . it is generally believed, but not at Court, that the papists have designed this and more . . . Here nothing almost is to be got that we have not in possession, bread, beer, meat, all in scarcity and many want it . . .

32 The Turn to Empirical Enquiry, 1667

(Thomas Sprat, *The History of the Royal Society of London, for the Improving of Natural Knowledge*, 1667 (1722 ed.), Dedication)

To the King. Sir, of all the kings of Europe, your majesty was the first who confirmed this noble design of experiments, by your own example, and by a public establishment. An enterprise equal to the most renowned actions of the best princes. For, to increase the powers of all mankind, and to free them from the bondage of errors, is greater glory than to enlarge empire, or to put chains on the necks of conquered nations.

What reverence all antiquity had for the authors of natural discoveries, is evident by the diviner sort of honour they conferred on them. Their founders of philosophical opinions were only admired by their own sects, their valiant men and generals did seldom rise higher than to demi-gods and heroes. But the gods they worshipped with temples and altars, were those who instructed the world to plough, to sow, to plant, to spin, to build houses, and to find out new countries. This zeal indeed, by which they expressed their gratitude to such benefactors, degenerated into superstition: yet has it taught us, that a higher degree of reputation is due to discoverers, than to the teachers of speculative doctrines, nay even to conquerors themselves.

Nor has the true God himself omitted to show his value of vulgar arts. In the whole history of the first monarchs of the world, from Adam to Noah, there is no mention of their wars, or their victories. All that is recorded is this, they lived so many years, and taught their posterity to keep sheep, to till the ground, to plant vineyards, to dwell in tents, to build cities, to play on the harp and organs, and to work in brass and iron. And if they deserved a sacred remembrance, for one natural or mechanical invention, your majesty will certainly obtain immortal fame, for having established a perpetual succession of inventors.

I am (may it please your majesty) your majesty's most humble, and most obedient subject, and servant,

Tho. Sprat

33 A Description of Westmoreland, 1671

(*Description of the County of Westmoreland by Sir Daniel Fleming of Rydal, A.D. 1671*, ed. G. F. Duckett (Cumberland and Westmoreland Antiquarian Society, Local Tract Series, I, 1882), pp. 1–11)

Beyond the farthest parts of Lancashire, more northward, lies another lesser country of the Brigantes, called by modern Latin writers Westmoria and Westmorlandia, in our tongue Westmoreland, bounded on the west and north with Cumberland and part of Lancashire, on the south with Lancashire, and on the east with Yorkshire and [the] bishopric of Durham, which, because it lies among moors and high hills, and was anciently for the most part unmanured, came by this name in our language, for such barren places which cannot easily, by the painful labour of the husbandman be brought to fruitfulness, the northern English men call *moors*, and Westmoreland is nothing else but a western moorish country.

The length thereof extending from Burton in her south to the joining Cumberland and the bishopric of Durham (in the mountains near the first rise of the two rivers Tees and Tyne) in her north part, is above thirty miles; the broadest part, from the east to west is from the Spittle on Stainmoor to the Shire-stones on Wreynose, containing about twenty-four miles; the whole circumference above 112 miles.

The air, in winter especially, is a little sharp and piercing, yet very healthful; the soil for a great part of it is but barren, being full of great moors and high mountains, called in the north fells, yet there are many fruitful valleys in it, abounding with good arable, meadows, and pasture grounds, and commended for plenty of corn and cattle.

The division thereof, according to its ecclesiastical government, is part (viz. the barony of Kendal) within the diocese of Chester, and part (viz. the bottom of Westmoreland) in Carlisle diocese; these two parts are divided into several deaneries, which are again divided into many parishes.

Its division according to the temporal government thereof, is into two great baronies, the one being divided from the other by a ridge of mountains . . . through which there are three common, but not very good passes, called Grayrigg-Hawse, Crook-dale Hawse, and Kirkstone, containing the south part of the county called Kendal-barony . . .

The barony of Kendal is divided into two wards, viz. Kendal-ward and Lonsdale-ward, which are subdivided into several constablewicks.

The other barony contains all the rest of the county, being the north part thereof, and called the barony of Westmoreland . . . This barony is also divided into two wards (there being no hundreds in this county, it being freed from all subsidies until King James I time, by reason of its no small charge in border service against the Scots), called the East and West wards, which are again divided into many constable-wicks.

In Lonsdale-ward are two market towns.

1. Burton, a town indifferently well built and procured to be a market since his majesty's happy restoration by Sir George Middleton, of Leighton, in Lancashire, Kt. and Bart., lord thereof, its market day every Tuesday, and fairs every 25th April and Whitsun-Monday.

2. Kirkby Lonsdale, anciently writ, Kirkby-in-Lonsdale, i.e., the church-town in Lonsdale; it's a fair market town, situate on the banks of the river Lon, which gives name to this place and to Loncaster, placed on the same river. This is a town of note, whither all the people round about repair to church and market, it being the greatest town, save Kendal, in this county; it is situate in a pleasant and rich vale called Lonsdale, and is beautified with a fair church, and a large bridge of stone. This town and lordship has several privileges, and was hereto-fore belonging to the Prestons of Holker, until of late it was sold to Sir John Lowther, of Lowther, Bart., who is now lord thereof. The market day is every Thursday, and the fairs on Ascension Day and St. Thomas Day[1] . . .

The market towns in Kendal-ward are two, viz.

1. Kendal, or rather Kirkby Kendale, writ anciently Kirkby in Kendale, i.e., the church town in Kendale. It is the chief town for largeness, neatness, buildings and trade in this county, and is most pleasantly seated, for the most part, on the west bank of the river Kent, so called from Kent-meer in this county, where its head is, which river gave name to a fruitful vale called Kent-dale, wherein this town is placed, and to Kent-Sands in Lancashire, this town gave name to the whole barony. Here was kept the sessions of the peace for this part of the county, as the sessions for the other part is held at Appleby, which two parts do comprehend the whole county, and do somewhat resemble the Ridings in Yorkshire. This town is seated in a very good air, and its healthful-ness is improved partly by the cleanliness of the people, and partly by its situation on a hill side, the river carrying away whatever filthiness the descending rain washes out of it. It has two broad and long streets, fairly built, crossing the one over the other, two large stone bridges, and one of wood. It has also a fair church, which does contain every Sunday as many people (almost) as any parish church in England, the advowson of it belongs to Trinity College, Cambridge, to which also

the impropriation of this parish does appertain . . . The present vicar is Mr Willm Brownsword, who has under him a curate, clerk, and six churchwardens. This town is a place of excellent manufacture, and for civility, ingenuity, and industry so surpassing, that in regard thereof it deservedly carries a great name. The trade of the town makes it populous, and the people seem to be shaped out for trade, improving themselves not only in their old manufactures of cottons, but of late of making of drugget, serges, hats, worsted, stockings, &c., whereby many of the poor are daily set on work, and the town much enriched. The inhabitants are generally addicted to sobriety and temperance, and express a thriftiness in their apparel, the women using a plain though decent and handsome dress, above most of their neighbours . . .

This corporation was anciently an alderman town, but being changed in King James I reign, it has ever since been a mayor town, and is now prudently governed by James Simpson Esq., Mayor thereof, Willm Guy, Edwd Turner, To. Towers, Tho. Fisher, Wm Potter, Tho. Jackson, John Park, Tho. Turner, Stephen Birkett, James Troughton, Willm Collinson, and John Jefferson, aldermen of the said town, with 20 common council men, assisted by Tho. Braithwaite Esq. Recorder, and Mr. Allan, Town-clerk, and two Attornies, who still attend at their sessions and courts of record; herein are also a sword-bearer, two serjeants-at-mace, two chamberlains, three constables, and six overseers for the poor. In this town are seven companies, viz. Mercers, Shearmen, Cordwainers, Tanners, Glovers, Taylors, and Pewterers, each of which companies has a Warden, chosen every year, and sworn to see their several trades, and the observation of their orders, having also each of them a several hall, or place belonging to the said companies. Here is quarterly a general sessions of the peace held for this town by the Mayor, Recorder, and two senior Aldermen, who are all justices of the peace for this corporation by their charter. Here, on the side of the churchyard, stands a free school, being a large building, and well endowed through the royal munificence of King Edward VI, Philip and Mary, and especially of Queen Elizabeth, who added to its former revenue out of her own revenues, whose royal example has been influential upon others, as upon Dr Airay, born in this parish, Mr George Fleming, and of late upon Mr James Jackson, formerly schoolmaster here for many years, who has given the interest of 100*l*, to the present school-master, Mr Richard Stewardson, and his successors for ever, besides Mr Henry Wilson, a great benefactor, Mr Charles Jopson, Mr Henry Park, and Mr John Smith, who bestowed good exhibitions for preferring poor scholars going from hence unto Queen's College, in

Oxford, and as charity has thus streamed out for the promoting of learning, so has it towards the poor of this town in many considerable gifts, amongst which that of Mrs Agnes Fleming, of Rydal, in this county, deserves to be mentioned, and that of Mr Thomas Sands (yet living in this town) is the most considerable, for he has lately upon his own charge built a large house, wherein eight ancient widows, skilled in wool work, have each of them a convenient lodging-room, and a room for work, and 4 marks a year in money towards their relief. There is also room for a school-master to read prayers to them, and to teach the poor children of the town, whose parents are not able to pay for their learning, and a yearly stipend settled upon him for the same; and lastly, there is a large room for a library, furnished already with many choice authors, both ancient and modern, to which he is daily adding more. It's a great market for all sorts of provision, &c., on every Saturday, and fairs for cattle on 25th April and 28th October. The country about this town is very pleasant and fruitful, abounding with corn and grass well enclosed, and well stored with good houses, woods, and rivers, divers of them empty themselves into Kent, and with it after a few miles travel incorporate with the ocean.

2. Ambleside, a market chiefly for wool and yarn, erected in the late times of rebellion, and ever since continued its market on every Wednesday, and fairs for cattle every Whitsun-Wednesday, and 18th October . . .

[1] 21 December.

34 A Nonconformist Divine's Account of his Father, 1675

(*The Rev. Oliver Heywood, B.A., 1630–1702. His Autobiography, Diaries, Anecdote and Event Books*, ed. J. Horsfall Turner (Brighouse, 1882), I, pp. 19–22)

An historical account of the family of my honoured father Richard Heywood of Little Leaver in Bolton parish in Lancashire: begun June 9 1675.

My dear and honoured father Richard Heywood was the first born son[1] of Oliver Heywood, by his wife Alice. He was born, as I suppose, about the year 1596.[2] He had a brother and a sister, his sister Mary being lame died about 40 years ago, his brother John is yet alive . . .

My father Richard Heywood, being brought up with his father in the ordinary way of working, and weaving fustians (the trade of that country, though his father was a carpenter), in process of time, God sent Mr Hubbert, a godly minister, to Cockey, a chapel about a mile distant, by whose preaching many were convinced and converted. It pleased the Lord to awaken the heart of my father at that time, and, I hope, to set his feet into the ways of peace, so that ever after that he associated himself with God's people, maintained days and duties of fasting and prayer, conference, and other Christian exercises, so that I can remember that in my childhood there were many days of that nature in my father's house, besides the real evidences he has given of practical piety, which I shall occasionally touch hereafter.

He married my mother, Alice Cretchlaw of Longworth in Bolton parish, about the year 1615, when he was about the age of 19, but my mother was 3 years older than he at their marriage. Good Mr Horrocks preached a nuptial sermon. After their marriage, God, that intended to build them high, laid their foundation low, by first taking from them their first-born son, John, when he was but about a year old. Then afterwards brought them into debt and danger, occasioned by his answering another's debt, whereby he was often forced to skulk in holes and flee. They removed one year from his house to the walk-mill at water-side, for secrecy and security, but it was a sad and afflictive year, partly for poverty, partly for debt and danger, partly for want of godly society. They fared bare, and worked hard, and were often put to shifts, but God had mercy on them, gave them more children, made his father kind to them, and many other friends whom he raised up beyond expectation, and at last the Lord was pleased to disengage and extricate them out of troubles. And my father being thrifty and careful, began to make fustians, which was then a very gainful calling, and after a while God opened a way for his trading to London, and raised up friends and brought him into acquaintance with one Mr Cotton in Milk street, and Mr Cary who was Mr Cotton's servant and afterwards married his daughter. These he traded with, many years, and several others. They got out of debt about the time I was born,[3] as I have oft heard my mother relate, and God did graciously bless them in matters of the world, so that he grew to a considerable estate, and things succeeded comfortably far beyond expectation, and 'tis very strange to consider how God increased him in the world, even while his family was increasing, so that he was carried on to do much beyond expectation, which I shall briefly touch.

1. The first thing he did was purchasing the house and land where he lives, formerly a tenement for lives, but now land, worth about 20*l* a year, which cost about 400*l*.

2. His building houses, barns, and several translations, which was very costly, and took much of his money and estate.

3. Sinking coal-pits in the land, though very costly, for I may say they lay in many hundreds of pounds, and brought little profit.

4. He had 4 daughters whom he married and gave them 60*l* a-piece, and something more, and they were well disposed.

5. Maintaining two sons at the University upon his own proper charges (for we had no preferment) for 4 years a-piece, which could not be less than 300*l* at least.

6. My eldest and youngest brothers who were sometime at London, and both wasteful, and lay him in well towards as much as we that were trained up scholars.

7. Besides all this he laid out a great deal of money, upon a paper-mill, which he confessed cost him 200*l*—besides a walk-mill, which cost much to put into frame, though for want of use it was presently lost.

8. He purchased large quantities of land, which he has since parted with as follows . . . so that the whole by computation of yearly rent or worth . . . which he had in his power comes to above 50*l* a year which he has thus disposed of, besides the land yet in his hands.

I must confess it is matter of great admiration to me to consider what an estate God gave my father that he might accomplish these works for the education of his children, and for training up my good brother and me at the University, and for doing God's service in His church, and when he had done that work He gave it him for, took it quite from him again. His entanglements and troubles in the world returned again upon him in his old age, after this manner. Whilst my own dear mother was living he saw that the fustian trade failed him, and he having a walk-mill in his hands, began to have an itching mind to be dealing with woollen cloth, which was an employment wherein he had not been versed. So he came to Ratchdale every Monday, bought cloth, got it milled, dressed, and sold it at London. He has often told me, he knew how he bought, and how he sold, and was confident he got abundance of money, and yet he says also that it went faster than it came, he saw it, but could not tell how to help it. For himself he has always been exceeding sparing, provident, and forecasting and witty enough for his calling, yet unawares was cast into 1,200*l* debt, which I confess is the strangest thing imaginable, and has been the wonder of many how it should come to pass . . .

[1] Heywood later added: 'I am informed since that my grandfather had an elder son than my father called John, but died young.'
[2] Heywood's father died in 1676.   [3] 1630.

35 The Condition of the Economy, 1676

(William Petty, *Political Arithmetick*, printed in *The Economic Writings of Sir William Petty*, ed. C. H. Hull (Cambridge, 1899), I, pp. 241–4)

Forasmuch as men, who are in a decaying condition, or who have but an ill opinion of their own concernments, instead of being (as some think) the more industrious to resist the evils they apprehend, do contrariwise become the more languid and ineffectual in all their endeavours, neither caring to attempt or prosecute even the probable means of their relief. Upon this consideration, as a member of the commonwealth, next to knowing the precise truth in what condition the common interest stands, I would in all doubtful cases think the best, and consequently not despair, without strong and manifest reasons, carefully examining whatever tends to lessen my hopes of the public welfare.

I have therefore thought fit to examine the following persuasions, which I find too current in the world, and too much to have affected the minds of some, to the prejudice of all, viz.

That the rents of lands are generally fallen; that therefore, and for many other reasons, the whole kingdom grows every day poorer and poorer; that formerly it abounded with gold, but now there is a great scarcity both of gold and silver; that there is no trade nor employment for the people, and yet that the land is under-peopled; that taxes have been many and great; that Ireland and the plantations in America and other additions to the Crown, are a burden to England; that Scotland is of no advantage; that trade in general does lamentably decay; that the Hollanders are at our heels in the race of naval power; the French grow too fast upon both, and appear so rich and potent, that it is but their clemency that they do not devour their neighbours; and finally, that the church and state of England, are in the same danger with the trade of England; with many other dismal suggestions, which I had rather stifle than repeat.

It is true, the expense of foreign commodities has of late been too great; much of our plate, had it remained money, would have better served trade; too many matters have been regulated by laws, which nature, long custom, and general consent, ought only to have governed; the slaughter and destruction of men by the late civil wars and plague have been great; the fire at London, and disaster at Chatham,[1] have begotten opinions in the *vulgus* of the world to our prejudice; the non-conformists increase; the people of Ireland think long of their settlement; the English there apprehend themselves to be aliens, and are forced to seek a trade with foreigners, which they might as well maintain with their own relations in England. But notwithstanding all this (the like whereof was always in all places), the buildings of London grow great and glorious; the American plantations employ four hundred sail of ships; actions in the East-India Company are near double the principal money; those who can give good security, may have money under the statute-interest; materials for building (even oaken-timber) are little dearer, some cheaper for the rebuilding of London; the Exchange seems as full of merchants as formerly; no more beggars in the streets, nor executed for thieves, than heretofore; the number of coaches, and splendour of equipage exceeding former times; the public theatres very magnificent; the king has a greater navy, and stronger guards than before our calamities; the clergy rich, and the cathedrals in repair; much land has been improved, and the price of food so reasonable, as that men refuse to have it cheaper, by admitting of Irish cattle; and in brief, no man needs to want that will take moderate pains. That some are poorer than others, ever was and ever will be: and that many are naturally querulous and envious, is an evil as old as the world.

These general observations, and that men eat, and drink, and laugh as they use to do, have encouraged me to try if I could also comfort others, being satisfied myself, that the interest and affairs of England are in no deplorable condition.

The method I take to do this, is not yet very usual; for instead of using only comparative and superlative words, and intellectual arguments, I have taken the course (as a specimen of the political arithmetic I have long aimed at) to express myself in terms of number, weight, or measure; to use only arguments of sense, and to consider only such causes, as have visible foundations in nature; leaving those that depend upon the mutable minds, opinions, appetites, and passions of particular men, to the consideration of others.

[1] Refers to the Dutch attack in June 1667. (CHH)

36 The Population and its Income, 1695, 1688

(Gregory King, *Natural and Political Observations and Conclusions upon the State and Condition of England*, 1696, appendix to G. Chalmers, *An Estimate of the Comparative Strength of Great Britain* (1804), pp. 33–6, 47)

Whereas the ensuing treatise depends chiefly upon the knowledge of the true number of people in England, and such other circumstances relating thereunto, as have been collected from the assessments on marriages, births, and burials, parish registers, and other public accounts: we shall first exhibit the calculation of the number of people, as they appear by the said assessments.

1st. As to the number of the people of England.

In this calculation, we shall consider,

1. The number of inhabited houses.
2. The number of people to each house.
3. The number of transitory people, and vagrants.

The number of houses in the kingdom, as charged in the books of the Hearth Office at Lady Day,[1] 1690, were . . . 1,319,215.

The kingdom increasing at this time about 9,000 people per annum, as will appear in the ensuing discourse, the increase of houses should be about 2,000 per annum; but, by reason of the present war with France, not much above 1,000 per annum: so that by the year 1695 the increase cannot have been above 6 or 7,000. Which makes the present number of houses, that is to say such as were so charged in the books of the Hearth Office, to be about . . . 1,326,000.

But whereas the chimney money being charged on the tenant or inhabitant, the divided houses stand as so many distinct dwellings in the accounts of the said Hearth Office; and whereas the empty houses, smiths' shops &c. are included in the said account, all which may very well amount to 1 in 36 or 37 (or near 3 per cent) which in the whole may be about 36,000 houses, it follows that the true number of inhabited houses in England, is not above 1,290,000.

Which however in a round number, we shall call 1,300,000
And shall thus apportion,

	Houses
London and the bills of mortality	105,000
The other cities and market towns	195,000
The villages and hamlets	1,000,000

In all 1,300,000

Having thus adjusted the number of inhabited houses, we come to proportion the number of souls to each house according to what we have observed from the said assessments on marriages, births, and burials, in several parts of the kingdom, viz.

That London within the walls produced at a medium almost	5½ souls per house
The 16 parishes without the walls full	4½ souls per house
And the rest of the said bills almost	4½ souls per house

That the other cities and market towns pro-
duced at a medium .... 4½ souls per house
And the villages and hamlets at a medium
about .... 4 souls per house
Accordingly the number of people computed
from the said assessments amounts to .... 5,318,100 souls
As by the following scheme:

	Inhabited houses	Souls per house	Number of souls
The 97 parishes within the walls	13,500	at 5·4	72,900
The 16 parishes without the walls	32,500	at 4·6	149,500
The 15 out parishes in Middlesex and Surrey	35,000	at 4·4	154,000
The 7 parishes in the city and liberty of Westminster	24,000	at 4·3	103,200
So London and the bills of mortality contain	105,000	at 4·57	479,600
The other cities and market towns	195,000	at 4·3	838,500
The villages and hamlets	1,000,000	at 4·	4,000,000
In all	1,300,000	at 4·9	5,318,100

But considering that the omissions in the said assessments may well
be,

In London and the bills of mor-
tality .... 10 per cent or 47,960 souls
In the cities and towns .... 2 per cent or 16,500 souls
In the villages and hamlets................. 1 per cent or 40,000 souls

In all 104,460 souls

it follows that the true number of people dwelling in the 1,300,000
inhabited houses should be 5,422,560 souls.

According to the following scheme

	People by the Assessments	Omissions in the Assessments	Number of people in all	
The 97 parishes	72,900	7,290	80,190	at almost 6 heads per house
The 16 parishes	149,500	14,950	164,450	at above 5 heads per house
The 15 parishes	154,000	15,400	169,400	at above 4·8 heads per house
The 7 parishes............	103,200	10,320	113,520	at almost 4¾ heads per house
The bills of mortality	479,600	47,960	527,560	at above 5 heads per house
The cities and towns	838,500	16,500	855,000	at almost 4·4 heads per house
The villages	4,000,000	40,000	4,040,000	at 4·4 heads per house
Total	5,318,100	104,460	5,422,560	at above 4·17 heads per house

Lastly, whereas the number of transitory people, as seamen and soldiers, may be accounted 140,000, whereof near one half, or 60,000, have no place in the said assessments; and that the number of vagrants, viz. hawkers, pedlars, crate carriers, gipsies, thieves and beggars, may be reckoned 30,000, whereof above one half, or 20,000, may not be taken notice of in the said assessments, making in all 80,000 persons.

It follows that the whole number of the people of England is much about .... 5,500,000 souls

viz. London and the bills of mortality .... 530,000 souls

The other cities and market towns .... 870,000 souls

The villages and hamlets .... 4,100,000 souls

In all 5,500,000 souls

* * *

The Annual Income and Expense of the Nation as it stood *Anno* 1688.

That the yearly income of the nation *anno* 1688 was .... 43,500,000 sterling

That the yearly expense of the nation was 41,700,000

That then the yearly increase of wealth was 1,800,000

That the yearly rent of the lands was about 10,000,000

of the burgage or housing about........................ 2,000,000

of all other hereditaments about 1,000,000

In all 13,000,000

That the yearly produce of trade, arts and labour was about 30,500,000

In all 43,500,000

That the number of inhabited houses being about 1,300,000

The number of families about 1,360,000

And the number of people about............ 5,500,000

The people answer to 4¼ per house, and 4 per family.

That the yearly estates or income of the several families answer

	l	s	d	
In common to about............	32	0	0	per family
And about	7	18	0	per head

That the yearly expense of the nation is about .... 7 11 4 per head

And the yearly increase about............ 6 8 per head

That the whole value of the kingdom in general is about .... 650,000,000 sterling

Viz.

The 13 millions of yearly rents, at about 18 years purchase .... 234,000,000 sterling

The 30 millions and a half per annum by trade, arts, labour &c. at near 11 years purchase (which being the value of the 5 millions and a half of people at 60*l* per head) comes to 330,000,000

The stock of the kingdom in money, plate, jewels and household goods about 28,000,000

The stock of the kingdom in shipping, forts, ammunition, stores, foreign or home goods, wares, and provisions for trade abroad, or consumption at home, and all instruments and materials relating thereunto 33,000,000

The livestock of the kingdom in cattle, beasts, fowl, &c............ 25,000,000

In all 650,000,000 sterling

[1] 25 March.

37 Limited Horizons of Countryfolk, 1698

(*The Journeys of Celia Fiennes*, ed. C. Morris (1949), p. 145)

Thence to Saxmunday [Saxmundham, Suffolk] 8 miles more, this is a pretty big market town, the ways are pretty deep, mostly lanes very little commons . . . so to Bathfort [Blyford] 8 miles . . . [from] thence I passed by some woods and little villages of a few scattered houses, and generally the people here are able to give so bad a direction that passengers are at a loss what aim to take, they know scarce 3 mile from their home . . .

38 The Foundations of Public Credit, 1711

(Joseph Addison, *The Spectator*, ed. D. F. Bond (Oxford, 1965), I, pp. 14–17)

In one of my late rambles, or rather speculations, I looked into the great hall where the bank is kept, and was not a little pleased to see the directors, secretaries, and clerks, with all the other members of that wealthy corporation, ranged in their several stations, according to the parts they act in that just and regular economy. This revived in my memory the many discourses which I had both read and heard concerning the decay of public credit, with the methods of restoring it, and which, in my opinion, have always been defective, because they have always been made with an eye to separate interests, and party principles.

The thoughts of the day gave my mind employment for the whole night, so that I fell insensibly into a kind of methodical dream, which disposed all my contemplations into a vision or allegory, or what else the reader shall please to call it.

Methought I returned to the great hall, where I had been the morning before, but, to my surprise, instead of the company that I left there, I saw towards the upper end of the hall, a beautiful virgin seated on a throne of gold. Her name (as they told me) was Public Credit. The walls, instead of being adorned with pictures and maps, were hung with many acts of Parliament written in golden letters. At the upper-end of the hall was the Magna Carta, with the Act of Uniformity on the right hand, and the Act of Toleration on the left. At the lower-end of the hall was the Act of Settlement,[1] which was placed full in the eye of the virgin that sat upon the throne. Both the sides of the hall were covered with such acts of Parliament as had been made for the establishment of public funds. The lady seemed to set an unspeakable value upon these several pieces of furniture, insomuch that she often refreshed her eye with them, and often smiled with a secret pleasure, as she looked upon them; but, at the same time, showed a very particular uneasiness, if she saw anything approaching that might hurt them. She appeared indeed infinitely timorous in all her behaviour: and, whether it was from the delicacy of her constitution, or that she was troubled with vapours, as I was afterwards told by one who I found was none of her well-wishers, she changed colour, and startled at every thing she heard. She was likewise (as I afterwards found) a greater valetudinarian than any I had ever met with, even in her own sex, and subject to such momentary consumptions, that in the twinkling of an eye, she would fall away from the most florid complexion, and the most healthful state of body, and wither into a skeleton. Her recoveries were often as sudden as her decays, insomuch that she would revive in a moment out of a wasting distemper, into a habit of the highest health and vigour.

I had very soon an opportunity of observing these quick turns and changes in her constitution. There sat at her feet a couple of secretaries, who received every hour letters from all parts of the world, which the one or the other of them was perpetually reading to her; and, according to the news she heard, to which she was exceedingly attentive, she changed colour, and discovered many symptoms of health or sickness.

Behind the throne was a prodigious heap of bags of money, which were piled upon one another so high that they touched the ceiling. The floor, on her right hand, and on her left, was covered with vast sums of gold that rose up in pyramids on either side of her: but this I did not so much wonder at, when I heard, upon enquiry, that she had the same virtue in her touch, which the poets tell us a Lydian king was formerly possessed of; and that she could convert whatever she pleased into that precious metal.

After a little dizziness, and confused hurry of thought, which a man often meets with in a dream, methought the hall was alarmed, the doors flew open, and there entered half a dozen of the most hideous phantoms that I had ever seen (even in a dream) before that time. They came in two by two, though matched in the most dissociable manner, and mingled together in a kind of dance. It would be tedious to describe their habits and persons, for which reason I shall only inform my reader that the first couple were Tyranny and Anarchy, the second were Bigotry and Atheism, the third the Genius of a Common-Wealth, and a young man of about twenty-two years of age,[2] whose name I could not learn. He had a sword in his right hand, which in the dance he often brandished at the Act of Settlement; and a citizen, who stood by me, whispered in my ear, that he saw a sponge in his left hand. The dance of so many jarring natures put me in mind of the sun, moon and earth, in the *Rehearsal*, that danced together for no other end but to eclipse one another.

The reader will easily suppose, by what has been before said, that the lady on the throne would have been almost frighted to distraction, had she seen but any one of these spectres; what then must have been her condition when she saw them all in a body? She fainted and died away at the sight.

There was as great a change in the hill of money bags, and the heaps of money, the former shrinking, and falling into so many empty bags, that I now found not above a tenth part of them had been filled with money. The rest that took up the same space, and made the same figure as the bags that were really filled with money, had been blown up with air, and called into my memory the bags full of wind, which Homer tells us his hero received as a present from Æolus. The great heaps of gold, on either side the throne, now appeared to be only heaps of paper, or little piles of notched sticks, bound up together in bundles, like bath-faggots.

Whilst I was lamenting this sudden desolation that had been made before me, the whole scene vanished: in the room of the frightful spectres, there now entered a second dance of apparitions very agreeably matched together, and made up of very amiable phantoms. The first pair was Liberty, with Monarchy at her right hand: the second was Moderation leading in Religion; and the third a person whom I had never seen,[3] with the Genius of Great Britain. At their first entrance the lady revived, the bags swelled to their former bulk, the piles of faggots and heaps of paper changed into pyramids of guineas: and for my own part I was so transported with joy, that I awaked, though I must confess I would fain have fallen asleep again to have closed my vision, if I could have done it.

[1] Guaranteeing the Protestant Succession, through the Electress Sophia and her descendants. (DFB)

[2] The Pretender. (DFB)

[3] George, son of the Electress, who had never visited Britain. (DFB)

39 The Trading Part of the People, 1726

(Daniel Defoe, *The Complete English Tradesman* (1726), pp. 372–7)

As to the wealth of the nation, that undoubtedly lies chiefly among the trading part of the people; and though there are a great many families raised within few years, in the late war by great employments, and by great actions abroad, to the honour of the English gentry; yet how many more families among the tradesmen have been raised to immense estates, even during the same time, by the attending circumstances of the war? such as the clothing, the paying, the victualling and furnishing, &c. both army and navy? And by whom have the prodigious taxes been paid, the loans supplied, and money advanced upon all occasions? By whom are the banks and companies carried on? And on whom are the customs and excises levied? Has not the trade and tradesmen borne the burden of the war? And do they not still pay four millions a year interest for the public debts? On whom are the funds levied, and by whom the public credit supported? Is not trade the inexhausted fund of all funds, and upon which all the rest depend?

As is the trade, so in proportion are the tradesmen; and how wealthy are tradesmen in almost all the several parts of England, as well as in London? How ordinary is it to see a tradesman go off of the stage, even but from mere shop-keeping, with, from ten to forty thousand pounds estate, to divide among his family? When, on the contrary, take the gentry in England from one end to the other, except a few here and there, what with excessive high living, which is of late grown so much into a disease, and the other ordinary circumstances of families, we find few families of the lower gentry, that is to say, from six or seven hundred a year downwards, but they are in debt and in necessitous circumstances, and a great many of greater estates also.

On the other hand, let any one who is acquainted with England, look but abroad into the several counties, especially near London, or within fifty miles of it. How are the ancient families worn out by time and family misfortunes, and the estates possessed by a new race of trades-men, grown up into families of gentry, and established by the immense wealth, gained, as I may say, behind the counter; that is, in the shop, the warehouse, and the counting-house? How are the sons of tradesmen ranked among the prime of the gentry? How are the daughters of tradesmen at this time adorned with the ducal coronets, and seen riding in the coaches of the best of our nobility? Nay, many of our trading gentlemen at this time refuse to be ennobled, scorn being knighted, and content themselves with being known to be rated among the richest commoners in the nation. And it must be acknowledged, that whatever they be as to court-breeding, and to manners, they, generally speaking, come behind none of the gentry in knowledge of the world.

At this very day we see the son of Sir Thomas Scawen matched into the ducal family of Bedford, and the son of Sir James Bateman into the princely house of Marlborough, both whose ancestors, within the memory of the writers of these sheets, were tradesmen in London; the first Sir William Scawen's apprentice, and the latter's grandfather a P . . . . . . upon, or near, London-Bridge.

How many noble seats, superior to the palaces of sovereign princes (in some countries) do we see erected within few miles of this city by tradesmen, or the sons of tradesmen, while the seats and castles of the ancient gentry, like their families, look worn out, and fallen into decay; witness the noble house of Sir John Eyles, himself a merchant, at Giddy Hall near Romford; Sir Gregory Page on Blackheath, the son of a brewer; Sir Nathaniel Mead near Wealgreen, his father a linen-draper, with many others, too long to repeat; and to crown all, the Lord Castlemain's at Wanstead, his father Sir Josiah Child originally a tradesman.

It was a smart, but just repartee of a London tradesman, when a gentleman, who had a good estate too, rudely reproached him in company, and bade him hold his tongue, for he was no gentleman; No, Sir, says he, but I can buy a gentleman, and therefore I claim a liberty to speak among gentlemen.

*　　*　　*

Trade is so far here from being inconsistent with a gentleman, that in short trade in England makes gentlemen, and has peopled this nation with gentlemen; for after a generation or two the tradesmen's children, or at least their grandchildren, come to be as good gentlemen, statesmen, parliament-men, privy counsellors, judges, bishops, and noblemen, as those of the highest birth and the most ancient families; and nothing too high for them. Thus the late Earl of Haversham was originally a merchant, the late Secretary Craggs was the son of a barber; the present Lord Castlemain's father was a tradesman; the great grandfather of the present Duke of Bedford the same, and so of several others. Nor do we find any defect either in the genius or capacities of the posterity of tradesmen, arising from any remains of mechanic blood, which it is pretended should influence them; but all the gallantry of spirit, greatness of soul, and all the generous principles, that can be found in any of the ancient families, whose blood is the most untainted, as they call it, with the low mixtures of a mechanic race, are found in these; and, as is said before, they generally go beyond them in knowledge of the world, which is the best education.

40 Riots at Coalbrookdale, 1756

(Letter of Hannah Darby, Rathbone MSS., printed in A. Raistrick, *Dynasty of Iron Founders. The Darbys and Coalbrookdale* (1953), pp. 78–9)   [n.d.]

My dear Aunt,

Being apprehensive that you may hear of the tumult which has happened here we are willing to inform you of the particulars, as such things generally gain much by carriage. The affair was this; this day week, the 1st inst. we were somewhat alarmed in the morning with an account that the colliers at Brewsley were rose and consternation was greatly increased soon by fresh accounts that the Madely Wood as well as our own colliers had joined them, and we plainly could hear the dismal sound of blowing of horns which is their signal. Their pretended reason for rising was to lower the price of corn so accordingly they went in a body to Wenlock market and there gave the farmers two hours to consider whether they would sell their wheat at 5s per bushel or have it took from them. Some of them refused the first proposition so they took it, but did not commit any great outrage that day. The next morning they went to Shiffnal market and in their way called at an old justice, Jourdans, and obliged him to ride in the midst of them to the market where they committed great outrages, they broke open houses, barns etc and took anything they could meet with. In this day's expedition some of our Dale workmen was with them. The next day was Brewsley market where they were if possible worse than ever; they got into the bakers' shops, took some bread and some threw it away; here the gentlemen read the proclamation. When they had done the mob gave a loud huzza and told them they neither valued them nor it. And today they began to visit us both in going and coming; they behaved pretty civil, only asking for meat and drink which we were glad to give them to keep them quiet; they threatened that they would destroy the Dale Works if our men would not join them the next day to go to Wellington market—to prevent which my father gave one of our clerks 20 guineas to have given the ringleaders had they offered such a thing, but they did not, he also deputed to stand with money in their hands to give them at our lower gate to prevent them coming up to the house for fear of frightening my mother. Where they were to have drink this did with a few but the numbers increased so fast that they all came running up like wild things where we employed several men in carrying them pailfuls of drink. This was as they went to Wellington where they became quite plunderers. They not only took from them that sold anything, but went into private peoples' houses and took away money, pewter, silver, plate or anything they could meet with. They also plundered farms' houses or any outhouses they met with. They came back in droves loaded with booty and I believe most of them called at our house but did not offer any violence—several hundreds had meat and drink this time. We baked bread three days together and sent several miles for it besides, for there was not a bit of bread nor corn nor flour to be had for money, for some miles about—so that the country was in the greatest distress. The mob gave themselves the title of levellers and so they were indeed. This night the gentlemen mustered up several hundred men, to suppress them, they were all armed and marched up our railway, they made a formidable appearance. They met with the mob at Ketley and they stood three fires before they fled. That morning they had agreed to plunder all our houses, they intended to have begun with our house and so have gone quite through, but through Divine favour were prevented. They have took many of them prisoners, and we hope it's all over, though we have had several alarms since. I intend to write again soon for can't say more now. We are pretty well. All join me in love to you.

Post waits.   H. Darby

2
The Agrarian Economy
1000–1485

England was widely settled by the eleventh century and agrarian activity remained the basis of the economy throughout the period and beyond. There were great regional variations in land use and methods of cultivation. Although parts of the country were subject to forest law (7), large areas of central England were covered by open fields which predated the Conquest (1). They comprised strips of land (5) and were worked in common (23). The emphasis was on cereal production but sheep farming was always important and from the later twelfth century the monastic houses of the North became leading wool producers (9). The arable economy was complemented by the keeping of livestock which, besides providing draught power, supplied manure which, in farming with rudimentary techniques, was essential as a fertiliser (17). In the thirteenth century the area under cultivation expanded at the expense of both waste and common pasture land in which enclosures were made (8). The frontiers of cultivation receded in the early fourteenth century as unprofitable marginal lands fell back into disuse. After the Black Death land was left uncultivated but in some areas the pressure of population on land was such that vacated holdings were taken up (20). At the end of the period there were moves to pastoral farming and stock rearing which were accompanied in limited parts of the Midlands by the enclosure of the open fields and depopulation (24).

Since most of the surviving records of agrarian life refer to the large estates of both lay and ecclesiastical landholders on which the lord's demesne was worked by dependent tenants, it is on these lands that we are best informed. The economic regime and level of tenant obligations varied considerably (1–4). In the twelfth century some estates were leased out (6) but with the rise of demesne farming by landholders in the thirteenth century greater pressure was placed on the tenants and commuted services were resumed (10). Nevertheless even at that time services might be commuted for cash payments (14). Wage labour was

D

drawn upon to supplement the enforced labour services during peak periods of activity in the agrarian calendar (*11*). Powers of lordship often conferred monopoly rights over milling and timber supplies (*18*). Many estates were cultivated on the basis of the individual manors (*13*) and were managed by a hierarchy of officers (*2*, *12*). From the late thirteenth century there was a tendency towards the leasing out of estates (*16*). In the fourteenth century tenants were reluctant to perform labour services (*21*) and the revenue of great rentier lords diminished (*22*). Many small landholders on the other hand prospered and built up estates.

1485–1760

The agrarian economy reveals most strongly the essential continuity of English economic life between 1485 and 1760. The pattern of land use, methods of cultivation, and the structure of landholding underwent change, but in the main very gradually. The passage of the seasons with their regular tasks—ploughing, sowing, lambing, haymaking, harvesting, threshing—gave an abiding rhythm to farming activity. The skills of shepherd, cattleman and ploughman (*29*), were traditional, sanctioned by time, passed on from one generation to the next.

Change and progress, however, are visible in the increasing volume and variety of agricultural output, in the achievement of a grain export surplus from the 1660s, and in the rise of local specialisms. Arable farming continued paramount, but sheep farming was profitable (**1**, *18*, **3**, *25*), and cattle and dairy farming both increased, subject like other branches of agriculture to fluctuating output (*48*). Market gardening (*37*) also figured more. Although villeinage was still to be found in the sixteenth century (*31*), the institutional fabric of the countryside, the system of landowning and landholding, became further modified over time. Private landowners gained at the expense of the Church and, less markedly, the Crown, and by the early eighteenth century a discernible trend existed towards larger estates. Estate stewards were important men, facing manifold problems (*38*, *49*). The more enterprising or commercial landlords, faced with expanding markets for agricultural goods, and pressed in the sixteenth and early seventeenth centuries by inflation and post-1660 by periods of downward-tending prices, maintained or improved their incomes by standing out against custom and themselves putting pressure on tenants and tenancies. Entry fines and rents were raised (*30*, *32*), leasehold was substituted for customary tenures (*27*, *50*), open fields were enclosed and commons expropriated

(*32, 35–6, 50*), measures often exciting opposition from those adversely affected. Tudor and early Stuart governments, whose anxiety over rural change was confined chiefly to questions of vagrancy and the food supply, made enquiries and legislated against the conversion of arable lands to pasture and the consequent depopulation (*28, 34–5*). But from the mid-seventeenth century, as the food supply improved and prices eased, so governmental interest in the countryside waned. Increasingly the division and enclosure of open fields was seen simply as a means to better farming (*43*), an improvement capable of achievement by consent (*45, 50*).

Persistent low wages due to an abundant labour supply—the annual hiring of farm servants was another landmark in the agrarian year (*40*) —discouraged mechanisation in farming. But by the mid-seventeenth century the investment of capital into the land and the adoption of better farming methods became more widely practised, inspired also by a search for income. Agricultural innovation took the form of land reclamation (*41*) and improvement (*42, 52*), convertible husbandry and the watering and floating of meadows (*39*), and the use of clover, artificial grasses and turnips in crop rotations, in the latter case Norfolk long being prominent (*52*). It is easy though to exaggerate movement in the English countryside before 1760, farming continuing to carry a great and inhibiting weight of customary practice and regulation (*33, 51*).

1 Extracts from the Laws of Ine, 688–94[1]

(Printed in *English Historical Documents*, I, ed. D. Whitelock (1955), pp. 365–71)

40. A ceorl's homestead must be fenced winter and summer. If it is not fenced, and his neighbour's cattle get in through his own gap, he has no right to anything from that cattle; he is to drive it out and suffer the damage.

* * *

42. If ceorls have a common meadow or other land divided in shares to fence, and some have fenced their portion and some have not, and [if cattle] eat up their common crops or grass, those who are responsible for the gap are to go and pay to the others, who have fenced their part, compensation for the damage that has been done there. They are to demand with regard to those cattle such reparation as is proper.

42.1. If, however, it is any of the cattle which breaks the hedges and enters anywhere, and he who owns it would not or could not control it, he who finds it on his arable is to seize it and kill it; and the owner is to take its hide and flesh and suffer the loss of the rest.

43. If anyone burns down a tree in the wood, and it is disclosed who did it, he is to pay full fine; he is to pay 60 shillings, for fire is a thief.

43.1. If anyone fells in the wood quite a number of trees, and it afterwards becomes known, he is to pay for three trees at 30 shillings each; he need not pay for more of them however many they were, for the axe is an informer, not a thief.

44. If, however, anyone cuts down a tree under which 30 swine could stand, and it becomes known, he is to pay 60 shillings.

*   *   *

49. If anyone finds swine on his mast-pasture without his permission he is to take then a pledge worth six shillings.

49.1. If, however, they were not there more often than once, the owner is to pay a shilling, and declare that they have not been there more often, by [an oath of] the value of the swine.

49.2. If they were there twice, he is to pay two shillings.

49.3. If one takes pannage in pigs, [one is to take] the third with the bacon three fingers thick, the fourth with it two fingers thick, the fifth with it a thumb thick.

*   *   *

60. The ceorl who has hired another's yoke [of oxen], if he has enough to pay for it entirely in fodder—let one see that he pays in full; if he has not, he is to pay half in fodder, half in other goods.

*   *   *

64. He who has 20 hides must show 12 hides of sown land when he wishes to leave.

65. He who has 10 hides, must show six hides of sown land.

66. He who has three hides is to show one and a half.

67. If anyone covenants for a yardland or more at a fixed rent, and ploughs it, if the lord wishes to increase for him the [rent of the] land by demanding service as well as rent, he need not accept it, if he does not give him a dwelling; and he is to forfeit the crops.

*   *   *

70.1. As a food-rent from 10 hides: 10 vats of honey, 300 loaves, 12 'ambers' of Welsh ale, 30 of clear ale, 2 full-grown cows, or 10 wethers,

10 geese, 20 hens, 10 cheeses, an 'amber' full of butter, 5 salmon, 20 pounds of fodder and 100 eels.

[1] These laws survive as a supplement to the laws of Alfred, 871–899.

2 Rights and Duties of All Persons, c.1000

(*Rectitudines Singularum Personarum*, Cambridge, Corpus Christi College MS. 383)

The Thegn's Law The thegn's law is that he be worthy of his book-right,[1] and that he do three things for his land, fyrdfare,[2] burhbote[3] and bridge-work. Also from many lands a greater land-service arises at the king's command, such as the deer-hedge at the king's abode and provision of warships and sea-ward and head-ward[4] and fyrd-ward, almsfee and churchscot, and many other diverse things.

The Geneat's Service Geneat-service is diverse according to the custom of the estate. On some he must pay land-gafol[5] and grass-swine[6] yearly, and ride and carry and lead loads, work and feast the lord, and reap and mow, and cut the deer-hedge and maintain it, build and hedge the burh,[7] bring strange wayfarers to the tun, pay churchscot and almsfee, keep head-ward and horse-ward, go errands far and near whithersoever he be told.

The Cottar's Service The cottar's service is according to the custom of the estate. On some he must work for his lord each Monday throughout the year and for three days each week in harvest. On some he works through the whole harvest every day and reaps an acre of oats for a day's work, and he shall have his sheaf which the reeve or lord's servant will give him. He ought not to pay land-gafol. It befits him to have 5 acres; more if it be the custom of the estate; and if it be less, it is too little, because his work shall be oft required; he shall pay his hearth-penny on Holy Thursday as all free men should; and he shall defend his lord's inland,[8] if he be required, from sea-ward and the king's deer-hedge and from such things as befit his degree; and he shall pay his churchscot at Martinmas.[9]

The Gebur's Services The gebur's services are diverse, in some places heavy, in others moderate; on some estates he must work two days at week-work at such work as is bidden him every week throughout the year, and in harvest three days at week-work, and from Candlemas[10] to Easter three. If he do carrying, he need not work while his horse is out. He must pay on Michaelmas[11] Day 10 gafol-pence, and on Martinmas Day 23 sesters of barley and two henfowls, at Easter a young sheep or two pence; and from Martinmas to Easter he must lie at the lord's fold as often as his turn comes; and from the time of the first ploughing to Martinmas he must plough an acre every week and himself fetch the seed in the lord's barn; also 3 acres at boonwork and 2 for grass-earth;[12] if he need more grass, he shall earn it as he shall be allowed; for his gafol-earth he shall plough 3 acres[13] and sow it from his own barn; and he shall pay his hearthpenny; two and two they shall feed a hunting-hound; and every gebur shall pay 6 loaves to the lord's swineherd when he drives his herd to mast. On the same lands where the above customs hold good, it belongs to the gebur that he be given for his landstock[14] 2 oxen and 1 cow and 6 sheep and 7 acres sown on his yardland; wherefore after that year he shall do all the customs that befit him; and he shall be given tools for his work and vessels for his house. When death befalls him, his lord shall take back the things which he leaves.

This land-law holds good on some lands, but, as I have said before, in some places it is heavier, in others lighter, for all land-customs are not alike. On some lands the gebur must pay honey-gafol, on some meat-gafol, on some ale-gafol. Let him who keeps the shire take heed that he knows what are the ancient uses of the land and what the custom of the people.

Of those who keep the Bees It belongs to the bee-churl, if he keep the gafol-hives, that he give as is customary on the estate. Among us it is customary that he give 5 sesters of honey for gafol; on some estates more gafol is wont to be rendered. Also he must be oft ready for many works at the lord's will, besides boon-ploughing and bedrips[15] and meadow-mowing; and if he be well landed, he must have a horse that he may lend it to the lord for carrying or drive it himself whithersoever he be told; and many things a man so placed must do; I cannot now tell all. When death befalls him, the lord shall have back the things which he leaves, save what is free.

Of the Swineherd It belongs to the gafol-paying swineherd that he give of his slaughter according to the custom of the estate. On many estates the custom is that he give every year 15 swine for sticking, 10 old and 5 young, and have himself what he breeds beyond that. To many estates a heavier swine-service belongs. Let the swineherd take heed also that after sticking he prepare and singe well his slaughtered swine; then is he right worthy of the entrails, and, as I said before of the bee-keeper, he must be oft ready for any work, and have a horse for his lord's need. The unfree swineherd and the unfree bee-keeper, after death, shall be worthy of one same law.

Of the Serf-Swineherd To the serf-swineherd who keeps the in-herd[16] belong a sucking-pig from the sty and the entrails when he has prepared bacon, and further the customs which befit the unfree.

Of Men's Board To a bondservant belong for board 12 pounds of good corn and 2 sheep-carcases and a good meat-cow, and wood, according to the custom of the estate.

Of Women's Board To unfree women belong 8 pounds of corn for food, one sheep or 3d for winter fare, one sester of beans for Lent fare, in summer whey or 1d.

To all serfs belong a mid-Winter feast and an Easter feast, a plough-acre[17] and a harvest handful, besides their needful dues.

Of Followers[18] It belongs to the follower that in 12 months he earn two acres, the one sown and the other unsown; he shall sow them himself, and his board and provision of shoes and gloves belong to him; if he may earn more, it shall be to his own behoof.

Of the Sower It belongs to the sower that he have a basketful of every kind of seed when he have well sown each sowing throughout the year.

Of the Ox-herd The ox-herd may pasture 2 oxen or more with the lord's herd in the common pastures by witness of his ealdorman;[19] and thereby may earn shoes and gloves for himself; and his meat-cow may go with the lord's oxen.

Of the Cow-herd It belongs to the cow-herd that he have an old cow's milk for seven days after she has newly calved, and the beestings[20] for fourteen nights; and his meat-cow shall go with the lord's cow.

Of Sheep-herds The sheep-herd's right is that he have 12 nights' manure at mid-Winter and 1 lamb of the year's increase, and the fleece of 1 bellwether and the milk of his flock for seven nights after the equinox and a bowlful of whey or buttermilk all the summer.

Of the Goat-herd To the goat-herd belongs his herd's milk after Martinmas Day and before that his share of whey and one kid of the year's increase, if he have well cared for his herd.

Of the Cheese-maker To the cheese-maker belong 100 cheeses, and that she make butter of the wring-whey[21] for the lord's table; and she shall have for herself all the buttermilk save the herd's share.

Of the Barn-keeper To the barn-keeper belong the corn-droppings in harvest at the barn-door, if his ealdorman give it him and he faith-fully earn it.

Of the Beadle It belongs to the beadle that for his office he be freer from work than another man, for that he must be oft ready; also to him belongs a strip of land for his toil.

Of the Woodward   To the woodward belongs every windfall-tree.

Of the Hayward   To the hayward it belongs that his toil be rewarded with land at the ends of the fields that lie by the pasture meadow; for he may expect that if he first neglects this, to his charge will be laid damage to the crops; and if a strip of land be allowed to him, this shall be by folk-right next the pasture meadow, for that if out of sloth he neglect his lord, his own land shall not be well defended, if it be found so; but if he defend well all that he shall hold, then shall he be right worthy of a good reward.

Land-laws are diverse, as I said before, nor do we fix for all places these customs that we have before spoken of, but we shew forth what is accustomed there where it is known to us; if we learn aught better, that will we gladly cherish and keep, according to the customs of the place where we shall then dwell; for gladly should he learn the law among the people, who wishes not himself to lose honour in the country. Folk-customs are many; in some places there belong to the people winter-feast, Easter-feast, boon-feast for harvest, a drinking feast for plough-ing, rick-meat,[22] mowing reward, a wainstick at wood-loading, a stack-cup[23] at corn-loading, and many things that I cannot number. But this is a reminder for men, yea, all that I have set forth above.

[1] The right conferred by his book or charter. (B, B, T, and other notes also)
[2] Military service.   [3] Repair of the king's castles or boroughs.
[4] Guard of the king's person.   [5] Rent.   [6] Payment for pasturing swine.
[7] The lord's house.   [8] i.e. acquit his lord's inland or demesne.
[9] 11 November.   [10] 2 February.   [11] 29 September.   [12] Pasture-land.
[13] i.e. he must plough 3 acres as his rent.   [14] Outfit.
[15] Reaping at the lord's command.   [16] The lord's herd.
[17] An acre for ploughing.   [18] A free but landless retainer.   [19] The reeve.
[20] The first milk of a milch-cow after calving.
[21] The residue after the last pressing of the cheese.
[22] A feast on the completion of the hayrick.
[23] Probably a feast at the completion of corn-stacking.

3 Labour Services at Hurstbourne Priors, c.1050[1]

(Printed in *Anglo-Saxon Charters*, ed. A. J. Robertson (Cambridge, 1939), p. 207)

Here are recorded the dues which the peasants must render at Hurst-bourne.[2] First from every hide [they must render] 40 pence at the autumnal equinox, and 6 church *mittan*[3] of ale and 3 sesters[4] of wheat for bread, and [they must] plough 3 acres in their own time and sow them with their own seed and bring it to the barn in their own time, and [give] 3 pounds of barley as rent, and [mow] half an acre of meadow as rent in their own time, and make it into a rick, and [supply] 4 fothers[5] of split wood as rent, made into a stack in their own time, and [supply] 16 poles of fencing as rent, likewise in their own time, and at Easter [they shall give] two ewes with two lambs—and we [reckon] two young sheep to a full-grown sheep—and they must wash the sheep and shear them in their own time, and work as they are bidden every week except three—one at midwinter, the second at Easter, the third at the Rogation Days.

[1] The document was included in a charter of Edward the Elder, dated 900.
[2] Hampshire.   [3] A measure of unknown quantity, containing two ambers.
[4] A dry or liquid measure.   [5] Cart-loads.

4 The Domesday Inquest, 1086

(a) The Form (*Inquisitio Eliensis, Domesday Book, Additamenta*, p. 497)

Here below is written the inquest of the lands, in what manner the king's barons enquire, to wit, by the oath of the sheriff of the shire, and of all the barons and their Frenchmen and of the whole hundred, of the priest, the reeve, six villeins of each town. Then how the manor is named; who held it in the time of King Edward; who holds it now; how many hides; how many ploughs on the demesne, and how many of the men; how many villeins; how many cottars; how many serfs; how many freemen; how many sokemen;[1] how much wood; how much meadow; how many pastures; how many mills; how many fishponds; how much has been added or taken away; how much it was worth altogether; and how much now; how much each freeman or sokeman there had or has. All this for three periods; to wit, in the time of King Edward; and when King William granted it; and as it is now; and if more can be had therefrom than is had.

[1] Tenants holding by socage, a free tenure involving the obligation of suit of court.

(b) The Manors of Barrington and Orwell, Cambridgeshire (*Domesday Book*, I, pp. 196–7, printed in *The Victoria County History of Cambridgeshire and the Isle of Ely*, I (1938), p. 382)

In Barrington Robert Gernon holds 7 hides and 2 and a half virgates. There is land for 11 ploughs. [There are] 3 and a half hides and two parts of a virgate in demesne, and there is 1 plough here and there might be another. Here 20 villeins with 7 bordars and 3 cottars have 9 ploughs. [There are] 2 serfs here and 1 and a half mills worth 32s, [and] meadow for 6 ploughs. In all it is worth 12l. When received [it was worth] 8l; in the time of King Edward [it was worth] 16l. There were 15 sokemen in this land who held 4 hides and 1 and a half virgates from King E[dward] and provided 12 and a half carrying-services and 4 watchmen, and 4 others, the men of Earl Algar, held 2 hides and half a virgate, and 3 others, the men of Asgar the Staller, held 1 hide. All these men could give and sell their land. Edric Pur also held 3 virgates of this land under King Edward and could sell [it], and the same Edric held half a virgate which on the day of King Edward's death pertained to the church of Chatteris. Robert Gernon usurped this in defiance of the abbess, as the men of the hundred bear witness.

In Orwell Robert holds 1 virgate. There is land for 3 oxen which are here with 2 bordars. [There is] meadow for 2 oxen, and 1 mill worth 12s. It is and always was worth 18s and 8d. One of King E[dward]'s sokemen held this land. He provided 1 carrying-service, and nevertheless could sell his land.

(c) The Manor of Rockland, Norfolk (*Domesday Book*, II, p. 164)

In Rockland Simon holds 3 carucates[1] of land which one freeman, Brode, held in the time of King Edward. Then as now 2 villeins and 12 bordars.[2] Then 4 serfs, now 1, and 8 acres of meadow; then as now 2 ploughs on the demesne and 1 plough among the men. Wood for 6 swine. Then 4 rounceys,[3] now none. Then 8 beasts, now 5. Then 30 swine, now 15. Then 100 sheep, and now likewise. And in the same [town] the same Simon holds 6 freemen and a half, whom the same Brode had in commendation only; 70 acres of land and 4 acres of meadow; then as now 1 plough and a half. Of these 6 freemen and a half the soke[4] was in the king's [manor of] Buckenham in the time of King Edward, and afterwards, until William de Warenne had it. Then and always they were worth 3l 10s.

After this there were added to this land 9 freemen and a half, 1 carucate of land, 54 acres, this is in demesne; then as now 9 bordiers and 8 acres of meadow; then as now 6 ploughs, and 2 half mills. The whole of this is [reckoned] for one manor of Lewes and is worth 3l 11s. Of four and a half of the 9 freemen the soke and commendation was in the king's [manor of] Buckenham in the time of King Edward, and afterwards, until William de Warenne had it, and the whole was delivered in the time of Earl Ralph. The whole is 1 league in length and a half in breadth, and [pays] 15*d* of geld.

[1] In the north and east of England, where Scandinavian influence was felt, land was measured in carucates and bovates. The carucate, the equivalent of the hide, comprised eight bovates or oxgangs.
[2] Bordars, like cottars, were small holders.
[3] Horses. (B, B, T)   [4] Jurisdiction.

(d) The Manor of Tavistock, Devon (*Exon. Domesday*, f. 177, printed in *The Victoria County History of the County of Devon*, I (1906), pp. 429–30)

The abbot of Tavistock has a manor called Tavistock which paid geld in the time of King Edward for 3 and a half hides. These 40 ploughs can till. Thereof the abbot has half a hide and 5 ploughs in demesne, and the villeins have thereof 1 and a half hides and 14 ploughs. There the abbot has 17 villeins, 20 bordars, 12 serfs, 1 rouncey, 26 beasts, 12 swine, 200 sheep, 30 goats, 1 mill for the service of the abbey, wood[land] 2 leagues in length by 1 in breadth, 16 acres of meadow, and pasture 10 furlongs in length by a like amount in breadth.

Of these 3 and a half hides 6 knights hold 1 and a half hides, which 4 thanes held of the abbot without being able to become independent of the church in the time of King Edward.

Thereof Ermenald has half a virgate. There Ermenald has 1 plough, and his villeins 1 plough, 7 beasts, and 40 sheep.

Ralf has thereof half a virgate, a villein, and 3 coscets,[1] and they have half a plough.

Hugh has half a hide, a third of a virgate, and 1 ferling,[2] and has in demesne 2 ploughs. He has there 1 villein, 6 bordars, and 2 serfs, who have 7 ploughing oxen. Hugh has there 10 beasts, 12 swine, and 60 sheep.

Rotbert has 1 virgate and 2 ferlings, and 1 and a half ploughs in demesne, and the villeins 1 and a half ploughs. There R[otbert] has 3 villeins, 6 bordars, 2 serfs, 12 beasts, 60 sheep, and 20 goats.

Ralf de Tilio has three quarters of a virgate and 1 plough, 1 villein, and 4 bordars, who have 2 oxen, 7 beasts, 30 sheep, and 10 goats.

Gosfrid has 1 ferling, and he has there 1 plough, 1 bordar, 6 beasts, and 30 sheep.

This manor is worth to the abbot 12 pounds a year, to the knights 100 shillings. When the abbot and the knights received it it was worth 14 pounds and 8 pounds respectively.

[1] Cottars.   [2] A quarter of a virgate.

5 An Exchange of Strip Holdings, c.1140–50

(*Documents Illustrative of the Social and Economic History of the Danelaw*, ed. F. M. Stenton (1920), pp. 140–1)

To all sons of Holy Church, present and to come, French and English, Hugh son of Eudes, greeting. Know you that I, with the consent and will of Robert, my son and heir, have granted and given to God and the church of St. Mary of Kirkstead and the monks serving God there half of my demesne arable land of Sturton[1] and half of my demesne meadow of the same vill. But because the strips of my demesne lie intermixed with the lands of my men and because the monks wish to dwell apart from other men, I have therefore gathered together the land of my demesne and the land of my men in the farthest part of the fields towards Minthinges, and I have given it to the monks to have in one place. I have given to my men of Sturton from land of my demesne an exchange for their share of the land, which they had, at their pleasure. Moreover all the land that lies from the outer boundary of the furlong of Thirna as far as the boundary of Baenburch and from the same boundary as far as the boundary of North Sturton, as the aforesaid boundaries march with the boundary of Minthinges, all this I give to the monks as half of my demesne of Sturton, but because that land is inferior I have given them more. All the land within the aforesaid boundaries I give them, except as much meadow as my men have in Domedala. I have also given them common pasture of the said vill and all easements of highways and byways. Similarly I have granted and given them whatever is of my fee within the curtilage of the mill above Beinam and in the millpool, and from the pool as far as *veterem* Beinam, and whatever Ralph the priest of Tateshala gave them of his land. I have given all the aforesaid things to God and the said monks in pure and perpetual alms, free and quit of all secular service and custom and all exaction, for my salvation and of my heirs and all my ancestors. Witnessed by Alan de Creun . . .[2]

[1] Great Sturton, Lincolnshire.   [2] And thirteen others named and many others.

6 Villein Services on a Leased Estate, 1183

(*The Boldon Book*, printed in *The Victoria History of the County of Durham*, I (1905), pp. 327–8)

In Boldon there are twenty-two villeins, every one of whom holds 2 bovates of land of 30 acres and renders 2 shillings and 6 pence of scotpenny and the half of a scot-chalder of oats and 16 pence of averpenny and five wagonloads of wood, and two hens and ten eggs, and works through the whole year three days in the week except Easter and Whitsunweek and thirteen days at Christmastide, and in his works he does in the autumn four boon-days at reaping with his entire household except the housewife and they reap moreover 3 roods of the standing crop of oats and he ploughs 3 roods of oat-stubble and harrows [it]. Every plough [team] of the villeins, also, ploughs 2 acres and harrows [them], and then they have once [only] a dole from the bishop and for that week they are quit of work, but when they make the great boon-days they have a dole. And in their works they harrow when it is necessary and they carry loads, and when they have carried them every man has a loaf of bread; and they mow one day at Houghton in their work until the evening, and then they have a dole. And every two villeins build one booth for the fair of St. Cuthbert. And when they are building lodges and carrying loads of wood they are quit of all other works.

There are twelve cottars there, every one of whom holds 12 acres, and they work through the whole year two days in the week, except at the three feasts aforenamed, and they render twelve hens and sixty eggs.

Robert holds two bovates of 36 acres and renders half a mark. The pinder[1] holds 12 acres and he has a thrave[2] of corn from every plough and he renders 40 hens and 500 eggs.

The mill renders $5\frac{1}{2}$ marks.

The villeins in their work in each year ought to make, if need be, a house 40 feet in length and 15 feet in breadth, and when they make it every man is quit of 4 pence of averpenny.

The whole vill renders 17 shillings of cornage and 1 milch-cow.

The demesne is at farm with stock of 4 ploughs and 4 harrows, and renders for 2 ploughs 16 chalders of wheat and 16 chalders of oats, and 8 chalders of barley, and for the other 2 ploughs 10 marks.

[1] A person in charge of the keeping of the pinfold or pound. (VCH)
[2] A shock or stook of corn. (VCH)

7 The Assize of the Forest, 1184

(W. Stubbs, *Select Charters*, ed. H. W. C. Davis (Oxford, 1913), pp. 186–8)

This is the English assize of the Lord King Henry, son of Maud, which he has made for the protection of his forest and forest game, with the advice and approval of the archbishops and bishops, and of the barons, earls, and nobles of England at Woodstock.

1, In the first place he forbids anyone to offend against him in any particular touching his forests or his forest game; and he desires that no one shall place confidence in the fact that he has hitherto been moderate in his punishment of offenders against his forests and forest game, and has taken from them only their chattels in satisfaction for their offences. For if anyone offends against him in the future and is convicted for his offence, the king will have from him the full measure of justice which was exacted in the time of King Henry, his grandfather.

2, He forbids that anyone shall have bows, arrows, hounds, or harriers in his forests, except by licence from the king or other duly authorised person.

3, He forbids any owner of a wood within King Henry's forest to sell or give away anything out of the wood to its wasting or destruction: but he allows that they may take freely from their woods to satisfy their own needs, provided that they do so without wasting, and under the supervision of the king's forester.

4, The king has commanded that all owners of woods within the boundaries of a royal forest shall appoint suitable foresters to their woods and go surety for them, or else find other suitable sureties capable of making satisfaction for any offences which the forester may commit in matters that concern the lord king. The owners of woods which are outside the forest regard[1] but in which the king's game is protected shall only have men as foresters or keepers of their woods as have sworn to uphold the lord king's assize and to protect his game.

5, The lord king commands his foresters to keep a watchful eye upon the forest holdings of knights and other owners of woods inside the boundaries of a royal forest, to make sure that these woods are not destroyed. If, despite their surveillance, the woods are destroyed, the owners of the woods may be well assured that satisfaction will be taken from no one else, but from their own persons or estates.

6, The lord king has commanded that all his foresters shall take an oath to uphold to the letter, and to the full extent of their powers, this assize which he has made for the protection of his forests, and not to obstruct the knights and other worthy owners when they seek to exercise within their own woods those rights which the king has allowed them.

7, The king has commanded that in every county where he has game, twelve knights shall be appointed as custodians of his game and of his vert[2] and generally to survey the forest; and that four knights shall be appointed to agist[3] his woods and to control and receive the dues from pannage.[4] The king forbids anyone to allow cattle to be pastured in his own woods, where these lie within the boundaries of a forest, before the agisting of the lord king's woods, which takes place during the fifteen days before and the fifteen days after Michaelmas.[5]

8, The king has commanded that where any of the demesne woods of the lord king are destroyed and the forester in charge of them is unable to account satisfactorily for their destruction, he shall not be fined, but shall answer with his body.

9, The king forbids any clerk in holy orders to offend against him in respect of his forests or of his forest game. He has given strict instructions to his foresters that they shall not hesitate to lay hands upon such persons, if they find them offending, in order to restrain them and secure their arrest; and he will cover them fully in their actions by his personal warrant.

10, The king has commanded that surveys shall be made of old and new assarts[6] and of purprestures[7] and of forest damage generally, and that each item of damage shall be separately recorded.

11, The king has commanded that earls, barons, knights, freeholders, and all men shall come when summoned by his master forester to hear the pleas of the lord king concerning his forests and to conduct his other business in the county court. If they fail to attend, they will be at the lord king's mercy.

12, At Woodstock, the king commanded that for a first and second forest offence a man shall give safe pledges, but that for a third offence no further pledges shall be taken from him, nor shall he be allowed any other manner of satisfaction, but he shall answer with his own body.

13, The king commands that all males over twelve years of age who live within an area where game is protected shall take an oath for the protection of game. Clerks in holy orders with lay holdings within the area shall not be exempt from taking the oath.

14, The king commands that wherever his wild animals are protected, or have customarily enjoyed protection, mastiffs shall be lawed.[8]

15, The king commands that no tanner or bleacher of hides shall be resident in his forests, except in a borough.

16, The king absolutely forbids that anyone in future shall hunt wild animals by night, with a view to their capture, in areas where his wild animals are protected or outside these areas in places where they are often to be found or where protection was formerly applied, on penalty of one year's imprisonment or the payment of a fine and ransom at the king's pleasure; or that anyone, at the risk of incurring this same penalty, shall set traps for the king's wild animals, using dead or live animals as bait, anywhere within the king's forests and woods, or within areas which used to form part of a forest, but were later disafforested by the king or his progenitors.

¹ A triennial inspection of woods within the forest bounds by 12 knights.
² Green vegetation which provided cover for deer etc.
³ To arrange the pasturing of livestock.   ⁴ Payment for feeding swine.
⁵ From 15th September to 14th October.
⁶ Woodland or waste cleared for cultivation.
⁷ Encroachment on forest waste or common land.
⁸ i.e. have the claws and three toes of their forefeet cut to prevent their being used in the forest.

8 The Taking-In of Waste Land, 1216–36

(*Thorney Red Book*, I, ff. 186v.–187, printed in E. Miller, *The Abbey and Bishopric of Ely* (Cambridge, 1951), p. 289)

Be it known to all faithful in Christ seeing or hearing this present writing that it has thus been agreed between the abbot and convent of Thorney on the one hand and Walter the son of Walter, Alan de Fitton', John the son of Geoffrey, William the son of Robert, Adam the son of Lewin, John the clerk, Geoffrey de Cruce, Peter the son of William, Robert de Fittun', Ralph Rote, Ellis the son of Geoffrey, Roger the son of Maud, Thomas the son of Walter, Thomas the son of Gothe, Adam the son of John, Alexander the son of Alured, Walter Rote, Adam de Cruce, Peter Franceys, Alan the son of Ralph, and Adam Catting and all their associates on the other in Leverington: namely that the aforesaid men and their associates have granted to the aforesaid abbot of Thorney 30 acres of land close to Trokenholt in the new purpresture, between the droveway that comes from the land of Gervase de Runmere and the old bank of Fulhilt, in name of the twenty-fifth part belonging to the abbot and convent in the same purpresture. And if the said men or their heirs shall make another purpresture in the marsh of Leverington between the old bank and the boundary between them and Wisbech, the said abbot and convent of Thorney and their successors will have their twenty-fifth part. The said men have also granted that all the demesne of the said abbot and convent around Trokenholt will be drained by the same sewer with which they drain their own lands. That the confirmation of this agreement will be observed faithfully and without fraud, Robert, by the grace of God, abbot of Thorney attached his seal together with the aforesaid seals of Walter and Alan, to this writing made in the manner of a chirograph. The aforesaid men took an oath, touching holy relics, for

themselves, their heirs and associates to observe this agreement faithfully. These witnesses, Sir Roger of Causton, then constable of Wisbech . . .[1]

[1] And twelve others named.

9 Monastic Sheep-Farming, 1221-35

(*Chronica Monasterii de Melsa*,[1] I, ed. E. A. Bond, *Rolls Series* (1866),
p. 430)

Meanwhile John, the son of John of Ockton, was harassing us in the
court of the lord king because we attempted to exercise the right of
pasture for 500 sheep in Ockton, besides the pasture belonging to our
land there. On the contrary the said John maintained that the right of
pasture granted to us for 500 sheep was the same pasture which belonged to our land there according to the custom of the place. Concerning which, when [our] differences had been settled, we released to
the aforesaid John in the court of the lord king the same pasture for
500 sheep, yet saving to us the pasture belonging to 30 bovates of land
which we possess there. And the aforesaid John confirmed to us three
carucates which we hold there of the fee of Godfrey of Harpham, and
the six bovates of land which we were holding of him, for which we
were accustomed to render foreign service, and he also released to us
in pure alms the service itself quit of all service, and he granted to us
as much common pasture in the same vill as belongs to the aforesaid
lands, namely the 30 bovates of land which we hold there.

[1] Meaux Abbey, Yorkshire.

10 Resumption of Labour Services, 1237-8

(*Bracton's Note Book*, III, ed. F. W. Maitland (1887), pp. 250-1)

The men of the prior and convent of St. Swithin of Crondall, Hurst-
bourne and Whitchurch, complained to the lord the king that whereas
they had been granted to the same prior and convent and their church
in pure and perpetual alms by the ancestors of the lord the king, the
prior and convent demanded of them other customs and services than
they used to do in the times in which they were in the hands of the
aforesaid predecessors . . .

And Oliver the steward and Horder come and say that they demand
no other services than the men used and ought to do, and that the lands

were never in the hands of the ancestors of the lord the king, because
two hundred years before the conquest of England they were given to
the prior and convent of St. Swithin and by others than kings, to wit,
earls and others . . . and then they owed and used to do whatever was
commanded them. But in process of time, when the priory was well
nigh destroyed by one Abbot Robert,[1] Bishop Richard came and for
the profit of the prior and convent disposed of their lands and manors
in such wise that he caused an inventory to be made of the holdings and
of the names of the tenants and their services, as well tenants in villeinage as in frank fee, and he demanded no other services than they
did then and were then set forth in the inventory. Afterwards however
when the lands were in the hand of farmers at one time and at one
time in the hand of the aforesaid villeins for forty years, the farmers
remitted to them certain services and customs for money. And when
the lands were in the hand of the aforesaid villeins they detained and
withheld the rent to the sum of 60s and more, and also a great amount
of corn, and withheld a great amount of the lands contrary to the
aforesaid enrolment made by the aforesaid Bishop Richard. And because the aforesaid men acknowledge that they are villeins, as is aforesaid, and because they cannot deny these things, they are told to do to
the prior and convent the services and customs which they used to do.
And the lord the king will not meddle with them since they were never
in the hand of him or his ancestors . . .

[1] 1174–88.

11 Wage Labour at Haymaking and Harvesting, c.1250

(*Hosebonderie*, printed in *Walter of Henley's Husbandry together with
an anonymous husbandry, Seneschaucie and Robert Grosseteste's Rules*,
ed. Elizabeth Lamond (1890), p. 69)

How one must pay labourers in August and in time of haymaking

You can well have three acres weeded for a penny, and an acre of
meadow mown for fourpence, and an acre of waste meadow for
threepence-halfpenny, and an acre of meadow turned and raised for a
penny-halfpenny, and an acre of waste for a penny-farthing. And know
that five men can well reap and bind two acres a day of each kind of
corn, more or less. And where each takes twopence a day then you
must give fivepence an acre, and when four take a penny-halfpenny a
day and the fifth twopence, because he is binder, then you must give
fourpence for the acre. And, because in many places they do not reap

by the acre, one can know by the reapers and by the work done what they do, but keep the reapers by the band, that is to say, that five men or women, whichever you will, who are called half men, make a band, and twenty-five men make five bands, and twenty-five men can reap and bind ten acres a day working all day, and in ten days a hundred acres, and in twenty days two hundred acres by five score. And see then how many acres there are to reap throughout, and see if they agree with the days and pay them then, and if they account for more days than is right according to this reckoning, do not let them be paid, for it is their fault that they have not reaped the amount and have not worked so well as they ought.

12 The Hayward and the Ploughman, c.1250

(*Seneschaucie*, printed in *Walter of Henley's Husbandry together with an anonymous husbandry, Seneschaucie and Robert Grosseteste's Rules*, ed. Elizabeth Lamond (1890), pp. 103–5, 111)

The hayward ought to be an active and sharp man, for he must, early and late, look after and go round and keep the woods, corn, and meadows and other things belonging to his office, and he ought to make attachments[1] and approvements[2] faithfully, and make the delivery by pledge before the provost,[3] and deliver them to the bailiff to be heard. And he ought to sow the lands, and be over the ploughers and harrowers at the time of each sowing. And he ought to make all the boontenants and customary-tenants who are bound and accustomed to come, do so, to do the work they ought to do. And in haytime he ought to be over the mowers, the making, the carrying, and in August assemble the reapers and the boon-tenants and the labourers and see that the corn be properly and cleanly gathered; and early and late watch so that nothing be stolen or eaten by beasts or spoilt. And he ought to tally with the provost all the seed, and boon-work, and customs, and labour, which ought to be done in the manor throughout the year, and what it amounts to the bailiff tallies and accounts for, and they ought to answer on the account for the rest.

*　　*　　*

The ploughmen ought to be men of intelligence, and ought to know how to sow, and how to repair and mend broken ploughs and harrows, and to till the land well, and crop it rightly; and they ought to know also how to yoke and drive the oxen, without beating or hurting them, and they ought to forage them well, and look well after the forage that it be not stolen nor carried off; and they ought to keep them safely in meadows and several pastures, and other beasts which are found therein they ought to impound. And they and the keepers must make ditches and build and remove the earth, and ditch it so that the ground may dry and the water be drained. And they must not flay any beast until some one has inspected it, and inquired by what default it died. And they must not carry fire into the byres for light, or to warm themselves, and have no candle there, or light unless it be in a lantern, and for great need and peril.

¹ The method of bringing a person under the control of a court of law by apprehending him, or by taking part or all of his property as pledge.
² Increasing the profit from the land.   ³ The reeve.

13 A Manorial Account, 1267–8

(Cambridge. Queen's College MS. Ad. 2. mm. 2–4, printed in *Wellingborough Manorial Accounts A.D. 1258–1323*, ed. F. M. Page (Northamptonshire Record Society, Publications, VIII, 1936), pp. 4–10)

Note that on St. John the Evangelist's day in the 13th year of the lord R[alph] the abbot, Richard, reeve of Wellingborough, renders his account of all receipts and expenses, from the Sunday after the feast of St. Luke the Evangelist in his 12th year, until the said day.¹

Receipts
From the term of All Saints² 6/7½.
From the term of St. Andrew³ 5*l* 15 2¾.
From the term of St. Guthlac⁴ 7*l* 13 8¼.
From the term of St. Botolph⁵ 5*l* 14 5¾.
From the term of St. Michael⁶ 4*l* 11 5¼.⁷
From two water mills for 5 terms 13*l* 6 8.
From one fulling-mill for the 5 aforesaid terms 16/8.
From the tithe of hay at the Gules of August⁸ 4*l*.
From wooding⁹ at two terms of St. Martin¹⁰ 27/-.
From soke wooding and 'longaverage'¹¹ at two Xmas terms 4/2½.
From pannage at Purification¹² 2/2.
From 'wara'¹³ at the Gules of August 2/9.
From the market throughout the year 6/8.
From works excused 36/-.
From carrying [excused] 4*l* 6 4½.
From four ovens for 5 terms 33/4.
From maltsilver¹⁴ at Purification 6/-.

From maltsilver at Pentecost 5/5.

From 'herbagium'[15] excused to the reeve by the lord, on account of service 2/-.

From harrowing excused 8/4½.

From foals sold 12d.

From the houses of Gilbert Takel for 3 terms 27d.

From the term of All Saints 6/7½.

From the term of St. Andrew 5l 15 2¾.

Total. 60l 15 6¼

Item from aid 16l 5 0. From fines and perquisites 11l 2 9. Item from one ox, 2 bulls, 3 cows, one this year's calf sold 66/4. Item from one heifer's hide, 2 hides of two-years-old bullocks dead of murrain 2/4½. Item from 9 pigs sold 19/8. Item from 50 wethers, 87 ewes sold 9l 4 0. Item from 2 pelts remaining 4d. Item from 4 pelts of ewes, 10 unsheared skins of hogasters[16] of which 4 are males 3/4. Item from 14½ quarters of barley sold 62/4. Item from 3 quarters of oats sold 8/-. From stubble sold 27/4. From white straw 8/-. From pea-straw 2/-. From hay sold 2/-. Item from the hay of Hardwick 6d. Item from 144 cheeses, making 4½ weighs with 26 collected after Michaelmas 38/10. From butter sold 4/8. Item from the garden 46/8. Item from 1020 pigeons sold 7/6. Item from the excusing of 60 hens 5/-. Item received from the lord 40/-. From the reeve of Addington 4l. From Gilbert Takel 66/8. Item from William Wilfrik' 6/8.

Total. 61l 9 11½.

Total of all receipts. 120l 45 5¾.

Expenses

Thence issued to the lord R de Well' by several tallies 31l 0 3¾d. Item to the same from the [proceeds of the] aid without tally 14l 0 0. Item issued to the lord Henry of Acolt for the expenses of the lord 15/6½. Item issued to brother Henry 8l 13 4. Item paid to the sheriff of Northampton to have an assize, 13/4. Item paid to the prior of St. Andrew's, Northampton, for the tithe of the churches of Wellingborough, Addington, and Elmington, given to the king, 6l 13 8¾. Item issued to the lord Nicholas of Whaplode from the [proceeds of the] mill for 3 terms with the tithe of hay at the Gules of August, 12l 10 0. Paid for the archdeacon's proctor 13/4. Paid to John le Seler' 26/3½. Item to William Launcelyn for rent 2/-. Item for the rent of Tingden (Finedon) 8d. For the whole upkeep of ploughs 7/4. For the whole upkeep of carts 29/10. For the wages of the smith for 2 terms with the shoeing of the horses of the *curia*[17] 14/-. For shoeing the horses of the supervisors 5/-. For one ploughing boon-work 5/-. In buying 12 geese 21¾*d*. In buying three dozen chickens to send to Croyland 2/-. For 3000 eggs sent to Croyland 6/3. Item for flock bought and sent to Croyland 2/-. Item [for] 12 *lingatores* sent to Croyland at the feast of St. James 3/-. Item for driving oxen and pigs to Croyland 7*d*. For the expenses of the lord Gilbert de Preston, the sheriff, and other supervisors, 23/11. For the expenses of the steward [and] his clerk on their visit 5/10. For the expenses of Gilbert the *serviens*, Master Nigel, 2 boys and 1 maid until Xmas together with the reeve 10/11½. For the expenses of Thomas the *serviens* from Xmas until the day of account 7/-. Item for three horses bought and three this year's foals 60/10½. Item for one bull 7/7. For coffers and lids sent to the lord G. de Preston' 2/6. For 12 cart saddles sent to Croyland 18*d*. Item for mending the grange and thatching [it] 4/7½. Item for mending the garden walls and the hall door 2/6. Item for thatching the fold and rods for the same 3/8. In buying 26 quarters of charcoal 5/4½. In hurdles for the kiln 2/8. For spreading manure 10*d*. Item for one new lock for the door together with the mending of the other locks broken by the depredators, mending the plumbing, mending the vats and other small things together with nails and wood for the loom, mending the fishing nets 8/7. For buying 60 saucers, 30 plates and sieves 2/10. Item for tallow bought throughout the year 2/3. Item for dressing one horse's hide brought forward from the [last] account, the hide of the horse of H. de Witering, 2 hides of two-year-old colts of which one was male, 2 hides of cows, one [hide] of a calf over a year old 20*d*. For garlic to plant 3*d*. For thressels, spades, threshing-sledges, hoes, sieves and a wheelbarrow 3/2. For the whole upkeep of the dairy 2/3. Item for milking the ewes 2/-. Item for sacks, that is to say 42 ells of canvas in gross 6/5½. Item for cutting the vine, the wages of the gardener, the meals of the ploughman and of a certain boy going to the ploughs at Cottenham 5/2½. Item for the hire of one cart going from Wansford to Croyland 9*d*. Item for 11½ quarters [and] 1 bushel of wheat bought for seed 78/4, item for 57 quarters 1 bushel of barley, item 30½ quarters and 1 bushel of oats, items 20½ quarters of barley-malt, item for 19½ quarters of drage-malt[18] 24*l* 13 0. For hoeing all the grain with meals to the *famuli*[19] 5/2. For two autumn boon-works for meat, herrings, and ale bought 11/10. For the expenses of the reeve and John from Xmas to Xmas 4/9½. For the wages of 8 ploughmen, 2 carters, one cowherd, 1 maid, 1 maltster, 1 shepherd, 1 swineherd from Michaelmas to Hoke day[20] 9/8. For the wages of the autumn workers, that is to say 2 stackers with 6 other servants in autumn 35/8. Item for [the hire of] one cart for 4 days 14*d*. Item for the allowance of rent to the reeve for 5 terms with 'herbagium' excused to him by the lord 7/-. Item for perquisites of the court excused by the lord 12/2.

	for 136 quarters of wheat	
Threshing	for 225 quarters of barley	together with
by	for 253 quarters of drage	winnowing
task.[21]	for 35½ quarters of bolmong[22]	4*l* 0 10½.
	for 12 quarters of peas	

	for 65 quarters of wheat and	
Threshing	rye	together with
of new grain	for 88½ quarters of barley	winnowing
	for 31½ quarters of oats	25/6
	for 8 quarters of bolmong	

Sum total of expenses 127*l* 5 9¼, and so the lord owes the reeve 5*l* 0 3½. Item the reeve should settle everything contained in this roll up to the day of account.

Issue of the Granary

Of wheat [threshed] by task 136 quarters. And of increment 21 quarters. Item by the work of the *famuli* 28½ quarters and ½ bushel. Item bought [wheat] 11½ quarters and 1 bushel. Of the hayward's grain 3½ quarters and ½ bushel.
Total 201 quarters.

Expenses

Thence in seed 29 quarters. Sent to Croyland 78 quarters. Baked for the lord on several visits 32 quarters. Item given away by the lord 7 quarters. Item baked in the *curia* throughout the year 15½ quarters 1 bushel. Item baked for the great boon-work and for the other boon-work 9½ quarters. Issued to 15 servants from the Sunday after the feast of St Laurence[23] to the Sunday after the feast of St. John before the Latin Gate[24] 14 quarters 1½ bushels. Item to the swineherd throughout the year 1 quarter. Item to two shepherds for 15 weeks 1 quarter 1 bushel. Item to six tithe-assessors, 2 tossers, 2 stackers, 3 quarters. Item to the gardener 1 bushel and so correct.

Rye

Of rye received from Croyland 29 quarters.

Expenses

Thence in seed 23 quarters. Sent to Addington 5 quarters. Baked for the lord's charity 1 quarter. Equal.

Barley

Of barley [threshed] by task 225 quarters. And of increment 36½ quarters 1 bushel. Item by the work of the *famuli* 32 quarters. Item bought [barley] 57 quarters 1 bushel. Total 371 quarters.

Expenses

Thence in seed 40 quarters and ½ bushel. Sent to Croyland 57 quarters. Sent to Langtoft 40 quarters. Sent to Addington 3 quarters. Issued for making malt in the vill 19 quarters. Sold 14½ quarters as above. Item as a gift of the lord 2 quarters. Brewed 176 quarters. And so correct.

Malt

Of the aforesaid 176 quarters brewed. And of increment 26 quarters. Item of *accomodato* as above 19 quarters. Item bought [malt] 40½ quarters as above. Total 261 quarters. Thence sent to Croyland 203 quarters and a half. Brewed for the lord 60 quarters for many visits. And so correct.

Issue of oats

Of oats [threshed] by task 253 quarters. And of increment 42½ quarters. Item by the work of the *famuli* 28½ quarters 1½ bushels. Item received from Croyland 26 quarters. Item of bought [oats] 30½ quarters 1 bushel as above. Total 381 quarters and ½ bushel.

Expenses

Thence in seed 60 quarters. Sent to Croyland 59 quarters. Brewed 67 quarters. For fodder for the lord['s horses] on his visits 75½ quarters. Sold 3 quarters. Item paid out for malt *accomodato* 8 quarters. For the fodder of the white horse which was stolen 20½ quarters. For the fodder of the cart horses of the *curia* and the stallions and of the horses of Morborne and Cottenham 58½ quarters 1 bushel. Item as a gift of the lord 5 quarters. For the fodder of John Spigurnel's horse 7½ quarters. For the fodder of the lord Thomas of Moulton, the dean of Lincoln, the parson of Swineshead, the parson of Morborne and other supervisors 11 quarters and ½ bushel. For oat-flour 3 quarters 1 bushel. For the fodder of the horse of G. the *serviens* 3 quarters. And so correct.

Oat-malt

Of the aforesaid 67 quarters brewed. Item of bought [malt] 19½ quarters. Item of *accomodato* 8 quarters as above. Total 94½ quarters.

Expenses

Thence sent to Croyland 84½ quarters. Item brewed for the lord 10 quarters. And so equal.

Bolmong'

Of bolmong [threshed] by task 35½ quarters, and of increment 5 quarters. Thence in seed 2 quarters. Issued for the *famuli* instead of barley 27 quarters 1 bushel. Item baked for the carrying of Langtoft 1 quarter 1 bushel. Item baked for dog-cake 6 quarters. Item to the gardener and husbandman 1 quarter. Issued for 5 *famuli* of Cottenham 2 quarters. For feeding the pigs 1 quarter. And so equal.

Issue of peas

Of peas [threshed] by task 12 quarters, and of increment 2 quarters. Thence in seed 5 quarters. Sent to Addington 4 quarters. For pottage for the *famuli* 3 quarters. Item issued to the cellarer of Croyland 1 quarter. Item given for the lord's charity 1 quarter. And so equal.

Stock

Item he accounts for 3 cart horses brought forward. Item bought 3 as above of which 3 were stolen. Item issued to Whaplode 1, and 2 remain. [Horses 2]. Item he accounts for 7 avers brought forward. Of which 1 was stolen. Sent to Addington 2. Sent to Croyland 3. And so none remain.

Two-year-old foals

Item he accounts for 8 foals of two years old brought forward, of which 2 are female. Whence in murrain 2 as above and there remain 6, of which 5 are male. Item he accounts for 3 mares brought forward. Item 1 filly now made a mare. Of which there were sent to Addington 2 as above. Sent to Croyland 2, and so none remain. Item he accounts for the issue of the said mares, 2 foals. Item bought 3 and so remain 5 foals of which . . . [This year's foals 5.] Item he accounts for 16 oxen brought forward. Item 3 young cattle now made oxen. Of which issued to the lord Nicholas del Pek 8. Sold 1 as above. In murrain 1, for the hide of which he answers above. Sent to Croyland 9. And so nothing remains. Item he accounts for 8 young cattle of over two years old brought forward. Of which 5 are males. Of which in murrain 2 male cattle for the hides of which he answers above, and so there remain 6 young cattle of which 3 are . . . [Two year old cattle 6.]

Item he accounts for 12 calves over a year old brought forward, of which in murrain 1, the hide of which was dressed as above, and so there remain 11, of which 7 are male. [Calves over a year old 11.]

Item he accounts for 13 cows brought forward and 2 bulls, and for 1 bull bought. Item for 6 young cattle now made cows, of which 3 were sold as above. Killed for the lord 1, for the dressing of whose hide he answers. In murrain 1, whose hide was dressed. And so there remain 14. [Cows 14.]

Item he accounts for 3 bulls as aforesaid, of which 2 were sold as above, and so there remains 1. [Bull 1.]

Item he accounts for the issue of the said cows, 11. Of which 1 was sold as above, and so there remain 10 of which 6 are male. [This year's calves 10.]

Item he accounts for 10 pigs brought forward, and all were sent to Croyland, of which one was a boar.

Item he accounts for 77 young pigs over a year old, of which 33 were killed for the lord last year. Sold 9, as above. Sent to Addington, 7. In the expenses of the lord this year for many visits, 17, of which one was a boar. Killed in the *curia*, 6. In murrain 5, and so there remain 6. [Pigs 6.]

Item he accounts for 5 sows brought forward and 1 boar, of which 1 had murrain, and so there remain 4 and one boar. Item of present [issue] 1. [Sows 4, and 2 boars.]

Item he accounts for the issue of the said sows, 64 young pigs. Of which in the expenses of the lord 10. In murrain 4, and so there remain 50. [Young pigs 50.]

Item he accounts for 52 wethers brought forward. Of which 50 were sold as above. Sent to Addington 2, and so none remain. Item he accounts for 38 hogasters now made wethers brought forward. Of which in murrain 4, for the skins of which he answers above and so there remain 34.[25] [Wethers 34.]

Item he accounts for 92 ewes brought forward. Of which 88 were sold as above. Killed in the *curia* 4, for the skins of which he answers above, and so none remain.

Item he accounts for 33 hogasters now made ewes brought forward. Of which 6 had murrain before shearing. For the skins of which he answers above, and so remain 17. [Ewes 17.][26]

Yield of the Dairy

Item he accounts for 4 cheeses brought forward. Item [cheeses] collected from the day of account until Mayday, 6. Item from the day of the apostles Philip and James[27] until Michaelmas making one cheese a day, 148. Item from the said day until Xmas of collected [cheeses] 32. Of which were sold 144 cheeses as above and of collected [cheeses] 26 as above. For the expenses of the lord on his visits, 5. Item to the lord's clerks going to Oxford, 2. For the expenses of the lord G. de Preston, 1. For the expenses of J. Lovel, 1. For the expenses of the *curia* 11, and so none remain.

Item he accounts for 15 ducks brought forward. And no issue, and all used in the expenses of the lord, and so none remain.

Yield of the goose-house

Item he accounts for 18 geese brought forward. Item from their issue 24. Item from rent of 2 terms, 4. Item received from Addington 6. Item bought 12 as above. Of which for expenses of the lord on several visits 25. For the expenses of the steward 2. For the expenses of the sheriff 2. For the expenses of the lord G. de Preston 2. For the expenses of the *curia* and for the Reapgoose and bedreap 6. For the expenses of the supervisors 2. In murrain 7, and so there remain 18, besides gifts.

Yield of the pigeon-cote

Of the pigeons 2250, of which 620 were sent to Croyland. Sold 800½.[28] For the expenses of the lord 200. For the expenses of the *curia* 230 and so equal.

Item he accounts for 16 hens brought forward. Item from the custom of the vill at two terms 230. Item from the villeins at 2 terms, 68. Bought 36 as above. Of which 60 were sold as above. Sent to Croyland 36. For the expenses of the lord 72. For the expenses of Gilbert the *serviens* 32, and so remain 150, besides presents. Item he accounts for 48 capons from assised rent for 2 terms, of which 12 were sent to Croyland. For the expenses of the steward and of the lord W. de Morborne 3. For the expenses of the *curia* and of Ralph de Litlebir 3, and so there remain 30 besides presents.

Implements

Item there remain in the *curia* 1 broken cart and another weak iron-[bound] one together with the iron-work of a third cart and the harness of three ploughs. Item 3 pairs of traces. Issued to the lord Nicholas 2 ploughs with the whole harness. Sent to Addington 2 with the whole harness. Item there remain in the *curia* without harness. Issued to lord Nicholas 2 crates. Item to Addington 2. Item 3 old ladders and 1 new. Item 2 manure-forks, ironed. Iron for 2. Item 3 iron spades. Item 5 iron threshing-sledges. Item 6 iron forks. Item 2 wheelbarrows and 3 baskets for carrying and 1 for sowing. Item 1 jar and 2 barrels. Item 12 old vats and 1 cover. Item 4 tins. Item 2 vats. Item 2 tubs. Item 1 brass bowl. Item 2 brass jugs. Item 3 brass plates. Item 1 wash-tub and 1 measure for grain and 2 tripods and 1 gridiron. Item 3 jars to mould cheese. Item 2 winnowing-fans. Item 2 tablecloths. Item 11 sacks. Item 2 covers for the kiln.

Note that the issue is made to the servants up to the Sunday before the Gules of August.

[1] The period of account given here is from about 18 October 1267 to about 27 December 1268 but the reeve accounted for the rents of assize only up to 29 September, the date on which the year of account usually ended.
[2] 1 November.   [3] 30 November.   [4] 11 April.   [5] 17 June.   [6] 29 September.
[7] The previous five items represent the rents of assize, fixed payments arising from a multiplicity of small sums of varying origins.
[8] 1 August.
[9] Possibly a payment commuting the timber-carrying service owed by the customary tenants.
[10] 11 November.
[11] Payments commuting the timber-carrying service owed by the toftsokemen and the service of driving three horses anywhere within the realm on the abbot's behalf.
[12] 2 February.
[13] Frangware—a payment by the full sokemen as a corporate unit, possibly given for the lord's personal favour and protection.
[14] Payment in lieu of making malt.   [15] Payment for rights of pasture.
[16] Hoggets—sheep of the second year.
[17] The enclosed area containing the farm buildings of the demesne.
[18] A mixture of oats and barley.
[19] The manorial servants attached to the lord's household.
[20] Second Tuesday after Easter.   [21] Piece-work.
[22] A mixture, usually of peas and beans but sometimes of peas and oats.
[23] 3 February.   [24] 6 May.
[25] This sentence, which in the manuscript is entered as a separate paragraph preceding the rest of the paragraph printed here, has been moved to make better sense of the text.
[26] Medieval clerks were not always accurate in their calculations.
[27] 1 May.   [28] i.e. 800 and a half of 800 which equals 1200.

14 Commutation of Services, 1269

(P.R.O. Inquisitions ad quod damnum, C 143/2/40)

Inquisition made before the sheriff on All Souls Day[1] in the 53rd year of the reign of King Henry son of King John, what and what sort of customs and services are due to the lord the king from two virgates of land with the appurtenances which Adam of Ardern holds of the aforesaid lord the king in Coverdine and Wallsworth, within the manor of the aforesaid lord the king of Barton without Gloucester, and how much those customs and services are worth yearly in money, if they were converted into money, and whether it would be to the damage of the aforesaid lord the king or to the injury of the manor aforesaid, if the lord the king should grant to the aforesaid Adam that for the customs and services aforesaid he should render to the aforesaid lord the king the value of the same yearly in money; and if it should be to the damage of the lord the king aforesaid or to the injury of the same manor, to what damage and what injury; by the oath of the below written persons, to wit, Philip of Hatherley[2] . . . Who say upon their oath that the aforesaid Adam holds of the aforesaid lord the king within the manor aforesaid in Coverdine a virgate of land with the appurtenances and renders 10*s* a year to the lord the king, and another virgate of land with the appurtenances in Wallsworth and renders 20*s* to the same lord the king, and for the aforesaid two virgates of land he owes suit to the court of the lord the king at the Barton aforesaid, and it is worth 2*s* a year, and he shall carry writs within the county and shall have no answering of the aforesaid writs, and it is worth 2*s* a year, and he ought to be tallaged for the two virgates of land aforesaid, when tallage is imposed, at the will of the lord the king. And if the aforesaid lord the king should grant to the aforesaid Adam to hold the aforesaid land for the aforesaid service,[3] it would not be to the damage of the lord the king nor to the injury of the manor aforesaid.

[1] 2 November.   [2] And twelve others named. (B, B, T)
[3] i.e. for the money-payments specified above. (B, B, T)

15 Complaints Against a Reeve, 1278

(P.R.O. Court Rolls, General Series, S.C. 2/179/4, m. 1d., printed in *Select Pleas in Manorial and other Seignorial Courts*, ed. F. W. Maitland (Selden Society, II, 1889), p. 95)

Elton.[1] *On the day of St. Clement in the said year*[2]

Michael the reeve complains of Richer son of Jocelin and Richard the reeve and his wife that when he was in the churchyard of Elton on the Sunday next before the feast of All Saints[3] in this year, there came the aforesaid Richer, Richard and Richard's wife and insulted him with vile words before the whole parish, charging him with having collected his own hay by the labour services due to the lord the abbot [of Ramsey], and with having reaped his own corn in autumn by the boon-works done by the abbot's customary tenants, and with having ploughed his land in Everesholmfeld with ploughs 'booned' from the town, and with having released to the customary tenants their labour services and carrying services on condition that they demised and leased their lands to him at a low price, and with having taken gifts from the rich tenants that they should not become tenants at a money rent, and with having put the poor tenants at a money rent. And the aforesaid Richard and Richer are present and deny . . . and ask for an enquiry by twelve jurors. Who come and say that the said Michael is guilty of none of the charges. Therefore the said Richard and Richer shall satisfy him, and for the trespass shall be in mercy; Richard's fine, 2s, pledge William son of James; Richer's fine, 12d, pledge, Jocelin. And the damages are taxed at 10s to be received from Richard the reeve, which sum Michael has released except 2s.

¹ Huntingdonshire.   ² 23 November 1278.   ³ 1 November.

16 Lease of a Manor to its Tenants, 1279

(*Cartularium Monasterii de Ramesia*, II, ed. W. H. Hart and P. A. Lyons, *Rolls Series* (1886), pp. 244–6)

To all Christ's faithful who shall see or hear the present writing, William, by the grace of God abbot of Ramsey, greeting in the Lord.

Know you that we have demised at farm to our men of Hemingford our manor of Hemingford from Michaelmas in the eighth year and beginning the ninth of the reign of King Edward, son of King Henry, until the end of seven years next following, for 40l sterling to be paid to us therefrom yearly at the four terms, to wit, at Michaelmas 10l, on St. Andrew's Day¹ 10l, at the Annunciation² 10l and at Midsummer 10l.

Our aforesaid men shall hold the aforesaid manor with all its appurtenances, except the gift of the church when it shall fall vacant, and our fishery, and the mill, which we have kept in our hand.

Also they shall have all profits of the town except our tallages, sheriff's aid, hundred aid, 'wardpenys', and scutage of the lord the king, and except the issues of causes which cannot be determined without us or our bailiffs, of the issue whereof they shall have a moiety, and except view of frankpledge and the Maunde acre and the acres of the reeve of Ramsey.

And be it known that if any customary tenant die without heir of his body, we will demise his land and his messuage to whomsoever we will and keep in our hand the gersum[3] arising thence.

Also no customary tenant shall make fine for relieving or marrying his daughters without our presence, but their gersums shall be made before us in the presence of the reeves or any of the farmers, who shall have and collect the said money towards their farm.

Nor may the said farmers demise house or land to any stranger or one of another's homage, without our special licence.

For we will that such gersums beyond the fixed farm be entirely paid to us.

Moreover the said farmers have received the following stock:—

The corn grange full of corn on either side the door by the door posts and by the beams beyond the door, and so sloping to the roof of the granary.

They have received also the oat barn full of oats by the east door post.

The breadth of the grange was 28 feet within, the length 39 feet, and the east end of the grange is round; the height in the middle is 19 feet; and at the side from the door to the curve of the round end the length of the wall is 30 feet, the height 5½ feet.

They have received also a heap of barley 36 feet in length, 11 feet in breadth, 11 feet in height, and 18 feet in breadth in the middle.

Moreover they shall be quit of a serjeant[4] in autumn every year except in the last year, in which they shall have a serjeant, by whose view, according to the custom of the abbey, the stock shall be made up.

They shall also be quit of our yearly lodging due, except that as often as we shall come there they shall find for us salt, straw and hay without an account.

And at the end of the seven years they shall render to us the aforesaid manor with the stock with which they received it.

Also they shall give back the land well ploughed twice.

And be it known that the fruits which were then in the barn ought to be counted for the first year, because they were of our stock.

In witness of which demise of the land and the manor we have caused our seal to be set to this present writing.

---

[1] 30 November.   [2] 25 March.   [3] Entry fine.
[4] i.e. free from the inspection and audit of the lord's officer. (B, B, T)

17 Manuring the Land, Late Thirteenth Century

(Anon., *Treatise on Rural Economy in England*, printed in G. Duby *Rural Economy and Country Life in the Medieval West*, translated C Postan (1968), p. 340)

Good sons, feed your dung heaps and raise your dung heap with good earth and mix it with dung. And every fortnight, marl the dung of your sheepfold with clay soil, if you wish or with good soil from cleaning out the ditches. . . . Your dung which is mixed with earth, put on sandy soil for summer weather is warm, the dung is warm and the sand is warm and when the three warmths come together, as the great heat withers the corn after St. John's Day,[1] and namely barleys which grow or sandy soil, and in the evening the earth mixed with dung cools the sandy soil and produces a dew which greatly saves the corn. You manured land, do not plough it too deep, so that the dung spoils in going down. Now you shall say rather that you shall have dung which is mixed with soil; if the dung is good and pure, it will last two years or three according to whether the soil is cool or warm, and dung mixed with soil will last twice as long. . . . You should know well that marl lasts longer than manure, for dung spoils in going down and marl in rising. And know that mixed dung will last longer than pure dung, fo dung and earth which are ploughed together, the earth supports the dung, so that it cannot spoil in going in. Your dung, when it is spread and watered a little, then is the time for it to be turned, and the earth and the dung will each take better together, and if you put your dung on the fallowed field, it shall be rather at the second plough turned under the soil and at sowing time shall be thrown up with the mixed earth; and if you put it on the second plough, then at sowing time it will be rather turned on the soil, and then it will be mixed with the earth; and it will not be too much.

[1] i.e. the feast of the Nativity of St. John the Baptist which fell on 24 June, Mid summer Day.

18 A Lord's Timber and Mill Rights, 1296

(*Pleas in the Manors of the Abbey of Bec*, printed in *Select Pleas in Manorial and other Seignorial Courts*, ed. F. W. Maitland (Selden Society, II, 1889), pp. 43–4, 47)

Ruislip.[1] *Court held on Friday next after the feast of St. Barnabas*[2] *in th twenty-fourth year of Edward I*

Adam of Ramsey was attached to answer the lord at the suit of Wil

liam Forester and William Reaper on the pledge of William of the
Exchequer and Robert Aliz in a plea of trespass, why when the said
Adam together with persons unknown had at Ruislip on the Friday in
Whitsunweek come with a cart upon the fee and franchise of the lord to
the house of Hugh Marleward the born bondman of the said lord and
there had caused to be carried away in the said cart certain timber cut
down by the said Hugh Marleward against the lord's prohibition (the
said prohibition so issued by the lord being known to the said Adam),
in order that against the lord's will the said timber might be removed
from the lord's franchise to the damage of the lord 100s, and when the
said William Forester and William Reaper as bailiffs of the lord had
come up and found the transport taking place and had on behalf of our
lord the king and of his [Adam's] lord commanded him not to remove
the said timber thus placed under the lord's prohibition from the said
place against the lord's will and to find pledges to answer the lord in
his court as to his having thus attempted to remove the said timber
from the lord's franchise against the lord's will, and had taken a horse
from the said Adam's cart by way of gage in order to attach him to
answer the lord for the said trespass, he the said Adam together with
persons unknown made an assault upon them [the two Williams] by
force and arms and would not permit himself to be attached in manner
aforesaid according to the law and custom of the realm, but to the
utmost of his power made rescue of the said horse which had been
attached, whereupon the said two Williams raised the hue against the
said Adam and his adherents who were thus making assault, and to the
hue there came Walter Savage tithingman of Eastcot with his whole
tithing, and the said Adam himself raising the hue bade them in the
king's name follow him with the hue saying that he while acting as
serjeant of our lord the king had been robbed of his horse by the said
two Williams against his will and against the king's peace, whereupon
the said Walter the tithingman with his whole tithing affrighted by the
command thus given in the king's name raised the hue and along with
Adam pursued after the said two Williams as though they were felons
unto the manor [house] of the lord, and moreover at the gate of the
said manor [house] the said Adam with those who were following him
raised the hue against the lord and his men, saying as aforesaid that he
had been robbed of his said horse by the said two Williams; [all of
which was] to the damage and dishonour of the lord to the amount of
100s and more; all of which things the said Adam did. Of all of which
trespasses thus in full court charged against him, the said Adam confesses himself in all respects guilty, and he puts himself in the lord's

E

mercy and finds pledges, to wit, Walter Savage, Robert Nothel, John Kevere and Hugh Marleward. Afterwards the amercement was affeered at two marks by Roger of Southcote, William of the Exchequer and Hugh of Combe free suitors of the court.

* * *

Ogbourne.[3] *Court held on the Saturday next after the feast of St. James*[4] *in the said year*

* * *

William Bigge and William Druladon are convicted by inquest of the court of wrongfully having millstones in their houses and taking toll and multure[5] to the great damage of the lord as regards the suit to his mill. Therefore be they in mercy and it is commanded that the said millstones be seized into the lord's hand.

[1] Middlesex.   [2] 11 June.   [3] Wiltshire.   [4] 25 July.
[5] Payment exacted for grinding of corn, often in kind as a proportion of the corn milled.

19 Villagers and their Stock, 1327

(P.R.O. Exchequer K.R. Subsidies, E 179/242/4, m. 25, printed in *Early Taxation Returns*, ed. A. C. Chibnall (Buckinghamshire Record Society, XIV, 1966), pp. 130–1)

   Upton in Dinton

Subtaxers: Robert Colles and
John West

Nicholas Bluet had 2 beasts 10s, 4 steers 26s 8d, 2 heifers 10s, 2 pigs 4s, 12 ewes 18s, 10 lambs 10s, 5 qr. wheat 15s, 6 qr. drage 14s, 2 qr. beans 5s 4d, hay and fodder 2s 10d.

   Sum   5l 15s 10d.   Thence 20th.   5s 9½d.

William Pymme had 1 cow 6s 8d, 1 steer 3s, 1 pig 2s, 1 qr. wheat 3s, 3 qr. drage 7s, ½ qr. beans 16d, hay and fodder 14d.

   Sum   24s 2d.   Thence 20th.   14½d.

Matilda of Kynggesbeuied had 6 qr. wheat 18s, 7 qr. drage 16s 4d, 2 qr. beans 5s 4d, hay and fodder 2s.

   Sum   41s 8d.   Thence 20th.   2s 1d.

John Walsh had 5 qr. wheat 15s, 6 qr. drage 14s, 2 qr. beans 5s 4d, 30 sheep 45s, 20 lambs 20s, hay and fodder 3s 2d.

   Sum   5l 2s 6d.   Thence 20th.   5s 1½d.

Geoffrey Barum had 1 beast 3*s*, 1 steer 6*s* 8*d*, 1 cow 6*s* 8*d*, 1 pig 2*s*, 1½ qr. wheat 4*s* 6*d*, 2 qr. drage 4*s* 8*d*, 4 bushels beans 16*d*, hay and fodder 19*d*.

          Sum   30*s* 5*d*.   Thence 20th.   18¼*d*.

Robert the smith had 1 cow 6*s* 8*d*, 6 sheep 9*s*, 6 lambs 6*s*, 4 b[ushels] wheat 18*d*, 1 qr. drage 2*s* 4*d*, hay and fodder 15*d*.

          Sum   27*s* 1*d*.   Thence 20th.   16¼*d*.

Robert Shartford had 1 beast 5*s*, 1 steer 6*s* 8*d*, 1 cow 6*s* 8*d*, 1 young steer 3*s*, 1 pig 2*s*, 8 sheep 12*s*, 8 lambs 8*s*, 3 qr. wheat 9*s*, 4 qr. drage 9*s* 4*d*, 1½ qr. beans 5*s*, hay and fodder 2*s*, chamber and vessels 3*s*.

          Sum   3*l* 11*s* 8*d*.   Thence 20th.   3*s* 7*d*.

John Randulf had 1 beast 4*s*, 1 steer 6*s* 8*d*, 2 cows 6*s* 8*d*, 1 calf 2*s*, 1 pig 2*s*, 4 sheep 6*s*, 3 lambs 3*s*, 2 qr. corn 6*s*, 3 qr. drage 7*s*, 1 qr. beans 2*s* 8*d*, hay and fodder 2*s*, vessels 2*s*.

          Sum   50*s*.   Thence 20th.   2*s* 6*d*.

Alice Randulf had 1 beast 5*s*, 1 steer 6*s* 8*d*, 1 cow 6*s* 8*d*, 1 pig 2*s*, 10 sheep 15*s*, 10 lambs 10*s*, 2 qr. wheat 6*s*, 4 qr. drage 11*s* 8*d*, 1 qr. beans 2*s* 8*d*, hay and fodder 2*s* 3*d*, chamber and vessels 2*s* 6*d*.

          Sum   3*l* 10*s* 5*d*.   Thence 20th.   3*s* 6¼*d*.

Jordan of Thame had 1 beast 4*s*, 1 cow 6*s* 8*d*, 1 bullock 4*s*, 1 pig 2*s*, 1 qr. wheat 3*s*, 2 qr. drage 4*s* 8*d*, 1 qr. beans 2*s* 8*d*, hay and fodder 20*d*, chamber and vessels 2*s* 2*d*.

          Sum   30*s* 10*d*.   Thence 20th.   18½*d*.

Denis Sterre had 1 beast 4*s*, 1 steer 6*s* 8*d*, 1 cow 6*s* 8*d*, 1 young steer 3*s*, 1 pig 2*s*, 2 qr. wheat 6*s*., 4 qr. drage 7*s*, 1 qr. beans 2*s* 8*d*, hay and fodder 2*s*, chamber and vessels 3*s* 4*d*.

          Sum   43*s* 4*d*.   Thence 20th.   2*s* 2*d*.

Richard Atwell had 1 beast 3*s*, 1 bullock 5*s*, [1 qr.] wheat 3*s*, 1 qr. drage 2*s* 4*d*, hay and fodder 12*d*.

          Sum   16*s* 8*d*.   Thence 20th.   10[*d*].

Isabella Polton had 1 cow 6*s* 8*d*, 6 bushels wheat 2*s* 3*d*, 6 bushels drage 21*d*, 2 bushels beans 8*d*, hay and fodder 14*d*.

          Sum   12*s* 6*d*.   Thence 20th.   6½*d*.

Robert le roos had 2 cows 13*s* 4*d*, 1 pig 2*s*, 1 qr. wheat 3*s*, 1 qr. drage 2*s*, ½ qr. beans 16*d*, fodder 11*d*.

          Sum   22*s* 11*d*.   Thence 20th.   13¾*d*.

Robert the cook had 1 beast 3s, 1 steer 13s 4d, 1 cow 5s, 1 young steer 3s, 6 lambs 6s, 2½ qr. wheat 7s 6d, 2½ qr. drage 10s 10d, 1 qr. beans 2s 8d, hay and fodder 2s 4d.

Sum   4l 1s 8d.   Thence 20th.   4s 1d.

William Bluet had 1 beast 4s, 1 cow 6s 8d, 1 bullock 5s, 1 qr. wheat 3s, 2 qr. drage 4s 8d, ½ qr. beans 16d, hay and fodder 19d.

Sum   26s 3d.   Thence 20th.   15¾d.

Sum of all the goods   38l 7s 11d.   Thence 20th.   38s 4¾d.

20 Customary Tenures after the Black Death, 1349

(P.R.O. Court Rolls, Duchy of Lancaster, D.L. 30/129/1957, m. 20)

Court of Bradford[1] held on Saturday, the eve of St. Lucy the Virgin, 23 Edward III[2]

Amy, daughter and heir of Roger of Oulesnape, came here into court and took a cottage and 4 acres of poor bondage land in the town of Stanbury after the death of the aforesaid Roger, to hold to her and her heirs according to the custom of the manor by the services . . . saving the right . . . And she gives to the lord 2s of fine for entry. Pledge, Roger son of Jurdan.

Entry, 2s.[3]

William Cooper, who held a cottage and 4 acres of bondage land there, is dead; and hereupon came Roger, his son and heir, and took those tenements, to hold to him and his heirs according to the custom of the manor by the services, etc., saving the right, etc. And he gives to the lord 2s of fine for entry. Pledge, Thomas of Keighley.

Entry, 2s.

Robert son of Roger son of Richard, who held a toft and 8 acres of bondage land there, is dead. And hereupon came John, his brother and heir, and took those tenements, to hold to him and his heirs according to the custom of the manor by the services . . . saving the right . . . And he gives to the lord 3s of fine for entry. Pledge, Roger son of Jurdan.

Entry, 3s.

Jordan of Stanbury, who held a messuage and ½ bovate of bondage land there, is dead. And hereupon came John, his son and heir, and took those tenements, to hold to him and his heirs by the services . . . saving the right . . . And he gives to the lord 5s of fine for entry. Pledges, John son of Roger and Roger son of Jurdan.

Entry, 5s.

John of Oldfield, who held a messuage and ½ bovate of bondage land there, is dead. And Alice, his daughter and heir, is of the age of half a year. And hereupon came John Swerd and took those tenements, to hold for a term of ten years next following fully complete, by the services . . . And he gives to the lord 2s of fine. Pledge, Adam of Oldfield.

Fine, 2s.

Adam Dickson came here into court and took a messuage and ½ bovate of very poor land, which was of Adam of Yate, to hold according to the custom of the manor, by the services . . . saving the right, . . . And he gives to the lord 2s of fine for entry. Pledge, John of Helwith.

Entry, 2s.

Roger Dickson, who held half a messuage and ½ bovate of land, is dead. And hereupon came Robert of Oldfield, next friend of William, son and heir of the aforesaid Roger, and took those tenements to the use of the said William, to hold to him and his heirs, according to the custom of the manor by the services . . . And he gives to the lord 5s of fine in the name of the said William. Pledge, John Swerd.

Entry, 5s.

John Barn of Manningham, who held a messuage and a bovate of bondage land there, is dead. And hereupon came Margery his wife and took those tenements, to hold according to the custom of the manor for the term of her life by the services . . . And she gives to the lord 2s of fine. Pledge, John of Yate.

Fine, 2s.

Margaret and Agnes, daughters and heirs of Hugh Browne, Alice, Joan and Juliana, daughters and heirs of John King, Juliana, who was the wife of Hugh King of Thornton, Robert son of John Bolling and Elizabeth his wife, Alice, who was the wife of William the Clerk of Clayton, Alice, daughter and heir of Robert of Manningham, and Thomas her husband, William, son and heir of Ellen Coke, and John (dead) son and heir of John of Windhill, came here into court and did their fealties, and they have a day at the next court to acknowledge their tenements and services ... and also to show their deeds ...

Fealties. Respite of acknowledgment of services.

Agnes Chapman came here into court and took a small house in Bradford called the Smithhouse, to hold at the will of the lord by the services. And she gives to the lord 18*d* of fine to have such estate ...

Fine, 12*d*. [*sic*.]

William Barn, who held 2 messuages and 2 bovates of bondage land in Manningham, is dead. And hereupon came Hugh, his brother and heir, and took the aforesaid tenements, to hold to him and his heirs according to the custom of the manor by the services ... saving the right ... And he gives to the lord 8*s* of fine for entry. Pledges, Thomas of Chellow and John his son.

Entry, 8*s*.

Richard Gilleson, who held there in the same manner 2 messuages and 2 bovates of land, is dead. And hereupon came John, his son and heir, and took those tenements, to hold to him and his heirs according to the custom of the manor by the services ... saving the right ... And he gives to the lord 10*s* of fine for entry. Pledges, Hugh Barn and the whole homage ...

Entry, 10*s*.

John son of Richard Gilleson came here into court and rendered into the hands of the lord 2 messuages and 2 bovates of very poor land there to the use of Thomas of Chellow for ever. Which tenements were afterwards granted to the same Thomas, to hold to him and his heirs according to the custom of the manor by the services ... saving the right ... And the same Thomas gives the lord 10*s* of fine for entry. Pledges, Hugh Barn and John Gilleson.

Entry, 10*s*.

William Wilkinson, who held there in like manner a messuage and a bovate of land, is dead, and Alice his daughter and heir is of the age of half a year. And hereupon came John Magson, her next friend, to whom ...[4] and took the wardship of the aforesaid land and heir until her full age ... by the services ... And he gives to the lord 2*s* of fine for entry. Pledges Hugh Barn and Thomas of Chellow.

Fine, 2*s*.

Thomas Newcomen, who held a messuage and a bovate of bondage land in Bradford, is dead. And hereupon came Margery, daughter and heir of the same Thomas, and took the aforesaid tenements, to hold to her and her heirs according to the custom of the manor by the services ... saving the right ... And the fine for entry is put in respite until the next court.

Fine respited.

William Tompsey of Bradford, the lord's bondman, who held a messuage and a bovate of bondage land in Bradford, is a runaway, because [he holds] other tenements in Morton by York by hereditary descent. Therefore he is distrained to dwell on the tenement here. Let the tenements at Morton be seized into the lord's hand ...

Distraint.   Tenements to be seized.

William Clerk of Clayton, who held a messuage and 2 bovates of land in Clayton by knight service, is dead. Let William, his son and heir, of the age of two years, together with the tenements aforesaid, be seized into the hands of the lord the earl. And hereupon comes Alice, who was the wife of the same William Clerk, and says that she was jointly enfeoffed of the aforesaid tenements with the aforesaid William, her husband, and craves a day at the next court to show her charters thereof, and has it. William, the son and heir, is committed to the wardship of the aforesaid Alice to be kept safely without a wife. Pledges, William son of Adam of Horton and Roger of Hollins.

Respite.

[1] Yorkshire.   [2] 12 December 1349.
[3] This and successive similar entries appeared as marginalia in the original document.
[4] i.e. to whom the inheritance cannot descend. (B, B, T)

21 Villeins Neglect their Services, 1352

(The History of Methley, ed. H. S. Darbyshire and G. D. Lumb (Thoresby Society, XXXV, 1937), p. 135)

Monday after the feast of St. Michael [26 Edward III]. The eighth day after. Fifty-one[1] villeins of Methley ought and are accustomed to mow the corn of the lord in autumn for 51 and a half bovates of land for as many days as 20 villeins of Horton and 15 of Castleford were accustomed to mow for 35 bovates of land there. The aforesaid 35 villeins of Horton and Castleford mowed for 12 days, and the aforesaid 53 villeins of Methley mowed only for nine and a half days during which the aforesaid 53 mowed at the same time at Hardwick on the eve of St. Bartholomew.[2] The aforesaid villeins of Methley were unwilling to mow so that a great part of the lord's oats growing there had been destroyed by the occurence of a tempest of wind. Amercement 17s 2d. Also that the aforesaid 53 villeins of Methley ought and are accustomed to scour a ditch called the Leighes. Through their default the said meadows were inundated to the damage of the lord.

[1] The figure should be 53 according to the sense of the following passage.
[2] i.e. on 23 August.

22 A Magnate's Declining Revenues, 1388

(P.R.O. Duchy of Lancaster Ministers' Accounts, D.L. 29/728/11975, printed in G. A. Holmes, *The Estates of the Higher Nobility in the Fourteenth Century* (1957), pp. 126–8)

As to the aforesaid values which are less than they used [to be] before this time in divers past years, the reasons will be certified in the following manner.

Because divers bailiffs of franchises in the counties of Cambridge, Huntingdon, Essex, Hertford, Surrey, Sussex, Bedford, Buckingham, Kent and Devon, who used to render account at the Savoy, have not accounted because the preceding accounts and all the memoranda relating to them were burnt at the Savoy by the rebels.[1] On this matter my very mistrusting lord and his council are taking consideration as it was certified in preceding years.

Because of the default of the green wax in the county of Nottingham during the [period of] office of Hugh Annesley,[2] which is not levied through the default of the bailiff who is not authorised to levy it, which in divers years amounted to a large sum.

Because the profits of the courts are less this year than previously, because the stewards are not holding the courts in person but by proxy without the assent of my lord or of his council.

Because the amercements of the brewers of the town of Leicester, called Cannemole,[3] are less this year than previously, for the reason that the 24 jurors of the town claim to be quit of amercements to the loss of my lord.

Because the fines and amercements of offenders there are not made as previously to the loss . . .

Because the husbandry of Higham Ferrers and Raunds[4] is of no value beyond the costs there, which are so great each year that the said husbandry is a great loss to my lord. The demesne lands should and can be leased at farm as in other places.

Because the windmill at Raunds, which used to be at 5 marks per annum, is leased this year at 36s.

Because the warrens and the fishery of the manor of Snettisham in Norfolk, which used to be leased at farm at 10 marks per annum, have raised nothing for the use of my lord through the default of the farmer. Wherefore discussion must be had with the steward on increasing the profit[5] and other things.

Because the courts of Hungry Hatch in Sussex and the courts of Castle Acre in Norfolk are not held by any steward as previously, to the loss of my lord . . . On this matter my lord, if he pleases, and his council will take consideration.

Because divers allowances and rewards are made to divers bailiffs and ministers, [who are] accountable this year, in default of the reeves and bailiffs, who used to perform their offices by custom for little or nothing, and now they refuse to hold their tenements by service and custom, as at Marchington, Scropton,[6] the wapentake of Wirksworth,[7] and in divers other places at Tutbury[8] and elsewhere.

Because the profits of agistments[9] and the amercements of attachments in the Peak are less this year than previously, in default of the administration of ministers there. On this matter my lord and his council will take consideration.

Because the manor of Gunthorpe,[10] which was part of the value of Leicester,[11] which is worth at farm 40 marks, is granted to Sir John Loudham out of my lord's hands for his annuity.

Because of the great costs expended this year for the repair of the mills at Higham, which were at farm and this year [are] in my lord's hands, and were decayed and for that reason repaired this year to the cost of my lord to the sum of 44l 5s 6d.

Because the stalls and shambles in the market in the town of Leicester are greatly decayed and are not put at such a high farm as they should if they were repaired.

Because the manor of Gimingham in Norfolk worth 210l in the hands of the earl of Gloucester, the manor of Soham[12] worth 125l in the hands of the earl of Derby, the hundred of Gallow worth 40l in the hands of Sir John Plaice, and the hundred of South Erpingham worth 20l in the hands of Sir Thomas Mandeville, and the manor of Rodmere[13] worth 8l in the hands of Brother John Feltwell as his annuity, are out of the hands of my lord for the term of the lives of the aforesaid persons.

Because the manor of Methwold in Norfolk, which was at farm in the preceding year at 80*l* and is this year in the hands of my lord for profit, is not worth more than 28*l* 11*s* 2*d* as it appears from the values this year, and besides this, the flock of sheep is dead from murrain and all the husbandry in great disarray, and the houses and the tenements of the tenants there in great ruin and mischief, and the rentals and extents, the custumals and evidences lost and burnt by the rebels in the time of rumour.

Because the manor of Snettisham in Norfolk, which was at farm at 86*l*, is this year in the hands of my lord for profit, which is not worth more than 50*l* 0*s* 8*d* as appears from the values, of which the demesne lands, which are cultivated this year, will be accounted for in the next year by a bailiff. For the costs of this husbandry my lord has paid this year 74*l* and the preceding year 11*l* 13*s* 4*d*.

Because the mills of Fakenham and Aylsham in Norfolk, which are in [the hands of my lord for] profit and not leased at farm, do not answer to my lord as was customary before this time for the low price of corn this year. On this matter the stewards there should be told that they can be leased at farm to the greater profit of my lord although the tenants claim that they will not be put to farm by the custom of the manor. On this matter the council of my lord will take consideration.

[1] John of Gaunt's palace, the Savoy in London, was ransacked by the rebels in 1381.

[2] Sheriff of Nottingham and Derby in 1380 and 1381 and the duke's steward and keeper of the fees in the honor of Nottinghamshire and Yorkshire in 1381 and 1382.

[3] A yearly payment for the right to sell ale.   [4] Northamptonshire.

[5] i.e. by taking into direct management.   [6] Staffordshire.   [7] Derbyshire.

[8] Staffordshire.   [9] Payments for grazing beasts.   [10] Norfolk.

[11] The manor was accounted for as part of the town.   [12] Cambridgeshire.

[13] Norfolk.

23 Regulation of Common Fields, c.1425[1]

(Historical Manuscripts Commission, *Report on the Manuscripts of Lord Middleton* (1911), pp. 106–9)

For neat pasture we ordain Orrow and Breches, Woldsyke and Wyloughbybroke, for to be broken[2] on Crowche messeday;[3] and whoso break this, every man shall pay for each beast that may be taken in any other several pasture a penny to the church; therefor to go a seven nightday.

Also, for the neat pasture, after that be eaten, all the wheatfield, to wit, Hardacre field namely, save Strete headlands, where they may not go for destroying of corn; this for to endure another sevennightday under the pain before said.

Also, on Holy Thursday eve we ordain the commons of the Peasfield for horses to be broken, and no other beasts to come therein. For if there be any man that have any horse that is feeble and may not do his work for fault of meat, and this may reasonably be known, let him relieve of his own, so that he save his neighbour from harm, for if any man may . . . which beasts 'lose' in corn or in grass, he shall for each beast pay a penny to the church, and make amends to his neighbour.

Also, on Whitsun eve every man [shall] break his several pasture as he likes, and no man tie his horse on other . . . his own for to be several till Lammas,[4] each man to eat his own, under the pain beforesaid.

Furthermore, if any man . . . plough-oxen for to be relieved on his several grass, let him tie them in his best manner or hold them in, as other men do their horses . . . on no other man's grass going to or fro abroad, as they will pay for each beast a penny to the church and make [amends] . . . to him that has the harm.

Also, if any man tie his horse or reach on any headlands or by brookside into any man's corn, he shall make amends to him that has the harm, and for each foot that is within the corn pay a penny to the church.

Also if any man shall be taken at night time destroying other corn or grass, he shall be punished as the law will, and pay 4d to the church.

Also, all manner of men that have any pease in the field when codding time comes, let them cod in their own lands and in no other man's lands. And other men or women that have no peas of their own growing, let them gather them twice in the week on Wednesday and on Friday, reasonably going in the land-furrows and gathering with their hands and with no sickles, once before noon and no more, for if any man or woman other that has any peas of his own and goes into any other, for each time [he shall] pay a penny to the church and lose his cods, and they that have none and go oftener than it is before said, with sickle or without, shall lose the vessel they gather them in and the cods, and a penny to the church.

Also, no man with common herd nor with shed herd [shall] come on the wold after grass be mown till it be made and led away, but on his own, and then let them go all together in God's name; and if they do, each man pay for his quantity of his beasts a certain to the church, that is for to say, a penny for each beast.

Also, if there be any man that throws in any sheaves on any land for to tie on his horses, he shall make a large amends to them that have the harm, and for each foot pay a penny to the church, but on his own. Furthermore, if any man tie his horse in any stubble and it be mown in reasonable time [he] shall pay the aforesaid pain.

Also, if any man may be taken at nighttime in the field with cart or with bearing of any other carriage in unreasonable time between bell and bell [he shall] pay 40d to the church, save as thus, if any man in peas harvest, he and his servants, in furthering of his work and saving of his corn, bind at morning or till it be moonshine, all other works at nighttime except, save this.

Also, all manner labourers that dwell in the town and have commons among us shall work harvest work and other works for their hire reasonable as custom is, and not to go to other towns but if they have no work or else no man speak to them, so that they may be excused, for if they do, they shall be chastised as the law will.

Also, no man or woman that works harvest work bear home no sheaves of no man's, but if they be given them well and truly, for if it may be wist, for each sheaf that they bear home without leave [they] shall pay a penny to the church.

Also, no man or woman glean no manner of corn that is able to work for his meat and twopence a day at the least to help to save his neighbour's corn; nor no other gleaners, that may not work, glean in no manner of wise among no sheaves, for if they do, they shall lose the corn and a penny to the church for each burden.

Also, neither common herd nor shed herd come in the wheat cornfield till the corn be led away, nor in the peas cornfield in the same wise till the peas be led away, and the common herd and shed herd may go together as they should do, on pain of each beast a penny to the church.

Also, that no man take away his beasts from the common herd from Michaelmas[5] tide to Yule to go in the wheatfield to 'lose' the wheat, for if any man may take any beast therein, they shall pay for each beast a penny to the church as often as they may be taken destroying the corn, and the herd [shall pay] his hire.

Also, if our hayward pen a flock of neat of the country, he shall take six pence, for a flock of sheep four pence, and for each horse a penny.

And that our wold be laid in several at Candlemas,[6] for if any herd let his beasts come thereon after, [he shall] pay for each time four pence to the church.

Also, whosoever has any meadows within the corns, my lord or any man else, let make them to 'dele' them out and take a profit of them on God's behalf, and whoso trespass, let make amends.[7]

[1] Of Wimeswould, Leicestershire.
[2] i.e. thrown open for grazing. (B, B, T)   [3] 14 September.
[4] 1 August.   [5] 29 September.   [6] 2 February.
[7] This document is defective and at best its bucolic English hard to interpret. (B, B, T)

24 Enclosure and Depopulation, Late Fifteenth Century

(*Domesday of Inclosures, 1517–18*, II, ed. I. S. Leadam (1897), pp. 431–2)[1]

Stretton super Street,[2] *Warwickshire*

And the aforesaid jurors say that Henry Smith was recently seised in his demesne as of fee of 12 messuages and 4 cottages, 640 acres of arable land to the annual value of 55*l* with appurtenances in Stretton super Street in the aforesaid county, and with each of the aforesaid messuages 40 acres of arable land, suitable for and ordinarily in cultivation, were accustomed to be let, farmed and occupied from time immemorial. Thus was the same Henry Smith seised on the 6th. December 9 Henry VII.[3] He enclosed the messuages, cottages and lands with ditches and banks and he wilfully caused the same messuages and cottages to be demolished and laid waste and he converted them from the use of cultivation and arable husbandry[4] into pasture for brute animals. Thus he holds them to this day, on account of which 12 ploughs that were employed in the cultivation of those lands are withdrawn and 80 persons, who similarly were occupied in the same cultivation, and who dwelled in the said messuages and cottages, were compelled to depart tearfully against their will. Since then they have remained idle and thus they lead a miserable existence, and indeed they die wretched. What is more to be lamented is [that] the church of Stretton on that occasion fell into ruin and decay, so that the Christian congregation, which used to gather there to hear the divine offices, is no longer held there and the worship of God is almost at an end. In the church animals are sheltered from the storms of the air and brute animals feed among the tombs of Christian bodies in the churchyard. In all things the church and burial-place are profaned to the evil example of others inclined to act in such a manner.

[1] This entry is an extract from the returns to the commission established in 1517 to enquire into enclosures. See **28**, p. 120.
[2] Stretton Baskerville.   [3] 1493.   [4] *Iconomie*.

25 Lease of a Royal Manor, 1485

(*Materials for a History of the Reign of Henry VII*, ed. W. Campbell (1873), I, p. 595)

4 December 1485   Lease for seven years to Sir John Fortescu of the site of the manor of Enfield, in county Middlesex, with the demesne lands, &c. from the postern of the park there to the head of Swinespound, with the pasture of Oldbury garden and Oldbury croft, and with the works of reaping corn, mowing the meadows, and the harvesting the corn arising from the customary tenants there not let to farm, and with the pasture called Lez lee, and of a certain stable, situate on the north part of the same manor, reserved for the king's auditor and receiver; also of a tenement in Enfield called Hakeneys, with the lands, meadows, &c. in anywise thereunto pertaining; and the profits of five quarters of grain and thirty quarters of wheat arising from the feefarm of the multure of the water-mill of Enfield; rendering annually for the said site of the manor, with the other premises, 22*l* 13*s* 4*d*; for the said tenement called Hakeneys, 4*l* 13*s* 4*d*; and for the said profits of the five quarters of grain and thirty quarters of wheat, 100*s*; with an improved rent of 20*d*, and keeping the said premises within the said site in repair at his own cost, except accidents arising through the wind or fire; and the said tenant is to have sufficient housebote, ploughbote, cartbote, haybote, and firebote, to be used within the site of the said manor, but not elsewhere.

26 A Cambridge College Acquires Land, 1507

(*Calendar of the Patent Rolls*, Henry VII, II, 1494–1509 (1916), p. 519)

28 November 1507. Westminster   Licence for the alienation in mortmain by Margaret, Countess of Richmond and Derby, of the manor of Dyseworth and 300 acres of land, 60 acres of meadow, 200 acres of pasture, 20 acres of wood and 10*l* of rent in Dyseworth, Keyworth, Hatharn and Whatton, county Leicester, and the advowsons of the churches of Kegworth and Sutton de Donyngton held of the king in chief and of the yearly value of 33*l* according to an inquisition taken before John Lee, escheator; the manors of Malketon, Melreth and Brache and 6 messuages, 22 tofts, 700 acres of land, 110 acres of meadow, 210 acres of pasture, 18 acres of wood and 43*s* 4*d* of rent in Malketon, Brache, Whaddon, Kneseworth, Hogyngton, Orwell and Baryngton and the advowson of the church of Malketon, county Cambridge, held of the king in chief and of the yearly value of 28*l* 13*s* 4*d* according to an inquisition taken before Edward Mynskyp, escheator; and the manor of Reydon and 20 messuages, 1,000 acres of land, 100 acres of meadow, 1,000 acres of pasture, 30 acres of wood and 5*l* of rent in Roydon, county Essex, held of the king in chief and of the yearly value of 40*l* according to an inquisition taken before John Steyke, escheator; to John Skylyng, Master or Warden of Christ's College, Cambridge, to hold as of the value of 104*l*, in part satisfaction of 107*l* yearly of land, which the master or warden and scholars of the said college had licence to acquire by letters patent of Henry VII.

27 Lease of a Manor to a Farmer, 1516

(*Historia et Cartularium Monasterii Sancti Petri Gloucestriae*, ed. W. H. Hart (1867), III, pp. 291–5)

This indenture made on the 5th day of October in the seventh year of King Henry VIII between William . . . Abbot of St. Peter . . . of the one part and Richard Cockes and Catharine his wife . . . and William and John, sons of the said Richard and Catharine, of the other part, witnesses, that the aforesaid abbot and convent . . . have leased, demised, and to farm let to Richard, Catharine, William, and John, the site of their manor of Ablode, situated in the county of Gloucester, with all its houses, buildings, arable lands, meadows, feedings and pastures, dovecotes, weir, waters, fishpools, and rabbit warrens, with all and everything thereto pertaining. And the said abbot and convent have leased to the aforesaid . . . divers goods and chattels, moveable, and immoveable, pertaining to the said manor. . . . Moreover the said abbot and convent have leased to the said . . . 320 sheep remaining for stock on the said manor, priced per head at 16*d*, which amounts in all to the sum of 21*l* 6*s* 8*d*, together with their meadows, pastures and all easements . . . needed for the support of the said sheep. . . . Furthermore the said abbot and convent have leased to the aforesaid . . . divers lands and demesne meadows belonging to the said manor, when the reversion thereof shall in any way have occurred, which lands and demesne meadows are now occupied by the customary tenants of the lord, as is plain from the rental drawn on the back of the present indenture. . . . And it shall be lawful for the aforesaid Richard, Catharine, William and John, or any of them to introduce at their pleasure new tenants on all those demesne lands aforesaid, now in the hands of the tenants there, whenever the aforesaid reversion shall have fallen in.

28 The Commission of Inquiry Touching Enclosures, 1517

(P.R.O. Patent Rolls, 9 Henry VIII, pt. 2, m. 6d.)

The king to his beloved and faithful John Veysy, dean of our Chapel, Andrew Wyndesore, knight, and Roger Wegeston, late of Leicester, greeting. Whereas of late in times past divers our lieges, not having before their eyes either God or the benefit and advantage of our realm or the defence of the same, have enclosed with hedges and dykes and other enclosures certain towns, hamlets and other places within this our realm of England, where many of our subjects dwelt and there yearly and assiduously occupied and exercised tillage and husbandry, and have expelled and ejected the same our subjects dwelling therein from their holdings and farms, and have reduced the country round the houses, towns and hamlets aforesaid, and the fields and lands within the same, to pasture and for flocks of sheep and other animals to graze there for the sake of their private gain and profit, and have imparked certain great fields and pasture and woods of the same in large and broad parks, and certain others in augmentation of parks for deer only to graze there, whereby the same towns, hamlets and places are not only brought to desolation, but also the houses and buildings of the same are brought to so great ruin, that no vestige of the same at the present is left, and our subjects, who have dwelt in the said places and there occupied and exercised tillage and husbandry, are now brought to idleness, which is the step-mother of virtues, and daily live in idleness, and the crops and breeding of cattle that were bred and nourished by the same tillers and husbandmen dwelling in the same towns, hamlets and places for human sustenance, are withdrawn and entirely voided from the same places, and the churches and chapels there hallowed are destroyed and divine services there taken away, and the memory of souls of Christians buried there utterly and wholly perished, and many other inestimable damages grow therefrom and daily hereafter will grow, to the greatest desolation and undoing of our realm and diminution of our subjects, unless an opportune remedy for the reformation of the same be swiftly and speedily applied: We, as we are duly bound, desiring to reform the aforesaid and wishing to be certified touching the same, what and how many towns and hamlets and how many houses and buildings have been thrown down from the feast of St. Michael the Archangel in the fourth year of the reign of the most illustrious lord Henry, late king of England, the Seventh, our father, and how many and how great lands which were then in tillage are now enclosed and converted to pasture, and how many and how great parks have been imparked for the feeding of deer since the same feast, and what lands have been enclosed in any parks or any park, which then were or was, for the amplifying and enlarging of such parks, have therefore appointed you and two of you to enquire by oath of good and lawful men of the counties of Oxford, Berks, Warwick, Leicester, Bedford, Buckingham, and Northampton, as well within liberties as without, and by other ways, manners and means whereby you shall or may the better learn the truth, what and how many towns, how many houses and buildings have been thrown down from the aforesaid feast, and how many and how great lands which were then in tillage are now converted to pasture, and how many and how great parks have been enclosed for the feeding of deer on this side the same feast, and what lands have been enclosed in any parks or any park, which then were or was, for the enlargement of such parks, and by whom, where, when, how and in what manner, and touching other articles and circumstances in any wise concerning the premises, according to the tenor and effect of certain articles specified in a bill to these presents annexed. And therefore we command you that you attend diligently to the premises and do and execute the same with effect. And by the tenor of these presents we command our sheriffs of the counties aforesaid that at certain days and places, which you shall cause them to know, they cause to come before you or two of you as many and such good and lawful men of their bailiwick by whom the truth of the matter may the better be known and enquired of; and that you certify us in our Chancery of what you shall do in the premises in three weeks from the day of St. Michael next coming, together with this commission.

29 On Ploughs and Ploughing, 1534

(*The Book of Husbandry, by Master Fitzherbert*, 1534d, edn., ed. W. W. Skeat (English Dialect Society, XXXVII, 1882), pp. 9–19)

1. Here begins the book of husbandry, and first whereby husband-men do live

The most general living that husbands can have, is by ploughing and sowing of their corn, and rearing or breeding of their cattle, and not the one without the other. Then is the plough the most necessary instrument that an husband can occupy. Wherefore it is convenient to be known, how a plough should be made.

2. Divers manners of ploughs

There are ploughs of divers makings in divers countries, and in like wise there are ploughs of iron of divers fashions. And that is because there are many manners of grounds and soils. Some white clay, some red clay, some gravel or chiltern, some sand, some mean earth, some meddled with marl, and in many places heath-ground, and one plough will not serve in all places. Wherefore it is necessary to have divers manners of ploughs. In Somerset, about Zelcester, the sharebeam, that in many places is called the plough-head, is four or five feet long, and it is broad and thin. And that is because the land is very tough, and would soke[1] the plough into the earth, if the sharebeam were not long, broad, and thin. In Kent they have other manner of ploughs, some go with wheels, as they do in many other places, and some will turn the sheldbred[2] at every land's end, and plough all one way. In Buckinghamshire, are ploughs made of another manner, and also other manner of plough-irons, the which me seem generally good, and likely to serve in many places, and especially if the ploughbeam and sharebeam be four inches longer, between the sheath and the plough-tail, that the sheldbred might come more a-slope: for those ploughs give out too suddenly, and therefore they are the worse to draw, and for no cause else. In Leicestershire, Lancashire, Yorkshire, Lincoln, Norfolk, Cambridgeshire, and many other countries, the ploughs are of divers makings, the which were too long process to declare how, &c. But howsoever they are made, if they are well tempered, and go well, they may be the better suffered ...

*   *   *

5. The necessary things that belong to a plough, cart and wain

But or he begins to plough, he must have his plough and his plough-iron, his oxen or horses, and the gear that belongs to them; that is to say, bows, yokes, lands, stylkings, wrething-temes.[3] And or he shall load his corn, he must have a wain, a copyoke, a pair of sleeves, a wain-rope, and a pitchfork. This wain is made of divers pieces, that will have a great reparation, that is to say, the wheels, and those are made of nathes, spokes, fells, and dowles, and they must be well fettered with wood or iron. And if they are iron bound, they are much the better, and though they are the dearer at first, yet at length they are better cheap; for a pair of wheels iron-bound will wear 7 or 8 pair of other wheels, and they go round and light after oxen or horses to draw. Howbeit on marreis ground and soft ground the other wheels are better, because they are broader on the soil, and will not go so deep. They must have an axle-tree, clout with 8 wainclouts of iron, 2 linchpins of iron in the axle-tree ends, 2 axle-pins of iron or else of tough hard wood. The body of the wain of oak, the staves, the nether rathes, the upper rathes, the cross somer, the keys and pike-staves.[4] And if he goes with a horse plough, then must he have his horses or mares, or both his hombers or collars, holmes whited,[5] traces, swingletrees, and togwith.[6] Also a cart made of ash, because it is light, and like stuff to it as to a wain, and also a cart saddle, back bands and belly bands and a cart ladder behind, when he shall carry either corn or kiddes[7] or such other. And in many countries their wains have cart ladders both behind and before. Also a husband must have an axe, a hatchet, a hedging bill, a pin-auger, a rest-auger, a flail, a spade, and a shovel. And howbeit that I give them these names, as are most commonly used in my country, I know they have other names in other countries. But hereby a man may perceive many things that belong to husbandry, to their great cost and charges, for the maintenance and upholding of the same. And many more things belong to husbands than these, as you shall well perceive, ere I have made an end of this treatise. And if a young husband should buy all these things, it would be costly for him: wherefore it is necessary for him to learn to make his yokes, ox-bows, stools, and all manner of plough-gear.

6. Whether is better, a plough of horses or a plough of oxen

It is to be known, whether it is better, a plough of horses, or a plough of oxen, and therein me seems ought to be a distinction. For in some places an ox-plough is better than a horse-plough, and in some places a horse-plough is better: that is to say, in every place whereas the husband has several pastures to put his oxen in when they come from their work, there the ox-plough is better. For an ox may not endure his work, to labour all day, and then to be put to the commons, or before the herdsman, and to be set in a fold all night without meat, and go to his labour in the morning. But if he be put in a good pasture all night, he will labour much of all the day daily. And oxen will plough in tough clay, and upon hilly ground, whereas horses will stand still. And whereas is no several pastures, there the horse-plough is better, for the horses may be tethered or tied upon leys, balks, or hades, where oxen may not be kept: and it is not used to tether them, but in few places. And horses will go faster than oxen on even ground or light ground, and are quicker for carriage: but they are far more costly to keep in winter, for they must have both hay and corn to eat, and straw for litter; they must be well shod on all four feet, and the gear that they shall draw with is more costly than for the oxen, and shorter while it will last. And oxen will eat but straw, and a little hay, the which is not half the cost that horses must have, and they have no shoes, as horses have. And if any sorance[8] comes to the horse, or he wax old, bruised, or blind, then he is little worth. And if any sorance comes to an ox, and he waxes old, bruised, or blind, for 2s he may be fed and then he is man's meat, and as good or better than ever he was. And the horse, when he dies, is but carrion. And therefore me seems, all things considered, the plough of oxen is much more profitable than the plough of horses . . .

*   *   *

8. How a man should plough all manner of land all times of the year

Now these ploughs are made and tempered, it is to be known how a man should plough all times of the year. In the beginning of the year, after the feast of the Epiphany,[9] it is time for a husband to go to the plough. And if you have any leys, to fallow or to sow oats upon, first plough them, that the grass and the moss may rot, and plough them a deep square furrow. And in all manner of ploughing, see that your eye, your hand, and your foot do agree, and be always ready one to serve another, and to turn up much mould, and to lay it flat, that it rear not on edge. For if it rear on edge, the grass and moss will not rot. And if you sow it with winter corn, as wheat or rye, as much corn as touches the moss will be drowned, moss does keep such wet in itself. And in some countries, if a man ploughs deep, he shall pass the good ground, and have but little corn: but that country is not for men to keep husbandry upon, but for to rear and breed cattle or sheep, for else they must go beat their lands with mattocks, as they do in many places of Cornwall, and in some places of Devonshire.

9. To plough for peas and beans

How to plough for peas and beans, were necessary to know. First you must remember, which is most clay-ground, and that plough first, and let it lie a good space, ere you sow it: because the frost, the rain, the wind, and the sun may cause it to break small, to make much mould, and to rig it. And to plough a square furrow, the breadth and the deepness all one, and to lay it close to its fellow. For the more furrows, the more corn, for a general rule of all manner of corn. And that may be proved at the coming up of all manner of corn, to stand at the land's end and look toward the other end; and then may you see how the corn grows.

10. *How to sow both peas and beans*

You shall sow your peas upon the clay ground, and your beans upon the barley-ground: for they would have ranker ground than peas. Howbeit some husbands hold opinion, that big and stiff ground, as clay, would be sown with big stuff, as beans; but I think the contrary. For if a dry summer comes, his beans will be short. And if the ground is good, put the more beans to the peas, and the better shall they yield, when they are threshed. And if it is very rank ground, as is much at every town-side, where cattle do resort, plough not that land, till you will sow it; for if you do, there will come up kedlokes and other weeds. And then sow it with beans; for if you sow peas, the kedlokes will hurt them; and when you see seasonable time, sow both peas and beans, so that they are sown in the beginning of March. How shall you know seasonable time? Go upon the land, that is ploughed, and if it sings or cries, or makes any noise under your feet, then it is too wet to sow: and if it makes no noise, and will bear your horses, then sow in the name of God. But how to sow? Put your peas into your hopper, and take a broad thong, of leather, or of garth-web of an ell long, and fasten it to both ends of the hopper, and put it over your head, like a leash; and stand in the midst of the land, where the sack lies, the which is most convenient for the filling of your hopper, and set your left foot before, and take an handfull of peas: and when you take up your right foot, then cast your peas from yourself all abroad; and when your left foot rises, take another handfull, and when the right foot rises, then cast them from yourself. And so at every two paces, you shall sow an handfull of peas: and so see that the foot and the hand agree, and then you shall sow even. And in your casting, you must open as well your fingers as your hand, and the higher and farther that you cast your corn, the better shall it spread, except it is a great wind. And if the land is very good, and will break small in the ploughing, it is better to sow after the plough than tarry any longer.

---

[1] Suck. (WWS, and other notes also)   [2] Shield board.   [3] Parts of harness.
[4] Parts of the wain.   [5] Cut to shape.   [6] Parts of harness.   [7] Faggots.
[8] Trouble.   [9] 6 January.

30 Of Rent Raisers, Mid-Sixteenth Century

(*The Select Work of Robert Crowley*, ed. J. M. Cowper (Early English
Text Society, Extra Series, XV, 1872), pp. 46–7)

> A man that had lands,
>   of ten pound by year,
> Surveyed the same,
>   and let it out dear.
> So that of ten pound
>   he made well a score,
> More pounds by the year
>   than other did before.
> But when he was told
>   what danger it was
> To oppress his tenants,
>   he said he did not pass.
> For this thing, he said,
>   full certain he wist,
> That with his own he might
>   always do as he list.
> But immediately, I trow,
>   this oppressor fell sick
> Of a voice that he heard,
>   'give account of thy bailiwick!'

31 Villeinage in the Reign of Elizabeth, 1561

(*The Records of the City of Norwich*, ed. J. C. Tingey, II (1910), p. 180)

Court of Mayoralty, 31 December 1561   Robert Ringwood brought in
a certain indenture wherein Lewes Lowth, the son of Thomas Lowth
of Attilburgh, was bound to him to serve as an apprentice for seven
years. And Mr John Holdiche came before Mr Mayor and other justices
and declared that the said Lewes is a bondman to my lord of Norfolk's
grace, and further that he was brought up in husbandry until he was
20 years old. Whereupon he was discharged of his service.

32 Petition for Tenant Rights, 1576

(P.R.O. Requests Proceedings, III, 24)

To the queen's most excellent majesty. In most humble wise shows unto your majesty your poor subject Thomas Langhorne, and other the inhabitants and residents of the lordship of Thornthwaite in your county of Westmoreland, that whereas your suppliant and other of the inhabitants and residents of the lordship aforesaid, and their ancestors time out of memory of man, have quietly had and enjoyed from heir to heir according to their ancient custom in consideration of their service to be in readiness with horse, harness and other furniture to serve your majesty at their own costs and charges in defence of your realm against the Scots, which custom has been sufficiently approved and allowed before your majesty's president and council at York, as by a decree ready to be shewed more at large it may appear. But so it is, and if it please your majesty, that Sir Henry Curwyn, knight, lord of the lordship aforesaid, has since the beginning of your majesty's reign expelled out of one piece of Shapps parish within the said lordship, where there was but thirteen tenants, twelve of them he has expelled and taken their land from them and enclosed it into his demesnes, whereby your majesty's service for the same is utterly taken away: and also the said Sir Henry Curwyn, lord of the lordship aforesaid, has of late surrendered over the same lordship to Nicholas Curwyn, gentleman, his son and heir, which Sir Henry and Nicholas do excessively fine the poor tenants and specially your orator, who was forced to pay them for the fine of his tenement, being but 13s 10d by year, 31l 6s 8d, and was admitted tenant to the said Nicholas Curwyn, who notwithstanding has contrary to all right and conscience granted a lease of your subject's tenement to one Henry Curwyn, servant to the same Nicholas, in the nature of an *ejection firm*[1] here at the common law, and has by your majesty's writ arrested your orator to appear in your highness' bench at Westminster to the utter undoing of your said poor subject, his wife and five children for ever, being not able to defend his rightful cause: May it therefore please your most excellent majesty that order may be set down by your majesty and your most honourable council that none of the lordship aforesaid may be expelled out and from their tenant rights until their said custom shall be tried and examined before the lord president of York for the time being, and that your majesty's said subject may not be constrained to answer any suit here at the common law concerning their tenant right . . .

[Endorsed.] 18 May, 1586.

Your humble subject Thomas Langhorne, one of the tenants of the lordship of Thornthwaite in the county of Westmoreland, being molested in their tenant right by one Henry Curwyn, servant unto Nicholas Curwyn, lord of the said manor, desire most humbly that all actions at the common laws here at Westminster might be stayed and the full hearing of the matter reserved to the Lord President at York.

25 May, 18 Elizabeth.

¹ i.e. an *ejectio firmae*, an action of ejectment. (B, B, T)

33 Customs of the Manor of High Furness, 1576

(P.R.O. Duchy of Lancaster, Special Commissions, 398)

For the queen

*   *   *

3. That the jury ought to present at the court after every tenant's death or alienation, and who is his heir, and which tenant has aliened, and to whom, and what, and who ought to be admitted tenant to the same, which presentment and admittance ought to be made in open court and be entered by the steward . . .

4. No person shall hereafter sell his customary tenement or any part of it, before he first be admitted tenant or come to court, and require to be admitted . . . offering his fine for the same.

The purchaser of any tenement shall publish the sale at the next court after the purchase, and cause it to be entered on the rolls, that her majesty may be duly answered of the fines, forfeitures and duties as well of the seller as the purchaser [penalty 20*s*]. Any purchaser not so coming to the second court after the purchase shall forfeit 40*s*, and the lands purchased shall be seized by the steward.

5. As heretofore dividing and portioning of tenements has caused great decay chiefly of the service due to her highness for horses, and of her woods, and has been the cause of making a great number of poor people in the lordship, it is now ordered that no one shall divide his tenement or tenements among his children, but that the least part shall be of the ancient yearly rent to her highness of 6*s* 8*d* and that before every such division there shall be several houses and ousettes for every part of such tenement.

Provided always that it be lawful for any one, who has bought any tenement or farmhold under the yearly rent of 6*s* 8*d* having houses and ousette upon it, which has been used as a dwelling house, [to leave it] to which of his children he thinks best.

And no person holding any part of any tenement shall bargain or put it away to any person except that person who is tenant of the residue of the tenement, if he will buy it at a reasonable price. If not, the tenant may sell it to any other customary tenant of the manor.

10. Every customary tenant and occupier shall uphold his houses according to our custom, forfeiting 6s 8d *toties quoties*.

11. No person shall fell timber without delivery of the bailiff, who shall deliver necessary timber to every tenant or occupier according to our custom.

12. No tenant or occupier shall sell underwood, &c., nor cut down any other man's wood in the lordship. Penalty 3s 4d, half to her highness, half to the party grieved. Every tenant so grieved may have his action for damages in the court of the lordship.

13. No tenant is to stop any common way nor turn aside a beck. Penalty 6s 8d.

For the tenants

1. Any tenant, lawfully seised of a messuage or tenement in fee to him and his heirs according to the custom of the manor, might and may lawfully give or sell the same by writing, and that the steward or his deputy ought to be made privy to it at or before next court under penalty of 20s.

The tenant may without the privity of the steward give his tenement in writing by his last will to which of his sons he thinks best, or any other person. If any customary tenant die seised of an estate of inheritance without a will or devise, then his eldest son or next cousin ought to have the tenement, as his next heir, according to the custom of the manor.

2. If any customary tenant die seised of a customary tenement, having no sons but a daughter or daughters, then the eldest daughter being unpreferred in marriage shall have the tenement as his next heir ...and she shall pay to her younger sister, if she have but one sister, 20 years' ancient rent, as is answered to her majesty; and if she have more than one sister, she shall pay 40 years' ancient rent to be equally divided among them.

3. The widow of any customary tenant having any estate of inheritance ought to have her widowright, viz., one-third of the same, as long as she is unmarried and chaste, according to our custom.

4. For the avoiding of great trouble in the agreements with younger brothers, it is now ordered that the oldest son shall pay to his brothers in the form following:—

If there is but 1 brother, 12 years' ancient rent.

If there are 2 brothers, 16 years' ancient rent, to be equally divided.

If there be 3 or more, 20 years' ancient rent, to be equally divided.

Provided that any father being a tenant may make a will dividing the money among his sons as he think best, provided he exceed not these sums and rates.

5. Whereas great inconvenience has grown by certain persons that at the marriages of sons or daughters have promised their tenements to the same son or daughter and their heirs according to the custom of the manor, and afterwards put the tenement away to another person, it is ordered, that whatever tenements a tenant shall promise to his son or daughter being his sole heir apparent at the time of his or her marriage, the same ought to come to them according to the same covenant, which ought to be showed at the next court.

6. If a tenant has a child, not his heir, an idiot or impotent, and die without disposition of his tenement, the same child shall be sustained out of the said tenement by direction of the steward or his deputy and 4 men sworn in court.

7. Finally be it agreed that no bye-law shall be any way prejudicial to her majesty.

34 Act for the Maintenance of Husbandry and Tillage, 1597–8

(39 Elizabeth, c. 2, *Statutes of the Realm*, IV, Part II (1819), pp. 893–6)

Whereas the strength and flourishing estate of this kingdom has been always and is greatly upheld and advanced by the maintenance of the plough and tillage, being the occasion of the increase and multiplying of people both for service in the wars and in times of peace, being also a principal means that people are set on work, and thereby withdrawn from idleness, drunkenness, unlawful games and all other lewd practices and conditions of life; and whereas by the same means of tillage and husbandry the greater part of the subjects are preserved from extreme poverty in a competent estate of maintenance and means to live, and the wealth of the realm is kept dispersed and distributed in many hands where it is more ready to answer all necessary charges for the service of the realm; and whereas also the said husbandry and tillage is a cause that the realm does more stand upon itself, without depending upon foreign countries either for bringing in of corn in time of scarcity, or for vent and utterance of our own commodities being in over great abundance; and whereas from the 27th year of King Henry VIII of famous memory, until the five and thirtieth year of her majesty's most happy reign, there was always in force some law which did ordain a conversion and continuance of a certain quantity and apportion of land in tillage not to be altered; and that in the last parliament held in the said five and thirtieth year of her majesty's reign, partly by reason of the great plenty and cheapness of grain at that time within this realm, and partly by reason of the imperfection and obscurity of the law made in that case, the same was discontinued; since which time there have grown many more depopulations, by turning tillage into pasture, than at any time for the like number of years heretofore: Be it enacted . . . that whereas any lands or grounds at any time since the seventeenth of November in the first year of her majesty's reign have been converted to sheep pastures or to the fattening or grazing of cattle, the same lands having been tillable lands, fields or grounds such as have been used in tillage by the space of twelve years together at the least next before such conversion, according to the nature of the soil and course of husbandry used in that part of the country, all such lands and grounds as aforesaid shall, before the first day of May which shall be in the year of Our Lord God 1599, be restored to tillage, or laid for tillage in such sort as the whole ground, according to the nature of that soil and course of husbandry used in that part of the country, be within three years at the least turned to tillage by the occupiers and possessors thereof, and so shall be continued for ever.

And be it further enacted . . . that all lands and grounds which now are used in tillage or for tillage, having been tillable lands, fields or grounds, such as next before the first day of this present parliament have been by the space of twelve years together at the least used in tillage or for tillage, according to the nature of the soil and course of husbandry used in that part of the country, shall not be converted to any sheep pasture or to the grazing or fattening of cattle by the occupiers or possessors thereof, but shall, according to the nature of that soil and course of husbandry used in that part of the country, continue to be used in tillage or for tillage for corn or grain, and not for waste. . . .

And be it enacted . . . that if any person or body politic or corporate shall offend against the premises, every such person or body politic or corporate so offending shall lose and forfeit for every acre not restored or not continued as aforesaid, the sum of twenty shillings for every year that he or they so offend; and that the said penalties or forfeitures shall be divided in three equal parts, whereof one third part to be to the queen's majesty, her heirs and successors to her and their own use [and] one other third part to the queen's majesty, her heirs and successors for relief of the poor in the parish where the offence shall be committed . . . and the other third part to such person as will sue for the same in any court of record at Westminster. . . .

Provided also, that this act shall not extend to any counties within this realm of England, but such only as shall be hereafter specified;

that is to say, the counties of Northampton, Leicester, Warwick, Buckingham, Bedford, Oxford, Berkshire, the Isle of Wight, Gloucester, Worcester, Nottingham, Hampshire, Wiltshire, Somerset, Dorset, Derby, Rutland, Lincoln, Hereford, Cambridge, Huntingdon, York, Pembroke in South Wales, and the bishopric of Durham, and Northumberland, and the counties of all the cities and corporations lying situate and being within the counties aforesaid, or confining to the same, and the Ainsty of the county of the city of York.

35 Enclosure Riots in the East Midlands, 1607–08

('The Journal of Sir Roger Wilbrahim', ed. H. S. Scott, *Camden Miscellany*, X (Camden Society, Third Series, IV, 1902), pp. 91–5)

In the middle of June 1607 Beggars and vagrants in the town of Northampton, angered at the enclosures made near the town, in bands during the night threw down a part thereof. And in as much as they are not put down—their numbers increase, both from this town and divers towns in the county and in the counties of Warwick, Leicester, &c., and for 20 days their numbers continue to increase, till 300 or more in one place night and day are throwing down the new enclosures, nor do they desist in spite of two proclamations made by the king on different occasions that they should have justice and mercy if they desisted. And yet they continue until Sir A. Mildmay with some horsemen using force slay some ten in hot blood; and thus they were put down. Afterwards at the assizes of the before mentioned several counties, two or 3 were hanged as an example. So that, as the king says, the punishment of a few may impress the majority with fear. Moreover the proclamation says that it is not a legal course for subjects to remedy their grievances by force, but that they should petition the king to be relieved according to justice. And the judges of assize in order to satisfy the common people inveigh against enclosers and depopulators; and inquire concerning them and promise reformation at the hands of justice. And this puts courage into the common people, so that with mutterings they threaten to have a more violent revenge if they cannot be relieved. On this the Council appoints select commissioners, learned in the law, in the six counties; to inquire concerning the acts of depopulation and conversion of arable into pasture land. And they report to the Council on December 6, 1607, to this effect. That in the counties of Lincoln, Leicester, Northampton, Warwick, Huntingdon, Bedford and Buckingham about 200 or 300 tenements have been depopulated; and a great number of acres have been converted from arable into pasture and. To wit, 9000 acres in Northamptonshire and a great number in the other counties. And that the people seek that their commons, appurtenant to the towns, should be disenclosed; but this point was not inquired into by the commissioners, but is referred to the law. And the depopulators offer reformation and submit themselves to the mercy of the king, and not the mercy of Sir H. Carey, patentee of the penal statute against depopulators.

On this directions were given to the learned counsel that the most notorious enclosers in each county should be summoned this Christmas for Hilary Term before the Star Chamber: and justice and mercy shown to them, so that they should not despair, nor should the common people insult them or be incited to make rebellion, whereof they are greatly suspected. Also the mayor of Northampton, the sheriff and the neighbouring justices who did not repress the outrages at the beginning should also be brought before the Star Chamber by reason of their remissness. And it is hoped that this public example may stay the fury of the common people. These deliberations I reported to the king at Newmarket on December 8th by order of the Council. And he seems to approve of this course, for the manifestation of his justice and the speedy reformation of oppression. And the earl of Salisbury advises the depopulators and enormous enclosers to submit themselves to the king, and make redress of the present offence.

February [*1608*] The Attorney General states that, after conference with all the judges, the law against depopulation is so variable and uncertain that no fixed punishment can be inflicted on depopulators, as can be on converters of tillage and pasturage, where the punishment is fixed. Therefore a provision was made for a commission to issue to divers lords of the Council, judges and Masters of Requests to make composition with the depopulators with the intent that they should persuade them to rebuild the houses with a view to giving visible satisfaction to the murmuring people; and to satisfy them rather than gain fines to the king.

36 Petition for Restoration of Rights of Common, temp. Charles I

(*The Topographer and Genealogist*, ed. J. G. Nichols, III (1858), pp. 22–5)

To the right honourable house of parliament now assembled. The humble petition of the mayor and free tenants of the borough of Wootton Basset in the county of Wiltshire.

Humbly shows to this honourable house, that whereas the mayor and free tenants of the said borough, by relation of our ancient predecessors, had and did hold unto them free common of pasture for the feeding of all manner of ruther beasts, as cows, &c., without stint, be they never so many, in and through Fasterne Great Park, which said park contained by estimation 2000 acres of ground or upwards; and in the second and third year of the reign of King Philip and Queen Mary, the manor of Wootton Basset aforesaid came by patent into the hands and possession of one Sir Francis Englefield, knight, who, in short time after he was thereof possessed, did enclose the said park; and in consideration of the common of pasture that the free tenants of the borough had in the said park, did grant, condescend and leave out unto the said free tenants of the said borough to use as common amongst them that parcel of the said Great Park which formerly was and now is called by the name of Wootton Lawnd, which was but a small portion to that privilege that they had before it, [and] does not contain by estimation above 100 acres; but the free tenants being therewith contented, the mayor and free tenants did equally stint the said ground or common, as follows (that is to say) to the mayor of the town for the time being two cows feeding, and to the constable one cow feeding, and to every inhabitant of the said borough, each and every of them, one cow feeding and no more, as well the poor as the rich, and every one to make and maintain a certain parcel of bound set forth to every person; and ever after that inclosure for the space of fifty and six years, or near thereabouts, any messuage, burgage or tenement that was bought or sold within the said borough, did always buy and sell the said cows-leaze together with the said messuage or burgage as part and member of the same, as does and may appear by divers deeds which are yet to be seen; and about which time, as we are informed and do verily believe, that Sir Francis Englefield, heir of the aforesaid Sir Francis Englefield, did by some means gain the charter of our town into his hands, and as lately we have heard that his successors now keep it; and we do believe that at the same time he did likewise gain the deed of the said common; and he thereby knowing that the town had nothing to show for their rights of common but by prescription, did begin suits in law with the said free tenants for their common, and did vex them with so many suits in law, for the space of seven or eight years at the least, and never suffer anyone to come to trial in all that space, but did divers times attempt to gain the possession thereof by putting in of divers sorts of cattle, in so much that at length, when his servants did put in cows by force into the said common, many times and present upon the putting of them in, the Lord in his mercy did send thunder and lightning from heaven, which did make the cattle of the said Sir Francis Englefield to run so violent out of the said ground that at one time one of the beasts was killed therewith; and it was so often that people that were not there in presence to see it, when it did thunder would say that Sir Francis Englefield's men were putting in their cattle into the Lawnd, and so it was; and as soon as those cattle were gone forth it would presently be very calm and fair, and the cattle of the town would never stir but follow their feeding as at other times, and never offer to move out of the way but follow their feeding. And this did continue so long, he being too powerful for them, that the said free tenants were not able to wage law any longer, for one John Rosier, one of the free tenants, was thereby enforced to sell all his land (to the value of 500*l*) with following the suits in law, and many others were thereby impoverished, and were thereby forced to yield up their right and take a lease of their said common of the said Sir Francis Englefield for term of his life. And the said mayor and free tenants have now lost their right of common in the said Lawnd near about twenty years, which this now Sir Francis Englefield, his heirs and his trustees, now detain from them.

Likewise the said Sir Francis Englefield has taken away their shops or shambles standing in the middle of the street in the market-place from the town, and has given them to a stranger that lives not in the town . . . and likewise he has taken away certain garden grounds, which are taken out of a bye-street . . . And he has altered and does seek ways and means to take the election of the mayor of our town to himself; for whereas the mayor is chosen at the law-day, and the jury did ever make choice of two men of the town, and the lord of the manor was to appoint one of them to serve, which the lord of the manor has refused, and caused one to stay in two years together divers times, which is a breach of our custom.

And as for our common we do verily believe that no corporation in England so much is wronged as we are. For we are put out of all the common that ever we had, and have not so much as one foot of common left unto us, nor never shall have any. We are thereby grown so in poverty, unless it please God to move the hearts of this honourable house to commiserate our cause, and to enact something for us, that we may enjoy our right again. And we your orators shall be ever bound to pray for your health and prosperity in the Lord.

[here follow 23 signatures.]

Divers hands more we might have had, but that many of them do rent bargains of the lord of the manor, and they are fearful that they shall be put forth of their bargains, and then they shall not tell how to live. Otherwise they would have set to their hands.

37 Market Gardening Around London, 1618

(*Calendar of State Papers, Venetian*, XV, 1617–19 (1909), pp. 318–19)

Report of Horatio Busino, chaplain to the Venetian ambassador

This island . . . is in great part gravelly to the depth of six or seven feet and upwards beneath the surface, its culture must therefore prove very sterile in such wise that unless aided by industry, the soil would yield no vegetables or very few, especially in the environs of London where they are needed. It is therefore customary to dig up this substance, which they employ not merely as ballast for the ships and for the repair of the muddy streets, but they incorporate its finer particles with building mortar. The voids thus formed in the fields are then filled up, to the depth of four or five feet with the filth of the city, which serves as excellent manure, rich and black as thick ink and which is conveyed at small cost by the innumerable carts which are bound to cleanse the streets, so that in a very short while many spots are improved and fertilized, their proprietors enclosing them immediately for their safe custody, in various ways, at small cost. Some effect this by means of palings; others sink very deep ditches; some again form the enclosure of soft mud mixed with half rotten straw, and this being raised to a sufficient height from the ground they surmount it with a thatch of rye straw, which serves for eaves. On the top of this thatch, which projects a foot on either side they place a parapet, also of mud, to consolidate the eaves and preserve this mud structure which soon becomes very hard. In these places, although the climate is not entirely favourable for them, they nevertheless raise a great quantity of vegetables. I will only mention their most beautiful and fine flavoured artichokes, of a sort different from ours, that is to say much larger and of a reddish tinge. Of these they gather an immense quantity during ten months of the year and sell them at a very cheap rate. I think I have already mentioned the size of the cabbages, which sometimes weigh 35 lbs the pair, to such an enormous size do they grow. But that is nothing; on this very day, the 19th of September, when his excellency went to inspect certain gardens and a sorry melon ground where the *sbotteghe* however cost us 35 pence a piece, we saw a number of cabbages weighing 28 lbs each, a marvellous thing. There are extremely white and very large potatoes, cauliflowers, parsnips, carrots, turnips etc. In these enclosures they endeavour to rear an immense number of suckers, which being subsequently engrafted are sold in due season to the curious to be planted in orchards or to embellish gardens. The apples are really very good and cheap, of various sorts and procurable all the year round. The pears are scarcely eatable and the other fruits most abominable, their taste resembling that of insipid masticated grass. The numerous sorts of cherries and egriots which one sees in Italy may well be desired in this kingdom, though certainly not enjoyed, for generally in the markets they only sell one single sort of very bad morella. Yet the English are extremely greedy of them, especially the women, buying them at the beginning of the season in bunches at the cost of an eye. Then these gentlewomen go with their squires to the fruit and flower gardens and orchards, to strive who can eat the most. It occurs to me here that a few months ago a leading lady ate 20 pounds of this fruit in competition with a cavalier who was scarcely seventeen. It is true that she ran the risk of her life, the exploit having confined her to her bed for many days.

38 A Steward's Grumble over Tenurial Complexities, c. 1630

(*The Book of John Rowe, Steward of the Manors of Lord Bergavenny, 1597–1622*, ed. W. H. Godfrey (Sussex Record Society, XXXIV, 1928), p. 93)

. . . All the residue of the tenants of this manor are copyholders; whose customs I find so variable, as that I can not certainly resolve myself thereof, much less satisfy others. For albeit I well know that there may be in one manor two several customs, some holding in fee, others for lives in several tenements and both good in law. Yet to hold in fee; for 3 lives successively; for 4 lives successively; for 2 or 3 lives successively and to theirs of one of them, and that in one and the same tenement as it often falls out in this manor and all of them very ancient . . . I think will hardly be found in any other manor of this realm the like confusion, except it be in the adjoining manor of Chiltington, whose customs as they are the same with Notborne, so I find their estates to be entangled with the like difficulties fitter for the reverend judges of this kingdom upon mature deliberation to resolve, than for mine insufficiency to determine.

F

39　Watering and Floating of Meadows, 1632

(Court Roll of the manor of Wylye, 1632, printed in *Surveys of the Manors of Philip, first Earl of Pembroke and Montgomery, 1631–2*, ed. E. Kerridge (Wiltshire Archaeological and Natural History Society, Records, IX, 1953), pp. 138–40)

It is ordered, concluded and agreed at this court between Sir Giles Mompesson, knight, and Guy Everley, freeholders within this manor, and others the tenants of the residue of the freeholders, and the customary tenants and others of this manor now present, and by and with the consent and approbation of the said William Kent, steward of this manor, of the one part, and John Knight of Stockton in the county of Wilts, for and concerning the watering and floating of the grounds within this manor called the Marsh, Nettlemead and the Moors, for the better improvement of them in yearly value as follows, videlicet.

First, the said John Knight has undertaken and does promise to draw a sufficient and competent quantity of water of the river of Wylye, out of the same river, sufficiently to water and float all the said grounds or so much thereof as by industry and art may be watered and floated, lying subject to the said river, before the feast of St. Andrew the Apostle[1] now next coming, and to continue the watering and floating thereof at all convenient times for one whole year to be ended at Michaelmas[2] 1633.

In consideration of which work, the said freeholders and tenants have agreed and do promise as follows: first, that they, the said freeholders and tenants, shall and will at their own proper costs and charges make and maintain all and all manner of timber works, flood-hatches and bays needful, necessary and useful for the work aforesaid. Item that the said freeholders and tenants and every of them respectively shall and will permit and suffer the said John Knight, his servants and assigns, to dig trenches and conduits for the said water and to make bays in all and every their several and particular grounds for the needful and necessary carriage and conducting of the said water for the intent aforesaid, without any their lets or interruptions. And further that whosoever shall molest, interrupt or disturb the said John Knight in doing and performing the work aforesaid, whereby the work may be impeached or the proceeding thereof hindered by the space of two days, shall forfeit to the lord of this manor for every such interruption 10*s.*

Item, the said freeholders and tenants do conclude, agree and promise to pay or cause to be paid to the said John Knight, for doing and performing the work aforesaid, for every acre of ground that by his art and industry shall be watered and floated according to the intent of the agreement aforesaid 14s of lawful money of England in manner and form following. That is to say, first, because it is conceived for the better improvement of the same grounds that it is more necessary that the same should be watered and floated at three several floatings and not altogether, they the said freeholders and tenants whose grounds shall first happen to be watered and floated, shall and will pay to the said John Knight the first day of the beginning of his work the one moiety of the said 14s for every acre so first to be watered and floated and so for a more or less quantity of ground a more or less part of the said 14s and shall also pay the other moiety of the said 14s the day when the water shall be taken off the said grounds. And the like payments to be made for the other two several waterings and floatings aforesaid by the owners of the grounds when they shall happen to be floated in a manner aforesaid.

And whereas it is agreed by and between the parties aforesaid and the said John Knight has promised yearly and every year during the space of six years to begin at the feast of St. Michael the Archangel which shall be in the year of our Lord 1633 to scour and cleanse the said trenches and amend the bays and banks thereof, and to float the said grounds in good, orderly and sufficient manner, they the said tenants and freeholders do promise to pay to the said John Knight yearly for every year of the said six years the sum of 2s for every acre so watered and floated, and after that rate for a more or less quantity of ground a more or less part of the said sum of 2s, the same to be paid at the feasts of St. Thomas the Apostle[3] and the Annunciation of the Blessed Virgin Mary[4] yearly by even and equal portions. And whosoever shall refuse to pay the said money or does not pay the same within six days next after reasonable request to be made by the said John Knight shall forfeit and pay to the lord of this manor for every time 3s 4d.

And lastly it is agreed by and between the said freeholders and tenants aforesaid that if any damage shall grow by any annoyances which may happen in and by the baying of the river for turning the water for the use aforesaid that then the damage of every such person and persons shall be recompensed, satisfied and paid to the party so damnified by the rest and residue of the inhabitants proportionably; which said agreement all the said parties at this court desired to have entered in the rolls of the court of this manor and that thereupon an order should be made for the binding all the said parties to perform this agreement upon pains and penalties to be therein expressed, being a business conceived to be very behooffull and beneficial to all the inhabitants of this manor. It is thereupon ordered at this court that whosoever shall refuse to perform the order and agreement aforesaid in manner and form before mentioned and expressed or shall impeach the said work or hinder the proceedings thereof contrary to the true intent and meaning of the said agreement, shall forfeit and pay to the lord of this manor for so refusing twenty pounds, and to every hindrance and interruption twenty shillings. And it is further ordered that the charges for all necessary work to be done by the said freeholders and tenants for finishing the work aforesaid shall be rated proportionably according to their several values of improvement at the court of the said manor by the steward there for the time being upon such pains and forfeitures as the said steward and the more part of the homage there present shall then think fit.

		ANTHONY BALLARD	
Assuratores	⎱	JOHN PEIRSON	⎰ *Jurati*
Curie	⎰	JOHN LOCK junior	⎱

[1] 30 November.   [2] 29 September.   [3] 21 December.   [4] 25 March.

40 Hiring of Farm Servants, 1641

(*Rural Economy in Yorkshire in 1641, being the Farming and Account Books of Henry Best*, ed. C. B. Robinson (Surtees Society, XXXIII, 1857), pp. 132–6)

We give usually to a foreman five marks per annum, and perhaps 2*s* or half a crown to a godspenny,[1] if he is such a one as can sow, mow, stack peas, go well with four horses, and has been used to marketing and the like; for now of late we employ and trust our foreman with the sowing of all our seed. We give usually 50*s* or four marks to another, and perhaps 2*s* or 2*s* 6*d* for a godspenny, providing he is such a one as can sow, mow, go well with a draught, and be a good ploughman, and him also we employ as a seedsman in haver seed time, when we come to sow old ardure,[2] and now and then send him to markets with the foreman. We give usually seven nobles to a third man, that is a good mower, and a good four horse-man, and one that can go heppenly with a wain, and lie on a load of corn handsomely. We give usually 35*s* or 36*s* to a fourth man, if the report go on him for a good ploughman, and that we perceive him to be of a good competent strength for carrying of pokes, forking of a wain, or the like. We give usually to a spaught[3] for holding of the ox plough four nobles or perhaps 30*s* per annum, if he is such a one as has been trained and been brought up at the plough, and is a wigger[4] and heppen youth for loading of a wain, and going with a draught. We give usually 20s to a good stubble boy for driving of the ox plough, and that can (in time of need) carry a mette[5] or three bushel peas out of the barn into the garner. We have usually two maid-servants, and we were wont that we could hire them for 18s per annum, and 12d or 1s 6d for a godspenny, but now of late we cannot hire a good lusty-maid servant under 24s wage, and sometimes 28s and 18d or 2s for a godspenny. Christopher Pearson had (the first year he dwelt here) 3l 5s wages per annum, and 5s to a godspenny: he had the next year 4l wage and 12d to a godspenny, and he was both a good seeds-man, and a very good mower, and did sow all our seed both the years. Henry Wise had the first year that he took wage 36s, he had the next year 50s and 4s to a godspenny; and the third year he had four marks and 2s to a godspenny, and was one that could both sow and mow indifferent well. Henry Pinder was not full sixteen years of age when he came to dwell here first, and he had 24s and the next year after he had five nobles and 12d to a godspenny, for going with the ox plough, and being an heppen lad for loading of a wain, and going with a draught. Thomas Smyth had (the first year he dwelt here) 20s for driving the ox plough, and the next year four nobles and 6d to a godspenny, and was to have a pair of old breeches. Priscilla Browne had (the first year she dwelt here) 18s wages and 12d to a godspenny, the next year 24s, the third year 28s and 2s to a godspenny, and might have had the fourth year 38s and 12d to a godspenny. We had (at this time in our own hands) all the lands belonging to the demesnes, all the lands be-longing to the West hall, all the lands belonging to the West house farm, and the four oxgang which appertain to John Bonwick's house; we kept constantly five ploughs going, and milked fourteen kine, wherefore we had always four men, two boys to go with the ox plough, and two good lusty maid-servants. Some servants will (at their hiring) condition to have an old suit, a pair of breeches, an old hat, or a pair of shoes; and maid-servants to have an apron, smock, or both, but it is but sometimes and with some servants that such things are desired.

In hiring of a servant you are first to make sure that he is set at liberty; after that to inquire of him where he was born, in what services he has been, with what labour he has been most exercised, and whether he can do such and such things; and after that to go to his master or some neighbour of his that you are acquainted with, and tell them that you are about to hire such a servant, and so know of them whether he be true and trusty, if he is a gentle and quiet fellow, whether he is addicted to company-keeping or no, and lastly to know what wages he had the year afore, but if he have any of the forenamed ill properties, the best way will be to forbear hiring of him. In hiring of maid-servants you are to make choice of such as are good milkers, and to have a care of such as are of a sluggish and sleepy disposition, for danger of fire; and never to hire such as are too near their friends, for *occasion* is said to *make a thief*; and, being hired, you are not to commit over much to their trust, but to see into all things yourself, and to keep as much as you can under lock and key. When you are about to hire a servant, you are to call them aside and to talk privately with them concerning their wage, if the servants stand in the church-yard, they usually call them aside, and walk to the back side of the church, and there treat of their wage; and so soon as you have hired them, you are to call to them for their tickets, and thereby shall you be secured from all future danger; their tickets cost them 2*d* a piece, and some masters will give them that 2*d* again, but that is in the master's choice, unless they condition so before the servant is hired. Some servants will condition to have so many sheep wintered and summered with their masters, and look how many sheep there is, we account that equal to so many eighteen pences.

About a fortnight or ten days afore Martinmas[6] the chief constable of every division sends abroad his precepts to all petty constables, willing them to give notice to all masters and servants within their several constabularies, how that he intends to sit at such a place on such a day, commanding every of them to bring in a bill of the names of all the masters and servants within their several constabularies. There are usually two, and sometimes three, sittings or statute-days for every division, whereof the first is a week or more afore Martinmas, and the next three or four days after that; for he perhaps sends one warrant to so many towns to meet him at such a place on such a day, and another to other towns to meet him again at another place, or perhaps at the same place on such a day; and the towns that are first called, are the most privileged; for masters that want servants, and servants that want masters, have the benefit of the next sitting to provide for themselves; whereas those towns that are not called till the latter sitting have but one day to provide themselves in, for the servants in these towns cannot be hired till the towns be called, that their masters, or some for them, be there to set them at liberty; the first thing that the chief constable does is to call the constables of every town, and to take in the bills, and then to call the masters by their names, in order as they are set in the bills, and to ask them if they will set such and such a servant at liberty; if the master will, then he makes the servant his ticket, and the servant gives him 2*d* for his pains; if the master will not set him at liberty, then the chief constable is to let them know what wages the statute will allow, and to set down a reasonable and indifferent wage betwixt them, and he is to have one penny of the master for every servant that stays two years in a place, or is not set at liberty, and this the petty constables are to do for him, viz; to send in bills of the names of all such servants as stay with their old masters, and to gather the money, and send it him. Our sittings were both at Kirkburn this year; the chief constable sat at Mr Whipp's, and the servants stood in the churchyard, there is always a sitting at Killam the morrow after All Saints day,[7] and usually another at Sledgmour, two or three days after.

A master cannot turn away his servant, nor a servant go from his master, without a quarter's warning; servants will usually give their old masters a day, some two days, and some will stay three days with their old masters, and go away on the fourth day after Martinmas. They stay usually two or three days with their friends, and then about the fifth or sixth day after Martinmas will they come to their new masters; they will depart from their old services, any day in the week, but their desire (hereabouts) is to go to their new masters either on a Tuesday, or on a Thursday; for on a Sunday they will seldom remove, and as for Monday, they account it ominous, for they say

Monday flit,

Never sit:

but as for the other days in the week they make no great matter. I heard a servant asked what he could do, who made this answer,

I can sow,

I can mow,

And I can stack,

And I can do,

My master too,

When my master turns his back.

They will say to a maid, when they hire her, that if she has but been used to washing, milking, brewing, and baking, they make no question but she can sweep the house and wash the dishes. When servants go to the sitting, they put on their best apparel, that their masters may see them well clad; they get their breakfasts, and so go to the sitting immediately, yet the towns are seldom called before ten or eleven of the clock, yet they will stay till it is almost dark, afore they come home, and then have they their dinners; and if they are hired, they are not to go to the latter sitting.

---

[1] An earnest of a bargain.   [2] Fallow.   [3] Youth.   [4] Strong.
[5] Measure of two bushels.   [6] 11 November.   [7] 1 November.

41 Draining of the Fens, 1649

(S. Wells, *A Collection of the Laws which form the Constitution of the Bedford Level Corporation* (1828), pp. 367–82)

May, 1649. An Act for the draining of the Great Level of the Fens, extending itself into the counties of Northampton, Norfolk, Suffolk, Lincoln, Cambridge, Huntingdon, and the Isle of Ely, or some of them.

Whereas the said Great Level, by reason of frequent overflowing of the rivers of Welland, Neane, Grant, Ouse, Brandon, Mildenhal, and Stoke, [has] been of small and uncertain profit, but (if drained) may be improved and made profitable, and of great advantage to the commonwealth and to the particular owners, commoners, and inhabitants, and be fit to bear coleseed and rapeseed in great abundance, which is of singular use to make soap and oils within this nation, to the advancement of the trade of clothing and spinning of wool, and much of it will be improved into good pasture for feeding and breeding of cattle, and of tillage to be sown with corn and grain, and for hemp and flax in great quantity, for making all sorts of linen cloth and cordage for shipping within this nation; which will increase manufactures, commerce and trading at home and abroad, will relieve the poor by setting them on work, and will many other ways redound to the great advantage and strengthening of the nation: And first, to the end it may be known what that Great Level is, and for the ascertaining the extent, bounds and limits thereof, and for prevention of all doubts, questions, and ambiguities touching the same, be it enacted, ordained, and declared by the authority of this present parliament, that the moors, marshes, fenny and low surrounded grounds [there follows a detailed list] be taken and esteemed to be the said Great Level, to be drained as hereafter is expressed . . . And whereas Francis late Earl of Bedford, in his life-time, did undertake the said work, and had ninety-five thousand acres, parcel of the said Great Level, decreed and set forth in October in the thirteenth year of the reign of the late King Charles in recompence thereof; and he and his participants, and the adventurers in the said work, and their heirs and assigns, have made a good progress therein with expence of great and vast sums of money, and so far proceeded as that the greatest part of the said ninety-five thousand acres was divided by twenty lots and shares amongst the said Francis Earl of Bedford, adventurers and participants, and their assigns; but by reason of some late interruptions, the works there made have fallen into decay, so that the intended benefit to the commonwealth has been in a great measure hitherto prevented and delayed: And whereas William now Earl of Bedford, son and heir of the said Francis, late Earl of Bedford, and the said participants and adventurers, their heirs and assigns, are content to proceed effectually in the said work of draining, and forthwith after the passing of this act to begin and prosecute the same without cessation or intermission, until the work be done, unseasonable times and extremity of weather only excepted; to the end therefore so public a work, proper for the care of a parliament, may continue, proceed, and be prosecuted with justice, equality and effect. Be it enacted and ordained . . . that the said William Earl of Bedford, the said participants and adventurers, and his and their heirs and assigns, be and are hereby declared to be the undertakers of the said work of draining the said Great Level, and shall at or before the tenth day of October, which shall be in the year of our Lord 1656, cause the same to be drained and embanked, without prejudice to the navigation in the said rivers or the parts adjacent; and all the said Level, except as hereafter is excepted, shall be made winter ground, in such manner as the said rivers or any of them shall not overflow the grounds within the said Level; breaches by inevitable accidents, which are in convenient time to be repaired and made good again by the said William Earl of Bedford, participants and adventurers, his and their heirs and assigns, only excepted; and except such lands and grounds, parcel of the said Level, which are not to exceed fifteen thousand acres at the most, which may be left in several places for receptacles and beds for the water upon sudden rains and floods, besides the meres, pools, and channels within the said Level which are not intended to be drained. And be it therefore further enacted and ordained, that the said William now Earl of Bedford, Edward Russell, Esq., Robert Henley, Esq. and Robert Castle, Esq. their heirs and assigns, upon the trusts hereafter following, and in recompence of the aforesaid charge and adventure, and for bearing the charge of draining and maintaining the works from time to time, shall have and enjoy the said whole ninety-five thousand acres . . .

42 Improving the Land, 1652

(W. Blith, *The English Improver Improved* (1652), pp. 131–47)

The fifth piece [of improvement] is a discovery of such simples and ingredients to be compounded with the earth, with the nature and use of them. In application whereof makes good the improvement promised, and meliorates the earth to all intents and purposes . . .

And in your tillage are these special opportunities to improve it, either by liming, marling, sanding, earthing, mudding, snail-codding,[1] mucking, chalking, pigeons' dung, hens' dung, hogs' dung, or by any other means, as some by rags, some by coarse wool, by pitch marks, and tarry stuff, any oily stuff, salt, and many things more, yea indeed anything almost that has any liquidness, foulness, saltness or good moisture in it, is very natural enrichment to almost any sort of land, all which as to all sorts of land, they are of an exceeding meliorating nature, and of most of these more particularly.

And first for liming, it is of most excellent use, yea so great that whole countries, and many counties that were naturally as barren as any in this nation, and had formerly (within less than half an age) [been supplied] with corn out of the fielden corn country, and now [are] and long have been ready to supply them, and do and have brought their land into such a posture, for bearing all sorts of corn, that upon land not worth above one or two shillings an acre, they will raise (well husbanded with lime) as good wheat, barley, and white and grey peas as England yields, yea they will take a parcel of land from off a lingy heath or common, not worth the having, nay many will not have it to husbandry it, and will raise most gallant corn, that naturally is so barren, worth five or six pound an acre . . .

. . . The land natural and suitable for lime is your light and sandy land, and mixed sound earth, so also is your gravel but not so good, and your wet and cold gravel is the worst, except your cold hungry clay, which is worst of all, but all mixed lands whatever are very good . . .

Marl is also a very gallant thing, I can say much for it, far more than I resolve to speak to, because others have spoken much thereof . . . It is commended of all men, and very highly almost by every writer that says anything in point of husbandry . . . And for the nature of it, it is also of a colder nature [like lime] because it saddens the land exceedingly, and very heavy it is, and will go downwards also, but being so much of substance cannot easily bury so soon as lime will. And the description of it is not so much in colour (as some say) as in the purity and uncompoundedness of it, for in my opinion be the colour what it will, if it be pure of itself that it will break into bits like a die, or but smooth like lead, without any composition of sand or gravel, and some others of it if it will slack like slate-stones, and then if it will purely slack after a shower of rain, question not the fruitfulness of it . . .

* * *

Now the lands upon which marl yields great increase is upon your higher sandy land mixed or gravelly, any sound land whatsoever, though never so barren, to whom it is as natural and nourishing as bread to man's nature, and will do well upon any of these, though somewhat mixed with clay, but strong clay in my opinion is most unsuitable . . .

As for sand's manure . . .

But as for your sands brought forth by the violence of strong land-floods, and cast upon hills and shelves in many meadows and other places, in them is fruit and virtue, and I question not but the application of them, either to corn or graze, will produce much fertility; especially being seasonably applied to such lands as are most different from the nature of itself . . .

But there is another sort of sand, and this is the richest of all, and that is your sand upon the sea coasts . . .

. . . give me leave to let you know the virtue and excellency the sea may yield as from sea-weeds also, which Cornwall and Devonshire and many other parts make great improvement of for the soiling and manuring of their land . . .

* * *

As for chalk, Sir Francis Bacon affirms it to be of an over-heating nature to the land, and is best for cold and moist land, but as it appears to me in Hertfordshire and other parts thereabout, there are great improvements to be made upon barren, gravelly, flinty lands, and it has great fruitfulness in it, but not having fallen under my own experience I dare affirm little therein, only advise any that have opportunity therein to be well resolved of the fruitfulness of the said chalk, or of the nature of the said lands, for there is some chalk, though not very much thereof, that is of so churlish a binding nature, that it will so fodder and bind, and hold the water upon the top of the earth so long till it destroy the corn, or work a sterility in the earth, that neither corn or ground shall yield but little fruit; but there is a chalk in thousand places of great fruitfulness for improvement . . .

And I also conceive that chalk, earth and manure, mixed together, makes an admirable, sure, and natural fruitful composition for almost any sort of lands, and is a very excellent, infallible remedy against barrenness, and raises corn in abundance, and enriches it also for grazing when you lay it down; many great countries in this nation are under this capacity.

Also the mud of old standing pools and ditches, the shovelling of streets and yards and highways, the overswarths of common lanes, or of commons near hedges, is very good both of itself, and compounded with other soil, manure, mud or straw. And very much account made thereof in some countries; nay more than this of manure that is made of horse or cow, for some sorts of land, and some sorts of corn, which I conceive is for lands very flinty, stony and gravelly, or a little mixed with clay amongst them; as also for wheat and barley it is very natural and is of constant use and great esteem in Hertfordshire, Essex, Sussex, and divers other countries thereabout . . .

Earth of a saltish nature is fruitful, especially all such earth as lies dry, covered with hovels or houses, of which you make saltpetre, is rich for land, so is old floors under any buildings.

There are many other gallant soils or manure, as your pigeons' dung, a load whereof is more worth than twenty shillings in many parts, your hens' and poultry dung, that live of corn, is very excellent. These being of a very hot or warm and brackish nature are a very excellent soil for a cold moist-natured land; two load hereof will very richly manure an acre; so is all dung, the more it is raised from corn or richer matter, the richer itself is usually by far; as where horses are highly corned, the richer is the dung than those only kept with hay.

*   *   *

As for sheep dung, cow dung and horse dung, such old ordinary soil I intend to say little, in regard the common use thereof . . .

[1] Using a river mud or sludge, containing shells.

43 The Benefits of Enclosure, 1669

(J. Worlidge, *Systema Agriculturae* (1669), pp. 10–12)

Enclosing of lands, and dividing the same into several fields, pastures, &c. is, and has been ever esteemed a most principal way of improvement, it ascertains every man his just and due propriety and interest, and prevents such infinity of trespasses and injuries, that lands in common are subject unto, occasioning so much of law, strife, and contention; it capacitates all sorts of land whatsoever for some of the improvements mentioned in the subsequent discourse, so that a good husband may plant timber, fruit, or other trees in his hedge-rows, or any other part of his lands, or may convert the same to meadows, pasture, arable, or gardens, &c. And sow or plant the same with any sorts or species, of grain, pulse, or other tillage whatsoever, without the check or control of his unthrifty or envious neighbours . . .

Enclosure with a good tall hedge-row, preserves the land warm, and defends and shelters it from the violent and nipping winds, that generally nip and destroy much of the corn, pulse, or whatsoever grows on the open field or champion grounds, and preserves it also from those drying and scorching winds more frequent in hot and dry springs, much damaging the champion lands; it much preserves that fertility and richness the land is either naturally subject unto, or that is by the diligent care and cost of the husbandman added. It furnishes the owners thereof with a greater burthen of corn, pulse, or whatever is sown thereon; also where it is laid down for meadow, or pasture, it yields much more of grass than the open field land, and the hedges being well planted with trees, affords shelter and shadow for the cattle both in summer and winter, which else would destroy more with their feet, than they eat with their mouths, and might lose more of their fat or flesh in one hot day, than they gain in three cool days; and affords the industrious husbandman plenty of provision for the maintenance of fire-boot, plough-boot, cart-boot; and (if carefully planted and preserved) furnishes him with timber, mast for his swine, and fruits for cider . . .

It is one of the greatest encouragements to good husbandry, and a good remedy against beggary; for it brings employment to the poor, by the continual labour that is bestowed thereon, which is doubly repaid by the fruitful crop it annually yields, and generally maintains treble the number of inhabitants or more than the champion, as you may easily perceive if you compare such counties and places in England, that are for the most part upon enclosure, with the champion, and chiltern counties or places; and compare also the difference of their manner and condition of living, and their food and apparel, &c. it must needs convince you that enclosure is much to be preferred above the champion, as well for the public as private advantage . . .

This great improvement meets with the greatest difficulties and impediments; amongst which none appears with a bigger face, than the several interests and diversity of titles and claims to almost every common-field or waste land in England; and although (by many) the greater part of the interested persons are willing to divide and enclose it, yet if but one or more envious or ignorant persons concerned oppose the design; or that some or other of them be not by the law under a capacity of assuring his interest to his neighbour, the whole must unavoidably cease, which has proved a general obstruction, and has been frequently complained of; for the remedy whereof, a statute to compel the minor party to submit to the judgement and vote of the major, and equally to capacitate all persons concerned for such an enterprise, would be very welcome to the country-man, wherein all particular interests might be sufficiently provided for, as well the lord of the soil, as the tenant, and the poor.

44 Farm Livestock and Poultry, 1669

(J. Worlidge, *Systema Agriculturae* (1669), pp. 149–52)

Our country farm is of little use and benefit to us, notwithstanding all our care, pains and cost in fencing, planting, or otherwise ordering the same, unless it be well stocked and provided with beasts and other animals, as well for labour and strength in tilling and manuring the ground, and facilitating other labours and exercises, as for the furnishing the market and kitchen.

Of the horse. The horse has the preeminence above all others, being the noblest, strongest, swiftest and most necessary of all the beasts used in this country for the saddle, for the plough and cart, and for the pack.

Where you have good store of pasture, either in several or in common, or in woods or groves, it is no small advantage to keep a team of mares for the breed; but where there is most of arable, and little of pasture land, horses or geldings are more necessary; which difference we may observe between the great breeding places for horses in the pastures and woodlands, and the naked corn countries; the one full of gallant lusty mares, the other of horses and geldings . . .

Of cows and oxen. These worthy sort of beasts are in great request with the husbandman, the ox being useful at his cart and plough, the cow yielding great store of provision both for the family and the market, and both a very great advantage to the support of the trade of the kingdom . . .

Of sheep. Next unto these the sheep deserves the chiefest place, and is by some preferred before any other, for the great profit and advantage they bring to mankind, both for food and apparel.

Whereof there are divers sorts, some bearing much finer wool than others . . .

Of swine. This beast is also of a very considerable advantage to the husbandman, the flesh being a principal support to his family, yielding more dainty dishes and variety of meat than any other beast whatsoever, considering them as pig, pork, bacon, brawn, with the different sorts of offal belonging to them . . .

*   *   *

The countryman's farm or habitation cannot be said to be completely stored or stocked without fowl, as well as beasts, yielding a considerable advantage by their eggs, brood, bodies and feathers. Amongst which the poultry seems to have the preeminence, being more universally kept than any other sort whatsoever, insomuch that any poor cottager that lives by the highway-side may keep of them, being able to shift for themselves the most part of the year, feeding on insects and on anything almost that's edible by any other sort of animal.

They are also kept to a very great advantage in the back-sides and at the barn-doors of great farms, and as I have been certainly informed, a good farm has been wholly stocked with poultry, spending the whole crop upon them, and keeping several to attend them, and that it has redounded to a very considerable improvement. It seems also consonant to reason, especially if within a day's journey of London, that they might have a quick return and a good market, being in a capacity to furnish the market throughout the year either with eggs, chickens, pullets, capons, or cocks and hens. Also the feathers must needs yield a considerable advantage, and the dung of poultry being of great use on the land, much exceeding the dung of any cattle whatsoever.

45 Difficulties with an Enclosure, 1671

(Entry Book on the Division of Commons, in Durham Court of Chancery, Book M, No. 482, 1671–76, original in P.R.O.)

October, 1671. Forasmuch as heretofore by order and decree of this court bearing date the fifteenth day of September last past, made between the parties above named, for the reasons then appearing to this court it was then ordered and decreed by the consent of all the said parties . . . that all the lands and grounds lying and being in the three common fields called the Hitherfield, Middlefield and Fairfield lying at Bishop Auckland, therein mentioned should . . . be forthwith measured and divided according to the agreements and consents of the said parties . . . and also that every of the said parties should have his and their particular shares, parts, and proportions therein particularly allotted and set forth in severalty unto him and them, to be by them respectively hedged, fenced, enclosed and enjoyed in severalty for ever thenafter for the better husbandry and improvement thereof. . . . And now upon the motion of Mr William Brabart . . . alleging that since the making of the said decree several of the parties thereunto, perceiving that some of the defendants, formerly being the chief opposers of the said intended division, have obtained their shares in the premises to be in such part thereof as themselves desired, their said parts being small and inconsiderable, they have therefore of late descended from their shares and parts of the premises formerly by them desired or consented unto and do now endeavour to have their proportionate parts to lie in other parts and places of the premises, to the great decay, hindrance, and obstruction of the said division, notwithstanding their former consents thereunto. It was therefore humbly prayed by the said counsel that a commission might be awarded out of this court to indifferent commissioners . . . as well for the hearing of all the said objections . . . as also to view and divide all the said premises and to appoint and set forth to every of the said parties their proportionable parts therein.

[*August, 1672, decree of the court.*]

Forasmuch as . . . every owner's share has been duly set out . . . and yet nevertheless one of the said defendants has endeavoured to obstruct the said division . . . it is therefore now thought fit and so ordered by the right honourable Sir Francis Goodriche Knight, Chancellor of the county of Durham and Sedbergh, that the award . . . shall stand absolutely confirmed and decreed unless good cause be shown to the contrary at the next sitting at Durham.

46 An Apprenticeship to Husbandry, 1692

(*Collections for a History of Staffordshire. The Gnosall Records, 1679 to 1837. Poor Law Administration*, ed. S. A. Cutlack (Staffordshire Record Society, 1936), pp. 116–17)

This indenture [of 24 November 1692] witnesses that Thomas Heele and John Taylor, churchwardens of the parish of Gnosall in the county of Stafford, with the consent of two of their majesties' justices of the peace for the said county according to the statute in the case made and provided, have placed and put forth John Stafford a poor fatherless and motherless child with Robert Shelley of Ingerstre in the county aforesaid, husbandman, to learn the art of husbandry, and with him after the manner of apprentice to serve from the date of this present indenture unto the full end and term of nine years . . . During which term the said apprentice his said master shall faithfully serve, his secrets keep, his lawful commandments everywhere gladly do. He shall do no damage to his said master nor see to be done of others but that he to his power shall act or forthwith give warning to his said master of the same. He shall not contract matrimony within the said term. He shall not haunt taverns nor absent himself from his master's service day nor night unlawfully but in all things as a faithful apprentice he shall behave himself towards his said master and all his during the said term. And the said churchwardens do covenant and grant by these presents for themselves and the succeeding wardens to and with the said Robert Shelley that [they] shall pay unto the said Robert Shelley his executors administrators or assigns the sum of seven pounds . . . in manner and form following, that is to say twenty shillings part thereof in hand before the insealing and delivery of these presents to buy clothes for the said apprentice and forty shillings more thereof upon the twenty fourth day of June next ensuing . . . And forty shillings more thereof which shall be in the year of our Lord 1694. And forty shillings more residue thereof upon the twenty fourth day of June which shall be in the year of our Lord 1695. And it is covenanted and agreed . . . that if the said apprentice shall happen to die before the first or second days of payment that then the said churchwardens shall pay unto the said Robert Shelley twelve pence a week for the time that he keeps him after either of the days of payment but if he happen to die before the third of payment then the said churchwardens shall pay to the said Robert sixpence a week. And the said Robert Shelley covenants and grants by these presents . . . to inform teach and instruct his said apprentice in the art of husbandry which he now uses finding unto his said apprentice sufficient meat drink apparel lodging washing laundering and all things fit for such an apprentice to have and at the end of the said term to give him two suits of apparel the one for holy days and the other for working days . . .

47 Dispute over Tithes, 1696

(Historical Manuscripts Commission, *The Manuscripts of the House of Lords*, New Series, II, 1695–1697 (1903), p. 262)

9 November 1696. Eastmond v Sandys. Petition and appeal of Joseph Eastmond, executor of Henry Eastmond, and Samuel Nayle.

Mr Sandys, Rector of Yeovilton in Somersetshire, brought a bill in the Court of Exchequer against petitioners for agistment tithes for the depasturing and fatting their oxen within the parish for ten years, and the Court decreed them liable for the value of the tithe herbage for feeding their oxen and unprofitable cattle not used for the plough within the parish, and, for those used for the plough and afterwards turned off and fattened in the aftermarshes or egrasses, during the time only when they were depastured in the pastures, but not in the after-marshes; and the Deputy Remembrancer accordingly reported them liable for 39*l* 11*s* 6*d*, and the costs are taxed at 75*l* against petitioners. Appeal against the report because it includes years not claimed for, because it charges them for the time when the oxen were ploughing and the rector had the tenths of the beasts' labour, and because it does not distinguish between the time when the oxen were worked and the time when they were turned off to depasture. [The appeal was dismissed with costs.]

Annexed.

(a) *30 November. Answer of Edwyn Sandys, clerk.*

The oxen were not charged during the time they were used for ploughing, as the decree expressly excepted that time, and there was no need for the report to specify the times for which they were not charged. Prays the appeal may be dismissed with exemplary costs.

48 An Outbreak of Cattle Disease, 1714

(B.M. Add. MSS 32704, f. 153, printed in E. Hughes, *North Country Life in the Eighteenth Century. The North-East, 1700–1750* (1952), pp. 148–9)

An account of what was done in 1714 on the breaking out of the distemper among the cows

The distemper first appeared in August 1714 at Islington and as soon as the Lords Justices had notice of it, the Lord Chancellor by their directions ordered four justices to take an account of the stocks of all the cowkeepers in or near the place who had any infected cows or calves and also to agree with them for all their cows and calves which were or should be taken ill.

This was done at 40*s* a cow and 10*s* a calf. On receiving information that the distemper was chiefly propagated by the selling of infected calves, the justices bought and killed all the calves, sick and well; they also appointed a slaughterman at 5*s* a day and proper surveyors who every day visited each cowherd, killing every cow as soon as it was taken ill, burying them ten foot deep with unslaked lime and covering them well with earth to prevent infectious steams. They also every week checked the accounts of the cowkeepers' stocks to prevent their buying in new cattle or old cows of small value which practices tended to increase the distemper.

By this management and other proper directions for separating the sound [animals] from the sick and even the sound from each other as soon as was possible, keeping them all in the fields and open air and drying up their milk as soon as could be, many were preserved and their distemper confined to Islington and Hogsden, where it first began, for more than a month. But then, the power of the justices being suspended by an accident or mistake for about five weeks, and afterwards while the Dutch medicine was trying, the cowkeepers were at liberty to do as they pleased and their cattle were suffered to live till they died of the distemper in a natural way, whereby it spread all round London, till on renewing the former powers, the former measures were renewed which kept the distemper from spreading further into the country and at last put a stop to it entirely.

All sorts of medicines were tried but without any success (the Dutch medicine only excepted of which I have the receipt by me) that cured 8 out of 50, but did much more harm than good by suspending the other method of killing as soon as they were taken ill and thereby, as there is a very good reason to believe being the occasion for the loss of several hundred cows that might otherwise have been saved, the distemper being always observed to rage with the greatest violence and most fatal effects whenever the cows were suffered to live any time after the distemper first seized them. The prodigious quantity of putrid effluvia emitted by them every time they breathed infected the air more strongly and carrying it further to other cows and herds.

9th April 1745   John Milner

49 An Estate Steward Reports to his Master, 1725

(*The Letters of Daniel Eaton to the third Earl of Cardigan, 1725–1732,* eds. J. Wake and D. C. Webster (Northamptonshire Record Society, XXIV, 1971), pp. 6–7)

[Saturday, 6 February, 1725]

My Lord,

I received yours of the second. I have delivered your lordship's orders to the tenants of Deenthorpe. I have sent your lordship's letter to Ward and have ordered him to be with me on Monday. I have sent Mr Whitwell's money today by Walt Harrisson. I have finished Mr John Billinge's account. I cannot find Wilcock's bond and Mr Lynwood is very positive he never had [it]. Mr Langtro was not at Weldon Sale. I intend to go to Kirby this afternoon.

I was at Wardly on Thursday and have examined into what your lordship ordered as follows: I find your lordship was misinformed as to the ploughing the land, for I am sure it could not have been done better. And for the cutting of the hedges, those that Mr Roberts has cut this year he promises both to cock-hedge and ditch; those that have been cut formerly in all the lordship have suffered very much, partly by the unskilfulness of labourers and then by the neglect of tenants after they have been cut, that a great many fine hedges are quite ruined. I think there ought to be a clause in every lease to oblige all tenants to cock-hedge and scour the ditches of all the hedges they plash.[1]

John Manton will give fifty pounds a year for his farm, and bear a third part of the tax, and be obliged to maintain his wife's mother, who has lived upon the farm this forty years, as long as she lives. I think that what he proposes is very reasonable, for I have looked upon all his land and I find that the close that is valued at 25s per annum is worth more, but the rest is dear enough of 18s per acre, take it altogether; for some of it (that has not been lately ploughed) I think is but indifferent land, and I do really think that it would not be let for 55l per annum together, for whosoever takes it will examine it thoroughly first. John Manton's wife died about a week since, and if he quits the town his wife's mother must of necessity fall upon the parish. I have got Harriss's lease.

I beg leave to advise your lordship to one thing, which I am sure will be of great advantage to Mr Brudenell, viz: that whereas the land that Mr Roberts is now a-ploughing, which I look upon to be about 50 acres, cannot recover itself under three years at least, and in the mean time cannot be worth above a mark an acre, now if his honour would be at the charge of sowing trefoil, which must be sown and rolled in immediately after Mr Roberts has sown his barley and oats, it will make the land worth 20s an acre the first year, and the trefoil will continue till the natural grass kills it, which will be four years at least. This, my lord, I will be bound to make good, for I think I never saw better land for trefoil than this is; but the soil is not so rich as the other side of the lordship is. The charge will not be very great; for Mr Dawson of Weldon has a large quantity of seed by him, which I believe for ready money I could buy for 2s a strike at the most.

The park sale came to 57l. Mr John Lynwood has contracted with Mr Worley for about 400 acres of land and another house in Benefield which was not proposed before, but it will be made a good house for him. Mr Worley will not let Jonas be his shepherd, but insists upon his employing John Harrisson, which I think is an hardship. Mr John Lynwood begs your lordship would assist him in this and write to Mr

Joy about it; but I have not agreed with Richard Harrisson, for fear that Jonas must stay at Deenthorp (from whence he cannot remove without a certificate). If so, I think he will be a better servant than the other.

J. Lummis and J. Hinks will be at Hamby tomorrow, when I will send Christopher Dexter's valuation of the alterations of Mr Lynwood's house, and on Monday I will take a particular of the moveable goods. The ant hills are laying on heaps. I have sent the hound whelps and spaniels to quarters and have put the hounds into the little kennel. I intend to draw a plan of Mr Lynwood's house, &c., and bring it with me, which I hope will be on Thursday next.

I am your
      lordship's most humble
      and most faithful servant,

DAN: EATON

I beg your lordship's commands about Manton, and likewise about the trefoil for fear it should be sold; I never knew any sold under 2s 6d a strike before.

[1] Plash, to bend, interweave branches.

50 Advice to Estate Stewards, 1731

(Edward Lawrence, *The Duty and Office of a Land Steward*, 3rd ed. (1731), pp. 25-6, 39)

A steward should not forget to make the best enquiry into the disposition of any of the freeholders within or near any of his lord's manors to sell their lands, that he may use his best endeavours to purchase them at as reasonable a price, as may be for his lord's advantage and convenience—especially in such manors, where improvements are to be made by enclosing commons and common-field; which (as every one, who is acquainted with the late improvement in agriculture, must know) is not a little advantageous to the nation in general, as well as highly profitable to the undertaker. If the freeholders cannot all be persuaded to sell, yet at least an agreement for enclosing should be pushed forward by the steward, and a scheme laid, wherein it may appear that an exact and proportional share will be allotted to every proprietor; persuading them first, if possible, to sign a form of agreement, and then to choose commissioners on both sides.

If the steward be a man of good sense, he will find a necessity for making a use of it all, in rooting out superstition from amongst them, as what is so great a hindrance to all noble improvements? The substance of what is proper for the proprietors to sign before an enclosure is to be made, may be conceived in some such form as follows.

'Whereas it is found, by long experience, that common or open fields, wherever they are suffered or continued, are great hindrances to a public good, and the honest improvement which every one might make of his own, by diligence and a seasonable charge: and, whereas the common objections hitherto raised against enclosures are founded on mistakes, as if enclosures contributed either to hurt or ruin the poor; whilst it is plain that (when an enclosure is once resolved on) the poor will be employed for many years, in planting and preserving the hedges, and afterwards will be set to work both in the tillage and pasture, wherein they may get an honest livelihood: And whereas all or most of the inconveniences and misfortunes which usually attend the open wastes and common fields have been fatally experienced at ——, to the great discouragement of industry and good husbandry in the freeholders, viz., that the poor take their advantage to pilfer, and steal, and trespass; that the corn is subject to be spoiled by cattle, that stray out of the commons and highways adjacent; that the tenants or owners, if they would secure the fruits of their labours to themselves, are obliged either to keep exact time in sowing and reaping or else to be subject to the damage and inconvenience that must attend the lazy practices of those who sow unseasonably, suffering their corn to stand to the beginning of winter, thereby hindering the whole parish from eating the herbage of the common field till the frosts have spoiled the most of it,' &c. &c.

* * *

To conclude this article upon commons, I would advise all noblemen and gentlemen, whose tenants hold their lands by copy of court roll for three lives, not to let them renew, except they will agree to deliver up their copy, in order to alter the tenure by converting it to leasehold on lives. This method will put a stop to that unreasonable custom of the widow holding a life by her free-bench, which is a fourth life, not covenanted for in the copy, but only pretended to by custom; which deprives the lord of an undoubted right of making the best, and doing what he will with his own.

51 Rules for Open Fields, 1750

(*Purefoy Letters, 1735–1753*, ed. G. Eland (1931), II, pp. 434–9)

Manor of Shalstone in co. Bucks. Rules and orders at this Court [Baron, 12 March 1750] made and agreed by the homage for the better regulation and good government of the fields within the said manor.

First, it is ordered that no person shall keep or depasture more than two cows or horned beasts, or two horses or mares for or in respect of one yardland, on pain to forfeit for every offence 3s 4d.

Also it is ordered that no person shall keep more than three ewes and lambs or five dry sheep for or in respect of one yardland in summer, and eight sheep for or in respect thereof in winter, when the least or Middle field lies fallow, and only four couples or six dry sheep in summer and eight sheep in winter for or in respect of one yardland when the biggest or East and West fields lie fallow. And that the stint thereof be made on or before the five and twentieth day of March in every year. On pain for each offence 3s 4d.

Also that the lot ground in the common fields shall be lotted yearly on or before the twentieth day of May, and that the same shall not be mowed (except only between Allhallowtide[1] and Candlemas[2]) but flit[3] with horses, upon pain for every offence 3s 4d.

Also that the cow pasture shall be hained[4] yearly at Candlemas and remain hained till the first day of June following in which time no beasts shall be suffered to go or depasture there (except only the hayward's cow till the fifteenth day of April and not longer) upon pain for every offence 3s 4d.

Also that the wheat field shall be hained yearly at the Feast of All Saints[5] upon pain for every offence 3s 4d.

Also that a good and sufficient bull shall be found and provided yearly until the next court is held for the service of the common herd by the occupiers of four of the farms of the open field land . . . the said Aaron Gibbs to find such bull for this next year, then the said John Franklin, William Scott, and John Boorton and Aaron Gibbs severally and alternately to find the same yearly afterwards till the next court is held . . . upon pain that every person making default herein . . . shall forfeit for every default the sum of 20s and that if any dispute shall at any time happen to arise touching the finding such bull the same shall be decided by the lord of this manor.

Also that every cow put or turned into the common or cow-pasture shall be tipped or nubbed on both horns at or before the age of 2 years and if any tip or nub come off to be put on again within 3 days upon pain for every offence 4d.

Also that the Herd's plot and the Church mead shall not be flit with any horses, mares or colts. Upon pain for every offence 3s 4d.

Also that for every cow put or turned into the common or cow-pasture shall be paid yearly to the fieldsmen on or before the 29th day of September in each year 6d, and that the fieldsmen shall collect the same of the respective commoners and forthwith pay the same to the owner of the bull for the time being. On pain each commoner for every default 3s 4d.

Also that no person shall fork or tie any cow before the common herd in the open field or cow pasture. Upon pain to forfeit for every offence 3s 4d.

Also that no person shall suffer any colt of a month old or upwards to go loose in the common fields till after the same fields are rid of corn and grain. Upon pain for every offence 3s 4d.

Also that no person shall bait or tie any cattle upon his own ground or elsewhere so as to prejudice or trespass on his neighbour till the harvest is inned. Upon pain for every offence 3s 4d.

Also that no person shall suffer his swine, hog or pig to go or be turned into the common fields till harvest is ended, or at anytime to go unringed there. Upon pain for every offence 3s 4d.

Also that no person shall mow his ground in the open field above or more than once in any one year. On pain for every offence 3s 4d.

Also that no horse common shall be let or set to any foreigner or persons not inhabitant of Shalstone. On pain for every offence 10s.

Also that the fieldsmen shall find a mole catcher yearly to be employed in the open fields and cow pasture, and that his wages shall be paid by the commoners proportionably on Easter Tuesday in every year, on pain each fieldsman or commoner making default herein 3s 4d.

Also that the fieldsmen do and shall yearly when and so soon as corn or grain in the open fields of Shalstone is ripe, hire a crow keeper to shoot and keep the crows and other vermin from destroying the same. On pain in default of 3s 4d.

Also that each person's leys and greensward ground, and such ground which has been lately ploughed further than usual in the open fields and cow pasture, shall be marked and meted out from the other by the jury or homage, or the major part of them, on or before the 1st day of May next. On pain each juryman making default the sum of 20s.

Also that all the jury or homage residing in Shalstone (except only such as shall be excused by the foreman for some reasonable cause) shall yearly in Easter week or the next week after go round the open fields and cowpasture and see that all the stakes, meteholes[6] and meerstones[6] be in good repair and in their right places, and fill up any vacant places where necessary. And in case a cart shall be wanted for carriage of stakes or meerstones for doing thereof the said jury shall hire such cart and the occupiers of the open field shall pay for the charge of the same in proportion to their land therein. On pain to the defaulter for each default 3s 4d.

Also that the hayward or cowkeeper for the time being do keep the cowpasture gate next the Wood green and that next Westbury Lane and the gate next the Woodway in good and sufficient repair, and shall be paid the charges thereof by the occupiers of the open field in proportion to their land therein. On pain to the defaulter for each default 3s 4d.

Also that every hayward or cowkeeper shall repair as often as necessary and keep in good repair the Evershaw Lane gate next Shalstone cowpasture at his own proper charges. And that the occupiers of the said open field land in proportion shall find timber for it. On pain for each defaulter to pay 3s 4d.

Also that the fieldsmen shall cause the cowpasture hedge to be well repaired before every five and twentieth day of March in each year, and so shall keep the same in repair until harvest be inned. On pain for each default 10s.

Also that the hayward shall be paid twopence for every horse, cow, bull, sheep, swine, or other beast he finds or catches trespassing in any of the said fields of Shalstone. And in default of payment thereof such hayward is hereby empowered to impound the same, and give notice and detain the same in the pound until the person injured be satisfied his damage for the trespass and also the hayward the said 2d per head.

Also that such person or persons who shall mow or trespass on another's grass or remove stakes or meerstones or stop up the meteholes shall forfeit and pay for each offence 3s 4d . . .

Also that when and as often as the lord of this manor shall cause any of the Shalstone Moors or other places in the open fields of Shalstone to be dug or trenched, then and so often the occupiers of the said slades, moors, or places so trenched shall within 3 weeks after trenching thereof remove the dirt or soil dug or thrown thereout and lay the same on heaps one pole distance from the trench, and carry away the same and lay it upon their respective ploughed lands before the first day of March next after the said trenching. And where the trenches shall lie between two owners or occupiers then each of them shall carry a like part to his land. On pain of each default to pay 20s.

Also that when and as often as the Lot Moors or fenny ground, by estimation 10 acres in the East field of Shalstone, shall be trenched the occupiers of the open field land for the time being shall in proportion of 3 poles to each yardland take away the soil to be dug and lay the same on a heap one pole distance from the trench within 3 weeks' time after the same shall be trenched as aforesaid, and carry away the same before the first day of August then next ensuing yearly to their respective ploughed lands as shall be directed by the lord of the manor. On penalty of each defaulter 20s.

Also that the said occupiers of the said open field, for the time being until the next court is held, shall in like proportion yearly and every year between the second day of November and second day of February in each year throw out the dirt and soil from the trenches in the said moors or fenny ground, and carry away the same before the second day of February yearly and lay it on their respective ploughed lands. On penalty of each default 20s.

Also that the said occupiers of the said open field for the time being shall yearly, and in every year between the second day of November and second day of February, throw out all the dirt and cleanse and preserve in like wideness and depth all the trenches on their respective lands and ground, as well those already made as those which hereafter shall be made thereon, and where the said trenches lie between two or more each of them shall do a proportionable part, on pain of each default 20s.

Also that every occupier shall plough his ground in the open field not further than where it has constantly or anciently been ploughed or should of right be ploughed, and shall on or before the twentieth day of May next lay down for greensward what ground thereof has been ploughed otherwise with grass seed as the jury shall mete out. On pain for each default 20s.

Also that the fieldsmen shall yearly make a rate or levy equal in proportion to and upon each yardland in the open field to reimburse the charges of repairs of the cowpasture hedges and their other charges and expenses in their said office, and the respective owners or occupiers of these lands shall pay the same. On pain in default of 20s.

Also that every fieldsman and hayward do take due care that the orders aforesaid be duly observed and kept. And in case of their refusal or neglect therein shall forfeit and pay for each offence 3s 4d.

Also that the lord of this manor, his heirs and assigns, with the consent and approbation of the majority of the said jury or homage then living in Shalstone, shall and may before another court create and make a new hayward and fieldsmen or jurymen or any of them in case of death or removal of the present hayward or fieldsmen, or turn them out for neglect.

Also that the fieldsmen or in their default the lord of this manor or his bailiff or other person he shall appoint shall and may have power until the next court to distrain the goods and chattels of every defaulter of keeping the said orders and to sell the said goods in like manner as goods distrained for rent to satisfy and pay the penalties. And that the fieldsmen shall after notice thereof within fourteen days collect or distrain for the penalties of each default of the due observance of these orders. Under pain for each offence 3s 4d . . .

Also that no ridgill[7] sheep or lamb shall lie in the open field after Holyrood Day[8] until St Andrew's Day.[9] Under pain for each offence 3s 4d.

Also that all the penalties of the breach of the aforesaid orders shall be equally divided between the lord of the said manor and the fieldsmen, viz[t] one moiety thereof to the lord and the other to the fieldsmen.

Fieldsmen chosen. John Franklin and Aaron Gibbs
Hayward chosen. William Harburd
Mole catcher. John Mumford

In witness whereof we the jury have herewith set our hands:

John Franklin	Aaron Gibbs	The mark of
The mark of	William Sinnell[?]	X
X	John Boorton	William Scott
William May		Richard Boorton

[1] 1 November. (GE, and other notes also)   [2] 2 February.
[3] To flit is to move a tethered animal.
[4] Meaning, cattle shall be excluded in order that grass may grow.
[5] 1 November.   [6] Measuring and boundary marks.
[7] Animals whose testicles have not descended.
[8] 14 September.   [9] 30 November.

52 Norfolk Husbandry, 1752

(*The Gentleman's Magazine*, XXII (1752), pp. 453–5, 502)

The state of husbandry in Norfolk. In a letter to a friend.

Sir, the improvements made in the county of Norfolk are talked of in all parts of the kingdom, and as I have frequently been asked about them; and am myself not altogether incurious in these affairs, I have taken some pains to become acquainted with their nature . . .

It is currently believed in London that the late Lord Townshend was the first inventor of marling, or claying lands in Norfolk; this has no other foundation than that worthy peer's readily embracing an opportunity of enriching his tenants, and almost doubling the value of a very great estate, by an expense few noblemen care to be at about estates they seldom see.

There are few great estates in England that will not pay 10*l* per cent. per ann. for many thousand pounds judiciously laid out, and though the absence of their possessors, and their attention to more captivating pursuits, prevents it for the most part, we frequently see men of the first quality turn their thoughts this way. The late Lord Townshend, when he retired into the country, following examples which he quickly eclipsed, created farmers in the middle of heath and sheep walks, and found means to make great crops of corn grow in fruitful enclosures, divided by luxuriant quickset hedges, upon ground that had always been thought too poor for the plough.

These improvements had already been carried great lengths in the western parts of this county. The first person supposed to have marled a great extent of ground was Mr Allen of Lynge House; before him it was common to clay or marl only two or three acres, beyond the memory of any one that has been living within forty or fifty years.

Marling of land in Staffordshire and Somersetshire is of great antiquity, and I question not is as ancient in the county I am writing of; for we have abundance of old pits, out of which it is evident somewhat has been dug, and the upper surface thrown in again, and many of them have gone by the name of marl-pits, and enclosures have been denominated from them above 200 years, as appears from writings in my own possession. To this may be added, that more than one ancient author mentions the searching of the bowels of the earth for materials to improve its surface.

Many great benefits accrued to England during the republican government of the long parliament. Among others I reckon the introduction of artificial grasses, which, though they did not become general for many years, yet then seem first to have gained a footing, as I judge from the writings of Mr Hartlib, and Captain Blith; it was in the succeeding reign the bounty upon corn was granted.

About the beginning of the present century, sowing turnips in fields for the feeding of cattle began.

The advantages arising from enclosures have been long understood in all parts of the kingdom, and it has become more feasible by the wearing out of small possessors, whose intervening lands prevented the fencing in large tracts. This had particularly been the case in Norfolk, wherein most of the townships formerly were unenclosed.

The soil of the county of Norfolk is mostly a light loam, generally pretty deep; the farmers of the western parts, for many years, made it a considerable part of their husbandry, to keep flocks of ewes for producing lambs, which they sold for stock to their neighbours. The price of wool has been decaying ever since the prohibition of its exportation. The price of sheep also, when our improvements began, being lower than they had been formerly, could not but help forward the new method of husbandry, which lessened these commodities, and increased corn, butter, and black cattle. To all these I may venture to add a remote cause, which probably had some effect at least by raising corn to a better price; every one knows the immense quantities of corn the Dutch used every year to bring from Poland, by way of Danzig; this having much decreased of late, partly from the destructive wars that laid waste that fertile kingdom; partly, perhaps, from a greater demand for grain in Sweden than formerly; the Russians, since the peace of Nystadt, remaining in possession of the only corn country that ever belonged to that crown, and suffering an exportation of it only when they please.

These two last causes could not but have the more sensible effect in Norfolk, as much land there had, in the reign of Queen Elizabeth, been converted from tillage for the use of keeping sheep, and as the coast of Norfolk is the most convenient for shipping corn for Holland, of any in England.

I have been enumerating the causes that helped forward the great improvements I have lately seen in this county, and have produced a course of husbandry utterly unlike that used 100 years ago, though gradually gaining ground since that time. This will be better understood by viewing its progressive state in several different farms, where the tenants to this day are not to be persuaded to quit a course of agriculture, that has subsisted themselves and their fathers, though it be to take up one that their neighbours have got estates by.

In the open-field-farms, of which some small ones still remain, there is no means of taking the benefit of clover and turnips, yet some of them have marled their grounds, but with success much short of their enclosed neighbours; their husbandry is precisely that of their great grandfather's grandfather. Wheat follows a summer fallow, and is succeeded by two, three or four crops of barley, oats, and pease, then comes the fallow again. Thus one year's rent in three, four, or five, is lost, and yet the land is always poor and foul. The best of it is let from 5s to 8s per acre, and no tenant can well live on it; some few will sow a little clover, but reap little benefit, being obliged to fother their cattle and when all turn their beasts in, it is every one's feed as well as theirs

Upon many enclosed estates the farmers and owners will not marl and sow little clover, taking their wheat or rye after a summer fallow yet they all sow turnips, but generally beggar their land by taking many successive, and consequently poor, crops. They who won't marl do not enclose their unenclosed lands, but there are many who marl yet never enclose, at least with a permanent fence; consequently canno enjoy the whole benefit of the clover and turnip husbandry.

I shall now proceed to show what this is, and what its advantage above all others with us. I have said the rent of our field land is mostly from 5s to 8s an acre; this, when a man can possess himself of an entire tract, is frequently the subject of the improvements we are speaking of, but more commonly it is upon our break lands we improve These let from 2s to 4s per acre, and have been used for sheep feed 7 10, 15 years, and being then broke up, yielded us a crop of rye that was generally followed by a crop of oats, or barley, after which the land took the rest again as sheep walk, and more of the same took its turn When this had laid some years it becomes covered with a thick short sward: on this we lay from 40 to 6 score cart loads per acre, of marl or rich clay, which last we generally reckon on the better the less tough it is mostly grey, but our marl is brown. The latter was formerl esteemed the only substance proper for this improvement, but exper ience has shown the former answers better on light warm land, and is besides more easily procured, every 30 or 40 acres affording us a new pit, which would otherwise be too remote, the carriage being so expen sive: these pits for the most part hold water, and become ponds, one of which we contrive to get in each enclosure, a benefit I have heard farmers say worth one-fourth of the rent of the land, when it is fed by cattle in summer, which is often 2 years in five. The fence is white thorn on a bank, in every rod we place an oak tree, many of which, planted since this late enclosing began, are become of a stature promising u timber in the next generation; white thorn thrives greatly with us, and our hedges with the trees form a shelter for both corn and cattle, ver conducive to their welfare.

Upon new improved land we seldom at first sow any thing but turnips, the hoeing these cleanses the soil from weeds, and helps t mix the new accession with the old surface; this is still more effectuall done by feeding cattle in the winter on these turnips, either first pulling them up with an instrument for that purpose, or leaving the beasts to help themselves; the former makes least waste, the latter mixes and meliorates the earth the most effectually; when the land is subject to be very wet in winter, they often carry off the turnips to another piece of ground, thus they go furthest; but as this ground is much benefitted, it is at the expense of that from whence the crop is brought. After turnips comes barley or oats, with these are sown clover seeds, which produce a crop the following year, and is either mown for hay or pastured with cattle. Wheat regularly succeeds clover, and thus no crop is lost; the land is sometimes ploughed three times for wheat, but very often but once, the clover being ploughed in, and the wheat harrowed in upon it, this would leave the land foul, but this ill consequence is prevented by the next crop of turnips. When the wheat crop is clean, barley is often sown after it . . .

I come now to the consequences of this method. First, we sow on these improved farms five times as many acres of wheat, twice as many of barley; of the former we grow three times as much on an acre, of the latter twice as much as formerly. The whole county has acquired a more cheerful appearance, and indeed more comfortable, from its numerous defences against the sun in summer, and bleak winds in winter. There is three times as much work for the labourers in ploughing, sowing, hedging, threshing, &c. This supports almost twice as many families, who have also twice as much work, yet the necessaries of life are cheaper. One farm is split into two, three, four, or more; new farm houses are erected; the old ones repaired; nothing but brick houses are to be seen here. Our towns on the coast, and market towns increase daily with the business done in them; our carpenters are twice as many; our masons ten times; our gentry have many of them doubled their estates; those whose lands were all capable of improvement have done more. Mr Morley of Barsham, a neighbouring gentleman, his estate of 800*l* per annum a few years ago, was let at 180*l*, but the most extraordinary instance is that of Mr —— who has at Sculthorpe about 240*l* per annum. I am told this was let to a warrener at 18*l* per annum. These instances are however rare, the improved lands are worth from 9*s* to 12*s* without tithes, and pay rent better than any other. Some farmers, on leases of 21 years have laid out their stock on lands, hired at old rents, and are become worth above 10,000*l* each . . .

53 Petition against a Rent Increase, 1753

(*Shardeloes Papers of the 17th and 18th Centuries*, ed. G. Eland (1947), pp. 113–14)

Duckington [Cheshire].
19 January 1753.

Honoured Sir,

I being incapable to write myself prevailed with a neighbour to presume in my behalf to trouble you with the subsequent lines. It is now upwards of forty years since my father and I first became tenants to you and yours; and when my father entered upon your estate the ground was most covered with gorse or furze, but he being lusty and willing strove daily to subdue it; and so constantly employed his mattock that it was a common saying (where a strict union was), 'as true as Thomas Leech to his mattock'. And one small close of two Cheshire acres and a quarter (after he had grubbed up the gorse), cost forty six pounds to have it marled. And for the house, it was, and is, chiefly clay walls, at first destitute of a glass window and all the outbuildings so shattered that a beast was in danger when tied up in any part of it, but repaired by my father. Since I have been subject to it, it has cost me forty pounds in improving the lands joining to the house; and to rebuild the old decayed mansion I have purposely made a kiln of brick and have already so repaired the outhouses that as to the improvement of the premises in general I will appeal to any one if my diligence does not merit encouragement.

I am informed your honour proposes to raise me ten pounds a year and liable to taxes and repairs. To speak ingenuously neither I nor any mortal can pay that rent from the premises, unless they can live on chopped furze and pounded fern, and I am sure no person can live more near or more frugally than myself to pay the present rent. As I was born upon the place I am willing to refer myself to your honour, no doubting but industry will meet with a reward from you, for all my aim and desire is to pay my landlord his rent.

If I could know your honour's inclination by a line from any servant directed for me, to be left at Hampton Post near Malpas, it shall ever be confessed by your poor tenant,

But very humble servant,
Mary Hopley

3

Industrial Activity
1000–1485

During the medieval period industrial activity was very limited and small in scale (*1*), being primarily inhibited by the low level of demand. Technological improvement was difficult to achieve (*7*). Local needs for manufactures were generally met by village craftsmen but by the late twelfth century towns were prospering as industrial centres (*2*). Urban industry was based on the workshops of individual craftsmen or masters who employed a few labourers and taught their craft. A trade was learned through apprenticeship (*16*), an institution open to abuse (*13*). In the later Middle Ages leading masters combined in craft gilds to regulate the affairs of their trade in their own interests (*14*).

The building trades employed many people. Much material and labour was absorbed by large projects which were organised by capitalist entrepreneurs and which required a high level of specialisation of labour (*5, 12*). The services of skilled workers were often secured by contract (*11*). The woollen textile manufacture served a wide market at home and abroad and was the pre-eminent industry. In the early Middle Ages cloth making was important in some towns of south and east England (*2*) and was sometimes under the control of leading merchant entrepreneurs (*6*). It was promoted by several monarchs, notably Edward III who encouraged skilled craftsmen to settle in England (*10*). In the later Middle Ages the restrictive practices of urban gilds (*14*) led to an expansion of the cloth making industry outside the towns and in East Anglia there were innovations in the types of cloth produced in the late fifteenth century (*17*). England's rich mineral resources were exploited quite widely in the early Middle Ages. Mining was promoted by grants of liberties freeing miners from manorial constraints (*4*) but in some areas mining activity was inhibited by landholders (*15*). Timber provided the main fuel for smelting of minerals and there were early complaints about the despoliation of woodland (*8*). Most mineral products were used locally but where water transport was available, as on Tyneside where coal was mined, wider markets were served (*9*).

1485–1760

Much industrial activity in these centuries, as earlier, was carried on by town and village craftsmen, such as smiths, millers and building workers (*39*), who met local needs. Of industries supplying wider markets woollen cloth making continued pre-eminent, its success based on the staple nature of its market and a capacity for product diversification, with the turn to the 'new draperies'. The growth of the industry in the early sixteenth century saw activity spread further into the countryside, with a continuing decline in the influence of gilds as elsewhere in industrial life. But little change occurred in the industry's organisation or techniques, Stumpe's bringing of weavers together (*18*) proving exceptional. Cloth making remained a household activity carried on by clothiers who varied much, locally and regionally, in the size and scatter of their work-force and in the working capitals they employed to finance wages and materials (*25*). By the mid-eighteenth century much of this industry was located in three principal areas, East Anglia, the West Country and the West Riding of Yorkshire (*36*). Of the remaining textile manufactures, linen, cotton and silk (*31*) were all expanding from the later seventeenth century, the Lombe silk mill of 1717 and after being a rare example of sizeable fixed investment in textiles (**8**, *35*).

Elsewhere in industry substantial fixed investment of capital was often needed. This was especially so in mining where much preparatory work as well as installations above and below ground were often necessary, as in the Tyneside coal industry (*34*) and Cornish tin mining (*23*). Appreciable fixed costs and great risk induced a variety of cost-sharing devices, leading to the establishment in copper mining of one of the first industrial joint-stock companies, the Mines Royal (*20*). Favourable mining licences were also helpful (*28*). Other industries needing costly plants were iron smelting (*22*) and salt making (*27*). Paper making (*31*) and shipbuilding, both prospering in the seventeenth century and after, were more labour intensive, although naval dockyards, such as that at Portsmouth, could be remarkable in their scale (*41*). In the establishment of 'new' industries in England, alien skills and capital were noteworthy and attractive to government (*30–1*), although sometimes productive of complaints from others (*26*). There was, of course, an obverse side to growth, the decline of once-flourishing trades (*24*).

Regulation of industrial activity by governments sprang chiefly from dislike of the disorder a growing wage-earning class could cause. Special concern was shown in the third quarter of the sixteenth century, as industrial unemployment rose with difficulties in foreign markets, resulting in the conservative Weavers Act of 1555 (*19*) and the detailed labour code enacted in 1563 (**8**, *18*). In later years occasional demonstrations by industrial workers against high food prices (**1**, *40*) or to raise wages (*29, 35*) inspired attempts to check labour combination (*38*). In accord with the rise of protectionist thinking, official intervention also sought to discriminate against Irish and American woollen production (*32*). The preoccupation of English ironmasters with colonial competition in the 1730s (*40*) had a similar end.

Continuing low wages for labour combined with intermittent and generally slow growth in markets at home and abroad meant traditional methods of manufacture remained broadly viable throughout the period. But some major technical advances were achieved, notably in industrial fuels with the widening resort to coal, and in mechanical power, with the Newcomen fire engine (*33, 37*). And by the mid-eighteenth century a spirit of mechanical invention was in the air (**8**, *35*).

1 Salt Making, 1086

(*Domesday Book*, I, p. 172, printed in *The Victoria County History of the County of Worcester*, I (1901), pp, 286–7)

To this manor[1] belong 13 saltpans in [Droit]wich and 3 salt-workers who render, from these saltpans, 300 'mits' of salt, for [making] which they used to be given 300 cart loads of wood by the keepers of the wood[land] in the time of King Edward. There are 6 leaden vats.

* * *

In [Droit]wich King Edward had 11 houses, and in 5 brinepits King Edward used to have his share. In one brine-pit, Upewic, [there are] 54 saltpans and 2 'hocci' [which] pay 6 shillings and 8 pence. In another brine-pit, Helperic, [there are] 17 saltpans. In a third brine-pit, Midelwic, [there are] 12 saltpans and two-thirds of a 'hoccus' [which] pay 6 shillings and 8 pence. In 5 other brine-pits there are 15 saltpans.

From all these King Edward used to have a ferm of 52 pounds.

In these brine-pits Earl E[a]dwine used to have 51½ saltpans, and from the 'Hocci' he used to have 6 shillings and 8 pence. All this used to pay a ferm of 24 pounds. Now King William has in demesne both what King Edward and what Earl E[a]dwine used to have. The sheriff [has] paid thence 65 pounds by weight and 2 'mits' of salt while he has had [the] wood.[2] For without the wood, he says, he could not possibly pay that [amount].

* * *

King William holds Tardebigg. King Edward held [it]. There are 9 hides. In [the] demesne is 1 plough and another can be employed. There are 2 villeins and 28 bordars with 12 ploughs. In [Droit]wich³ are 7 saltpans and 2 lead vats, and they pay 20 shillings and 100 'mits' of salt.

¹ The king's manor of Bromsgrove, Warwickshire.   ² For the saltworks.
³ i.e. belonging to this manor.

2 Payments by Town Gilds, 1179–80

(Extracts from *Pipe Roll. 26 Henry II* (Pipe Roll Society, XXIX, 1908), pp. 26–153)

The weavers of Oxford render account of 6*l* for their gild. They have delivered it into the treasury.   And they are quit.

The corvesers of Oxford render account of 15*s* for an ounce of gold for their gild. They have delivered it into the treasury.

And they are quit.

The weavers of Huntingdon render account of 40*s* for their gild. They have delivered it into the treasury.   And they are quit.

The weavers of Lincoln render account of 6*l* for their gild. They have delivered it into the treasury.   And they are quit.

The weavers of York render account of 10*l* for their gild. They have delivered it into the treasury.   And they are quit.

The same sheriff [of York] renders account of 2 marks from the gild of glovers and curriers. In the treasury is 1 mark.

And they owe 1 mark.

The same sheriff renders account of 20*s* from the gild of saddlers for [customs which they exact unjustly]. In the treasury is 10*s*.

And it owes 10*s*.

The same sheriff renders account . . . of 1 mark from the gild of hosiers by way of mercy . . .   And he is quit.

* * *

The weavers of Winchester render account of 2 marks of gold for their gild. In the treasury are 12*l* for 2 marks of gold.

And they are quit.

The fullers of Winchester render account of 6*l* for their gild. They have delivered it into the treasury.   And they are quit.

The weavers of Nottingham render account of 40*s* for their gild. They have delivered it into the treasury.   And they are quit.

The weavers of London render account of 12*l* for their gild. They have delivered it into the treasury. And they are quit.

Amercements of Adulterine Gilds in the City of London.

The gild whereof Goscelin is alderman owes 30 marks.

The gild of pepperers whereof Edward is alderman owes 16 marks.

The gild of St. Lazarus whereof Ralph le Barre is alderman owes 25 marks.

The gild of goldsmiths whereof Ralph Flael is alderman owes 45 marks.

3 Grant of Wood for Charcoal, 1195

(Bodleian Library Rawlinson MS B 449, f. 150*v.*, printed in H. R. Schubert, *History of the British Iron and Steel Industry from c. 450 B.C. to A.D. 1775* (1957), p. 341)

William de Stutevill to his bailiffs and foresters of Knaresborough and to all his friends seeing and hearing these letters greeting. Know you that I have granted and in this charter confirm to the master smith of Fountains charcoal for burning in my forest of Knaresborough wherever, and as much as, he wishes from dead wood, both standing and fallen, and for taking wherever he wishes within my forest and without. Therefore I will and order that he and his men may burn charcoal and may take it where they wish in peace as it is aforesaid without any impediment. Rendering thence to me ten shillings and three dacres[1] of horse shoes per annum. The aforesaid smith will burn this charcoal for as long as he wishes by the aforesaid rent. The term of this agreement begins at Easter in the 1195th year from the Incarnation of the Lord.

[1] i.e. sixty.

4 Charter of Liberties to Tin Miners, 1201

(P.R.O. Charter Roll, 36 Henry III, m. 18, printed in G. R. Lewis, *The Stannaries. A Study of the English Tin Miner* (Harvard Economic Studies, III, 1924), p. 238)

The king to the archbishops . . . greeting. We have inspected the charter which the Lord King John, our father, made to our tin miners in Cornwall and Devon in these words:— John, by the grace of God, king of England . . . to the archbishops, bishops, abbots, earls, barons, judges, sheriffs, foresters and to all our bailiffs and faithful people, greeting. Know you that we have granted that all tin miners in Cornwall and Devon are free of pleas of neifs as long as they work for the profit of our farm or of the marks of our new tax, for the stannaries are on our demesne. And they may dig for tin and for turf for smelting it, at all times freely and peaceably without hindrance from any man, everywhere on the moors and in the fiefs of bishops, abbots and earls, as they have been accustomed to do. And they may buy faggots to smelt the tin, without waste of forest, and they may divert streams for their work in the stannaries just as they have been accustomed to do by ancient usage. Nor shall they desist from their work by reason of any summons, except those of the chief warden of the stannaries or his bailiffs. We have granted also that the chief warden of the stannaries and his bailiffs have plenary power over the miners to do justice to them and to hold them to the law. And if it should happen that any of the aforesaid miners ought to be seized or imprisoned for any breach of the law they should be received from them[1] in our prisons; and if any of them should become a fugitive or outlaw his chattels shall be delivered to us by the hands of the warden of the stannaries because the miners are our farmers and always in our demesne. Moreover, we have granted to our treasurer and the weighers, so that they might be more faithful and attentive to our service in the receiving and guarding of our treasure in market towns, that they shall be quit in all towns in which they stay of aids and tallages as long as they are in our service as treasurers and weighers; for they have and can have nothing else throughout the year for their services to us. These witnesses, W., earl of Salisbury,[2] . . . Given by the hand of S. Archdeacon of Wells at Bona Villa super Tokam the 29th day of October in the third year . . .

And we, ratifying and approving the aforesaid grant, grant and confirm it for us and our heirs as the aforesaid charter reasonably testifies. These witnesses . . . Given by our hand at Merton, the 2nd day of April.

[1] The chief warden and his bailiffs.   [2] And four others named.

5 Building Work at Westminster Abbey, 1253

(P.R.O. Exchequer K.R. Accounts, E 101/467/1, printed in *Building Accounts of King Henry III*, ed. H. M. Colvin (Oxford, 1971), pp. 249–51)

From 28 April to 11 May 1253

The first week after Easter. Containing the feast of the Apostles Philip and James[1] on Thursday which is the lord king's and the feast of the Invention of the Holy Cross[2] on Saturday which is the masons'.

For wages of 39 white cutters,[3] 14 marblers, 20 layers, 32 carpenters together with John at St. Albans, 3 painters, 13 polishers, 19 smiths, 14 glaziers, and 4 plumbers, 14*l* 12*s*.

For wages of 150 labourers, with keepers, clerks, and [the charges of] two carts daily, 6*l* 16*s*.

　　　Total wages 21*l* 8*s*.

Purchases

To Henry the smith.

To Bernard of St. Osyth for cutting 588 feet of ashlars[4] by task, 14*s* 8*d*.

And to Henry of Carshalton for cutting six hundredweight and a half of chalk for the vaults by task, 2*s* 2*d*.

And to Nicholas Scot and his fellows for portage of stone, 6*s* 7*d*.

And for 36 hundredweight of freestone,[5] 10*l* 16*s*.

To Roger of Reigate for 10 hundredweight of freestone, 65*s*, for two shiploads of ragstone,[6] 13*s* 3*d*.

And for five hundredweight of lime, 25*s*.

To Adam the timber merchant for timber, boards, and laths, 33*s* 10*d*.

And to James the joiner for tables for the chambers of the lord king and the queen and for panels for the lord king's bed, 64*s* 2*d*.

And to Richard of Eastcheap for withies and hurdles, 4*s* 6*d*.

And to Richard Ogul for hurdles, 5*s*.

To Richard the cooper for buckets, 3*s* 6*d*.

To Walter Box for cords, 8*s* 6*d*.

To Henry of Bridge for a whetstone to sharpen mauls, 4*s*.

And to the aforesaid Henry for iron nails, 13*s*.

To Richard of the cellar for 24 hundredweight of tough Gloucester iron, 4*l* 16*s*.

And for carriage of the same iron, 3*s* 4*d*.

And to Michael Tony for 23 chars of lead, 50*l*.

And to Pain for smelting lead ashes, 40*s*.

And to John Sige for 13,500 tiles together with portage and tile-pins, 28s 11d.

> Total purchases, 27l 12s 4d.[7]
> Sum total of the week, 49l 0s 4d.

The second week after Easter containing the feast of the blessed John before the Latin Gate[8] on Tuesday which is the lord king's.

For wages of 39 white cutters, 15 marblers, 26 layers, 32 carpenters together with John and his fellow at St. Albans, two painters with a servant, 13 polishers, 19 smiths, 14 glaziers, and four plumbers, 15l 10s 1d.

For wages of 176 labourers, with keepers, clerks, and [the charges of] two carts daily, 9l 17s 2d.

> Total wages, 25l 7s 3d.

Purchases. To Master Aubrey for the arrears owed for tracery and ......, 66s, for 53 feet of parpent stone at 4d a foot, 59 feet of voussoirs with fillets at 3½d a foot, 221½ feet at 3d a foot, 50 *assises* at 5d each, 42 jambs, 22 feet of mullions, 243 feet of *cerches*,[9] 9 feet of *bosseus*, and seven steps cut by task, 7l 13s 1d.

And for 9 capitals, 68 feet of skew-stones, 1,591 feet of *cerches*, 54s 4d.

And for 25¾ hundredweight of chalk for the vaults, 8s 7d.

And for 22 hundredweight and three quarters of freestone, 6l 16s 6d.

To Roger of Reigate for eight hundredweight and a quarter of freestone, 53s 7½d.

To Richard the lime-burner for three hundredweight of lime, 15s.

To Agnes for two hundredweight and a half of lime, 12s 6d.

And to Richard of Eastcheap for two dozen hurdles together with withies, 9s 7d.

To Richard Oggol for five dozen hurdles together with withies, 12s 6d.

To Henry of Bridge for iron nails and whetstones, 19s 8d.

To Benedict for carriage, portage, and pesage of 23 chars of lead, 9s 4d.

To Richer for straw, 1s 6d.

> Sum total of the purchases, 27l 12s 10½d.
> Sum total of the week, 53l 0s 1½d.

---

[1] 1 May.   [2] 3 May.   [3] Freemasons.
[4] Hewn stones used in facing rubble walls.
[5] A fine-grained sandstone or limestone that could be cut or sawn easily.
[6] Coarse rough stone supplied in this case from Kent.
[7] Figures in accounts such as these do not always tally.   [8] 6 May.
[9] These appear to have been stones cut so as to form a segment of a circle.

6 Regulation of the Leicester Cloth Industry, 1254–65

(Second Merchant Gild Roll, Box 1, No. 2, printed in *Records of the Borough of Leicester*, I, ed. M. Bateson (1899), pp. 69, 89–91, 101, 105)

21 January, 1254

William of Aylstone charged that many times he sold the wool of the men of Hinckley and Coventry by weight and scale[1] against the commune of the gild. He pledged 60*s*, to wit so that he will give 6*s* 8*d* now and the rest is put in respite: and he abjured trespass of this kind, and if he be again convicted of any trespass of this sort against the commune of the gild, he shall lose every kind of gild trade for a year and a day: pledges [named]: and thereof 3*s* are allowed to the said William, which he lent for the redemption of Bridgesilver, and he owes 3*s* 8*d* of which he paid to Henry of Ruddington now 1*s* 10*d*, and he will pay at the sitting of the commune of the gild after Easter 1*s* 10*d*. He paid and is quit.

* * *

1260

Henry of Ruddington being then Mayor of Leicester, 44 Hen. III., these customs were agreed to in the gild of merchants with the consent of the merchants and the weavers and the fullers.

The weavers swore that they will conceal no infidelity in their work and that they will have three shuttles in their work, and will not weave at night.

The fullers swore that they will not full unfaithful cloth without showing their defects to the mayor and bailiffs, and that they will not full coloured cloths in argol and lye and that they will not use beetles on dry cloth, and that they will not hold any morningspeech except in the presence of two merchants of the gild of merchants who shall have been chosen for this purpose from the community of the gild, and accordingly these two are chosen for this purpose, James Motun and Nicholas the burgess . . . the fullers shall not make among themselves a fixed assize how much each of them will take for a yard of . . . of cloths. And that they will full cloth well and of one sort without any default. And when cloths shall have been calendered and cottoned,[2] and those to whom these cloths belong . . . if they should find defective fulling, these cloths shall be shown to four merchants of the gild of merchants, who shall have been appointed for this purpose by the community of the gild, and by these four the defects of fulling shall be presented to the mayor and the community: Peter the White, Henry Houhil, Philip

Leveriz and Simon of Cotes are the four now appointed for this purpose. If any of the fullers act against any article aforesaid, he shall make satisfaction therefor to . . . by those cloths . . . if he has whereof he can pay therefor . . . and at the first trespass he shall be in mercy of the gild at half a mark; and at the second one mark, and at the third he shall abjure fulling work for a year and a day. It is provided and agreed by the community of the gild of merchants that none of them shall keep . . . a fulling mill outside the town of Leicester unless it be by the consent of the community [and of him to whom] the cloth belongs and of the fuller of Leicester [who shall full the cloth].

* * *

1262–3

William of Shilton, fuller, convicted of the defective fulling of a blue cloth to the great damage of Richard of Shilton whose cloth it was: he pledged half a mark to the gild. Pledges. The first trespass of this W.; 8d thereof are pardoned to him and he shall pay 6s at three sittings . . .

* * *

21 January, 1265

In full morningspeech held on St Agnes' day, it was provided and agreed and published that the weavers who wish to weave in Leicester may weave both by night and by day, but so that no defect may be in their work: and they shall take for each yard of whatever kind of cloth $\frac{1}{2}d$, except for all russets; and shall take for each yard of russet $\frac{3}{4}d$: and they shall not weave any cloth of country villages as long as they may be able to have enough work from the men of Leicester, and if they should have a scarcity of work from the men of Leicester, they shall point out this scarcity to two men of the gild of Leicester who shall be appointed for this purpose, and by their view, when there is a scarcity of Leicester cloth, they shall weave the cloth of strangers.

Roger of Kilsby, weaver, for defective weaving of a cloth belonging to Mary the ostler pledged mercy of the gild on Friday next after the octave of Epiphany 49 Hen. III. and it is put in respite on account of poverty, but let it be exacted when he has anything to pay with.

---

[1] The probable meaning is that he sold wholesale. (MB)
[2] The meaning of this passage is unclear. (MB)

7 An Attempt at Improvement in Milling, 1295

(*Annales Prioratus de Dunstaplia*, ed. H. R. Luard, *Annales Monastici*, III, *Rolls Series* (1866), p. 402)

In the same year[1] brother J[ohn] the carpenter made a new mill of an original and until then unheard-of construction, promising that it could be drawn by a single horse. But when the mill had been completed and should have ground [corn], four powerful horses could scarcely set it in motion. Consequently it was abandoned and the old horse-mill was again taken [into use].

[1] 1295.

8 The Wastage of Timber, 1306

(*Rotuli Parliamentorum*, I, p. 198)

[We] wish our lord, the king, to hear that lord Anthony, bishop of Durham,[1] wastes and destroys all the woodland belonging to his church in the bishopric of Durham, by gift, sale and bad supervision and by setting up forges of iron and lead to burn charcoal. And furthermore he burdens the bondsmen of the church with divers exactions[2] and tallages, also with damages which the prior of Durham and other persons have claimed against him before the justices of our lord the king, for which trespass he was attainted, as well as with other manner of tallages, so that they are so impoverished that they are not able to hold their land, wherefore if our lord the king, who is advocate of the aforesaid church, does not give remedy thereon, the aforesaid church will be disinherited and impoverished to the prejudice of our lord the king, and of his regalian rights[3] and of the chapter of Durham.

[Reply] It is replied thus, that it be forbidden by writ of Chancery to the bishop and his officials to make waste of the things contained in the petition.

[1] Anthony Bek, 1284–1311.   [2] *Mises.*   [3] *Corone.*

9 Sea-Coal and Pollution, 1307

(*Calendar of Close Rolls, 1302–7*, p. 537)

June 12. Carlisle

[To the sheriff] of Surrey. Order to cause proclamation to be made in the town of Southwark that all who wish to use kilns in that town or its confines, shall make their kilns of brushwood or charcoal in the usual way, and shall not use in any way sea-coal hereafter, under pain of heavy forfeiture, and the sheriff shall cause this order to be observed inviolably hereafter, as the king learns from the complaint of prelates and magnates of his realm, who frequently come to London for the benefit of the commonwealth by his order, and from the complaint of his citizens and all his people dwelling there and in Southwark that the workmen in the city and town aforesaid and in their confines now burn them and construct them of sea-coal instead of brushwood or charcoal, from the use of which sea-coal an intolerable smell diffuses itself throughout the neighbouring places and the air is greatly infected, to the annoyance of the magnates, citizens and others there dwelling and to the injury of their bodily health.

10 Flemish Cloth Workers Encouraged to Settle, 1331

(P.R.O. Patent Roll, 5 Edward III, pt. 2, m. 25)

[Letters] of protection for John Kempe of Flanders

The king to all his bailiffs . . . to whom . . . greeting. Know you that since John Kempe of Flanders, weaver of woollen cloths, will come to stay within our realm of England to exercise his mystery here, and to instruct and teach those wishing to learn therein, and will bring with him certain men, servants and apprentices of that mystery, we have taken John and his aforesaid men, servants and apprentices, and their goods and chattels into our special protection and defence. Therefore we charge you to maintain, protect and defend John, his aforesaid men, servants and apprentices and their aforesaid goods and chattels and that without any calumny you permit the same John to exercise freely without any impediment his aforesaid mystery within the same realm, both in cities and boroughs and elsewhere in the same realm where for his own convenience he shall see it to be more advantageous, and to instruct and teach those who shall wish to learn the aforesaid mystery, [you] not bringing against them or permitting to be brought injury, vexation, loss or burden, and if anything shall be forfeited by them [you] are to cause it to be amended to them without delay. We promise that we are obliged to make our similar letters of protection for other men of that mystery, and for dyers and fullers wishing to come from foreign parts to stay within our realm for the aforesaid reason. In [testimony] of which thing . . . to last as long as it shall please the king. Witnessed by the king at Lincoln the 23rd day of July.

11 Building Contract for a Tavern, 1342

(London Bridge Estate Deeds, G17, printed in E. Rickert, *Chaucer's World*, ed. C. C. Olson and M. M. Crow (1948), p. 8)

Covenant of Richard of Felstead, carpenter, with William Marbrer, taverner, to build upon the land of the said William in Paternoster Row, between the room beneath the gate of the tavern of Thomas Legge which is held by John of Oakbrook, chaplain, on the east and the tenement of the said Thomas on the west and south, a new house with two gabled roofs toward the street, each with two jetties; and above the two storeys, beneath the one roof, a garret with puncheons six feet in height, and beneath the other roof, towards Paternoster Row, a room on the highest storey, and at one end thereof, towards the north, a buttery and a kitchen; and all the partitions throughout the whole house; and upon the lowest floor above the vault a partitioned room, and on the rest of the same floor thirty seats for the tavern; and a partition extending along the whole length of the said lowest floor; and on the second floor above, thirty seats for the tavern; and in the room a bay window towards the street and on either side thereof a linteled window; and in the bedroom another bay window, with other such linteled windows on either side; and everywhere windows, doors, and steps as they are required; and in the bedroom the canopy over the bed; the said William supplying the timber and 'le syer' of timber, and the said Richard receiving for his carpenter's work 24*l* and a gown worth 20*s* or its value in money.

12 Work Conditions at York Minster, c.1352

(*The Fabric Rolls of York Minster*, ed. J. Raine (Surtees Society, XXXV, 1858), pp. 172–3, translated in L. F. Salzman, *Building in England down to 1540: a Documentary History* (Oxford, 1967), pp. 56–7)

That the masons, carpenters and other workmen ought to begin to work, on all working days in the summer, from Easter to Michaelmas,[1] at sunrise and ought to work from that time until the ringing of the bell of the Blessed Virgin Mary, and then they should sit down to breakfast in the lodge of the works, if they have not breakfasted, for the space [of time that it takes to walk] half a league; and then the masters, or one of them, shall knock upon the door of the lodge, and all shall at once go to their work; and so they shall diligently carry out their duties until noon, and then they shall go to their dinner. Also in winter, from Michaelmas to Easter, they shall come to their work at dawn and everyone when he comes shall immediately start work, and so continue in the said way until noon. From the feast of the Invention of the Holy Cross[2] to the feast of St. Peter's Chains,[3] they ought to sleep in the lodge after dinner; and when the vicars come out from the canons' hall the master mason, or his deputy, shall cause them to rise from slumber and get to their work; and so they ought to work until the first bell for vespers, and then they shall sit and drink in the lodge, from the said first bell to the third bell, both in summer and winter. Also from the [1 August] to the [3 May], they shall return to their work immediately after their dinner, for which a reasonable time shall be taken, without waiting for the return of the vicars from the canons' hall; and so they shall work until the first bell for vespers and then they shall drink in the lodge until the third bell has rung, and shall return to their work, and so they shall work until the ringing of the bell of St. Mary's Abbey which is called le Langebell, namely, every working day from the feast of St. Peter's Chains to Michaelmas, and from Michaelmas to the said feast of St. Peter, they shall continue to work as long as they can see by daylight. Also each mason shall take less for the week in winter, that is from Michaelmas to Easter, than in summer by one day's wage. Also when two feast days happen in one week, each loses one day's wage and when three occur, half that week. Also on vigils and on Saturdays, when they rest after noon, out of respect for the next day, then they shall work until noon strikes. Also the said two master masons and the carpenter of the works shall be present at every pay-day, and there shall inform the warden and controller of the works of any defaults and absence of masons, carpenters, and other workmen, and according to his lateness or absence deductions shall be made from each man's wages, both for a whole day and a half day, as is reasonable. Also the said two master masons and carpenter, for the time being, ought faithfully to observe the said regulations, in virtue of the oath which they take, and they shall see that they are kept by the other masons and workmen working there, on pain of dismissal. And if anyone refuse to work in the said manner, let him be dismissed at once and not taken back again on to the works until he is willing to keep the rules in every detail.

[1] 29 September.   [2] 3 May.   [3] 1 August.

13 Abuse of Apprenticeship, 1369

(*Calendar of Plea and Memoranda Rolls, A.D. 1364–1381,* ed. A. H. Thomas (Cambridge, 1929), p. 107)

John Catour of Reading brought a bill of complaint against Ellis Mympe, embroiderer of London, to whom his daughter Alice had been apprenticed for five years, for beating and ill treating the girl, and failing to provide for her.

The parties were summoned to appear on March 3, when they announced that they had come to an agreement on terms that the defendant should pay the complainant 13*s* 4*d* and release the girl from her apprenticeship. Thereupon he released her.

The defendant was then asked why he took the girl for less than seven years, and had not enrolled the indentures, according to the custom of the city and his oath. He put himself on the mercy of the mayor and the aldermen, who gave judgment exonerating the said Alice from her apprenticeship. By order of the court the indentures were surrendered for cancellation.

14 Ordinances of the Bristol Dyers, 1407

(P.R.O. Patent Roll, 13 Henry IV, pt. 2, m. 31)

These are the petition, ordinances and articles, which are granted and confirmed to the masters, burgesses of the craft of dyeing of the town of Bristol . . . by the assent and advice of the whole Common Council . . . held in the Guildhall of Bristol . . . the 8th year of the reign of King Henry the Fourth after the Conquest, to endure for ever, as well for the honour of the town of Bristol as for the profit and amendment of the said craft; the tenor of which petition and ordinances follows hereafter:

To the honourable and discreet sirs, the mayor, sheriff and bailiffs of the town of Bristol, and to all the honourable folk of the Common Council, the said masters make supplication: Whereas certain persons of the said town of divers crafts, not cunning in the craft of dyeing, who were never apprentices nor masters of the said craft, take upon them divers charges and bargains to dye cloths and wools of many folk of the same town and the country round, which cloths and wools have been divers times ill dressed and worked through their ignorance and lack of knowledge, to the great damage of the owners and scandal of the whole craft aforesaid and of the drapery of the same town; whereupon, most wise sirs, please it your special grace to grant to the said suppliants the ordinances underwritten, to put out and bring to nought all deceits and damages which could hereafter befall within the craft aforesaid, and this for God and as a work of charity.

First, be it ordained and assented that each year two masters of the said craft be elected by the common assent of all the masters of the same craft in the town of Bristol, and their names presented to the mayor of Bristol in full court of the Guildhall of the same town, and there to be sworn on the Holy Gospels within the quinzaine of Michaelmas at the latest to survey well and lawfully all manner of defects which shall be made henceforward as well in dyed cloths as in wools put in woad within the franchise of Bristol. And if any damage is done to any person through defect of dyeing by any man or woman of the said craft, that then he shall pay sufficient amends to the parties damaged according to the discretion of the said two masters and of four other indifferent persons elected by the mayor and his council, as the trespass demands. And if it so be that any man or woman will not abide by the ordinance and award of the said two masters and other indifferent persons elected by the mayor as before is said, that then the mayor and his council for the time being shall cause them to be compelled to pay and satisfy the said persons so damaged of all that is adjudged by them. And in case that the said two masters after their oath made be negligent in executing their office touching their said mystery, that they be punished and amerced according to the advice of the mayor and of the court aforesaid to the use of the chamber and to the common profit as is aforesaid.

Further, that no servant or apprentice of the said mystery be henceforth admitted to the liberties of Bristol to be a burgess sworn to exercise the said mystery until it be testified to the court before the mayor of Bristol by the said two masters that they are able and well learned in the said craft of dyeing, to save and keep the goods of the good folk who are wont to be served for their money in the exercise of the mystery aforesaid. And if any master of the said mystery make any such servant or apprentice, if he be not able and well learned in the said craft, as before is said, he shall incur the penalty of 20s for each time, to wit, to the use and profit of the commonalty, as before is said, 13s 4d, and to the masters for their light, 6s 8d, without any pardon, provided always that the mayor of the town of Bristol have his power and jurisdiction to accept and make burgesses of each person presented to him, as has been used and accustomed before these times, these ordinances notwithstanding.

Further, forasmuch as often before these times divers folk, as well those who have not been apprentices, servants or masters of the said mystery, as other folk who are of other mysteries, not cunning nor having knowledge in the aforesaid art of dyeing, have taken upon them to dye cloths and wools put in woad, as well of good folk of the town as of the country round, which, by reason of ill management and through lack of knowledge of the said folk, are greatly impaired of their colours and many other defects to the great loss and damage of the owners of the said cloths and great scandal of the town and shame of the whole craft aforesaid, whereby the masters and apprentices of the said craft of dyeing go vagrant for lack of work, because the said folk of other crafts have been occupied in their said craft, to their great mischief and undoing, therefore it is ordained and assented that henceforward no manner of man of the same craft nor any other mystery do dye any cloth or wool, unless it be presented by the said masters that he be good and able and sufficiently learned in the said craft, upon pain of paying to the mayor and bailiffs of the chamber for the use and common profit, as before is said, at the first default 6s 8d, at the second default 13s 4d, at the third default 20s, and for each default after the said three defaults 20s, without any pardon, so that the said masters have for their labour the third part arising from the said defaults for their light, provided always that all the burgesses of this town may make their profit for dyeing in their houses their own cloths, as has been used before these times, these ordinances notwithstanding.

And after the view of the said petition and ordinances aforesaid by the mayor and Common Council, it was assented that all the masters of the said mystery of dyeing dwelling within the franchise of Bristol should come before the mayor to hear their said ordinances and whether they would assent thereto and grant them or not. And by command of the . . . mayor, Ralph Dyer . . . and many others of the mystery aforesaid came in their own persons, to whom all the said ordinances were published and declared, and every of them in the presence of the mayor aforesaid granted and assented to all the ordinances and pains aforesaid, praying of their common assent that the ordinances and pains aforesaid be ratified, confirmed and enrolled of record in the papers of the Guildhall of Bristol, and be put in due execution for ever, saving always to the jurisdiction of the mayor and Common Council of the town of Bristol that if any ordinance or any new addition hereafter touching the mystery aforesaid which may be profitable as well for the town as for the aforesaid mystery, that then by the advice and ordinance of the mayor of Bristol for the time being and the Council of the town and also of the masters of the said mystery, they shall be corrected and amended according to good faith and reason and put in due execution, the ordinances aforesaid notwithstanding. Provided also that the dyers abovesaid be bound by these ordinances to make the assay of woad and to work wools and cloths as well in woad as in madder of the goods of all merchants and burgesses of Bristol, taking for their labour reasonably as has been accustomed and used before these times. In witness whereof, at the special prayer and request of the said masters to keep and maintain their ordinances aforesaid, we have put hereto the seal of the office of the Mayoralty of the town of Bristol. Given in the Guildhall of the same town 17 March, 8 Henry IV.

15 A Lease of Coal Mines, 1447

(*Historiae Dunelmensis Scriptores Tres*, ed. J. Raine (Surtees Society, IX, 1839), pp. cccxii–cccxiii)

This indenture made between William the prior of Durham on the one part, and John Brown of Tudhoe, Bertram Gaythird, Alexander Belfield, William Lethom, Rallyn Brownsmith of Middleham and William Brown of Durham, flesh-hewer, on the other part, witnesses that the said prior has granted and let to farm to the said John, Bertram, Alexander, William, Rallyn and William a waste toft and 28 acres of land with the appurtenances in Trillesden, and with a coal-pit in the same land, to work therein and win coal every working day with three picks, and each pick to win every working day 60 scoops, to have and to hold the said toft and land with the appurtenances, and with the said coal-pit from the feast of St. Cuthbert in September next coming for the term of a year then next following, giving to the said prior for the said toft and land with the appurtenances 24s and for the said coal-pit 10 marks of good English money, at the feasts of the Invention of the Holy Cross[1] and the Nativity of St. John the Baptist[2] next coming, by even portions. And the said John, Bertram, Alexander, William, Rallyn and William shall work the said mine in a workmanlike fashion, to save the field standing, by the sight of certain viewers assigned by the said prior as often as he wishes to appoint them within the same year to search the same mine. Also the said prior has granted and let to farm to the said John Brown, Bertram Gaythird, Alexander Belfield, William Lethom, Rallyn Brownsmith and William Brown a coal-pit on the north side of Spennymoor, to work therein and win coal with three picks every working day, & every pick winning every working day 60 scoops of coal, to have and to hold the said coal-pit in

Spennymoor from the feast of St. Cuthbert in September next coming after the date of this indenture unto the end of a year then next following, paying therefore to the said prior at the feasts of the Invention of the Holy Cross and the Nativity of St. John the Baptist above written by even portions 20*l* of good English payment. And the said John, Bertram, Alexander, William, Rallyn and William shall work the said mine in a workmanlike fashion, and save the field standing, by the sight of certain viewers thereto assigned by the said prior as often as he wishes to appoint them within the same year to search the same mine. Also the said John, Bertram, Alexander, William, Rallyn and William shall of their own costs and expense labour and win a water-gate[3] for winning of coal in the same coal-pit of Spennymoor, and the same watergate, like as they win it, they shall leave it at the year's end by the sight of the said viewers. And the said prior shall warrant to the said John, Bertram, Alexander, William, Rallyn and William the said toft and land with appurtenances and with the coal-pit in Trillesden, and also the coal-pit in Spennymoor, for the year aforesaid. In witness of which agreement the parties aforesaid have interchangeably set their seals to this indenture. Written the last day of August, the year of our sovereign and gracious Lord Jesus 1447.

[1] 3 May.   [2] 24 June.   [3] A drainage channel.

16 Indenture of Apprenticeship, 1459

(P.R.O. Ancient Deeds, A 10022)

This indenture made between John Gibbs of Penzance in the county of Cornwall of the one part and John Goffe, Spaniard, of the other part, witnesses that the aforesaid John Goffe has put himself to the aforesaid John Gibbs to learn the craft of fishing, and to stay with him as apprentice and to serve from the feast of Philip and James[1] next to come after the date of these presents until the end of eight years then next ensuing and fully complete; throughout which term the aforesaid John Goffe shall well and faithfully serve the aforesaid John Gibbs and Agnes his wife as his masters and lords, shall keep their secrets, shall everywhere willingly do their lawful and honourable commands, shall do his masters no injury nor see injury done to them by others, but prevent the same as far as he can, shall not waste his master's goods nor lend them to any man without his special command. And the aforesaid John Gibbs and Agnes his wife shall teach, train and inform or cause the aforesaid John Goffe, their apprentice, to be informed in the craft of fishing in the best way they know, chastising him duly and finding for the same John, their apprentice, food, clothing linen and woollen, and shoes, sufficiently, as befits such an apprentice to be found, during the term aforesaid. And at the end of the term aforesaid the aforesaid John Goffe shall have of the aforesaid John Gibbs and Agnes his wife 20s sterling without any fraud. In witness whereof the parties aforesaid have interchangeably set their seals to the parts of this indenture. These witnesses:— Richard Boscawen, Robert Martin and Robert Cosin and many others. Given at Penzance, 1 April in the 37th year of the reign of King Henry the Sixth after the Conquest of England.

¹ 1 May.

17 Act for the Improvement of Worsted Making, 1467

(9 Edward IV, c.1., *Statutes at Large*, II (1763), pp. 20–1)

For that there be as well within the city of Norwich, as elsewhere within the county of Norfolk, divers persons which do make untrue wares of all manner of worsteds, not being of the assise in length nor in breadth, nor of good stuff and right making as they ought to be, and of old time were accustomed, and the sleyes and yarn pertaining to the same not well made and wrought, in great deceit as well of denizens as of strangers inhabiting or repairing to this realm, which have used and do use to buy such merchandises, trusting that they were within as they seemed without, where indeed it is contrary: and for that the worsteds in times past were lawfully wrought, and merchandise well liked, and greatly desired and esteemed in the parts beyond the sea; now because they be of no right making, nor good stuff, they be reported and esteemed deceitful and unlawful merchandise, and of little regard, to the great damage of our lord the king, and great prejudice of his loyal subjects: Our said lord the king, by the assent of the lords spiritual and temporal, and at the request of his commons being in the said parliament, and by authority of the said parliament, for the wealth of his people, and the perpetual amendment of the said worsteds, and eschewing and avoiding all manner of deceits to be done and wrought in worsteds by them that work the same, and are the means thereof, has ordained and established, that men of the said craft within the said city shall have power every year, the monday next after the feast of Pentecost, to choose four wardens within the said city of the same craft; and also that artificers of the same craft likewise out of the city, that is to say, within the county of Norfolk, shall have power every year at the same day to choose four wardens within and of the said county, of the same craft: And the aforesaid wardens in the said county and city, to come before the mayor of the said city for the time being, upon the monday next after the feast of Corpus Christi then next following, and then to be sworn before the mayor of the said city, and the steward of the Duchy of Lancaster within the said county for the time being, if it happen him within the said county then to be present, or else before the said mayor only, the said steward then being absent. And that all the said wardens, as well within the said city as without, or else the greatest part of them, under this form before recited chosen and sworn, shall have full power for the year then next following, to survey the workmanship of the said artificers, and that they make and work rightfully and well, and of good stuff, and to ordain such rules and ordinances within the said craft, as often as it shall seem needful or necessary for the amendment of the said worsteds and craft; and that all such rules and ordinances, so made and ordained by them, shall be obeyed and kept by the said artificers.

Or otherwise four of the said wardens, calling to them six of the most discreet of the said artificers within the said city, and six of the same artificers within the said county, by the discretion of the said mayor and steward, or one of them, shall punish such of the said artificers which breaks, or does contrary to any of their said rules and ordinances.

18 Stumpe of Malmesbury, 1542

(*The Itinerary of John Leland in or about the Years 1535–43*, ed. L. Toulmin Smith (1907), I, p. 132)

Malmesbury has a good quick market kept every Saturday.

There is a right fair and costly piece of work in the market place made all of stone and curiously vaulted for poor market folks to stand dry when rain comes.

There are 8 great pillars and 8 open arches: and the work is 8 square: one great pillar in the middle bears up the vault. The men of the town made this piece of work in *hominum memoria*.

The whole loggings[1] of the abbey are now belonging to one Stumpe, an exceedingly rich clothier that bought them off the king.

This Stumpe's son has married Sir Edward Baynton's daughter.

This Stumpe was the chief cause and contributor to have the abbey church made a parish church.

At this present time every corner of the vast houses of office that belonged to the abbey are full of looms to weave cloth in, and this Stumpe intends to make a street or two for clothier[s] in the back vacant ground of the abbey that is within the town walls.

There are made now every year in the town a[bout] 3000 cloths.

[1] Lodgings.

19 An Act Touching Weavers, 1555

(2 and 3 Philip and Mary, c. 11, *Statutes of the Realm*, IV, Part I (1819), pp. 286–7)

Forasmuch as the weavers of this realm have, as well at this present parliament as at divers other times, complained that the rich and wealthy clothiers do many ways oppress them, some by setting up and keeping in their houses divers looms, and keeping and maintaining them by journeymen and persons unskilful, to the decay of a great number of artificers which were brought up in the said science of weaving, their family and household, some by ingrossing of looms into their hands and possession, and letting them out at such unreasonable rents as the poor artificers are not able to maintain themselves, much less their wives, family and children, some also by giving much less wages and hire for the weaving and workmanship of [cloth] than in times past they did, whereby they are enforced utterly to forsake their art and occupation wherein they have been brought up: it is therefore, for remedy of the premises, and for the avoiding of a great number of inconveniences which may grow (if in time it be not foreseen) ordained, established and enacted, by authority of this present parliament, that no person using the feat or mystery of clothmaking and dwelling out of a city, borough, market town or corporate town, shall from the feast of St. Michael the Archangel[1] now next ensuing, keep, retain or have in his or their house or possession any more or above one woollen loom at one time, nor shall by any means directly or indirectly receive or take any manner profit, gain or commodity by letting or setting any loom, or any house wherein any loom is or shall be used and occupied, which shall be together by him set or let, upon pain of forfeiture for every week that any person shall do contrary to the tenor and true meaning hereof 20*s*.

And be it further ordained . . . that no woollen weaver using or exercising the feat or mystery of weaving, and dwelling out of city, borough, market town or town corporate, shall after the said feast have or keep at any time above the number of two woollen looms, or receive any profit, gain or commodity, directly or indirectly as is aforesaid, by any more than two looms at one time, upon pain to forfeit for every week that any person shall offend or do to the contrary 20s.

And it is further ordained . . . that no person which shall after the said feast, use, exercise or occupy only the feat or mystery of a weaver, and not clothmaking, shall during the time that he shall use the feat or mystery of a weaver, keep or have any tucking mill, or shall use or exercise the feat or mystery of a [tucker] or dyer, upon pain to forfeit for every week that he shall so do 20s.

And it is further enacted . . . that no person which after the said feast shall use, exercise or occupy the feat or mystery of a tucker or fuller, shall during the time that he shall so use the said feat or mystery, keep or have any loom in his house or possession, or shall directly or indirectly take any profit or commodity by the same, upon pain to forfeit for every week 20s.

And it is further ordained . . . that no person whatsoever, which heretofore has not used or exercised the feat, mystery or art of cloth-making, shall after the said feast, make or weave or cause to be made or woven any kind of broad white woollen cloths, but only in a city, borough, town corporate or market town, or else in such place or places where such cloths have been used to be commonly made by the space of ten years next before the making this act; upon pain of forfeiture for every cloth otherwise made five pounds.

Provided always . . . that it shall not be lawful to any person or persons being a weaver, or that does or shall use the art or mystery of a weaver or weaving, dwelling out of a city, borough, town corporate or market town, to have in his and their service any more or above the number of two apprentices at one time; upon pain to forfeit for every time that he shall offend . . . the sum of ten pounds.

And further be it enacted . . . that it shall not be lawful to or for any person or persons to set up the art or mystery of weaving, after the said feast of St. Michael, unless the same person or persons so setting up the same art or mystery of weaving, have been apprentice to the same art or mystery, or exercised the same, by the space of 7 years at the least; upon pain of twenty pounds to be forfeited to the king and queen's majesties, her grace's heirs or successors, the one moiety of all which forfeitures shall be to the king and queen's highnesses, heirs [and] successors, and the other moiety to him or them that will sue for the same in any court of record by action of debt, bill, plaint or informa-tion, wherein no wager of law, essoigne or protection shall be admitted or allowed for the defendant.

Provided always . . . that this act or anything therein contained shall [not] in any way extend or be prejudicial to any person or persons that does or shall dwell in the counties of York, Cumberland, Northumberland or Westmoreland; but that they and every of them shall and may have and keep looms in their houses, and do and exercise all and every thing and things for or concerning spinning, weaving, clothworking and clothmaking in the said counties, as they or any of them might have done or exercised lawfully before the making of this statute; anything contained in this statute to the contrary in any way notwithstanding.

[1] 29 September.

20 Charter of the Mines Royal, 1568

(Patent Rolls, 10 Elizabeth, pt. v, printed in C. T. Carr, ed., *Select Charters of Trading Companies, 1530–1707* (Selden Society, XXVIII, 1913), pp. 4–15)

Elizabeth by the grace of God . . . To all unto whom these presents shall come, greeting:

Where we by our letters patent bearing date at Westminster the tenth day of October in the sixth year of our reign have, for the considerations therein mentioned, given and granted full power, licence and authority to Thomas Thurland, clerk, one of our chaplains and master of our hospital of the Savoy, and to Daniel Houghsetter, a German born, their heirs and assigns and every of them forever, by themselves, their servants, labourers and workmen or any of them to search, dig, open, roast, melt, stamp, wash, drain, or convey waters or otherwise work for all manner of mines or ores of gold, silver, copper and quicksilver within our counties of York, Lancaster, Cumberland, Westmoreland, Cornwall, Devon, Gloucestershire and Worcestershire, and within our principality of Wales, or in any of them.

And the same to try out, convert and use to their most profit and commodity and the commodity of every of them forever, as well within our own lands, grounds and possessions as also within the lands, grounds and possessions of any of our subjects set, lying or being within our said counties and principalities or in any of them, without any let or perturbation of us our heirs or successors or of any other person or persons whatsoever . . .

And whereas our pleasure intent and meaning in our said letters patent was that, for the better help and more commodity of the said Thomas Thurland and Daniel Houghsetter and their several assigns, they and every of them might from time to time and at their pleasure grant, convey and assign parts and portions of the said licences, privileges, powers, authorities, benefits and immunities. And thereupon their several assignees have since the making of our said letters patent for divers good considerations granted, assigned and conveyed to our right trusty and right wellbeloved cousins and counsellors William, Earl of Pembroke and Robert, Earl of Leicestershire, and to our trusty and wellbeloved James, Lord Mountjoy and to our right trusty and wellbeloved counsellor, Sir William Cecil, knight, our principal secretary, and to John Tamworth and John Dudley, esquires, Lionel Duckett, citizen and alderman of London, Benedict Spinola of London, merchant, John Lover, William Winter, Antony Duckett, of the county of Westmoreland, esquires, Roger Wetherall of Lincoln's Inn in the county of Middlesex, gentleman, Richard Springham, Jeffery Duckett, Richard Barnes, William Patten, Thomas Smyth, William Bird, Daniel Ulstett a German born, Mathew Felde, George Nedham and Edmond Thurland, divers parts and portions of the licences, powers, authorities, privileges, benefits and immunities aforesaid.

By force whereof the said Thomas Thurland and Daniel Houghsetter and their said assignees, by virtue of our said letters patent and by the skilful direction of the said Daniel Houghsetter, have travailed in the search, work and experiment of the mines and ores aforesaid to their very great charge and expenses and have now brought the said work to very good effect, whereby great benefit is like to come to us and this our realm of England, which also will the rather come to pass if the persons now and hereafter having interest in the privileges aforesaid might by our grant be incorporated and made a perpetual body politic, thereby to avoid divers and sundry great inconveniences which by the several deaths of the persons abovesaid or their assigns should else from time to time ensue.

Know you therefore that we, minding and carefully intending the furtherance and advancement of the said mineral works so prosperously and with great charge begun . . . by these presents for us our heirs and successors do give and grant, to the aforenamed William, Earl of Pembroke [and names as above with Thomas Thurland and Daniel Houghsetter] that they by the name of Governor, Assistants and Commonalty for the Mines Royal shall be from henceforth forever one body politic in itself incorporate and a perpetual society of themselves both in deed and name . . .

21 The Fishing Industry of Yarmouth, Later Sixteenth Century

(The Official Papers of Sir Nathaniel Bacon of Stiffkey, Norfolk, as Justice of the Peace 1580–1620, ed. H. W. Saunders (Camden Society, Third Series, XXVI, 1915), pp. 44–5)

The answer of the town of Yarmouth unto the motion of the fishmongers for the repealing of a statute made for the maintenance of navigation.[1]

Since the statute of navigation is increased for trial whereof, especially in the coast towns of Norfolk and Suffolk that give themselves to trading in fisher fare these hard and dangerous days, as Aldborough Southwold, Yarmouth and Wells, and besides the great quantity that other towns have brought in, there is brought into Yarmouth this year about 400,000 fish taken in Iceland and north seas besides their small fish and offal that poor men keep their houses withal, and also a commodity of oil made of the livers of that fish, which said fish being valued at 30*l* per 1,000 will amount to 12,000*l*, the taking whereof does not only help greatly to the serving of the land with fish but does also besides the breeding up of many seafaring men in those towns set on work many people both in town and country for the making of provision for that trade.

Fetching in of fish does employ little shipping and few persons to that which is employed in the taking of it (the one setting on work five times as many persons as the other) so that to decay our own taking of fish by and for the fetching of it in is a thing hurtful to the increase of navigation.

Whereas the strangers having now the greater employment of themselves by taking of it and a double vent for their fish (their own liberty to bring in and our to fetch in) their shipping and their wealth is increased with the decay of ours.

As the offering of commodity and bringing it makes it cheaper so the fetching in of fish beyond the seas and seeking for it either does or will in time as the buyers grow wise to see our regard of it grow dearer, so that their allegations that charge the statute with the raising of the prices of holland lings does not justly touch us, the great price not proceeding from the statute but by reason of the great vent for ling that the Hollander has unto the Spaniard now over that he had when the Spaniard himself trading to Newfoundland (as now they do) was not able to provide himself without them by reason whereof as this land is served by them the dearer, so by the good vent they have in Spain we are also served with the worst.

Whereas the suffering of fish to be fetched in under pretence of the necessity of it for the use of the land does decay our trade if men of ability having great shipping and besides for their other voyages great hoys, would (as they do now employ them for the fetching of coals) employ themselves in part for the taking of fish both the land should be served without any such need of the stranger our shipping should grow stronger our people much more employed. A great quantity of our money and our commodity kept within the land for other uses and by reason that they should know the charge and adventure of fish (as poor fishermen do) the trade of fishermen should be in more account.

If the fish which our men do take in the coasts of Suffolk and Norfolk (which comes not so little yearly as in quantity to 1,000,000 fish and in price to 30,000*l*) with all the rest of the fish taken in all part of England besides be but the tenth part of that which the land spends (as the fish-monger do allege), then it would be considered both how great quantity of money and commodity there goes out of the land without any such necessity, and how needful it were that by the employment of our own men that money and commodity were kept within the land especially having joined with it the setting of so many of our own poor people on work, both in town and country, as the preparation and performing of the trade of taking fish will require.

[1] Act of 1564.

22 The Cost of Iron Making, 1571

(Historical Manuscripts Commission, *Report on the Manuscripts of Lord Middleton* (1911), pp. 494–5)

To the right worshipful . . . Mr Francis Willoughby, esquire, at Nottingham.

It may please your worship to understand . . . I have spoken with the iron-men about Walsall [of] whom I have knowledge, of the prices of their tra[de] . . . as follows:

First, their stone is worth at the [pit] ready gotten 4*s* every load; from the pit to Middleton is . . . miles, every load carriage will cost 3*s* or thereabout; every load of stone will make a bloom; the bloomer will have for every bloom 16*d*; the bloom is made in 12 hours. Then the brander will have for every brand 6*d*. Every bloom makes 2 brands, which will be wrought in 4 hours; 8 blooms will make a ton of iron, and then there is allowed to the burning of every ton 8 load of coals, which is valued every load at 6*s* 8*d*; and every ton of iron is worth when it is branded 7*l* or thereabout. These charges are certain, besides other for common workmen, as need shall require. For the taking or purchasing of any ground where the stone is got, it is very hard to come by, for it is daily laid for by my Lord Paget, and has been long, but he can neither take nor purchase, as I am credibly informed by honest men. Thus much I did learn upon Saturday last by very honest men, who were in hand with me very earnestly to buy wood for the same purpose, and gladly would bestow a hundred pounds or more if that may please your worship to consider hereof. It is thought by them that have travailed long in the aforesaid trade that your woods will be better sold, and more gain to you, than if you should set up smithies, considering the great charge and trouble that do belong unto them. And further they say if you should set them up, your woods would not serve you 4 years, and your wood being gone, there is not any left in the country to be bought, except it be Drayton lordship.

From Middleton, the 6 of December, 1571.

By your obedient servant,

John Tyror.

23 Tin Mining in Cornwall, 1602

(Richard Carew, *The Survey of Cornwall*, ed. F. E. Halliday (1953), pp. 91–5)

When the new found work entices with probability of profit, the discoverer does commonly associate himself with some more partners, because the charge amounts mostly very high for any one man's purse, except lined beyond ordinary, to reach unto; and if the work do fail, many shoulders will more easily support the burden. These partners consist either of such tinners as work to their own behoof, or of such adventurers as put in hired labourers. The hirelings stand at a certain wage, either by the day, which may be about eightpence, or for the year, being between four and six pound, as their deserving can drive the bargain, at both which rates they must find themselves.

If the work carry some importance, and require the travail of many hands, that has his name, and they their overseer whom they term their captain . . .

The captain's office binds him to sort each workman his task, to see them apply their labour, to make timely provision for binding the work with frames of timber if need exact it, to place pumps for drawing off water, and to give such other directions. In most places their toil is so extreme as they cannot endure it above four hours in a day, but are succeeded by spells; the residue of the time they wear out at quoits, kayles,[1] or like idle exercises. Their calendar also allows them more holidays than are warranted by the church, our laws, or their own profit.

Their ordinary tools are a pickaxe of iron about sixteen inches long, sharpened at the one end to peck, and flat-headed at the other to drive certain little iron wedges wherewith they cleave the rocks. They have also a broad shovel, the utter part of iron, the middle of timber, into which the staff is slopewise fastened.

Their manner of working in the load mines is to follow the load as it lies, either sidelong or downright; both ways the deeper they sink the greater they find the load. When they light upon a small vein, or chance to lose the load which they wrought, by means of certain strings[2] that may hap to cross it, they begin at another place near hand and so draw by guess to the main load again. If the load lie right down they follow it sometimes to the depth of forty or fifty fathom . . . From some of their bottoms you shall at noonday descry the stars. The workmen are let down and taken up in a stirrup by two men who wind the rope.

If the load lie slopewise, the tinners dig a convenient depth and then pass forward underground so far as the air will yield them breathing, which, as it begins to fail, they sink a shaft down thither from the top to admit a renewing vent, which notwithstanding, their work is most by candle-light. In these passages they meet sometimes with very loose earth, sometimes with exceeding hard rocks, and sometimes with great streams of water.

The loose earth is propped by frames of timber-work as they go, and yet now and then falling down, either presses the poor workmen to death or stops them from returning. To part the rocks they have the forementioned axes and wedges, with which, mostly, they make speedy way, and yet (not seldom) are so tied by the teeth as a good workman shall hardly be able to hew three feet in the space of so many weeks. While they thus play the moldwarps, unsavoury damps do here and there distemper their heads, though not with so much danger in the consequence as annoyance for the present.

For conveying away the water they pray in aid of sundry devices, as adits, pumps, and wheels driven by a stream and interchangeably filling and emptying two buckets, with many such like, all which notwithstanding, the springs so encroach upon these inventions as in sundry places they are driven to keep men, and somewhere horses also, at work both day and night without ceasing, and in some all this will not serve the turn. For supplying such hard services they have always fresh men at hand.

They call it the bringing of an adit, or audit, when they begin to trench without, and carry the same through the ground to the tin work somewhat deeper than the water does lie, thereby to give it passage away. This adit they either fetch athwart the whole load, or right from the branch where they work, as the next valley ministers fittest opportunity for soonest cutting into the hill . . . Surely the practice is cunning in device, costly in charge, and long in effecting, and yet when all is done many times the load falls away and they may sing with Augustus' bird, *Opera et impensa periit*.[3] If you did see how aptly they cast the ground for conveying the water, by compassings and turnings to shun such hills and valleys as let[4] them by their too much height or lowness, you would wonder how so great skill could couch in so base a cabin as their (otherwise) thickclouded brains.

As much almost does it exceed credit that the tin, for and in so small quantity, dug up with so great toil, and passing afterwards through the managing of so many hands ere it come to sale, should be any way able to acquit the cost; for being once brought above ground in the stone, it is first broken in pieces with hammers, and then carried either in wains or on horses' backs to a stamping-mill, where three, and in some places six great logs of timber, bound at the ends with iron, and lifted up and down by a wheel driven with the water, do break it smaller. If the stones be over moist they are dried by the fire in an iron cradle or grate.

From the stamping-mill it passes to the crazing-mill, which between two grinding stones, turned also with a water wheel, bruises the same to a fine sand. Howbeit, of late times they mostly use wet stampers, and so have no need of the crazing-mills for their best stuff, but only for the crust of their tails.

The stream, after it has forsaken the mill, is made to fall by certain degrees, one somewhat distant from another, upon each of which at every descent lies a green turf, three or four foot square and one foot thick. On this the tinner lays a certain portion of the sandy tin, and with his shovel softly tosses the same to and fro, that through this stirring the water which runs over it may wash away the light earth from the tin, which of a heavier substance lies fast on the turf. Having so cleansed one portion, he sets the same aside and begins with another, until his labour take end with his task. The best of those turfs (for all sorts serve not) are fetched about two miles to the eastward of St. Michael's Mount, where at a low water they cast aside the sand and dig them up . . . After it is thus washed, they put the remnant into a wooden dish, broad, flat, and round, being about two foot over and having two handles fastened at the sides, by which they softly shog the same to and fro in the water between their legs as they sit over it, until whatsoever of the earthy substance that was yet left be flitted away. Some of later time, with a sleighter invention and lighter labour, do cause certain boys to stir it up and down with their feet, which works the same effect. The residue, after this often cleansing, they call black tin,[1] which is proportionably divided to every of the adventurers when the lord's part has been first deducted upon the whole.

Then does each man carry his portion to the blowing-house, where the same is melted with charcoal fire, blown by a great pair of bellows moved with a water-wheel, and so cast into pieces of a long and thick squareness, from three hundred to four hundred pound weight, at which time the owner's mark is set thereupon. The last remove is to the place of coinage, which I shall touch hereafter. I have already told you how great charge the tinner undergoes before he can bring his ore to this last mill, whereto if you add his care and cost in buying the wood for this service, in felling, framing, and piling it to be burned, in fetching the same when it is coaled, through such far, foul, and cumber-some ways to the blowing-house, together with the blowers' two or three months' extreme and increasing labour, sweltering heat, danger of scalding their bodies, burning the houses, casting away the work, and lastly their ugly countenances tanned with smoke and besmeared with sweat: all these things (I say) being duly considered, I know not whether you would more marvel either whence a sufficient gain should arise to countervail so manifold expenses, or that any gain could train men to undertake such pains and peril . . .

---

[1] Skittles. (FEH, and other notes also).   [2] A thin vein of ore.
[3] It perished from work and expense.   [4] Hinder.

24 A Declining Trade, 1607

Journals of the House of Commons, I, 1547–1628, pp. 356–7)

30 March 1607.

To the honourable assembly of the commons of England, now assembled in the high court of parliament: the humble petition of the armour-makers, gun-makers, and of the like artificers, inhabiting within the city of London, and the suburbs thereof.

Shewing, that where our late sovereign lord King Henry the VIIIth (out of his royal care for the good of this realm) did not only direct his gracious letters to certain princes in Germany, for the sending over into this realm of artificers of the aforesaid arts, but also, upon their coming hither, did give unto them large allowances, during their abode here in this realm; intending thereby that his majesty's subjects might learn of them the making of munition fit for the wars, that thereby this realm in future times might be sufficiently furnished with serviceable armour and weapons that should be made within the same, according to his majesty's said intention; his majesty's subjects were so careful in learning the said trades, that this realm through their great industries has ever since been furnished with sufficient store of good armour and weapons, and at lesser prices than any other nation has of many years been. The which trades having been ever since continued within this realm, in the time of our late sovereign, Queen Elizabeth, there were thirty-five armour-makers within the city of London, and the suburb thereof, who kept servants and shops; and who being now greatly decayed for want of sale of their armours, there remain only five of them who do exercise the same trade, all which do keep but one servant not being able to keep more, for want of employment and means of maintenance for them; the which are like utterly to decay, and the said trade with them to be extinguished, by reason that the statute, made in the fourth and fifth years of King Phillip and Queen Mary (which authorized magistrates to enjoin a provision of armour, and other weapons) is repealed by a statute made in the first year of his majesty' reign, unless, by your honourable care and providence, some course be taken whereby the said trades may be continued.

Your suppliants, in their bounden duty, thought it meet to certify you thereof; hoping that, by your wisdoms' care for the safety of this flourishing kingdom, some good law may be provided whereby the same may be continually furnished with serviceable armour and weapons, as it has formerly been, and the said trades still continued within this realm; all which, the now final remainder of the artificers of that kind do humbly and truly protest, is sincerely and truly intended for the future safety of the realm, the most of us, for want of employment in this kind, having already betaken ourselves to live by other means and the residue shall be forced so to do. And therefore have presumed, in this humble sort, to inform your honours, how the case stands, and most humbly leave it to your judgments to do therein as shall seem, in your wisdoms, most convenient for the safety of your selves and your posterity to God's good and gracious pleasure.

25 The Organisation of the Woollen Industry, c.1615

(P.R.O. State Papers Domestic, James I, LXXX, 13, printed in G. Unwin, *Industrial Organisation in the Sixteenth and Seventeenth Centuries* (Oxford, 1904), pp. 234–6)

The breeders of wool in all countries are of three sorts.

1. First those that are men of great estate, having both grounds and stock of their own, and are beforehand in wealth. These can afford to delay the selling of their wools and to stay the clothiers' leisure for the payment to increase the price. The number of these is small.

2. Those that do rent the king's, noblemen's and gentlemen's grounds and deal as largely as either their stock or credit will afford. These are many and breed great store of wool; most of them do usually either sell their wools beforehand, or promise the refusal of them for money which they borrowed at the spring of the year to buy them sheep to breed the wool, they then having need of money to pay their Lady-day[1] rent and to double their stock upon the ground as the spring time requires, and at that time the clothiers disburse their stock in yarns to lay up in store against hay-time and harvest when their spinning fails. So that these farmers and clothiers have greatest want of money at one time.

3. The general number of husbandmen in all the wool countries that have small livings, whereof every one usually has some wool, though not much. These are many in numbers in all countries and have great store of wool, though in small parcels. Many of these also do borrow money of the wool merchant to buy sheep to stock their commons. Their parcels being so small, the times of selling so divers, the distance of place so great between the clothier and them, it would be their undoing to stay the clothier's leisure for the time of their sale, or to be subject to him for the price . . .

These wools are usually converted by four sorts of people.

1. The rich clothier that buys his wool of the grower in the wool countries, and makes his whole year's provision beforehand, and lays it up in store, and in the winter time has it spun by his own spinsters and woven by his own weavers and fulled by his own tuckers, and all at the lowest rate for wages. These clothiers could well spare the wool buyers that they might likewise have wool at their own prices, and the rather because many of them be brogging clothiers and sell again very much, if not most, of the wool they buy.

2. The second is the meaner clothier that seldom or never travels into the wool country to buy his wool, but borrows the most part of it at the market, and sets many poor on work, clothes it presently, and

H

sells his cloth in some countries upon the bare thread, as in Devonshire and Yorkshire, and others dress it and sell it in London for ready money, and then comes to the wool market and pays the old debt and borrows more. Of this sort there are great store, that live well and grow rich and set thousands on work; they cannot miss the wool chapman, for if they do they must presently put off all their work-folk, and become servants to the rich clothier for 4d or 6d a day, which is a poor living.

3. The third sort are such clothiers that have not stock enough to bestow, some in wool and some in yarn, and to forbear some in cloth as the rich clothiers do, and they buy but little or no wool, but do weekly buy their yarn in the markets, and presently make it into cloth and sell it for ready money, and so buy yarn again; which yarn is weekly brought into the markets by a great number of poor people that will not spin to the clothier for small wages; but have stock enough to set themselves on work, and do weekly buy their wool in the market by very small parcels according to their use and weekly return it in yarn, and make good profit thereof, having the benefit both of their labour and of the merchandise, and live exceeding well. These yarn-makers are so many in number that it is supposed by men of judgment that more than half the cloths that are made in Wiltshire, Gloucester, and Somerset is made by the means of these yarn-makers and poor clothiers that depend weekly upon the wool chapman, who serves them weekly with wool either for money or credit.

4. The fourth sort is of them of the new drapery, which are thousands of poor people inhabiting near the ports and coasts from Yarmouth to Plymouth, and in many great cities and towns, as London, Norwich, Colchester, Canterbury, Southampton, Exeter, and many others. These people by their great industry and skill do spend a great part of the coarse wools growing in the kingdom, and that at as high a price or higher than the clothiers do the finest wools of this country . . .

[1] 25 March.

26 Complaints about Aliens, 1622

(*Lists of Foreign Protestants Resident in England, 1618–1688*, ed. W. D. Cooper (Camden Society, O.S., LXXXII, 1862), pp. 25–7)

Colchester. Complaints of the English against the Dutch strangers

Michael Cock, alien born, bay and saymaker; buys and sells says to foreigners besides those that he makes.

Frances Toispill, alien; does the like.

Isaac Size, born here of Dutch parents; apprentice to a card maker and does use the same trade, and sells aliens' goods brought from beyond the seas as a factor for them.

Samuel de Heame, born here of Dutch parents; by profession and trade a comb maker, who, upon his promise to deal with nothing but that which concerns his trade, because he had been troubled by informers, obtained to be a free man of this town, yet he now keeps a common shop in his house, and sells all manner of linen cloth and haberdashers' wares by retail.

Thomas Benne, born here of Dutch parents; his trade a bay and say-maker and weaver, he is now a beer brewer, a maltster, a farmer, a maker of bay cheans and sends them [to] Sandwich, and farms lands about 100*l* per annum.

Jasper Vanhulst, an alien born; a saymaker, and is a merchant and factor for strangers.

John Valender, born here of Dutch parents; a baymaker by his profession, and is a factor for strangers.

Hugh de Lobell, an alien born; a saymaker; he is a merchant and factor for strangers.

Samuel de Gavake, born here of Dutch parents; he has erected and set up a new brewhouse; he makes vinegar and aquevita; he is a dyer, a merchant, and factor for strangers.

John Miller; he is by profession a scholar, brought up in the university, and is now a merchant and factor for strangers.

Josias Snace, a bay and saymaker; his wife sells black, brown, and white thread, all sorts of bone lace, valure gardes, and other commodities which they receive out of Holland.

Isaac Bowman, an alien born; by his profession a surgeon, and uses the same; he is a merchant and factor for strangers, sells in his house all manner of linen cloth, stuffs, bone laces, and such like, oils, hops, and other commodities, to the great grievance and hindrance of the free burgesses.

Charles Toispill, an alien born, and a single man about the age of 22 years; he is a merchant and factor for strangers.

Michael de Groate, an alien born; using the trade of a fringe-maker by the space of 25 years, and before that a baymaker, and now a beer brewer, a maltster, and a farmer.

The English tailors within this corporation, being about fourscore, complain that divers strangers born do much hinder them in using the trade within this town, contrary to law, and do desire reformation by suppressing of them.

The English wiredrawers complain that they are much hindered in their trade, and cannot set themselves on work to maintain themselves and family by reason the strangers do send for such quantities of wire ready wrought from beyond the seas, and do work some of it into cards, and a great part they sell to others; whereof they do humbly desire reformation, and that the strangers may be restrained.

WILLIAM MOTT,   } Bailiffs.
THOMAS THURSTON, }

27 Salt Making at Shields, 1635

(*North Country Diaries, Second Series*, ed. J. C. Hodgson (Surtees Society, CXXIV, 1915), pp. 16–19)

Journal of Sir William Brereton, 23 June 1635

I took boat about 12 o'clock [from Newcastle] and went down to Tynemouth and to the Shields, and returned about 7 o'clock. It is about 7 miles. Here I viewed the salt-works wherein is more salt works, and more salt made than in any part of England that I know, and all the salt here made is made of salt water: these pans which are not to be numbered being placed in the river mouth: and wrought with coals brought by water from Newcastle pits.

A most dainty new saltwork lately here erected: which is absolutely the most complete work that I ever saw.

In the breadth whereof is placed 6 ranks of pans: 4 pans in a rank: at either out-side the furnaces are placed in the same manner as are my brother Booth's: under the grate of which furnaces the ashes fall: and there is a lid or cover for both: and by the heat of these ashes: there being a pan made in the floor betwixt every furnace which is made of brick: for which also there is a cover: there is boiled, and made into lumps of hard and black salt which is made of the brine which drops from the new-made salt, which is placed over a cistern of lead: which cistern is under the floor of the storehouse: which is in the end of the building. These great lumps of hard black salt are sent to Colchester to make salt upon salt: which are sold for a greater price than the rest: because without these at Colchester, they cannot make any salt.

These 24 pans have only 12 furnaces, and 12 fires: and are erected in this manner: all being square, and of like proportion. They are placed by two and two together one against each other. The 6 pans in the highest rank, the bottom equal with the top of the lower.

The highest pans are thrice filled, and boiled till it begins to draw towards salt: then a spigot being pulled out, the brine thus prepared, runs into the lower pans; which brings it to a larger proportion of salt, than otherwise: gains time and saves fire: because it must be longer boiled in the other pans, and would spend fire: which is saved by reason of the heat which derives from the furnace of the upper pan, which by a passage is conveyed under the lower pan: which passage is about half a yard broad in the bottom, and is, at the top, of the breadth of the pan which rests upon a brick wall which is of the thickness of one brick at top: and this concavity under the lower pans is shaped slope-wise like unto a kiln: narrow in the bottom, and broad at the top: and this heat, which is conveyed under, and makes the lower pans to boil, comes together with the smoke, which has no other passage, under these pans [than] through loop holes, or pigeon holes, which is conveyed into a chimney: a double rank whereof is placed in the middle of this building: betwixt which is a passage for a man to walk in. In the middle of every these chimneys there is a broad iron plate, which is shaped to the chimney: which as it stops, and keeps in the heat, so it being pulled out abates the heat.

It is to be observed that the 12 lower pans are only to be drawn twice in 24 hours: and by that time they are ready to be drawn: the brine in the higher pans will be sufficiently boiled, and prepared to be let into the lower: which are only to be drawn, and that twice in 24 hours. They yield every of them every draught two bolls,[1] which is worth 2s a boll; and sometimes 2s 4d. So every pan yielding every day 4 bolls at two draughts which comes to 8s 0d: all 12 pans are worth every day 4l 16s 0d. So as all the 12 pans in a week make salt worth 28l a week: which in the year amounts to 1,400l, accounting 50 weeks to the year.

Two men and one woman to get out ashes, and one to pump their brine, manage and tend this whole work. The men's wage is 14s a week: besides he that pumps. This salt is made of salt-water which, out of a brine pit made, which is supplied at full sea, is pumped and by pipes of lead conveyed into every pan. The wall of this house is stone and the roof of this, and all the rest of the houses wherein are brine-pans, are boards . . .

Here at the Shields are the vastest saltworks I have seen, and by reason of the convenience of coal, and cheapness thereof, being at 7s a chaldron[2] which is 3 wain load.

Here is such a cloud of smoke, as amongst these works you cannot see to walk. There are (as I was informed) about 250 houses, poor ones and low built, but all covered with boards. Here in every house is erected one fair great iron pan, 5 yards long, 3 yards and a half broad.

The bottom of them made of thin plates nailed together, and strong square rivets upon the nail heads about the breadth of the ball of your hand. These pans are 3 quarters of a yard deep. Ten great bars there are placed on the inner-side of the pan, 3 square 2 inches thick. Every of these great pans (as Dobson informed me) cost about 100*l* and cannot be taken down to be repaired with less than 10*l* charge.

Every pan yields four draughts of salt in a week, and every draught is worth about 1*l* 10*s*. Spent in coal, 10 chaldron of coal at 7*s* a chaldron, which amounts to 3*l* 10*s* 0*d* in coals. Deduct out of 6*l* there remains 2*l* 10*s* 0*d* besides one man's wages.

So as in these 250 pans there is weekly spent in coals 775*l*.[3] Every pan yielding 6*l* weekly: being 250, total of the worth of the salt made in them amounts to 1,500*l*, gained 735*l*.[4] Deduct of this 120*l* workmen's wages for making it, 120: clear gain about 600*l*[5] a year.

A wain load of salt is here worth about 3*l* 10*s* 0*d*, and a chaldron of coal, which is worth 7*s*, is 3 wain load.

[1] In Northumberland salt, corn, coal, lime and some other things were sold by the measured boll. The 'old boll' contained six bushels, the 'new boll' two bushels. (JCH)

[2] A Newcastle chaldron at this time was about 51 cwt.

[3] Should be 875*l*.   [4] Should be 625*l*.   [5] Should be 505*l*.

28 Licence for Lead Mining, 1635

(Historical Manuscripts Commission, *Calendar of the Manuscripts of the Dean and Chapter of Wells*, II (1914), p. 412)

April 16

[The dean and chapter] unanimously authorised (as much as in them lies) Thomas Bakehouse and Thomas Sergeaunt of Wells, groviers, Nicholas Sexton, gent., Edward Browning and Cornelius Watts of Wells aforesaid, to dig and search for lead ore within their manor of Winscombe and in every or any part of their waste ground, and particularly in the enclosed [? grounds] of Mr Henry Tripp, their tenant there, and shall forthwith set on the said work, with consent of the said Tripp. Provided and on condition that they shall pay unto the dean and chapter aforesaid the seventh part of the said lead ore for their part, as being lords of the said grounds where the said lead ore is to be found, and also the tenth part or lottlead to the said dean and chapter as being the chief lords royal of the soil. But if the ore expected and hoped for do not arise so plentifully as to defray the workmen's wages and necessary charges, then the dean and chapter is to have but the eighth part, and the said lottlead or 10th part of the ore that shall be found in the said grooves. Which agreement is to be confirmed on the next chapter day, and that the said Tripp, for his suffering his grounds to be broken up, shall be saved harmels[2] from the dean and chapter abovesaid.

[1] Miners.   [2] Liability.

29 Trowbridge Workmen Parade for More Wages, 1677

(*Records of the County of Wilts., being extracts from the Quarter Sessions Great Rolls of the Seventeenth Century*, ed. B. H. Cunnington (Devizes, 1932), pp. 259–60)

The information of William Brewer of Trowbridge, clothier, taken upon oath the 25th day of June 1677

Who says that being in his house in Trowbridge the day aforesaid he heard an uproar in the street and going forth he saw a great company of men following a fiddler and one of them made a kind of proclamation that 'whosoever was of their side should follow them'. Afterwards, hearing that they were at an alehouse near the bridge, he went thither with the constables where he heard Aaron Atkins say that he was the man who made the proclamation and that the intention thereof was to engage as many as he could to combine for the raising of their wages sixpence per week, and that Samuel Bowden (and others) affirmed the same and were with him in the street upon the same design, and Atkins said that he had a sword and wished that he had had it with him.

Taken before William Brewer

Samuel Bowden confesses that he was amongst the others today and being demanded for what reason so many were assembled in such a manner with a fiddle before them and calling those that were on their side to come to them, said it was to raise their wages to six and sixpence for working twelve hours in a day.

30 Huguenot Immigration, 1681

(*Savile Correspondence*, ed. W. D. Cooper (Camden Society, O.S., LXXI, 1858), p. 236)

To Mr Secretary Jenkins.

[Paris]. September 21, '81.

Sir, I send this in favour of a Protestant linen draper, who with all his substance is resolved to retire into England, in order to which he has packed up his shop and sent it in specie to Dunkirk, having paid all the duties and customs on this side for exportation; but, being now told that his religion will not hinder the confiscation of his goods, he goes first to London himself before he will hazard his effects. This being his case, he desires a recommendation to you, begging your favour and assistance, which I hope you will please to afford him as far as the law will permit, which if stretched a little upon the account of religion, will not I believe give offence to the most rigorous legislators.

This man will be able also to give you some lights into the method of bringing the manufacture of sail cloth into England (the project I have always appeared so fond of), which may entitle him to some favour, though I need not doubt but he will from your bounty find all the regular assistance desired on his behalf by, sir, your most faithful and most humble servant,

Hen. Savile.

Here is a Protestant haberdasher in the same trouble about carrying his effects. Pray instruct me what to say to such people upon the like occasions. I assure you it is worth a serious consideration, for if you refuse to take substantial tradesmen with their ware, they will go into Holland, so that they will get the rich merchants and we only the poor ones.

31 Canterbury's Industries, 1697

(*The Journeys of Celia Fiennes*, ed. C. Morris (1949), pp. 123–4)

[Canterbury is] a flourishing town, good trading in the weaving of silks. I saw 20 looms in one house with several fine flowered silks, very good ones, and it's a very ingenious art to fix the warps and chain in their looms to cast their work into such figures and flowers. There stands a boy by every loom and pulls up and down threads which are fastened to the weaving and so pulls the chain to the exact form for the shuttle to work through.

There are also paper mills which dispatch paper at a quick rate; they were then making brown paper when I saw it. The mill is set agoing by the water and at the same time it pounded the rags to mortar for the paper, and it beat oatmeal and hemp and ground bread together, that is at the same time. When the substance for the paper is pounded enough they take it in a great tub and so with a frame just of the size of the sheets of paper, made all of small wire just as I have seen fine screens to screen corn in, only this is much closer wrought, and they clap a frame of wood round the edge and so dip it into the tub and what is too thin runs through. Then they turn this frame down on a piece of coarse woollen just of the size of the paper and so give a knock to it and it falls off, on which they clap another such a piece of woollen cloth which is ready to lay the next frame of paper, and so till they have made a large heap which they by a board on the bottom move to a press, and so lay a board on the top and so let down a great screw and weight on it, which they force together into such a narrow compass as they know so many sheets of paper will be reduced, and this presses out all the thinner part and leaves the paper so firm as it may be taken up sheet by sheet, and laid together to be thoroughly dried by the wind. They told me white paper was made in the same manner only they must have white woollen to put between. There is a great number of French people in this town which are employed in the weaving and silk winding. I meet them every night going home in great companies, but then some of them were employed in the hopping, it being the season for pulling them.

32 Discrimination against Irish and Colonial Woollen Interests, 1699

(10 and 11 William III, c. 10, *Statutes at Large*, IV (1763), pp. 9–12)

Forasmuch as wool and the woollen manufactures of cloth, serge, bays, kerseys, and other stuffs made or mixed with wool, are the greatest and most profitable commodities of this kingdom [of England], on which the value of lands, and the trade of the nation do chiefly depend: and whereas great quantities of the like manufactures have of late been made, and are daily increasing in the kingdom of Ireland, and in the English plantations in America, and are exported from thence to foreign markets, heretofore supplied from England, which will inevitably sink the value of lands, and tend to the ruin of the trade, and the woollen manufactures of this realm. For the prevention whereof, and for the encouragement of the woollen manufactures within this kingdom, be it enacted . . . that no person or persons whatsoever, from and after [24 June 1699] shall directly or indirectly export . . . or cause or procure to be exported . . . out of, or from the said kingdom of Ireland, into any foreign realm, states, or dominions, or into any parts or places whatsoever, other than the parts within the kingdom of England, or the dominion of Wales, any the wool, woolfells, shortlings, mortlings, woolflocks, worsted, bay, or woollen yarn, cloth, serge, bays, kerseys, says, frizes, druggets, cloth-serges, shalloons, or any other drapery stuffs or woollen manufactures whatsoever, made up or mixed with wool or woolflocks, or shall directly or indirectly load, or cause to be loaded upon any horse, cart, or other carriage, or load or lay on board, or cause to be laden or laid on board in any ship or vessel, in any place or parts within or belonging to the said kingdom of Ireland, any such wool, woolfells [and other commodities as before] to the intent or purpose to export . . . the same, or cause the same to be exported . . . out of the said kingdom of Ireland, or out of any port or place belonging to the same, or with intent or purpose, that any person or persons whatsoever should so export . . . the same out of the said kingdom of Ireland, into any ports or places, except as aforesaid.

II   And be it enacted . . . that all and every of the offender and offenders, offence and offences aforesaid, shall be subject and liable to the respective pains, and penalties, and forfeitures hereafter following (that is to say) the said wool, woolfells [and other commodities as before] so exported . . . or loaded, contrary to the true intent and meaning of this act, shall be forfeited; and that every of the offender and offenders therein shall likewise forfeit the sum of five hundred pounds for every such offence; and all and every ship, vessel, barge, boat, or other bottom whatsoever, wherein any of the said commodities are or shall be shipped or laid on board, contrary to the true intent and meaning of this act, shall be forfeited, with all her tackle, apparel, and furniture to them and every of them belonging; and the masters and mariners thereof, or any porters, carriers, waggoners, boatmen, or other persons whatsoever, knowing such offence, and wittingly aiding and assisting therein, shall forfeit forty pounds; of which one moiety shall be to him or them that shall sue for the same by bill, plaint, or information in any of his majesty's courts of record in England, or Ireland, and the other moiety thereof to the encouragement of setting up the linen manufactures in Ireland, to be disposed of by the court of exchequer there for that use only . . .

*   *   *

XIX   And for the more effectual encouragement of the woollen manufacture of this kingdom; be it further enacted . . . that from and after [1 December 1699], no wool, woolfells, shortlings, mortlings, woolflocks, worsted, bay, or woollen yarn, cloth, serge, bays, kerseys, says, frizes, druggets, cloth-serges, shalloons, or any other drapery stuffs or woollen manufactures whatsoever, made or mixed with wool or woolflocks, being of the product or manufacture of any of the English plantations in America, shall be loaded or laid on board in any ship or vessel, in any place or parts within any of the said English plantations, upon any pretence whatsoever; as likewise that no such wool, woolfells, [and other commodities as before] being of the product or manufacture of any of the English plantations in America, as aforesaid, shall be loaded upon any horse, cart, or other carriage, to the intent and purpose to be exported . . . to any other of the said plantations, or to any other place whatsoever; upon the same and like pains, penalties, and forfeitures, to and upon all and every the offender and offenders herein, within all and every of the said English plantations respectively, as are prescribed and provided by this act for the like offences committed within the kingdom of Ireland . . .

33 Newcomen and the Steam Engine, c.1700

(Marten Triewald, *A Short Description of the Fire and Air Machine at the Dannemora Mines* (Stockholm, 1734), printed in L. T. C. Rolt, *Thomas Newcomen. The Prehistory of the Steam Engine* (Dawlish, 1963), pp. 51, 56, 61)

Now it happened that a man from Dartmouth, named Thomas Newcomen, without any knowledge whatever of the speculations of Captain Savery, had at the same time also made up his mind, in conjunction with his assistant, a plumber by the name of Calley, to invent a fire-machine for drawing water from the mines. He was induced to undertake this by considering the heavy cost of lifting water by means of horses, which Mr Newcomen found existing in the English tin mines. These mines Mr Newcomen often visited in the capacity of a dealer in iron tools with which he used to furnish many of the tin mines.

For ten consecutive years Mr Newcomen worked at this fire-machine which never would have exhibited the desired effect, unless Almighty God had caused a lucky incident to take place. It happened at the last attempt to make the model work that a more than wished-for effect was suddenly caused by the following strange event. The cold water, which was allowed to flow into a lead-case embracing the cylinder, pierced through an imperfection which had been mended with tin-solder. The heat of the steam caused the tin-solder to melt[1] and thus opened a way for the cold water, which rushed into the cylinder and immediately condensed the steam, creating such a vacuum that the weight, attached to the little beam, which was supposed to represent the weight of the water in the pumps, proved to be so insufficient that the air, which pressed with a tremendous power on the piston, caused its chain to break and the piston to crush the bottom of the cylinder as well as the lid of the small boiler. The hot water which flowed everywhere thus convinced the very senses of the onlookers that they had discovered an incomparably powerful force which had hitherto been entirely unknown in nature,—at least no one had ever suspected that it could originate in this way.

*   *   *

.... Later on Mr Newcomen erected the first fire-machine in England in the year 1712, which erection took place at Dudley Castle in Staffordshire.

The cylinder of this machine measured 21 inches in diameter, and was 7 feet 10 inches high. The boiler was 5 feet 6 inches in diameter and 6 feet 1 inch high. The water in the boiler stood 4 feet 4 inches high and contained 13 hogsheads; besides, the machine delivered at every rise or lift (12 lifts in a minute) 10 English gallons of water, and the mine was 51 yards or 25½ fathoms deep.

[1] Steam at no more than atmospheric pressure would not have been hot enough to melt the solder, that the flux had not 'taken' in the blow-hole is more than likely. (LTCR)

34 The Newcastle Coal Industry, c.1713

(Printed in E. Hughes, *North Country Life in the Eighteenth Century. The North-East, 1700–1750* (1952), pp. 156–8)

Reflections on the coal trade from its first rise

The country adjacent to Newcastle affords variety of seams or veins of coal some of which are to be found and wrought from 10 to 73 fathoms from the surface of the earth, and generally speaking, the deeper the vein lies, the better and stronger is the coal. The thickness of the vein is in some places a yard, in others ½ yard, it is in some few near two yards.

Where the seam lies deep you are always attended with vast quantities of water which must be drawn by horses and at a prodigious expense from 500*l* to 1500*l* yearly. To add to this infirmity you generally are disturbed with sulphurious damps which for want of circulation of air to purge them are very apt to take fire and frequently (though the nicest care to prevent be used) does blow up numbers of workmen, and consequently where this hazard is run men will have a proportionate addition of price for the working. These collieries generally lie near the river, and by that means the shortness of land carriage does in some measure put them upon a balance with other collieries that lie at a distance from the river.

The charges of winning a colliery thus attended and situated is known to be seldom less than 4 sometimes 7000*l*. Nay frequent instances within this 20 years make it appear that sometimes the undertaker loses his venture and [is] never able to compass the working of the seam. But suppose he should, your sum is actually sunk; then to manage the work of such a concern, a less sum than that cannot be supposed to be advanced and lies dead. *Quaere*. What interest one might reasonably expect for hazard of monies? At least 20 per cent; so that if 10,000*l* should be required to manage such a concern the profit should be 2000*l* yearly profit. The charges of work, the sinking the pit and drawing the coals above the ground at 70 fathoms may be computed, [for] 17 chaldrons[1] Newcastle measure (as follows).

17 cha[ldron] work[ing]	4*l*		17 chaldron [selling]	
Drawing water		10*s*	price at 10*s* 6*d*	8*l* 18*s* 6*d*
Rent		15*s*	Fittage and owner's	
Leading		15*s*	wages to be deducted	
Repair of ways		7*s* 6*d*	at least 1*s* 6*d* per cha.	1*l* 5*s* 6*d*
Wayleaves, servants'				
wages, charges at the pit		10*s*		7*l* 13*s*
			[Deduct cost]	6*l* 17*s* 6*d*
		6*l* 17*s* 6*d*	[Leaves]	15*s* 6*d*

Where the pits are so deep you may be supposed to raise from 500 to 800 of these tens, the profit of which is little more than 600*l* for the interest of your monies, supposing no loss in the way of dealing by the [ship] masters' notes and failing of your fitters. Nay, if you do not sell that quantity and at the price near, you are actually running out your principal stock.

As the seams are of several depths and sorts so are the veins of each coal, some proper for smiths where only the strongest caker is sought for, and others of a lesser strength are fittest for brewers, glass, sugar bakers, lime, and those that are still more open are the most coveted by the housekeepers.

Till of late years fitters, that is people employed per the owners to sell the master coal, had so much per chaldron and one owner would give leave to 10 or 12 fitters to use his steath, and these fitters perhaps had the liberty of vending from as many different steaths: by this means there was a general mixture, insomuch that no consumer could rely upon any commodity that was brought up to market as entirely fit for his purpose, upon which continued complaints were made. To prevent which the . . . [chief] coal owners came to an agreement to work the best of their several seams and send them unmixed with an account of each vessel's loads, and employ several lightermen to encourage and recommend these best sort of coals to their customers, and for their pains are content to allow them a small recompense of the nature of factorage. These dealers are actually losers by the bargain for having formerly used to buy ordinary coals at an easy rate and mixing them with the best, sold at the top of the market and this was put in their pockets, but the consumer being disappointed was the sole sufferer.

It is matter of fact that at some concerns that are led by wain or cart carriage, the price of each ch[aldron] led is advanced $\frac{1}{3}$, others $\frac{1}{4}$, not any less than $\frac{1}{6}$, and this is not solely owing to the dearth of provisions, but also to the great demand of carriage of pan coal.

The prices of working and drawing are considerably advanced on account of the price of corn which is double the price at least of former years, and it cannot be supposed that a man's family can be maintained with less than formerly, the price being double, he accordingly sets a value upon his labour and all this goes out of the coalowner's pocket. Nay, I am certain that one with another all charges to the steath, the owner is [the] sufferer by [the] additional charge at least 14 or 15d per cha[ldron] Newcastle measure, the master has his 53 [cwt] with only [an] advance of sixpence in price, while at Sunderland they have raised theirs at least 12d per chaldron within this two years.

[1] A Newcastle chaldron at this time weighed 53 cwt.

35 A Combination amongst Journeymen Tailors, 1721

(*Select Documents illustrating the History of Trade Unionism. I. The Tailoring Trade*, ed. F. W. Galton (1896), pp. 1–4)

The case of the master tailors residing within the cities of London and Westminster, in relation to the great abuses committed by their journeymen. Humbly offered to the consideration of Parliament.

The journeymen tailors in and about the cities of London and Westminster, to the number of seven thousand and upwards, have lately entered into a combination to raise their wages, and leave off working an hour sooner than they used to do; and for the better carrying on their design, have subscribed their respective names in books prepared for that purpose, at the several houses of call or resort (being public houses in and about London and Westminster) where they use; and collect several considerable sums of money to defend any prosecutions against them.

At this time there are but few of them come to work at all, and most of those that do, insist upon, and have, twelve shillings and ninepence per week (instead of ten shillings and ninepence per week, the usual wages), and leave off work at eight of the clock at night (instead of nine, their usual hour, time out of mind), and very great numbers of them go loitering about the town, and seduce and corrupt all they can meet: to the great hindrance and prejudice of trade.

Upon complaint made to some of his majesty's justices of the peace, they have issued out their warrants against these offenders as loiterers; by virtue whereof some of them have been bound over to the sessions, and others have been taken up, and bound over to appear in his majesty's Court of King's Bench at Westminster, and the subscription books seized by virtue of the Secretary of State's warrant. Yet they still continue obstinate, and persist not only in putting the abovesaid difficulties upon their masters, to the great prejudice of trade in general; but also in collecting great sums of money to support their unlawful combinations and confederacies.

This combination of the journeymen tailors is and may be attended with many very ill consequences: inasmuch as the public is deprived of the benefit of the labour of a considerable number of the subjects of this kingdom, and the families of several of these journeymen thereby impoverished, and likely to become a charge and burden to the public. And the very persons themselves who are under this unlawful combination, choosing rather to live in idleness, than to work at their usual rates and hours, will not only become useless and burdensome, but also very dangerous to the public; and are of very ill example to journeymen in all other trades; as is sufficiently seen in the journeymen curriers, smiths, farriers, sail-makers, coach-makers, and artificers of divers other arts and mysteries, who have actually entered into confederacies of the like nature; and the journeymen carpenters, bricklayers and joiners have taken some steps for that purpose, and only wait to see the event of others.

These journeymen tailors, when there is a hurry of business against the king's birthday, or for making of mourning or wedding garments (as often happens) or other holidays, and always the summer seasons, are not content with the unreasonable rates they at present insist upon; but have demanded, and have had, three and four shillings a day, and sometimes more; otherwise they will not work; and at such times some will not work at all; which is a great disappointment to gentlemen, and an imposition to the masters; and, if suffered to go on, must increase the charge of making clothes considerably.

As to the said houses of call, or public-houses, there are a great number of them in London and the suburbs, where these journeymen tailors frequently meet and use, and spend all or the greatest part of the monies they receive for their wages; and the masters of these houses of call, support, encourage and abet these journeymen, in their unlawful combinations for raising their wages, and lessening their hours.

The laws now in being for regulating of artificers, labourers, and servants, were made in the fifth of Queen Elizabeth, and might be well adapted for those times; but not altogether so proper for the trade of London and Westminster, &c., as it is now carried on.

Therefore, the masters humbly hope this honourable house will take such measures, by passing of a law for redress of the public grievances aforesaid, or grant such other relief, as in their great wisdom shall seem meet.

36 The West Riding Cloth Industry, 1724-6

(Daniel Defoe, *A Tour through England and Wales*, 1724-6 (Everyman ed., 1928), II, pp. 193-6)

From Blackstone Edge to Halifax is eight miles, and all the way, except from Sorby to Halifax, is thus up hill and down; so that, I suppose, we mounted to the clouds and descended to the water level about eight times, in that little part of the journey.

But now I must observe to you, that after having passed the second hill, and come down into the valley again, and so still the nearer we came to Halifax, we found the houses thicker, and the villages greater in every bottom; and not only so, but the sides of the hills, which were very steep every way, were spread with houses, and that very thick; for the land being divided into small enclosures, that is to say, from two acres to six or seven acres each, seldom more; every three or four pieces of land had a house belonging to it.

Then it was I began to perceive the reason and nature of the thing, and found that this division of the land into small pieces, and scattering of the dwellings, was occasioned by, and done for the convenience of the business which the people were generally employed in, and that, as I said before, though we saw no people stirring without doors, yet they were all full within; for, in short, this whole country, however mountainous, and that no sooner we were down one hill but we mounted another, is yet infinitely full of people; those people all full of business; not a beggar, not an idle person to be seen, except here and there an alms-house, where people ancient, decrepit, and past labour, might perhaps be found; for it is observable, that the people here, however laborious, generally live to a great age, a certain testimony to the goodness and wholesomeness of the country, which is, without doubt, as healthy as any part of England; nor is the health of the people lessened, but helped and established by their being constantly employed, and, as we call it, their working hard; so that they find a double advantage by their being always in business.

This business is the clothing trade, for the convenience of which the houses are thus scattered and spread upon the sides of the hills, as above, even from the bottom to the top; the reason is this; such has been the bounty of nature to this otherwise frightful country, that two things essential to the business, as well as to the ease of the people are found here, and that in a situation which I never saw the like of in any part of England; and, I believe, the like is not to be seen so contrived in any part of the world; I mean coals and running water upon the tops of the highest hills: This seems to have been directed by the wise hand of Providence for the very purpose which is now served by it, namely, the manufactures, which otherwise could not be carried on; neither indeed could one fifth part of the inhabitants be supported without them, for the land could not maintain them. After we had mounted the third hill, we found the country, in short, one continued village, though mountainous every way, as before; hardly a house standing out of a speaking distance from another, and (which soon told us their business) the day clearing up, and the sun shining, we could see that almost at every house there was a tenter, and almost on every tenter a piece of cloth, or kersie, or shalloon, for they are the three articles of that country's labour; from which the sun glancing, and, as I may say, shining (the white reflecting its rays) to us, I thought it was the most agreeable sight that I ever saw, for the hills, as I say, rising and falling so thick, and the valleys opening sometimes one way, sometimes another, so that sometimes we could see two or three miles this way, sometimes as far another; sometimes like the streets near St. Giles's, called the Seven Dials; we could see through the glades almost every way round us, yet look which way we would, high to the tops, and low to the bottoms, it was all the same; innumerable houses and tenters, and a white piece upon every tenter.

But to return to the reason of dispersing the houses, as above; I found, as our road passed among them, for indeed no road could do otherwise, wherever we passed any house we found a little rill or gutter of running water, if the house was above the road, it came from it, and crossed the way to run to another; if the house was below us, it crossed us from some other distant house above it, and at every considerable house was a manufactury or work-house, and as they could not do their business without water, the little streams were so parted and guided by gutters or pipes, and by turning and dividing the streams, that none of those houses were without a river, if I may call it so, running into and through their work-houses.

Again, as the dyeing-houses, scouring-shops and places where they used this water, emitted the water again, tinged with the drugs of the dyeing fat, and with the oil, the soap, the tallow, and other ingredients used by the clothiers in dressing and scouring, &c. which then runs away through the lands to the next, the grounds are not only universally watered, how dry soever the season, but that water so tinged and so fattened enriches the lands they run through, that 'tis hardly to be imagined how fertile and rich the soil is made by it.

Then, as every clothier must keep a horse, perhaps two, to fetch and carry for the use of his manufacture, (viz.) to fetch home his wool and his provisions from the market, to carry his yarn to the spinners, his manufacture to the fulling mill, and, when finished, to the market to be sold, and the like; so every manufacturer generally keeps a cow or two, or more, for his family, and this employs the two, or three, or four pieces of enclosed land about his house, for they scarce sow corn enough for their cocks and hens; and this feeding their grounds still adds by the dung of the cattle, to enrich the soil.

But now, to speak of the bounty of nature again, which I but just mentioned; it is to be observed, that these hills are so furnished by nature with springs and mines, that not only on the sides, but even to the very tops, there is scarce a hill but you find, on the highest part of it, a spring of water, and a coal-pit. I doubt not but there are both springs and coal-pits lower in the hills, 'tis enough to say they are at the top; but, as I say, the hills are so full of springs, so the lower coal-pits may perhaps be too full of water, to work without drains to carry it off, and the coals in the upper pits being easy to come at, they may choose to work them, because the horses which fetch the coals, go light up the hill, and come laden down.

Having thus fire and water at every dwelling, there is no need to enquire why they dwell thus dispersed upon the highest hills, the convenience of the manufactures requiring it. Among the manufacturers' houses are likewise scattered an infinite number of cottages or small dwellings, in which dwell the workmen which are employed, the women and children of whom, are always busy carding, spinning, &c. so that no hands being unemployed, all can gain their bread, even from the youngest to the ancient; hardly any thing above four years old, but its hands are sufficient to itself.

This is the reason also why we saw so few people without doors; but if we knocked at the door of any of the master manufacturers, we presently saw a house full of lusty fellows, some at the dye-fat, some dressing the cloths, some in the loom, some one thing, some another, all hard at work, and full employed upon the manufacture, and all seeming to have sufficient business.

I should not have dwelt so upon this part, if there was not abundance of things subsequent to it, which will be explained by this one description, and which are needful to be understood by any one that desires a full understanding of the manner how the people of England are employed, and do subsist in these remoter parts where they are so numerous; for this is one of the most populous parts of Britain, London and the adjacent parts excepted.

37 Mine Pumps and Coal Transport, 1725

(Historical Manuscripts Commission, *Journeys in England, by Lord Harley, Report on the Manuscripts of his Grace the Duke of Portland*, VI (1901), pp. 103–4)

5 May 1725

. . . From Chester[-le-Street, Durham] we go about half a mile to the left where is a very large fire engine for draining the coal pits there.

The boiler holds eighty hogsheads.

The fire stove consumes five fothers, or sixty bushels of coals in twenty-four hours.

The brass barrel or cylinder is nine feet long. Its diameter two feet four inches.

Thickness of the brass—one inch and a half. From the surface of the ground to the bottom of the water is twenty-four fathoms or forty-eight yards.

The water in the pit is two yards deep. From the surface of the water to the drift or level where the engine forces it out is twelve fathoms.

It discharges two hundred and fifty hogsheads in one hour; it strikes (as they term it) or makes a discharge fourteen times in one minute.

In the same place are two other engines for draining, called bob-gins, and are moved by water turning a wheel.

They all belong to Mr Headworth, dean of the church, and Mr Allan. The weekly expense of these three engines is 5*l* paid by the owners of the colliery to Mr Potter the undertaker of the fire engine, the owners allowing whatever coals are expended.

Coming from this engine towards Newcastle we pass over two way leaves which cross the great road. These way leaves are an artificial road made for the conveyance of coal from the pit to the steaths on the riverside; whereby one horse shall carry a greater burden than a whole team on a common way, and as they generally pass through the grounds of several proprietors, are very expensive to the coal owners, who pay very high prices for their trespass on that occasion. The nearest to Chester is a single one and belongs to Mr Allan's colliery, the other about half a mile further is a double one, and belongs to Dean Headworth; the loaded cart goes upon one, and the empty one returns upon the other. The whole length of these two way leaves from the coal pits to the place from whence the coals are loaded into the lighters or keels at Sunderland, is five miles.

38 Act to Prevent Unlawful Combinations of Woollen Workmen, 1725

(12 George I, c. 34, *Statutes at Large*, V 1763, p. 604)

Whereas great numbers of weavers, and others concerned in the woollen manufactures in several towns and parishes in this kingdom, have lately formed themselves into unlawful clubs and societies, and have presumed, contrary to law, to enter into combinations, and to make by-laws or orders, by which they pretend to regulate the trade and the prices of their goods, and to advance their wages unreasonably, and many other things to the like purpose: and whereas the said persons so unlawfully assembling and associating themselves have committed great violences and outrages upon many of his majesty's good subjects, and by force protected themselves and their wicked accomplices against law and justice; and it is absolutely necessary that more effectual provision should be made against such unlawful combinations, and for preventing such violences and outrages for the future, and for bringing all offenders in the premises to more speedy and exemplary justice; may it therefore . . . be enacted . . . that all contracts, covenants or agreements, and all by-laws, ordinances, rules or orders, in such un-

lawful clubs and societies, heretofore made or entered into, or hereafter
to be made or entered into, by or between any persons brought up in or
professing, using or exercising the art and mystery of a woolcomber or
weaver, or journeyman woolcomber or journeyman weaver, in any
parish or place within this kingdom, for regulating the said trade or
mystery, or for regulating or settling the prices of goods, or for ad-
vancing their wages, or for lessening their usual hours of work, shall
be and are hereby declared to be illegal, null and void to all intents and
purposes; and further, that if any woolcomber or weaver, or journeyman woolcomber or journeyman weaver, or other person concerned in
any of the woollen manufactures of this kingdom shall, at any time or
times after the twenty-fourth day of June [1726] keep up, continue, act
in, make, enter into, sign, seal or be knowingly concerned in any contract, covenant or agreement, by-law, ordinance, rule or order of any
club, society or combination by this act declared to be illegal, null and
void, or shall presume or attempt to put any such illegal agreement,
by-law, ordinance, rule or order in execution, every person so offending
being thereof lawfully convicted upon the oath or oaths of one or more
credible witness or witnesses, before any two or more justices of the
peace for the county, city, town or place where such offence shall be
committed, upon any information exhibited or prosecution within
three calendar months after the offence committed . . . shall, by order of
such justices, at their discretion be committed either to the house of
correction, there to remain and be kept to hard labour for any time not
exceeding three months, or to the common gaol of the county, city,
town or place where such offence shall be committed, as they shall see
cause, there to remain, without bail or mainprize, for any time not
exceeding three months . . .

39 Some Building Costs, 1729

(*The Letters and Papers of the Banks Family of Revesby Abbey, 1704–
1760*, ed. J. W. F. Hill (Lincoln Record Society, XLV, 1952), p. 106)

An account of the expense of building the ten almshouses at Revesby,[1]
finished March 1729

	l	s	d
For 940 foot of timber used in this work, measured and delivered by Wm. Banks..	47	0	0
Per Simon Flint, carpenter, his bill for work done as carpenter	33	0	0

	l	*s*	*d*
To Mich: Gibbons, bricklayer, for 116 rood and half of brick work at 3s 6d	20	7	9
And for laying 10 floors 30 yards each at 1½d	1	17	6
Bricks used in the walls reckoning 1100 to the rood is 27,600 at 16s per m.	102	1	0
Bricks in each floor 900, ten floors 8,900..	7	1	6
To Mr Young for 23 chalder of lime delivered at 1/4.0..	27	12	0
For 63 hundred of reed at 4s per hundred	12	12	0
2 hundred and half farmarling at 1/6.0	3	5	0
To Holgarth, thatcher, for thatching the whole rushrope etc. as by bill	9	17	3
Ten locks and ten pair hinges and staples at 4s 6d each door	2	5	0
Nails of all kinds	1	15	0
Tom Kirkham, glazing the windows	2	17	0
Smith's work, done by John Nelson		17	0
To carriage of all the timber, bricks, sand and other materials, being a summer's work for 2 draughts attended by 3 or 4 labourers	66	13	4
To levelling the ground	2	0	0
To Mr Ball, cutting the inscription	1	1	0
To leading the thatch, being 32 load at 5s per load ..	8	0	0

TOTAL...	350*l* 2*s* 4*d*	

¹ Lincolnshire.

40 Colonial Competition in Ironwares, 1736

(*Journals of the House of Commons*, XXII 1732–7, p. 776)

7 March 1736

A petition of sundry iron-masters and ironmongers, on behalf of themselves, and many others trading to his majesty's plantations in America, was presented to the House, and read; setting forth, that the inhabitants of New England have, within these few years, erected several forges and slitting-mills, and do annually make a great deal of bar iron, and manufacture the said iron into axes, nails, and sundry other species, and do now not only supply themselves with great part of their nails and iron ware, but export great quantities to many other of his majesty's plantations; to the great decay and prejudice of the iron trade in this kingdom, which, at this time employs more people, and especially of the poor laborious sort, than any other trade, that of the woollen manufacture only excepted; and that, unless their slitting-mills are destroyed, and some stop put to their manufacturing, our trade must soon be utterly ruined, and great numbers of people employed in the making and manufacturing of iron will be unavoidably deprived of the means of their subsistence. And praying the House to take the case of the petitioners into consideration, and grant them such relief as to the House shall seem reasonable.

A petition of sundry iron-masters and ironmongers, concerned in the iron manufactory of the county of Worcester, on behalf of themselves, and others, was also presented to the House, and read; setting forth, that, in that and other adjacent counties, there has long been established the greatest manufactory of iron ware in this kingdom; and that their manufactory owes its original, as well to the several forges erected in the neighbourhood, for making bar iron suitable to particular purposes, as to the great plenty of pit coal, and the conveniency of Severn for exportation; and that their trade has always increased and flourished, until lately, in proportion to the American plantations, but now greatly declines, for want of its usual demands; and that they can ascribe this to nothing but the making of iron and iron wares in that part of the world; and that many of their artificers and workmen have, of late, gone off, and, as it is to be feared, have removed themselves thither; and that they are apprehensive, by a free importation of bar iron from America, the evil complained of will be rather increased than remedied. And therefore praying the House to take their case into consideration.

And the said petitions were severally ordered to lie upon the table, until the adjourned debate of Thursday last, upon the question proposed for referring to a committee the petition of the merchants and ironmongers of this kingdom, on behalf of themselves, and many others trading to his majesty's plantations in America, be resumed.

41 Portsmouth Dockyard, 1754

(*The Travels through England of Dr. Richard Pococke*, II, ed. J. J. Cartwright (Camden Society, New Series, XLIV, 1889), pp. 114–16)

On the 23rd [September] I went from Havant . . . and came into the road from London to Portsmouth . . . and going over Portsdown came to the island of Portsea, to which there is a passage by a bridge, it being an island when the tide is in: to the east of it is a harbour called

Langston Haven; there is a fort to defend it lately built, called Cumberland Fort, and there are works to defend the entrance of the island . . . At the south-west part of it is Portsmouth, which was burnt by the French in the time of Richard II. The fortifications were begun by Edward IV, and improved by Henry VII, King Charles II, King James II, and now of late years brought to much greater perfection by new works, especially in this present reign, which are still carrying on, as it is looked on as the key to England. The eastern entrance of the harbour is defended by South Sea Castle, built by Henry VIII, and on Gosport side by four forts and a platform of twenty cannons. It is a fine harbour, and extends almost as far as Porchester, and it is said will hold a thousand men of war . . . The governor has a handsome house and chapel in the town, and there is a large brewhouse, bakehouse, and cooperage for the dock, and barracks for the invalids who are here in garrison . . . Although there is a chapel in the dock, yet they have built another near it for the large suburb, which is made by the workmen of the dock, who pay a chaplain to officiate; and near it is a handsome music room for a weekly concert, chiefly performed by gentlemen. They are supplied with water from pumps about half a mile out of town, which is brought in hogsheads and never fails; they have a well also in the dock at which the ships water. The great curiosity of this place is the dock, where first we saw the gun wharf, in which are two Chinese pagods seven feet high, with the heads of lions, as on a sort of a pillar, all of one piece of grey granite, brought by Commodore Anson and placed here.

Most of the docks are lined with Portland stone, and are staunched with the clay brought from Estamsay near. They have from 1,000 to 1,500 men employed in the yard; it is curious to see them go out at the toll of a bell at noon and night, when every one may take out any useless pieces of wood and chips, as much as they can carry under the arm, and small chips in bags, which are examined with a wooden crow, and all of them observed to see that they do not take out any iron, or anything valuable. It is curious also to see the forges where they make the anchors; the largest weigh about 80 hundred weight, that is four tons, which are worked with machines to move them. The ropeyard is 102 fathoms in length; they join three lengths to make the longest cable, which is 306 fathoms, and 23 inches round, consequently about eight inches in diameter, consists of 3,000 threads, and weighs five tons. The main-yard of a first rate man-of-war is $23\frac{3}{4}$ inches in diameter and 33[1] long, and the bowsprit is 36 inches in diameter, and the main-mast 38. The house of the commissioner, who is the head officer of the dock and of all the other officers, is on the east side of the dock. The academy is a handsome building for fifty youths to be instructed in the theory and practice of navigation, where they are lodged, dieted, and wear the sea officers' uniform, blue turned up with white . . . From the commissioner there goes up an account every week to the Navy Board of all the work that is done in the dock. On the Gosport side is lately built of brick part of a very noble hospital for the sick and wounded sailors; it is to make four sides of a square court, one of which only as yet is finished, which is 574 [feet] long and 100 deep . . . It consists of four floors above ground and one under ground for certain offices [and] is divided into several wards, with many beds in them, as other hospitals, and there is a kitchen at each end.

¹ [Feet?]

4

Internal Trade and Transport
1000–1485

Local commerce was widespread in foodstuffs and other commodities such as cloth (*8*). Domestic trade in medieval England was however greatly curtailed by the bad state of roads and bridges (*14*), the upkeep of which depended on private enterprise and acts of piety (*7*). Lawlessness further threatened road traffic (*5*). As a result much use was made of waterways but water-borne trade suffered from hindrances through building of weirs and other constructions (*11*). Another obstruction to internal trade was the levying of tolls (*4*). In some cases the proceeds were devoted to road maintenance (*10*). The countryside had a network of rural markets and fairs which were under the control of the leading landholders (*6*). The growing towns, especially London, provided a market for foodstuffs (*9, 13*). The growth of the towns as centres for trade was encouraged by grants of autonomy from manorial controls (*1*) and led to exchange between town and country. Those towns which were ports served a wider hinterland as points for the distribution of imported goods (*15*). In the early Middle Ages urban trade was regulated by leading merchants (*2*) who were sometimes organised into merchant gilds (*3*). Some trade was later controlled by craft gilds and increasing protectionism suggests that domestic trade declined in the later Middle Ages (*17*). Nevertheless the wool trade flourished in the late fifteenth century and the needs of the London-based wool-exporting merchants of the Staple encouraged the activity of middlemen in the countryside (*16*). The development of trade rested on a credit system which was legally protected after 1283 (*6, 9*) and on the provision of a sound coinage (*6, 1*) and a reliable system of weights and measures (*12*).

1485–1760

By 1485 England was already very much an exchange economy, despite the largely self-sufficing nature of many households, especially in the countryside. Most commercial transactions were local, but there were regional and nationwide flows of trade, especially in grain, coal and other primary products, and in textiles and some imported goods, which grew impressively to 1760. The expansion of domestic trade was governed in the first instance by developments in demand and production, both at home and abroad, but the means of transport available were also crucial. Land carriage for goods was generally difficult and costly (*31*), even near the metropolis (*40*). Public and private attempts were made to improve matters, the statute of 1555 putting the responsibility for road repairs on the parishes (*21*), whose deficiencies in the performance of their duties were glaring (*34*). Public authorities also attempted to cope with bridge maintenance (*22*). The great step forward in road improvement was the turnpike trust (*37*) which had transformed some roads by the mid-eighteenth century. Costly land transport meant water traffic, by river (*18*) or coast, remained highly competitive for many branches of trade, especially the more distant and bulky. Hence official concern over impediments to river navigation (*27*), and the urging of some for river improvements (*36*). A number of navigations were in fact improved during the seventeenth and early eighteenth centuries, private action on river schemes being rewarded with preferential rights (*32*). A great variety of goods was carried in river and coastal trade (*23*).

Towns and other authorities kept a close watch on local trade and markets (*24–5*), licensing dealers (*30*) and easing restrictions in time of dearth (*41*). Central and local governmental interest in this vital area of supply is seen too in attempts to check unfair dealing (*20*), in a sometimes urgent concern for food supplies (*8, 14, 27*), and in the banning of fairs in time of plague (*26*). Domestic trade and the wealth it generated could cause bad feeling against merchants (*19*), or between rival groups of merchants (*29*). By the mid-eighteenth century specialised forms of business practice existed as in the corn trade (*38*), accompanied by a growing financial sophistication and the widespread use of the bill of exchange (*35*). The volume of trade fluctuated from year to year, primarily because of variations in output and demand, but also in war years through the action of enemy privateers (*5, 30*). Aiding the advance of domestic commerce was the creation of a national postal system (*33*), and the improvement of passenger traffic, regular coaching services being in operation by the early eighteenth century (*39*).

1 The Liberties of the Bristol Burgesses, 1188

(*Bristol Charters 1155–1373*, ed. N. D. Harding (Bristol Record Society Publications, I, 1930), pp. 9–13)

John, count of Mortain,[1] to all men and to his friends, French and English, Welsh and Irish, present and to come, greeting. Know you that I have granted and by this present charter have confirmed to my burgesses of Bristol dwelling within the walls and without the walls unto the metes of the town, to wit, between Sandbrook and Bewell and Brightneebridge and the spring in the way near Aldebury of Knowle, all their liberties and free customs, as well, freely and entirely, or more so, as ever they had them in my time or in the time of any of my predecessors. Now the liberties which have been granted to them are these, to wit:—That no burgess of Bristol shall plead without the walls of the town concerning any plea except pleas of exterior tenements which do not pertain to the hundred of the town. And that they shall be quit of murder within the metes of the town. And that no burgess shall wage battle except he have been appealed concerning the death of a foreign man who has been killed in the town and who was not of the town. And that no one shall take a hospice within the walls by assize or by livery of the marshals against the will of the burgesses. And that they shall be quit of toll and lastage[2] and passage[3] and pontage[4] and of all other customs throughout all my land and power. And that none shall be adjudged to be in mercy as to his money except according to the law of the hundred, to wit, by forfeiture of forty shillings. And that the hundred shall be held only once in the week. And that in no plea shall any be able to sue by miskenning.[5] And that they shall have justly their lands and tenures and their pledges and debts throughout all my land whosoever shall owe to them. And that concerning lands and tenures which are within the town, right shall be done to them according to the custom of the town. And that concerning debts which have been contracted in Bristol and concerning pledges made in the same place pleas shall be held in the town, according to the custom of the town. And that if anyone anywhere in my land shall take toll of the men of Bristol if he have not restored it after he shall have been required to restore [it], the reeve of Bristol shall take thereupon a distress at Bristol and shall distrain to restore [it]. And that no strange merchant shall buy within the town of any strange man hides or corn or wool except of the burgesses. And that no stranger shall have a tavern except in a ship, nor shall he sell cloths for cutting except in the fair. And that no stranger shall tarry in the town with his wares in order to sell his wares except for forty days. And that no burgess anywhere in my land or power shall be attached or distrained for any debt except he be debtor or pledge. And that they shall be able to marry themselves and their sons and daughters and widows without licence of their lords. And that none of their lords on account of foreign lands shall have custody or gift of their sons or daughters or widows, but only custody of their tenements which are of their fee until they shall be of age. And that there shall be no recognition in the town. And that none shall take tine in the town except for the use of the lord count, and that according to the custom of the town. And that they shall be able to grind their corn wheresoever they will. And that they shall have all their reasonable gilds as well as, or better than, they had them in the time of Robert and William his son, earls of Gloucester. And that no burgess shall be compelled to repledge anyone except he himself will, although he be dwelling upon his own land. I have granted also to them all their tenures within the walls and without the walls unto the aforesaid metes in messuages, in gardens, in edifices upon the water and elsewhere wheresoever they be in the town to hold in free burgage, to wit:—by service of landgable which they render within the walls. I have granted also that everyone of them shall be able to make improvement as much as he be able in making edifices everywhere upon the bank and elsewhere without damage to the borough and town. And that they shall have and possess all lands and void places which are contained within the aforesaid metes to be built on at their will. Wherefore, I will and firmly command that my aforesaid burgesses of Bristol and their heirs shall have and shall hold all their aforesaid liberties and free customs as is above written of me and my heirs as well and entirely, or more so, as ever they had them at what time they have been effectual, well and in peace and honourably without all impediment or molestation which any one shall do to them thereupon. Witnesses: Stephen Ridel, my Chancellor . . . At Bristol.

[1] Before becoming king in 1199, John was Count of Mortain.
[2] Payment due for loading a ship.
[3] Charge or custom levied upon passengers.
[4] Toll, the proceeds of which were applied to the maintenance of bridges.
[5] A mistake or variation in pleading before a court.

2 Restrictions on the Sale of Cloth, c.1209

(*Beverley Town Documents*, ed. A. F. Leach (Selden Society, XIV, 1900), pp. 134–5)

This is the law of the weavers and fullers at Winchester. Be it known that no weaver or fuller may dry or dye cloth nor go outside the city to sell it, nor may they sell their cloth to any foreigner,[1] but only to merchants of the city. And if it happens that one of the weavers or fullers wishes to go outside the city to sell in order to enrich himself, it is lawful for the honest men of the city to take his merchandise[2] and bring it back to the city and to deal with it as forfeit by the view of the sheriffs and the honest men of the city. And if any weaver or fuller sells his cloth to a foreigner, the foreigner shall lose it, and the other shall remain in the mercy of the city for as much as he has. Neither the weaver nor the fuller who has not made agreement with the sheriff may buy anything except that which belongs to his trade. No freeman can be attainted by a weaver or a fuller, nor can they [the weavers and fullers] bear witness [against a freeman]. If any of them enriches himself so that he wishes to give up his trade, he may forswear it and turn his tools out of his house, and do so much towards the city that he might be admitted to the franchise.[3] They have this law of the liberty and customs of London, as they say.

[1] i.e. outsider.   [2] The text has 'chattel'. (AFL)
[3] The text has 'he might be in the franchise'. (AFL)

3 Regulation of Trade by a Merchant Gild, 1257–73

(Second Merchant Gild Roll, Box I, No. 2, printed in *Records of the Borough of Leicester*, I, ed. M. Bateson (1899), pp. 72–3, 79–80, 114)

6 February, 1257

William of Barkby of Newton found buying six woolfells in Leicester: he said he was in the Gild Merchant, and this was attested by others; and the fells were attached and shewn in the morningspeech, the said William being there present. And it was adjudged by the community of the gild that, though he were in the gild, he cannot practise gild trade unless he return to Leicester and live there and bear the burden and answer with others of the gild: and because he bought the said fells unlawfully and against gild liberties and customs, he pledged mercy and the said fells remain in the custody of Richard the reeve.

*   *   *

1 March, 1258

Memorandum that on Friday next after the feast of St Matthias, Apostle, 42 Hen. III, Henry of Ruddington being mayor, in full morningspeech it was provided and agreed by all the community of the gild that all merchants of Leicester, who at the time of Stamford fair next following shall come to Stamford with cloth or wool or with fells, shall cause this merchandise to be carried to the shops, in which the merchandise of Leicester is usually kept, and there cause the said merchandise to be unloaded and opened in the presence of the neighbours and shall keep the same there (except the fells) for at least a day and a night, and if they should wish to move this merchandise elsewhere, they shall be allowed to carry them well and without hindrance wherever they may wish, and each of them shall give for each cloth 3*d* and for each sack of wool 6*d* and for a hundred fells 3*d*. So that if any of them should contravene this in any way he shall fully discharge one shop.[1]

* * *

29 November, 1273

Be it known that if any of the community or liberty of Leicester go to Chester or Shrewsbury or any other market town to carry on trade and be distrained for the debt of any neighbour of his and not for his own debt, he may come home and point this out to the bailiffs of the lord earl, and the bailiffs shall give warning to him who owes the debt, once, and again, and if he should not make delivery of the distrained goods of his neighbour, distrained on his account, let the bailiffs close his house, whoever he may be, with bolts, and forbid him ingress until he shall have delivered his neighbours and shall have made satisfaction for his debt, and this was granted and [held] for judgment by Sir Ralph of Hengham, Walter of Hopton, judges of the Lord King Edward in the hall of the earl of Leicester at the castle, on Wednesday next after the feast of St Clement, 2 Ed. I.

* * *

(Portmanmoot Roll, Box I, No. 25, printed in *Records of the Borough of Leicester*, I, ed. M. Bateson (1899), pp. 123–4)

c.1260

Whereas at one time the merchants from foreign parts went out into the county of Leicester and bought wool in places where they ought not, and caused wool to be carried to Leicester and were convicted thereof that they were very guilty against the community, for which they were heavily amerced and punished, therefore it was provided by assent and consent of all the community and chiefly at the petition of the merchants, that the places should be enrolled and publicly announced where they may buy without hindrance, and the places are written, to wit these, Melton, Loughborough, Breedon, Hinckley, Bosworth, Lutterworth, Lilbourne, and afterwards they are announced: wherefore it was determined that if any strange merchant should henceforth ever be convicted of committing such a trespass to the prejudice of the lord earl and against the provision of the community, he should be more heavily amerced than before the determination and provision of the agreement was settled.

[1] ? Pay the whole seldage or rent of a shop. (MB)

4 Tolls on Riverine Trade, 1275

(*Rotuli Hundredorum*, I, p. 320)

The township of Lincoln. 3 Edward I

Item we say that William of Hepham and Jordan son of Giles, then bailiffs of Lincoln, extorted from every cart coming to Lincoln with hay, to wit from each cart 2*d* where they were accustomed to give only 1½*d*, and they took approximately 1 mark, by what warrant we do not know and they have the common custom of the city.

Item the same William and Jordan by reason of their office extorted from every ship coming to Lincoln with turves and faggots 4*d*, and [they took] approximately 10*s* four years ago, by what warrant we do not know and [they have] the common custom of the city.

*   *   *

Item Robert of Dunham, bailiff of Lord William de Valence, by the authority of his office took 12 years ago an undue custom from all ships crossing by way of Foss Dyke[1] from Lincoln towards Dunham, to wit from each ship ½*d*, or more or less at his will, and he thus took approximately half a mark per annum[2] to the prejudice of the king, by what warrant we do not know.

Item Roger, bailiff of Lady Devorgilla of Torkesy, by the authority of his office has extorted fines from the men of Lincoln and the surrounding countryside coming with their merchandise to Torksey in ships for 5 years and more so that they cannot load or unload their ships until they have fined with him for the sake of gain, by what warrant we do not know.

¹ A waterway connecting Lincoln with the river Trent at Torksey.
² This sum suggests 160 ships at least passing annually along Foss Dyke, but it does not include those ships passing down river from Torksey.

5 Act for the Securing of Towns and Highways, 1285

(The Statute of Winchester, cc. 4–5, P.R.O. Statute Roll, I, m. 41)

And for the greater security of the country the king has commanded that in the great towns, which are enclosed, the gates be shut from sunset until sunrise; and that no man lodge in the suburbs, or in any foreign part of the town save only in the daytime, nor yet in the daytime, if the host will not answer for him; and that the bailiffs of towns every week, or at the least every fortnight, make enquiry as to all persons lodging in the suburbs, and in foreign parts of the towns; and if they find any who receives or lodges in any manner persons who may be suspected of being against the peace, the bailiffs shall do right therein. And it is commanded that from henceforth watches be kept, as has been used in times past, that is to say, from the day of the Ascension to the day of St. Michael,¹ in every city by six men at every gate; in every borough by twelve men; in every town by six men or four, according to the number of the inhabitants who dwell [in the town], and that they keep watch continually all night, from sunset to sunrise. And if any stranger pass by them, he shall be arrested until morning; and if no suspicion be found, he shall go quit; and if they find cause of suspicion, he shall be delivered to the sheriff forthwith, and he shall receive him without danger, and keep him safely, until he be delivered in due manner. And if they will not suffer themselves to be arrested, hue and cry shall be levied against them, and those who keep watch shall follow with all the town, with the towns near, with hue and cry from town to town, until they be taken and delivered to the sheriff, as before is said; and for the arrest of such strangers none shall be called in question.

And further, it is commanded, that highways from one market town to another be enlarged, where there are woods, hedges, or ditches, so that there be neither ditches, underwood, nor bushes wherein a man may lurk to do hurt, near the road, within two hundred feet on the one side, and two hundred feet on the other side, provided that this statute extend not to oaks, or to great woods, so as it be clear underneath. And if by default of the lord who will not abate the ditch, underwood, or

I

bushes in the manner aforesaid, any robberies be done, that the lord be answerable therefor; and if murder be done, that the lord make fine at the king's pleasure. And if the lord be not able to clear away the underwood, that the country aid him in doing it. And the king wills, that in his demesne lands and woods, within his forest and without, the roads be enlarged as aforesaid.

And if, perchance, a park be near the highway, it is requisite that the lord of the park diminish his park, so that there be a space of two hundred feet from the highway, as before said, or that he make such a wall, ditch, or hedge, that evil doers will not be able to pass or return, to do evil.

[1] 29 September.

6 Grant of a Market, 1293

(*Cartularium Monasterii de Rameseia*, II, ed. W. A. Hart and P. A. Lyons, *Rolls Series* (1893), pp. 298–9)

Edward by the grace of God king of England, lord of Ireland and duke of Aquitaine, to archbishops, bishops, abbots, priors, earls, barons, justices, sheriffs, reeves, ministers and all his bailiffs and faithful, greeting. Know you that we have granted and by this our charter confirmed to our beloved in Christ, the abbot and convent of Ramsey, that they and their successors for ever have a market every week on Monday at their manor of St. Ives in the county of Huntingdon, unless that market be to the nuisance of neighbouring markets. Wherefore we will and straitly command, for us and our heirs, that the aforesaid abbot and convent and their successors for ever have the aforesaid market at their manor aforesaid with all the liberties and free customs to such market pertaining, unless that market be to the nuisance of neighbouring markets, as is aforesaid. These witnesses:—the venerable fathers John, of Winchester, Anthony, of Durham, William, of Ely, bishops, William de Valence, our uncle, Roger le Bigod, earl of Norfolk and marshal of England, John de Warenne, earl of Surrey, Henry de Lacy, earl of Lincoln, William de Beauchamp, earl of Warwick, Robert de Tibetot, Gilbert de Thornton, John of Mettingham, Robert of Hertford, Robert Malet, and others. Given by our hand at Westminster on the fourteenth day of May in the twenty-first year of our reign.

7 An Indulgence for Road Repairs, 1314

(*Registrum Palatinum Dunelmense*, I, ed. T. D. Hardy, *Rolls Series* (1873), p. 507)

To all etc. Believing that the minds of the faithful turn to works of piety more readily when aroused more beneficially by the more noble grants of indulgences, and trusting in the mercy of almighty God and in the merits and prayers of the glorious Virgin, his mother, and of the Blessed Peter and Paul, and of the most holy confessor Cuthbert, our patron, and of all the saints, to all our parishioners, and to outsiders, of whom the diocesans have approval and acceptance, truly repenting and confessing of their sins, who, towards the making or repair of the causeway between Brotherton and Ferrybridge,[1] where there is a frequent passage of people, contribute any gifts of charity, or support that work with their bodily labour, or similarly help to support it, 40 days of indulgence awarded to them, etc. In testimony of which thing etc.

[1] Yorkshire.

8 A Prior Purchases Cloth and Corn, 1318–23

(*Literae Cantuarienses. The Letter-Books of the Monastery of Christ Church Canterbury*, I, ed. J. Brigstocke Sheppard, *Rolls Series* (1887), pp. 41, 113)

24 February, 1318

I[1] beg you to send by the bearer of this letter, samples of the cloths which you have for sale: that is to say, two pieces and a half of well dyed for clerks, the price of each piece seventy-three shillings and four-pence. Also, a sample of two pieces of coloured cloth, and of two pieces with broad stripes of concordant colours, for esquires, the price of each piece seventy shillings. Also, a sample of four pieces with broad stripes, or of a good particolour, for keepers and knaves, the price of each piece four marks. Also, a sample of four pieces of striped cloth, or of good particolour, for grooms, the price of each piece forty shillings. And when I have seen the samples of your cloth, and the price, I will send a man to you to choose the pieces and to bring them to Canterbury. God be with you, to keep you and all belonging to you. Given at Canterbury the 24th of February.

*   *   *

1323

To his very dear and well-beloved in God Sir John Pecche, constable of Dover, Henry prior of the Church of Canterbury, greeting, and enduring health. Respecting that which you requested of us lately in your letters, [namely] that we should advance you twenty quarters of wheat, and as many of barley in our manor of Eastry, or in that of West Cliffe, the money to be paid at Midsummer next, know, Sir, that one half of our estates lie so far away from us outside of this county in the direction of Oxford[shire], and Devonshire, and elsewhere, that hence it behoves us to sell our own corn in those parts, and to purchase other in this district. And know, Sir, that all the corn that we possess (beyond the seed corn for our lands), between Sandwich and Rochester, does not by any means suffice for the maintenance of our convent, and our household beyond Whitsuntide, and therefore we are obliged to buy a thousand quarters of corn and even more, every year, in this district. I commend you to God, who keep you and whatever belongs to you.

[1] The writer, Henry of Eastry, is writing to a cloth merchant.

9 The Supply of Corn and Malt to London, c.1323–4

(*Liber Albus*, ed. H. T. Riley (1861), p. 372)

Proclamation as to the places where the corndealers shall stand

Let proclamation be made, that all those who bring corn or malt unto the city of London for sale, bring the same solely unto the markets in the said city for the sale thereof, at the places from of old used therefor, that is to say; that those from the counties of Cambridge, Huntingdon, Bedford, and those who come by Ware, bring all the corn and malt which they shall bring unto the said city for sale unto the market upon the pavement at Gracechurch, and there stand for the purposes of sale, and nowhere else, without fraud or evil intent, and without placing or selling any thereof in secret places; and that the same corn and malt be not mixed, in deceit of the people, under pain of forfeiture of the said corn and malt in the said condition, as to which any person shall be attainted.

And that those who come from the parts towards the west of the said city, as from Barnet, and those who have to come by that way and by way of other places, bringing corn or malt unto the said city for sale, bring the same solely unto the market upon the pavement before the Friars Minor, in Newgate, and there stand for the purposes of sale, and nowhere else, without placing or selling any part thereof in secret; and that the same corn or malt be not mixed, in deceit of the people, under pain of forfeiture of the said corn and malt in the said condition, as to which any person shall be attainted.

10 Pavage Tolls on Goods Entering Newark, 1328

(P.R.O. Patent Roll, 2 Edward III, pt. 1, m. 5)

The king to the venerable father in Christ H. by the same grace bishop of Lincoln, greeting. Know you that we have granted to you, in aid of paving your town of Newark, that from the day of the making of these presents to the end of three years completed next following you take in the same town, by those whom you shall think fit to depute hereto and for whom you will be answerable, the underwritten customs on things for sale coming to the same town, to wit, on each quarter of corn for sale $\frac{1}{4}d$, on each horse and mare for sale $\frac{1}{2}d$, on each hide of horse and mare, ox and cow, fresh, salted and tanned, for sale $\frac{1}{4}d$, on each cart carrying meat, salted or fresh, for sale $1\frac{1}{2}d$, on 5 bacons for sale $\frac{1}{2}d$, on each salmon, fresh or salt, for sale $\frac{1}{4}d$, on each 100 mackerel for sale $\frac{1}{2}d$, on each lamprey for sale $\frac{1}{2}d$, on 10 sheep, goats or swine for sale $1d$, on 10 fleeces for sale $\frac{1}{2}d$, on each 100 woolfells of sheep, goats, stags, hinds, bucks and does for sale $1d$, on each 100 fells of lambs, kids, hares, rabbits, foxes, cats and squirrels $\frac{1}{2}d$, on each cart-load of sea-fish for sale $2d$, on each horse-load of sea-fish for sale $\frac{1}{2}d$, on each truss of cloths brought by cart $3d$, on each horse-load of cloth for sale or other diverse and minute things for sale coming to the same town $\frac{1}{2}d$, on each cart-load of iron for sale $1d$, on each 100 of steel for sale $\frac{1}{4}d$, on each cart-load of tin for sale $\frac{1}{2}d$, on each quarter of woad $2d$, on each tun of wine for sale $2d$, on each sack of wool for sale $2d$, on each horse-load of wool $1d$, on each horse-load of apples, pears or nuts for sale $\frac{1}{4}d$, on each 100 of linen web and canvas for sale $\frac{1}{2}d$, on each 100 of linen for sale $\frac{1}{4}d$, on each new cart for sale $\frac{1}{4}d$, on each cart laden with timber for sale $\frac{1}{2}d$, on each 1000 laths $1\frac{1}{2}d$, on each 100 stockfish and Aberdeen fish $\frac{1}{2}d$, on each cart laden with hay or grass for sale $\frac{1}{4}d$, on each cart carrying rushes for sale $1d$, on each cart-load of heath for sale $\frac{1}{2}d$, on each truss of chalons[1] for sale $\frac{1}{2}d$, on each horse-load of glass $\frac{1}{2}d$, on each horse-load of garlic for sale $\frac{1}{2}d$, on each 1000 herrings for sale $\frac{1}{4}d$, on each 100 boards for sale $1d$, on each cart-load of faggots for sale $\frac{1}{4}d$, on each quarter of salt for sale $\frac{1}{4}d$, on each dozen horse-loads of coals for sale $\frac{1}{2}d$, on each cart-load of coals for sale $\frac{1}{2}d$, on each cart-load of brushwood for sale $\frac{1}{2}d$, on each horse-load of brushwood for sale by the week $\frac{1}{4}d$, on each 1000 nails for house gables for sale $\frac{1}{4}d$, on each 100 horse shoes for horses and clout-nails for carts $\frac{1}{2}d$, on 2000 of all manner of nails for sale except nails for carts and house gables $\frac{1}{4}d$, on each truss of every kind of ware for sale coming to the same town and exceeding the value of $2s$, $\frac{1}{4}d$. And therefore we command you that you take the customs aforesaid until the end of the said three years in the form aforesaid, and that after the term of the said three years be complete the said customs wholly cease and be annulled. In witness whereof . . . to endure for the aforesaid three years. Witness the king at Northampton, 8 May.

By the king himself.

[1] Coverlets made at Chalons-sur-Marne.

11 A River Obstruction Disrupts Local Trade, 1331

(*Cartularium Monasterii de Rameseia*, III, ed. W. H. Hart and P. A. Lyons, *Rolls Series* (1893), pp. 141–2)

12th May, 1331
Verdict of the county of Norfolk
The jurors of the county of Norfolk . . .[1] say on their oath that Walter of Langton, once bishop of Coventry and Lichfield, by reason of the draining of his aforesaid manor of Coldeham about thirty years ago, obstructed the course of the said river[2] at Outwell, with the result that men, wishing to cross [the fenland] there in their boats and small craft with their goods and merchandise frome Holme, Yaxley and from other inland parts to the said port of Lynn Episcopi[3] in the county of Norfolk, and also men, wishing to return directly from the said port to Holme, Yaxley, the borough of St. Peter[4] and elsewhere inland, could not travel across there in their boats and small craft as they were previously accustomed before the said obstruction, but they were obliged to cross by skirting around by a longer way, namely *via* Oldwelness and Littleport, which is fifty leagues and more for the return journey, with the result that corn, timber, wool, sedges, reeds, turves, peat and other merchandise are dearer and fish, herrings and other victuals are, by reason of the said detour, dearer and spoiled.

The damage and hurt to the men of the county of Norfolk each year is two hundred pounds . . .

[1] The names of the twelve jurors.   [2] The Nene.
[3] King's Lynn.   [4] Peterborough.

12 The Rebuilding of a Balance, 1344

(*Calendar of Letter-Book F, c.1337–1352*, ed. R. R. Sharpe (1904), pp. 113–14)

Thursday the morrow of the Nativity of Blessed Mary, 18 Edward III,[1] it was ordained by John Hamond, the mayor, and the aldermen,[2] with the assent of the more discreet and wealthier men of the mystery of mercery, that the small balance be remade with new weights appertaining to the same small balance, for the common benefit as well of buyers as of sellers, and that the tongue of the beam of the same balance be pierced through in the middle of the said tongue of the beam. So that when the article for sale is placed in one end of the said balance and the weight appertaining to the said balance in the other end of the same, the top of the tongue of the beam of the said balance shall stand up direct and equally under the cleft of the said balance, declining neither towards the thing to be sold nor to the weight of the said balance; but the top of the tongue of the said beam, as aforesaid, shall stand even without any declining towards either extremity of the said balance, lest buyers or sellers of articles of commerce weighed by the said small balance be in any way deceived by the keeper of the said small balance.

It was also ordained the same Thursday that the weight of a pound of silk should contain only 20 ounces. And the same day the office of the said small balance was granted by the said mayor and aldermen, with the assent of the said good men of the mystery of mercery, to Thomas of Deophan, who was sworn to exercise the said office well and faithfully so long as he remained therein.

[1] 8 September 1344.   [2] Of London.

13 Municipal Regulation of the Sale of Meat and Fish, 1365–1409

(*Beverley Town Documents*, ed. A. F. Leach (Selden Society, XIV, 1900), pp. 28–30)

Orders as to the butchers' market

Also, it was ordered, A.D. 1365, by Richard Holme . . . keepers or governors of the town of Beverley, that no market should be held for selling meat anywhere in Beverley except in the ancient butchers' market and in Barleyholme, fair and market days only excepted.

Of meat kept or sold out of season

Also, it was ordered in the year last mentioned, that if a butcher sell, or put out for sale, meat maggoty or kept beyond the proper time, or dead of murrain, or carrion, for every time any of them has been duly convicted of any of the crimes or offences aforesaid, he should pay, without remedy, to the community 6s 8d.

Of blood or any tainted matter placed in the streets

Also, it was ordered by the community that if a butcher or any of his men put offal, blood or any tainted thing in the high streets or Walkerbeck, or any other place except where they have been appointed by the community, everyone so offending pay to the community 40d.

Of the custody of butchers' dogs

Also, because of divers complaints made about butchers' dogs it was ordered, A.D. 1367, by the keepers of the town of Beverley, that if any butcher's dog be found in the road without a keeper, or if he bite a stranger's pig or dog, he whose dog commits the offence pay to the community 40d.

Of meat for sale

Also, proclamation was made in the Lord Archbishop's court on Monday, St. Mary Magdalen's day,[1] A.D. 1370, that every butcher was to sell meat killed by himself in his own shop, and not to send it to another butcher to sell, under penalty of forfeiting the same.

Of the same

Also, that every butcher must sell his meat within four days from the time of killing, or on the fourth day put it in salt, under the penalty aforesaid.

Of the market of butchers and fishmongers

Also, that town butchers stand at one end of the lord's market to be chosen by them, and strange butchers at the other end; so that the fish market may be between them on market day; so that the butchers do not intermeddle with each other.

4 May, A.D. 1409, it was ordered that no cook was to buy fish in the market, or poultry at the cross, before 8 a.m. for the future, under penalty of 3s 4d, to be paid to the community; and on fair-days they may buy earlier, but moderately so, under the same penalty.

[1] 22 July.

14 A Dilapidated Bridge, 1376

(*Rotuli Parliamentorum*, II, p. 350)

Item pray the Commons of the counties of Nottingham, Derby and Lincoln and of the town of Nottingham that whereas there is a great bridge over the river Trent by the town of Nottingham called Heybe-thebrigg, to the making or repairing of which no one there is bound save only by alms, over which all men coming or going between the regions of the South and North should have their passage, and because the said bridge cannot be maintained without great costs from year to year, and at which passage, when one could not cross on the said bridge because of its ruined state, several persons were often drowned, men on horse and well as carts, men and harness, that when he has knowledge of this,[1] that it please our lord the king to grant by his letters patent to the said Commons, that the said Commons of Nottingham and the town may be empowered to choose two perpetual wardens of the said bridge, one from the said town and the other from the said county of Nottingham, who may be empowered to purchase and receive lands, tenements and rents to themselves and their successors, without any other licence whatsoever, for the upkeep and maintenance of the said bridge, for God and as a work of charity.

[1] *et quant il y avoit.*

15 The Carting of Goods from a Port, 1443

(*The Brokage Book of Southampton 1443–1444*, ed. O. Coleman (Southampton Record Series, IV, 1960), pp. 3–4)

Wednesday, October 2nd

From John Chavon, junior, carting towards Wilton with 1 cask of oil of Margery Hill,[1] free of custom, and 1 balet of woad of John Soper of Salisbury, custom ½d, brokage 4d, pontage 1d.

From John Chavon, senior, carting towards Salisbury with 8 barrels of black soap of William Warwick, custom 8d, brokage 4d, pontage 1d.

From William Hekle of Bursledon, carting towards London with 8 bales of dates, 3 bales of pepper of Simon Spenell,[2] custom by sea,[3] brokage 8d, pontage 1d.

From William Rylford carting towards London with 9 bales of almonds of Simon Spenell', custom by sea, brokage 8d, pontage 1d.

From John Walton carting towards Winchester with 4 balets of woad of Laurence Trygge, free of custom, brokage 1d, pontage 1d.

From John Chappe carting towards Wickham with 5 measures of

pippins[4] of John Dowse, custom 5*d*, one hundred of pepper, custom 4*d*, half a hundred of wax, custom 1*d*, brokage nothing, pontage 1*d*.

From John Cruse carting towards Salisbury with 4 balets of woad sent by Walter Fetplace, custom 4*d*, brokage 2*d*, pontage 1*d*.

From John Rook entering with 3 quarters of malt, custom 1½*d*, and departing towards Salisbury with 4 balets of woad, sent by Walter Fetplace, custom 4*d*, brokage 2*d*, pontage 1*d*.

From John Brook carting towards Sherborne with 2 wains carting with 1 cask of oil and 2 butts of wine of John Tucker, custom 2 shillings, brokage 16*d*, pontage 2*d*.

[1] Of Wilton.   [2] An Italian of Genoa.
[3] i.e. already paid to the water-bailiff on entry to the port.
[4] ? *vagis pipys*.

16 Buying Wool on Credit, 1478–9

(*The Cely Papers, selected from the Correspondence and Memoranda of the Cely Family, Merchants of the Staple, 1475–88*, ed. H. E. Malden (Camden Society, Third Series, I, 1900), p. 11)

1478

Item the 24th day of November I have bought of William Midwinter[1] of Northleach[2] 40 sacks of good Cotswold wool, good wool and middle wool of the same 40 sacks, price the sack of both good wool and middle wool 12 marks, the refuse wool to be cast to William Midwinter by the wool packer at the packing of the foresaid wool at Northleach, and the foresaid wool to be weighed at the Leadenhall[3] at the king's beam, and the reckoning made and the 3rd penny paid in hand, and the other 3rd penny, the second payment, [on] the last day of May next coming, and the rest, the last payment, the last day of September next coming, this bill ending between both parties. I, Richard Cely, merchant of the staple of Calais, write with my hand.

Item, the 24th day of January I have delivered to William Midwinter in part payment—20*l*.

Item the 2nd day of April I have delivered to William Midwinter in part payment—20*l* sterling.

[1] Midwinter was a prominent middleman in the Cotswold wool trade.
[2] Gloucestershire. An important centre of the Cotswold wool trade.
[3] London. The Leadenhall was appointed for the weighing of wool in 1463.

17 A Craft Gild Acts against an Interloper, 1475–80, 1483–5

(P.R.O. Early Chancery Proceedings, C 1/66/364)

To the reverend father in God, the bishop of Lincoln, chancellor of
England.

Meekly beseeches your gracious lordship your poor orator Robert
Clement, skinner. Where that he, not being able now of [the] power to
keep a shop of [the] skinner's craft, goes about to gentlemen and pro-
vides for them such furs as be necessary to them for reasonable price
better than they should buy in a skinner's shop, and by these means
gets his poor living, by occasion whereof the Craft of Skinners of
London, having indignation to your said poor orator thereof, have
caused one Hugh Byrd, citizen and skinner of London and parish clerk
of Saint Mary, Staining in London, to take surety of peace and an
action of trespass against your poor orator before the sheriffs of
London without any cause or matter God knows, but only it is intended
to keep him in prison, namely against and in this holy time of Christmas
so that he should not let the said skinners, after their intent, of their
excessive lucre. And so he is now cast in prison for the said cause to the
utter undoing of your said poor orator without your gracious lordship
be shewed to him in this behalf. Please it therefore the same your
lordship, in consideration of the premises, to grant a writ of *certiorari*
to be directed to the sheriffs of London, commanding them by the
same to bring up the said causes before the king in his Chancery at a
certain day by your lordship to be limited, and then and there such
direction to be had herein by your lordship as shall be thought to the
same according to reason and conscience, and this for the love of God
and in way of charity.[1]

[1] Transcription of document kindly provided by Elspeth Veale.

18 The Advantage of Water Carriage, 1505–6

(Historical Manuscripts Commission, *Calendar of the Manuscripts of
the Dean and Chapter of Wells*, II (1914), p. 187)

Shows unto your masterships the merchants and other occupiers,
tenants and inhabitants unto our lord bishop of Winchester of his
town of Taunton, that where we, the said tenants, occupiers and inhabitants and all other merchants, tenants and inhabitants of the same
town, out of time of mind, in the right of our said lord, have peaceably
used and had course, recourse and free passage upon the water of

Toon, Bathpolemill and Bridgwater, for all manner of merchandises, corn, coal, stones, and all other stuff by us bought and sold, unto the time a mill called Hammill, which of time past was raised and new made by the prior of Montacute and the dean and chapter of Wells, by reason whereof your said petitioners be stopped and letted of their said carriages, so that in default thereof in the winter season we can have no carriage, the ways be so foundered by overflowing of the water. Whereas if the said mills had not [been] made, we should have had our carriages by water, and that in every ton better cheap by 2s than the carriage is to carry it by land, to our great charge, loss and hindrances for lack of conveying of our merchandise and stuff, and many times of our premises to such persons as we buy and sell with, for lack of carriage, by occasion aforesaid. Wherefore it will please your masterships, in the way of charity, to provide for the reformation of the premises, and we shall pray for the prosperity as well of our said lord as of your said masterships, long to endure.

19 A Coal Merchant, 1550

(*The Select Works of Robert Crowley*, ed. J. M. Cowper (Early English Text Society, Extra Series, XV, 1872), p. 20)

Of the Collier of Croydon

It is said, that in Croydon
    there did sometime dwell
A collier, that did
    all other colliers excel.
For his riches this collier
    might have been a knight;
But in the order of knighthood
    he had no delight.
Would God all our knights
    did mind coaling no more,
Than this collier did knighting,
    as is said before!
For when none but poor colliers
    did with coals mell,[1]
At a reasonable price,
    they did their coals sell;
But since our knight colliers
    have had the first sale,

We have paid much money
and had few sacks to tale.
A load that of late years
for a royal[2] was sold,
will cost now 16s
of silver or gold.
God grant these men grace
their polling[3] to refrain,
Or else bring them back
to their old state again.
And especially the collier
that at Croydon doth sell;
For men think he is cousin
to the collier of hell.

[1] Meddle.   [2] In the reign of Henry VIII a royal was valued at 11s 3d.
[3] Robbing or cheating.

20 An Act against Unfair Dealing, 1552

(5 and 6 Edward VI, c. 14, *Statutes of the Realm*, IV, Part I (1819), pp. 148–50)

Albeit divers good statutes heretofore have been made against fore-stallers of merchandise and victuals, yet for that good laws and statutes against regraters and ingrossers of the same things have not been here-tofore sufficiently made and provided, and also, for that it has not been perfectly known what person should be taken for a forestaller, regrater or ingrosser, the said statutes have not taken good effect according to the minds of the makers thereof: therefore be it enacted . . . that whatsoever person or persons that after the first day of May next com-ing shall buy or cause to be bought any merchandise, victual or any other thing whatsoever, coming by land or by water toward any market or fair to be sold in the same, or coming toward any city, port, haven, creek or road of this realm or Wales from any parts beyond the sea to be sold, or make any bargain, contract or promise for the having or buying of the same or any part thereof so coming as is aforesaid, before the said merchandise, victuals or other things shall be in the market, fair, city, port, haven, creek or road ready to be sold, or shall make any motion by word, letter, message or otherwise to any person or persons for the enhancing of the price or dearer selling of any thing or things above mentioned, or else dissuade, move or stir any person or persons coming to the market or fair to abstain or forbear to bring or convey any of the things above rehearsed to any market, fair, city, port, haven, creek or road to be sold as is aforesaid, shall be deemed, taken and adjudged a forestaller.

Further be it enacted . . . that whatsoever person or persons that after the said first day of May shall by any means regrate, obtain or get into his or their hands or possession, in any fair or market, any corn, wine, fish, butter, cheese, candles, tallow, sheep, lambs, calves, swine, pigs, geese, capons, hens, chickens, pigeons, conies or other dead victual whatsoever, that shall be brought to any fair or market within this realm or Wales to be sold, and do sell the same again, in any fair or market held or kept in the same place, or in any other fair or market within four miles thereof, shall be accepted, reputed and taken for a regrater or regraters.

And be it also enacted . . . that whatsoever person or persons that after the said first day of May shall ingross or get into his or their hands by buying, contracting or promise taking, other than by demise, grant or lease of land or tithe, any corn growing in the fields, or any other corn or grain, butter, cheese, fish or other dead victual whatsoever within the realm of England to the intent to sell the same again, shall be accepted, reputed and taken an unlawful ingrosser or ingrossers.

And if any person or persons shall at any time after the said first day of May offend in any of the things before recited, and being thereof duly convicted or attainted by the laws of this realm or after the form hereafter mentioned, shall for his or their first offence have and suffer imprisonment by the space of two months without bail or mainprise, and shall also lose and forfeit the value of the goods, chattels and victual so by him or them bought or had: and if any person lawfully convicted or attainted of or for any the offences abovesaid, be thereof *eftsones* lawfully convicted or attainted, that then every person or persons so offending shall have and suffer for his said second offence imprisonment by the space of one half year without bail or mainprise, and shall lose the double value of all the goods, chattels and victual so by him bought or had as is aforesaid; and if any person being lawfully twice convicted or attainted of or for any of the said offences shall *eftsones* offend the third time and be thereof lawfully convicted or attainted, that then every such person for the said third offence shall be set in the pillory in the city, town or place where he shall then dwell and inhabit, and lose and forfeit all the goods and chattels that he or they have to their own use, and also be committed to prison there to remain during the king's majesty's pleasure . . .

21 The Statute for the Mending of Highways, 1555

(2 and 3 Philip and Mary, c. 8, *Statutes at Large*, II (1763), pp. 491–2)

For amending of highways, being now both very noisome and tedious to travel in, and dangerous to all passengers and carriages.

Be it enacted by the authority of this present parliament, that the constables and churchwardens of every parish within this realm, shall yearly upon the Tuesday or Wednesday in Easter week call together a number of the parishioners, and shall then elect and choose two honest persons of the parish to be surveyors and orderers for one year, of the works for amendment of the highways in their parish leading to any market town; the which persons shall have authority by virtue hereof, to order and direct the persons and carriages that shall be appointed for those works, by their discretions; and the said persons so named shall take upon them the execution of the said offices, upon pain every of them making default, to forfeit twenty shillings.

II And the said constables and churchwardens shall then also name and appoint four days for the amending of the said ways, before the feast of the Nativity of Saint John Baptist[1] then next following; and shall openly in the church the next Sunday after Easter give knowledge of the same four days; and upon the said days the parishioners shall endeavour themselves to the amending of the said ways; and shall be chargeable thereunto as follows; that is to say, every person for every plough-land in tillage or pasture that he or she shall occupy in the same parish, and every other person keeping there a draught or plough, shall find and send at every day and place to be appointed for the amending of the ways in that parish, as is aforesaid, one wain or cart furnished after the custom of the country with oxen, horses or other cattle, and all other necessaries meet to carry things convenient for that purpose, and also two able men with the same, upon pain of every draught making default, ten shillings; and every other householder, and also every cottager and labourer of that parish, able to labour, and being no hired servant by the year, shall by themselves or one sufficient labourer for every of them, upon every of the said four days, work and travail in the amendment of the said highways, upon pain of every person making default, to lose for every day twelve pence. And if the said carriages of the parish, or any of them, shall not be thought needful by the supervisors to be occupied upon any of the said days, that then every such person that should have sent any such carriage, shall send to the said work for every carriage so spared two able men, there to labour for that day, upon pain to lose for every man not so sent to the said work, twelve pence. And every person and carriage abovesaid shall have and bring with them such shovels, spades, picks, mattocks, and other tools and instruments, as they do make their own ditches and fences withal, and such as be necessary for their said work. And all the said persons and carriages shall do and keep their work as they shall be appointed by the said supervisors, or one of them, eight hours of every of the said days, unless they shall be otherwise licensed by the said supervisors, or one of them. And be it enacted . . . that the steward and stewards of every leet or law day shall therein have full power and authority to enquire by the oaths of the suitors, of all and every the offences that shall be committed within the leet or law day, against every point and article of this statute, and to assess such reasonable fines and amercements for the same, as shall be thought meet by the said steward. And in default of such inquiry or presentment, the justices of peace of every place or county shall have authority to enquire of the same offences which shall be committed within the limits of their commission at every their quarter sessions, and to assess such fines therefore as they or two of them, whereof one to be of the quroum, shall think meet . . .

*   *   *

IV   And be it enacted . . . that all fines, amercements and forfeitures, which shall be due for any offence against the purview of this statute, shall be to the churchwardens of every parish wherein the offences shall be committed, to be bestowed on the highways in the said parishes . . .

[1] 24 June.

22 Repair of Rochester Bridge, 1557

(*Calendar of the Patent Rolls*, Philip and Mary, III, 1555–7 (1938), p. 368)

21 May 1557   Whereas Rochester bridge in Kent, one of the most notable occupied bridges in the realm, and a wall or wharf of stone leading from the bridge under the castle by the great violence and force of the water is fallen into great decay; commission to Sir George Cobham, K.G., Lord Cobham, and Sir Thomas Moile, knight, wardens of the bridge, to oversee and from time to time repair as need shall require the bridge, stone wall and wharves, and power to them and their deputies appointed by their writing under the seal of the bridge to levy towards the charges of the said repairs during the next four years the tolls following, viz. for every cart passing and repassing over the bridge,

4*d*; every horseman and his horse, 1*d*; every pack horse, 2*d*; every horse being led or driven, 1*d*; every head of meat (bull, ox, cow, steer, bullock or heifer), 1*d*; every calf without his dam, ½*d*; every 4 sheep, 1*d*; every sow, hog, boar or yelt,[1] ½*d*; every boat passing and repassing through the bridge with oysters or other lading between one and six tons burden, 2*d*; every boat or lighter above six and not above twelve tons laden with merchandise, 4*d*; all manner of hoys or other vessels above twelve tons and laden with iron, wood, coal, grain, etc., ½*d* a ton. Power also to ask and receive once a year during the said four years the charitable alms of all dwelling within the county with the consent and help of the curate and churchwardens of every parish.

[1] Young female pig.

23 Rye's Coastal Trade, 1574

(*Rye Shipping Records, 1566–1590*, ed. R. F. Dell (Sussex Record Society, LXIV, 1965–6), pp. 19–20)

Port Book of the Controller of Rye for Coastal Shipments, May 1574

In the *Nicholas* of Rye, burden 20 tons, of which John Emmery is master, went out the 4th day of May.

From Thomas Browne and John Wigsell, native merchants, for 14 tuns of unsweet wine to London.

In the *Marie Fortune* of Rye, burden 16 tons, of which John Awood is master, entered the same day of May.

From Richard Daniel, native, for 6 tons beer and 600 lb of lead, 5 barrels of pitch and tar, and one load of utensils, 2 chests of apparel, 2 baskets of groceries, from London per cocket dated 30th April.

In the *John* of Meaching [Newhaven], burden 14 tons, of which Richard Tomsett is master, entered 21st day of May.

From Robert Farley of Rye, native, for 12 hogsheads of copperas, 3 tons of ordinary cast iron, 20 flitches of bacon, 4 barrels of peas. And for Saunder Courtupp, native, 10 hogsheads copperas, 19 bags of woad, from Meaching to Rye per cocket dated 14th May.

In the *Christopher* of Folkestone, burden 16 tons, of which John Tillereman is master, went out 24th day of May.

From John Wells of Dover, native, for 9,000 barrel boards to Dover.

In the *Samuel* of Meaching, burden 20 tons, of which Simon Nicolles is master, went out the same day.

From John Webb of London, native, 18 ton fairre[1] and 2,000 billets to London.

In the *Mary Catherine* of Colchester, burden 40 tons, of which Howard Johns is master, entered the same day.

From the same master, native, for 25 chaldrons coal from Newcastle to Rye per cocket bearing date at Newcastle aforesaid 20th April.

In the *Jesus* of Rye, burden 18 tons, of which John Tiler is master, entered the same day.

From Guy Harrison, native, for 4 pieces fairre containing 2,000 lb, 9 baskets and 10 chests of groceries, 3 loads of utensils, 8 barrels of soap, 2 anchors containing 5 cwt, 30 iron beds, 6 hogsheads vinegar, 2 barrels tar, 6 bolts of poldaves,[2] from London to Rye by cocket dated 6th May.

In the *Jesus* of Rye, burden 30 tons, of which Mark Sariant is master, entered 27th of May.

From Robert Weeks, native, for 3 millstones, 4 baskets and 3 trusses of groceries and haberdashery wares, one tierce of aquavita, 3 pieces of raisins, 10 firkins of soap, one hogshead vinegar, 6 wainscotts, 4 bedposts, one tun wine from London to Rye by cocket bearing date at London aforesaid the 18th day of May.

In the *Jesus* aforesaid, Mark Sariant master, entered the same day.

From John Mercer of Rye, native, for 100 quarters siliginis Aug[usti] called rye from London to Rye by cocket bearing date at London aforesaid the 21st day of May.

In the *Nicholas* of Rye, burden 20 tons, of which John Emmery is master, entered the same day.

From Robert Farley, native, for 4 tuns ship beer, 4 tons fern ashes, one butt sack, 2 doz. picks, 18 oars from London to Rye by cocket dated 18th day of May.

In the *Jesus* of Rye, burden 18 tons, of which John Tiler is master, went out the same day.

From Thomas Duffrett, native merchant, for 10 tons fairre towards London.

[1] Possibly from *fer*, iron.   [2] A coarse canvas.

24 Regulation of Local Corn Markets, 1576

(*Wiltshire County Records. Minutes of Proceedings in Sessions, 1563 and 1574 to 1592*, ed. H. C. Johnson (Wiltshire Archaeological and Natural History Society, Records, IV, 1949), p. 21)

Easter Sessions, 1576. Warminster It is ordered at this court that no foreigner or outdweller shall buy any corn in Warminster market or any other market within Wiltshire before 11 of the clock in the forenoon of the said market day. And that no farmer or any other sell[er] shall be suffered to lay in their corn into any man's house but shall sell their corn in the market or else bear it home again. And that the poorer sort of the town and country shall first be suffered to buy before badgers and other strangers. And that no badger shall house any corn in the town of Warminster or in any other market town in the market day until the country be served. And that the justices of peace within every division or the township of every market town do appoint 2 or more to view whether the premises be observed on the market day yea or no.

25 Municipal Regulation of the Candle Trade, 1587

(*Court Leet Records*, eds. F. J. C. and D. M. Hearnshaw (Southampton Record Society, Publications, I, Part II, 1905), p. 256)

Presentments Item, we present that Mr Barwycke, who as it is said was bound unto your worships for the serving of the inhabitants of this town with candles at 2*d* the lb., having all the tallow of the victuallers to this town at a price reasonable to his good liking and great commodity many years, restraining all others from having any part thereof by virtue of his grant from your worships as aforesaid, a scarcity of tallow now happening for one year, does presently refuse to serve the inhabitants at any reasonable price, and the best cheap that is to be had is 3*d*, and many times 4*d* the lb.; a happy man that can make his bargain so well to take it when there is profit and to leave or refuse to serve when the profit fails, and to raise it at his own will for his best advantage, and to tie all men and himself to be at liberty; the artificers and the poorer sort of people are most of all pinched, wherewith they, with the rest, find themselves aggrieved, and so desire your worships thoroughly to consider thereof.

26 Prohibition of Fairs in Time of Plague, 1603

(*Stuart Royal Proclamations*, I, *Royal Proclamations of King James I, 1603–1625*, eds. J. F. Larkin and P. L. Hughes (Oxford, 1973), pp. 46–7)

The spreading of the infection in our city of London, and in the places next about it, does give us just cause to be as provident as a careful prince can be, to take away all occasion of increasing the same . . . And forasmuch as there are at hand two notable fairs, unto which there is usually extraordinary resort out of all parts of the kingdom, one in

Smithfield near our city of London, commonly called Bartholomew fair, and the other near Cambridge commonly called Stourbridge fair, which if they should be held at the usual times, would in all likelihood be the occasion both of the increase, and of dispersing of the contagion into all the parts of our realm: We have thought good . . . to enjoin to the lords of the said fairs, and others interested therein, and of all other fairs within fifty miles of our city of London, that they shall not hold the said fairs, nor anything appertaining to them, at the times accustomed, nor any time till they shall be licensed by us, upon pain of such punishment, as for a contempt so much concerning the universal safety of our people, they shall be adjudged to deserve . . . And we do further charge and enjoin under like penalty, to all citizens and inhabitants of our city of London, that none of them shall repair to any fairs held within any part of this realm, until it shall please God to cease the infection now reigning amongst them.

27 Impediments to Navigation of the Tyne, 1613

(*Acts of the Privy Council of England, 1613–14* (1921), pp. 142–4)

20 July. A letter to the mayor of the town of Newcastle

Complaint has been made unto us by the Master, Wardens and Assistants of the Trinity House, that the river of Tyne is of late much impaired, and daily does decay more and more, by reason of divers disorders and abuses suffered and done there to the utter ruin and decay of the said river, if some timely course be not taken for the prevention thereof. Amongst which they first complain that there are one hundred and twenty salt pans upon that river, the ashes and cinders whereof, and other things proceeding from them, are suffered to fall into the same. Secondly, that the wharfs for ballast are not sufficiently built, but left open at the ends, whereby the ballast falls into the river; besides also that in some places the ballast is cast on shore without any wharf at all. Thirdly, that quarries for grindstones are digged so near the river side, as the rubbish and earth does and is suffered to fall and wash into the river. Lastly, that the ballast taken out of ships that lade at the Shields into keels or lighters, to be carried to shore, is by the keel-men cast into the river. By all which means the river is so decayed, as it will in a short time be no way fit for navigation.

And although we did expect to have found better care in you, the mayor, that pretend to be conservator of that river, and are trusted with the execution of such laws and orders as are ordained for the maintenance thereof, if not out of public consideration, yet in respect of the benefit of that town, and the ample trade that is drawn thither by the commodity of that river, than to suffer so famous a river, so fit for navigation, to be stopped up and choked through such gross negligence as is not to be excused, and whereof we purpose to take further notice: yet forasmuch as it is grown to this extremity of inconvenience, as it needs the direction of this board to amend and repair the same: we have therefore thought meet hereby to will and require you to take notice of this complaint, and to put in due execution, without favour or connivancy, all such ordinances and laws as are made for the conservancy of that river of Tyne, and likewise to order some present course to remedy the falling in of such cinders, ballast, and rubbish, as by the means aforesaid do wash into that river . . .

And whereas it is not only thought expedient to give a remedy to these abuses, which have so far prevailed to the prejudice of trade and navigation there, but also to consider of some means for the amendment of such shelves and shallows that are grown in that channel, and to bring the river to that depth and state as it was heretofore, we do also in like manner require you to send some fit persons of that town up hither by the beginning of the next term, to confer with the masters of the Trinity House concerning the amendment of that which is already past and has impaired the river, and brought it to that state as now it is, and in the mean time that you certify us of your proceedings touching this reformation now required.

28 The Carts of London, 1618

(*Calendar of State Papers, Venetian*, XV, 1617–19 (1909), p. 247)

Report of Horatio Busino, chaplain to the Venetian ambassador

To return to the carts of London, there is such a multitude of them, large and small, that is to say on two wheels and on four, that it would be impossible to estimate them correctly. Those which circulate in the city are for the most part on two broad and high wheels like those of Rome, and serve for the conveyance of sundry articles such as beer, coal, wood etc.; but among them are some very filthy ones, employed solely for cleansing the streets and carrying manure, and it is precisely the drivers of these who are usually the most insolent fellows in the world. The other four-wheeled waggons come up from the country bringing goods and passengers higgledy-piggledy, precisely like Marghera boats, and they are drawn by seven or eight horses in file, one behind the other, with plumes and bells, embroidered cloth coverings, and their stamping in the centre of the deep rut renders travelling on narrow roads in the country so inconvenient that it is impossible to get on with a coach and four. So we, who lately took a distant journey, broke the carriage and harassed the mares cruelly, although they were very fresh and spirited.

29 The York Merchants and their Grievances, 1623

(P.R.O. State Papers Domestic, James I, CXXXVIII, printed in *Chapters in the History of Yorkshire*, ed. J. J. Cartwright (Wakefield, 1872), pp. 285–9)

The Mayor, &c., of York to the Privy Council

To the right honourable the lords of his majesty's most honourable Privy Council.

The humble petition of the mayor and citizens of the city of York as well for themselves as for others of that country praying relief against the grievances and wrongs done unto them by the mayor and burgesses of the town of Kingston-upon-Hull.

First, divers of that corporation calling themselves contractors and combining together have, for their own private lucre and gain, bought and ingrossed all the corn brought in by strangers, as namely, this last year thirty thousand quarters, and have sold the same to country chapmen at 3, 4, and 5s profit in a quarter, not suffering the merchants of York to buy any part thereof, contrary to a branch of certain articles mutually agreed upon under the seals of both the said corporations, and made by the mediation of the right honourable Henry, late Earl of Huntingdon, Lord President of the North in June 1578, 20 Eliz. R. By which it was agreed that the mayor and citizens of York might buy in Hull of all foreigners and strangers the moiety or under of all commodities brought thither to be sold within the space of ten days after the ship entered, and after ten days to buy all or part as the buyer and seller could agree, cloth and lead only excepted.

Secondly, it has been practised of late years by them of Hull (by way of forestalling the market) that when they hear tell of any corn brought in by strangers and coming up Humber, they send down pilots to meet the ships ten or twelve miles off, with commission to buy their corn, and the master or factor upon such invitation coming to Hull before the ship, they do usually bargain for the corn before the ship be entered. By which means the merchants of York are prevented in their said privilege, of buying; the strangers' price is advanced, and the country injured and damnified.

Thirdly, the merchants of York having within 13 months last past shipped out 50000 kerseys and above, and for the same bringing in great quantities of corn to their port of Hull, the late mayor Joshua Hall and divers others of that corporation (to enforce them to sell the said corn unto them, that they might vent it again for their own profit at higher prices into the country) have not permitted the said merchants of York to sell the said corn to the country chapmen of Yorkshire and Lincolnshire, who attended the market there to transport the same by the rivers of Trent, Aire, Don, and other rivers into divers parts of those countries; but have against the law made seizures of such corn as they sold to the said country chapmen as forfeited for foreign bought and sold, and have threatened the country chapmen with seizures and suit, contrary to the ancient privilege and right of the said merchants of York, who have used time out of mind to sell great quantities of their corn so imported to the country chapmen attending their markets there, as by the certificates of several towns and of the justices of the peace of county of York, may appear; to the great hindrance of the vent of the cloth of that country, and the encouraging of strangers to bring in greater quantities of corn, who for the same export the monies out of the realm; to the utter decay of navigation in those parts.

Fourthly, when they have bought divers ships lading of corn as aforesaid, they by practice and combination and for their own private lucre and gain (setting their servants aboard the ships) set a certain rate and price upon the said corn, with caution that no man sell under that stinted rate, nor any to sell any corn upon the shore till those ships' loadings should be sold. And so they force the merchants of York (having such privilege of buying a moiety of corn and other goods as aforesaid) to buy corn off them to furnish the city of York and the country thereabouts; by reason whereof the country is enforced to pay dearer for their corn, than otherwise they should have done.

Fifthly, whereas by a schedule annexed to the articles aforesaid the merchants of York are to pay certain rates to them of Hull for taking up, weighing, houseroom, and striking of their lead at Hull, when there is occasion so to take up the same, &c. And whereas their lead being weighed at Bawtry and York, and carried down in their keels and boats (the customers being agreed withal) is for expedition and to save their markets hoisted out of the keels and boats into the ships. Those of Hull by colour of the said articles, but in truth to hinder their voyages and to lay a charge upon their lead, to the end they of Hull may undersell them at the markets, do enforce them to take up and weigh their said lead with them, and to pay the said rates. And (for not doing the same in the case aforesaid) the mayor of Hull about three years since seized divers pigs of lead of the said merchants of York to the number of 20 or 30 which they detain or keep from them till this day.

Sixthly. Some of their aldermen by consent or connivance of the mayor have for these ten years last past bought and ingrossed all the herrings that came into the port, sometimes five or six ships loading at once, and would not permit any merchant or fishmonger of York to have any part of the said herrings unless they would buy of them. And further have and do condition with the ships, that what they buy not, shall be carried away out of the port, that no man else may buy any there, or that otherwise they will buy none at all themselves, and so the shippers lose some part of their market. By reason whereof the prices of herrings have been enhanced from 15s a barrel to 27s to the great prejudice of the country, especially the poorer sort of people.

Seventhly, when the ships laden with Newcastle coals come to Hull to serve the country, those of Hull will not permit either the merchants or mariners of York to buy any coals out of the said ships until such time as they have bought for themselves and the parts of the country thereabouts, as many of the said coals as they think good, to the great prejudice of the said merchants and mariners whose keels lie there at great charge, and sometimes lose their spring tides for their voyage to York, and to the great damage and disappointing of the city and country about York.

30 Licensing of Badgers in Somerset, 1630

(*Quarter Sessions Records for the County of Somerset, II, Charles I, 1625–1639*, ed. E. H. Bates Harbin (Somerset Record Society, XXIV, 1908), pp. 118–19)

General Sessions, Wells, 7 January 1630. Licenses granted

To Edith Doddington of Hilbishopps, widow, to be a badger of butter and cheese and to carry the same into the counties of Wilts, Hampshire, Dorset and Devon, and to return again laden with corn, and to sell it again in any fair or market within this county during one whole year now next ensuing; and she is not to travel with above three horses, mares or geldings at the most part; for performance whereof Mr Symes is to take her recognizance, granted by John Horner, John Symes, John Harington.

To Thomas Rawlings of Lympsham to buy corn in the counties of Wilts and Somerset to sell the same again in the city of Bristol, Mr Harington to take the recognizance. Ro. Phelipps, Pa. Godwyn.

To Anthony Banbury of Pitney to buy barley and oats, and the same to convert into malt, and to sell again in any fair, and to travel not with above two horses, geldings or mares at the most. Ro. Phelipps, He. Berkley, Pa. Godwyn, John Harington.

* * *

This court taking notice of the great prices of corn and butter and cheese and all other commodities, it was ordered that from henceforth no badger whatsoever be licensed but in open sessions and shall first enter into recognizance . . . And also that all maltsters do the like before any justice do sign and seal his licence.

31 Difficulties and Drawbacks of Road Transport, 1633

(*Worcestershire County Records. Division I, Documents relating to Quarter Sessions. Calendar of the Quarter Sessions Papers, I, 1591–1643*, ed. J. W. Willis Bund (Worcester, 1900), p. 528)

Grievances exhibited to his majesty's justices of the peace by William Smith, Parson of Alvechurch, 1633

The parish of Alvechurch has many roadways and thoroughfares for travellers both on horseback and for carriages, by wains and carts, and other common highways to divers market towns through sundry parts of the said parish, but all generally so ill and negligently repaired that divers enormities redound therefrom not only to many of the parishioners themselves but also to many others travelling by those ways. In particular myself in this harvest time riding about my lawful and necessary occasion of tithes have been twice fast set in the mire in common roads and market ways not without danger. By occasion of these ill repaired highways I am forced to sell much of my tithes far under value. Much of this ill repair is caused by some who staunch up water in ditches and turning them out of their course to water and overflow the adjoining ground and some of the roads formerly used for passage on horseback and loaded wagons and cattle cannot be used for passage on horseback without danger [of] getting fast and miring.

32 Enterprise in River Improvement, 1636

(Patent 12 Charles I, p. 21, n. 2, printed in T. Rymer, *Foedera, Conventiones, Literae*, 3rd ed., IX (The Hague, 1744), Part II, p. 6)

De commissione speciali Edwardo Vicecomiti Campden & aliis

Charles, by the grace of God, &c.

To our right trusty and right well beloved cousin, Edward Lord Viscount Campden, and to our trusty and well beloved, Thomas Lord Windsor, William Lord Spencer, Robert Lord Brooke, William Lord Craven, and to our trusty and well beloved, Thomas Coventry esquire, Robert Barkeley knight, one of our justices of our Court of King's Bench, John Bridgeman knight, our Chief Justice of Chester, Richard Tracy knight and baronet, Thomas Puckering knight and baronet, Walter Devereux knight and baronet, William Russell baronet, Edward Littleton baronet, Sir Thomas Lucy knight, Sir James Pitt knight, Sir John Rous knight, Sir Robert Lee knight, Sir Edward Peyto knight, Sir Edward Underhill knight, Sir Robert Tracy knight, Sir Robert Cooke knight, William Smith doctor of divinity, Rowley Ward sergeant at law, William Curteen esquire, Walter Overbury esquire, William Sheldon of Beely esquire, Richard Creswell esquire, Humfrey Salway esquire, William Barkley esquire, and John Keyt esquire, greeting.

Whereas our well beloved and faithful subject William Sandys of Flatbury in the county of Worcester esquire, has undertaken at his own charge to make the river of Avon and some other streams falling into the same, passable for boats, barges, trows and other vessels of reasonable burden, from Severn, where that river falls in near Tewkesbury, as it runs through our counties of Warwick, Worcester and Gloucester, by the several boroughs and market towns of Warwick, Stratford, Bedford, Evesham, Pershore and Tewkesbury, unto or near our city of Coventry, and for the effecting thereof, has already been at great charge, as well in purchasing and buying in estates, of most of the mills standing upon that stream, as otherwise for the bringing of that work to perfection, and that he, the said William Sandys, intends likewise at his own costs, to make passable for boats, barges, trows and other vessels of reasonable burden, a good part of the river of Teme, lying on the west side of Severn towards our town and castle of Ludlow in our said county of Worcester, whereby our counties aforesaid may from those parts be better supplied with wood, iron, pit coal and other commodities which they now want, and that this work shall be effected without the detriment or prejudice of any person or persons, in his or their lands, mills, trees, bridges or other things, more than what shall be recompensed and paid for, according to the true value thereof; our intentions being that the said William Sandys in recompense of his great charge and hazard in a work of this nature, shall have the benefit of the water carriages, as in such cases is usual.

Know you that we, being willing to advance works of this kind, and well approving the enterprise and endeavours of the said William Sandys in these his undertakings, tending so much to the public good of those counties, in opening a passage by water in an inland country, whereby the common trade and commerce of our subjects in those parts of our kingdom, which now by reason of the length and foulness of the ways, is (as we are informed) much interrupted and hindered, will be greatly furthered and enlarged; and being minded to give the said William Sandys all possible encouragement in his proceedings, in so commendable a work, have, with the advice of our Privy Council, assigned, made and constituted you to be our commissioners, and do hereby give unto you, or any four or more of you, full power and authority to take view of and survey the said river of Avon, and the streams falling thereunto, and the said river of Teme so intended by the said William Sandys to be made passable as aforesaid, as well in the channel and streams, as in the banks thereof, and of the impediments, wants and defects thereof and therein, whereby the same are now unfit for the carriage and passage of boats, barges and other vessels of burden, for the transporting and conveying of corn, victual, wood, iron, coal and other commodities, and to consider how the said wants, impediments and defects may be removed, remedied and supplied, and a passage opened through the said rivers and streams for boats and other vessels of indifferent burden, as well by cleansing, scouring or enlarging the same, in the shallow places and banks thereof, as by heightening, widening or enlarging of bridges, or making of locks sluices, wharfs or new cuts, upon or through the land and soil of any person or persons, adjoining to the said rivers and streams, through which it is necessary the same should pass, or be made for the more convenience and commodiousness of the passage of boats and other vessels . . .

33 Establishment of General Post Office, 1657

(*Acts and Ordinances of the Interregnum, 1642–1660*, eds. C. H. Firth and R. S. Rait (1911), II, pp. 1110–11)

Whereas it has been found by experience that the erecting and settling of one General Post Office, for the speedy conveying, carrying and re-carrying of letters by post, to and from all places within England, Scotland and Ireland, and into several parts beyond the seas, has been, and is the best means, not only to maintain a certain and constant intercourse of trade and commerce betwixt all the said places, to the great benefit of the people of these nations, but also to convey the public dispatches, and to discover and prevent many dangerous and wicked designs, which have been and are daily contrived against the peace and welfare of this Commonwealth, the intelligence whereof cannot well be communicated but by letter of escript.

Be it enacted by his highness the Lord Protector and the Parliament . . . that from henceforth there be one General Office, to be called and known by the name of the Post Office of England. And one officer from time to time to be nominated . . . under the name and style of Post-master General of England, and Comptroller of the Post Office; which said officer, and his deputies by him thereunto sufficiently authorized, and no other, shall have the receiving, taking up, ordering, sending forward and delivering of all letters and packets which shall from time to time come and go to and from all parts and places of England, Scotland and Ireland, where he shall settle posts, and from all the said parts and places of England, Scotland and Ireland, unto any the parts and places beyond the seas, excepting such letters as shall be sent by common known carriers, and by them conveyed along with their carts, waggons, and pack-horses, and letters of advice of merchants, which shall be sent by masters of any ship, barque or other vessel of merchandize, or any of their company or passengers therein, immediately from any port town of England, Scotland and Ireland, by them to be conveyed along with such ship, barque or other vessel to any other port town within any of the same, or into the parts beyond the seas, or from the parts beyond the seas to any port town of England, Scotland and Ireland, or members thereof, and no further. And excepting a letter or more sent by a messenger on purpose for his or their own affairs, who is, or are, the sender or senders thereof, or by any friend to any place or places within the said nations of England, Scotland or Ireland . . .

34 The Finance of Road Repairs, 1692

(Warwick County Record Office, Quarter Sessions Records, QS40/1/6, ff. 256–7)

Michaelmas Sessions, 1692

Whereas it appears . . . unto this court, as well by a certificate under the hands of many of the inhabitants of the parish of Birmingham in this county as by other good evidence, that the street called Digbath Street in Birmingham aforesaid being a very great road is by reason of the daily passing and repassing of great numbers of waggons, carts and other carriages loaded with coals, ironwares and other ponderous goods become a hollow way and very much out of repair and dangerous to such as pass the same, which street cannot otherwise be sufficiently amended and repaired by means of the laws now in force without the help of the late act of parliament[1] . . . wherein the said inhabitants prayed the assistance of this court. It is therefore . . . ordered by this court by virtue of the said act of parliament that the constables of the parish of Birmingham aforesaid, and the surveyors of the highways there . . . shall forthwith upon public notice make one assessment upon all and every the inhabitants, owners and occupiers of lands, houses, tenements, and hereditaments and upon all estates usually rateable to the poor within the said parish . . . so as the said assessment does not exceed the rate of six pence in the pound of the yearly value of any lands . . . so assessed nor the rate of six pence for twenty pounds in personal estate. And it is further ordered that after such assessment made the constables of the parish . . . shall forthwith collect the several sums of money so assessed and upon receipt thereof from time to time pay over the same unto the surveyors of the highways of Birmingham aforesaid and to John Cotterell, Henry Porter, William Weeley and Joseph Carelesse . . . who are hereby directed and appointed to employ and lay out so much of the said money towards the amending and repairing the said hollow way in Digbath Street as shall be needful. And if there shall be any overplus of the said money remaining after . . . Digbath Street shall be sufficiently amended and repaired, that then the said surveyors and other persons aforesaid shall employ and lay out the same towards the amending and repairing the common high ways in Bull Street in the said town of Birmingham and at a certain place there called Parsonage Stile, which highways this court is fully satisfied to need also the help of the said act of Parliament . . . And in case any person or persons shall refuse to pay the sum or sums . . .

respectively assessed ... then the said constables ... are ... to levy the same by distress and sale of the goods of every person so assessed not paying the same within ten days after demand, rendering the overplus of the value of the goods so distrained to the owner and owners thereof ...

[1] 3 William and Mary, c. 12.

35 The Form of an Inland Bill of Exchange, 1697

(E. Hatton, *The Merchants's Magazine*, 4th ed. (1701), p. 238)

Norwich, June 1. 1697
At four days sight pay unto Mr Miles Moneylove, or his order, one hundred thirty two pounds, value received of Edmund Easie, and place it to account as per advice of

Your humble servant,
David Drawwell

To Mr Paul Punctual at
the Ship in Gracechurch
Street, London.

36 Houghton on Making Rivers Navigable, 1698

(John Houghton, *A Collection for the Improvement of Husbandry and Trade* (1727 ed.), II, pp. 284–7)

Friday, April 22. 1698 Num. CCC

At Ware in Hertfordshire have been 300,000 quarters of malt at one time. How many barges, and what they carry on that river. Some brought by land, and why: difference between land and water carriage. Objections against navigable rivers, and answers.

In my last I spoke about excise on barley, &c. now something on its carriages, which are very great by land in carts and waggons, even to the town of Ware in Hertfordshire, where, I have been assured, have been laid up at one time 300,000 quarters; and upon that little river of Lea, that comes from thence into the Thames. Below Blackwall are twenty six barges, twenty four whereof come from Ware; and, as I have been informed, bring twelve score quarters each about two and fifty times in a year; for although sometimes they cannot make a voyage in a week, at other times they do more; and all these amount to 299,520 quarters, beside what is brought by cart to serve the north side of London. For although there is a great disproportion between land and water carriages, yet considering those about Old Street and Shoreditch (for instance) may have it brought by water to the wharf much cheaper; yet the landing and carrying home by cars over the stones of London, and charges attending, besides the certainty of coming at set times (for in the river sometimes they want water, and sometimes have too much ice), for these reasons, I say, these north-side folk think it worth their while to have a great deal brought by land from so short a cut as Ware. But I hear of none that comes from Reading, Newbury, Abingdon or Oxford, or from the distant places in Kent, but by water; and I have been told, they will bring that for ten pence three hundred miles down the river Thames, which will cost three shillings to bring by cart from Hitchin, which is but thirty miles. Wherefore 'tis to be wished that we had more navigable rivers; and those were lengthened and improved that we have, which I hope I may live to see; because the parliament seems well disposed towards such things.

I know there are some objections against making rivers navigable; as 'twill decrease the use of horses, carts and men. But the like objection may be made against printing, and all sorts of engines, yea, against horses, ploughs, and carts; for they hinder the employment of men, supposing a certain quantity was to be carried. But this will make things so dear, that the people will be able to sell almost nothing, and they must live poor and meanly, eating up their own product; for others will out-sell them; and if by births they should increase, many would run away or be starved, because their product will not keep them, as 'tis in Hudson's-Bay and other places. When as by help of engines and other helps, as water-carriage, &c. they produce abundance, can sell all, and employ vast numbers more of people; and this do more and more, according to the easiness of the contrivances.

Another objection is, that 'twill bring up cheap corn, and spoil the price of what grows in the up-lands. Have not the going down stream the advantage of going up; and if they keep their corn dearer, than those they must pass by, must they not bring it home again, and eat it themselves? 'Twill make them produce thrice the quantity; and if they sell abroad three bushels for three shillings the bushel, they shall grow richer than if they sell one bushel for six shillings.

Yours,
John Houghton, F.R.S.

Friday, April 28 [sic]. 1698   Num. CCCI

More objections for making rivers navigable, and answers. The difference of land and water-carriage. Some proposals about rivers.

There are other objections against making rivers navigable, as that 'twill spoil the growing of willows by the river-side, the barge-men will steal the sheep and the poultry, and do a great many more such little things, which is a shame to name; but I know they were used against my Lord Bullinbrook, when he endeavoured to make the river navigable to Bedford.

Without doubt the bringing grocery and tobacco to these places cheap, will over-balance all these damages; and the like arguments may be brought against high-ways, for some inconveniences attend them; and I think these people deserve no better answer.

But the main objection is, that it will take away men's land at over small values, and damnify some other places that have the trade now.

Seeing it is for a public good, I cannot see why a very good recompense should not be given. But the land owners are also to consider that their land will be meliorated; for 'twill cause more building and popularity thereabout, and they may have the advantage of wharfs, fetching and carrying, beside dung, many other things; and who grows so rich as they that live nigh navigation? And if the pulling down of one town makes a better, where is the hurt? But perhaps it may put both to a greater industry, and that will be good for the whole. But supposing the contrary, if the greater good must not be done for fear of the lesser evil, farewell all new arts and fashions, and a law may be made to put a stop to all industry. I presume the parliament meet to consider what's best for England, not for any private place to the damage of the whole; if any such be, I wish some more public spirited gentlemen may next time be chosen in their room.

37 A Turnpike Act, 1722

(9 George I, c. 31, Gloucester City Library, Gloucestershire Collection, JF 9.22)

Whereas the highways or roads leading from the city of Gloucester, to the top of Birdlip-hill, (being the road to London) and from the foot of the said hill, to the top of Crickley-hill, being the road to Oxford, are become very ruinous and almost impassable, and are very dangerous to travellers; which roads cannot be effectually repaired by the ordinary course appointed by the laws and statutes of this realm, without some other provision made by parliament for the raising of money to be applied for that purpose.

For remedy whereof, and to the intent the said highways may with all convenient speed be effectually amended, and hereafter kept in good and sufficient repair.

May it please your majesty, that it may be enacted . . . that for the better surveying, ordering, enlarging, repairing and keeping in repair the said highways or roads leading from the said city of Gloucester to the top of Birdlip-hill, and from the foot of the said hill, to the top of Crickley-hill aforesaid; that it shall be in the power of the right honourable Thomas Lord Viscount Gage in the kingdom of Ireland; Sir John Guise, Sir Richard How, barts [and 43 others]; who are hereby nominated and appointed commissioners and trustees for putting this act in execution, and the survivors of them, or any five or more of them, or such person or persons as they or any five or more of them, shall authorize and appoint, to erect, or cause to be erected, a gate or gates, turnpike or turnpikes, in or cross any part or parts of the said highways or roads, and to receive and take for every coach, chariot, berlin, chaise or calash before they shall be permitted to pass through the same, one shilling; and for every waggon, cart or carriage, one shilling; and for every saddle-horse, mare or gelding, not drawing any coach, cart or carriage, one penny; and for every pack-horse, mare or gelding, ass or mule, one penny; and for every drove of oxen or neat cattle, eight pence per score, and so proportionably for any greater or lesser number exceeding four; and for every drove of hogs, two pence half penny per score, and so in proportion for any greater or lesser number exceeding four; and for every drove of sheep or lambs, two pence half penny per score, and so in proportion for any greater or lesser number exceeding four, in the name of or as a toll . . .

Provided always, that no person or persons having occasion to pass the place where the toll is taken, and return the same day before twelve of the clock at night, between the months of March and September, and before ten of the clock at night during the other months of the year, with the same coach, waggon, cart or other carriage, horse, mare or gelding, shall be compelled the same day to pay the said toll a second time; other than and except where a waggon or cart shall pass the said turnpike twice in one day, loaden with different goods or loading.

And further also, that all and every person and persons passing through the place appointed for the receiving the toll aforesaid, and coming from any parish or township wherein the said road lies, or any parish or township next adjoining to the said road respectively, shall have liberty to drive any cattle, and drive or ride any horse, mare or gelding to water or pasture, and to carry through the place where the said toll is to be received and taken, in any cart or carriage, any quantities of stone, sand, lime or gravel, for the mending the said roads, or dung, mould or compost, of any nature or kind whatsoever, brick or

K

chalk, or any wood not going to any market, hay, and corn in the straw, ploughs, harrows, and other implements of husbandry, materials for building, and all other things whatsoever employed in husbandry, manuring and stocking of their several and respective lands, in the said several and respective parishes, or in building of any house or houses, or other buildings therein. And that it shall and may be lawful also, for all and every soldier and soldiers upon their march, and all carts and waggons attending them, and also all carts and waggons travelling with vagrants sent by passes, and also any carrier or his servant, in respect of any horse, mare or gelding they shall ride on in driving any waggon or cart, to pass through the said places where the said toll is to be collected, without paying anything for their passing; anything in this act contained to the contrary thereof in any wise notwithstanding.

38 Defoe's Account, of the Corn Trade, 1726

(Daniel Defoe, *The Complete English Tradesman* (1841 ed.), II, pp. 177–82)

As the corn trade is of such consequence to us, for the shipping off the overplus, so it is a very considerable business in itself; the principal people concerned in it, as a trade, are, though very numerous, yet but of four denominations;—

1. Cornfactors;	3. Maltsters;
2. Mealmen;	4. Carriers.

1. Cornfactors; these, as corn is now become a considerable article of trade, as well foreign as inland, are now exceeding numerous; and though we had them at first only in London, yet now they are also in all the great corn markets and ports where corn is exported through the whole island of Britain; and in all those ports they generally correspond with the corn factors in England.

Those in the country ride about among the farmers, and buy the corn even in the barn before it is threshed; nay, sometimes they buy it in the field standing, not only before it is reaped, but before it is ripe. This subtle business is very profitable; for, by this means, cunningly taking advantage of the farmers, by letting them have money beforehand, which they, poor men, often want, they buy cheap when there is a prospect of corn being dear; yet sometimes they are mistaken too, and are caught in their own snare; but indeed, that is but seldom; and were they famed for their honesty, as much as they generally are for their understanding in business, they might boast of having a very shining character.

2. Mealmen; these generally live either in London or within thirty miles of it, that employment chiefly relating to the markets of London; they formerly were the general buyers of corn, that is to say, wheat and rye, in all the great markets about London, or within thirty or forty miles of London, which corn they used to bring to the nearest mills they could find to the market, and there have it ground, and then sell the meal to the shopkeepers, called mealmen, in London.

But a few years past have given a new turn to this trade, for now the bakers in London, and the parts adjacent, go to the markets themselves, and have cut out the shopkeeping mealmen; so the bakers are the mealmen, and sell the fine flour to private families, as the mealmen used to do. And as the bakers have cut out the meal shops in London, so the millers have cut out the mealmen in the country; and whereas they formerly only ground the corn for the mealmen, they now scorn that trade, buy the corn, and grind it for themselves; so the baker goes to the miller for his meal, and the miller goes to the market for the corn.

It is true, this is an anticipation in trade, and is against a stated wholesome rule of commerce, that trade ought to pass through as many hands as it can; and that the circulation of trade, like that of the blood, is the life of the commerce. But I am not directing to what should be, but telling what is; it is certain the mealmen are, in a manner, cut out of the trade, both in London and in the country, except it be those country mealmen who send meal to London by barges, from all the countries bordering on the Thames, or on any navigable river running into the Thames west; and some about Chichester, Arundel, and the coast of Sussex and Hampshire, who send meal by sea; and these are a kind of meal merchants, and have factors at London to sell it for them —either at Queenhithe, the great meal-market of England, or at other smaller markets.

By this change of the trade, the millers, especially in that part of England which is near the Thames, who in former times were esteemed people of a very mean employment, are now become men of vast business; and it is not an uncommon thing to have mills upon some of the large rivers near the town, which are let for three or four hundred pounds a year rent.

3. Maltsters; these are now no longer farmers, and, as might be said, working labouring people, as was formerly the case, when the public expense of beer and ale, and the number of alehouses, was not so great, but generally the most considerable farmers malted their own barley, especially in the towns and counties, from whence they supplied London, and almost every farmhouse of note.

As the demand for malt increased, those farmers found it for their purpose to make more and larger quantities of malt, than the barley they themselves sowed would supply; and so bought the barley at the smaller farms about them; till at length the market for malt still increasing, and the profits like-wise encouraging, they sought far and near for barley; and at this time the malting trade at Ware, Hertford, Royston, Hitchin, and other towns on that side of Hertfordshire, fetch their barley twenty, thirty, or forty miles; and all the barley they can get out of the counties of Essex, Cambridge, Bedford, Huntingdon, and even as far as Suffolk, is little enough to supply them; and the like it is at all the malt-making towns upon the river of Thames, where the malt trade is carried on for supply of London, such as Kingston, Chertsey, Windsor, High Wycombe, Reading, Wallingford, Abingdon, Thame, Oxford, and all the towns adjacent; and at Abingdon in particular, they have a barley market, where you see every market-day four or five hundred carts and wagons of barley to be sold at a time, standing in rows in the market-place, besides the vast quantity carried directly to the maltsters' houses.

The malt trade thus increasing, it soon came out of the hands of the farmers; for either the farmers found so much business, and to so much advantage, in the malting-trade, that they left off ploughing, and put off their farms, sticking wholly to the malt; or other men, encouraged by the apparent advantage of the malting-trade, set it up by itself, and bought their barley, as is said above, of the farmers, when their malt trade first increased; or both these together, which is most probable; and thus malting became a trade by itself.

Again, though the farmers then generally left off malting in the manner as above, yet they did not wholly throw themselves out of the profit of the trade, but hired the making of their own malt; that is, to put out their barley to the malthouses to be made on their account; and this occasioned many men to erect malthouses, chiefly to make malt only for other people, at so much per quarter, as they could agree; and at intervals, if they wanted full employ, then they made it for themselves; of these I shall say more presently.

Under the head of corn factors, I might have taken notice, that there are many of those factors who sell no other grain than malt; and are, as we may say, agents for the maltsters who stay in the country, and only send up their goods; and assistants to those maltsters who come up themselves.

The mentioning these factors again here, naturally brings me to observe a new way of buying and selling of corn, as well as malt, which is introduced by these factors; a practice greatly increased of late, though it is an unlawful way of dealing, and many ways prejudicial to the markets; and this is buying of corn by samples only. The case is thus:—

The farmer, who has perhaps twenty load of wheat in his barn, rubs out only a few handfuls of it with his hand, and puts it into a little money-bag; and with this sample, as it is called, in his pocket, away he goes to market.

When he comes thither, he stands with his little bag in his hand, at a particular place where such business is done, and thither the factors or buyers come also; the factor looks on the sample, asks his price, bids, and then buys; and that not a sack or a load, but the whole quantity; and away they go together to the next inn, to adjust the bargain, the manner of delivery, the payment, etc. Thus the whole barn, or stack, or mow of corn, is sold at once; and not only so, but it is odds but the factor deals with him ever after, by coming to his house; and so the farmer troubles the market no more.

This kind of trade is chiefly carried on in those market-towns which are at a small distance from London, or at least from the river Thames; such as Romford, Dartford, Grays, Rochester, Maidstone, Chelmsford, Malden, Colchester, Ipswich, and so down on both sides the river to the North Foreland, and particularly at Margate and Whitstable, on one side; and to the coast of Suffolk, and along the coast both ways beyond, and likewise up the river. Also,

At these markets you may see, that, besides the market-house, where a small quantity of corn perhaps is seen, the place mentioned above, where the farmers and factors meet, is like a little exchange, where all the rest of the business is transacted, and where a hundred times the quantity of corn is bought and sold, as appears in sacks in the market-house; it is thus, in particular, at Grays, and at Dartford: and though on a market-day there are very few wagons with corn to be seen in the market, yet the street or market-place, nay, the towns and inns, are thronged with farmers and samples on one hand, and with mealmen, London bakers, millers, and cornfactors, and other buyers, on the other. The rest of the week you see the wagons and carts continually coming all night and all day, laden with corn of all sorts, to be delivered on board the hoys, where the hoymen stand ready to receive it, and generally to pay for it also: and thus a prodigious corn trade is managed in the market, and little or nothing to be seen of it.

39 A Stage Coach Service, 1731

(Printed in H. W. Dickinson, *Mathew Boulton* (Cambridge, 1936), p. 18)

Advertisement for the first regular stage coach service between Birmingham and London

Birmingham Stage Coach. In two days and a half; begins May the 24th 1731.

Sets out from the Swan Inn in Birmingham every Monday at six a clock in the morning, through Warwick, Banbury and Aylesbury, to the Red Lion Inn in Aldersgate Street, London, every Wednesday morning. And returns from the Red Lion Inn every Thursday morning at five a clock the same way to the Swan Inn in Birmingham every Saturday, at 21 shillings each passenger, and 18 shillings from Warwick, who has liberty to carry 14 pounds in weight and all above to pay one penny a pound.

Performed (if God permit) by Nicolas Rothwell.

40 State of a London Road, 1737

(Robert Phillips, *A Dissertation concerning the Present State of the High Roads of England, especially of those near London* (1737), pp. 44–6)

I shall conclude these considerations with an account of Tyburn Road. It appears by the new foundation dug out for a new street on the north side, and several on the south side, that the soil is the same as the Park, Grosvenor Street and Square, and that the clay or loam in most places was not above four feet deep before they came to a gravel. And had this been considered at first, by digging off the clay they might have saved a great many thousand pounds, and might have had, for a great many years past, a good road instead of a very bad one. This is well known by travellers; for in the summer, though the road be level and smooth, yet they are suffocated and smothered with dust; and towards the winter, between wet and dry, there are deep ruts full of water, with hard dry ridges, which make it difficult for passengers to cross by one another without overturning; and in the winter they are all mud, which rises, spews, and squeezes into the ditches; so that the ditches and roads are full of mud and dirt all alike, and all of a level. And in the spring they dig out what is in the ditches, and fling it into the middle of the road, covering over the high hard ridges, and deep wet ruts; and what with the fresh gravel laid on, and mixed with it, the road then becomes more difficult, troublesome and dangerous than any part of the year, so that it may be said, there is not one part of the year that is pleasant to travel in such roads.

41 Easing of Town Regulations in Time of Dearth, 1756

(*Records of the Borough of Leicester, V, Hall Books and Papers, 1689–1835*, ed. G. A. Chinnery (Leicester, 1965), p. 186)

23 December

In order to prevent the ill consequences of any unlawful combinations amongst the bakers within this borough, and that the town may be supplied with bread in this time of scarcity and dearness of corn, it is ordered that such of the country bakers as Mr Mayor and the justices shall think fit may have the liberty of bringing their bread and selling the same within this borough without being molested until the first day of May next, provided they keep the assize in weight and goodness, and observe all other regulations relating thereto according to the laws and statutes of this realm in such case made and provided.

5

Foreign Trade and Enterprise
1000–1485

Overseas trade had but a slight role in English economic life in the early Middle Ages but there was commerce between England and the Continent even before the Conquest (*2*). The principal commodity of English trade at that time was wool, upon which the Flemish cloth manufacturers depended heavily (*5*). Trade was carried on in ships usually chartered by several merchants and carrying mixed cargoes (*6*). Trade with north-western Europe probably increased after 1066 and the import of wine from Gascony and Anjou was important throughout the period (*6, 10*). The flow of specie from the country was a problem to which medieval government addressed itself (*8*). After 1350 new areas of commerce were opened up to the benefit of certain ports. Direct trade with the Mediterranean led to the rise of Southampton (*11*) and increased Atlantic coastal trade favoured the prosperity of Bristol, which had for long traded with Ireland (*15*). In the fifteenth century ships sailed from east coast ports such as Scarborough to the Icelandic fishing grounds (*12*). Such expansion was probably based on advances in nautical technology and a growth of native shipping, the importance of which was recognised in 1381 (*10*). Trade was also expedited by better credit facilities (*16*).

Early medieval overseas trade was largely in the hands of foreign merchants. They traded in London before the Conquest (*1*) and Scandinavian traders were in commerce with English ports as late as the mid-twelfth century (*3*). Foreigners were encouraged to do so by grants of privileges (*4*). In 1303 they were freed from exorbitant taxes in return for certain tolls (*7*). In the later Middle Ages the rising native merchant class resented the privileges of the aliens, particularly those enjoyed by members of the Hanseatic League (*13*), and the activity of foreigners was increasingly regulated (*14*). The establishment of staple towns in order to control the export of wool and to ensure that customs revenue was not lost by the Crown, encouraged native trade (*9*). By the fifteenth century native merchants were becoming important in the cloth trade, which itself was of rising significance (*3, 17*).

1485–1760

Between 1485 and 1760 English overseas trade grew impressively if irregularly. For much of the sixteenth century it was focussed on the Low Countries, until the 1550s predominantly on a London-Antwerp axis. The involvement of foreigners, still striking at the beginning of the century, had declined considerably by its end, partly owing to official discrimination (*18*). The English Company of Merchant Adventurers had come to exercise a large measure of control over trade with the Low Countries, its members exchanging woollen cloth and some minerals for other manufactures, raw materials, and spices (*23*). Before 1550 direct trades with the rest of Europe, including the wine trade with France (*19*), remained small. From the mid-century though, inspired partly by difficulties in the Low Countries connection, occurred a remarkable if gradual widening of English commercial horizons. A series of voyages—of which the earlier Cabot voyages to Newfoundland were forerunners (*17*)—and new companies opened up trading relations with northern Europe and the eastern Mediterranean, West Africa, Asia and the Americas, although the volume of trade transacted, particularly outside Europe, was slow to grow. Hakluyt's collections chronicle these achievements, and the benefits hoped for from new plantations (*20*). Hazardous and costly long-distance ventures implied corporate organisation, with valuable rights (*29*).

The main rivals to English commercial enterprise in the early seventeenth century were the Dutch, in the Baltic (*25*) as elsewhere. Given the value contemporaries attached to foreign trade as a means to wealth and power (**8**, *25*), nationalist policies were soon to develop further, a landmark being the Navigation Act of 1660 (*26*). While it satisfied the tenets of mercantilist thinking and vested English interests, the planters of Virginia and Maryland were quick to see how it could harm them (*27*). After 1660, and again after 1740, trade growth was considerable. In the mid-eighteenth century, although the bulk of transactions was still with the Continent, a description of English trade shows how diverse and world-wide it had become (*34*). The plantation trades in sugar and tobacco, with their associated re-exports to the Continent and return trades to the Americas, had become a main dynamic of growth. The West African slave trade (*32*) was a vital prop to this system and Liverpool, its chief organising port, a place of much civic pride (*35*). Smuggling trades flourished alongside legal English commerce, notably in wool from England (*28*) and in tea and other high duty imports (*33*).

Foreign trade experienced fluctuations, like other parts of the

economy, in accord with the rhythm of agricultural production. Trade
depressions though could spring from official acts of policy or through
wartime disturbances (*30*), the pressing of merchant seamen into the
navy (*24*) at times seriously disrupting navigation. War, however,
offered alternative outlets for maritime enterprise, in the speculative
pursuit of privateering (*22, 36*).

1 The Port of London, 978–1016[1]

(*Toll of London, temp.* Ethelred, printed in H. I. Adelson, *Medieval
Commerce* (Princeton, 1962), pp. 158–9)

Aldgate and Cripplegate, those are the gates which the guards watch.

At Billingsgate, if a ship should come, one *obol*[2] should be given for
the toll; if it was large and had sails, a penny; if a long ship or a round
cargo vessel should come, and it should anchor there, four pennies
[should be paid] for the toll. From a ship full of timber one [piece] of
timber [should be paid] as the toll. During the week the toll [should be
collected on] three days, Sunday, Tuesday, and Thursday. Whoever
should come to the bridge with a boat wherein there are fish, that
merchant should give one *obol* as toll, and for a large ship, one penny.
The men of Rouen who come with wine and grampus should give the
correct [sum], six *solidi* for a large ship and a twentieth part of the
same grampus. The Flemings, and men of Ponthieu, and Normandy,
and France should show their goods and pay the toll. [The men of]
Huy, Liège, and Nivelles, who journey through the lands, should show
their goods and [pay] the toll. And the men of the [Holy Roman]
Emperor, who come in their ships, should be held worthy of good laws
just as we are; besides uncarded wool, let it be permissible for them to
purchase both weak ointment and three live pigs in their ships, and let
it not be permissible for them to commit any crime against the burghers
and to pay the toll. And on holy Christmas [let them give] two cloaks
of squirrel fur, and one hauberk, and ten pounds of pepper, and five
[pairs] of men's gloves, and two hogsheads filled with vinegar, and the
same on Easter. For a basket of chickens, one chicken [should be paid]
as toll, and for a basket of eggs, five eggs [should be paid] as toll, if they
come to market. The butterwomen, who sell cheese and butter [should
pay] one penny fourteen days before Christmas and another one seven
days before Christmas.

---

[1] N. S. B. Gras dates the document to 978–1016 or to the last third of the 11th
century: *Early English Customs System*, pp. 154–5.

[2] Probably a half-penny.

2 Aelfric's Merchant, c.1000

(*Aelfric's Colloquy*, printed in S. H. Gem, *An Anglo-Saxon. Aelfric of Eynsham* (Edinburgh, 1912), p. 189)

Master   What have you to say, Merchant?

Merchant   I maintain that I am useful to the king, and to the nobles, and to the wealthy, and to the whole people.

Master   How so?

Merchant   I go on board ship, with my merchandise. I sail to regions beyond the sea, and sell my goods, and buy valuable produce that is not made in this country, and I bring it you here. I face great dangers in crossing the ocean and sometimes I suffer shipwreck, with the loss of all my goods, hardly escaping with my life.

Master   What kinds of things do you bring us?

Merchant   Purple and silk, precious stones and gold, various sorts of clothing, pigments, wine and oil, ivory, copper, brass and tin, sulphur and glass, and the like.

Master   Are you willing to sell your things just as you bought them there?

Merchant   By no means. If I did so, what good would my labour be to me? I wish to sell dearer here, than I bought there, that I may gain some profit, to keep myself, and my wife and son.

3 Scandinavian Traders at East Coast Ports, 1155–75

(*Calendar of Charter Rolls, 1300–26*, p. 7)

Henry, king of the English, duke of the Normans and of the men of Aquitaine and count of the Angevins, to all Norsemen who come to the port of Grimsby or to other ports of Lincolnshire, greeting. I order you to pay my reeves of Lincoln all the rights and customs which you were wont to pay to the reeves of Lincoln in the time of King Henry, my grandfather.[1] And I forbid any one of you to withold his toll or any other custom unjustly, upon a forfeiture of ten pounds. Witness W. son of John, at Worcester.

[1] Henry I, 1100–1135.

4 The Liberties of the Merchants of Douai, 1250

(P.R.O. Charter Roll, 45 Henry III, m. 4, no. 32)

The king to archbishops . . . Know you that we have granted and by this our charter have confirmed for us and our heirs to our beloved burgesses and merchants of Douai that for ever throughout the whole of our land and power they have this liberty, to wit, that they or their goods, found in any place soever in our power, shall not be arrested for any debt for which they are not sureties or principal debtors, unless by chance such debtors be of their commune and power, having goods wherefrom they can make satisfaction for their debts in whole or in part, and unless the burgesses of Douai, by whom that town is governed, fail in justice to those who are of our land and power, and this can be reasonably ascertained; and that the said burgesses and merchants for ever be quit of murages on all their goods, possessions and merchandise throughout our whole realm; and that the burgesses and merchants aforesaid shall not lose their chattels and goods found in their hands or deposited elsewhere by their servants, so far as they can sufficiently prove them to be their own, for the trespass or forfeiture of their servants; and also if the said burgesses and merchants or any of them die within our land and power testate or intestate, we or our heirs will not cause their goods to be confiscated so that their heirs should not entirely have them, so far as the same be proved to be the chattels of the said deceased, provided that sufficient knowledge or proof be had touching the said heirs; and that they with their merchandise may safely come into our land and power and stay there, paying the due and right customs; so also that if at any time there be war between the king of the French or others and us or our heirs, they be forewarned to depart from our realm with their goods within forty days. Wherefore we will and straitly command, for us and our heirs, that the aforesaid burgesses and merchants and their heirs for ever have all the liberties aforewritten throughout the whole of our land and power. And we forbid, upon our forfeiture of 10*l*, that any man presume to molest or annoy them in aught unjustly contrary to this liberty and our grant. These witnesses:—the venerable father H., bishop of London, Richard de Clare, earl of Gloucester and Hertford, Humphrey de Bohun, earl of Hereford and Essex, Hugh le Bigod, Philip Basset, Hugh le Despenser, our justiciar of England, James de Audley, Roger de Mortimer, John Maunsell, treasurer of York, Robert Walerand, and others. Given by our hand at Westminster, 24 November in the 45th year of our reign.

The burgesses and merchants of Douai give the king 100 marks for this charter, which sum should be allowed in the 90*l* in which the king is bound to them, whereof there is the king's writ of *liberate* at the king's Exchequer; and the writ should be searched for and the 100 marks noted therein.

5 The Flanders Trade Affected by an International Dispute, 1273

(*Calendar of Patent Rolls, 1272–81*, pp. 13–14)

17 January 1273. Westminster

Licence, until Easter, for James de Vetula, Atynus Previdal, Bonachamus de Philippo, and Petrinus Decanus, merchants of Piacenza, to take 180 sacks of their own wool, which they have in the kingdom, which they bought for their own use of others than Flemings or Hainaulters, and which they can reasonably show to be their own, to any parts beyond seas, except such as are within the power of the countess of Flanders, the said merchants having made oath before the king's lieutenants in England that they will not take out of the kingdom wools or other goods into Flanders or elsewhither within the power of the countess of Flanders during the contention between the king and the said countess which recently arose between Henry III and herself, and that they will not sell such wool or other goods to Flemings or others of the power of the said countess, nor make exchange with them thereof, nor deal by art or craft so that the said wools or other goods may come into the hands of the subjects of the said countess, nor receive any money from the Flemings for trading with wools or other merchandise to the behoof of the said Flemings, nor avouch their goods nor those of any other subjects of the said countess, the king with his council having ordained that if they attempt anything against their said oath, he will take into his hands, as forfeited, their wools or other goods found in the kingdom.

The like for the following to export the following number of sacks:—
John Donedeu, merchant of Cahors, 30.
Robert of Arras, citizen and merchant of London, 20
Thomas de Micheldever, merchant of Winchester, 20.
Ellis Westman, merchant of Winchester, 20.
Nicholas of Merewell, merchant of Winchester, 20.
Copinus of Troyes, merchant of London, 20.
Bernard of Hampton and John le Long of Cardiff, merchants of Southampton, 200, by 10 pairs of letters.

William Bonenfaunt, merchants of St. Quentin, 20.

John of Newbury, citizen and merchant of Winchester, 20.

William Fressevede, merchant of London, 40.

Bertram Malewyn, merchant of Gascony, 20.

William Bonenfaunt, merchant of St. Omer, 20.

John de Bek, merchant of Gascony, 20.

Lambert Reyner and Bartholomew Jacobi, merchants of Florence.

John Lilyun of Malling, merchant of Brabant, 20.

Lambert of Malines, merchant of Brabant, 40 by 2 pairs, and afterwards he had 2 pairs for 40 sacks.

Thomas of Basing, citizen of London, 20.

Nicholas Teste and Peter de Wirhale, merchants of Lucca, for 20 sacks by one writ, and 20 sacks by another, and 20 sacks by a third writ.[1]

_____
[1] Similar entries for a large number of merchants follow.

6 The Export of Wool and Hides from Newcastle, 1296

(P.R.O. Exchequer K.R. Customs Accounts, E 122/105/3, printed in J. Conway Davies, _The Wool Customs Accounts for Newcastle upon Tyne for the reign of Edward I_ (Archaeologia Aeliana, Fourth Series, XXXII, 1954), pp. 281–3)

The Roll of Adam of York, clerk of the king's New Customs,[1] Newcastle upon Tyne, from 29 July 22 Edward I [1294] to 16 October 25 Edward I [1297] for wool, hides and wool-fells.

[The 24th Year 1295–1296]

The ship of Hugh, son of Henry of Middelburgh, which left the port of Newcastle, licensed, on 2 January, 24 Edward I [1296], with the goods of the merchants who follow:

John Dinard had in the same ship in two sarplers,[2] two sacks one stone of wool, whereupon the custom 4_l_ 18½_d_. Also he had in the same ship one last[3] six dickers[4] of hides, whereon the custom 4_l_ 6_s_ 8_d_.

Walter of Windsor had in the same one last of hides, whereon the custom 66_s_ 8_d_.

Hugh Gerardin had in the same one and a half lasts of hides, whereon the custom 100_s_.

Roger le Dounbeor and Adam of Durham had in the same one and a half dickers of hides, whereon the custom 5_s_. Increase and counterfeit money, nothing.

Of the same John, Walter, Hugh and Roger for tronage[5] and the Coket[6] 9d, whereof for tronage 1d.

Totals:		
Wool, 2 sacks 1 stone	4l	0s 18½d.
Hides, 3½ lasts 7½ dickers	12l	18s 4d.
Tronage and the Coket		9d.
Sum Total. 17l 0s 7½d.	Certified.	

The ship of Simon, son of Enoce of Middelburgh, called *Middelburgh*, which left . . . 13 February with the goods of the merchants, etc.:

Simon Roland, Henry le Pessoner and Lupus, his fellow, merchants of Brabant, had in the same ship in seventy sarplers, seventy and a half sacks eight stones of wool, by weight, whereof the customs 141l 12s 4d. Peter le Graper had in the same in seven sarplers, seven sacks of wool, by weight, whereon the custom 14l.

William Casse of Cortekin had in the same in one sarpler, one sack and one stone of wool, by weight, whereon the custom 41s 6½d. Of increase by weight 2s, by statute. Of the same Simon, Peter and William for tronage and the Coket 3s 8½d, whereof for tronage 3s 2½d.

Totals:		
Wool, 78½ sacks 9 stones	157l	13s 10½d.
Increase		2s 0d.
Tronage and the Coket		3s 8½d.
Sum Total. 157l 19s 7d.	Certified.	

The ship of Lambert, the son of William of West Chapel, which left . . . called *Northman*, 1 May with the goods, etc.:

Hermann Molle of Lübeck had in the same in twelve sarplers and two bags, twelve sacks one stone of wool, whereon the custom 26l 0s 18½d. The same had in the same four and a half lasts and five hides, whereon the customs 15l 0s 20d. Also he had in the same a hundred and fifty wool-fells, whereon . . . 20s.

Arnald Keseling of the same had in the same ship in fourteen sarplers and one bag, fourteen sacks and five stones of wool, whereon the custom 28l 7s 8½d.

Henry Lescot of Newcastle had in the same in two sarplers, two sacks three stones of wool, whereon the custom 4l 4s 7½d.

Corandin of Germany had in the same in one sarpler, one sack of wool, whereon the custom 40s.

And the same Hermann, Arnald, Henry and Corandin for tronage and the Coket 23d, whereof for tronage 15d.

Totals:		
Wool, 30 sacks 9 stones	60l	13s 9½d.
Hides, 4½ lasts 5 hides	15l	0s 20d.

Wool-fells, 150		20s 0d.
Tronage and the Coket		23d.
Sum Total. 76l 17s 4½d.	Certified.	

The ship of Robert of Orneham, called *The Blith of Yarmouth*, which left . . . 24 May with the goods . . .

Hugh Gerardin had in the same in one bag, twenty two stones of wool, whereon the custom 33s 10½d. And he had in the same five and a half lasts one dicker and three hides, whereon the custom 18l 10s.

James of Auangate of the Society of the Mozzi of Florence had in the same in twelve sarplers, twelve sacks of wool, whereon the custom 24l. Certified. Of the same for tronage and the Coket 10d, whereof for tronage 6d.

Totals: Wool, 12½ sacks 9 stones	25l 13s 10½d.	
Hides, 5½ lasts 1 dicker 3 hides	18l 11s 0d.	
Tronage and the Coket	10d.	
Sum Total 44l 5s 8½d.	Certified.	

The ship of Richard, son of Walter of Yarmouth, called *The Margerie*, which left . . . 24 May as above:

Hugh Gerardin had in the same five lasts four dickers 8 hides, whereon the custom 17l 9s 4d.

The said James of Auangate had in the same in sixteen sarplers, sixteen sacks of wool by weight, whereon the custom 32l. Of the same for tronage and the Coket 12d, whereof for tronage 8d.

Totals: Wool, 16 sacks	32l 0s 0d.	
Hides, 5 lasts 4 dickers 8 hides	17l 9s 4d.	
Tronage and the Coket	12d.	
Sum Total. 49l 10s 4d.	Certified.	

[1] Granted in 1275 on the export of wool, wool-fells and hides. The rates were increased between 1294 and 1297.
[2] Containers.   [3] A last contained 20 dickers.
[4] A dicker contained 10 hides.
[5] A payment exacted for weighing by the tron and chargeable on wool.
[6] The seal used on receipts for customs monies received by the collectors.

7 Privileges Granted to Foreign Merchants, 1303[1]

(P.R.O. Charter Roll, 2 Edward III, m. 11, no. 37)

Edward by the grace of God King of England, Lord of Ireland and Duke of Aquitaine, to archbishops, bishops, abbots, priors, earls, barons, justices, sheriffs, reeves, ministers, and all his bailiffs and faithful, greeting. Touching the good estate of all merchants of the underwritten realms, lands and provinces, to wit, Almain, France, Spain, Portugal, Navarre, Lombardy, Tuscany, Provence, Catalonia, our duchy of Aquitaine, Toulouse, Quercy, Flanders, Brabant, and all other foreign lands and places, by whatsoever name they be known, coming to our realm of England and staying there, an especial anxiety weighs upon us, in what wise under our lordship a means of tranquillity and full security may be devised for the same merchants for times to come: in order therefore that their desires may be rendered apter to the service of us and our realm, we, favourably inclining to their petitions, for the fuller assurance of their estate, have deemed fit to ordain and to grant to the said merchants for us and our heirs for ever as follows: First, to wit, that all merchants of the said realms and lands, safely and securely, under our defence and protection, may come into our said realm of England and everywhere else within our power with their merchandise whatsoever free and quit of murage, pontage and pavage,[2] and that within the same our realm and power in cities, boroughs and market-towns they may traffic in gross only[3] as well with denizens or inhabitants of the same our realm and power aforesaid as with aliens, strangers or friends,[4] so nevertheless that the wares which are commonly called mercery and spices may be sold at retail as before was wont to be done, and that all the aforesaid merchants may cause their merchandise, which they chance to bring to our aforesaid realm and power or to buy or otherwise acquire within the same our realm and power, to be taken or carried whither they will as well within our realm and power aforesaid as without, except to lands of manifest and notorious enemies of our realm, paying the customs which they shall owe, wines only excepted, which it shall not be lawful for them in any wise to take away from the same our realm or power after they shall have been brought within the same our realm or power, without our will and special licence.

Further, that the aforesaid merchants may lodge at their will in the cities, boroughs and towns aforesaid, and stay with their goods at the pleasure of those to whom the inns or houses belong.

Further, that every contract entered upon by those merchants with any persons soever, whencesoever they be, touching any sort of merchandise, shall be valid and stable, so that neither of the merchants can withdraw or retire from that contract after God's penny shall have been given and received between the principal contracting persons; and if by chance a dispute arise on such a contract, proof or inquisition shall be made thereof according to the uses and customs of the fairs and towns where the said contract shall happen to be made and entered upon.

Further, we promise to the aforesaid merchants for us and our heirs for ever, granting that we will in no wise make or suffer to be made henceforth any prise or arrest or delay on account of prise of their wares, merchandise or other goods by us or another or others for any necessity or case against the will of the same merchants, save upon immediate payment of the price for which the merchants can sell such wares to others, or upon satisfaction otherwise made to them, so that they hold themselves contented; and that no valuation or estimation be set by us or our ministers on their wares, merchandise or goods.

Further, we will that all bailiffs and ministers of fairs, cities, boroughs and market-towns do speedy justice to the merchants aforesaid who complain before them from day to day without delay according to the Law Merchant touching all and singular plaints which can be determined by the same law; and if by chance default be found in any of the bailiffs or ministers aforesaid whereby the same merchants or any of them shall sustain the inconveniences of delay, although the merchant recover his damages in principal against the party, nevertheless the bailiff or other minister shall be punished in respect of us as the guilt demands, and that punishment we have granted by way of favour to the merchants aforesaid to hasten justice for them.

Further, that in all sorts of pleas, saving the case of crime for which the penalty of death shall be inflicted, where a merchant shall be impleaded or shall implead another, of whatsoever condition he who is impleaded shall be, stranger or native, in fairs, cities, or boroughs, where there shall be a sufficient number of merchants of the aforesaid lands, and inquest should be made, one moiety of the inquest shall be of the same merchants, and the other moiety of other good and lawful men of that place where that plea shall happen to be, and if a sufficient number of merchants of the said lands be not found, there shall be put on the inquest those who shall be found there fit, and the residue shall be of other men good and fit of the places in which that plea shall be.

Further, we will, ordain and decree that in each market-town and fair of our realm aforesaid and elsewhere within our power our weight be set in a certain place, and before weighing the scales shall be seen to be empty in the presence of buyer and seller, and that the arms be level, and that then the weigher weigh level, and when he have put the scales on a level, forthwith move his hands away, so that it remain level; and that throughout our whole realm and power there be one weight and one measure, and that they be marked with the mark of our standard, and that each man may have scales of a quarter and less, where it shall not be against the lord of the place or a liberty granted by us or our ancestors, or against the custom of towns or fairs hitherto observed.

Further, we will and grant that a certain loyal and discreet man resident in London be assigned as justice for the said merchants, before whom they may specially plead and speedily recover their debts, if the sheriffs and mayors do not full and speedy justice for them from day to day, and that a commission be made thereon granted out of the present charter to the merchants aforesaid, to wit, of the things which shall be tried between merchants and merchants according to the Law Merchant.

Further, we ordain and decree, and for us and our heirs for ever we will that that ordinance and decree be straitly observed, that for each liberty which we or our heirs shall hereafter grant, the aforesaid merchants shall not lose the above written liberties or any of them. But for the obtaining of the aforesaid liberties and free customs and the remission of our prises to them, the said merchants, all and singular, for them and all others of their parts, have granted to us with one heart and mind that on each tun of wine which they shall bring or cause to be brought within our realm or power, whereon they shall be bound to pay freight to the mariners, they shall pay to us and our heirs by name of custom 2s beyond the ancient customs due and accustomed to be paid in money to us or others within forty days after the said wines be put ashore out of the ships; further, on each sack of wool which the said merchants or others in their name shall buy and take or cause to be bought and taken from our realm, they shall pay 40d of increment beyond the ancient custom of half a mark which had before been paid; and for a last of hides to be carried out of our realm and power half a mark above that which before was paid of ancient custom; and likewise on 300 wool-fells to be taken out of our realm and power 40d beyond the . . . sum which had before been given of ancient custom; further, 2s on each scarlet and cloth dyed in grain; further, 18d on each cloth wherein part of the grain is intermixed; further, 12d on each other cloth without grain; further, 12d on each quintal of wax.

And whereas some of the aforesaid merchants deal in other merchandise as avoir-du-pois and other fine goods, such as cloths of Tars, silk, cendals and other diverse wares, and horses also and other animals, corn and other goods and merchandise which cannot easily be put at a fixed custom, the same merchants have granted to give us and our heirs on each pound of silver of the estimation or value of such goods and merchandise, by what name soever they be known, 3d in the pound at the entry of those goods and merchandise into our realm and power aforesaid within fifteen days after such goods and merchandise shall have been brought into our realm and power and there unladen or sold; and likewise 3*d* on each pound of silver at the export of any such goods and merchandise bought in our realm and power aforesaid, beyond the ancient customs before given to us or others; and touching the value and estimation of such goods and merchandise whereon 3*d* on each pound of silver, as is aforesaid, are to be paid, credit shall be given to them by the letters which they shall show from their lords or fellows, and if they have no letters, it shall stand in this behalf by the oaths of the merchants, if they be present, or of their yeomen in the absence of the same merchants. It shall be lawful, moreover, for the fellows of the fellowship of the merchants aforesaid to sell wools within our realm and power aforesaid to other their fellows, and likewise to buy from the same without payment of custom, so, nevertheless, that the said wools come not to such hands that we be defrauded of the custom due to us.

And furthermore it is to be known that after the said merchants shall have once paid in the form aforesaid in one place within our realm and power the custom above granted to us for their merchandise, and have their warrant thereof, they shall be free and quit in all other places within our realm and power aforesaid of payment of such custom for the same merchandise or wares by the same warrant, whether such merchandise remain within our realm and power or be carried without, except wines which shall in no wise be taken out of our realm and power aforesaid without our will and licence, as is aforesaid. And we will, and for us and our heirs we grant that no exaction, prise or prest or any other charge be in any wise imposed on the persons of the merchants aforesaid, their merchandise or goods, against the form expressed and granted above. These witnesses:—the venerable fathers, Robert, archbishop of Canterbury, primate of all England, Walter, bishop of Coventry and Lichfield, Henry de Lacy, earl of Lincoln, Humphrey de Bohun, earl of Hereford and Essex and constable of England, Aymer de Valence, Geoffrey de Geneville, Hugh le Despenser, Walter de Beauchamp, steward of our household, Robert de Bures and others. Given by our hand at Windsor, 1 February in the 31st year of our reign.

[1] These customs were known as the petty custom and this charter as the *Carta Mercatoria*. (B, B, T, and other notes also)

[2] Tolls for the repair of walls, bridges and streets.

[3] i.e. wholesale.   [4] *Privatis.*

8 Action against the Export of Money, 1303

(P.R.O. Chancery Miscellanea, C 47/60/5/153)

To the most excellent lord, the lord prince Edward, by the grace of God king of England, lord of Ireland, duke of Aquitaine, his humble and devoted mayor and bailiffs of the town of Southampton, obedience, reverence and honour. We have received your command in these words:

Edward, by the grace of God, king of England, lord of Ireland and duke of Aquitaine, to his mayor and bailiffs of Southampton, greeting. Because we have learnt by an inquisition which we lately caused to be made by our beloved and trusty Robert of Glamorgan and John Lee, that Pelegrin de Castello, our merchant of Bayonne, wished to take the 24*l*—which you, believing that he wished to carry the same to parts beyond the sea against our prohibition that no man should carry any money or silver in bullion out of our realm, arrested on that account in a ship in our port of Southampton—to the parts of Devon and Cornwall to buy there lead and tin and other merchandise, and not to parts beyond the sea against the prohibition aforesaid, as you charged against him: We command you, as we have before commanded, that, if the aforesaid 24*l* have been arrested for the cause aforesaid and no other, then you cause the same to be delivered without delay to the aforesaid Pelegrin, or that you signify to us the cause wherefor you have refused or were unable to execute our command before directed to you thereon.

Wherefore we signify to you that the searchers of the town of Southampton aforesaid, by your writ of the wardrobe sealed with your privy seal directed to the said searchers on 7 January commanding the said 24*l* to be brought to Odiham and delivered there into your said wardrobe [paid and delivered the same], of which payment and delivery of the said 24*l* so made the aforesaid searchers have a due acquittance of receipt. And by the tenor of these presents we signify that for no other cause were the aforesaid 24*l* arrested, save only in the form aforesaid. In witness whereof we transmit to you these our letters sealed with our seal. Given at Southampton, 9 March.

Wherefore the same Pelegrin sues for a writ of the lord the king to be directed to the keeper of the wardrobe of the lord the king, for satisfaction to be made to him according to the form of the return of the writ.

9 The Staple System, 1326

(P.R.O. Patent Roll, 19 Edward II, pt. 2, m. 8)

Edward . . . to the mayor of our city of London, greeting. We command you, straitly enjoining, that the things below written, ordained by us and our council for the common profit and relief of the people of all our realm and power, you cause to be proclaimed and published and straitly kept and observed in our city aforesaid and everywhere in your bailiwick.

First, that the staple of the merchants and the merchandise of England, Ireland and Wales, namely, of wools, hides, wool-fells and tin, be held in the same lands and nowhere else, and that too in the places below written, that is to say, at Newcastle upon Tyne, York, Lincoln, Norwich, London, Winchester, Exeter, and Bristol, for England, Dublin, Drogheda and Cork, for Ireland, Shrewsbury, Carmarthen and Cardiff, for Wales. And for the tin of Cornwall, at Lostwithiel and Truro. And for the tin of Devonshire, at Ashburton, and not elsewhere in England, Ireland or Wales.

And that all alien people there and not elsewhere in England, Ireland or Wales, may freely buy and seek wools, hides and fells and other merchandise, and tin in Ashburton, Lostwithiel and Truro, and not elsewhere, and when they have bought their merchandise at the said places and in the form abovesaid and paid their customs, and have thereon letters sealed with the seal of the cocket, they may carry the said wools, hides, fells, tin and other merchandise into what land soever they will, if it be not into a land that is at war or enmity with us or our realm. And that the merchant strangers be warned hereof.

And that no alien by himself or another privily or openly may buy elsewhere wools or other merchandise abovesaid except at the said places, upon forfeiture of the wools or other merchandise abovesaid which he shall have so bought.

And that the merchants of England, Ireland and Wales, who wish to carry wools, hides, fells or tin out of the staples to be sold elsewhere, may not carry them from the staples out of our power until they have remained fifteen days at any of the staples to sell them, and then they may go with the said merchandise whither they will, without making or holding a staple anywhere out of the said lands or within the said lands elsewhere than at the places abovesaid.

And that all people of England, Ireland and Wales, may sell and buy wools and all other merchandise anywhere that they will in the said lands, so that the sale be not made to aliens except at the staple. And that wools, hides, fells and tin be nowhere carried out of the said lands by aliens or denizens except from the staples aforesaid.

And that the merchants of our power make not among themselves any conspiracy or compact to lessen the price of wools or other merchandise abovesaid, or to delay merchant strangers in the purchase or sale of their merchandise, and that those who shall do so and can be attainted hereof be heavily punished according to the ordinance of us and of our good council. And that every man be admitted on our behalf who will sue to attaint and punish such, and that such suit be made before our chief justices or others whom we will assign hereto and not elsewhere. And that the merchants and the people of Gascony and of the duchy of Aquitaine, who now are or for the time shall be of the fealty and obedience of us or of our son and heir,[1] be held as denizens and not as aliens in all these affairs.

And that all merchants, native and strangers, be subject to the Law merchant in all things that touch trafficking at the places of the staples.

And that no man or woman of a borough or city, nor the commons of the people outside a borough or city in England, Ireland or Wales, after Christmas next coming, use cloth of their own buying that shall be bought after the said feast of Christmas, unless it be cloth made in England, Ireland or Wales, upon heavy forfeiture and punishment, as we by our good council will ordain hereon. And be it known that by the commons in this case shall be understood all people except the king and queen, earls and barons, knights and ladies and their children born in wedlock, archbishops and bishops and other persons and people of Holy Church, and seculars, who can spend yearly from their rents 40*l* sterling, and this so long as it please us by our good council further to extend this ordinance and prohibition.

And that every man and woman of England, Ireland and Wales, may make cloths as long and as short as they shall please.

And that people may have the greater will to work upon the making of cloth in England, Ireland and Wales, we will that all people know that we shall grant suitable franchises to fullers, weavers, dyers and other clothworkers who live mainly by this craft, when such franchises be asked of us.

And that it be granted to the wool-merchants that they have a mayor of the staples abovesaid.

And that all merchant strangers may have the greater will to come into our power and may the more safely stay and return, we take them, their persons and goods, into our protection. And we forbid, upon heavy forfeiture, that anyone do them wrong or injury in person or goods, while they be coming, staying or returning, so that if anyone do them injury contrary to this protection and prohibition, those of the town to which the evildoers shall belong shall be bound to answer for the damages or for the persons of the evildoers, and that the mayor or bailiffs of the town where the shipping is take surety for which they will answer at their peril from the sailors of the same shipping every time that they shall go out of the havens, that they will not do evil or misbehave towards any man contrary to these articles.

In witness whereof we have caused these our letters to be sealed with our seal. Given at Kenilworth, 1 May.

[1] Prince Edward was created Duke of Aquitaine on 16 September 1325. (B, B, T)

10 An Early Navigation Act, 1381–2

(5 Richard II, c. 3, *Statutes of the Realm*, II, p. 18)

Also, to increase the navy of England, which is now greatly diminished, it is assented and accorded that none of the king's liege people do from henceforth ship any merchandise in going out or coming within the realm of England, in any port, but only in ships of the king's liegance; and every person of the said liegance, which after the feast of Easter next ensuing, at which feast this ordinance shall first begin to hold place, do ship any merchandise in any other ships or vessels upon the sea, than of the said liegance, shall forfeit to the king all his merchandise shipped in other vessels, wheresoever they be found hereafter, or the value of the same; of which forfeiture the king wills and grants that he, that duly espies and duly proves that any person has any thing forfeited against this ordinance, shall have the third part for his labour, of the king's gift.

11 Italian Ships at Southampton, 1430

(*The Port Books of Southampton, 1427–1430*, ed. P. Studer (Southampton Record Society, 1913), pp. 108–9)

596. Enter the 12th day of January 2 galleys of Florence, masters Piere Vespouche and Bernard Caruesek, anchorage, keelage and wharfage 20s.:

Poul Morel: 22 bales of dates—custom, pontage 4s 1½d;
             33 bales of aniseed—custom 5s 6d, pontage 8¼d;
             6 bales of grain[1] weight 8 hundred, worth 98l 13s 4d—
                custom 24s 8d, pontage 3d;
             9 barrels of oil—custom 3s, pontage 2d;

2 cases of confection,[2] worth 26s—custom 4d, pontage ½d;

98 small baskets of raisins—custom 2s ½d, pontage 2d;

9 barrels of succade,[3] worth 40s—custom 6d, pontage 2d;

4 cases, containing 12 pieces of silk cloth, 4 pieces of velvet, 1 piece of gold cloth, 8 pieces of damask, 1 piece of velvet, worth 246l 16s 8d—custom 3l 20½d, pontage 2d.

Gregore Catan: 2 bales of grain,[1] weight 2 hundred and a quarter, worth 28l 15s—custom 7s 2¼d, pontage 1d.

Luke de Ancone: 4 small barrels of oil—custom, pontage 10d.

Antony de Lovente: 8 quarters of figs—custom 3d.

597. Clearing the aforesaid galleys:

Poul Morel: 1026 pokes[4] of wool—custom 8l 11s, pontage 42s 9d;

130 pieces of tin—custom 21s 8d, pontage 2s 8½d;

120 pieces of lead, containing 28 fothers—custom 14s, pontage 5s;

30 bales of Guildford cloth, containing 670 cloths, 18 yards—custom 5l 11s 9½d, pontage 2s 6d;

23 bales, 4 coffers, 20 bundles, containing 630 cloths, 4 yards—custom 5l 5s, pontage 3s 4d;

7 beds, worth 18l—custom 4s 6d;

5 pieces of worsted—custom 10d;

5 dozens of hures,[5] worth 4 nobles—custom 4d . . .

[1] For dyeing cloth. [2] Preserved fruit. [3] Sweetmeat. [4] Small sacks. [5] Hairy caps.

12 The Icelandic Trade, c.1436

(*The Libelle of Englyshe Polycye. A Poem on the Use of Sea-Power 1436*, ed. G. Warner (Oxford, 1926), p. 41)

> Of Iceland to write is little need
> Save of stockfish; yet forsooth indeed
> Out of Bristol and coasts many one,
> Men have practised by needle and by stone[1]
> Thitherwards within a little while,
> Within 12 years, and without peril
> Have gone and returned, as men were wont of old
> Of Scarborough unto the coasts cold.

[1] The use of lodestone with a needle served as a primitive compass. The mariner's compass, used by the Italians in the Mediterranean in the 14th century, was not employed in the north until the late 15th century.

13 English Complaints against the Hanseatic League, 1440

(T. Rymer, *Foedera, Conventiones, Literae*, V, printed and trans. in *English Historical Documents*, IV, ed. A. R. Myers (1969), pp. 1036–7)

Grievances about which the merchants, subjects of the king of England, have complained against the master of Prussia and against the governor and officials of the town of Danzig in Prussia.

First, although neither the merchants of England nor any others were of old accustomed to pay any tribute or custom for their ships in the land of Prussia, nevertheless the Master of Prussia often compelled the king's subjects to value their ships between entry and departure, receiving from them for each mark of Prussian money nine pence, and the English are compelled to pay this, against the custom of ancient time, under penalty of forfeiture of their ships.

Also, the merchandise of the king's subjects is appraised when it comes in and the merchants are compelled, under pain of forfeiture of the same, to pay for each twenty shillings of English money two new shillings Prussian, and are compelled to pay on exit, according to the price, for every Prussian mark four new pennies.

Also, the governors of the town of Danzig compel the English merchants to pay uncertain taxes and tribute and such sums as they wish to impose upon them at their will.

Also, when the dues, albeit unjust, are paid, many of the ships of the same merchants, prepared and ready to sail, are not permitted to leave, but are maliciously kept, so that on this account losses of ships and other evils happen to those Englishmen in their goods, as lately occurred to the ships of John Church, citizen of London.

Also, the governors of the town of Danzig and other burgomasters of the land have compelled the English who dwell in the land and town of Prussia to leave their accustomed lodgings against ancient custom and against the agreements made in this matter.

Also, Thomas Chapman, a citizen of York, John Forster of Hull, John Hereford of Newcastle, and other lieges of our lord the king, against the last agreement made in this matter, by untrue suggestions and pretended actions on account of transgressions which were untruthfully claimed to have been committed outside the land of Prussia, when they were not guilty but entirely innocent, were taken in the town of Danzig and were led by the executioner of those condemned to death, ignominiously, with their hands tied, as thieves and murderers, into the presence of the justice there and by fear of death were compelled to pay heavy and burdensome sums of money, contrary to the agreements formerly made and often renewed.

Henry ... to the noble and distinguished men, the burgomasters, proconsuls and consuls ... of the city of Lübeck, and others of the common cities of the Teutonic Hanse ...

We marvel at the complaints of the merchants of our realm of England, which repeatedly assault our ears, about the oppressions, injuries, and hurts inflicted on them by you against the tenor of the agreements, who have lamentably shown to us that after the agreements on this matter and after you have consented to be bound by them, you acted wrongly. For Thomas Griffin of Lynn, Peter Gascoyne of Sandwich, and Thomas Gadon of Ipswich, and several other subjects who were in the town of Stettin, and John Newenton of Hull, in the town of Koslin, were unlawfully thrown into prison, and despoiled of the money which they had on them and mulcted of heavy ransoms and fines.

14 Aliens in the Wine and Cloth Trades, 1442

(P.R.O. Exchequer K.R. Accounts, E 101/125/31, m. 15)

This is the view of William Chervyle, surveyor and host ordained and deputed by Robert Clopton, late mayor of the city of London, upon John Mantell, captain of a carrack coming to Sandwich, and James Ryche, scrivan[1] of the said carrack, and James Douhonour, merchants, coming from Sandwich with the said carrack, to survey as well their merchandise found in their keeping and also coming afterwards, as the employment of the same, to wit, the said John Mantell and James Ryche between the 18th day of January, and James Douhonour between the 25th day of January in the 20th year of the reign of our sovereign lord King Henry the Sixth, until the feast of Michaelmas next following.

The merchandise coming and found in the said carrack of the said John Mantell and James Ryche and James Douhonour—
First, 14 butts of sweet wine.
Further, 30 barrels of the same sweet wine.
Further, 144 butts of sweet wine.
Further, 10 butts of currant raisins.

The merchandise sold by the said John Mantell, James Ryche and James Douhonour:—
First, sold in the month of February to the prior of
    Canterbury, 1 butt for.. .. .. 4*l* 6*s* 8*d*.
Further, to John Brockley, 2 butts for .. .. .. 8*l* 6*s* 8*d*.

Further, to Andrew Tye, 2 butts for .. .. .. 8*l.*
Further, to John Style, 4 butts for .. .. .. 14*l.*
Further, to Davy Selly, 3 butts for .. .. .. 12*l.*
Further, to Richard Tremaine, 2 butts for .. .. 8*l.*
Further, to John Chippenham, 30 barrels for .. 16*l.*

Further, sold in the month of March to Simon Eyre,
    101 butts for .. .. 305*l.*
Further, to John Style, 20 butts for .. .. .. 75*l.*
Further, to John Style, 10 butts for .. .. .. 40*l.*
Further, to Davy Selly, 4 butts for .. .. .. 16*l.*
Further, to Thomas Grey, 3 butts for .. .. .. 11*l* 10*s.*
Further, to John Attwood, 2 butts for .. .. 7*l.*
Further, to John Bale, 4 butts for .. .. .. 16*l.*
Further, to Harry Purchase, 3 butts of currant raisins
    for .. .. 29*l.*
Further, to John Gibb, 3 butts for .. .. .. 29*l.*
Further, to Nicholas Wyfold, 3 butts for .. .. 31*l.*
Further, to John Peacock, 1 butt [for] .. .. 9*l* 10*s.*
                Sum of the said sales .. .. .. 639*l* 13*s* 4*d.*

The purchases made by the said John Mantell and James Ryche and
James Douhonour for the employment of the merchandise aforesaid:—
    First, bought of Simon Eyre, 200 cloths "westrons" for .. 305*l.*
    Further, of John Brockley, 40 yards of murrey in grain .. 18*l.*
    Further, of Henry Kempe, 5 cloths "Northamptons" .. 40*l.*
    Further, of Philip Malpas, 60 cloths "westrons" .. .. 90*l.*
    Further, of John Bale, 60 pieces of Suffolk "streyts" for .. 38*l.*
    Further, of William Dyllowe, 10 cloths "Northamptons".. 60*l.*
    Further, of John Andrew, 8 cloths "Ludlowes" .. .. 16*l.*
    Further, of Thomas Grey, 1101 quarters of pewter for .. 15*l.*
    Further, of William ——, 40 cloths "westrons" .. .. 60*l.*
    Further, of John Attwood, 20 cloths "westrons" for .. 32*l.*
    Further, of John Style, 80 Suffolk "streyts" for .. .. 46*l.*
                Sum of the purchases aforesaid .. .. .. 745*l.*

The scrivan (i.e. writer) had charge of the merchandise on board. (B, B, T)

15 A Bristol Ship and its Trade, 1453–5

(P.R.O. Early Chancery Proceedings, C 1/24/211, printed in *The Overseas Trade of Bristol in the Later Middle Ages*, ed. E. Carus-Wilson (Bristol Record Society, Publications, VII, 1967), pp. 106–8)

To the right high good and gracious lord, the Earl of Salisbury, Chancellor of England

Beseeches meekly John Heyton of Bristol, merchant, that where one Clement Bagot of the said town was possessed of a ship called the *Julian* of Bristol, in the which one John White was master, accord and agreement was had the sixth day of February of [the] year of the reign of the king our sovereign lord that now is the 31st[1] at Bristol [afore]said between your said beseecher and the said Clement that he should freight and charge the said ship with divers merchandise at his pleasure, except and reserved to the said Clement 10 tuntight[2] and to the said John White 6 tuntight and to one Nicholas Moody 5 tuntight, which ship so freighted with the said merchandise should sail to Lisbon in Portugal and there to be discharged of all that merchandise of your said beseecher and by your said beseecher to be recharged with 85 tuns[3] [of] wine, 15 tuns [of] honey and the residue of the said charge to be in salt, and from thence to sail unto *legge de Breon*,[4] Sligo and to Galway in Ireland or to one of them at the election of your said beseecher, paying for every tun and tunload, accounting 1 tun for 1 tun, 2 pipes for the tun, 4 hogsheads for the tun and 5 quarters [of] salt for the tun of the measure of Bristol, 20*s* of [the] lawful money of England, that is to say at one of the said 3 places in Ireland in which it happens the said ship to arrive, 20 marks of the said freight to be paid unto the mariners in the said ship being within 6 weeks after the arrival of the said ship according to a charter party made between your said beseecher and the said John White by the assent and agreement of the said Clement, and there the said ship to be discharged of the said honey, wine and salt and recharged with hides and from thence the said ship to sail to the port of Plymouth in England there to tarry 3 tides and so to Harfleur in Normandy or to Middelburg in Z[eeland] or unto Bur[. . .] or to Nantes in Brittany at the choice of your said beseecher, paying for freight of every last of hides to the said Clement, his factors or attorneys 40*s* of good and lawful mone[y] of England; by force of which accord and agreement the said ship sailed from the said port of Bristol unto Lisbon [a]foresaid and so unto Ireland and so unto

Plymouth, and at the said port of Plymouth the 8th day of November
the said year your said beseecher assigned the said master to sail with
the said ship to Middelburg in Zeeland, and from the said port of
Plymouth the said ship sailed in his right course unto the port of
Winchelsea intent and so to Sandwich [and] there the said master by
[the] commandment of the said Clement discharged the said ship of all
the merchandise of your said beseecher being within the said ship,
contrary to the said charter party, compelling your said beseecher there
to sell 1 last [of] hides of his said merchandise within the price that they
might have been sold at Middelburg to the value of 400 marks and
more, to pay and content the whole freight of the said ship unto the
said master to the great loss and undoing of your said beseecher without
your gracious help and succour be had in this party to him. Please it
your gracious lordship, the premises tenderly considered and that your
said beseecher has no remedy by the course of the c[om]mon law, to
grant a writ under a pain,[5] by your lordship limited, directed to the
said Clement to appear before you in [the] Chancery of our sovereign
lord at a certain day to answer to the premises and to every of them as
conscience requires and he shall ever pray to God for you.

[1] 6 February 1453.
[2] A tuntight was originally the space occupied by a tun of wine, about 56 cubic
feet.
[3] A tun was a large cask, hence a measure of capacity for wine etc., containing
252 gallons.
[4] Probably Burrishoole, Co. Mayo. (EC-W)   [5] A writ of *subpoena*.

16 Foreign Exchange Transactions, 1487

(*The Cely Papers, selected from the Correspondence and Memoranda of
the Cely Family, Merchants of the Staple, 1475–88*, ed. H. E. Malden
(Camden Society, Third Series, I, 1900), pp. 159–61)

*William Cely in Calais to Richard and George Cely, merchants of the
staple of Calais, in London at Mark Lane*

Right worshipful sirs and my reverent masters after all due recommendation preceding I lowly recommend me unto your masterships.
Furthermore please it your masterships to understand that I have
received of John Delowppys upon payment of the bill, which is sent me
by Adlyngton, but 300*l* fleming, whereof I have paid to Gnyott Strabant
84*l* 6*s* 6*d* fleming. Item, I have made you over by exchange with Benyngne
Decasonn, Lombard, an 180 nobles sterling, payable at usance.[1] I
delivered it at 11*s* 2½*d* fleming the noble. It amounts—100*l* 17*s* 6*d*

fleming. Item, I have made you over by exchange in like wise with Jacob van de Base 89 nobles and 6s sterling, payable at London at usance in like wise. I delivered it at 11s 2d fleming for every noble sterling. It amounts—50l fleming, and the rest of your 300l remains still by me for I can make you over no more at this season, for here is no more that will take any money as yet. And money goes now upon the bourse at 11s 3½d the noble and no other money but Nimueguen groats, crowns, Andrew guilders and Rhenish guilders and the exchange goes over the longer worse and worse. Item, sir I send you enclosed in this said letter the 2 first letters of the payments of the exchange above written. Benyngne Decasonn's letter is directed to Gabryell Defuye and Petyr Sanly, Genoese, and Jacob van de Base's is directed to Anthony Corsy and Marcy Strossy, Spaniards, in Lombard Street. You shall hear of them . . .

Written at Calais the 12th day of September.

By your servant William Cely.

[1] Interest.

17 Letters Patent Granted to the Cabots, 1496

(P.R.O. Patent Rolls, 4 Edward VI, p. 6)

The king to all to whom . . . greeting. It is manifest to us by inspection of the rolls of our Chancery that the Lord Henry the Seventh, late king of England, our dearest grand father, caused his letters patent to be made in these words:

Henry by the grace of God King of England and France and lord of Ireland, to all to whom the present letters shall come, greeting. Be it known and manifest that we have given and granted, and by these presents we do give and grant for us and our heirs to our beloved John Cabot, citizen of Venice, and Lewis, Sebastian and Sanctus, sons of the said John, and the heirs and deputies of them and every of them, full and free authority, faculty and power to sail to all parts, regions and gulfs of the sea, east, west and north, under our banners, standards, and ensigns, with five ships or boats of whatsoever portage or kind they be, and with as many sailors and men as they wish to take with them in the said ships at their own and the others' costs and expenses, to find, discover and search out any isles, countries, regions or provinces of heathens and infidels whomsoever set in any part of the world soever, which have been before these times unknown to all Christians. We have granted also to the same and to every of them and to the heirs and deputies of them and every of them, and given licence for them to affix our aforesaid banners and ensigns in any town, castle, isle or solid land soever newly found by them; and that the aforenamed John and his sons or heirs and the deputies of the same may subjugate, occupy and possess any such towns, castles and islands found by them which can be subjugated, occupied and possessed, as our vassals and governors, lieutenants and deputies of the same, acquiring for us the lordship, title and jurisdiction of the same towns, castles, islands and solid land so found; so nevertheless, that of all fruits, profits, emoluments, commodities, gains and obventions arising from such voyages, the aforesaid John and his sons and heirs and their deputies be held and bound to pay to us for every voyage, as often as they touch at our port of Bristol, at which alone they are held and bound to touch, after deducting the necessary costs and expenses made by them, a fifth part of their capital gain made whether in wares or in money; giving and granting to them and their heirs and deputies that they be free and immune from all payment of customs on all and singular goods and wares which they bring back with them from those places so newly found. And further we have given and granted to the same and to their heirs and deputies that all lands, farms, isles, towns, castles and places whatsoever found by them, as many as shall be found by them, may not be frequented or visited by any other our subjects soever without licence of the aforesaid John and his sons and their deputies, under pain of loss as well of the ships or boats as of all goods whatsoever presuming to sail to those places so found; willing and most straitly commanding all and singular our subjects set as well on land as on sea that they give good assistance to the aforesaid John and his sons and deputies and show all their favour and aid as well in manning the ships or boats as in provision of equipment and victuals to be bought for their money and all other things to be provided for them to be taken for the said voyage. In witness whereof we have caused these our letters patent to be made. Witness myself at Westminster, 5 April in the 11th year of our reign.

And we, because the letters aforesaid have been lost by mischance, as the aforesaid Sebastian, appearing in person before us in our Chancery, has taken a corporal oath, and that he will restore those letters to us into the same our Chancery to be cancelled there, if he shall find them hereafter, have deemed fit to exemplify by these presents the tenor of the enrolment of the letters aforesaid, at the request of the same Sebastian. In witness whereof these our letters . . . Witness the king at Westminster, 4 June.

18 Revocation of the Hansards' Privileges, 1552

(*Acts of the Privy Council of England*, New Series, III, 1550–1552 (1891), pp. 487–9)

In the matter touching the information exhibited against the merchants of the Hanse, commonly called merchants of the Steelyard, upon good consideration as well of the said informations as also of the answer of the said merchants of the Steelyard, and of such records, writings, charters, treaties, depositions of witnesses and other evidences and proofs as has been exhibited on both parts, it was found apparent to the king's majesty's Privy Council as follows:

First, it is found that all liberties and privileges pretended to be granted to the said merchants of the Hanse be void by the laws of this realm, for so much as the same merchants of the Hanse have no sufficient corporation to take the same.

It appeared also that such grants and privileges as the said merchants of the Hanse do claim to have do not extend to any persons or towns certain, and therefore uncertain what persons or which towns should enjoy the said privileges, by the reason of which uncertainty they have and do admit and appoint to be free with them whom and as many as they list, to the great prejudice and hurt of the king's majesty's custom and yearly hindrance of 20,000*l* or nigh thereabouts, besides the common hurt to the whole realm.

It appears also that if the said pretended grants were good by the laws of this realm, as indeed they be not, yet the same were made upon condition that they should not avow or colour any foreigner's goods or merchandises, which conditions the said merchants of the Hanse have not observed, as may appear by office found remaining of record in the king's majesty's Exchequer, and by other sufficient proofs of the same.

It appears also that one hundred years and more after the pretended privileges granted to them, the foresaid merchants of the Hanse used to transport no merchandise out of this realm but only into their own countries, neither to bring into this realm any wares or merchandises, but only such as were commodities of their own countries; where at this present they do not only convey the merchandises and commodities of this realm into the base countries of Brabant, Flanders and other places nigh adjoining, and there sell the same, to the great damage and subversion of the laudable order of the king's majesty's subjects trading those parts for merchandise and commodities, but also do bring into this realm the merchandise and commodities of all foreign countries, contrary to the true meaning of the grants of their privileges declared

L

by the ancient usages of the same, by means whereof the king's majesty has not only lost much in his customs, but also it is contrary to the condition of a recognisance made in the time of King Henry the Seventh . . .

* * *

In consideration of which the premises and such other matter as has appeared in the examination of this matter, the lords of the king's majesty's Privy Council, on his highness' behalf, decreed that the privileges, liberties and franchises claimed by the foresaid merchants of the Steelyard shall from henceforth be and remain seized and resumed into the king's majesty's hands until the said merchants of the Steelyard shall declare and prove better and more sufficient matter for their claim in the premises; saving, nevertheless, and reserving to the said merchants of the Steelyard all such and like liberties of coming into this realm and other the king's dominions, buying, selling and all manner of traffic or trade of merchandise in as large and ample manner as any other merchant strangers have or of right ought to have within the same, this order aforesaid or anything therein contained to the contrary notwithstanding.

This decree was made and given at Westminster, the 24th of February, in the sixth year of the reign of our sovereign lord, King Edward the Sixth.

19 A Ship's Charter Party, 1577

(*Rye Shipping Records, 1566–1590*, ed. R. F. Dell (Sussex Record Society, LXIV, 1965–6), pp. 6–7)

In the name of God amen. This charter party indented and made the 13th day of September 20th ye[ar] of the reign of our sovereign lady Elizabeth . . . Between Richard Holdbrooke of the ancient town of Rye in the county of Sussex, mariner, master of a barque named the *Elizabeth Bonaventure* of Rye, of the burden of fifty and eight tons or thereabouts, of the one party, and Thomas Bromrick and Richard Killingback of the city of London, merchants, of the other party. Witnesses that the said Richard Holdbrook has let out to freight the aforesaid barque being strong and staunch and well manned with 9 men and 2 boys besides the said master and also well victualled, tackled and apparelled in all points necessary and meet for a voyage (by God's grace) to be made from Rye aforesaid with the next meet and apt wind which God shall send after the date hereof unto Bordeaux in the dominion of the king of France, and being arrived at Bordeaux there the said master and company to stay with the said barque by the space of sixteen days after the wines of Graves be ready to be laden, if he arrive there before they be ready to be laden, and there to take in so many tuns of wines or other goods as the said barque can reasonably carry away, always accounting two pipes to a tun, three puncheons to a tun, four hogsheads to a tun and six tierces to a tun, pesterable goods only excepted. And so being laden to return and directly to sail to London with as much convenient speed as may be, there to make his full and right discharge in so short time after his arrival at London aforesaid as may reasonably be. The said merchandise and wines to be well conditioned (the casualties of the seas only excepted).

During all which voyage a competent number of mariners and ship boys shall be attendant with their longboat upon the said merchants, their factors and assigns to and from London as occasion shall serve. All which the foresaid premises on the part of the said master and his company to be performed and kept, he the said master for himself, his executors and assigns covenants and grants to and with the said merchants . . . well truly and justly to observe, fulfil, keep and perform.

20 The Advantages of Colonies, 1583

(Richard Hakluyt, *The Principal Navigations, Voyages, Traffiques and Discoveries of the English Nation*, VIII (Glasgow, 1904), pp. 89–120)

A true report of the late discoveries and possession, taken in the right of the crown of England of the Newfound Lands, by that valiant and worthy gentleman, Sir Humphrey Gilbert, knight. Wherein is also briefly set down her highness's lawful title thereunto, and the great and manifold commodities that are likely to grow thereby, to the whole realm in general and to the adventurers in particular: together with the easiness and shortness of the voyage. Written[1] by Sir George Peckham, knight, the chief adventurer and furtherer of Sir Humphrey Gilbert's voyage to the Newfound Land.

* * *

By occasion of this history I drew myself into a more deep considera-tion of this late undertaken voyage, whether it were as pleasing to almighty God, as profitable to men: as lawful, as it seemed honourable: as well grateful to the savages, as gainful to the Christians. And upon mature deliberation I found the action to be honest and profitable . . .

Now whereas I do understand that Sir Humphrey Gilbert, his adherents, associates and friends, do mean with a convenient supply (with as much speed as may be) to maintain, pursue and follow this intended voyage already in part performed, and (by the assistance of almighty God) to plant themselves and their people in the continent of the hither part of America, between the degrees of 30 and 60 septentrional latitude . . .

* * *

The fourth chapter shows how that the trade, traffic, and planting in those countries is likely to prove very profitable to the whole realm in general.

Now to show how the same is likely to prove very profitable and beneficial generally to the whole realm. It is very certain that the greatest jewel of this realm, and the chief strength and force of the same, for defence or offence in martial matter and manner, is the multitude of ships, masters, and mariners ready to assist the most stately and royal navy of her majesty, which by reason of this voyage shall have both increase and maintenance. And it is well known that in sundry places of this realm ships have been built and set forth of late days for the trade of fishing only; yet, notwithstanding, the fish which is taken and brought into England by the English navy of fishermen will not suffice for the expense of this realm four months, if there were none else brought of strangers. And the chief cause why our English men do not go so far westerly as the especial fishing places do lie, both for plenty and greatness of fish, is for that they have no succour and known safe harbour in those parts. But if our nation were once planted there or near thereabouts, whereas they now fish but for two months in the year, they might then fish for so long as pleased themselves . . . Which being brought to pass shall increase the number of our ships and mariners . . .

Moreover, it is well known that all savages . . . so soon as they shall begin but a little to taste of civility, will take marvellous delight in any garment, be it never so simple, as a shirt, a blue, yellow, red, or green cotton cassock, a cap, or such like, and will take incredible pains for such a trifle . . . Which being so, what vent for our English cloths will thereby ensue, and how great benefit to all such persons and artificers, whose names are quoted in the margin, I leave to such as are discreet . . .

To what end need I endeavour myself by arguments to prove that by this voyage our navy and navigation shall be enlarged, when as there needs none other reason than the manifest and late example of the near neighbours to this realm, the kings of Spain and Portugal, who, since the first discovery of the Indies, have not only mightily enlarged their dominions, greatly enriched themselves and their subjects, but have also, by just account, trebled the number of their ships, masters and mariners, a matter of no small moment and importance?

Besides this, it will prove a general benefit unto our country, that, through this occasion, not only a great number of men which do now live idly at home, and are burdenous, chargeable, and unprofitable to this realm, shall hereby be set on work, but also children of twelve or fourteen years of age, or under, may be kept from idleness, in making of a thousand kinds of trifling things, which will be good merchandise for that country. And, moreover, our idle women (which the realm may well spare) shall also be employed on plucking, drying, and sorting of feathers, in pulling, beating, and working of hemp, and in gathering of cotton, and divers things right necessary for dyeing. All which things are to be found in those countries most plentifully. And the men may employ themselves in dragging for pearl, working for mines, and in matters of husbandry, and likewise in hunting the whale for train [oil], and making casks to put the same in, besides in fishing for cod, salmon and herring, drying, salting and barrelling the same, and felling of trees, hewing and sawing of them, and such like work, meet for those persons that are no men of art or science.

Many other things may be found to the great relief and good employment of no small number of the natural subjects of this realm, which do now live here idly, to the common annoy of the whole state. Neither may I here omit the great hope and likelihood of a passage beyond the Grand Bay into the South Seas, confirmed by sundry authors to be found leading to Cataia, the Moluccas and Spiceries, whereby may ensue as general a benefit to the realm, or greater than yet has been spoken of, without either such charges or other inconveniences, as, by the tedious tract of time and peril, which the ordinary passage to those parts at this day does minister . . .

I must now, according to my promise, show forth some probable reasons that the adventurers in this journey are to take particular profit by the same. It is, therefore, convenient that I do divide the adventurers into two sorts, the noblemen and gentlemen by themselves, and the merchants by themselves. For, as I do hear, it is meant that there shall be one society of the noblemen and gentlemen, and another society of the merchants; and yet not so divided, but that each society may freely and frankly trade and traffic one with the other.

And first to bend my speech to the noblemen and gentlemen, who do chiefly seek a temperate climate, wholesome air, fertile soil, and a strong place by nature whereupon they may fortify, and there either plant themselves or such other persons as they shall think good to send to be lords of that place and country. To them I say that all these things are very easy to be found within the degrees of 30 and 60 aforesaid, either by south or north, both in the continent and in islands thereunto adjoining, at their choice . . . and in the whole tract of that land, by the description of as many as have been there, great plenty of mineral matter of all sorts, and in very many places both stones of price, pearl and crystal, and great store of beasts, birds, and fowls, both for pleasure and necessary use of man are to be found . . .

And now for the better contentation and satisfaction of such worshipful, honest-minded and well-disposed merchants as have a desire to the furtherance of every good and commendable action, I will first say unto them, as I have done before to the noblemen and gentlemen, that within the degrees aforesaid is doubtless to be found the most wholesome and best temperature of air, fertility of soil, and every other commodity or merchandise, for the which, with no small peril, we do travel into Barbary, Spain, Portugal, France, Italy, Muscovy and Eastland . . . And yet, to the end my argument shall not altogether stand upon likelihoods and presumptions, I say that such persons as have discovered and travelled those parts do testify that they have found in those countries all these things following, namely:—[a list of beasts, birds, fishes, trees, minerals, etc.] . . .

Now for the trial hereof, considering that in the articles of the society of the adventurers in this voyage there is provision made that no adventurer shall be bound to any further charge than his first adventure, and yet notwithstanding keep still to himself, his children, his apprentices and servants, his and their freedom for trade and traffic, which is a privilege that adventurers in other voyages have not; and in the said articles it is likewise provided that none other than such as have adventured in the first voyage, or shall become adventurers in this supply, at any time hereafter are to be admitted in the said society, but as redemptionaries, which will be very chargeable; therefore, generally, I say unto all such, according to the old proverb, Nothing venture, nothing have.

* * *

The sixth chapter shows that the traffic and planting in those countries shall be unto the savages themselves very beneficial and gainful . . .

. . . First and chiefly, in respect of the most happy and gladsome tidings of the most glorious gospel of our Saviour Jesus Christ, whereby they may be brought from falsehood to truth, from darkness to light, from the highway of death to the path of life, from superstitious idolatry to sincere Christianity, from the devil to Christ, from hell to heaven. And if in respect of all the commodities they can yield us (were they many more) that they should but receive this only benefit of Christianity, they were more than fully recompensed.

But hereunto it may be objected that the Gospel must be freely preached, for such was the example of the apostles. . . . Yet for further answer we may say with St. Paul; If we have sown unto you heavenly things, do you think it much that we should reap your carnal things? And withal, the workman is worthy of his hire. These heavenly tidings which those labourers our countrymen (as messengers of God's great goodness and mercy) will voluntarily present unto them, do far exceed their earthly riches. Moreover, if the other inferior worldly and temporal things which they shall receive from us be weighed in equal balance, I assure myself that, by equal judgment of any indifferent person, the benefits which they then receive shall far surmount those which they shall depart withal unto us. And admit that they had (as they have not) the knowledge to put their land to some use: yet being brought from brutish ignorance to civility and knowledge, and made then to understand how the tenth part of their land may be so manured and employed as it may yield more commodities to the necessary use of man's life than the whole now does, what just cause of complaint may they have? And in my private opinion I do verily think that God did create land to the end that it should by culture and husbandry yield things necessary for man's life.

But this is not all the benefit which they shall receive by the Christians: for, over and beside the knowledge how to till and dress their grounds, they shall be reduced from unseemly customs to honest manners, from disordered riotous routs and companies to a well governed commonwealth, and withal, shall be taught mechanical occupations, arts and liberal sciences; and which stands them most upon, they shall be defended from the cruelty of their tyrannical and blood sucking neighbours the cannibals, whereby infinite number of their lives shall be preserved. And lastly, by this means many of their poor innocent children shall be preserved from the bloody knife of the sacrificer, a most horrible and detestable custom in the sight of God and man, now and ever heretofore used amongst them. Many other things could I here allege to this purpose, were it not that I do fear lest I have already more than half tired the reader . . .

[1] Gilbert was drowned in the *Squirrel* on 9 September 1583. This document purports to have been written after the return of the *Golden Hind*, but before the loss of the *Squirrel* was certainly known. (B, B, T)

21 The Supply of Sea Fish From Abroad, 1584

(*York Civic Records, Vol. VIII*, ed. A. Raine (Yorkshire Archaeological Society, Record Series, CXIX, 1963), pp. 92–3)

The copy of a certain note delivered to my Lord President the sixteenth of February, 1584

Whereas heretofore the merchants of York, Hull, Newcastle, Lynn and Boston with other creeks and havens of the north part were accustomed to bring into the north parts of this realm great quantity of staple fish, lings and cod, every year to the value of three hundred thousand and more from the parts beyond the seas, viz. from Holland, Friesland, Shetland, Hamburg, Bremen and other parts; and also great quantity of salted herrings from Zeeland, Holland, Malstrande and Scotland, to the number of 15 or 20 hundred last or more every year; whereby all the north parts of this realm, viz. Lincolnshire, Nottinghamshire, Derbyshire, Leicestershire, Yorkshire, bishopric of Durham, Northumberland, Westmorland, Cumberland and a great part of Lancashire were served at a reasonable price, that is; lings, which were at 3*l* or near thereabouts the hundred, the like thereof is not now to be had for 5*l*; staple fish for 50*s* or four marks the hundred, the like whereof is not now to be had for 4*l* 6*s* 8*d*, and white salted herrings sold commonly for 13*s* 4*d* or 15*s* the barrel, and is now dearer than 18*s* and 20*s*; and no quantity to be had to serve these north parts withal, by reason men are restrained from the bringing of any the said fish and herrings into the said north parts, as they have been always accustomed to do. The experience of this scarcity was very well seen in these north parts this last year, and is like to be much more this year, and especially amongst the poor sort of people, which is not able to make provision for victuals aforehand, which is thought to be reason of a statute[1] made in the 23rd year of her majesty's reign against the bringing into this realm of such salted fish and herrings.

[1] An Act for the Increase of Mariners, 23 Elizabeth, c. 7.

22 Prizes Taken at Sea, 1590

(Books of Examinations and Depositions, 1570–1594, eds. G. H. Hamilton and E. R. Aubrey (Southampton Record Society, 1914), p. 73)

The examination of Henry Rasmont of Fowey, in the county of Cornwall, of the age 22 or thereabouts, taken the 13th of July, 1590

First the said examinant says that he was shipped a ship of this town called carvel by name of the *Hare*, of the burden of 30 tons or thereabouts. And the owners thereof are Denys Rowse of the town of Southampton, merchant, and Thomas Exton of the same town, gentleman, captain's name he knows not. And being examined how many prizes they took says that they took certain prizes against St Malo, whereof one with 10 or 11 packs of linen whereof it fell to 7 ells to a single share, and says there was of soldiers and mariners aboard 30 men. And the owners had their shares of the ships and victuals accordingly. And also took one other prize which had a quantity of butter, but how much he knows not. After that they took these two [merchant] men which they brought into the port of the town of Southampton laden with salt. To the apparel and furniture of ships he can say nothing. Being demanded what commission he serves at any time, says that he heard that they had a commission out of the town.

23 The Company of Merchant Adventurers, 1601

(J. Wheeler, *A Treatise of Commerce* (Middelburg, 1601), pp. 22–9)

Of the state and government of the Company of Merchants Adventurers, and of such benefits as grow to the realm by the maintenance thereof

The Company of Merchants Adventurers consists of a great number of wealthy, and well experimented merchants, dwelling in divers great cities, maritime towns and other parts of the realm, to wit, in London, York, Norwich, Exeter, Ipswich, Newcastle, Hull &c. These men of old time linked and bound themselves together in company, for the exercise of merchandise, and sea-fare, trading in cloth, kersey and all other, as well English as foreign commodities vendible abroad, by the which they brought unto the places, where they traded, much wealth, benefit, & commodity, and for that cause have obtained many very excellent, & singular privileges, rights, jurisdictions, exemptions & immunities, all which those of the aforesaid fellowship equally enjoy after a well ordered manner, and form, and according to the ordinances, laws, and customs denized, and agreed upon by common consent of all the merchants, free of the said fellowship, dwelling in the above mentioned towns, and places of the land: the parts, and places which they trade unto, are the towns, and ports lying between the rivers of Somme in France and the Scawe in the German sea: not into all at once, or at each man's pleasure, but into one, or two towns at the most within the abovesaid bounds, which they commonly call the mart town, or towns:[1] for that there only they stapled the commodities, which they brought out of England, and put the same to sale, and bought such foreign commodities, as the land wanted, and were brought from far by merchants of divers nations, and countries flocking thither, as to a fair, or market to buy and sell. And albeit through the troubles, and alteration of times, the M.M. Adventurers have been forced to change and leave their old mart towns and seek new . . . yet wheresoever they seated themselves, thither presently repaired other strangers, leaving likewise the places whence the English merchants were departed, and planting themselves where they resided: so that as long as the company continued their mart, or staple in a place, so long grew and prospered that place, but when they forsook it, the welfare, and good estate thereof seemed withal to depart, and forsake it, as in old time has been seen in Bridges [Bruges], and in our time in some others, and no marvel. For diligent enquiry being made in the year 1550 by the commandment of the Emperor Charles the Fifth, what benefit, or commodity came to his state of the low countries by the haunt, and commerce of the English merchants, it was found, that in the city of Antwerp alone, where the company of M.M. Adventurers was at that time residing, were at least twenty thousand persons fed and maintained for the most part by the trade of the M.M. Adventurers: besides thirty thousand others in other places of the low countries likewise maintained and fed partly by the said trade, partly by endraping of cloth, and working in wool and other commodities brought out of England. In confirmation whereof, I have heard ancient merchants say, that at the time when the above said company was entirely resident at Antwerp, a little before the troubles which fell out in the years '63 and '64 there were fed, and maintained in the low countries sixty thousand souls (and some have said a great many more) by the English trade, and by the wares bought in the low countries to be carried into England, which no doubt was the cause, that the princes of the low countries have been so favourable to the above said company, and so loath to forgo or lose them, as knowing that therewithal they should lose a very fair flower of their garland, yea a sure root, and foundation of their wealth. For on the one side, such is the value, profit, and goodness of the English commodities, that all nations of these parts of Europe, and elsewhere, desire them, and on the other side, the English merchants buy up, and carry into England so great a quantity of foreign wares, that for the sale thereof, all strange merchants do, and will repair unto them. Now what these English commodities are, and how they be so profitable, may appear by the particulars following:

First, there is shipped out yearly by the abovesaid company at least sixty thousand white cloths, besides coloured cloths of all sorts, kerseys short and long, bays, cottons, northern dozens, and divers other kinds of coarse cloths: the just value of these sixty thousand white cloths can not well be calculated, or set down, but they are not less worth (in my opinion) then six hundred thousand pounds sterling, or English money.

The coloured cloths of all sorts, bays, kerseys, northern dozens, and other coarse cloths, I reckon to arise to the number of forty thousand cloths, at least, and they be worth one with another four hundred thousand pounds sterling, or English money.

There goes also out of England, besides these wool cloths, into the low countries, wool, fell, lead, tin, saffron, conyskins, leather, tallow, alabaster stones, corn, beer, and divers other things, amounting unto great sums of money. By all which commodities, a number of labouring men are set on work, and gain much money, besides that which the merchant gains, which is no small matter. Hereunto add the money which shippers, and men that live upon the water, get by freight, and portage of the foresaid commodities from place to place, which would amount to a great sum, if the particulars thereof were, or could be exactly gathered: hereby in short may be seen, how great and profitable the company of M.M. Adventurers trade has been, and is in the places, where they hold their residence, besides the profit raised upon the chambers, cellars, and packhouses, which they must have for four or five hundred merchants, whereby rents are maintained and kept up, and the great expenses otherwise, which the said merchants are at for their diet, apparel, &c. to say nothing of the princes', or generality's profit, and revenues by their tolls, convoys, imposts, excises, and other duties . . . it follows to show, what the M.M. Adventurers buy for return, of strange nations, and people frequenting their mart towns, and bringing their country commodities thither.

Of the Dutch, and German merchants, they buy Rhenish wine, fustians, copper, steel, hemp, onion-seed, copper and iron wire, latten, kettles, and pans, linen cloth, harness, saltpetre, gun-powder, all things made at Nuremberg, and in sum, there is no kind of ware, that Germany yields, but generally the M.M. Adventurers buy as much, or more thereof, than any other nation.

Of the Italians, they buy all kind of silk wares, velvets, wrought and unwrought, taffetas, satins, damasks, sarsenettes, Milan fustians, cloth of gold and silver, grograins, chamlettes, satin and sowing silk, organzine, orfoy, and all other kind of wares either made, or to be had in Italy.

Of the Easterlings they buy flax, hemp, wax, pitch, tar, wainscot, deal boards, oars, corn, furs, cables, and cable yarn, tallow, ropes, masts for ships, soap ashes, estridge wool, and almost whatsoever is made, or grown in the East countries.

Of the Portingales, they buy all kind of spices, and drugs: with the Spanish and French, they had not much to do, by reason that other English merchants have had a great trade into France and Spain, and so serve England directly from thence with the commodities of those countries.

Of the low country merchants, or Netherlanders, they buy all kind of manufacture, or handwork not made in England, tapestry, buckrams, white thread, incle, linen cloth of all sorts, cambricks, lawns, mather, and an infinite number of other things, too long to rehearse in particular, but hereby I hope it sufficiently appears, that it is of an exceeding value, which the M.M. Adventurers buy, and carry into England, in so much, that I have heard it credibly reported, that all the commodities, that come out of all other countries, besides England, were not wont to set so many people on work in the low countries, as the commodities which came out of England only did, neither that any other two of the greatest nations, that frequented the said low countries for trade, did buy, or carry out so much goods in value, as the Merchants Adventurers. The knowledge, and consideration whereof has made them thought worthy to be made of, cherished, and desired by princes, states and commonwealths, and it would not hurt the state of the empire a whit, to hold friendship, and entertain so profitable a company, and trade, as this, whereby great multitudes of their poor people, might be set on work, and get their living, and in process of time grow rich thereby, as the men of Antwerp, and others of the low countries have done, which by the practices of the Pope, and King of Spain, and the unreasonable dealing of the Hanses, is in a manner kept from them.

[1] In 1601 the mart town was Middelburg.

24 Privy Council Injunctions on the Impressing of Seamen, 1620

(*The Official Papers of Sir Nathaniel Bacon, 1580–1620*, ed. H. W. Saunders (Camden Society, Third Series, XXVI, 1915), pp. 72–4)

Privy Council to the justices of Norfolk.[1] 12 July 1620

After our very hearty commendations, whereas the expedition which his majesty has been moved, at the instance of his merchants, to cause to be prepared against pirates and therein to employ six of his own royal ships is now in good forwardness and will be ready to set forth to sea by the first of August next. And that the time does now require to prest and take up such mariners and seafaring men as are requisite for the furnishing of this fleet. We have thought well for the avoiding of such oppression, abuse and corruption, as has heretofore been practised by ordinary prestors to the prejudice of his majesty's service and the great injury and wrong of many poor men, to make special choice of you for the presting of 80 mariners and seafaring men in that county of Norfolk. And do hereby pray and require you to give order for the present presting of the aforesaid number according to the directions contained [below].

To send your precepts to every constable within your precincts to warn and summon all mariners and seafaring men as well fathers and masters as sons and servants to appear personally before you at a certain day and place to be appointed, as they will answer for their contempt at their perils before the judges of assize.

To require the said constables to deliver every one respectively unto you at the same place and time a roll or book of the proper and surnames of all the mariners and seafaring men dwelling or abiding within their several precincts to be sent together with the prest roll to the Office of the Navy that his majesty's service may be more equally carried by the knowledge thereof.

If any seaman be omitted in that book or be not summoned to appear before you or being summoned shall make default, to bind over the said constables so offending: and to cause the said parties not appearing to be apprehended and bound over, in like manner to appear at the next assizes to answer their contempt.

At the time and place of appearance by your best judgments or by the advice of men experienced in sea service to choose out and prest your appointed number of men of such only as are seamen or fishermen or that are practised in seafaring and no unskilful, weak, decrepit, impotent, maimed or unfit persons for his majesty's service.

To deliver to every one whom you prest their prest and conduct monies at his majesty's usual rates, together with a ticket or note in writing containing the name and description of the party, the place whence he was prested, the monies paid unto him, with commandment in his majesty's name to appear one such a day before the Clerk of the Checque at Chatham to be appointed by him in what ship he shall serve.

To take but one or two men at most out of the company of any small barque and generally to use such discretion in the choice that his majesty may be served, and yet trade and fishing as little hindered as may be.

To charge fathers and masters to be answerable for the appearance and service of their sons and servants, and to give warning to all prest men that if they appear not at Chatham according to their tickets, or depart from the service without lawful discharge, they shall from henceforth upon process to be sent against them out of the Court of the Admiralty be apprehended and undergo the penalty of the law.

To cause a book to be drawn of all the names of those whom you prest describing therein their persons by their age, stature, complexion or other pregnant mark to know them by agreeable to their tickets, and setting down the monies delivered for their prest and conduct, the place and day of their presting, and the time appointed for their appearance, and to send the said book signed under your hands to the commissioners of his majesty's navy at London or the treasurer's office at Deptford that present order may be taken for the repayment of the monies, and for allowing of reasonable charge to the party whom to that end you put in trust.

[1] Similar letters were sent to a number of other counties at this time. (HWS)

25 Dutch Competition in the Baltic Trades, 1620

(P.R.O. S.P. 14/115/109, printed in R. W. K. Hinton, *The Eastland Trade and the Common Weal in the Seventeenth Century* (Cambridge, 1959), pp. 168–70)

Petition of the Eastland merchants 1620

To the king's most excellent majesty.

The humble petition of your faithful subjects the merchants trading to the eastern parts.

Humbly show unto your majesty that whereas in time past the English merchants have had an ample trade into those parts whereby they sold great numbers of dyed and dressed cloths and other English commodities in those countries, and have in return thereof laden great numbers of English shipping to the increase of the navigation of this kingdom and vent of their commodities, but now of late years the Netherlanders by reason of their great shipping and cheap freight have much decayed the navigation of this land and in short time if some good course be not taken by your majesty they are like to carry the whole trade and in their own shipping, to the damage and undoing of your majesty's loving subjects and the great increase of the strangers' wealth and strength in navigation.

In tender consideration whereof they humbly beseech your majesty by your royal proclamation to forbid both English and others not to bring into this land any pitch, tar, hemp, flax, ashes, deal boards, spars, masts, or any other eastern goods except the native commodities of their own several countries but in English ships. And they shall according to their bounden duties daily pray to God for the long and prosperous reign of your highness over us.

Reasons to induce the granting of the said petition.

Inprimis the Netherlanders have eaten out the shipping belonging to the eastern cities, who have left the trade wholly to the Hollanders for transportation of their native commodities into other countries, so that now themselves have only small barques who trade within their lands from port to port.

The Netherlanders by their practice, as in the aforesaid petition, have much decayed the trade and shipping of this land and will also in time bring our shipping into utter decay.

There is employed in that trade about 200 sail of ships yearly in bringing into this land hemp, flax, cordage, pitch, tar, corn, ashes, copper, wax, Polish wool, yarn, poldavis,[1] coarse linen, masts, deals, spars, wood of divers sorts and divers other commodities.

The Netherlanders return little or no commodities for the goods they bring in, other than coin, gold or silver, as well for their freight as the proceed of their goods, which may by circumstance be proved for that they return their ships empty without employment of their money in any commodities, and heretofore they have for their goods and freight made their bargain to receive groats, pieces of ninepence and such other coins as have best fitted their profit.

The Netherlanders buy the aforesaid goods at the same market the English buy, and with their ready money they carry they buy 30 in the hundred better cheap than the English, because the English carry cloths and other native commodities which they have heretofore given in barter for the eastern commodities, whereby they overthrow the English merchants and shipping, and besides they have a great advantage in the cheapness of their freight.

Heretofore the English merchants have vented in the eastern parts yearly 25,000 cloths worth 250,000*l*, whereby [whereas] now they vent not above 7,000 or 8,000 cloths which are sent from London, Ipswich, Newcastle, York, Hull and the western ports.

More the English have sent in conyskins and other peltry ware, 8,000*l*. More in white leather, coals, lead and other English commodities for above 6,000*l*. More in foreign commodities to the value of 8,000*l*.

The proceed whereof was wholly returned in the commodities of the eastern countries before named. For bringing home thereof there has yearly been employed at least 100 sail of English ships, beside the English have yearly freighted there at least 100 sail of Netherlanders to bring in the gross commodities of that country. But now of late the Netherlanders are fallen into that trade for this country and bring hither all those commodities better cheap than the English can by the reasons aforesaid.

For prevention whereof we are of opinion that his majesty may for the strengthening and increasing of his decayed navigation by proclamation forbid all strangers whatsoever to bring any gruff goods into these dominions other than in English ships except the native commodities of their countries, so shall the English be encouraged to build shipping and set his majesty's subjects on work and thereby breed and increase mariners for the general occasion when it shall be needful.

In general.

The Netherlanders beside this trade aforesaid take freight from one foreign part to another and carry commodities, the least their own but of other countries, whereby they do not only weaken all other nations in their shipping but so in exceeding manner they increase their own, which makes them so strong at the seas that they neglect the respect they owe to their neighbour princes and make them bold to offer many insolent wrongs.

And lastly the Netherlanders bring as many foreign commodities as they can, ready wrought. As mainly heretofore flax has been brought into this land undressed which now they bring ready dressed to the spinner's hand, the dressing whereof has here in London and in the suburbs maintained above 300 households who did maintain in each household some 6, some 8, and some 10 servants, which now for want of the aforesaid work are fallen into great poverty.

[*Subscribed in another hand*] The consideration of this petition is by his majesty referred unto Sir Thomas Smyth, Sir John Wolstenholme, Sir William Russell, Nicholas Leatt and Thomas Stile, who are to report to his majesty their opinions therein. June 26, 1620.

G. Buckingham

¹ A coarse canvas.

26 Navigation Act, 1660

(12 Charles II, c. 18, *Statutes at Large*, III (1763), pp. 182–4)

For the increase of shipping and encouragement of the navigation of this nation, wherein, under the good providence and protection of God, the wealth, safety and strength of this kingdom is so much concerned; be it enacted . . . that from and after [1 December 1660] no goods or commodities whatsoever shall be imported into or exported out of any lands, islands, plantations or territories to his majesty belonging or in his possession, or which may hereafter belong unto or be in the possession of his majesty, his heirs and successors, in Asia, Africa, or America, in any other ship or ships, vessel or vessels whatsoever, but in such ships or vessels as do truly and without fraud belong only to the people of England or Ireland, dominion of Wales or town of Berwick upon Tweed, or are of the build of and belonging to any the said lands, islands, plantations or territories, as the proprietors and right owners thereof, and whereof the master and three fourths of the mariners at least are English; under the penalty of the forfeiture and loss of all the goods and commodities which shall be imported into or exported out of any of the aforesaid places in any other ship or vessel, as also of the ship or vessel, with all its guns, furniture, tackle, ammunition and apparel; one third part thereof to his majesty, his heirs and successors; one third part to the governor of such land . . . or territory where such default shall be committed, in case the said ship or goods be there seized, or otherwise that third part also to his majesty . . . and the other third part to him or them who shall seize, inform or sue for the same in any court of record . . .

II . . . no alien or person not born within the allegiance of our sovereign lord the king . . . or naturalised, or made a free denizen, shall from and after the [1 February 1661] exercise the trade or occupation of a merchant or factor in any the said places; upon pain of the forfeiture and loss of all his goods and chattels, or which are in his possession . . .

III And it is further enacted . . . that no goods or commodities whatsoever, of the growth, production or manufacture of Africa, Asia or America . . . be imported into England, Ireland or Wales, islands of Guernsey and Jersey, or town of Berwick upon Tweed, in any other ship or ships, vessel or vessels whatsoever, but in such as do truly and without fraud belong only to the people of England or Ireland, dominion of Wales, or town of Berwick upon Tweed, or of the lands, islands, plantations or territories in Asia, Africa or America, to his majesty belonging, as the proprietors and right owners thereof, and whereof the master, and three fourths at least of the mariners are English; under the penalty of the forfeiture of all such goods and commodities, and of the ship or vessel in which they were imported. . . .

IV   . . . no goods or commodities that are of foreign growth, production or manufacture, and which are to be brought into England, Ireland, Wales, the islands of Guernsey and Jersey, or town of Berwick upon Tweed, in English-built shipping, or other shipping belonging to some of the aforesaid places, and navigated by English mariners, as aforesaid, shall be shipped or brought from any other place or places . . . but only from those of the said growth, production or manufacture, or from those ports where the said goods and commodities can only, or are, or usually have been, first shipped for transportation, and from no other places or countries . . .

V   . . . any sort of ling, stock-fish, pilchard, or any other kind of dried or salted fish, usually fished for and caught by the people of England, Ireland, Wales, or town of Berwick upon Tweed; or any sort of cod fish or herring, or any oil or blubber made or that shall be made of any kind of fish whatsoever, or any whale fins or whale bones, which shall be imported into England, Ireland, Wales, or town of Berwick upon Tweed, not having been caught in vessels truly and properly belonging thereunto as proprietors and right owners thereof, and the said fish cured, saved and dried, and the oil and blubber aforesaid (which shall be accounted and pay as oil) not made by the people thereof, and shall be imported . . . shall pay double aliens custom.

VI   . . . from henceforth it shall not be lawful to any person or persons whatsoever, to load or cause to be loaded and carried in any . . . vessels whatsoever, whereof any stranger or strangers born (unless such as shall be denizens or naturalised) be owners, part-owners or master, and whereof three fourths of the mariners at least shall not be English, any fish, victual, wares, goods, commodities or things, of what kind or nature soever the same shall be, from one port or creek of England, Ireland, Wales, islands of Guernsey or Jersey, or town of Berwick upon Tweed to another port or creek of the same . . .

VIII . . . no goods or commodities of the growth, production or manufacture of Muscovy . . . as also that no sort of masts, timber or boards, no foreign salt, pitch, tar, rosin, hemp or flax, raisins, figs, prunes, olive-oils, no sorts of corn or grain, sugar, pot-ashes, wines, vinegar, or spirits called aquavitae, or brandy-wine, shall from and after [1 April 1661] be imported into England, Ireland, Wales, or town of Berwick upon Tweed, in any . . . vessels whatsoever, but in such as do truly and without fraud belong to the people thereof, or some of them, as the true owners and proprietors thereof, and whereof the master and three fourths of the mariners at least are English: and that no currants nor commodities of the growth, production or manufacture of . . . the Othoman or Turkish empire . . . shall from and after [1 September 1661] be imported into any the afore-mentioned places in any ship or vessel, but which is of English build, and navigated, as aforesaid, and in no other, except only such foreign ships and vessels as are of the build of that country or place of which the said goods are the growth, production or manufacture respectively, or of such port where the said goods can only be, or most usually are, first shipped for transportation, and whereof the master and three fourths of the mariners at least are of the said country or place.

*   *   *

XVIII . . . from and after [1 April 1661], no sugars, tobacco, cottonwool, indigoes, ginger, fustick, or other dyeing wood, of the growth, production or manufacture of any English plantations in America, Asia or Africa, shall be shipped . . . from any of the said English plantations to any land . . . or place whatsoever, other than to such other English plantations as do belong to his majesty . . . or to the kingdom of England or Ireland, or principality of Wales, or town of Berwick upon Tweed, there to be laid on shore . . .

XIX . . . for every ship or vessel, which from and after [25 December 1660] shall set sail out or from England, Ireland, Wales, or town of Berwick upon Tweed, for any English plantation in America, Asia or Africa, sufficient bond shall be given with one surety to the chief officers of the custom house of such port or place from whence the said ship shall set sail, to the value of one thousand pounds, if the ship be of less burden than one hundred tons; and of the sum of two thousand pounds, if the ship shall be of greater burden; that in case the said ship or vessel shall load any of the said commodities at any of the said English plantations, that the same commodities shall be by the said ship brought to some port of England, Ireland, Wales, or to the port or town of Berwick upon Tweed, and shall there unload and put on shore the same, the danger of the seas only excepted. And for all ships coming from any other port or place to any of the aforesaid plantations, who by this act are permitted to trade there, that the governor of such English plantations shall before the said ship or vessel be permitted to load on board any of the said commodities, take bond in manner and to the value aforesaid, for each respective ship or vessel, that such ship or vessel shall carry all the aforementioned goods that shall be laden on board in the said ship to some other of his majesty's English plantations, or to England, Ireland, Wales, or town of Berwick upon Tweed. And that every ship or vessel which shall load or take on board any of the aforesaid goods, until such bond [be] given to the said governor, or certificate produced from the officers of any custom house of England, Ireland, Wales or of the town of Berwick, that such bonds have been there duly given, shall be forfeited. . . .

27 An Attack on the Navigation Act, c.1663

(Printed in *Virginia Magazine of History and Biography*, I, No. 2 (Richmond, Virginia, 1893), pp. 142–55)

To the king's most excellent majesty

The humble remonstrance of John Bland of London, merchant, on the behalf of the inhabitants and planters in Virginia and Maryland. Most humbly representing unto your majesty the inevitable destruction of those colonies, if so be that the late Act for increase of trade and shipping be not as to them dispensed with: for it will not only ruinate the inhabitants and planters, but make desolate the largest, fertilest, and most glorious plantations under your majesty's dominion; the which, if otherwise suspended, will produce the greatest advantage to this nation's commerce and considerablest income to your majesty's revenue, that any part of the world does to which we trade.

*   *   *

. . . I pray that the state of Virginia and Maryland, as they now are in may be considered.

Virginia and Maryland are colonies, which though capable of better commodities, yet for the present afford only these, tobacco chiefly, then in the next place corn and cattle, commodities almost in every country whatever to be had; withal they are such commodities, that except purchased in those plantations so cheap as not elsewhere so to be had, none would ever go thither to fetch them, no not we ourselves. Which being so, then certainly it cannot stand with wisdom to hinder the Hollanders from going thither, for unless what is there produced be fetched from thence, the planters will have little encouragement to manure the ground, or trouble themselves to take so much pains as they do, for what, when obtained, they know not what to do therewith. Does it not then hence appear, that unless as some plant, others go to buy what is planted, there can be no trade or commerce in such a place? Seeing what the commodities of Virginia and Maryland are is it not a great advantage to those colonies to have them by everybody fetched thence? and on the contrary, must it not needs be a disadvantage to the commerce there, not to do it? If therefore then we debar the Hollanders from going thither, see the inconveniences that will arise thereby.

The Hollander began to plant tobacco in his own territories, as soon as the Act for their prohibition from Virginia and Maryland in the Long Parliament was obtained, will he not proceed to plant greater quantities, and so totally supply himself by his own labour? do we not force him to this ourselves, and so thereby cut off our own trade? will he, after accustomed to the tobacco of his own growth, ever regard that which is in Virginia? will he ever afterwards be induced to fetch it thence, when he finds his profit higher at home? and will he ever buy that of us, when by passing so many hands, and so much charge contracted thereon, is made so dear, that he can have it cheaper in his own territories? (Surely no.) Therefore it clearly appears, that being so, of necessity we must lose that trade and commerce.

And if it be alleged, that tobacco planted in Holland is not so good as what comes from Virginia, none will buy gold too dear, and being once used to bad, the best is not regarded; what grows in Holland for present spending is as good as any. . . .

Again, if the Hollanders must not trade to Virginia how shall the planters dispose of their tobacco? the English will not buy it, for what the Hollander carried thence was a sort of tobacco, not desired by any other people, nor used by us in England but merely to transport for Holland. Will it not then perish on the planters' hands? which undoubtedly is not only an apparent loss of so much stock and commodity to the plantations, who suffer thereby, but for want of its employment, an infinite prejudice to the commerce in general.

Then again, if you keep thence the Hollanders, can it be believed, that from England more ships will be sent than are able to bring thence what tobacco England will spend? if they do bring more, must they not lose thereby both stock and block, principal and charges? the tobacco will not vend in England, the Hollanders will not fetch it from England; what must become thereof? even flung to the dunghill. Is not then this a destruction to the commerce? for if men lose their estates, certainly trade cannot be increased.

A further prejudice does evidently attend the commerce by this Act, not only in debarring Hollanders from trading to those colonies, but thereby we do likewise debar ourselves; for by the Act, no English ships can load any goods in Virginia and Maryland to transport to any country but our own territories. Is not this absolutely against the very essence and being of trade and commerce, and cuts off all industry or ingenious designs, and is in a manner quite against, and contrary to the intent of the Act itself, which I conceive is to find out a means, that the Hollanders' cheap sailing should not overthrow our markets, our shipping going dearer set to sea than theirs? . . .

Now as this is a prejudice to the commerce of Virginia and Maryland, so in the like it will hold in all our American plantations; but I am, and it is my business at present only, to plead for Virginia and Maryland, and to show its disadvantages to those colonies. Will not this contract a great deal of needless charges and hazardous voyages, and that upon such goods and commodities as Virginia and Maryland afford, which will not keep in long and tedious voyages? does it not hereby then appear to be an absolute hindrance of trade and commerce, not only to those places, but to ourselves here in England?

I demand then, if it would not be better to let our English ships, loading in these colonies, when laden, to go whither they please, and pay in the places where they do lade, (if it will not be dispensed with otherwise) the same customs to your majesty as they should have done in England, or give bills from thence to pay it in England? certainly this would be more beneficial to the commerce, and security both for the ships and goods and advantageous to your majesty . . .

Does it not plainly appear, that foreign nations trading into a country make the people industrious, and their industry makes that nation rich, and so by wealth come countries to be inhabited, which increases trade, and the more trade the more need of shipping to manage it? so that I am of the judgment, that the freer foreign nations be admitted to those colonies, it will the more increase navigation that way, and the contrary will lessen it. For if once the inhabitants be destroyed and ruinated, where is your trade? and then, how shall we employ our shipping? . . .

28 The Illicit Export of Wool, 1664

(*Calendar of State Papers, Domestic Series, Charles II, 1663–1664*, ed. M. A. E. Green (1862), pp. 531–2)

Captain John Strode, Dover Castle, to William Prynne, chairman of a committee of the House of Commons, March 27 1664

Vast quantities of wool are transported at night along the coast from Sandwich to Newhaven, and the persons so strong, that none dare meddle with them without five files of soldiers. Nobody before looked into it, for more wool has been seized this year than in many years before; now they have spies about the castle, so that if the gates be opened, they take the alarm, and return their wools to the houses, and, pretending to be woolcombers and weavers, it cannot be seized there, though they hardly make a piece a year. They have threatened and beaten most of the officers of customs, and go disguised on dark nights, so that no one can swear to them; 200,000 pistoles worth of wool have been this year landed at French seaports, besides what has gone for Flanders and Holland. The Walloons at Canterbury are great traders in it, and all this side of England. Names of the chief offenders. Many could depose to injuries inflicted upon them because they happened to go by when the wool was shipping.

29 The East India Company and Interlopers, 1684

(*The Diary and Consultation Book of the Agent Governor and Council of Fort St. George, 1684*, ed. A. T. Pringle, First Series, III (Madras, 1895), p. 49.)

To Sir John Wetwang, commander of ship Royal James, 6 June 1684

His majesty the king of England our sovereign lord, having granted the honourable East India Company full power and authority to enter into any ship or vessel, and to make seizure of the same, that shall be found in these parts of the East Indies, contrary to his royal will and pleasure . . . we therefore, the Agent and Council of Fort St. George, for the said honourable East India Company, do . . . (there being now an interloper's ship, the *Constantinople Merchant*, John Smith, master, at Covelon), require you immediately to repair aboard your ship, weigh anchor, and set sail for that port of Covelon, and there seize upon the said interloper's ship and bring her into this road of Madras . . . Captain Nicholson in the *Beaufort* is to accompany you, and to follow your orders, and you may take along with you the sloops *Charles* and

Rochester, whose commanders are also to follow your orders, and the soldiers aboard you are to obey your commands as formerly.

30 A Lancaster Merchant on the Effects of War, 1689

(*The Autobiography of William Stout of Lancaster, 1665–1752*, ed. J. D. Marshall (Manchester, 1967), pp. 94–5)

. . . And this was the beginning of the war which was soon after proclaimed in England, France and our allies aforesaid. And immediately after, the sea was overspread with the French privateers and ships of war, which quite put a stop to the commerce by sea betwixt London and this county, as also all commerce with France, and a prohibition of all their produce and manufactures.

Before this war with France, it was computed that we paid to [that] nation at least one million of money sterling for their fashions, products and manufactures over and above what they took from us of our products and manufactures; and although it was evident during the first year of this war they took from us at least five hundred of our ships, which was computed at half a million in value more than we took of their ships—which losses were great to particular persons or merchants —yet the nation got or saved yearly one million of money this year to carry on the war with France, by being prohibited trade with them, and put us upon the silk, linen, paper and many other of their manufactures, to the enriching this nation; and particularly in the south of this county, in making canvas in imitation and as good as their Normandy canvas and Brittany linen. As to wine and salt, we now had them from Portugal and Spain, who took from us the double value in goods of what we had from them. Also, at this time, the salt rock was found in Cheshire, from the brine of which they formerly made fine salt. But now they dug out the rock and carried it by sea to all parts of England and Ireland, and melted it in sea water and boiled it up into a strong salt as good [as] French [and] Spanish salt.

Also abundance of stills were set up for extracting good and strong spirits from malt, molasses, fruit and other materials, instead of French brandy. Some thousand tons of prunes used to be brought yearly from France to England, and commonly sold three pounds for fourpence— and now not to be had at 40s a hundred, which now turned to the butcher's[1] profit. Resin from France, usually sold for ten shilling a hundred, now advanced to 6 or 8d a pound till got from New England, where it was in few years extracted in as great plenty as cheap and fine as French.

We had now no carriage from London but by land, and the cheese of Lancashire and Cheshire, which used to employ at least twenty ships yearly to carry cheese from Liverpool and Chester to London, were now no more employed, but all the cheese sent by waggon to London. And for back carriage brought groceries and other merchandize into the country, by whom we got our goods to Standish at the rate of 3s to 5s a hundred in summer, they choosing to bring them thither in order to [carry] coals or cannel back into Cheshire. And we usually gave 1s 6d a hundred bringing them from Standish to Lancaster. But all our goods from 20s a hundred and under, we got them elsewhere; iron from the bloomeries in Cartmel and Furness, there being then no furnaces erected there for refining it, and what Swedish iron we got, it was from York or Leeds by land. Tobacco, we had always one or more ships yearly hither from Virginia importing it, where we had opportunity to buy small bundles off the sailors at moderate prices; but at the beginning of the war it was high, most ships being taken. Our neighbour John Hodgson sent a ship with a cargo about two hundred pounds value, which purchased about 200 hogsheads, [and] got well home, by which he gained at least one thousand five hundred pounds, tobacco being then near 12d a pound. And in Virginia then 20s worth of English goods here would purchase one hogshead of good tobacco there. It was then permitted to be imported in bulk or small parcels to stow close. The said John Hodgson had then, and some years before, a sugar house in Lancaster for refining sugar, which supplied us with refined sugar and molasses. But as no natural sugar was then imported here, he got his from Bristol or Liverpool, from whom we got ours. There was then no copperas works erected at Liverpool to supply this country, and alum works in Yorkshire, and many other manufactories to answer what we formerly had from London and foreign parts to the ease and benefit of this country.

[1] Middleman's. (JDM)

31 Bristol's Import Trade, 1699–1700

(B.M. Add. MSS 9764, ff. 115–16, printed in *The Trade of Bristol in the Eighteenth Century*, ed. W. E. Minchinton (Bristol Record Society, Publications, XX, 1957), p. 5)

List of ships arrived in the port of Bristol, 25 June 1699–25 June 1700, coasting vessels not included

Number of ships	Of what burden (tons)	From whence they arrived	With what goods chiefly laden
29	4270	Virginia	Tobacco
28	2435	Antigua, Nevis, Montserrat and St Kitts	Sugar, cotton, ginger, molasses, fustick, lignum vitae &c.
18	2060	Jamaica	Sugar, logwood, cotton, indigo, pimento, and dyeing wood
9	675	Barbados	Sugar, cotton, ginger, molasses
22	1450	Lisbon, Bilbao, St Sebastian, Oporto, Faro, Canaries	Wine, oil, fruit and salt, iron and wool
8	195	St Malo, Murlaix and other ports in France	Linen cloth, wine and brandy, pitch, rosin, cork and towe[1]
16	1115	Hamburg and Rotterdam	Linen cloth, Rhenish wine, old iron, earthenware
9	390	Carolina, Newfoundland, New England, Bermuda	Train oil and fish, rice, skins, furs and timber
5	460	Baltic, as Stockholm, Riga, Koningsburg	Pitch, tar, iron, hemp, wire and planks
10	2500	Norway and Gothenburg	Deals, balks, masts and spars
18	2100	Cadiz, St Lucar, Malaga, and up the Streights[2]	Wine, oil and fruit
172	17650	*Total*	
68	2228	Ireland	Wool, woollen yarn and worsted, linen cloth, frieze, tallow, hides and pelts, fish, and cooper's timbers

[1] Coarse part of hemp and flax.
[2] Used to denote unspecified ports in the Mediterranean. (WEM)

32 Instructions for a Slaving Captain, 1725

(*Documents illustrative of the History of the Slave Trade to America,
II, The Eighteenth Century,* ed. E. Donnan (New York, 1969), pp.
327-9)

Bristol, October 7th, 1725

Capt. Wm. Barry, As the wind is inclining to be fair you are ordered
with your men (which we allow to be 20 in number, yourself included)
to repair on board the *Dispatch* brigantine, of which you are continued
commander, and to lose no time but sail directly taking the pilot with
you so far as the Holmes, and at his return let us be advised whether all
the hands are on board and what else may be material.

You must make the best of your way to the coast of Africa, that is to
that part of it called Andony[1] (without touching or tarrying at any
other place) where you are to slave entirely, but as our brigantine
draws deep water, we are not inclinable you should proceed over the
bar, but rather that you anchor as usual in the best and [most] convenient place for safety [as] well as slaving.

The cargo of goods are of your own ordering, and as it's very good
in kind and amounts to thirteen hundred and thirty pounds eight
shillings and $2\frac{1}{4}d$ we hope 'twill purchase you 240 choice slaves, besides
a quantity of teeth[2] the latter of which are always to embrace provided
they are large, seeing in that commodity there's no mortality to be
feared. As to the slaves let your endeavours be to buy none but what's
healthy and strong and of a convenient age—none to exceed the years
of 25 or under 10 if possible, among which so many men, and stout
men boys as can be had seeing such are most valuable at the plantations.

Let your care be in preserving so well as in purchasing, in order to
which let their provisions be well and carefully looked after and boiled
and that it's given them in due season, to see the sailors don't abuse
them which has often been done to the prejudice of the voyage. So soon
as you begin to slave let your netting be fixed breast high fore and aft
and so keep them shackled and hand bolted fearing their rising or
leaping overboard, to prevent which let always a constant and careful
watch be appointed to which must give the strictest charge for the
preservation of their own lives, so well as yours and on which the
voyage depends, which per sleeping in their watch has often been fatal
and many a good voyage (which otherwise might been made) entirely
ruined. You have said that their large canoes will bring the slaves
below the bar for a small matter, which charge had rather be at than

fatigue the men to row so many leagues, which frequently has hurried them into sickness and fevers.

If any redwood can be purchased there, and they'll bring it on board, may take in what can conveniently stow.

Notwithstanding you are ordered directly to Andony and there to slave wholly, yet if you find there many ships and believe can do better at any other part in the Bight, that is at Old Calabar or Bandy, you have liberty to proceed.

When you are fully slaved make the best of your way to Princess, where you are to water and get other recruits that may want, and there may dispose of all your returned goods for gold, as also so many or all of the slaves provided [you] can get 10 moidores[3] or upwards per head round, which if so make the best of your way directly hither. But in case you can't then proceed to Antigua, where expect our further orders in the hands of Capt. John Turnell, which if should not find then repair to Nevis at Mr John Woodleys, where if should also miss thereof, or either of the islands, then make the best of your way to South Carolina and d'd all the slaves to Mr. Jos. Wragg, who shall have directions for the further proceedings.

Your coast commission is 4 from every 104*l* of the net proceeds of the slaves etc, your privilege slaves 2, provided you purchase them with your own goods and mark them in the presence of both mates. Mr Ross, the chief mate, has the same privilege for his encouragement, but you must supply him with goods to do it, which you are to take an account of, as he must be debited for it here at home after knows what 'tis, his slaves must also be marked in your presence and 2nd mate, and as for teeth we can't allow to any. You must pay the half wages abroad according to act of parliament, and in all your passages keep a good and constant look out, and trust no sail you see, fearing pirates. See your officers do their duty in their several stations, and with them and the men keep a good harmony and decorum without too much familiarity or austerity, seeing the voyage depends on good conduct.

You have copies of the invoice, the cargo, portlidge bill, stores and provisions, all which think is complete and sure enough. Of all which stores and provisions desire your utmost care and inspection to see how they are made use of, and to observe there's no waste or want.

In case of your mortality (which God forbid) then it's our directions Mr Jno. Ross take up and follow these our instructions and after him Mr Willm. Pine, 2nd mate.

We can't break off without recommending to you dispatch, which is the life of the voyage, and as you know that *Commerce* is ready and

bound the same way, therefore endeavour what in you lies to get there
before her, and to see you are not outdone in the slaving by other
commanders.

Be careful of fire and in fine of all committed to your charge, and
keeping us advised by all opportunities of all material occurrences [in]
what immediately offers. But recommending you to the Good God
Almighty's protection, and wishing you a good voyage, we remain,

> Your affectionate friends
> Isaac Hobhouse
> No. Ruddock
> Wm. Baker

I acknowledge the above to be a true copy of my orders delivered me
from Messrs. Isaac Hobhouse and Co., owners of the *Dispatch*, which
I promise to perform (God willing) to the utmost of my power.

> William Barry

[1] Andoni, on the Bight of Biafra, north of Fernando Po. (ED)
[2] Elephant tusks.
[3] The moidore, or Portuguese *moeda do ouro*, was worth 27s 6d.

33 Smuggling from the Isle of Man, 1732

(*Customs Letter-Books of the Port of Liverpool, 1711–1813*, ed. R. C.
Jarvis (Chetham Society, Third Series, VI, 1954), p. 41)

*Board of Commissioners, London, to the Collector of Customs, Liverpool,
6 April 1732*

Mr Jackson, the Collector of Beaumaris, having acquainted the Commissioners that he has an account from Captain Richmond, who
commands the Custom House sloop at Liverpool, who put into Beaumaris from the Isle of Man, that he has found there no less than thirty
sail of vessels lading brandies and other goods which he apprehended
were intended for North Britain and Ireland, and that there has lately
[been] imported into that island a considerable quantity of tea from
Flanders and Holland which [is] in order to be run into this kingdom
or Ireland: the Commissioners direct that you give it in strict charge to
the several preventive officers on shore as well as on the water-guard
diligently to look out for the said vessels in order to prevent their
running their cargoes.

34 The Composition of Overseas Trade, 1747

(R. Campbell, *The London Tradesman* (1747), pp. 289–92)

To take a view of our imports and exports.

We export to Jamaica, and the rest of the sugar colonies, all manner of materials for wearing apparel, household furniture of all sorts, cutlery and haberdashery wares, watches, jewels and toys, East-India goods of all sorts, some French wines, English malt liquor, linen cloths of the growth of Scotland, Ireland, and Germany, and our ships generally touch in Ireland and take in provisions, such as beef, pork, and butter. The returns from thence are rum, sugar, cotton, indigo, some fine woods, such as mahogany, lignum vitae, &c. and some dyeing woods, particularly logwood.

We export to New England, New York, Pennsylvania, and the rest of our northern colonies, the same articles mentioned in the last paragraph; in a word, every article for the use of life, except provisions. We have in return, wood for shipping, corn and other provisions for the southern colonies: some furs and skins, flax, rice and flax-seed from the provinces of Georgia and Pennsylvania, and fish from New England, for the Levant market.

We export to Virginia and Maryland every article mentioned before, and have in return tobacco and pig-iron. From all the colonies we have ready money, besides the goods sent them, which they procure by the illicit trade carried on between our island and the Spanish main.

We export to Ireland the growth of our plantations, sugar and tobacco, East-India goods of all sorts, silks of the manufacture of England, and raw-silk, the production of Italy; broad-cloths, hats and stockings, gold and silver lace, and many other articles of the production of this country; for which we take nothing from them in return but ready money, except some linen cloth, and provisions for our southern colonies. The balance paid by Ireland in exchange of goods, and the money spent by their gentry and nobility in England, amount at least to one million sterling per annum, which is a greater advantage than we reap from all our other branches of commerce; yet we grudge these people the common privileges of subjects, despise their persons, and condemn their country, as if it was a crime to be born in that kingdom from whence we derive the greatest part of our wealth.

We export to Holland and Flanders some woollen goods, Birmingham and Sheffield goods, coal, lead, tin, and lead-ore; sometimes corn, butter, cheese, and hides from Ireland; some leather, tobacco, and sugar. From thence we have holland, cambric, paper, whale-fin, and whale-oil, delft and earthen-ware, thread and thread-laces, and a monstrous quantity of East-India goods run in upon our coast by the smugglers. The Dutch have scarce any export of commodities peculiar to themselves; the ground of their commerce is East-India goods and fish caught upon the coast of Britain; with these two articles they purchase all the production of the earth, and are more masters of the American wealth than the proud monarch, whose property it is.

We send to Germany, some woollen goods; but fewer of late years than formerly; some lead, leather, and tin. And in return have linen cloths, for our home consumption, and the use of our plantations; and pay a large balance in ready money.

We export to France scarce anything but lead and tin, some tobacco to Dunkirk, and some salmon from Scotland; but we import wine, brandy, silks of various sorts, cambrics, laces of thread and of gold and silver, paper, cards, and an innumerable quantity of trifling jewels and toys; for all which we pay an annual balance of one million and a half. In reckoning up the imports from France, I should have mentioned pride, vanity, luxury, and corruption; but as I could make no estimate by the custom-house books of the quantity of these goods entered, I choose to leave them out.

We export to Sweden and Denmark some woollen goods, tobacco, sugar, and a few East-India goods; but this last article is daily decaying. We send them soap and salt, and some fish; but the Dutch monopolise that branch. We receive in return deal, iron, copper, and oaken-planks; and pay them a great balance in ready money.

We send to the East Country much the same goods last mentioned, and receive in return naval stores of all sorts, some linen cloth, and some goods of the growth of Persia, brought through Russia by land.

We used to send to Spain woollen goods of various fabrics and furnished their plantations with the same articles we send to our own; we furnished them with negroes from the coast of Guinea. For all which we had in return, some wines of the growth of Spain, fruits, oil, and olives, and a large remittance in gold and silver; but this trade has now dwindled to nothing, the French have engrossed it wholly to themselves.

We send to Portugal lead, tin, woollen goods, goods for their plantations in the Brazils, and have our returns in wines, oils, and ready money.

We send to Italy, fish from New England and Newfoundland, lead, tin, some woollen goods, leather, tobacco, sugar, and East-India goods;

and have, in return, some rich wines, currants, silks wrought and raw, oil, olives and pickles.

To the East-Indies we send out some woollen goods, lead, watches, clocks, fire-arms, hats; but our chief export is silver bullion. For which we receive in exchange, gold, diamonds, spices, drugs, tea, porcelain or china-ware, silk wrought and raw, cotton-cloths of different kinds, salt-petre, &c. A great part of these goods are consumed at home and in our plantations, and the remainder is exported to other countries of Europe; the return of which makes amends for the bullion exported.

To Guinea we send some woollen and linen goods, cutlery ware, firearms, swords, cutlasses, toys of glass and metal, &c. and receive in return negroes for the use of our plantations, gold dust, and elephant's teeth.

To Turkey we send woollen goods of all sorts, lead, tin, East-India goods, sugar, &c. and receive in return, coffee, silks, mohair, carpets, &c. This is a beneficial branch of trade; the imports and exports being near upon a par.

35 A Description of Liverpool, 1753

(*The Liverpool Memorandum Book for the Year 1753*. Printed for R. Williamson. Liverpool Record Office, 920 MD 407. Preface)

Liverpool . . . is situated on the east side of the river Mersey, about three miles from the mouth of the river, being of late years the most flourishing sea-port (next to the mother port) in Great Britain. The inhabitants are universal merchants, and trade to all foreign parts, but Turkey and the East Indies. It shares the trade to Ireland and Wales with Bristol, and engrosses most of the Scotch trade. It is both a con-venient and very much frequented passage to Ireland and the Isle of Man, there being always vessels going and coming from thence. Ships of any burden may come up with their full lading, and ride before the town, which is quite open and unfortified, and vessels of eighteen feet draught of water may go into the docks, which are not inferior to any in Great Britain. On the 14th of September, 1749, the first stone of a new exchange was laid, which is now near finished; and, for its size, is not to be paralleled in Europe.

36 A Bideford Privateer, 1756

(Advertisement in *Felix Farley's Bristol Journal*, September, 1756, printed in J. W. Damer Powell, *Bristol Privateers and Ships of War* (Bristol, 1930), opp. p. 184)

Bideford, August 30, 1756. On a cruise, the *Tigress*, privateer, a prime sailer, William Burch, commander, burden about 200 tons, 16 six and four pounders, and 120 men, will sail in 30 days, having a protection for the ship's company. All sailors and able-bodied landsmen who are disposed to enter on board the said privateer, let them repair to the Town Arms, on the key at Bideford, where they shall meet with all proper encouragement.

M

6

Finance, Private and Public
1000–1485

The maintenance of a sound coinage was vital to the flow of private and royal transactions in medieval times. Before 1066 the minting of the coinage was already firmly under the control of the monarchy (*1*), but problems of forgery and clipping persisted despite the later strengthening of royal government (*5*). The quality of the coinage was also affected by the movement of specie in foreign trade (*11*).

At every level of society individuals had recourse to loans. Moneylenders were to be found in the villages (*13*). In the late twelfth and early thirteenth centuries the Jews were among the chief suppliers of credit (*3*). In the later thirteenth century they were superseded by Italian financiers, members of associations of merchant capitalists, who provided banking facilities and credit to the better-off (*8*). In the later Middle Ages prosperous merchants and others in the towns also provided loans (*9*). Such private transactions facilitated the growth of trade and economic activity. Landholders also borrowed from the merchants and high rates of interest were charged (*15*). Despite Church teachings against the taking of interest usurious agreements were common (*19*).

In the Middle Ages public finance was a matter of royal finance. In the eleventh century the monarch could draw on the wealth of the realm in the form of the geld, a tax assessed on land (*2*). Crown revenue after the Conquest was principally derived from Crown lands, the administration of justice and feudal incidents. Royal revenues were collected by the sheriff who accounted annually at the Exchequer, a distinct court by the mid-twelfth century (*4*). Such sources were inadequate and the Crown relied increasingly on extraordinary taxes on land and also the personal wealth of its subjects (*12*). From the later thirteenth century Italian bankers financed much of government expenditure (*6*) until the Crown reneged on its debts in the mid-fourteenth century. In the thirteenth century customs were introduced to tap the flourishing wool trade (*7*). In the following centuries royal revenue declined for a variety of reasons (*10*). The monarch, exhorted by Parliament, attempted to live of his own (*18*) but was forced to adopt various measures including exploiting feudal incidents, borrowing from native merchants (*14*) and debasing the coinage (*17*).

1485–1760

There were some outstanding advances in financial activity in this period. Expanding wealth, production and trade promoted a growing volume of financial transactions which in turn inspired an increasing sophistication of practice. Such growth and innovation was paralleled in, and linked with developments in, state finance.

The borrowing of funds and obtaining of credit by individuals, for business or personal reasons, became even more extensive. Among the better-off the device of the mortgage was often employed (*26*, *27*), while in the lower reaches of society recourse was normally had to lesser money-lenders and pawn-brokers (*41*). Medieval hostility to the taking of interest gradually waned, more relaxed attitudes being apparent in comment (*25*) as in legislation. Men, though, were still prosecuted for usury early in the seventeenth century (*28*). Although the use of credit instruments, such as the bill of exchange, was already widespread by the sixteenth century, the coinage, and hence the activity of the royal mint (*20*), was vital to the flow of transactions. Deficiencies or alterations in the coinage could disturb trade and prices, as with the debasements of the 1540s (*22–3*), or the clipping and counterfeiting that preceded the silver recoinage of 1696 (*37*). By the later seventeenth century private paper instruments serving as money were being supplemented by a growing amount of government paper, and by the notes of the emergent private banks (*33*). The foundation of the Bank of England in 1694 (*36*) strengthened these developments, its creation being part of a remarkable boom in joint stock ventures. A rising market in stocks fed the contemporary love of speculation (*38*), a proclivity attaining frenetic proportions in the 'bubble' of 1720 (*39*).

The evolution of public finance before 1760 stemmed largely from the increasing inadequacy of traditional sources of royal supply, seen most acutely in wartime, and the rising wealth of the nation. Sixteenth-century governments sought funds additional to income from royal estates and the customs, by levying subsidies on certain kinds of property (*24*) and by loans raised at home and abroad (*21*). Gresham's analysis of the role of the exchanges in public finance demonstrates the expertise available to the Crown (*23*). The difficulties of early Stuart times (*29*) culminated in a striking move to modernity, in the introduction of excise duties (*30*)—long to be unpopular (*42*), the greater use of the customs, and the ending of feudal incidents (*31*). In the later seventeenth century short-term loans from private banks and, from 1693–4, the rise of long-term borrowing from the Bank of England and the public, further aided public finance. These developments underpinned the unprecedentedly high spending of the War of the League of Augsburg (*35*). Increasing resort in the early eighteenth century to a specific land tax aroused the plaint of the landed (*40*). Massie's estimates of 1756 of the tax burden of all classes (*43*) reveal that all paid and the poorer proportionately least.

Seventeenth- and eighteenth-century England was attractive to Dutch investors (*32*). English funds too went abroad, principally to the colonies and in the finance of foreign trade, while in wartime appreciable sums were disbursed on the Continent, by 1760 there being a highly efficient mechanism for such transfers (*44*).

1 Pre-Conquest Laws on the Coinage, Tenth and Early Eleventh Centuries

(Printed in *English Historical Documents*, I, ed. D. Whitelock (1955), pp. 384, 420)

(a) *Athelstan's Laws at Grately, 924–939*

*   *   *

14. Concerning moneyers. Thirdly, that there is to be one coinage over all the king's dominion, and no one is to mint money except in a town.

14.1. And if a moneyer is convicted, the hand with which he committed the crime is to be struck off, and put up on the mint. And if, however, there is an accusation, and he wishes to clear himself, he is then to go to [the ordeal of] hot iron, and redeem the hand with which he is accused of having committed the crime; and if he is convicted at the ordeal, the same is to be done as it [is] said here above.

14.2. In Canterbury [there are to be] seven moneyers; four of the king, two of the bishop, one of the abbot; in Rochester three, two of the king, one of the bishop; in London eight; in Winchester six; in Lewes two; in Hastings one; another at Chichester; at Southampton two; at Wareham two; [at Dorchester one];[1] at Exeter two; at Shaftesbury two; otherwise in the other boroughs one.

(b) *Laws of Cnut, 1020–1023*

*   *   *

8. And also let us all take thought very earnestly about the improvement of the peace and the improvement of the coinage; about the improvement of the peace in such a way as may be best for the householder[2] and most grievous for the thief; and about the improvement of the coinage in such a way that one coinage is to be current throughout all this nation without any debasement, and no man is to refuse it.

8.1. And he who after this coins false money is to forfeit the hand with which he coined the false money, and he is not to redeem it at any price, neither with gold nor with silver.

8.2. And if the reeve is accused, that it was with his permission that he coined the false money, he is to clear himself with the three-fold process of exculpation; and if this exculpation fails, he is to incur the same sentence as he who coined the false money.

[1] From the *Quadripartitus* of *c*.1114. (DW)
[2] *Bonda*, peasant proprietor—in this context any law-abiding member of society. DW)

2 The Northamptonshire Geld Roll, 1068–83

Anglo-Saxon Charters, ed. A. J. Robertson (Cambridge, 1939), pp. 231–3)

To Sutton Hundred belong 100 hides, as was the case in King Edward's time, and of these 21 hides and two-thirds of a hide have paid geld and 40 hides are in demesne and 10 hides are the king's own food-rent land and 28 hides and one-third of a hide are waste.

To Warden Hundred belong 100 hides, as was the case in King Edward's time, and of these 18 hides less one yardland have paid geld and 40 hides are in demesne and 41 hides and 1 yardland are waste.

To Cleyley Hundred belong 100 hides, as was the case in King Edward's time, and of these 18 hides have paid geld and 40 hides are in demesne and 42 hides are waste.

* * *

To *Egelweardesle* Hundred belong 100 hides, as was the case in King Edward's time, and of these 16 hides and half a hide have paid geld and 40 hides are in demesne and from 6½ hides at Norton not a penny has been received—Osmund, the king's secretary, owns that estate—and 37 hides are waste.

* * *

To Willybrook Hundred belong 62 hides, as was the case in King Edward's time, and of these 7 hides have paid geld and 11 hides are in demesne and 13 hides are waste. All this belongs to half the hundred and the king owns the half hundred which has paid no geld.

To the double hundred of Upton Green belong 108½ hides, as was the case in King Edward's time, and of these 50 hides have paid geld and 27 hides are in demesne and 29 hides and half a hide are waste and of the 100 hides 2½ hides have not paid geld, and that estate is owned by Richard Engayne.

To the double hundred of *Navereslund* belong 160 hides, as was the case in King Edward's time, and the amount of land belonging to this double hundred which has paid geld is 29 hides and 1 hide and 59 hides are in demesne and 11½ hides are waste, and of these 160 hides 8 hides have not paid geld, and that estate is owned by the Lady, the king's wife.

3 A Religious House in the Grip of a Money-Lender, 1174-82

(*Chronica Jocelini de Brakelonda de rebus gestis Samsonis Abbatis Monasterii Sancti Edmundi*, ed. H. E. Butler (Nelson's Medieval Texts, 1949), pp. 1-3)

Discipline and religion and all things pertaining to the Rule were zealously observed within the cloister; but outside all things were badly handled, and every man did, not what he ought, but what he would, since his lord[1] was simple and growing old. The townships of the abbot and all the hundreds were given out to farm; the woods were destroyed, the houses of the manors threatened to fall in ruin, and day by day all things went from bad to worse. The abbot found but one remedy and one consolation—to borrow money, that thus at least he might be able to maintain the honour of his house. No Easter nor Michaelmas came round during the eight years before his death but that one or two hundred pounds were added to his debt; the bonds were continually renewed, and the interest as it grew was turned into capital. This infirmity spread from the head to the members—from the superior to his subjects. And so it came about that each obedientiary had his own seal and bound himself in debt to Jews and Christians as he pleased. Often silken copes and flasks of gold and other ornaments of the church were placed in pawn without the knowledge of the convent. I saw a bond given to William son of Isabel for one thousand and forty pounds, and have never known the why or the wherefore. I saw another bond given to Isaac the son of Rabbi Joce for four hundred pounds, but I know not why; and yet a third to Benedict the Jew of Norwich for eight hundred and fourscore; and the cause of this last debt was as follows: our chamber was fallen in ruin, and the sacrist, willy-nilly, undertook to restore it, and secretly borrowed forty marks at interest from Benedict the Jew and gave him a bond sealed with the seal that used to hang from the feretory of St. Edmund, and with which the instruments of the gilds and fraternities used to be sealed: it was broken up afterwards, at the bidding of the convent, but all too late. Now when this debt had increased to one hundred pounds, the Jew came with letters from our lord the king concerning the sacrist's debt, and at last that which had been hidden from the abbot and the convent was revealed. The abbot was angry and would have deposed the sacrist, alleging a privilege granted him by the Lord Pope, enabling him to depose William his sacrist when he would. But someone came to the abbot and speaking on the sacrist's behalf, so deluded the abbot that he allowed a bond to be given to Benedict the Jew for four hundred pounds, to be paid at the end of four years, to wit, for the hundred pounds already accumulated at interest and another hundred pounds which the said Jew had lent the sacrist on the abbot's behalf. And the sacrist undertook in full chapter to repay the whole debt, and a bond was given sealed with the convent's seal: for the abbot dissembled and would not set his seal to the bond, as though the debt was no concern of his. But at the end of four years there was not the wherewithal to pay the debt, and a new bond was made for eight hundred and four-score pounds, to be paid off at stated times at the rate of fourscore pounds a year. The same Jew also held a number of bonds for smaller debts and one that was of fourteen years' standing, so that the total debt due to him amounted to twelve hundred pounds not counting the accumulated interest . . .

[1] Abbot Hugh, 1157–82. (HEB)

4 The Sheriff's Account at the Exchequer, c.1177

(Richard, son of Nigel, *Dialogus de Scaccario*, ed. C. Johnson (Nelson's Medieval Texts, 1950), pp. 6–8, 29–31)

Scholar What is the Exchequer?

Master The exchequer[1] is an oblong board measuring about ten feet by five, used as a table by those who sit at it, and with a rim round it about four finger-breadths in height, to prevent anything set on it from falling off. Over the exchequer is spread a cloth, bought in Easter term, of a special pattern, black, ruled with lines a foot, or a full span, apart. In the spaces between them are placed the counters, in their ranks, as will be explained in another place. But though such a board is called 'exchequer,' the name is transferred to the court in session at it; so that if a litigant wins his case, or a decision on any point is taken by common consent, it is said to have happened 'at the Exchequer' of such a year. But where we now say 'at the Exchequer,' they used to say 'at the Tallies.' . . . here too the struggle takes place, and battle is joined, mainly between two persons, to wit, the treasurer and the sheriff who sits at his account, while the rest sit by as judges to see and decide . . .

Scholar Is the Exchequer where this conflict takes place the only Exchequer?

Master No. For there is a Lower Exchequer, also called the Receipt, where the money received is counted and entered on rolls and tallies, in order that the account may be made up from them in the Upper Exchequer. But both spring from the same root, because whatever is found in the Upper Exchequer to be due, is paid in the Lower, and what is paid in the Lower is credited in the Upper.

*   *   *

The duty of the scribe who sits next to the treasurer is to prepare the Rolls (which for a certain reason are of sheepskin) for writing. The length of the Rolls[2] is that of two membranes, larger than the average and carefully chosen for the purpose, but their width is a little more than a span and a half.[3] They are ruled from the top nearly to the bottom, on both sides, with a reasonable space between the lines. At the head of the Roll, are entered the names of the county and bailiwicks of which the account is rendered below. A space of three or four finger-breadths is left blank. Then in the middle of the line is written the name of the county which is to be dealt with first. Then, at the head of the next line, the name of the sheriff is engrossed, and after it the following formula: 'So-and-so the sheriff renders account of such-and-such a county.' Farther on in the same line: 'In the Treasury.' But no more is added till the closing of the account for an urgent reason which is made clear in business of the sheriff. Then, at the head of the next line is set down how much has been spent in fixed alms and tithes, and how much in payments out of the farm of the county. After this at the head of the line below, as 'Lands granted,' are noted the gifts which royal liberality has made to churches, or to those who served them, out of the lands which are assigned to the Crown, some blanch, some by tale.

Scholar It excites my curiosity that you should say that some lands are given 'blanch' and some 'by tale.'

Master Let us, for the present, proceed with the duty of the scribe.

You can question me on this point when we come to the business of the sheriff. After the 'Lands granted' a line is left blank to indicate a change of subject, and then are noted the payments which have been made by order of the king's writs, because these are not fixed, but casual. Also certain payments which are allowed without writ, by the custom of the Exchequer, as will be explained below; and so concludes the account of the farm of the county

Next, after leaving a blank space of six or seven lines, comes the account of purprestures and escheats in these words: 'The same sheriff renders account of the farm of purprestures and escheats.' After this, furthermore, in their proper order, are placed all the accounts of farms of manors and cess of woods, except certain cities, towns and bailiwicks whose accounts are longer, because they have their own fixed alms and liveries, and lands granted, and special summonses are sent to their keepers for the debts due to the king. Their accounts are entered after the complete closing of the accounts of the counties in which they are. Such are Lincoln, Winchester, Meons, Berkhamstead, Colchester and several others.

Scholar I am surprised at your calling some fixed rents 'farms' and others 'cesses.'

Master Manors have farms; only woods have cesses. For the income from manors, since they are renewed and come back every year by cultivation, and besides have fixed rents established by ancient custom, is rightly called 'farm,' being firm and unchangeable. But that due annually from woods, which are daily cut down and perish, from which there is no firm and unchangeable profit, but a constant, though not annual, ascent and descent, is called 'cess,' and by a similar dropping of the first syllable those rents are said to be 'sessed'. But some people think that 'cess' is what is paid by individuals, but 'farm' the sum to which these amount; so that 'farm' is a collective noun like 'crowd.' The reason, they think, why it is thus 'assessed,' is to show that it is annual, but not fixed.

After these fixed farms, and another blank space, comes the account of the debts about which the sheriff has been summoned, above which are written as a title the names of the judges responsible for determining them.

Finally the chattels of fugitives from justice and of those mutilated for their crimes are brought to account. And when this is finished the sheriff's account comes to an end.

But the scribe must be careful not to write anything of his own in the Roll, but only what the treasurer has dictated. But if from carelessness, or from some other accident, he makes a clerical error, in a name, a number or an account, in which details the main value of the Roll consists, he must not venture to make an erasure, but must cancel by drawing a fine line underneath and write the correct version on the line after the cancellation. For the writing of the Roll has this in common with charters and other engrossed documents, that it ought not to contain any erasure. And that is why it has been provided that the 'pipes' should be made of sheepskin, on which it is difficult to make an erasure without its showing plainly.

[1] *Scaccarium*, chess board.
[2] The 'pipes' or sheets of which the Roll is made up. (CJ)
[3] About 13 in. (CJ)

5 Problems of Clipped and Counterfeit Coinage, 1248

(Matthew Paris, *English History*, II, translated J. A. Giles (1853), pp. 262–5)

About this time, the English coin was so intolerably debased by money-clippers and forgers, that neither natives nor foreigners could look upon it with other than angry eyes and disturbed feelings. For it was clipped round almost to the inner part of the ring, and the border which bore the letters was either entirely destroyed or enormously defaced. Proclamation was therefore made by herald in the king's name in all cities, boroughs, and markets, that no penny should be taken which was not of legitimate weight and circumference, nor be received in any way, either in buying, selling, or exchange, and that all transgressors of this order would be punished. Great diligence was used to discover the aforesaid false dealers, that, if found guilty of the crime, they might meet with condign punishment, according to the decision of a court. A careful inquisition, therefore, was made, and there were found to be guilty of this crime certain Jews and notorious Caursins, and also some Flemish wool-merchants. The French king also ordered all persons guilty of this crime who were found in his kingdom to be suspended on gibbets and exposed to the winds.

* * *

Of the trouble and vexation of the people, owing to the changing of the money

In the course of this year the people were so troubled by divers precepts of the king concerning the receiving of money, proclaimed by the voice of a herald throughout the cities of England, that they would rather a measure of corn had cost more than twenty shillings; for exchange was carried on but in few cities; and when they got there, they received a certain weight of new money for a certain weight of old, and were obliged to pay thirteen pence on every pound for the smith's work, or moneying, which was commonly called whitening. The form of this money differed from the old, insomuch that a double cross traversed the border where the letters were marked; but in other respects, namely, as to weight, chief impression, and the lettered characters, it remained as before. The people were therefore reduced to great straits, and suffered no slight injury, inasmuch as twenty shillings could scarcely be obtained from the money-changer's table for thirty, without a trouble and expense of several days' duration and tedious expectation. As a great increase of profit accrued to the king by these matters, his brother, Earl Richard, to whom he was deeply indebted, came to him, like another Jacob and a subtle supplanter, and said to him, "My king and brother, pay me the debts you owe me." And as he perseveringly continued to press his demand, the king replied, "My only brother by the same parents, you see my necessities on all sides. The very small portion of territory which remains to me on the continent is exposed to peril and injury. Gascony is protected by the shield of Bordeaux alone; to liberate which province I find it necessary to expend a no small sum of money." The earl, however, with an insolently loud voice, demanded satisfaction for his debt out of the profits arising from the money coinage; and as he unceasingly reiterated his demands with importunity, he obtained a promise that he should receive the profits arising from the coinage, which, according to the exchangers, would continue for seven years, and the profits themselves would amount to twenty thousand pounds, a third portion of the proceeds only being reserved to the king; and thus he was freed from his debt to the earl. The earl, having obtained this, procured preceptory letters from the king, that no coin which had been clipped should be passed in England,—indeed, that all clipped money should be bored through; and if any exchanger should be anywhere discovered giving two pence for one, or three for two, that he should be taken and severely punished, both in his property and person, as being an offender against the king, and a transgressor of the royal precept.

6 The Crown Borrows from Florentine Merchants, 1257

(*Calendar of Patent Rolls, 1247–58*, pp. 562–3)

Bond by the King, Queen Eleanor and Edward their first-born son, to Maynettus Spine, Rustikellus Cambii, Hugucio Simonetti called Macce, Hugettus, brothers, Deuteycttus Gwillelmi, and their fellows, citizens and merchants of Florence, in 10000 marks of good, new and lawful sterlings, counting 13s 4d to the mark, which money they acknowledge has been paid to them renouncing all exceptions, with promise singly and jointly, to pay the same before Midsummer, 1258, at the New Temple, London. If however it be not paid fully by them at that term they promise to pay every two months 1 mark for every 10 marks as compensation for losses, interest and expenses in the recovery of the same. They will believe the amount of such losses on the simple oath of them, or each of them or their proctor, and they will not retain the said debt under pretext of such compensation beyond the term aforesaid. And for the payment of this they bind themselves, the realm, their heirs and all their goods, to wit, more particularly the fruits, rents and profits arising from void archbishoprics, bishoprics, abbeys and priories in England, wardships, sale of woods or forests and marriages of women except the marriage granted to Sir Robert Walerand, the escheats of the Jewry and the money which the king has now or shall have hereafter, the obventions arising from the tenth of ecclesiastical revenues and from the fruits of void benefices, and from certain other apostolic graces granted to the king for the prosecution of his vow, of all which they cannot make any grant to any other purpose until the said merchants are fully paid, except wardships under the value of 50 marks and escheats of inheritances which the king has promised to William de Valence, his brother, and to Simon de Montfort, Earl of Leicester, and 3000 marks which ought to be paid out of the sale of woods to certain other of the king's creditors, and except also the void churches of Ely and Carlisle, and the monastery of St. Edmunds. And this done, the said merchants shall, out of the said money received up to next All Saints, first satisfy the king's envoys to the court of Rome to the amount of 10000 marks. And the king and his son Edward swear on the gospels that nothing shall prevent this from being done, and if the said money be not then paid, the bishops of London, Salisbury and Worcester shall place the king and his chapels under an ecclesiastical interdict when they receive a papal mandate for this, and they shall not revoke such sentence until the money is fully paid with the expenses, interest and damages; they renounce all exceptions and especially that of crusaders. And they grant that if any letters of indulgence or privilege shall be obtained from the apostolic see whereby the premises can be prevented or retarded, these shall be of no force, and promise that such letters shall not be used in any proceedings, which if they do they promise to give the said merchants or one of them 1000*l* sterling by the name of a penalty; and grant that the said merchants can convene them before any judge whether in or out of England. And for the greater security hereof at their prayers Richard Earl of Gloucester, William de Valence, Robert Walerand, Philip Lovel the treasurer, and Henry of Wingham the chancellor, have sworn on the gospels to see that these conditions are kept. Witnesses, the said Robert, William, Robert, Philip and Henry.

7 The Custom on Wool, 1275

(P.R.O. Fine Roll, 3 Edward I, m. 24)

For the new custom which is granted by all the great men of the realm and at the prayer of the communities of the merchants of all England, it is provided that in every county in the largest town where there is a port two of the more lawful and able men be elected, who shall have one piece of a seal in keeping, and one man who shall be assigned by the king shall have another piece; and they shall be sworn that they will lawfully receive and answer for the king's money, that is to say, on each sack of wool ½ mark, and on each 300 fells which make a sack ½ mark, and on each last of hides 1 mark, that shall go out of the realm, as well in Ireland and Wales as in England, within franchise and without. Furthermore in every port whence ships can sail there shall be two good men sworn that they will not suffer wools, fells or hides to leave without letters patent sealed with the seal which shall be at the chief port in the same county; and if there is any man who goes otherwise therewith out of the realm, he shall lose all the chattels which he has and his body shall be at the king's will. And forasmuch as this business cannot be performed immediately, it is provided that the king send his letters to every sheriff throughout all the realm, and cause it to be proclaimed and forbidden through all the counties that any man, upon forfeiture of his body and of all his chattels, cause wools, fells or hides to be taken out of the land before the feast of Trinity this year, and thereafter by letters patent sealed with the seals as is aforesaid, and not otherwise, upon the aforesaid forfeitures. And the king has granted of his grace that all lordships, through the ports whereof wools or hides shall pass, shall have the forfeitures when they are incurred, each in its port, saving to the king ½ mark on each sack of wool and fells, and 1 mark on each last of hides.

8 Italian Merchant-Bankers and the Wool Trade, 1284

(P.R.O. Exchequer Plea Roll, E 13/26, m. 23, printed in *Select Cases concerning the Law Merchant*, II, ed. H. Hall (Selden Society, XLVI, 1930), pp. 69–70)

The morrow of St. Andrew, 31–32 Edward I[1]

The prioress of Arden[2] was attached to answer to Coppus Cotenni, yeoman of William bishop of Coventry and Lichfield, treasurer of the lord king, on a plea that she do render to him ten pounds which she owes to him and unjustly detains; and whereupon the said Coppus proffered a certain writing which he says is the deed of Margaret, formerly prioress of Arden, the predecessor of the now prioress, in which is contained that the prioress of Arden and the convent of the same place acknowledge that they have sold to Coppus Cotenni, Chynus Thyfang and John Wlpus and to their fellows, merchants of the society of the Friscobaldi of Florence, all the wool of the aforesaid house of Arden for the year of Our Lord 1291, and for nine years next following, fully completed, namely every sack for eleven marks and a half. And the aforesaid wool shall be well prepared and weighed according to the use and custom of the house aforesaid, without cooked and black guard, grey scab, clacked and all vile fleeces. And that the aforesaid merchants shall pay to the said prioress and convent in hand, as earnest money,[3] ten pounds of good sterlings, whereof the aforesaid ten pounds in the last year shall be fully allowed to the same merchants. And the aforesaid merchants shall pay to them in hand, as earnest money, ten pounds every year during the term within the Quindisme next after the Feast of S. Michael at Arden, and the whole residue in consideration of the aforesaid wool the said merchants shall pay to the said prioress and convent at the issue and delivery of the wool aforesaid. And they shall find sarpler-makers and packers of the said wool at their expense. And the same prioress and convent at their expense shall carry the said wool to Thorpe, to the wool-house of Byland,[4] every year during the term. And this wool, well prepared and weighed, the said prioress and convent promise and are bound by legal stipulation to issue and deliver to the said merchants, or to one of them, or to their regular attorney, at

Thorpe, at the wool-house of the house of Byland, at the Feast of the Nativity of S. John the Baptist[5] in the year of Our Lord 1291, and so from year to year until the ten years shall be fully completed. And for this they bind themselves and their successors and all their goods, etc. In witness whereof the seal of the chapter of the said house is appended to the said writing. Dated at Arden the day of S. Bartholomew, in the year of grace 1284.

And whereupon the same Coppus says that whereas, according to the form of agreement of the aforesaid writing, the aforesaid ten pounds ought to have been allowed to him in the last year of the aforesaid ten years in the issue of the aforesaid wool, Margaret then prioress did not deliver the wools of the same last year to the said Coppus or to any of his fellows or to the attorneys of the same, nor did she cause them to be carried to the wool-house of Byland at Thorpe, according to the form of the aforesaid agreement, but kept them in her hands; wherefore he says that she injuriously detains the aforesaid ten pounds to the loss of the said Coppus 20*l* . . .

[1] 1 December 1303.
[2] Benedictine nunnery in Cleveland, Yorks. (HH)
[3] The payment of earnest money bound a mercantile bargain.
[4] Cistercian monastery in Cleveland, Yorks.
[5] 24 June

9 The Recovery of a Debt, 1293

(P.R.O. Chancery Files, 415)

To the reverend and discreet and their dearest lord, J. de Langton, chancellor of the illustrious king of England, Robert le Venur, guardian of the city of Lincoln, and Adam son of Martin of the same city, clerk, deputed to receive recognisances of debts, greeting. With all reverence and honour we make known to your reverend discretion by these presents that Simon le Sage of Scarborough and William Kempe of the same town, of the county of York, and each of them for the whole sum, acknowledged before us that they owe to William le Noyr of Lincoln 28*s* sterling to be paid to him or his attorney at the feast of St. Michael in the twenty-first year of the reign of King Edward, according to the form of the statute of the said lord the king published at Westminster. And because the aforesaid Simon and William have not kept the term of their payment at all, we beseech your reverend discretion humbly and devoutly, that you will order a writ to be sent to the sheriff of York to compel the same Simon and William to pay the said money according to the form of the statute aforesaid. May your reverend discretion prosper long and well. Given at Lincoln on Friday next after the feast of St. Martin in the year aforesaid.[1]

[1] This procedure was first authorised by the Statute of Acton Burnel, 1283, devised to expedite the collection of debts by merchants. The Statute of Merchants, 1285, further strengthened the creditor's security by providing that a defaulting debtor should be committed to prison.

10 A Decline in Customs Revenue from Wine, 1330

(P.R.O. Exchequer, K.R. Accounts, E 101/78/4a, printed in N. S. B. Gras, *The Early English Customs System* (Harvard Economic Studies, XVIII, 1918), pp. 211–12)

The reasons why the wine customs do not yield as much now as previously.

Richard de la Pole delivered this schedule on the 23rd of February in the fourth year of the reign of King Edward the Third after the Conquest.

Because the Gascons are not wont to import wine [into England] if they are not refused in Normandy, Picardy and Flanders, into which parts they now import to a greater degree than they do into England.

Also because formerly wines were imported into England by foreign merchants who pay custom and not much wine was imported by merchants of England, who now bring more wine into England in one year than all the foreign merchants in two, and they are quit of custom.

Also when William of Trent was butler and the wine custom together with the small custom was assigned to him in aid of his office, all the denizen merchants paid the said wine custom as well as the foreign merchants by which the said custom was worth much more.

Also at that time the custom was levied at Berwick-upon-Tweed, where it now ceases, and at Newcastle, Hartlepool and Yarmouth the said custom was good but it is now worth little or nothing, for the reason that the land is wasted and impoverished by the war, that was had there, that merchants still abandon those parts.

Also at that time custom was levied in the port of Kingston upon Hull which was and is one of the better ports of England, where now no custom is taken at all because the Archbishop of York has recovered, by judgment in parliament, the prise of wine there, whereupon the king's butler, who now is, was ordered to cease levying both customs and prises there and to make restitution to the said archbishop of the prises and to the merchants of the customs that he had taken from them.

Also William of Trent in his time levied custom in all the ports in Cornwall where the officers of Queen Isabel do not allow the butler, who now is, or his officers to levy custom. And in like manner act the officers of the earl marshal in the port of Chepstow to the great damage of the king.

Also the citizens[1] of London are now enfranchised by our lord the king so that they pay neither custom nor prise, who when William of Trent was butler used to pay both the one and the other.

Also the same citizens enfranchise other foreign citizens, namely Lombards, Gascons and Picards who used to pay custom but who now pay nothing by reason of their franchise.

Also the citizens of Sandwich have now enfranchised of new four Gascons, namely Peter of Garfis, William Turgian, Arnaud of Sauncz and John of Sastet', who each year import into England 1,000 casks of wine or more, on which they pay no custom because the citizens of Sandwich avow them for their fellow citizens.[2] In like manner it is done at Winchelsea and elsewhere throughout the ports to the great damage of the king.

[1] *Les gentz.*   [2] *Combarons.*

11 Provisions to Maintain the Currency, 1335

(P.R.O. Fine Roll, 9 Edward III, m. 10)

The king to the sheriff of York, greeting. Forasmuch as we have heard that many folk beyond the sea strive to counterfeit our good money, the sterling of England, with worse money, and to send this bad money into our realm, to the deception of us and the damage and oppression of our people if a remedy be not set thereto; we, willing to prevent such damages and oppressions, and to provide a suitable remedy hereon and that our said good money may be multiplied within our realm and the lands of our power, to the profit of us and our subjects, by assent of the prelates, earls and barons of our said realm assembled in our Parliament held at York on the morrow of the Ascension last past, have ordained and established the things that ensue in the manner under-written:—

First, it is provided that no man of religion or other henceforth carry the sterling out of the realm of England, nor silver in plate, nor vessels of gold or silver, on pain of forfeiture of the money, plate or vessel that he shall carry, without special licence from us.

Further, that no false money nor counterfeit sterling be brought into the realm or elsewhere in our power, on pain of forfeiture of the money; so always that all folk of what realms or power soever they be, may safely bring to the exchanges for bullion and not elsewhere silver in plate, vessels of silver and all manner of moneys of silver, of what value soever they be, save false money and counterfeit sterling, and there receive good and suitable exchange.

And that no sterling halfpenny or farthing be molten to make a vessel or other thing by goldsmiths or others on pain of forfeiture of the money so molten, and that the goldsmith or other who shall have so molten it, be put in prison and there stay until he shall have rendered to us the moiety of that which he shall have so molten, notwithstanding charter or franchise granted or used to the contrary.

And that all manner of black money now commonly current in our realm and power be utterly excluded, so that none be current after the month next after proclamation be made, on pain of forfeiture of the same money.

And that every man who will sue for us against such as shall commit fraud against this ordinance be admitted hereto and have the fourth penny of that which shall be so deraigned at his suit to our profit.

And that the mayor or bailiffs in every port where merchants and ships are take oath of the merchants and masters of ships going and returning that they will commit no fraud against this ordinance in any point.

And that there be a table of exchange at Dover and elsewhere where and when it shall seem good to us and our council to make exchanges. And that the wardens of the said tables make exchanges by testimony of the controllers whom we will appoint there.

And that no pilgrim pass out of our realm to the parts beyond the sea except at Dover, on pain of imprisonment for a year. And that good ward and strict be made in all places on the seacoast in ports and elsewhere where there is any manner of landing, by good and lawful men sworn, who in our name shall cause diligent search to be made that none, of what condition or estate soever he be, take sterling money, silver in plate, or vessel of gold or silver out of our realm without our licence, nor bring into the said realm or power false money or counterfeit sterling, as is aforesaid, on the pains and forfeitures aforesaid. And the money, vessel or plate so forfeited shall be delivered at our exchanges by indenture, whereof the one part remaining with the searchers shall be delivered at the Exchequer, and by the same indentures the warden of the exchanges shall be charged with that which he shall have received.

And that the searchers have of our gift for all their work the fourth penny of as much as they find so forfeited. And if the searchers make release or show favour to any and be attainted hereof they shall be liable to forfeiture of as much as they shall have in goods; and that the hostlers in every port where there is passage shall be sworn to make search upon their guests in like manner as the searchers shall do, and shall have the fourth penny of that which they find forfeit to us, as the said searchers shall have. And it is our intention that the said searchers have power to search the hostels and to inform themselves of the doings of hostlers; and that the hostlers, in case they be found deceitful against the said articles, shall be punished and incur the forfeiture aforesaid.

Wherefore we command you, straitly enjoining, that forthwith upon sight of these letters you cause all the articles and points aforesaid to be cried and published in cities and boroughs, market towns, ports and all other places within your bailiwick, as well within franchise as without, where you shall see fit so to do; and that in all other places within your bailiwick where need shall be, except the places where such wardens and searchers shall be deputed by us, you cause such searchers and wardens to be established and sworn to keep and observe this our ordinance in the form aforesaid, on the pains contained in this form; and that you certify the Treasurer and Barons of our Exchequer without delay of the names of those who shall be hereafter assigned by you as searchers and wardens. Given under our great seal at York, 6th June in the 9th year of our reign.

In like manner command is given to the several sheriffs throughout England. . . .

The oath of the searchers.—You shall swear that you will well and lawfully make search of all the things contained in your commission whereof search ought to be made according to the commission, and that you will lawfully perform all the other things contained in the same, and that you will lawfully charge yourself with that which you shall find forfeited to the king and will make a lawful indenture thereof and render a lawful account, and that you will spare none for love or for favour, to have private gain, whereby the king may be a loser. So help you God and his saints.

12 Form of the Taxation of a Fifteenth and Tenth, 1336

(P.R.O. Fine Roll, 10 Edward III, m. 13)

This is the form which the assessors and taxers of the fifteenth, granted to our lord the king in his Parliament held at Westminster on the

Monday next after Sunday in mid-Lent last past, in the tenth year of his reign, by the earls, barons, freemen and the commonalties of all the counties of the realm, and also of the tenth there granted to our said lord the king in all the cities, boroughs and the ancient demesnes of the king, of the same realm, from all their goods which they had on the day of the said grant, ought to observe, and thereby to assess, tax, collect and levy the same fifteenth and tenth in the counties of Northumberland, Cumberland and Westmoreland, to wit, that the chief taxers without delay cause to come before them from each city, borough and other town of the counties, within franchise and without, the more lawful and wealthier men of the same places in such number that therefrom the chief taxers may sufficiently choose four or six of each town, or more if need be, at their discretion, by whom the said taxation and that which pertains thereto to be done may best be done and accomplished; and when they shall have chosen such, then they shall cause them to swear on the Holy Gospels, to wit, those of each town by themselves, that those so sworn will lawfully and fully enquire what goods each man of the same towns had on the said day within house and without, wheresoever they be, without any favour, upon heavy forfeiture, and will lawfully tax all those goods, wheresoever they have come from then till now by sale or otherwise, according to the true value, save the things below excepted in this form, and will cause them to be listed and put on a roll indented quite fully as speedily as they can, and to be delivered to the chief taxers one part under their seals, and retain by themselves the other part under the seals of the chief taxers, and when the chief taxers shall have in such wise received the indentures of those who shall be sworn to tax in cities, boroughs and other towns, the same chief taxers shall lawfully and minutely examine such indentures, and if they discover that there is any defect they shall forthwith amend it, so that nothing be concealed, neither for gift nor for reward of a person taxed less than reason requires; and the king wills that the chief taxers go from hundred to hundred and from town to town, where need shall be, to survey and enquire that the subtaxers in the same towns have fully taxed and valued the goods of every man, and if they find anything concealed, amend it forthwith and cause the Treasurer and Barons of the Exchequer to know the names of those who shall have so trespassed, and the manner of their misdeed; and the taxation of the goods of the subtaxers of the towns shall be made by the chief taxers and by other good men whom they choose so to do, so that their goods be well and lawfully taxed in the same manner as those of others. The taxation of the goods of the chief taxers and of their clerks shall be reserved to the Treasurer and Barons of the Exchequer. And the chief taxers, as soon as they shall have received the presentment of the subtaxers shall cause the fifteenth and tenth to be levied to the use of the king without delay and without doing favour to any man, in the form which is enjoined upon them by the commission. And they shall cause to be made two rolls of the said taxation agreeing in all points, and retain the one by them to levy the taxation and have the other at the Exchequer at the feast of St. Peter's Chains next coming, on which day they shall make their first payment. And be it known that in this taxation of the goods of the commonalty of all the counties there shall be excepted armour, mounts, jewels and robes for knights and gentlemen and their wives, and their vessels of gold and silver and brass, and in cities and boroughs shall be excepted a robe for the man and another for his wife and a bed for both, a ring and a buckle of gold or silver, and a girdle of silk, which they use every day, and also a bowl of silver or of mazer from which they drink. And the goods of lepers, where they are governed by a superior who is a leper, shall not be taxed or taken, and if the lepers be governed by a sound master, their goods shall be taxed like those of others. And be it remembered that from people of counties out of cities, boroughs and the king's demesnes whose goods in all exceed not the value of 10s, nothing shall be demanded or levied; and from the goods of people of cities, boroughs and the king's demesnes, which exceed not the value of 6s in all, nothing shall be demanded or levied.

13 A Village Money-Lender, 1367

(Cambridge, Queen's College MS. Dd. 3, M. 13 (6), printed in F. M. Page, *The Estates of Crowland Abbey* (Cambridge, 1934), p. 172)

Henry Denning, plaintiff, appears against William the herring-monger, and his wife Ida and John Pepiz, executors of the will of John Pepiz the elder, deforciants, on a plea of debt. In which he complains that the aforesaid William, Ida and John owe him and unjustly withold 20s of silver which the same Henry, on the feast of Michaelmas in the 27th year of the reign of King Edward the Third,[1] handed over to the aforesaid John Pepiz, the elder, whose executors are the aforesaid Ida and John. And the aforesaid John [Pepiz, the elder,] received them for trading and for making profit[2] to be paid to the same Henry at the next feast of Michaelmas with the whole profit arising therefrom. On which day of payment the same John did not pay [either the sum] or the profit arising therefrom, nor has he paid yet. Neither have the aforesaid

Ida and John, executors of the same John, paid but they withold and still withold to the loss of Henry 100*s* and from thence etc. And the aforesaid William, Ida and John deny . . . etc. and they say that they owe him nothing nor do they withold as he accuses them and on this they place themselves on an inquisition. Therefore make 12 to come at the next [court].

[1] 1353.   [2] *Ad martandizandum et proficiendum.*

14 The Crown and the Staplers, c.1436

(P.R.O. Early Chancery Proceedings, C 1/11/289)

To the reverend father in God the bishop of Bath, chancellor of England.

Meekly beseeches your servant, Hugh Dyke, that whereas our lord the king on the second day of December in the fourteenth year of his reign, considering the great kindness which the said Hugh, William Eastfield and Hammond Sutton did to him, and specially for that they then granted to lend to our said lord the king the sum of 8,000 marks, and our said lord the king wishing graciously to favour the same William, Hammond and Hugh in this behalf, by his letters patent, by the advice and assent of his council in his Parliament, granted and gave licence to the same William, Hammond and Hugh, that in the sale of their wools at the town of Calais they should be preferred before all other merchants there to the value of the sum aforesaid, and that they and every of them, or others in their name whom the said William, Hammond and Hugh would name hereto, might freely sell their wools aforesaid to the value aforesaid within your said town to what person soever and in what manner soever they should wish, before the other merchants aforesaid, and retain by them the sums forthcoming thence without any restriction or partition to be made thereof in the Staple of Calais among the merchants of the same, any statute or ordinance made to the contrary notwithstanding, as is more fully contained in the said letters; and although one Thomas Ketyll, servant to the said Hugh, at the commandment and will of his master, sold a sarpler of wool to a stranger for the sum of 12*l* 5*s*, to have and enjoy to him without any restriction or partition to be made thereof, as parcel of the sum aforesaid, nevertheless Thomas Thurland of Calais, because the said Thomas Ketyll would not deliver the said sum of 12*l* 5*s* to put the same in partition in the Staple, put him in prison and detained him for a long time contrary to the tenor of the letters aforesaid to the prejudice of our lord the king and the great damage and loss of the said Hugh and

Thomas Ketyll. Wherefore please it your benign grace to grant a writ of *subpoena* directed to the said Thomas Thurland to appear before you in the Chancery of our lord the king upon pain of 30*l* to answer as well our lord the king as the said Hugh and Thomas Ketyll touching the premises, and to do right to the parties, by way of charity.

15 A Merchant Loan to a Landowner, 1453

(*Calendar of Plea and Memoranda Rolls, A.D. 1437–1457*, ed. P. E. Jones (Cambridge, 1954), pp. 134–5)

2 Aug. 1454 Inquisition taken before the mayor and aldermen at Guildhall concerning all manner of contracts of false chevisance and usury made within the City, by the oath of Richard Wyldbore, Robert Collins, John Twigg, John Day, John Routh, Laurence Hay, Thomas Basset, John King, John Claymond, Thomas Knolles, John Shopman, John Halman, John Mader, Robert Fisher, William Butler, John Blaunche, Robert Drayton, Thomas Bryce, Richard Hayward, Robert West and John Hubbard.

The jurors say upon oath that William Bertram, attorney of Richard Woodville, Lord Rivers, applied to Alexander Brook, salter, in the parish of All Hallows, for a loan of 400*l* for a term of six months from 7 Jan. 1453, but the said Alexander refused to lend the money for so long a term save in consideration of 59*l* interest. William, in his great necessity and perplexed by great affliction of heart, chose what he thought to be the lesser evil and accepted the conditions imposed, receiving from the said Alexander only 300*l* and giving goods of his master to the value of 700*l* by way of pledge and a bond for 59*l* in the name of Thomas Coly, skinner, as security for payment of that sum as interest at the end of six months. On the expiration of the term William Bertram was unable to repay the loan, whereupon Alexander allowed him a further six months' grace on condition that he made out to him a letter of sale for certain jewels of the said Lord Rivers which he held in pledge for the sum of 98*l* owed to divers creditors, and also gave security for the payment of a further 50*l pro accommodacione* by a bond in the name of a certain John Gille. Thus the said Alexander by his said false chevisance made a damnable profit of 59*l* for the loan of 300*l*, besides retaining jewels to the value of 700*l* for the same, and also 50*l* for the loan of 98*l*, together with other jewels to the value of 200*l*.

Alexander denied the charge and put himself upon a jury of the aforesaid parish, viz. William Woodward, Robert Butler, John Lambard, John Polhill, John Crow, Oliver Caston, Edward Warmington,

Richard Snowdon, John Book, John Neale, Nicholas Marshall and John Rokley, who returned a verdict of not guilty.

16 The Repayment of a Royal Debt, 1461

(*Paston Letters. 1422–1509*, II, ed. J. Gairdner (Edinburgh, 1910), pp. 33–5)

The king to all to whom . . . greeting. As we are indebted to John Paston, esquire, and Thomas Hows, clerk, in seven hundred marks of the legal money of the realm of England, to be paid to the same John and Thomas after the form of a certain bill, signed with our hand, the tenor of which follows in these words:—

Edward,[1] King of England and of France, Lord of Ireland, records and acknowledges that we have received of John Paston, esquire, and Thomas Hows, clerk, by the assent of our trusty and well-beloved cousin Thomas, archbishop of Canterbury, [and] Master John Stokes, clerk, an ouche[2] of gold with a great pointed diamond set upon a rose enamelled white, and an ouche of gold in [the] fashion of a ragged staff with 2 images of [a] man and woman garnished with a ruby, a diamond and a great pearl, which were laid to pledge by our father,[3] whom Christ assoil, to Sir John Fastolff,[4] knight, for 487*l* [?]; and also an obligation whereby our said father was bound to the said Sir John Fastolff in 100 marks; for which we grant and promise in the word of a king to pay to the said John Paston and Thomas Hows, clerk, or to their assigns, 700 marks of [the] lawful money of England at the days underwritten. That is to say, at the feast of All Saints[5] then next following after the date of this bill 200 marks, and another 200 marks at the feast of All Saints then next following, and another 200 marks at the feast of All Saints then next following and 100 marks at the feast of All Saints then next following. And also we grant that the said John Paston and Thomas Hows shall have an assignment to them, agreeable for the said payment. And if it fortune that the same John and Thomas be unpaid by the said assignment of any of the said payments at any of the said feasts then we grant, upon notice made to us thereof by the same John or Thomas, to pay them or their assigns that payment so behind and unpaid out of our coffers without delay. In witness whereof we have signed this bill with our hand the 12th day of July, the first year of our reign.[6]

We, wishing the payment of that sum to be made and had to the aforesaid John and Thomas, as we are bound, grant and by the presents we concede to the same John Paston and Thomas Hows seven hundred marks of the aforesaid money to be received in the following manner and form, namely, a hundred marks annually to be received of the first money coming and arising from the fee farm of our city of Norwich and from all other farms, issues, profits and returns arising from the same city by the hand of the mayor, custodian, sheriffs, citizens or bailiffs of the same city for the time being, or of other receivers, farmers of approvers of the same fee farms, issues, profits and returns of the said city for the time being, and a hundred marks annually to be received from the farms, rents, issues, profits and other sources whatsoever arising from our counties of Norfolk and Suffolk by the hand of the sheriff of the same counties for the time being, until the seven hundred marks shall have been paid full to the same John Paston and Thomas Hows. In testimony of which etc. Witness the king at Westminster the 27th day of July.

[1] Edward IV.   [2] Buckle, clasp.   [3] Richard, duke of York, d. 1461.
[4] A kinsman of Sir John Paston.   [5] 1 November.   [6] 1461.

17 Coinage Debasement and its Consequences, 1464–5

(*The Historical Collections of a London Citizen*, ed. J. Gairdner (Camden Society, New Series, XVII, 1876), p. 227)

And this year it was ordained that the noble of 6s 8d[1] should go for 8s 4d. And a new coin was made. First they made an angel[2] and it went for 6s 8d, and half an angel for 40d, but they made no farthings[3] of that gold. And then they made a greater coin and named it a royal,[4] and that went for 10s, and half the royal for 5s, and the farthing for 2s 6d. And they made new groats, not so good as the old, but they were worth 4d. And then silver rose to a greater price for an ounce of silver was set at 3s and better of some silver. But at the beginning of this money men grudged passing sore, for they could not reckon that gold as quickly as they did the old gold. And men might go throughout a street or a whole parish before he might change it. And some men said that the new gold was not so good as the old gold was, for it was alloyed.

[1] A gold coin, first minted in 1344.
[2] The device portrayed the archangel Michael.
[3] i.e. no quarter angels.   [4] Another gold coin.

18 The King Proposes to Live of his Own, 1467

(*Rotuli Parliamentorum*, V, p. 572)

John Say, and you Sirs, coming to this my Court of Parliament for the Commons of this my land. The cause why I have called and summoned this my present Parliament is, that I purpose to live upon mine own, and not to charge my subjects but in great and urgent causes, concerning more the weal of themselves, and also the defence of them and of this my realm, rather than mine own pleasure, as heretofore by Commons of this land has been done and borne unto my progenitors in time of need; wherein I trust that you Sirs, and all the Commons of this my land will be as tender and kind unto me in such cases, as heretofore any Commons have been to any of my said progenitors. And for the good will, kindness, and true hearts that you have borne, continued and showed unto me at all times heretofore, I thank you as heartily as I can, as so I trust you will continue in time coming; for the which by the grace of God, I shall be to you as good and gracious king, and reign as right wisely upon you, as ever did any of my progenitors upon Commons of this my realm in days past; and shall also, in time of need, apply my person for the weal and defence of you, and of this my realm, not sparing my body nor life for any jeopardy that might happen to the same.

19 Interest on a Commercial Loan, c.1480

(P.R.O. Early Chancery Proceedings, C 1/64/291)

To the right reverend father in God, the bishop of Lincoln and chancellor of England.

Right humbly beseeches unto your lordship your orator William Elrington of Durham, mercer, that whereas he now 4 years past and more had for a stock of one Richard Elrington the sum of 30*l*, wherefore your said orator was by his obligation bound unto the said Richard in 40*l* and odd silver; which sum of 30*l* your said orator should have to be employed in merchandise, during the space of 7 years, yielding yearly unto the said Richard, for the loan thereof 4*l* of lawful money of England, and at the 7 years' end to yield whole unto the said Richard the said sum of 30*l*; whereupon your said suppliant occupied the said sum by the space of 2 years, and paid yearly unto the said Richard 4*l*; and after that your said orator, remembering in his conscience that that bargain was not godly nor profitable, intended and proffered the said Richard his said sum of 30*l* again, which to do he refused, but would that your said orator should perform his bargain. Nevertheless, the said Richard was afterward caused, and in manner compelled, by spiritual men to take again the said 30*l*, whereupon before sufficient record the said Richard faithfully promised that the said obligation of 40*l* and covenants should be cancelled and delivered unto your said orator, as reason is. Now it is so that the said Richard owes and is indebted by his obligation in a great sum of money to one John Saumpill, which is now mayor of Newcastle, wherefore now late the said Richard, by the mean of the said mayor, caused an action of debt upon the said obligation of 40*l* to be affirmed before the mayor and sheriff of the said town of Newcastle, and there by the space almost of 12 months has sued your said orator, to his great cost, and this against all truth and conscience, by the mighty favour of the said mayor, by cause he would the rather attain unto his duty, purposes now by subtle means, to cast and condemn wrongfully your said orator in the said sum of 40*l*, to his great hurt and undoing, without your special lordship be unto him shewed in this behalf, wherefore please it your said lordship to consider the premise, thereupon to grant a *certiorari*, direct unto the mayor and sheriff of the said town, to bring up before you the cause, that it may be there examined and ruled as conscience requires, for the love of God and in way of charity.

20 Instructions to the London Mint, 1490

(*Materials for a History of the Reign of Henry VII*, ed. W. Campbell (1877), II, p. 522)

29 October 1490. The king to his trusty counsellor Giles Lord Daubenay and Bartholomew Reed, of London, goldsmith, masters and workers of the king's monies within the tower of London.

Greeting. We for certain considerations us moving will and charge you that of such bullion of gold as shall be brought unto you into our mint within our said tower you make or do to be made a new money of gold according to the print and form of a piece of lead to this our present letters annexed; and the same money of gold to be of the fineness of the standard of our monies of gold of this our realm of England, according to the indenture between us and you in that party made; and we will that every piece of gold of the said money be of double the weight of the piece of gold called royal, of which pieces 22 and a half shall make a pound weight tour; and the same piece of gold shall be called the sovereign, and shall go and have course in receipt and payment of money for 20*s* sterling; and in every pound weight of

gold that shall be made within our said tower, we will that you make
or warrant and discharge at all times against us in this behalf.

21 Royal Agreement with the Fuggers, 1546

(*Acts of the Privy Council of England*, New Series, I, 1542–1547 (1890),
pp. 488–90)

The agreement between Christopher Haunsell for and in the name of
Antony Fugger and his nephews on the one part, and the king his
majesty's council for his behalf on the other part.

That where the king his majesty is indebted to the said Fuggers for
divers sums of money and other things to his majesty's use delivered
and furnished at Antwerp, in the sum of 152,180*l*, Flemish, payable the
15th day of August next, as by several obligations of the city of London
and letters patents of his majesty appears; it is agreed between his
majesty's council and the said Christopher in the name of the said
Fuggers in this wise; that is to say, the said Fuggers at his majesty's
request [are] content to take and receive of the said debt of a hundred
fifty and two thousand, one hundred and four score pounds, Flemish,
the sum of 92,180*l*, Flemish, to be paid in Antwerp the said 15th day of
August next, and for the rest which is 60,000*l*, Flemish, the same
Fuggers are content to respite his majesty for 6 months with the interest
of 6½ in the 100, to be paid in Antwerp the 15th day of February next,
upon such like obligations of the city of London and letters patents of
security of his majesty as heretofore have been made; and furthermore
the said Christopher, for and in the name of the said Fuggers, has
bargained and sold to his majesty eight thousand five hundred three
score and eleven quintals and 43lb of copper, after the rate of one
hundred pound weight of the weight of Antwerp for the quintal, and
for the price of 46*s* 8*d*, Flemish, for the quintal; which amounts in all
to 20,000*l*, Flemish, to be paid in Antwerp without any interest the 15th
day of August in the year of our Lord God [1547], by such like obligations of the city of London and letters patents of his majesty as is
aforesaid; and the said Fuggers to deliver the said copper in Antwerp
at all times upon his majesty's request of such goodness as is a sample
of 2 pieces; viz. one bowlet and another plate remaining in the custody
of Sir John Gresham, knight; that is to say two parts thereof; viz.
5,714 quintals and 29lb in bowlets, and the other third part, 2,857
quintals and 14lb in plate copper, either round or square; nevertheless
if the same Fuggers lawfully approve that they cannot deliver the said
third part in plate copper, then the same Fuggers shall stand bound but

for the delivery only of one fourth part; viz. 2,142 quintals and 85lb in plate copper, and the other in bowlets. And it is further condescended and agreed between the king's majesty's council and the said Christopher that the said 8,571 quintals of copper shall be spent within this realm of England and not be transposed to any other realm to be sold. All the which premises either of the said parties promise to observe, and in witness thereof to the one part of this writing indented the king his majesty's council have signed, and to the other part the said Christopher has subscribed, the 10th day of July, 1546.

22 Latimer on Debasement of the Coinage, 1549

(*Master Hugh Latimer. Seven Sermons before Edward VI*, ed. E. Arber (Birmingham, 1869), pp. 34–5)

We have now a pretty little shilling, indeed a very pretty one. I have but one, I think, in my purse, and the last days I had put it away almost for an old groat, and so I trust some will take them. The fineness of the silver I cannot see. But therein is printed a fine sentence: . . . the fear of the Lord is the foundation of life or wisdom. I would God this sentence were always printed in the heart of the king in choosing his wife, and in all his officers.

23 Gresham on Managing the Exchanges, 1558

(Printed in J. W. Burgon, *The Life and Times of Sir Thomas Gresham* (1839), I, pp. 483–6)

To the queen's most excellent majesty

It may please your majesty to understand, that the first occasion of the fall of the exchange did grow by the king's majesty, your late father, in abasing his coin from 6 ounces fine to 3 ounces fine. Whereupon the exchange fell from 26*s* 8*d* to 13*s* 4*d* which was the occasion that all your fine gold was conveyed out of this your realm.

Secondly, by the reason of his wars, the king's majesty fell into great debt in Flanders. And for the payment thereof they had no other device but pay it by exchange, and to carry over his fine gold for the payment of the same.

Thirdly, the great freedom of the Steelyard and granting of licence for the carrying of your wool and other commodities out of your realm, which is now one of the chief points that your majesty has to foresee in this your common weal; that you never restore the steads called the Steelyard again to their privilege, which has been the chief point of the undoing of this your realm, and the merchants of the same.

Now, for redress of these things, in anno 1551 the king's majesty, your late brother, called me to be his agent, and reposed a more trust in me, as well for the payment of his debts beyond the seas, as for the raising of the exchange, being then at 15s and 16s the pound; and your money current, as it is at this present, being not in value 10s. First, I practised with the king and my lord of Northumberland to overthrow the Steelyard, or else it could not be brought to pass, for that they would keep down the exchange by this consideration; whereas your own mere merchants pay outwards 14d upon a cloth custom, they pay but 9d; and likewise, for all such wares as were brought into your realm, your own mere merchants pay 12d upon the pound, the Steelyard paid but 3d upon the pound, which is 5s difference upon the hundredth: and as they were men that ran all upon the exchange for the buying of their commodities, what did they pass to give a lower price than your own merchants, when they got 5l in the hundred by your custom? Which in process of time would have undone your whole realm, and your merchants of the same.

Secondly, I practised with the king's majesty, your brother, to come in credit with his own mere merchants: and when time served, I practised with them at a set shipping, the exchange being still at 16s, that every man should pay the king 15s upon a cloth in Antwerp, to pay at double usage 20s in London; which the king's majesty paid them royally, which did amount to the sum of 60,000l. And so, 6 months after, I practised the like upon their commodities for the sum of 70,000l to pay for every pound sterling 22s: so by this means, I made plenty of money, and scarcity, and brought into the king's hands, which raised the exchange to 23s 4d. And by this means I did not only bring the king's majesty, your brother, out of debt, whereby I saved him 6 or 7s upon the pound, but saved his treasure within the realm, as therein Mr Secretary Cecil was most privy unto.

Thirdly, I did likewise cause all foreign coins to be unvalued, whereby it might be brought into the mint to his majesty's most fordle;[1] at which time the king your brother died, and for my reward of service, the Bishop of Winchester sought to undo me, and whatsoever I said in these matters I should not be credited: and against all wisdom, the said bishop went and valued the French crown at 6s 4d and the pistole at 6s 2d, and the silver royal at $6\frac{1}{2}d$. Whereupon, immediately, the exchange fell to 20s 6d and 21s and there has kept ever since. And so consequently after this rate and manner, I brought the queen's majesty, your sister, out of debt of the sum of 435,000*l*.

Fourthly, by this it may plainly appear to your highness, as the exchange is the thing that eats out all princes, to the whole destruction of their common weal, if it be not substantially looked unto, so likewise the exchange is the chief and richest thing only above all other, to restore your majesty and your realm to fine gold and silver, and is the mean that makes all foreign commodities and your own commodities with all kind of victuals good cheap, and likewise keeps your fine gold and silver within your realm. As, for example to your highness, the exchange being at this present at 22*s*, all merchants seek to bring into your realm fine gold and silver; for if he should deliver it by exchange, he disburses 22*s* Flemish to have 20*s* sterling: and to bring it in gold and silver he shall make thereof 21*s* 4*d*—whereby he saves 8*d* in the pound: which profit, if the exchange should keep but after this rate of 22*s* in few years you should have a wealthy realm, for here the treasure should continue for ever; for that all men should find more profit by 5*l* in the hundred to deliver it per exchange, than to carry it over in money. So consequently the higher the exchange rises, the more shall your majesty and your realm and common weal flourish, which thing is only kept up by art and God's providence; for the coin of this your realm does not correspond in fineness not 10*s* the pound.

Finally, and it please your majesty to restore this your realm into such state, as heretofore it has been; first, your highness has no other ways, but when time and opportunity serves, to bring your base money into fine of 11 ounces fine, and so gold after the rate.

Secondly, not to restore the Steelyard to their usurped privileges.

Thirdly, to grant as few licences as you can.

Fourthly, to come in as small debt as you can beyond seas.

Fifthly, to keep [up] your credit, and specially with your own merchants, for it is they must stand by you at all events in your necessity. And thus I shall most humbly beseech your majesty to accept this my [poor writing in good] part; wherein I shall from time to time, as opportunity does serve, put your highness in remembrance, according to the trust your majesty has reposed in me; beseeching the Lord to give me the grace and fortune that my service may always be acceptable to your highness; as knows Our Lord, whom preserve your noble majesty in health, and long to reign over us with increase of honour.

By your majesty's most humble and faithful obedient subject,

Thomas Gresham, *Mercer*

[1] Fordeal, or advantage. (B, B, T)

24 An Act of Subsidy and Fifteenths and Tenths, 1558

(1 Elizabeth, c. 21, *Statutes of the Realm*, IV, Part I (1819), pp. 384–96)

The case which we do perceive your majesty has, most noble and re-doubted sovereign, to reduce this realm . . . now lately so sore shaken, so impoverished, so enfeebled and weakened, into the former estate, strength and glory, does make us not only to rejoice much in the great bounteousness of Almighty God, who has so marvellously and beyond all wordly expectation preserved your majesty in these late difficult and dangerous times, but also to study and bend all our wits and force of understanding how we may, like loving and obedient subjects, follow our head in this so noble and so necessary an enterprise; and consider-ing with ourselves that the decay has been, besides many other things, especially in these three, first, wasting of treasure, abandoning of strength, and in diminishing of the ancient authority of your imperial crown; we do most earnestly and faithfully promise to your highness that there shall lack no good will, travail nor force on our behalf to the redress of all this . . . Since it does so manifestly appear to us all, what inestimable wasting and consumption of the treasure and ancient revenues of this realm has been of late days, and what great new charges and intolerable expenses your highness is forced now to sustain . . . we your most obedient and loving subjects the lords spiritual and tem-poral, and the commons in this present parliament assembled . . . have condescended and agreed with one voice . . . to make your highness at this time a present . . . be it enacted that your highness . . . shall have . . . two whole fifteenths and tenths to be paid, taken and levied of the movable goods, cattle and other things usual to such fifteenths and tenths to be contributory and chargeable within the shires, cities, boroughs, towns and other places of this your majesty's realm, in manner and form afore time used; except the sum of twelve thousand pounds thereof fully to be deducted . . . in relief, comfort and discharge of the poor towns, cities and boroughs of this your said realm wasted, desolate or destroyed, or overgreatly impoverished, after such rate as was and has afore this time been had and made unto every shire . . . And the said two whole 15ths and tenths . . . to be paid in manner and form following, that is to say, the first whole fifteenth and tenth . . . to be paid to your highness in the receipt of your highness' exchequer, before the 10th day of November next coming; and the said second 15th and 10th . . . to be paid . . . before the 10th day of November [1560] . . .

* * *

IV   And furthermore . . . we . . . give and grant to your highness . . . one entire subsidy to be rated, taxed, levied and paid at two several payments, of every person spiritual and temporal, of what estate or degree he or they be . . . in manner and form following, that is to say, as well of every person born within this realm of England, Wales or other the queen's dominions, as of all and every fraternity, guild, corporation, mystery, brotherhood and commonalty, corporated or not corporated, within this realm . . . being worth five pounds, for every pound as well in coin and the value of every pound that every such person, fraternity . . . has of his or their own or any other to his or their use, as also plate, stock of merchandises, all manner of corn and blades, household stuff and of all other goods movable, as well within the realm as without, and of all such sums of money as to him or them is or shall be owing . . . except . . . such sums of money as he or they owe . . . and except also the apparel of such persons, their wives and children, belonging to their own bodies (saving jewels, gold, silver, stone and pearl) shall pay to and for the first payment of the said subsidy 20*d* of every pound, and to and for the second payment of the said subsidy 12*d* of every pound . . .

V   And be it further enacted . . . that every person born under the queen's obeisance and every corporation, fraternity . . . for every pound that every of the same person and every corporation, fraternity . . . or any other to his or their use has in fee simple, fee tale for term of life, term of years, by execution, wardship or by copy of court roll, of and in any honour's castles, manors, lands, tenements, rents, services, hereditaments, annuities, fees, corrodies, or other yearly profits of the yearly value of 20*s* as well within ancient demesne and other places privileged or elsewhere, and so upwards, shall pay to and for the first payment of the said subsidy 2*s* 8*d* of and for every pound, and to and for the second payment of the said subsidy 16*d* of and for every pound . . .

*   *   *

XII   Provided always, that every such person which shall be set or taxed for payment of and to this subsidy for and after the yearly value of his lands, tenements and other real possessions or profits at any of the said taxations, shall not be set and taxed for his goods and cattle or other movable substance at the same taxations; and that he that shall be charged or taxed for the same subsidy for his goods, cattle and other movables at any of the said taxations, shall not be charged, taxed or chargeable for his lands or other real possessions and profits abovesaid

N

at the same taxations; nor that any person be double charged for the said subsidy, neither set or taxed at several places by reason of this act . . .

25 The Businessman's View of Interest-Taking, 1572

(Thomas Wilson, *A Discourse upon Usury*, ed. R. H. Tawney (1925), pp. 249–51)

Gromel Gayner's or the Merchant's Oration

To say and do are two things. I will not directly speak in the favour of usury, but rather, if you will have me, I am contented to speak against it. Mary, not to use my money for my benefit, call it what you will, I can hardly allow thereof. You have said meetly well, master lawyer, that you will suffer exchange within certain bounds. Others talk so much (I wote[1] not how) that in the end they will mar all. Poor merchants cannot be suffered to thrive amongst them. And I, for my part, am against you all that will have no usury, or will make the gain over little. For, I pray you, what trade or bargaining can there be among merchants, or what lending or borrowing among all men, if you take away the assurance and the hope of gain? What man is so mad to deliver his money out of his own possession for naught? or who is he that will not make of his own the best he can? or who is he that will lend to others and want himself? You see all men now are so wise, that none will lend for moonshine in the water; and therefore, if you forbid gain, you destroy intercourse of merchandize, you overthrow bargaining, and you bring all trading betwixt man and man to such confusion, as either man will not deal, or else they will say they cannot tell how to deal one with another.

I have been a doer in this world these 30 winters, and as fresh an occupier as another, and yet never found I better or more assured gain than by putting out my money for gain, the same being always the best and easiest trade that could be in the world. And in a dead time when there is no occupying, either by restraint or through wars, what would you merchants to do otherwise than to turn the penny and to live by their money? For if they should spend still on the stock without lending it for gain, or barratting[2] any whit at all, I do fear the best of us all (I mean such as live by our money) would soon shut up our doors, and play the bankrupts, which were a most abominable shame, and a great dishonour to this realm. Do not you know that we are ever called upon in time of need, to lend to the prince, for maintenance of the state?

Have not noble men money of us, and all other gentlemen of service, whensoever they have need? And when is it that they have not need of us, great need, God wotes, full oft and many a time? Yea, need must always be, and men shall ever have need. And where is money to be had in time of need, if the city should fail? . . .

We lend not for usury, but for interest, and by exchange, and I think no man can disallow either interest or exchange. I pray you, if an ambassador shall have cause to travail in the affairs of the state, or the queen's agent occasion to pay great sums of money abroad in other countries beyond the seas, what will you have done, if the exchange were not? How can great masses of money be carried to far countries, if bills of exchange be not current? Or who will be so mad to pay thousands in another country for moonshine in the water, to have nothing for his pains, but only his labour for his travail? Hope of gain makes men industrious, and, where no gain is to be had, men will not take pains. And as good it is to sit idle and do nothing, as to take pains and have nothing. Merchants' doings must not be thus overthwarted by preachers and others, that cannot skill of their dealings. And this over great curiosity of some to meddle in other mens' matter, I must tell you plain, it is even the very right way to undo all in the end. Therefore say what you will, I will live and amend, so as I may live every day better and better, by any means, I care not how. Yea, I will make hard shift with the world, and strain my conscience narrowly before I will either starve or beg, both I and my children after me. Provided always that I will not come within the compass of positive laws: and this I wote well, that by all laws a man may take as much for his own wares as he can get, and it is no sin for one man to deceive another in bargaining, so that it be not too much beyond God's forbode, and a bargain is a bargain, let men say what they list. Such your straight prohibitions and strange preciseness, my masters, do make men weary of their lives. You may as well forbid buying and selling, as forbid taking interest for money: for, I pray you, what difference is there betwixt the one and the other? I do buy a piece of land for 500*l* this day, and sell it tomorrow, or within six months after, for 600*l*; and I do lend likewise 500*l* at the same time that I do buy land, and do receive within six months after 600*l* again for my 500*l* so lent. What difference is there betwixt these two dealings? God amend you, my masters of the clergy, and you civilians also.

---

[1] Know.   [2] Charging.

26 Aristocratic Borrowing on Mortgage, c.1576

('Devereux Papers with Richard Broughton's Memoranda, (1575–1601)', ed. H. E. Malden, *Camden Miscellany XIII* (Camden Society, Third Series, XXXIV, 1924), pp. 19–20)

This indenture made . . . between the right honourable Walter, Earl of Essex . . . on the one part, and Thomas Gresham, knight, the queen's majesty's agent, Thomas Aldersey, of the city of London, merchant, William Denham, citizen and goldsmith of London, Richard Broughton, of the Inner Temple, London, gentleman, John Stedman, and William Barrell, gentleman, servants of the said earl, on the other part, witnesses that whereas the said earl intends by the grant and pleasure of her highness, an exploit and enterprise in warlike sort within the north part of the realm of Ireland, and for and in consideration of the better maintenance of the said earl in his said enterprise the said earl has of an especial trust elected, chosen and requested his right well-beloved friends the said Sir Thomas Gresham [and the others] and every of them in the necessary business of the said earl, to take up by way of loan to the use of the said earl such sum and sums of money as to the said Richard Broughton, John Stedman and William Barrell, or any two of them, shall be thought requisite or necessary. And for the saving harmeles[1] of the said Thomas Gresham [and the others] and every of them and for the repayment to be made of for and concerning all and singular such sum and sums of money as the said Thomas Gresham [and the others] or any of them, shall lend, disburse or take up by way of loan to and for the use, business or behalf of the said earl as aforesaid, the said earl by these presents has given, granted, demised, and assigned to the said Sir Thomas Gresham [and the others] all those his estates, interests, possessions, and terms of years, of and in all and singular those lands, pastures, and possessions called Uttoxeter Moors and Moorhead in the county of Stafford, and also all his term of years, estates, possessions and interests, of and in the parsonage of Colwich, in the said county of Stafford, and of and in all and singular the lands, tenements, corn, grain, oatmeal and other customs and possessions belonging to the late monastery of Strata Florida, in the county of Cardigan, with appurtenance which the said earl holds for term of years, to have and to hold all and singular the said possessions, lands, pastures, estates and terms of years to the said Sir Thomas Gresham [and the others] and the survivors and survivor of them during all the estates and terms of years which the said earl has of, in, or to the same.

[1] Harm or loss.

27 Renewal of a Mortgage, 1603

(Printed in R. Meredith, 'The Eyres of Hassop, 1470–1640', *Derbyshire Archaeological Journal*, LXXXIV (1964), p. 43)

Memorandum that upon the 23rd of December 1603 there has been a reckoning between Richard Leech and Roland Eyre in the presence of these persons whose names are underwritten. And the said Richard Leech does acknowledge and confess that he owes unto the said Roland Eyre and his sons the whole and just sum of 233*l* 7*s* of lawful English money. For the true payment of which he stood bound unto them; and has forfeited his land. Yet nevertheless the said Roland Eyre is contented that if the said Richard Leech does pay him at the six years end after 10*l* in the hundred and the said sum of 233*l* that then he shall have the land in Litton and Tydswall again to himself and his heirs. And also to pay yearly during the said time 13*l* 6*s* 8*d* . . . And the said Richard, his wife, his sons and his father in law are contented that if they do fail of the payment of the said rents at the said days, that then the said Roland and his sons shall make the best of it that they can and expel them and put them forth. And moreover the said Richard or his assignees shall pay one hen at Candlemas[1] and one capon at Easter yearly during the said term. Memorandum that the true meaning is that the rent received is to be made but after 10*l* in the hundred if it be redeemed.

[1] 2 February.

28 A Usurer Presented to the Justices, 1606

(*Quarter Sessions Records*, ed. J. C. Atkinson (North Riding Record Society, County of York, I, 1884), p. 46)

Richmond, 14 July 1606 [Presented by the jury].

Christopher Paycock of Newby-super-Wiske for being a great usurer—*in haec verba*, viz. has received of Tho. Catterick of Brompton beside Allerton excessive usury contrary to the statute,[1] that is to say, for the loan of 4*l* for one year, 13*s* 4*d*, and for the loan of the same for a year next after, other 14*s* 4*d*, in *malum exemplum* &c.

[1] 13 Elizabeth, c. 8.

29 The Crown in Financial Difficulty, 1640

(*Calendar of State Papers*, Venetian, XXV, 1640–1642 (1924), pp. 37–85, *passim*)

Giovanni Giustinian, Venetian ambassador in England, to the Doge and Senate

27 April 1640

Parliament was opened in state on Monday. His majesty went to open it . . . He gave a significant account to the members of the continued disobedience of the Scots and the need of bringing them to their duty by force. He asked for prompt contributions for this most just cause . . .

4 May 1640

Parliament has not so far come to any decision about granting the contributions demanded by his majesty. They have spent the whole of this week in an enquiry into the misconduct of several ministers, all the disorders of the present government, and the introduction of fresh gabelles . . . The king . . . sent for the members two days ago, and repeated with emphasis his request that they should vote without delay the subsidies he asked for, admonishing them not to spend time on other matters, but postpone the discussion of them to a more opportune moment when he will be ready to give just satisfaction to his people and in particular to suspend ship money . . .

11 May 1640

. . . the Upper Chamber at length voted in favour of gratifying the king's demands before receiving the satisfaction claimed from him . . . the Lower Chamber [refused] to concur in these sentiments . . .

18 May 1640

The insuperable reluctance of the Lower Chamber to vote the subsidies asked for has at length forced the king to dismiss them . . . A decree has already issued obliging everyone strictly to make a loan for the expenses of the levy . . . against the Scots.

25 May 1640

[The king] has demanded a loan of 200,000*l* from this city.[1] As this has been openly refused, he now proposes, in great wrath, to compel the most substantial merchants to pay it down. For this he sent for the aldermen, so that they may divide it out among the richest; but as they declined he has had them imprisoned,[2] amid universal murmurs . . .

1 June 1640

. . . The king seized with serious fears [about] the discontent of his people [has] turned to conciliating the good will of his subjects once more. To this end he has promptly released the aldermen . . . and it is reported that he will soon, by a public declaration, relieve the kingdom of the payment of many duties recently imposed . . . This city, to show its appreciation of his majesty's good will, has spontaneously granted a loan of 50,000*l* of their money, to use for present emergencies.

15 June 1640

Negotiations have been opened with Genoese merchants to induce them to advance a loan to the king. In addition to a security he offers them interest at the rate of 8 per cent per annum . . .

29 June 1640

In order to make the burden of the soldiers' pay tolerable, they have reduced the pay of the cavalry . . . The men complain bitterly and threaten to desert . . .

The securities offered to the Genoese for their loan do not satisfy them and so they talk of the Court negotiating with Amsterdam merchants for a considerable sum in cash raised upon jewels or some other consignment. They have at length arranged with the customs officials to have a prompt loan of 100,000*l* of their money, and they are also getting together a certain sum by the sale of titles and appointments, but not enough to meet present needs.

27 July 1640

This week the king has come more than once from Oatlands to this city to take part in long consultations with the ministers . . . upon the ways of providing a certain amount of money to meet the present expenses, which have reduced the treasures of the crown to the last extreme. After many conferences they decided to avail themselves of the third part of the silver at present in the mint, brought there by individuals to be coined into money, granting them in compensation 8 per cent per annum, with a promise on the customs as security for the capital and the king's word to pay it off within six months, which is not believed.

This new plan, which does not receive general approval is deeply resented by the interested parties, who have represented in writing the very serious prejudice which will result to the mart here . . .

Besides this measure they have decided to coin 500,000 of their pounds with three parts of copper and only one of silver, to be of the same value as those which are all silver. They are now devoting their ingenuity to find a way to put this in practice. Everyone recognizes the harmful consequences and those who are most skilled believe that it will involve insuperable difficulties, for as the people here are not accustomed to use such base money it will be difficult to oblige them to take it . . .

In order to reduce expenditure as much as possible they have cut down the original assignment to the queen mother by one half. With great perturbation of spirit her majesty has had to dismiss a good number of her household, and to arrange to live a more frugal life.

3 August 1640

His majesty remains at Oatlands with the majority of the ministers. Their most anxious concern is to facilitate the success of the decision to introduce copper money into this kingdom . . .

17 August 1640

After careful enquiry into the disadvantages that might follow the introduction of copper money, and hearing the determined statements of the merchants that they will not take it, the execution of the order has been postponed. With the ever pressing need of money the king has taken the step of asking this city, for the third time, for a loan of 200,000*l* promising, in order to make the way easier, that it shall not be used for warlike purposes, but to establish a beneficial peace in this kingdom. All the same the Council met and by a unanimous vote answered frankly that they could not satisfy the demands of his majesty, as the grant of money ought to depend on the judgment of Parliament alone and not on this city only and a small member of that body . . .

31 August 1640

. . . the Scots . . . crossed the river Tweed on Saturday with a force of 20,000 men . . .

On the arrival of this evil news . . . the Council met and . . . it was decided that without loss of time his majesty should proceed to York. He did so yesterday . . .

. . . The extreme scarcity of money greatly augments the difficulties and his majesty had to leave with no more than 19,000*l* lent by individual merchants. He has suspended the stipends of all the officials of the crown and to save expense has cut down his own table.

7 September 1640

Fresh requests for loans have been made of this city, but have met with no better response than before, and they have definitely refused to contribute without a vote of Parliament. Not knowing where else to go they have tried to obtain on credit from the India Company all the pepper brought by the ships, which have recently arrived, amounting to 70,000*l* with the idea of selling it afterwards to the merchants at a loss, who will readily supply the money. But when negotiations were opened with the interested parties and the heads of the Company, they showed no inclination to entrust their capital to the king, and unless they take it by force, as was done before with the money which lay in the Tower, it seems likely that this last expedient will fail also . . .

His majesty has unexpectedly issued a proclamation to the sheriffs whose duty it is to collect the last tax known as ship money, which the people have been unwilling to pay in the past, although under pressure, informing them that they must satisfy the Treasury within a month, under pain of severe penalties, as he is determined to have prompt obedience and full payment. These, on the contrary, claim that the royal authority does not extend to the imposition of the greater charges, and they refuse to pay. Dissatisfaction constantly increases . . .

14 September 1640

Upon the promise of the customers and of many men of credit, the India Company has at last agreed to grant the king the sale of the pepper as asked. The ministers have hastened to complete the bargain, but so far they have not been able to find anyone willing to take it up, the calamities of the time inducing everybody to proceed with great caution in a matter which may give general offence.

28 September 1640

The ministers here have sold at a loss of 30 per cent the pepper taken on credit for the king, and they have sent the money to the army.

---

[1] London.   [2] Four aldermen were sent to prison.

30 Ordinance Establishing an Excise, 1643

(*Acts and Ordinances of the Interregnum, 1642–1660*, eds. C. H. Firth and R. S. Rait (1911), I, pp. 202–14)

[*22 July 1643*] An ordinance for the speedy raising and levying of monies, set by way of charge or new impost, on the several commodities mentioned in the schedule hereunto annexed; as well for the better securing of trade, as for the maintenance of the forces raised for the defence of the king and parliament, both by sea and land, as for and towards the payment of the debts of the commonwealth, for which the public faith is, or shall be, given.

The lords and commons now assembled in parliament, taking into their serious consideration the great danger that this kingdom lies under, through the implacable malice and treachery of papists, and other malignant persons, who have, and daily do wickedly practise, and endeavour the utter ruin and extirpation of the protestant religion, the privilege of parliament, and the liberty of the subject: insomuch, that there is no probable way left them for the preservation of this nation how to prevent the said malicious practices, but by raising of monies for the purposes first above-mentioned, until it shall please almighty God in his mercy to move the king's majesty's heart to confide in, and concur with both his houses of parliament, for the establishing of a blessed and happy peace, which by both houses is much desired and prayed for. And forasmuch as many great levies have been already made for the purposes first above-mentioned, which the well-affected party to the protestant religion, have hitherto willingly paid, to their great charge; and the malignants of this kingdom have hitherto practised by all cunning ways and means how to evade and elude the payment of any part thereof. By reason whereof the lords and commons do hold it fit, that some constant and equal way for the levying of monies for the future maintenance of the parliament forces, and other great affairs of the commonwealth may be had and established, whereby the said malignants and neutrals may be brought to and compelled to pay their proportionable parts of the aforesaid charge, and that the levies hereafter to be made for the purposes aforesaid, may be borne with as much indifference to the subject in general as may be.

I Be it therefore ordered . . . that the several rates and charges in a schedule hereunto annexed and contained; shall be set . . . upon all and every the commodities in the said schedule particularly expressed . . .

II And be it further ordained . . . that for the better levying of the monies hereby to be raised, that an office from henceforth [be] appointed in the city of London, called or known by the name of the Office of Excise or New Impost, whereof there shall be eight commissioners to govern the same . . . with several registers, collectors, clerks, and other subordinate officers, as the eight commissioners . . . nominate and appoint . . .

* * *

V That the like office, and so many of such officers shall be . . . appointed in all and every the counties of the realm of England, dominion of Wales, and town of Berwick, and in all other the cities, and such other places thereof, as the said eight commissioners . . . think fit to nominate . . .

* * *

VII That the said office in all places where it shall be placed, shall be kept open in the week days, from eight of the clock in the morning till eleven, and from two till five of the clock in the afternoon, for the entering and registering of the names and surnames, as well of the sellers, buyers, and makers of all and every the commodities in the said schedule mentioned, and of the several quantities thereof, as for the receiving of all monies as shall be due upon the sale or making of the same, in such manner as by the said schedule is appointed . . .

* * *

X That all and every the merchants and importers of any of the several foreign commodities in the schedule mentioned, and all ale and common beer brewers shall weekly cause to be entered into the said office a true and perfect list or account, as well of all and every the several commodities by them respectively and weekly sold, as of the names of the buyers thereof, and of those to whose use the same is bought, and that they shall not deliver any of the said commodities, unto any of the buyers thereof, or other person or persons until the same shall be so entered, and that the buyer have procured a ticket, under the hand of the treasurer for the time being, signifying that he has paid the rates set upon the said commodities, or given security for the same.

XI That if any of the sellers of the said commodities shall refuse or neglect to make a true entry of the said commodities, according to the next precedent article, or do anything contrary to the said article, that then he or they . . . shall forfeit to the use of the commonwealth four times the true value or worth of the goods and commodities . . .

XII   That if any common brewer, alehouse-keeper, cider or perry maker, in the country or in any city, town, or place therein, which does brew ale or beer, or make cider and perry, in their houses or elsewhere, do not make a true entry in manner aforesaid . . . then they shall incur the like penalty . . .

XIII   That all and every person and persons whatsoever, that keep or shall keep private houses and families, as well in the city of London, and suburbs thereof, as in all other parts of the kingdom . . . which brew, or shall cause to be brewed, their own ale, and beer for the sustenance of their families, or do make, or cause to be made, any cider and perry, for the purposes aforesaid, shall monthly cause the like entries to be made of all such quantities of ale and beer, cider and perry . . . on the like penalties . . .

*   *   *

XX   That the said commissioners . . . shall have power and authority to call before them any person or persons whom they shall think fit, to inform or testify touching the premises, and to examine them upon oath for the better discovery of any fraud or guile in the not entering, or not payment of the rates of excise, or new impost herein mentioned . . .

XXI   That the said commissioners . . . shall from time to time appoint any officer or officers belonging to the said office, to enter into the cellars, shops, warehouses, storehouses, or other places of every person or persons that sells, buys, or spends any of the said commodities, to search and see what quantities of any of the said commodities every such has on his hands, or any other person or persons to his use.

*   *   *

In this schedule is contained the charge and excise which by the ordinance hereunto annexed is set and imposed, to be paid on the several commodities hereafter mentioned.

For every pound of tobacco, which is not of the English plantation, over and above all customs due for the same, to be paid by the first buyer thereof from the merchant or importer, four shillings.

For every pound of tobacco of the English plantation abroad, or made in the land, over and above all customs due for the same, to be paid by the first buyer thereof from the merchant or importer, two shillings.

For every ton of wine containing four hogsheads, being here retailed over and above all customs due for the same, to be paid by the first retailer thereof . . . six pounds.

For every ton of wine here bought for private use, over and above all customs due for the same, to be paid by the first buyer from the merchant, three pounds . . .

That the wine merchant shall pay for every ton of wine that he spends in his house, over and above all customs due for the same, three pounds . . .

For every hogshead of cider and perry here sold, to be paid by the first retailer, two shillings . . .

For every barrel of strong beer and ale, of eight shillings a barrel or upwards, here sold, to be paid by the first retailer, two shillings.

For every barrel of strong beer or ale, of eight shillings the barrel and upwards, and for every hogshead of cider and perry bought for private use to be paid by the first buyer for every of them, one shilling.

For every barrel of strong beer or ale, of eight shillings the barrel or upwards, which any private housekeeper brews in his house for his own spending, one shilling.

For every hogshead of cider and perry, that every private housekeeper makes for his own spending, one shilling.

For every barrel of ale and beer that any alehouse-keeper, vintner or innholder shall brew and sell in his house or elsewhere, to be paid by the alehouse-keeper, innholder, or vintner, two shillings.

For every barrel of six shillings beer, sold to be spent as well in private houses, as in victualling houses, to be paid by the common brewer thereof, as also by all others that do brew and spend the like beer in their private houses, six pence.

Grocery Imported

Malaga, and other raisins of the growth of Spain, over and above all customs due for the same, to be paid by the first buyer thereof from the merchant, for every pound, one farthing.

Raisins of the sun imported, over and above all customs due for the same to be paid by the first buyer thereof from the merchant, for every pound, one half penny.

For every pound of figs, a farthing.

For every pound of currants, one penny.

For every pound of Saint Thome and Pannellis sugar, one half penny.

For every pound of muscovado sugar, one penny.

For every pound of white sugar, two pence.

For every pound of double or single refined loaf sugar, four pence.

For every pound of pepper, two pence.

[Rates of excise are given also for imported silks, furs, hats, lace, leather, linen, thread, iron, steel, wire, &c.]

That the excise hereby set upon every the foreign commodities above mentioned, is to be paid by the first buyer of the commodity from the merchant, or importer thereof, unless it be otherwise appointed by these presents. And all commodities here rated, which are first imported and then exported (*bona fide*) shall be free, so that it be exported within three months next after the passing of the ordinance hereunto annexed.

31 Reform of Royal Finance, 1660

(12 Charles II, c. 24, *Statutes at Large*, III (1763), pp. 192–8)

An act for taking away the Court of Wards and Liveries, and tenures *in capite*, and by knights-service, and purveyance, and for settling a revenue upon his majesty in lieu thereof.

Whereas it has been found by former experience, that the Courts of Wards and Liveries, and tenures by knights-service, either of the king or others, or by knights-service *in capite*, or socage *in capite* of the king, and the consequents upon the same, have been much more burdensome, grievous and prejudicial to the kingdom, than they have been beneficial to the king: And whereas since the intermission of the said court, which has been from [24 February 1645] many persons have by will and otherwise made disposal of their lands held by knights-service, whereupon divers questions might possibly arise, unless some seasonable remedy be taken to prevent the same; Be it therefore enacted . . . that the Court of Wards and Liveries, and all wardships, liveries, primer seisins and ousterlemains, values and forfeitures of marriages, by reason of any tenure of the king's majesty, or of any other by knights-service, and all mean rates, and all other gifts, grants, charges incident or arising, for or by reason of wardships, liveries, primer seisins or ousterlemains to be taken away and discharged, and are hereby enacted to be taken away and discharged, from the said [24 February 1645]; any law, statute, custom or usage to the contrary hereof in any wise notwithstanding: And that all fines for alienations, seizures and pardons for alienations, tenure by homage, and all charges incident or arising, for or by reason of wardship, livery, primer seisin or ousterlemain, or tenure by knights-service, escuage, and also *Aid pur file marrier*, and *Pur fair fitz chivalier*, all other charges incident thereunto, be likewise taken away and discharged . . . And that all tenures by knights-service of the king, or of any other person, and by knights-service *in capite*, and by socage *in capite* of the king, and the fruits and consequents thereof, happened or which shall or may hereafter happen or arise thereupon or thereby, be taken away and discharged . . . and all tenures of any honours, manors, lands, tenements or hereditaments, or any estate of any inheritance at the common law, held either of the king, or of any other person or persons, bodies politic or corporate, are hereby enacted to be turned into free and common socage, to all intents and purposes . . .

*   *   *

XII And whereas by like experience it has been found, that though divers good, strict, and wholesome laws have been made in the times of sundry his majesty's most noble progenitors, some extending so far as to life, for redress of the grievances and oppressions committed by the persons employed for making provisions for the king's household, carriages and other purveyance for his majesty and his occasions; yet divers oppressions have been still continued, and several counties have submitted themselves to sundry rates and taxes and compositions, to redeem themselves from such vexations and oppressions: And forasmuch as the lords and commons assembled in parliament do find that the said remedies are not fully effectual, and that no other remedy will be so effectual and just, as to take away the occasion thereof, especially if satisfaction and recompense shall be therefore made to his majesty, his heirs and successors, which is hereby provided to his majesty's goodliking and content; his majesty is therefore graciously pleased, that it may be enacted . . . that from henceforth no sum or sums of money or other thing shall be taken, raised, taxed, rated, imposed, paid or levied, for or in regard of any provision, carriages or purveyance for his majesty, his heirs or successors.

*   *   *

XIV And be it further enacted, that no pre-emption shall be allowed or claimed in the behalf of his majesty or of any his heirs or successors, or of any the queens of England, or of any the children of the royal family for the time being, in market or out of market; but that it be for ever hereafter free to all and every of the subjects of his majesty, to sell, dispose or employ his said goods to any other person or persons as himself lists, any pretence of making provision or purveyance of victual, carriages or other thing for his majesty, his heirs and successors, or of the said queens or children, or any pretence of preemption in their or any of their behalfs notwithstanding . . .

XV Be it therefore enacted . . . that there shall be paid unto the king's majesty, his heirs and successors for ever hereafter, in recompense as aforesaid, the several rates, impositions, duties and charges herein after expressed, and in manner and form following: that is to say,

XVI For every barrel of beer or ale above six shillings the barrel, brewed by the common brewer or any other person or persons who does or shall sell or tap out beer or ale publicly or privately, to be paid by the common brewer or by such other person or persons respectively, and so proportionably for a greater or lesser quantity, one shilling three pence.

XVII For every barrel of six shillings beer or ale or under, brewed by the common brewer or any other person or persons who does or shall sell or tap out such beer or ale publicly or privately . . . three pence.

XVIII For all cider and perry made and sold by retail, upon every hogshead, to be paid by the retailer thereof . . . one shilling three pence.

XIX For all metheglin or mead sold, whether by retail or otherwise, to be paid by the maker thereof, upon every gallon, one half-penny.

XX For every barrel of beer, commonly called vinegar-beer, brewed by any common brewer or in any common brewhouse, six pence.

XXI For every gallon of strong-water or aqua-vitae made and sold, to be paid by the maker thereof, one penny.

XXII For every barrel of beer or ale imported from beyond the seas, three shillings.

XXIII For every ton of cider or perry imported from beyond the seas . . . five shillings.

XXIV For every gallon of spirits made of any kind of wine or cider imported, two pence.

XXV For every gallon of strong-water perfectly made, imported from beyond the seas, four pence.

XXVI For every gallon of coffee made and sold, to be paid by the maker thereof, four pence.

XXVII For every gallon of chocolate, sherbet and tea, made and sold, to be paid by the maker thereof, eight pence.

32 Conflicting Evidence on Dutch Money in England, 1669

(*Historical Manuscripts Commission, 8th Report*, Pt. I (1881), *Calendar of House of Lords Manuscripts*, 1665–1671, ff. 133b–34b)

28 October 1669 Minutes of proceedings of the House of Lords committee appointed to consider of the causes and grounds of the fall of rents

and decay of trade within these kingdoms. Evidence given by members of the Council of Trade.

* * *

Mr Titus says a great part of the money used in trade and for the building of London is Dutch money.

Mr Child does not believe there is 10,000*l* of foreign money here.

* * *

1 December 1669   Evidence given before Committee of the whole House of Lords, with regard to the question of reducing the rate of interest.

. . . On the question of what foreign money there is in England, it is stated that Alderman Bucknell had above 100,000*l* in his hands, Mr Meynell above 30,000*l*, Mr Vandeput at one time 60,000*l*, Mr Dericost always near 200,000*l* of Dutch money, lent to merchants at 7, 6, and 5 per cent when money was at 8 per cent. On the other side it is said that Dutch merchants, who are the usual lenders of Dutch money, say there is no considerable quantity of Dutch money in England; and on the general question of the reduction it is contended that trade has increased since the withdrawal of foreign money and the lowering of interest from 8 per cent . . .

33 Dudley North and the Goldsmith Bankers, Late Seventeenth Century

(*The Lives of the Norths by the Hon. Roger North*, ed. A. Jessopp (1890), II, pp. 174–5)

Living in this way, he applied himself wholly to business and did not dream of any thing to happen that might divert him. He found divers usages in London very different from what had been practised in his time there, or in any other place where he had lived: as, first, touching their running cash, which, by almost all sorts of merchants, was slid into goldsmith's hands; and they themselves paid and received only by bills; as if all their dealings were *in banco*. He counted this a foolish, lazy method and obnoxious to great accidents; and he never could bring himself wholly to comply with it. For, having taken an apprentice, one Fairclough, the son of a Presbyterian old usurer, he paid and received all by his cash-keeper in his own counting house, as merchants used to do. But, at length, he was prevailed on to use Benjamin Hinton, a Lombard-street man; and, for acting therein against his conscience, was punished with the loss of about fifty pounds. But others lost great sums by this man; and his breaking made a great shake upon the

Exchange. I remember, he has come home (for, at first, he was, as I said, with us) in great amazement at his own greatness; for the banking goldsmiths came to him upon the Exchange, with low obeisances, 'hoping for the honour'—'should be proud to serve him,' and the like; and all for nothing but to have the keeping of his cash. This pressing made him the more averse to that practice; and, when his acquaintance asked him where he kept his cash, he said, 'At home; where should he keep it?' They wondered at him, as one that did not know his own interest. But, in the latter end of his time,[1] when he had left the city and dealt more in trusts and mortgages than in merchandise, he saw a better bottom, and used the shop of Sir Francis Child, at Temple-bar, for the paying and receiving all his great sums.

[1] Sir Dudley North died in 1691.

34 Political Crisis and the Banks, 1688

(*Letters written during the Years 1686, 1687, 1688, and addressed to John Ellis, Esq.*, ed. Lord Dover (1831), II, pp. 234–5)

London, Oct. 2nd, 1688

I apprehend this will be the last I shall write to you from hence for some time, the wind having been fair all night and to-day from Holland. Our Admiral is gone on board, and weighed anchor, with order to attend the Dutch wherever they go. The King will up with his standard and march upon the first tidings of their landing. The City of London had their Old Charter promised this evening, and great help is hoped from them, as the reward of such a favour. It was time; for Lombard-street stared yesterday, Moor and Thomas[1] having given way, viz. shut up, and all their shops have been crammed this four days, and the merchants' accounts all agree in an invasion. Great confusion, all our noblemen out of town, and in uncertainty where they are. What I wrote on Saturday to you, was real measures taken, though most since retracted; but ere the next Saturday, I think all will again be made good.

For John Ellis, Esq. Secretary of His
    Majesty's Revenue in Ireland, Dublin.

[1] Two bankers. (D)

35 Public Income and Expenditure, 1693–4

(*Parliamentary Papers*, *House of Commons*, XXXV, Part I (1869), pp. 10–11)

Net public income and expenditure of Great Britain, and of other receipts into and issues from the Exchequer, &c. in the year ended 29th September 1694.

	l	*s*	*d*	*l*	*s*	*d*
ʙALANCES in the Exchequer on 29th September 1693	–	–	–	256,892	15	10
ɴET RECEIPTS of Public Income, deducting Drawbacks, &c., and Charges of Collection and Management, viz.:						
Customs	891,948	8	10			
Excise	879,015	19	3			
Stamps	44,548	–	5			
Post Office	59,972	14	9			
Arrears of Hearth Money	1,612	1	10			
Land and Assessed Taxes, and Duties on Pensions, Offices, Personal Estates, &c. (including also Duty on Joint Stocks, per 4 Will. & Mary, c. 15, 21,609*l* 10*s*)	1,914,496	16	7			
Poll Taxes	156,510	1	3			
Crown Lands, including 3,700*l* from Duchy of Cornwall	15,916	8	4			

Miscellaneous, viz.:	*l*	*s*	*d*			
First Fruits and Tenths .	15,893	–	3			
Tenths of Prizes from the Mogul	18,000	–	–			
Other Small Branches and Casualties . . .	4,734	10	11			
Imprest Moneys repaid .	1,150	–	–			
	39,777	11	2			
TOTAL NET INCOME				4,003,798	2	5

ᴏTHER RECEIPTS, viz.:						
Raised by Loan from the Bank of England, in part of 1,200,000*l*; Loan at Annuity of 100,000*l*, from 1 June 1694, per 5 Will. & Mary, c. 20	600,000	–	–			
„ to complete 1,000,000*l* by Life Annuities at 14 per cent, from 24 June 1694, per 4 Will. & Mary, c. 3, and 5 Will. & Mary, c. 5	118,506	5	10			
„ by Contributions under the 1,000,000*l* Lottery Act, 5 Will. & Mary, c. 7, for Annuities at 14 per cent. for 16 years from 25 March 1694.	934,485	17	5			
Ditto for Exchequer Annuities, for one, two, or three Lives, per 5 Will. & Mary, c. 20	300,000	–	–			
„ by Loans in anticipation of Duties, &c. .	3,188,801	15	9			
TOTAL raised by CREATION OF DEBT . .				5,141,793	19	–
				9,402,484	17	3

	l	*s*	*d*	*l*	*s*
INTEREST and MANAGEMENT of the Public Debt, viz.:					
Bank of England, on their Annuity of 100,000*l*, at					
8*l* per cent., including Management, 4,000*l* .	12,000	–	–		
Exchequer Annuities	110,812	16	2		
Interest on Loans in anticipation of Duties, &c. .	319,366	3	1		
				442,178	19
CIVIL GOVERNMENT, viz.:					
Privy Purse	39,795	–	–		
H.M.'s Household	184,228	–	3		
Works and Gardens	35,008	4	8		

Pensions and Annuities, viz.:	*l*	*s*	*d*				
The Queen	64,000	–	–				
Queen Dowager (out of Hereditary Gross Revenues)	10,709	15	2				
Prince and Princess of Denmark (ditto). . .	47,000	–	–				
Other Civil List Pensions and Annuities (including 20,945*l* 10*s* paid out of Hereditary Gross Revenues)	55,566	15	8				

	l	*s*	*d*	*l*	*s*
				177,276	10	10
Royal Bounty	29,714	6	11		
Secret Service	43,606	7	9		
Fees and Salaries	83,551	5	3		
British Ministers Abroad	26,281	1	8		
Contingent and Miscellaneous Charges, Civil List	42,680	5	7		
TOTAL CIVIL LIST	662,141	2	11		
Mint Expenses	7,225	–	–		
TOTAL CIVIL GOVERNMENT				669,366	2
ARMY SERVICES	2,119,404	9	6		
NAVY SERVICES	2,131,693	17	7		
ORDNANCE SERVICES	239,307	6	8		
				4,490,405	13
TOTAL EXPENDITURE	.	.	.	5,601,950	15
Issued to Pay off Loans in anticipation of Duties, &c.	3,573,169	8	7		
TOTAL applied to REDUCTION of DEBT				3,573,169	8
BALANCES in the Exchequer on 29th September 1694	–	–	–	227,364	12
				9,402,484	17

36 Foundation of the Bank of England, 1694

(5 William and Mary, c. 20, *Statutes at Large*, III (1763), pp. 558–68)

An act for granting to their majesties several rates and duties upon tonnage of ships and vessels, and upon beer, ale, and other liquors, for securing certain recompenses and advantages in the said act mentioned, to such persons as shall voluntarily advance the sum of fifteen hundred thousand pounds, towards the carrying on the war against France.

Most gracious sovereigns, we your majesties' most dutiful and loyal subjects, the commons assembled in parliament, for the further supply of your majesties' extraordinary occasions, for and towards the necessary defence of your realms, do humbly present your majesties with the further gift of the impositions, rates, and duties herein after mentioned; and do beseech your majesties that it may be enacted . . . that for and during the term of four years, commencing from [1 June 1694] there shall be throughout the kingdom of England, dominion of Wales, and town of Berwick upon Tweed, raised . . . for the use of their majesties, their heirs and successors, for and upon the tonnage of all ships and vessels, wherein at any time or times, and for every time during the said term of four years, there shall be imported any goods or merchandises into this kingdom . . . from any the parts, places, or countries hereafter mentioned, &c. Several rates. East Indies ships, &c. 30*s.* Italy, Turkey, 15*s.* Portugal, Spain, 10*s.* West Indies, 10*s.* Holland, &c., 3*s.* Norway, &c., 5*s.* Ireland, Scotland, 2*s.* Streights, 15*s.* Guinea, Africa, 20*s.* Hudson's Bay, 20*s.* Canaries, 10*s.* Greenland, 10*s.* Coasters, 6*d* . . .

* * *

X And whereas by an act of parliament made in the second year of their majesties' reign, entitled, An act for granting to their majesties several additional duties upon beer, ale, and other liquors for four years . . . it was enacted, that from and after [17 November 1691] there should be throughout their majesties' kingdom of England, dominion of Wales, and town of Berwick upon Tweed, raised, levied, collected, and paid, unto their majesties, their heirs and successors, during the space and term of four years, and no longer, for beer, ale, cider, and other liquors therein mentioned, by way of excise, over and above all other duties, charges, and impositions, by any former act or acts, which should be then unexpired, set, and imposed, in such manner as therein is mentioned; which rates and duties aforesaid, by act of parliament made in the third and fourth years of their now majesties' reign, are continued until [17 May 1697]: be it further enacted, that for the further encouragement of such persons who shall voluntarily contribute towards the raising and paying into their majesties' exchequer any sum or sums, not exceeding in the whole the sum of fifteen hundred thousand pounds, upon the several terms and recompenses herein after mentioned, that from and after [17 May 1697] there shall be throughout their majesties' kingdom ... raised, levied, collected and paid unto their majesties, their heirs and successors, for beer, ale, cider, and other liquors, herein after expressed, by way of excise, over and above all duties, charges, and impositions, by any former act or acts then unexpired, set, and imposed, one moiety or half part of the several rates and duties of excise granted by the said last mentioned act, in manner and form following ...

*   *   *

XVII   And be it further enacted . . . that yearly and every year, reckoning the first year to begin from [1 June 1694] the full sum of one hundred and forty thousand pounds, by or out of the monies to arise by the said several duties upon the tonnage of ships and vessels, and by the said rates and duties of excise hereby granted . . . shall be the whole and entire yearly fund . . . for and towards the answering and paying off the several and respective annuities herein after mentioned, and for other the purposes hereafter in this act expressed . . .

*   *   *

XIX   And be it further enacted . . . that it shall and may be lawful to and for their majesties, by commission under the great seal of England, to authorise and appoint any number of persons to take and receive all such voluntary subscriptions as shall be made on or before [1 August 1694] by any person or persons, natives or foreigners, bodies politic or corporate, for and towards the raising and paying into the receipt of exchequer the said sum of twelve hundred thousand pounds, part of the sum of fifteen hundred thousand pounds, and that the yearly sum of one hundred thousand pounds, part of the said yearly sum of one hundred and forty thousand pounds . . . shall be applied, issued, and directed, and is hereby appropriated, to the use and advantage of such person and persons, bodies politic and corporate, as shall make such voluntary subscriptions and payments, their heirs, successors, or assigns . . .

XX   And be it further enacted, that it shall and may be lawful to and for their majesties . . . to limit, direct, and appoint, how and in what manner and proportions, and under what rules and directions, the said sum of twelve hundred thousand pounds . . . and the said yearly sum of one hundred thousand pounds . . . may be assignable or transferable, assigned or transferred, to such person or persons only, as shall freely and voluntarily accept of the same, and not otherwise; and to incorporate all and every such subscribers and contributors, their heirs, successors, or assigns, to be one body corporate and politic, by the name of 'The Governor and Company of the Bank of England' . . .

XXI Provided always . . . that in case the whole sum of twelve hundred thousand pounds . . . shall not be advanced and paid into the receipt of exchequer before [1 January 1694] that then the subscribers and contributors . . . shall only have and receive so much, and such part and proportion of the said sum and sums so respectively paid and advanced, as shall be after the rate of eight pounds per centum per annum . . .

* * *

XXIII Provided always . . . that no person or persons, bodies politic or corporate, shall . . . subscribe or cause to be subscribed, for and towards the raising and paying the said sum of twelve hundred thousand pounds, any sum or sums of money, exceeding the sum of twenty thousand pounds . . .

* * *

XXVII And to the intent that their majesties' subjects may not be oppressed by the said corporation, by their monopolizing or engrossing any sort of goods, wares, or merchandises, be it further declared and enacted . . . that the said corporation to be made and created by this act, shall not at any time, during the continuance thereof, deal or trade, or permit or suffer any person or persons whatsoever either in trust or for the benefit of the same, to deal or trade with any of the stock, monies, or effects, of or any ways belonging to the said corporation, in the buying or selling of any goods, wares, or merchandises whatsoever . . .

XXVIII Provided, that nothing herein contained shall any ways be construed to hinder the said corporation from dealing in bills of exchange, or in buying or selling bullion, gold or silver, or in selling any goods, wares, or merchandise whatsoever, which shall really and *bona fide* be left or deposited with the said corporation for money lent and advanced thereon, and which shall not be redeemed at the time agreed on, or within three months after, or from selling such goods as shall or may be the produce of lands purchased by the said corporation.

37 The Need for a Recoinage, 1696

(H. Haynes, 'Brief Memoirs Relating to the Silver and Gold Coins of England', B. M. Lansdowne MSS, 801, temp. Anne, ff. 33–48)

The silver moneys of England as well as the coins of all other countries are liable to abuse by these three following methods:

1st, by alteration of the standard appointed by public authority.

2nd, by melting them down and converting the metal to other uses.

3rd, by exporting them into foreign countries, to carry on a trade . . .

And by all those methods was the whole stock of the cash of this kingdom excessively impaired before the late grand coinage.

For 1st. the standard of our silver moneys appointed by the government was notoriously violated. By standard is here meant that particular weight and fineness in the silver moneys which was settled by Queen Elizabeth and continued all her time, and after it, through the reigns of all her several successors down to her present majesty,[1] and was lately confirmed by act of parliament . . .

These were the just weights, and the legal fineness of our silver moneys coined with the hammer, of which sort the far greater part of the cash of the whole kingdom did consist; but they were very liable to be clipped and diminished in their weight, because very few of these pieces were of a just assize when they first came out of the Mint. So many pieces, I suppose, were by the moneyers cut out of a bar of standard silver, as did pretty exactly answer the pound weight troy; and the tale of the pieces required in that weight, by the indenture of the Mint: but though all the pieces together might come near the pound weight or be within remedy; yet divers of them compared one with the other were very disproportionable, as was too well known to many persons, who picked out the heavy pieces, and threw them into the melting pot, to fit them for exportation, or to supply the silver smiths.

According to the best observation of goldsmiths and others the clipping of our coins began to be discoverable in great receipts a little after the Dutch war in 1672, but it made no great progress at first for some years: and the silver moneys of Queen Elizabeth were very little diminished . . . But the yearly loss by clipping made terrible advances every year from 1686 . . . In the later end of 1695 the public loss upon all the clipped money then actually current (if one may judge of the whole . . .) was at least 45 per cent. by mere clipping and light counterfeit pieces, which upon the whole running silver cash of the kingdom amounts to 2,250,000*l* . . .

The whole kingdom was in a general distraction by the badness of the silver coin and the rise of guineas, for no body knew what to trust to; the landlord knew not in what to receive his rents, nor the tenant in what to pay them. Neither of them could foretell the value of his moneys to-morrow. The merchant could not foresee the worth of his wares at two or three days distance, and was at a loss to set a price upon his goods. Everybody was afraid to engage in any new contracts, and as shy in performing old ones, the king subsisted his forces in foreign parts at the disadvantage of seven or eight per cent. interest and five per cent. premio for money borrowed here, besides the loss by the exchange abroad: and how to provide for the next year's expense, was a mystery.

[1] Anne.

38 A Speculation in Bank Stock, 1710

(Jonathan Swift, *Journal to Stella*, ed. H. Williams (Oxford, 1948), I, pp. 73–140)

1710. 26 October . . . If the fellow that has your money will pay it, let me beg you to buy Bank stock with it, which is fallen near thirty per cent. and pays eight pounds per cent. and you have the principal when you please: it will certainly soon rise. I would to God Lady Giffard would put in the four hundred pounds she owes you, and take the five per cent. common interest, and give you the remainder. I will speak to your mother about it when I see her. I am resolved to buy three hundred pounds of it for myself, and take up what I have in Ireland; and I have a contrivance for it, that I hope will do, by making a friend of mine buy it as for himself, and I'll pay him when I can get in my money. I hope Stratford will do me that kindness. I'll ask him to-morrow or next day.

8 November . . . Your mother is still in the country, I suppose, for she promised to see me when she came to town. I wrote to her four days ago, to desire her to break it to Lady Giffard, to put some money for you in the Bank, which was then fallen thirty per cent. Would to God mine had been here, I should have gained one hundred pounds, and got as good interest as in Ireland, and much securer. I would fain have borrowed three hundred pounds; but money is so scarce here, there is no borrowing, by this fall of stocks. 'Tis rising now, and I knew it would: it fell from one hundred and twenty-nine to ninety-six . . .

13 November. I dined today in the city . . . My business [there] was to thank Stratford for a kindness he has done me . . . My project was this: I had three hundred pounds in Ireland; and so I wrote to Mr Stratford in the city, to desire he would buy me three hundred pounds in Bank stock, and that he should keep the papers, and that I would be bound to pay him for them; and if it should rise or fall, I would take my chance, and pay him interest in the mean time. I showed my letter to one or two people, who understand those things; and they said, money was so hard to be got here, that no man would do it for me. However, Stratford, who is the most generous man alive, has done it: but it costs one hundred pounds and a half, that is ten shillings, so that three hundred pounds cost me three hundred pounds and thirty shillings. This was done about a week ago and I can have five pounds for my bargain already. Before it fell it was one hundred and thirty pounds, and we are sure it will be the same again . . .

23 December . . . Bank stock is 105, so I may get 12*l* for my bargain already . . .

24 December . . . When I came from church I went up to Court again, where Sir Edmund Bacon told me the bad news from Spain[1] which you will hear before this reaches you; as we have it now, we are undone there . . .

25 December . . . Bank stock will fall like stock-fish by this bad news, and two days ago I could have got 12*l* by my bargain; but I don't intend to sell, and in time it will rise . . .

[1] On 9 December, N.S., at Brihuega, Stanhope and 4,000 British troops surrendered to Vendôme. (HW)

39 The South Sea Bubble, 1720

(*Exchange Alley: or, the Stock Jobber turn'd Gentleman. A Tragi-Comical Farce* (1720), preface)

The whim of the stocks in this kingdom is of late so far cultivated and improved, from a foreign example, that one might reasonably conclude, the numerous inhabitants of this great metropolis, had for the most part deserted their stations, businesses, and occupations; and given up all pretensions to industry, in pursuit of an imaginary profit.

If your occasions be never so urgent for a mercer, a tailor, a shoemaker, &c. they are no where to be met with but at the Royal Exchange. If you resort to any public office, or place of business, the whole enquiry is, how are the stocks? If you are at a coffee-house, the only conversation turns on the stocks, even the scandal of the tea-table is forgotten; if you repair to a tavern, the edifying subject (especially to a philosopher) is the South-Sea Company; if you wait on a lady of quality, you'll find her hastening to her house of intelligence in Exchange Alley; and what is stranger and wonderful, her very dress, diamond shoe buckles and garters, neglected for the stocks.

Even smocks are deposited to help make up the security for cash; jewels pawned to raise money for the purchase of ruin—and, perhaps, wives and daughters have been mortgaged for the very same purpose. To that degree of lunacy are the people of this age arrived, that they'll be nowhere eased of the burden of their cash, but in Exchange Alley; twenty per cent is parted with for a bare week's loan of one hundred pounds, in expectation of a miser's gain; (though the consequence be further loss;) and if fame be not a great calumnator, some persons of distinction have generously condescended to lay in limbo their st—s and g—rs.

When these extraordinary events are considered, and women of the town are become dealers in the stocks, valets de chambre, footmen, and porters, (as well as merchants, tradesmen, and pick-pockets) walk on the Exchange, and ride in their coaches, at the same time some good natured gentlemen have quitted them; projectors successfully bubble the public in all their schemes; sharpers leave their gaming tables in Covent Garden, for more profitable business at Jonathan's coffee house; and even poets commence stock jobbers, it is high time to pronounce Exchange Alley truly a F A R C E.

40 A Spokesman for the Landed Interest, 1733

(*The Gentleman's Magazine*, III (1733), p. 450)

Debate on the motion to take 500,000l from the Sinking Fund

Joseph Danvers, M.P. for Bramber.

I am so far from seeing any inconvenience in what the hon. gentleman has proposed that, considering how little occasion there is at present for paying off any of the public debts, I am surprised at his modesty in asking so little from the Sinking Fund; for if he had asked the whole, it would have been reasonable for us to have given it him, since it is for the support of a government under which we enjoy so many blessings, more particularly that of the free exercise of our holy religion. The landed gentlemen bore the greatest share of the late war; by that they have been loaded with many heavy taxes; by that were all those funds created out of which the plumb men of the City of London have made most of their estates, by which they are enabled to deck their wives in velvets and rich brocades, while poor country gentlemen are hardly able to afford their wives a gown of lindsey woolsey. The landed interest has long laboured under the greatest distress, and therefore we ought to embrace every opportunity of giving them relief.

41 The Pawn-Broker, 1747

(R. Campbell, *The London Tradesman* (1747), pp. 296–7)

The pawn-broker is a kind of broker for the poor, and though esteemed by some not very reputable, yet I must do these people that justice, they are so necessary to the poor labouring tradesman in this metropolis, I cannot comprehend almost how they can live without the pawn-broker. He is reckoned an usurer, that he takes too much for the loan of small sums, and encourages thieving; but I apprehend there may be such a thing as a pawn-broker, without being chargeable with any of these crimes. As to his being an usurer, if we consider him merely as a lender of money the charge is true; but we must state it in a different light. First, he must serve a seven years apprenticeship to learn his business, and that is rather too little to become judge of the almost infinite number of goods he is obliged to receive as pledges. He must have a large stock of ready-money, pay shop and warehouse rent, maintain a journeyman and apprentices, employ his whole time in attending his business and customers. Now will any man in his senses contend, that a man in this situation ought to have no more than legal interest for his money? Does not he employ skill, time, and necessary expense, besides his money; And is it not reasonable he should be paid for that, as well as any other tradesman? Suppose any tradesman employs one thousand or fifteen hundred pounds in trade, bestows his skill, labour, and attendance, will he be content with five or fifteen per cent at the year's end. No, he expects twenty, or perhaps twenty-five per cent; at least, he would not think himself an usurer could he procure it. And I take him and a pawn-broker of the same stock to be in similar circumstances. As to encouragement of thieves, a pawn-broker of credit is as cautious as any other man; it is much his interest to be so, and I do not apprehend that he is liable to more mistakes than others who have a more reputable name. The trade is undoubtedly profitable, and requires a great deal of judgement and acuteness to become thoroughly master of it. He must write a plain quick hand, and ought to be master of figures. A lad may be bound about fourteen or fifteen, and when out of his time may have twenty pounds a year, bed and board.

42 Dr Johnson's Definition of 'Excise', 1755

(Samuel Johnson, *A Dictionary of the English Language* (1755), I)

EXCI'SE. *n.s.* [*acciis*, Dutch; *excisum*, Latin.] A hateful tax levied upon commodities, and adjudged not by the common judges of property, but wretches hired by those to whom excise is paid.

The people should pay a rateable tax for their sheep, and an *excise* for every thing which they should eat.   *Hayward*

Ambitious now to take *excise*
Of a more fragrant paradise.   *Cleaveland.*

Excise,
With hundred rows of teeth, the shark exceeds,
And on all trades like Cassawar she feeds.   *Marvel.*

Can hire large houses, and oppress the poor,
By farm'd *excise*.   *Dryden's Juvenal, Sat. 3.*

43 Some Estimates of Taxes Paid, 1756

(J. Massie, *Calculations of Taxes for a Family of each Rank, Degree or Class: for one Year* (1756), pp. 5–46)

Introduction Calculations of the taxes paid by a private family of each rank, degree, or class, seem to be of no other use than to amuse a few curious men; as any person, who is desirous of knowing how much money he pays for taxes, may satisfy himself without much trouble, or difficulty.

But notwithstanding the facility of making such calculations, it is difficult for any person to find out how much money he pays for, or in consequence of, taxes; and this difficulty seems to have been increased by the manner in which the subject has been treated, by several persons who have written upon the taxes of this kingdom.

These persons say, that the money paid for taxes, or in the increased prices of commodities, and of labour, caused thereby, amounts to twelve or fourteen shillings in the pound, on the incomes, or expenses, of the people of England: but how those persons could find out the several things which are necessary to ascertain what number of shillings in the pound are paid for, or in consequence of, taxes, by all the people in this nation, is to me a mystery.

For in order to determine this matter, it is requisite to know, what number of people there are in the nation; how much money their incomes, or expenses, amount to; how much the prices of commodities, and of labour, have been increased by means of taxes; and how much money is annually paid for taxes by the whole kingdom:— of which four things, I cannot find that more than one of them is yet certainly known, and that is, the amount of the money annually paid for taxes by the whole kingdom . . .

The recollection of some general facts concerning the prices of living and of labour, fully satisfied me that the payments for, or in consequence of, taxes, could not possibly amount to fourteen, or twelve shillings in the pound, upon the incomes, or expenses, of the people of this nation; and it required very little thinking to find out the ill consequences which either have attended, or may attend a general belief that the payments for, or in consequence of, taxes, take a much greater part of every person's income, than they really do.

Asserting that the payments for, or in consequence of, taxes, take twelve, or fourteen shillings in the pound, out of the incomes, or expenses, of the people of England; is asserting in other words, that they have no more than eight, or six shillings in the pound, out of their incomes, for their own proper uses and benefits.

And though asserting one or other of these things does not prove them to be true, yet while such assertions have the same weight as proof, with all such persons as believe them; and the effects wrought thereby, in the minds of such persons, will be the same in quality and degree, as if they were produced by fact instead of fiction.

By such assertions, the value of many estates in this kingdom may be depreciated in the opinions of the gentlemen who own them.

By such assertions, people of the middle or inferior classes, may be prevented from pursuing with assiduity the means to make future provision for their families.

By such assertions, industry may be slackened, and labour discouraged, among manufacturers and working people.

By such assertions, people are induced to entertain unhappy opinions concerning government.

By such assertions, and inferences drawn from them, people have been made uneasy about the trade of the nation, and induced to believe it is in danger of being ruined by those very laws which are a principal means of preserving it.

And by such assertions, the ability of the nation to maintain war, is diminished in the opinion of the people.

Such are the ill consequences which may result from publicly asserting, that people pay much more money for, or in consequence of, taxes, than they really do pay; and the possibility of any such things happening, seemed to me a sufficient reason for contributing my mite to prevent them, by making and publishing *Calculations of the Taxes paid by one Family of each Rank, Degree or Class* . . .

As to the payments in consequence of taxes, I cannot see any reason for thinking they make more than one part in five of the payments for taxes, and the payments in consequence of taxes, when added together: by which I mean, that for every four pounds, or shillings paid for taxes on consumable commodities, one pound, or shilling must be added, for payments in consequence of taxes; but this addition is not to be made on the land-tax as that is out of the question . . .

[Calculations of taxes paid].

No. 4   A nobleman, or gentleman, who has an estate of six thousand pounds a year in land

	l	*s*	*d*
For malt, hops, beer and cider	23	8	0
Salt	1	10	0
Sugar, raisins, currants and spices	2	14	0
Leather	1	4	0
Soap and candles	5	8	0
Coals, in London	4	16	0
Houses and windows	9	4	0
Drugs, tobacco, glass, paper, parchment, stamp duties, postage of letters, coaches and chairs, &c.	150	0	0
Land-tax four shillings in the pound	1,200	0	0
	1,398	4	0
Foreign wines, arrack, rum, brandy, coffee, tea and chocolate	450	0	0
Foreign manufactured silks, linens, cottons, &c.	75	0	0
Total of taxes	1,923	4	0

The taxes amount to six shillings and five pence in the pound upon the annual income.

*   *   *

No. 9   A gentleman who has an estate of six hundred pounds a year in land

	l	s	d
For malt, hops, beer and cider	8	9	0
Salt		10	10
Sugar, raisins, currants and spices		19	6
Leather		8	8
Soap and candles	1	19	0
Coals, in London	2	0	0
House and windows	2	12	0
Drugs, tobacco, glass, paper, parchment, stamp duties, postage of letters, coach or chair, &c.	15	0	0
Land-tax four shillings in the pound	120	0	0
	151	19	0
Foreign wines, arrack, rum, brandy, coffee, tea and chocolate	45	0	0
Foreign manufactured silks, linens, cottons, &c.	7	10	0
Total of taxes	204	9	0

The taxes amount to six shillings and ten pence in the pound upon the annual income.

*   *   *

No. 16   A farmer who expends one hundred pounds a year

	l	s	d
For malt, hops, beer and cider	3	10	0
Salt		6	8
Sugar, raisins, currants and spices		7	0
Leather		4	8
Soap and candles		13	8
House and windows		9	0
Drugs, tobacco, glass, paper, parchment, stamp duties, postage of letters, &c.		11	1
	6	2	1

	l	s	d
Foreign wines, rum, brandy, tea, &c.	1	13	4
Foreign linens, &c.		5	7
Total of taxes	8	1	0

The taxes amount to one shilling and seven pence in the pound upon the annual expenses.

*   *   *

No. 21 A tradesman in London, who expends one hundred pounds a year

	l	s	d
For beer and cider	3	5	0
Salt		3	4
Sugar, raisins, currants and spices		7	6
Leather		3	4
Soap and candles		15	4
Coals	2	0	0
House and windows	1	2	0
Drugs, tobacco, glass, paper, parchment, stamp duties, postage of letters, &c.	1	2	3
	8	18	9
Foreign wines, rum, brandy, coffee tea, &c.	3	6	8
Foreign manufactured silks, linens, cottons, &c.		11	1
Total of taxes	12	16	6

The taxes amount to two shillings and six pence in the pound upon the annual expenses.

*   *   *

No. 28 A manufacturer of wood, iron, &c. in the country, whose wages may be nine shillings a week, which amounts to twenty three pounds eight shillings a year

	l	s	d
For beer		13	4
Salt		2	6
Sugar, &c.		3	0
Leather		1	11
Soap and candles		3	10

Drugs, tobacco, &c.	5	0
Window tax	2	4
Total of taxes	1 11	11

The taxes amount to one shilling and four pence in the pound upon the annual income.

* * *

No. 30   A husbandman, or labourer, in the country, whose wages may be five shillings a week, which amounts to thirteen pounds a year

	l	*s*	*d*
For beer		4	7
Salt		3	4
Sugar, &c.		2	0
Leather		2	2
Soap and candles		1	3
Drugs, tobacco, &c.		2	6
Total of taxes		15	10

The taxes amount to one shilling and three pence in the pound upon the annual income.

44 Wartime Transfers to the Continent, 1760

(B.M. Add. MSS 32,806, printed in C. Wilson, *Anglo-Dutch Commerce and Finance in the Eighteenth Century* (Cambridge, 1941), pp. 159–60)

Letter to James West, a Financial Secretary to the Treasury, London 13 March 1760

Sir, In answer to your favour of yesterday will you please to acquaint the Duke of Newcastle that we give our bills to the pay office on the day we receive the money, ⅓rd at 8 days' sight and the other ⅓rd at one month date, and allowing six days for the passage of the mail to Holland, and they generally pass in three, the Deputy Paymaster at Amsterdam receives the moneys of 100,000*l*, viz. 66,000*l* in 14 days after the issue from the pay office here, 33,000*l* 5 weeks after, and I do not well conceive how such large sums could be remitted quicker consistent with the interest of government in the support of the exchange. All the public remittances were made in the same manner last war, and I never heard of any inconveniency from it. What time is necessary for converting the amount of our bills into specie proper for the payment of the army and sending it there from Amsterdam I cannot precisely say, but cannot think many days are necessary, or that giving our bills at shorter date would forward that operation in the least because when the Deputy Paymasters receive our bills and are sure of the money they may provide the specie by buying ducats at some days' credit without any difficulty or inconvenience.

I remain with the sincerest regard, Sir,
Your most obedient humble servant,
Joshua van Neck.

7

Living Conditions, Poverty and its Relief
1000–1485

Direct evidence on living conditions in the medieval period is hard to find but it is clear that there were great differences in the standard of living. The Anglo-Saxon landed aristocracy was small but wealthy (*2*) but like its Norman successor it did not enjoy the comfort and luxury open to the rich of the later Middle Ages. Great landholders in medieval times were constantly on the move visiting their estates (*5*). Up to the mid-fourteenth century the diet of substantial landholders lacked variety (*10*) but after 1350 a new range of imported luxury goods became available (*13*). In the late fifteenth century even a modest country gentleman could enjoy a comfortable standard of living (*16*). For most people however life was dominated by long hours of work in the fields in harsh conditions (*3*). Their diet was deficient in protein but was occasionally relieved by feasts at important dates in the agrarian and religious calendars (*8*). The standard of living for many peasants improved in the later fourteenth century (*12*). There were few towns of any notable size apart from London where overcrowding, rickety buildings and the danger of fire had become problems by the mid-twelfth century (*4*). Town life too was characterised by poor sanitation, which worsened as numbers grew (*7*). By the later fourteenth century the rising expectations of the prospering urban patriciate and of lesser men too led to legislative attempts to halt social mobility by preserving class distinctions (*11*).

Although alms-giving was a function of religious houses (*1*) poverty and destitution were such in medieval England that monastic aid was quite inadequate. The main provisions for the care of the elderly and infirm were made within the family (*6*). Lay piety expressed itself in charitable grants, and in the later Middle Ages private provision for the relief of the poor became more important (*15*). In town and country religious gilds were founded in part to perform a social function in caring for their members (*14*).

1485–1760

In an age of low productivity and great inequalities in the distribution of income stark differences in living conditions were inevitable. A meagre diet, mean and cold housing and long hours of work interspersed with periods of unemployment, were the common lot of the labourer and his family. And when injuries occurred, health failed, or old age brought infirmity, matters could be much worse. In contrast were the opulent circumstances of a minority of noblemen and rich townsmen. However, a small but growing class of men with more middling incomes—made up of lesser landowners, farmers, artisans, tradesmen and professional men—helped to blur the sharpness of social division. And there was a noticeable if slight improvement in the condition of wage-earners in the century after 1660, with the more fortunate trend of food prices. On the state of the least well-off we can consider a census of some of the poor in one parish in 1570 (*18*), a labourer's possessions in 1620 (*27*), a workhouse dietary (*38*), the condition of Irish vagrants awaiting passage to Ireland (*41*), a view of the London poor in the mid-eighteenth century (*44*), and the lot of a weaver's family of the same period (*45*). In turn, consider a Tudor nobleman's household expenses (*24*), the house and fittings of the late sixteenth century better-off Englishman (*21*), a farmer's and a rector's possessions (*22, 27*), a Frenchman's view of the middling Englishman's table in the 1690s (*37*), and the Christmastime fare of prosperous folk in 1759 (*46*).

Although for most people life was normally hard and uncertain there were the occasional feasts (*29*). A feature of English life, noteworthy for the acceptance of change, was the aspiration of many to emulate the living style of their betters (*42*). Some improvements were made in the condition of towns (*30–1*) but in London more died than were born (*35*).

While private aid to the poor went on through this period (*23, 26, 40*) there was, from the mid-sixteenth century, an outstanding development of public provision. Civic attempts (*17, 19*) prepared the way for national action in 1572 (*20*), 1576 and 1601 (*25*). Prevalent attitudes among the better-off towards the poor remained harsh, as witness the Settlement Act of 1662 (*33*) and the policies of the Huntingdonshire justices in the mid-1670s (*34*). The desperation with which a settlement right to relief was sought tells its own story (*43*). It does not seem that in the century before 1760 the better-off became noticeably more sympathetic towards the less fortunate.

1 Monastic Distribution of Alms, c. 970

(*Regularis Concordia Anglicae Nationis Monachorum Sanctimonialiumque*, ed. Dom. T. Symons (Nelson's Medieval Texts, 1953), pp. 61–2)

The Maundy, in which we follow the Lord's example as also the admonition of the Holy Rule, shall—apart from that which the brethren carry out among themselves—be administered with the greatest care to the poor, in whom Christ shall be adored Who is received in them. Therefore let there be a place set apart for the reception of the poor, where daily[1] and without fail the service of the Maundy may be rendered to three poor men chosen from among those who are wont to receive their support from the monastery; and let the same foods of which the brethren partake that day be given to them. Let this Maundy, then, be attended to in the following manner: on Saturday the children of the right hand choir with their master shall carry it out, and on the following Sunday the other children, those of the left hand choir, with the other master; and thenceforth on each day of the week let so many of the brethren be deputed to this duty that, apart from the abbot, no one shall be excused from the obligation of this service. As for the abbot, let him devote himself to this office not only once but as often as leisure or opportunity suggests.

Moreover, when poor strangers arrive, the abbot and such of the brethren as he shall choose shall render to them the service of the Maundy in accordance with the ordinance of the Rule. Wherefore whenever he can, the father himself,[2] no less than each of the brethren, shall be most zealous in providing every kind service in the guesthouse; nor, seduced by boastful pride or deceived by idle thoughtlessness, shall he foolishly neglect anything commanded by the Rule in this regard. One point, however, must be firmly kept in mind, namely the decision made by the holy fathers at a synodal council[3]—not indeed out of contempt of the Rule but for the good of souls and the safeguard of virtues—that, of those who dwell in a monastery, neither the abbot himself nor any of the brethren shall eat or drink outside the refectory except in the case of sickness. All other duties, as we have said, the abbot shall fulfil most faithfully and with great gladness of heart; nor let him who is the vicar of the eternal Christ be slow and cold in the guesthouse of the monastery nor delay or neglect his ministrations to the poor while in the management of transitory affairs he shows himself swift and fervent in his desire to serve the rich. For the rest, wayfarers shall on their departure be provided with a supply of victuals according to the means of the house.

[1] The daily Maundy of the poor was of general observance. (TS)
[2] The abbot.   [3] The Council of Aix, 817. (TS)

2 An Anglo-Saxon Will, 984–1016

(*Anglo-Saxon Wills*, ed. D. Whitelock (Cambridge, 1930), pp. 63–5)

I, Wulfwaru, pray my dear lord King Ethelred, of his charity, that I may be entitled to make my will. I make known to you, Sire, here in this document, what I grant to St Peter's monastery at Bath for my poor soul and for the souls of my ancestors from whom my property and my possessions came to me; namely then, that I grant to that holy place there an armlet which consists of sixty mancuses[1] of gold, and a bowl of two and a half pounds, and two gold crucifixes, and a set of mass-vestments with everything that belongs to it, and the best dorsal that I have, and a set of bed-clothing with tapestry and curtain and with everything that belongs to it. And I grant to the Abbot Ælfhere the estate at Freshford with the produce and the men and all the profit which is obtained there.

And I grant to my elder son Wulfmær the estate at Claverton, with produce and with men and all profits; and the estate at Compton with produce and men and all profits; and I grant him half the estate at Butcombe with produce and men and all profits, and half of it I grant to my younger daughter Ælfwaru, with produce and men and all profits. And they are to share the principal residence between them as evenly as they can, so that each of them shall have a just portion of it.

And to my younger son Ælfwine I grant the estate at Leigh, with produce and men and all the profits; and the estate at Holton, with produce and men and all profits; and the estate at Hogston, with produce and men and all profits; and thirty mancuses of gold.

And I grant to my elder daughter, Gode, the estate at Winford, with produce and men and all profits; and two cups of four pounds; and a band of thirty mancuses of gold and two brooches and a woman's attire complete. And to my younger daughter Ælfwaru I grant all the women's clothing which is left.

And to my son Wulfmær and my second son Ælfwine and my daughter Ælfwaru—to each of the three of them—I grant two cups of good value. And I grant to my son Wulfmær a hall-tapestry and a set of bed-clothes. To Ælfwine my second son I grant a tapestry for a hall and tapestry for a chamber, together with a table-cover and with all the cloths which go with it.

And I grant to my four servants Ælfmær, Ælfweard, Wulfric and Wulfstan, a band of twenty mancuses of gold. And I grant to all my household women, in common, a good chest well decorated.

And I desire that those who succeed to my property provide twenty freedmen, ten in the east and ten in the west; and all together furnish a food-rent for Bath every year for ever, as good as ever they can afford, at such season as it seems to all of them that they can accomplish it best and most fittingly. Whichever of them shall discharge this, may he have God's favour and mine; and whichever of them will not discharge it, may he have to account for it with the Most High, who is the true God, who created and made all creatures.

¹ A mancus was equivalent to thirty silver pieces.

3 The Hard Life of Agricultural Labourers, c.1000

(*Aelfric's Colloquy*, printed in S. H. Gem, *An Anglo-Saxon Abbot. Aelfric of Eynsham* (Edinburgh, 1912), pp. 184–5)

Master What do these companions of yours know?

Scholar Some are ploughboys, some shepherds, some oxherds, some also are huntsmen, some fishermen, some fowlers, some chapmen, some tailors, some salters, some bakers in the place.

Master What do you say, Ploughboy, how do you carry on your work?

Ploughboy O Master, I have to work far too much; I go out at dawn, driving the oxen to the field, and I yoke them to the plough; I dare not in the severest weather lie hid at home, for fear of my lord; and when I have yoked the oxen together, and fastened the ploughshare to the plough, I have to plough a whole acre every day, or more.

Master Have you any companion?

Ploughboy I have a boy who threatens the oxen with a goad, and he is also hoarse with the cold and his shouting.

Master What more do you perform in the day?

Ploughboy Certainly I do more besides that. I have to supply the mangers of the oxen with hay, and give them water, and carry their dung outside.

Master O indeed! This is a great labour.

Ploughboy Yes, it is a great labour that I have to fulfil, for I am not free.

Master What do you say, Shepherd, have you any work?

Shepherd Indeed, I have. In early morning I drive my sheep to the pastures, and I stand by them, in heat and cold, with dogs, lest the wolves should devour them, and I bring them back to their folds, and milk them twice a day, and I move their folds besides. I also make butter and cheese, and I am faithful to my lord.

Master Oxherd, what do you work at?

Oxherd O Master, I labour much. When the ploughman unyokes the oxen, I lead them to the pastures, and all night I stand by them watching against thieves, and then, early in the morning, I give them over to the ploughman, well fed and watered.

4 Building in Timber and Stone in London, 1189

FitzElwyne's Assize of Buildings, printed in *Liber Albus*, ed. H. T. Riley (1861), pp. 284–5)

Of the ancient manner of building houses

It should be remarked, that in ancient times the greater part of the city was built of wood, and the houses were covered with straw, stubble, and the like.

Hence it happened, that when a single house had caught fire, the greater part of the city was destroyed through such conflagration; a thing that took place in the first year of the reign of King Stephen, when, by reason of a fire that broke out at London Bridge, the church of Saint Paul was burnt; from which spot the conflagration extended, destroying houses and buildings, as far as the church of Saint Clement Danes.

After this, many of the citizens, to the best of their ability to avoid such a peril, built stone houses upon their foundations, covered with thick tiles, and [so] protected against the fury of the flames; whence it has often been the case that, when a fire has broken out in the city, and has destroyed many buildings, upon reaching such houses, it has been unable to do further mischief, and has been there extinguished; so that, through such a house as this the houses of the neighbours have been saved from being burnt.

Hence it is, that in the aforesaid ordinance, called the 'Assize,' it was provided and ordained, in order that the citizens might be encouraged to build with stone, that every one who should have a stone wall upon his own land sixteen feet in height, might possess the same as freely and meritoriously as in manner already stated; it always being the duty, that is to say, of such man's neighbour, to receive upon his own land the water falling from the house built upon such wall, and at his own cost to carry off the same; and if he shall wish to build near the said wall, he is bound to make his own gutter under the eaves of the said house for receiving the water therefrom. And this, to the end that such house[1] may remain secure and protected against the violence of fire when it comes, and so, through it, many a house may be saved and preserved unharmed by the violence of the flames.

[1] i.e. a house flanked by a stone wall. (HTR)

5 Advice to a Lord on How to Live off his Estates, c.1240

(*Les Reules Seynt Roberd*, printed in *Walter of Henley's Husbandry together with an anonymous husbandry, Seneschaucie and Robert Grosseteste's Rules*, ed. Elizabeth Lamond (1890), pp. 127–9, 145)

The fourth rule teaches how a lord or lady can further examine into their estate, that is to say, how he or she can live yearly of their own

In two ways by calculation can you inquire your estate. First this, command strictly that in each place at the leading of your corn there be thrown in a measure at the entrance to the grange the eighth sheaf of each kind of corn, and let it be threshed and measured by itself. And by calculating from that measure you can calculate all the rest in the grange. And in doing this I advise you to send to the best manors of your lands those of your household in whom you place most confidence to be present in August at the leading in of the corn, and to guard it as is aforesaid. And if this does not please you, do it in this way. Command your seneschal that every year at Michaelmas[1] he cause all the stacks of each kind of corn, within the grange and without, to be valued by prudent, faithful, and capable men, how many quarters there may be, and then how many quarters will be taken for seed and servants on the land, and then of the whole amount, and of what remains over and above the land and the servants, set the sum in writing, and according to that assign the expenses of your household in bread and ale. Also see how many quarters of corn you will spend in a week in dispensable bread, how much in alms. That is if you spend two quarters a day, that is fourteen quarters a week, that is seven hundred and fourteen quarters a year. And if to increase your alms you spend two quarters and a half every day, that is seventeen quarters and a half in the week, and in the year eight hundred and fifty three quarters and a half. And when you have subtracted this sum from the sum total of your corn, then you can subtract the sum for ale, according as weekly custom has been for the brewing in your household. And take care of the sum which will remain from sale. And with the money from your corn, and from your rents, and from the issues of pleas in your courts, and from your stock, arrange the expenses of your kitchen and your wines and your wardrobe and the wages of servants, and subtract your stock. But on all manors take care of your corn, that it be not sold out of season nor without need; that is, if your rents and other returns will suffice for the expenses of your chamber and wines and kitchen, leave your store of corn whole until you have the advantage of the corn of another year, not more, or at the least, of half [a year].

* * *

The twenty-sixth rule teaches how at Michaelmas you may arrange your sojourn for all the year

Every year, at Michaelmas, when you know the measure of all your corn, then arrange your sojourn for the whole of that year, and for how many weeks in each place, according to the seasons of the year, and the advantages of the country in flesh and in fish, and do not in any wise burden by debt or long residence the places where you sojourn, but so arrange your sojourns that the place at your departure shall not remain in debt, but something may remain on the manor, whereby the manor can raise money from increase of stock, and especially cows and sheep, until your stock acquits your wines, robes, wax, and all your wardrobe, and that will be in a short time if you hold and act after this treatise as you can see plainly in this way. The wool of a thousand sheep in good pasture at the least ought to yield fifty marks a year, the wool of two thousand a hundred marks, and so forth, counting by thousands. The wool of a thousand sheep in scant pasture ought at the least to yield forty marks, in coarse and poor pasture thirty marks.

* * *

The twenty-eighth rule teaches you at what times in the year you ought to make your purchases

I advise that at two seasons of the year you make your principal purchases, that is to say your wines, and your wax, and your wardrobe, at the fair of St. Botolph, what you shall spend in Lindsey and in Norfolk, in the Vale of Belvoir, and in the country of Caversham, and in that at Southampton for Winchester, and Somerset at Bristol; your robes purchase at St. Ives.

[1] 29 September.

6 A Son Supports His Widowed Mother, 1281

(*Court Rolls of the Manor of Hales 1272–1307, Part I*, ed. J. Amphlett (Worcestershire Historical Society, 1910), pp. 166–8)

Court of Hales on the day of the Apostles Simon and Jude in the ninth year of King Edward[1]

This is the agreement made between Agnes, the widow of Thomas Brid of Ridgacre in Hales, on the one part and Thomas her elder son on the other in the ninth year of the reign of King Edward, on the Thursday next before the feast of the Apostles Simon and Jude.[2] Namely that the said Agnes surrendered to the said Thomas all her land that she held in the same vill of Ridgacre with all its appurtenances in all things and places on condition that the said Thomas will honourably and fully provide for the said Agnes, as long as she lives, in all necessities, in the following manner. The said Agnes shall first receive from the same Thomas on the feast of Michaelmas,[3] in the tenth year of the reign of the aforesaid king, a quarter of wheat, a quarter of oats and a measure[4] of peas. On the feast of All Saints[5] next following she shall receive five cart-loads of sea-coal from the same; on the eighth day before Christmas a quarter of wheat, a quarter of oats and a measure of peas; on Good Friday a quarter of wheat and a quarter of oats; at Pentecost five shillings of good money; and on the day of the Nativity of St. John the Baptist[6] half a quarter of wheat and a quarter of oats. Also the said Thomas is obliged to build at his own expense a house, suitable for Agnes to inhabit, comprising 30 feet in length between the walls and 14 feet in width within the ambit of the walls with the posts and with three suitable new doors and two windows. And Agnes shall receive fully from the same Thomas everything aforesaid at the above mentioned terms for each year as long as she lives. And the said Thomas shall cause those things to be carried to the house of the said Agnes at the said terms by himself or by one of his household. And Thomas, himself, will answer to the lord for all customs and services which are known to belong to the said land. And if it happens that the said Thomas does not have the corn on time, he must satisfy the same Agnes in money according to the price in the market of the better grain, apart from that chosen for seed. And if it happens that he does not observe the said agreement at the aforesaid terms, as it is laid out above, the said Thomas binds himself to pay half a mark to the pittancer[7] of the convent of Hales as many times as the said Agnes, with the testimony of two lawful men, shall find it necessary to invoke the power of the lord abbot and convent of Hales for that. And that from then, the said Agnes may be at liberty to resume that land with all its appurtenances as her own and to deal therein in all things as she pleases, the recorded agreement notwithstanding in anything. And for the perpetual force of all the aforesaid things and for faithful testimony, everything, before being recited in the full court of Hales, was written down word for word in the rental of the lord abbot and convent for everlasting memory, Lord Nicholas then being abbot, before Brother Geoffrey, then cellarer there.

[1] 28 October 1281.   [2] i.e. 23 October 1281.   [3] 29 September.
[4] *modius*, a peck.   [5] 1 November.   [6] 24 June.
[7] The officer in a religious house charged with distributing charitable gifts, allowances of food, etc.

7 Regulations for London's Streets, 1297

(*Memorials of London and London Life in the XIIIth, XIVth and XVth Centuries*, ed. H. T. Riley (1868), pp. 34–5)

On Thursday next after the feast of the Exaltation of the Holy Cross,[1] in the 25th year of the reign of King Edward, by Sir John Bretun, warden, and the aldermen, the following proclamation was ordered for maintaining the peace of our lord the king.—

On behalf of the king and his son and their council, the warden and the aldermen ordain that no person shall be so daring as to be found walking through the streets after curfew rung at St. Martin's le Grand, and that every one, under the penalty that is awarded thereto, shall come when he is summoned to the watch, as well at the city gates as in the streets, armed and arrayed as he ought to be.

And that every one shall keep clean the front of his tenement, that so the streets be delivered from all incumbrances before Friday next at Vespers; and where incumbrances shall be found after the time aforesaid, let the owner be amerced in half a mark.

And that the stands[2] be removed forthwith before vespers.

And that on Sunday every alderman in his own ward shall take such stands as shall be found in the streets, and do his will therewith; and if after that time any stand shall be found in the streets, the warden shall do his will therewith.

And that no taverner or brewster shall keep the door open after curfew rung as aforesaid; and that whosoever shall be convicted thereof shall be amerced in half a mark, which shall be expended in repairing the walls and the gates of the city.

And that fullers' implements shall be forthwith removed,[3] before Vespers.

And that pentices which are too low shall be forthwith pulled down, so that persons may ride on great horses[4] beneath.

And also that pig-sties that are in the streets shall be speedily removed; and that no swine shall be found in the streets, on pain of forfeiture thereof, in aid of making the walls and gates.

[1] 14 September.
[2] *Trounckes*; boxes placed in the streets for the sale of wares. (HTR)
[3] Fulling, like some other trades, was probably carried on in the streets. (HTR)
[4] Chargers or war-horses. (HTR)

8 The Peasants' Christmas Feast at North Curry, 1314

(Historical Manuscripts Commission, *Calendar of the Manuscripts of the Dean and Chapter of Wells*, I (1907), p. 332)

North Curry

Custumal of the lands and tenements of the homage of the king's ancient demesne, made 1314 by oath of William Hughet[1] . . . chosen by the said homage.

Hundredman.

John of Knapp and Margaret his wife, Adam le Henr' and Margery his wife and their tenants, 2½ virgates with messuages, curtilages, gardens, woods, pastures and meadows adjoining: the said John is the king's bailiff in the hundred of North Curry, receives and executes his writs, and returns them by William Colne, Richard Fry, and the heirs of Walter French: of every prisoner in the Stockhouse he shall have 4*d* of his outer garment, of every man or knave of the out hundred entering in an assize his hundred penny; also his *gestum* at Christmas with two others, namely two white loaves, as much beer as they will drink in the day, a mess of beef and of bacon with mustard, one of browis of hen, and a cheese, fuel to cook his food and that of the other tenants of the king's ancient demesne, and to burn from dinner time till even and afterwards, and two candles of assize to burn out while they sit and drink one after the other if they will sit so long, and if he come not he may send three men in his stead, or send for the bread, beef and bacon and two gallons of beer; and the next day immediately after noon his medale with one man, as much beer as he will drink till even; also common for all manner of his beasts on all common moors in the hundred of North Curry quit of herbage: to do suit to the hundred court twice a year, and at any court when there be a plea upon the king's writ, or judgments be in suspense for lack of suitors, and at gaol deliveries: heriot at his decease, his best beast.[2]

[1] And nine others.

[2] The custumal then lists the services of the various tenants (writ-servers, socmen and villeins), most of whom, apart from several socmen, received the *gestum* and medale. Many villeins were obliged to thresh corn at the *gestum*.

9 A Tenant Unable to Pay His Rent, 1318

(*The Court Baron*, ed. F. W. Maitland and W. P. Baildon (Selden Society, IV, 1890), pp. 124–5)

Littleport. Court there on Wednesday before the feast of S. Gregory in the eleventh year of King Edward the Second and the second of John of Hotham.[1]

John of Elm, who held of the demesne of the lord 6 acres of land newly set to rent by the service of 12*s* a year, has left the said land fresh and uncultivated on account of his poverty and the excessive heaviness of that rent, and is not able for the future to maintain or discharge the said land, as is found by the whole homage. And now comes the said John and surrenders the said land into the lord's hand. And Robert Carter came and took the said land from the lord to hold for four whole years from Michaelmas last. The fine is forborne.

[1] i.e. 8 March 1318.

10 Christmas Week in the Household of a Norfolk Knight, 1347

('A Roll of Household Accounts of Sir Hamon le Strange of Hunstanton, Norfolk, 1347–8', ed. Hamon le Strange, *Archaeologia*, LXIX (1917–18), pp. 112–13)[1]

Expenses of the house of Sir John de Camoys and Hamon le Strange in residence at Hunstanton, with the lady de Camoys, her damsel and maid, and with Hamon le Strange and his wife, with her damsel and maid, and with the free servants living with the aforesaid John and Hamon—that is to say, Richard the chaplain, the butler, the cook, with the groom, two boys, and one lad of the aforesaid Hamon, from the feast of St. Michael in the 21st year of Edward III to the feast of St. Peter's Chains next following, in the 22nd year of the said king.

* * *

Sunday. For flesh of oxen with one quarter of mutton, and for flesh of calf and pig bought by John the cook, 16*d*. For eggs bought by the said John, 1½*d*. For mustard bought by the said John, 1*d*. In store, one hen.

Monday in the Vigil of Christmas. For wheaten bread, 1 quarter of wheat and 3 bushels of mixtelyn. For beer brewed 1½ quarters of malt of barley, price the quarter 6*s*. For plaice and sprats bought by John the cook, 1¾*d*. In store, 1 cheling.

Tuesday. Christmas day. For bread bought for the kitchen by John the cook, ½*d*. For 2 gallons of wine bought at Heacham by the lord, 12*d*. In store, 1 porker for the larder, price 4*s*; 1 small pig, price 6*d*; 1 swan from the lord John Camoys, price . . . . 2 hens of rent. And received from Gressenhall 6 rabbits, and 2 rabbits from John of Somerton as a gift. Whereof consumed 5 rabbits and one ham. For provender for 4 horses of the lord John Camoys for 2 days and nights preceding, 12 pecks of oats; and for one horse of Richard, the servant of John de Docking, for one day and one night, 2 pecks.

Wednesday on the feast of St. Stephen. For one gallon of wine bought by John Camoys. For spices bought of John the grocer at Lynn, 12*s* 1*d*. Also at the same place 3 lb. of wax, bought of the same John the grocer, 15*d*. In store, 1 rabbit; 1 goose, price 3*d*; 1 capon, price 2*d*; 2 hens of rent. For provender for 4 horses of the lord John de Camoys, 12 pecks of oats, and for 1 horse of the hayward of Lexham, 1 peck of oats.

Thursday on the feast of St. John the Evangelist. For 1 bushel of peas bought for soup by Richard the bailiff, 8*d*. For eggs bought by John the cook, ½*d*. In store, 1 goose, price 3*d*; 2 hens of rent and 2 rabbits. For provender for 4 horses of the lord John de Camoys, 12 pecks of oats.

Friday. For plaice bought by John the cook, ½*d*. In store, 2 fish, viz. 1 ling and 1 cheling.

Saturday. On the feast of St. Thomas the Martyr. In store, 1 kymp of herrings. For sprats bought by John the cook, ½*d*. For provender for 2 horses of the lord through the whole preceding week, 4 bushels, 2 pecks of oats.

Total of money, 21*s* 11¼*d*. Whereof paid by John the cook 22¼*d*.

Total of corn, 1 quarter of wheat and 3 bushels of mixtelyn.

Total of malt, 1½ quarters.

Total of store, 1 porker, price as above; 1 small pig, price as above; 2 geese, 1 capon, & 6 hens of rent, as above.

Total of oats, 1 quarter, 2 bushels, 1 peck. Of which for the lord's horses, 4 bushels, 2 pecks; and for horses of the lord John Camoys, 4 bushels, 12 pecks.

One kymp of herrings.

[1] A few alterations to the translation as printed in *Archaeologia* have been made by the present editors.

11 Sumptuary Legislation, 1363

(37 Edward III, *Statutes of the Realm*, I, pp. 378–83)

III   Also, for the great dearth that is, in many places, of poultry; it is ordained, that the price of a young capon shall not pass 3*d* and [that] of an old [capon] 4*d*, [that] of an hen 2*d*, [that] of a pullet 1*d*, [that] of a goose 4*d*, and in places where the prices of such victuals be less, they shall hold without being enhanced by this ordinance; and that in the towns and markets of uplands, they shall be sold at a less price, according as may be agreed between the seller and the buyer: and justices shall be thereupon assigned by commission to put the thing duly in execution.

*   *   *

VIII   Also, for the outrageous and excessive apparel of divers people against their estate and degree, to the great destruction and impoverishment of all the land; it is ordained that grooms, as well as servants of lords as they of mysteries and artificers, shall be served to eat and drink once a day of flesh or of fish, and the remnant of other victuals, as of milk, butter, and cheese and other such victuals, according to their estate. And that they have clothes for their vesture, or hosing, whereof the whole cloth shall not exceed two marks, and that they wear no cloth of higher price, of their buying, nor otherwise, nor anything of gold nor of silver embroidered, enamelled, nor of silk, nor anything pertaining to the said things; and their wives, daughters and children of the same condition in their clothing and apparel, and they shall wear no veils passing 12*d* a veil.

IX   Also, that people of handicraft and yeomen, shall neither take nor wear cloth of a higher price for their vesture or hosing than within forty shillings the whole cloth by way of buying, nor otherwise; nor stone, nor cloth of silk nor of silver, nor girdle, knife, button, ring, garter, nor ouche, ribbon, chain, nor any such other things of gold or of silver, nor any manner of apparel embroidered, enamelled, nor of silk in any way; and that their wives, daughters and children be of the same condition in their vesture and apparel; and that they wear no veil of silk, but only of yarn made within the realm, nor any manner of fur, nor of budge,[1] but only lamb, coney, cat and fox.

X Also, that esquires and all manner of gentlemen under the estate of a knight which have not land or rent to the value of a hundred pounds a year shall not take nor wear cloth for their clothing or hosing of a higher price than within the price of four marks and a half the whole cloth, by way of buying or otherwise; and that they wear no cloth of gold, nor silk, nor silver, nor any manner of clothing embroidered, ring, button, nor ouche of gold, ribbon, girdle, nor any other apparel, nor harness of gold nor of silver, nor anything of stone, nor any manner of fur; and that their wives, daughters and children be of the same condition, as to their vesture and apparel, without any turning up or purfle;[2] and that they wear no manner of apparel of gold, or silver, nor of stone. But that esquires, which have land or rent to the value of 200 marks a year and above may take and wear cloths of the price of 5 marks the whole cloth, and cloth of silk and silver, ribbon, girdle and other apparel reasonably garnished of silver; and that their wives, daughters and children may wear fur turned up of miniver,[3] without ermine or lettice[4] or any manner of stone, but for their heads.

XI Also, that merchants, citizens, and burgesses, artificers, people of handicraft, as well within the city of London, as elsewhere, which have clearly goods and chattels to the value of 500 pounds, and their wives and children, may take and wear in the same manner as the esquires and gentlemen which have land and rent to the value of 100*l* a year; and that the same merchants, citizens and burgesses, which have clearly goods and chattels to the value of 1000*l* and their wives and children, may take and wear in the same manner as esquires and gentlemen which have land and rent to the value of 200*l* a year; and no groom, yeoman, or servant of merchant, artificer, or people of handicraft shall wear otherwise in apparel than is above-ordained of yeomen of lords.

XII Also, that knights, which have land or rent within the value of 200*l* shall take and wear cloth of 6 marks the whole cloth, for their vesture, and of none higher price: and that they wear not cloth of gold, nor cloth, mantle nor gown furred with miniver nor sleeves of ermine, nor any apparel embroidered of stone, nor otherwise; and that their wives, daughters and children be of the same condition; and that they wear no turning up of ermine nor of lettice, nor any manner of apparel of stone, but only for their heads. But that all knights and ladies, which have land or rent over the value of 400 marks a year to the sum of 1000*l* a year shall wear at their pleasure, except ermine and lettice, and apparel of pearls and stone, but only for their heads.

XIII Also, that clerks, which have degree in any church, cathedral, collegial, or schools, or clerk of the king, that has such estate that requires fur, shall do and use according to the constitution of the same; and all other clerks, which have above 200 marks of land[5] a year, shall wear and do as knights of the same rent; and other clerks within the same rent, shall wear as the esquires of 100*l* of rent: and that all those, as well knights as clerks, which by this ordinance may wear fur in the winter, in the same manner shall wear lawn[6] in the summer.

XIV Also, that carters, ploughmen, drivers of the plough, oxherds, cowherds, shepherds, swineherds, dairymen, and all other keepers of beasts, threshers of corn, and all manner of people of the estate of a groom, attending to husbandry, and other people that have not forty shillings of goods nor of chattels, shall not take nor wear any manner of cloth but blanket and russet, of wool, worth not more than twelve-pence; and shall wear girdles of linen according to their estate; and that they come to eat and drink in the same manner that pertains to them, and not excessively. And it is ordained that if any wear or do contrary to any of the points aforesaid, that he shall forfeit to the king all the apparel that he has so worn against the form of this ordinance.

XV Also, to the intent that this ordinance as to the price and wearing of cloths be maintained and kept in all points without blemish, it is ordained that all the makers of cloths within the realm of England, as well men as women, shall conform them to make their cloths according to the price limited by this ordinance, and that all the drapers shall buy and purvey their sorts according to the same price, so that so great plenty of such cloths be made and set to sale in every city, borough and merchant town,[7] and elsewhere within the realm, that for default of such cloths the said ordinance be in no point broken; and to that shall the said clothmakers and drapers be constrained by any manner [of]

way that best shall seem to the king and his council. And this ordinance
of new apparel shall begin at Candlemas next coming.

¹ Lambskin.   ² Embroidered border of the edge of a garment.
³ Fur used as a lining or trimming.   ⁴ A whitish grey fur.
⁵ Rent in the French.   ⁶ A fine linen.   ⁷ *Ville marchande.*

12 Langland on the Lot of the Peasantry, c.1377–9

(William Langland, *Piers the Ploughman*, transl. J. F. Goodridge (1966),
pp. 89–90)

'Good gracious!' said Hunger, 'I'm not going yet—not until I've had
a square meal and something to drink.'

'I haven't a penny left,' said Piers, 'so I can't buy you pullets or
geese or pigs. All I've got is a couple of fresh cheeses, a little curds and
cream, an oat-cake, and two loaves of beans and bran which I baked
for my children. Upon my soul, I haven't a scrap of bacon, and I
haven't a cook to fry you steak and onions. But I've some parsley and
shallots and plenty of cabbages, and a cow and a calf, and a mare to
cart my dung, till the drought is over. And with these few things we
must live till Lammas time, when I hope to reap a harvest in my fields.
Then I can spread you a feast, as I'd really like to.'

Then all the poor folk came with peas-cods, and brought beans and
baked apples by the lapful, and spring onions and chervils and hundreds
of ripe cherries, and offered these gifts to Piers, to satisfy Hunger.

Hunger soon gobbled it all up and asked for more. So the poor folk
were afraid, and quickly brought up supplies of green leeks and peas,
and would gladly have poisoned him. But by that time the harvest was
approaching, and new corn came to market. So the people took comfort, and fed Hunger royally—Glutton himself couldn't wish for better
ale. And so they put him to sleep.

And then Waster would not work any more, but set out as a tramp.
And the beggars refused the bread that had beans in it, demanding
milk loaves and fine white wheaten bread. And they would not drink
cheap beer at any price, but only the best brown ale that is sold in the
towns.

And the day-labourers, who have no land to live on but their shovels,
would not deign to eat yesterday's vegetables. And draught-ale was not
good enough for them, nor a hunk of bacon, but they must have fresh
meat or fish, fried or baked and *chaud* or *plus chaud* at that, lest they
catch a chill on their stomachs!

And so it is nowadays—the labourer is angry unless he gets high wages,[1] and he curses the day that he was ever born a workman. And he won't listen to wise Cato's advice—'Bear the burden of poverty patiently.' But he blames God, and murmurs against Reason, and curses the king and his council for making statutes on purpose to plague the workmen!—Yet none of them ever complained while Hunger was their master, nor quarrelled with *his* statutes, he had such a fierce look about him.

But I warn you labourers, work while you have the chance, for Hunger is coming fast, and shall awake with the floods to deal justice on wastrels . . .

[1] A reference to the rise in the level of wages enjoyed by labourers in the latter half of the 14th century.

13 A Monastic Cellarer's Account, 1385–6

(*Accounts of the Cellarers of Battle Abbey 1275–1513*, ed. E. Searle and B. Ross (Sydney, 1967), pp. 80–2)

Account of the office of cellarer of Battle from Michaelmas in the ninth year of the reign of King Richard the Second after the Conquest to the same feast next following in the tenth year of the same king by Brother Thomas Elham.

Profits of the Cellarer He answers for 66s 8d received from the mill of Pipringey. And for 65s 10d from the hides of cattle. And for 33s 2d from the entrails of cattle. And for 42s received from sheepskins. And for 10s from wool sold. And for 11s 6d from tallow sold. And for 66s from the pig-fold. And for 10s from the produce of the garden. From oats in Winyarde, nothing this year because they are sown. And for 26s received from Ratt' and Sharpeham. And for 23s 4d from Forelonde. And for 7s from the farm of Chittecombe for Northrode.

Total   20l 2s 4d

Receipt of money And for 153l 22½d [16s 8½d: *crossed out*] received from the lord abbot. And for 84l 10s 9d received both from the manors of Wy, Alciston', Lullyngton', Bernehorne, Ikelsham, Westfeld', Apuldreham and Dengemersshe and from the beadlry of Battle.

Total   237l 12s 7½d.

SUM TOTAL OF RECEIPTS 257l 14s 11½d.

Wine From which he accounts for 2 tuns and 2 pipes of red wine bought at Sandwicum, 19l 6s 8d. For 1 tun of Osey[1] bought at Canterbury, 8*l.* For 1 tun of red wine bought from Patrick of Winchelsey, 6*l* 3*s* 4*d.* For 1 butt of Malvesye[2] bought in the aforesaid year and delivered, for the expenses of this as appears in the great account, 6*l* 13*s* 4*d.* To the convent for wine at Martinmas, Christmas, and the Assumption of the Blessed Virgin Mary, 17*s* 2*d.* For those being bled in Advent and Lent, 8*s.* For expenses incurred towards the carriage of the said wine, 40*s* 2*d.*

Total   43*l* 8*s* 8*d.*

Spice   For pepper, saffron, rice and almonds bought at London, 66*s* 7*d.* For 21 gallons oil bought, 28*s.* For 7 qr. 4 bz. salt bought, 40*s* 8*d.* For wax bought, 13*s* 4*d.* For cotton bought, 3*s* 8*d.* For figs bought, 16*s.* For O Clavis David,[3] 16*s.*

Total   9*l* 4*s* 3*d.*

Meat   For beef bought this year both from the manor and the neighbourhood, 24*l* 2*s.* For mutton bought in the same way, 26*l* 14*s.* For pork bought in the same way, 12*l* 9*s* 8*d.* For veal bought in the same way, 6*l* 15*s* 3½*d.* For lamb bought in the same way, 7*l* 2*s.* For sucking pig bought in the same way, 6*l* 3*s* 8*d.* For poultry and birds bought this year, 11*l* 14*d.*

Total   94*l* 7*s* 9½*d.*

Fish   For salt fish, stockfish, salmon', red and white herrings bought at London and elsewhere this year together with expenses towards the carriage of the same, 41*l* 9*s.* For fresh fish bought at Hastings', Winchelsey, Dengemersshe and at the gate this year, 30*l* 16*s.* For eels bought at Dengemersshe and at the gate this year, 33*s* 6*d.*

Total   73*l* 18*s* 6*d.*

Eggs   For eggs bought this year, 10*l* 17*s* 4*d.* For mustard seed bought, 10*s* 11*d.* For white peas bought, 12*s* 4*d.* For milk, cheese, cream and butter bought this year, 52*s* 8*d.*

Total   14*l* 13*s* 3*d.*

Wages and salaries   For all the staff's wages and salaries this year, 35*l* 19*s.*

Total   35*l* 19*s*

Necessaries   For the staff's gifts on Christmas and Easter Days, 28*s* 3*d.* For straynores and bolting-cloth bought, 7*s* 4*d.* For canvas bought for the cooks, 14*s.* For saccloth bought, 9*s.* For bolts, nails, clowts [4] broddis⁵ and priggis⁶ bought, 19s 6d. For castrating pigs, 2s 8d. For wheels made this year, 9s 2d. For gifts to those working in the quarry on occasions, 3s.

Total 4l 12s 11d.

Works For scything Bodyham meadow and other meadows and for lifting and gathering the hay thence this year, 44s 2d. For making kindling and faggot' this year, 51s 3d. For hay bought at Merlee and elsewhere this year, 26s 8d. For mending various necessities within the court this year, 18s 4d. For shoeing the horses with Thomas Smith, 26s 8d. For 1 plumber hired to repair the chapel of the Blessed Virgin Mary, 20s. Also 1 plumber for mending les guteres above the stable, 10s. Also to the plumber for making a certain portion of new pipe, 108s 10d.

Total 15l 5s 11d.

TOTAL OF ALL EXPENSES 291l 10s 3½d.

And so he exceeds 33l 15s 4d. From which 50s is owed to John Claydon fishmonger, London. And 16s 8d to Thomas Aytone, merchant of Northwyc. And 118s to the Bailiff of Bexle and 118s to William Brekele-sham, 3s 4d to the Dean of Battle, 11s 4d to Walter Offinton, 10l 7s 4d to William Battiford. And 100s 8d to Robert Baker.

¹ Osey wine.   ² Malmsey wine.
³ 20 December, on which day the antiphon *O Clavis David* was sung.
⁴ Clouts.   ⁵ Bradnails.   ⁶ Variety of small nails.

14 Benefits Provided by a Village Gild, 1389

(P.R.O. Chancery Miscellanea Gild Certificates, C 47/38/30)

Certificate of the gild of St. John the Baptist founded and continued in the church of the Blessed Virgin Mary at Stow by Quy,¹ diocese of Ely, made by virtue of the proclamation by the king's writ, and delivered in Chancery before the king's council by John Saffrey, warden of the same gild on the last day of January 12 Richard II.

Firstly the said gild was begun by the devotion of divers men of the same village in the said church of Blessed Mary in the same village thirty years and more ago. It is continued and exists in honour of the feast of the Nativity of St. John the Baptist and was ordered in this form. The warden of the gild and all his brethren ought to come to-gether on the vigil of the said feast to hear the first vespers devotedly, and similarly on the said feast of the Nativity of St. John to hear high mass and then each of them according to his will will offer a penny or a half penny, but the said warden a penny of his own certainly.

Item if any brother or sister of the gild should emigrate from this world within seven leagues from the said village of Stow, the warden and his brethren will bury the corpse in the said church or churchyard according to the wish of the dead man [and] at the expense of the deceased if his goods suffice otherwise at the expense of the gild. Each of the brothers and sisters should be present at the burial of the deceased if they can do this conveniently and at the mass celebrated for him on his anniversary in the said church at the expense of the gild.

Item if any brother or sister of the gild comes to such indigence and poverty arising from any misfortune, and cannot live honestly by his means according to his former estate, then he shall receive every week 7*d* from the warden out of the goods of the gild until death or until he comes to a better estate by divine ordinance without fraud. If any devout man or woman [wishes] to enter the gild, he shall then give four bushels of barley, or the value thereof, at his entry for the maintenance of the gild, promising that he will aid and keep faithfully all the aforesaid articles in so far as he can. If any of them are found to default or to be fraudulent in the premises, then for that default he shall give a pound of wax, or the value thereof, to maintain the candle burning before the image of St. John in the said church on all feast days at the proper hours, unless he has a reasonable excuse.

Item it is ordained by the warden and brethren of the gild that each year on the day of the said feast after nones the goods and chattels belonging in any way to the gild by gift, bequest or acquired by any other legitimate means, shall be inspected and when the said articles, works and charities specified above have been fulfilled, acquitted and perfected, the residue of them may, at the good discretion of the brethren, be distributed faithfully by the warden towards the fabric and use of the said church and not for anything else.

It is to be noted that the warden and brethren of the gild have no land, tenements or rents belonging to the gild in any way or acquired for its use. But the warden and brethren have 22*s* 4*d*.

---

[1] Stow cum Quy, Cambridgeshire.

15 A Charitable Bequest by a Merchant, 1434

(*The Little Red Book of Bristol*, I, ed. F. W. Bickley (1900), pp. 174–7)

Covenant concerning the bequest of Mark William, late merchant and burgess of Bristol, of 100 marks to be employed in purchasing corn for the use of the town, when there shall be a scarcity. Dated 9 April, 12 Hen. VI.

This indenture made between John Fisher, mayor of the town of Bristol and the commonalty of the same town on the one part, and Agnes William, relict of Mark William late burgess and merchant of the town aforesaid, and Richard Arvas, burgess and merchant of the same town, executors of the will of the said Mark on the other part, witnesses, whereas the said Mark lately in his lifetime in his last will and testament bequeathed and assigned to the mayor and commonalty of the aforesaid town and their successors for ever one hundred marks sterling of good and lawful English money, on this condition, that the said mayor and commonalty before their receipt of the said hundred marks shall furnish to the executors of the said Mark sufficient security that the mayor and commonalty and their successors once a year hereafter for ever should have and put the said hundred marks in the common chest of St. George in the Guildhall, and that the mayor and commonalty or their successors should dispose of and administer the said hundred marks according to the last will of the said Mark and not otherwise; to wit, the said Mark willed and ordained that the said hundred marks should be placed in the common chest of St. George aforesaid under four locks and kept there safe and sound, under the condition following, viz., that when there shall have arisen a scarcity of corn then with that sum or part thereof a certain quantity of corn, as shall be fit and necessary in the discretion of the mayor of the town of Bristol, and the good men of the Common Council of the town for the time being, ought to be provided and purchased in those parts where there is very great abundance, and where it is of moderate and less price, for the use of the commonalty of the said town, provided always that neither the aforesaid sum of money nor any part of it ought to be sent out of the kingdom of England, nor in any way to be adventured or lessened as is more fully contained in the aforesaid will. And the aforesaid Agnes and Richard wishing to fulfil the last will of the said Mark, the testator, received security from the mayor and commonalty before the receipt of the aforesaid sum as more fully appears in the form hereunder written, viz. that the said mayor and commonalty or their successors by these presents bind themselves to the said Agnes and Richard, executors of the said Mark, in one hundred marks of good and lawful money of England to carry out the last will of the said Mark in the manner and form above expressed. Upon which security being received according to the force, form, effect and tenor of the will of the aforesaid Mark, the aforesaid Agnes and Richard executors aforesaid delivered on the day of the making of these presents in the Guildhall of the town of Bristol to the aforesaid mayor and commonalty the said hundred marks of good English money. To have to the mayor and commonalty and their successors to their use and to do therewith according to the force, form and effect of the abovesaid will and in no other way whatsoever; which hundred marks the aforesaid mayor and commonalty received and had then and there from the aforesaid Agnes and Richard to the use of the mayor and commonalty of the aforesaid town, and of their successors for ever, to place these moneys in the aforesaid chest and to keep them safe and secure to the use of the commonalty of the aforesaid town in all the ways and methods as is above said and not otherwise. In testimony whereof the said mayor and commonalty have put the common seal of the town of Bristol to one part of the indented writing remaining in the hands of the said Agnes and Richard, and to the other part remaining in the possession of the mayor and commonalty the said Agnes and Richard have put their seals. Dated in the Guildhall, Bristol, the ninth day of the month of April, the twelfth year of the reign of King Henry the Sixth after the Conquest of England.

16 Purchases for a Country Gentleman, 1482

(*The Stonor Letters and Papers, 1290–1483*, II, ed. C. L. Kingsford (Camden Society, Third Series, XXX, 1919), pp. 146–7)

Hugh Unton to Sir William Stonor, 11 May, 1482

Right worshipful Master I recommend me unto you. . . . Sir, as for wine I have sent you by John Somer, to be delivered to John Baker at Henley, 2 hogsheads of claret wine, a hogshead of red wine, a hogshead of white wine. And as for spices I spoke to Master Rush. He looks for a galley coming now in, as he says, and then he will buy by the gross, and then you shall have with him as much as you will, but he will lay down now no money for none. And as for candle we can have none such as you sent for, as Tailbois can tell your Mastership. And as for fish I can none buy without money. And *rysshes* and soap I have sent you by

John Somer's barge, which will be at Henley upon Sunday or Monday at the furthest. . . .

Your own servant H. Unton.

To my worshipful Master, Sir William Stonor, knight for the body.

17 Regulations Made at Chester as to Beggars, 1539

(Printed in R. H. Morris, *Chester in the Plantaganet and Tudor Reigns* (Chester, ?1894), pp. 355–6)

Henry Gee, Mayor, 31 Henry VIII Forasmuch as by reason of the great number of multitude of valiant idle persons and vagabonds which be strong and able to serve and labour for their livings, and yet daily go on begging within the same city, so that the poor impotent and indigent people and inhabiting within the same city and having no other means to get their living but only by the charitable alms of good Christian people daily want and be destitute of the same, to the great displeasure of Almighty God and contrary to good conscience and the wholesome statute and laws of our sovereign lord the king in such case made and provided; for reformation whereof it is ordained and established by the said city . . . that the number and names of all indigent and needy mendicant people shall be searched, known and written, and thereupon divided in 15 parts, and every of them assigned to what ward they shall resort and beg within the said city, and in no other place within the same, and their names to be written in a bill and set up in every man's house within every ward for knowledge to whom they shall give their alms and to no other. And if any other person or persons come to any man or woman's door, house or person to beg, not having his name in the bill within that man's or woman's houses, then the same man or woman to give unto the same beggar no manner alms or relief but rather to bring or send him to the stocks within the same ward, or else to deliver him to the constable of the same ward or the alderman's deputy within the same ward, and he to put him in the stocks, there to remain by the space of a day and a night; and yet, every man and woman that shall offend in using themselves contrary to this ordinance concerning such valiant beggars shall for every such offence forfeit 12*d* to be levied to the use of the common box by the commandment of the alderman of the same ward, and for default of payment thereof the same man or woman so offending to be committed to the ward by the mayor till it be paid.

And if any of the indigent and poor needy beggars [beg] at any time in any other place within this city out of the ward to them assigned as is aforesaid, then the same beggar so offending to be punished by the mayor's discretion. And further it is ordered that all manner of idle persons, being able to labour abiding within the said city and not admitted to live by alms within the said city, shall every workday in the morning in the time of winter at 6 of the clock, and in time of summer at 4 of the clock, resort and come unto the high cross of the said city, and there to offer themselves to be hired to labour for their living according to the king's laws and his statutes provided for labourers; and if any person or persons do refuse so to do, then he or they so refusing to be committed to ward by the mayor of the said city for the time being, there to remain unto such time he or they so refusing have found sufficient sureties to be bound by recognisance before the said mayor in a certain sum, so to do accordingly to the king's laws and statutes aforesaid.

18 Some of the Poor in a Norwich Parish, 1570

(*The Norwich Census of the Poor, 1570*, ed. J. F. Pound (Norfolk Record Society, XL, 1971), pp. 23–4)

South Consforth Ward, St. Peter of South gate[1]

Richard Rich of 35 years, a husbandman that works with Mr Cantrell, and keeps not with his wife but at times and helps her little, and Margaret, his wife, of 40 years, she spins white warp, and Joan, their daughter of 12 years, that spins also the same, and Simond, their son of 8 years, that goes to school, and Alice and Fader, the eldest of 4 and the other 8 years. They have dwelt here two years and since Whitsuntide, and have dwelt most at Banham where they were married, and since at Swanton next North Walsham and Amringhall.
The house of Mr Robert Suckling. No alms and very poor. Able to work. To go away.

Peter Brown, porter, a cobbler of 50 years, has little work, and Agnes his wife, of 60 years, that works not but has been sick since Christmas, but in health she spins white warp; three daughters of 18, 16, of 14 years who all spin when they can get it, but now they are without work. They have dwelt here above 20 years, and they have one daughter, Elizabeth, who is idle and sent from service with William Naught of Thorp, where she dwelt three quarters of a year. [able].
The house of the gates. 4d a week and very poor. Able to work. Non spare.

Ralph Claxton, boatwright, abroad at work, and comforts his wife to his power, and is of 43 years, and Anne, his wife, of 27 years; and two sons, the eldest of 4 years, she spins white warp. He has dwelt here ever, and she now does lie in childbed, and they be indifferently stuffed. [able].
The house is his own, but now in mortgage. 4d a week. Indifferent.

Thomas Mathew, labourer, gone from his wife, of 40 years, from whom she has no help, and Margaret, his wife, of 32 years, and no children. She spins white warp and has dwelt here ever, and she knows not where her husband is, and has not dwelt here 3 years. [to go away].
The house of Wm. Joys. No alms. Very poor.

Thomas Maxwell of 40 years, labourer, and Isabel, his wife, of 40 years; and four children, the eldest 9 years.[2] [able to work].
None spare.

Harry Risbrook, mason, of 26 years, and Elizabeth, his wife, of 30 years; and two sons, the eldest 3 years. She spins white warp, and spare 15 years here.
John Monfors. Poor. No alms. Able to work.

Robert Warner, tailor, of 40 years, and Joan, his wife, of 43; two sons, the eldest 7 years. She spins white warp; dwelt here 6 years. [able to work].
John Monforth. No alms. Indifferent.

William Bridges of 40 years, a labourer, and Joan, his wife, of 23 years. She spins white warp; a son and a daughter, the eldest 8 years old. They keep together and have dwelt here 8 years.
In the first tower. No alms. Very poor. Able to work.

Also there is Thomas Gared and his wife [he dwells at St. Giles, to go away] Joys and his wife; but they live upon their labour. [able to work] 2 spare.
John Monfor. Indifferent.

James Taylor, a tailor of the age of 30 years, now in prison in the guild hall, and Margery, his wife, of 30 years, who spins white warp, and she was Linses wife, that was so long in prison; and one child, a son of 7 years. They have dwelt here since Michaelmas last, but she

lives off his labour, and dwells within Garode at Monforths. [They go to St. Stevens].
At Garodes. No alms. Very poor. Indifferent. Able to work. 1 spare.

Thomas Wilson of 30 years, a basket maker, and Katherine, his wife, of 25 years, who makes buttons; two daughters, the eldest 5 years. They have dwelt here ever. [able to work.]
Balistons house. Indifferent. No alms. 2 spare.

Michael Coke of 40 years, a labourer, and . . . his wife, of 50 years. They live together, and have dwelt here above 3 years. [able].
Edward Paulins house. No alms. Indifferent.

Nicholas Field of 30 years, labourer, sometime a painter, and Rose, his wife, of 30 years, who spins white warp; and two sons, the eldest 6 years. They keep together and work, and have dwelt here ever. [able].
Paulins house. Very poor. No alms.

Also John Soule of 40 years, labourer, and Alice, his wife, of 60 years, who spins white warp, and no child, and they live together, and dwelt here ever. [able]. [gone to St. Stevens].
Indifferent. No alms. Very poor.[3]

John Bundy of 60 years, labourer, and Elizabeth, his wife, of 40 years, who spins her own wool; and one son of 12 years that is idle and a daughter of 12 years that spins wool. They dwell together, and have dwelt here ever.
Paulins house. Very poor. Skouldes.

Walter Field of 64 years, smith, and Agnes, his wife, of 60 years; she spins linen. They keep together, and have dwelt here 40 years.
2d a week. Very poor.

Thomas Frances of 30 years, a smith and boatman, with Margaret, his wife, of 28 years, who spins white warp. They have dwelt here above a year and before in Yarmouth, and now they dwell together: and one son of 1 month old. [to go away].
No alms. Very poor.

Robert Barwick of the age of 60 years, that is and has been long in prison for debt, and Anne, his wife, of 40 years, that has no exercise

ut travels daily on her husband's behalf: and has at their charge 8
children, all idle, and live upon the labour of others, and the biggest of
them keeps the bowling alley. [able].

Edward Paulins house. No alms. Very poor.

[1] Marginalia to the original text are printed in italics. Comments probably inserted
subsequent to the first draft of the ms. are placed in square brackets. (JEP)
[2] This entry was later deleted.   [3] 'Very poor' was later deleted.

19 Poor Relief at Norwich, 1571

Printed in E. M. Leonard, *The Early History of English Poor Relief*
(Cambridge, 1900), pp. 311–15)

Orders for the poor [3rd May, 1571]

1. First, that no person or persons old or young shall be suffered to
go abroad after a general warning given, or be found a-begging in the
streets at the sermon or at any man's door or at any place within the
city, in pain of six stripes with a whip.

2. That not any person or persons shall sustain or feed any such
beggars at their doors, in pain of such fine as is appointed by statute,
and further to pay for every time fourpence, to be collected by the
deacons, and to go to the use of the poor of the said city.

3. Item, that at the house called the Normans in the convenientest
place therefore, shall be appointed a working place, as well for men as
for women, viz. for the men to be prepared fourteen malt querns to
grind malt and such exercises; and for the women to spin and card and
such like exercises.

Which working place shall contain to set twelve persons or more
upon work, which persons shall be kept as prisoners to work for meat
and drink for the space of twenty and one days at the least, and longer
if cause serve, and they shall not eat but as they can earn (except some
friend will be bound for them), that the city shall no more be troubled
with them; with this proviso that such persons as shall be thither committed shall be such as be able to work and daily notwithstanding will
not work but rather beg, or be without master or husband, or else be
vagabonds or loiterers.

Which persons shall begin their works at five of the clock in summer,
viz. from our Lady the Annunciation[1] until Michaelmas,[2] and shall end
their works at eight of the clock at night, and in winter to begin at six
of the clock from Michaelmas to our Lady, and to end at seven of the
clock at night or half an hour past, with the allowance of one half
hour or more to eat and a quarter of an hour to spend in prayer.

And every one sent thither shall be by warrant from the mayor or his deputy or deputies to the bailiff there, upon which warrant the bailiff shall be bound to receive everyone so sent and set them a-work.

And those that shall refuse to do their works to them appointed or keep their hours, to be punished by the whip at the discretion of the wardens or bailiff of the house.

*   *   *

For the bailiff of Bridewell

Item, upon the said authority be also appointed another officer, to be called the bailiff of Bridewell, who is to be resident there with his wife and family, who shall take the charge by inventory from the wardens of all bedding and other utensils delivered unto him to the use of the workfolks, who shall yearly account with the wardens for the same.

And also shall take charge of such vagabonds, men and women, as to them shall be committed, enforcing them to work by the hours aforesaid. The men to grind malt and other works, and the women to use their hand-deed and, except that they work, not to eat.

And to take of them for their victual, and fuel, or other necessaries as the price shall be rated and there set up. And to allow them for their work by the pound (or otherwise) as shall be rated and set up, and shall use such correction as is aforesaid.

And also shall receive all stuff thither brought and see the same truly and well used and safely delivered.

And he to provide him of such servants as in his absence or his wife's shall see the works done as it ought to be, and to do the house business, as washing, making of beds, baking and also to be expert in hand-deed to spin, card, etc.

And also to provide one officer surveyor, to go daily about the city, with a staff in his hand, to arrest whom that is apt for Bridewell and bring them to master mayor or to any of the committees be commanded thither.

And as he goes abroad he shall certify how the works in every ward are ordered and occupied, and shall inform master mayor, the committees or his master thereof.

And he shall resort to the deacons in every ward, and be aiding unto them to bring such as be newcomers into the city to master mayor, the same presently to be sent away again to the place they came from. And likewise shall bring all disordered persons to be punished to Bridewell if such shall dwell in any ward, and shall give his whole attendance thereupon.

And the said bailiff shall be allowed for himself, his wife, servants and surveyors, (if he shall be charged with his whole number of prisoners,) for meat, drink and wages thirty pounds by year, whereof he shall pay forty shillings a year to a priest to minister service to them twice a week, or else, if he have less charge, to have after the rate as by the discretion of the committees and wardens of Bridewell shall be thought convenient or as they can agree.

*   *   *

Orders for children and others in wards

Item, that there be also appointed by the committees or commissioners for every single ward so many select women as shall suffice to receive of persons within that ward, viz. of women, maidens or children that shall be appointed unto them by the committees or deacons, to work or learn letters in their house or houses, of the most poor children whose parents are not able to pay for their learning or of women and maids that live idly or be disordered to the number of six, eight, ten or twelve at the most in any one of their houses.

The same to be driven to work and learn, by the hours appointed in Bridewell and with such corrections, till their hands be brought into such use and their bodies to such pains as labour and learning shall be easier to them than idleness, and as they shall of themselves be able to live of their own works with their families as others do.

And every such select woman appointed to take charge of such aforesaid, shall see that such as to them be committed shall do their works truly and workmanly and be learned profitably, or else to lay sharp correction upon them; and every such select woman doing her duty to teach or cause to be taught or set a-work, to have for her pains in that behalf twenty shillings by year every one of them so appointed and nominated.

And whosoever select woman so appointed shall refuse the same being thereunto appointed, shall suffer imprisonment by the space of twenty days at the least.

*   *   *

Orders for the deacons

Item, that in every single ward within this city be also appointed in that order, form and time aforesaid, two civil and expert men that will be painful, the same to be called deacons, which two in every petty

P

ward appointed, shall have the oversight of the poor of that ward, and have the names of them as well of men, women and children. And such as have not remained three years in the city, to certify the committees thereof, to be presently sent away with their families, and also to have a continual eye that no more such strangers be suffered here to inhabit as be not able to live of themselves, or be like to be chargeable to the city, for the which they shall make search every one in their ward once in a month at the least, upon pain of three shillings and four pence for every time done the contrary.

And such as shall have need and remain and that the alms cannot suffice, to certify the said committees of their state from time to time, as they may be provided for.

And the rest that can work, to see that they run not about a-begging, but rather to be set a-work.

And all those that can and will not work to see them placed with such select women as shall be charged with them, and to keep their hours to them appointed, or else to see correction upon them as at Bridewell (if they shall refuse the correction of their dames).

And also to certify the number of disordered persons to be punished weekly.

And also that the number of children under age (not able to work) and that their parents are not able to sustain, to certify as well of their names, ages as places inhabiting, to be considered thereof.

And also to certify the number of such big wenches or boys as may do service, not able to be kept of their parents, to be put to service according to the statute, and the rest to work with their parents so as they go not idly about.

And whosoever old or young going about to beg, the same to be punished as aforesaid.

Also what vagabonds or idle loiterers, drunkards or disordered persons, do in that ward remain, that they be certified to be punished also.

And that all money, wood or other things whatsoever given or to be given to be distributed to the poor may by them within every ward be truly done and recorded, and the committees made privy thereunto.

And every one to this office appointed and shall refuse to do his duty (in all the premises) both truly and faithfully, shall forfeit the sum of forty shillings the same to go to the use of the poor.

Of the which two, one of the same shall ever continue for two years before he shall go off, to the end to instruct the other.

Item, it is also ordered that the poor in every ward shall receive such sums of money as is to them weekly assigned at the hands of every of the foresaid deacons.

Item, it is also ordered that all gifts, collections, legacies or benevolences given or bequeathed to the use of the poor, shall go to the use aforesaid, and as else hereafter shall be thought meet, to prepare wood or other fuel to sustain the poor in winter or to prepare them houses to dwell in or for any other necessity, or to purchase some certainty of lands to maintain the same.

[1] 31 March.   [2] 29 September.

20 The First Act Requiring a Compulsory Poor Rate, 1572

(14 Elizabeth, c. 5, *Statutes of the Realm*, IV, Part I (1819), pp. 590–98)

An act for the punishment of vagabonds, and for the relief of the poor and impotent

*   *   *

And forasmuch as charity would that poor, aged and impotent persons should as necessarily be provided for, as the said rogues, vagabonds and sturdy beggars repressed, and that the said aged, impotent and poor people should have convenient habitations and abiding places throughout this realm to settle themselves upon, to the end that they nor any of them should hereafter beg or wander about; It is therefore enacted . . . that the justices of peace of . . . the shires of England and Wales . . . and all other justices of the peace, mayors, sheriffs, bailiffs, and other officers of all and every city, borough, riding and franchises within this realm . . . shall at or before the . . . feast of St. Bartholomew[1] next coming . . . make diligent search and enquiry of all aged, poor, impotent and decayed persons born within their . . . divisions and limits, or which were there dwelling within three years next before this present parliament, which live or of necessity be compelled to live by alms . . . and shall . . . make a register book containing [their] names and surnames . . . And when the number of the said poor people forced to live upon alms be by that means truly known, then the said justices . . . and other officers shall within like convenient time devise and appoint, within every their said several divisions, meet and convenient places by their discretions to settle the same poor people for their habitations and abidings, if the parish within the which they shall be found shall not or will not provide for them; and shall also within like convenient time number all the said poor people within their said several limits, and thereupon (having regard to the number) set down what portion the weekly charge towards the relief and sustentation of the said poor people will amount unto within every their said several divisions and limits; and that done, they . . . shall by their good discretions tax and assess all and every the inhabitants, dwelling in all and every city, borough, town, village, hamlet and place known within the said limits and divisions, to such weekly charge as they and every of them shall weekly contribute towards the relief of the said poor people, and the names of all such inhabitants taxed shall also enter into the said register book together with their taxation, and also shall by their discretion within every their said divisions and limits appoint or see collectors for one whole year to be appointed of the said weekly portion, which shall collect and gather the said proportion, and make delivery of so much thereof, according to the discretion of the said justices . . . and other officers, to the said poor people, as the said justices . . . and other officers shall appoint them: and also shall appoint the overseers of the said poor people by their discretions, to continue also for one whole year; and if they do refuse to be overseers, then every of them so refusing to forfeit ten shillings for every such default . . .

[1] 24 August.

21 The Better-off Englishman's House and Furniture, 1577–87

(William Harrison, *The Description of England, 1577, 1587*, ed. G. Edelen (New York, 1968), pp. 195–202)

The greatest part of our building in the cities and good towns of England consists only of timber, for as yet few of the houses of the commonalty (except here and there in the West Country towns) are made of stone, although they may (in my opinion) in divers other places be built so good cheap of the one as of the other. In old time the houses of the Britons were slightly set up with a few posts and many raddles,[1] with stable and all offices under one roof, the like whereof almost is to be seen in the fenny countries and northern parts unto this day, where for lack of wood they are enforced to continue this ancient manner of building. It is not in vain, therefore, in speaking of building, to make a distinction between the plain and woody soils; for as in these our houses are commonly strong and well-timbered—so that in many places there are not above four, six, or nine inches between stud and stud—so in the open and champaign countries they are enforced for want of stuff to use no studs at all but only frank posts,[2] rasens,[3] beams, prick posts,[4] groundsels,[3] summers (or dormants),[5] transoms,[6] and such principals, with here and there a girding,[7] whereunto they fasten their splints or raddles, and then cast it all over with thick clay to keep out the wind, which otherwise would annoy them . . . In like sort, as every country house is thus apparelled on the outside, so is it inwardly divided into sundry rooms above and beneath; and where plenty of wood is, they cover them with tiles [shingles], otherwise with straw, sedge, or reed, except some quarry of slate be near-hand, from whence they have for their money so much as may suffice them.

The clay wherewith our houses are impanelled is either white, red, or blue; and of these the first does participate very much with the nature of our chalk, the second is called loam,[8] but the third eftsoons changes colour so soon as it is wrought, notwithstanding that it look blue when it is thrown out of the pit. Of chalk also we have our excellent asbestos or white lime made in most places, wherewith, being quenched, we strike over our clay works and stone walls in cities, good towns, rich farmers' and gentlemen's houses; otherwise, instead of chalk (where it wants, for it is so scant that in some places it is sold by the pound), they are compelled to burn a certain kind of red stone as in Wales, and elsewhere other stones and shells of oysters and like fish found upon the seacoast, which being converted into lime does naturally (as the other) abhor and eschew water, whereby it is dissolved, and nevertheless desire oil, wherewith it is easily mixed, as I have seen by experience. Within their doors also such as are of ability do oft make their floors[9] and parget[10] of fine alabaster burned, which they call plaster of Paris, whereof in some places we have great plenty and that very profitable against the rage of fire.

In plastering likewise of our fairest houses over our heads, we use to lay first a lain or two of white mortar tempered with hair upon laths, which are nailed one by another (or sometimes upon reed or wickers, more dangerous for fire, and made fast here and there with sap-laths, for falling down), and finally cover all with the aforesaid plaster, which beside the delectable whiteness of the stuff itself is laid on so even and smoothly as nothing in my judgment can be done with more exactness. The walls of our houses on the inner sides in like sort be either hanged with tapestry, arras work, or painted cloths, wherein either divers histories, or herbs, beasts, knots, and suchlike are stained, or else they are ceiled [panelled] with oak of our own or wainscot brought hither out of the East countries, whereby the rooms are not a little commended, made warm, and much more close than otherwise they would be. As for stoves, we have not hitherto used them greatly, yet do they now begin to be made in divers houses of the gentry and wealthy citizens, who build them not to work and feed in, as in Germany and elsewhere, but now and then to sweat in, as occasion and need shall require it.

This also has been common in England, contrary to the customs of all other nations and yet to be seen (for example, in most streets of London), that many of our greatest houses have outwardly been very simple and plain to sight, which inwardly have been able to receive a duke with his whole train and lodge them at their ease. Hereby moreover it is come to pass that the fronts of our streets have not been so uniform and orderly built as those of foreign cities, where (to say truth) the utterside of their mansions and dwellings have oft more cost bestowed upon them than all the rest of the house, which are often very simple and uneasy within, as experience does confirm. Of old time our country houses instead of glass did use much lattice, and that made either of wicker or fine rifts [strips] of oak in checkerwise . . . I read also that some of the better sort in and before the times of the Saxons . . . did make panels of horn instead of glass and fix them in wooden calms [frames]. But as horn in windows is now quite laid down in every place, so our lattices are also grown into less use, because glass is come to be so plentiful and within a very little so good cheap, if not better than the other.

* * *

Heretofore also the houses of our princes and noblemen were often glazed with beryl (an example whereof is yet to be seen in Sudley Castle) and in divers other places with fine crystal . . . But now these are not in use, so that only the clearest glass is most esteemed; for we have divers sorts, some brought out of Burgundy, some out of Normandy, much out of Flanders, beside that which is made in England, which would be so good as the best if we were diligent and careful to bestow more cost upon it, and yet as it is each one that may will have it for his building. Moreover the mansion houses [dwellings] of our country towns and villages (which in champaign ground stand all together by streets and joining one to another but in woodland soils dispersed here and there, each one upon the several grounds of their owners) are built in such sort generally as that they have neither dairy, stable, nor brewhouse annexed unto them under the same roof (as in many places beyond the sea and some of the north parts of our country) but all separate from the first and one of them from another. And yet for all this they are not so far distant in sunder but that the goodman lying in his bed may lightly hear what is done in each of them with ease and call quickly unto his meinie [household] if any danger should attach [seize] him.

The ancient manors and houses of our gentlemen are yet, and for the most part, of strong timber, in framing whereof our carpenters have been and are worthily preferred before those of like science among all other nations. Howbeit, such as be lately built are commonly either of brick or hard stone or both, their rooms large and comely, and houses of office further distant from their lodgings. Those of the nobility are likewise wrought with brick and hard stone, as provision may best be made, but so magnificent and stately as the basest house of a baron does often match in our days with some honours of princes in old time. So that if ever curious building did flourish in England, it is in these our years, wherein our workmen excel and are in manner comparable in skill with old Vitruvius, Leon Battista, and Serlio. Nevertheless, their estimation, more than their greedy and servile covetousness, joined with a lingering humour, causes them often to be rejected and strangers preferred to greater bargains, who are more reasonable in their takings and less wasters of time by a great deal than our own.

The furniture of our houses also exceeds and is grown in manner even to passing delicacy; and herein I do not speak of the nobility and gentry only but likewise of the lowest sort in most places of our South Country that have anything at all to take to. Certes in noblemen's houses it is not rare to see abundance of arras, rich hangings of tapestry, silver vessel, and so much other plate as may furnish sundry cupboards, to the sum oftentimes of 1,000*l* or 2,000*l* at the least, whereby the value of this and the rest of their stuff does grow to be almost inestimable. Likewise in the houses of knights, gentlemen, merchantmen, and some other wealthy citizens, it is not geason [uncommon] to behold generally their great provision of tapestry, Turkey work,[11] pewter, brass, fine linen, and thereto costly cupboards of plate, worth 500*l* or 600*l* or 1,000*l* to be deemed by estimation. But as herein all these sorts do far exceed their elders and predecessors, and in neatness and curiosity the merchant all other, so in time past the costly furniture stayed there, whereas now it is descended yet lower, even unto the inferior artificers and many farmers, who, by virtue of their old and not of their new leases, have for the most part learned also to garnish their cupboards with plate, their joint beds[12] with tapestry and silk hangings, and their tables with carpets and fine napery, whereby the wealth of our country (God be praised therefore and give us grace to employ it well) does infinitely appear. Neither do I speak this in reproach of any man, God is my judge, but to show that I do rejoice rather to see how God has blessed us with His good gifts; and whilst I behold how that, in a time wherein all things are grown to most excessive prices and what commodity soever is to be had is daily plucked from the commonalty by such as look into every trade, we do yet find the means to obtain and achieve such furniture as heretofore has been impossible.

There are old men yet dwelling in the village where I remain which have noted three things to be marvellously altered in England within their sound remembrance . . . One is the multitude of chimneys lately erected, whereas in their young days there were not above two or three, if so many, in most uplandish towns of the realm (the religious houses and manor places of their lords always excepted, and peradventure some great personages), but each one made his fire against a reredos in the hall, where he dined and dressed his meat.

The second is the great (although not general) amendment of lodging, for (said they) our fathers, yea, and we ourselves also, have lain full oft upon straw pallets, on rough mats covered only with a sheet, under coverlets made of dagswain or hapharlots[13] (I use their own terms), and a good round log under their heads instead of a bolster or pillow. If it were so that our fathers or the goodman of the house had within seven years after his marriage purchased a mattress or flock-bed,[14] and thereto a sack of chaff to rest his head upon, he thought himself to be as well lodged as the lord of the town, that peradventure lay seldom in a bed of down or whole feathers, so well were they contented and with such base kind of furniture, which also is not very much amended as yet in some parts of Bedfordshire and elsewhere further off from our southern parts. Pillows (said they) were thought meet only for women in childbed. As for servants, if they had any sheet above them it was well, for seldom had they any under their bodies to keep them from the pricking straws that ran oft through the canvas of the pallet and razed their hardened hides.

The third thing they tell of is the exchange of vessel, as of treen [wooden] platters into pewter, and wooden spoons into silver or tin. For so common were all sorts of treen stuff in old time that a man should hardly find four pieces of pewter (of which one was peradventure a salt) in a good farmer's house, and yet for all this frugality (if it may so be justly called) they were scarce able to live and pay their rents at their days without selling of a cow or an horse or more, although they paid but 4l at the uttermost by the year.[15] Such also was their poverty that if some one odd farmer or husbandman had been at the alehouse, a thing greatly used in those days, amongst six or seven of his neighbours, and there in a bravery to show what store he had did cast down his purse, and therein a noble or 6s in silver, unto them (for few such men then cared for gold, because it was not so ready payment, and they were oft enforced to give a penny for the exchange of an angel), it was very likely that all the rest could not lay down so much against it; whereas in my time, although peradventure 4*l* of old rent be improved to 40*l*, 50*l*, or 100*l*, yet will the farmer, as another palm or date tree,[16] think his gains very small toward the end of his term if he have not six or seven years' rent lying by him, therewith to purchase a new lease, beside a fair garnish of pewter on his cupboard, with so much more in odd vessel going about the house, three or four feather beds, so many coverlets and carpets of tapestry, a silver salt, a bowl for wine (if not an whole nest), and a dozen of spoons to furnish up the suit.

[1] Flexible sticks or branches woven between posts to support clay or plaster. (GE, and other notes also)
[2] Apparently angle posts.
[3] Horizontal timbers at the base and top of posts.
[4] Secondary, side posts.   [5] Horizontal bearing timbers.
[6] Crosspieces.   [7] Girder, joist.
[8] Clay mixed with water, sand, dung, straw, etc., used in plastering.
[9] Ceilings.   [10] Plastered walls.
[11] Turkish tapestry, or imitation of it.
[12] Beds made by joiners, more ornamental than carpenters' work.
[13] Coverlets of coarse, shaggy material.
[14] A mattress stuffed with coarse tufts of wool or cotton.
[15] 'This was in the time of general idleness.' (H)
[16] In reference to the proverb, 'The heavier the weight the palm tree bears, the taller it grows.'

22 Personal Estate of an Oxfordshire Farmer, 1584

(*Household and Farm Inventories in Oxfordshire, 1550–1590*, ed. M. A. Havinden (1965), pp. 169–70)

John Coxe, of Deddington, husbandman, taken 28th April 1584, by Philip Lodwell, clerk, Edward Marsh and Richard Skrogges

	l	*s*	*d*
In the hall.			
2 tables, 2 forms, a cupboard, 2 shelves, 2 spits, a pair of pothangings and hooks, and one chair		6	8
4 platters, 3 pewterdishes, 4 saucers, 4 candlesticks, a latten[1] basin and a yore,[2] a salt and a chafing-dish[3]		8	0
Also three brasspots, one posnet,[4] and two small kettles		10	0

	l	*s*	*d*

In the chambers.

4 bedsteads, a flockbed, four bolsters, two pillows, 4 coverlets and one blanket		19	0
8 pair of sheets, 3 tablecloths, 6 tablenapkins, 2 towels and a pair of pillowberes[5]	1	2	0
2 brasspans and 2 bottles		6	8
Three coffers, 3 lomes,[6] one tub, a covell,[7] two pails and a yeoting vat[8]		8	0
The crop in the fields, both of wintercorn, barley, pease and oats	6	13	8
Five horses and their gear	5	6	8
Two kine and a heifer	3	0	0
Two ironbound carts	2	0	0
2 hovels, wood in the yard, and 2 ladders	1	0	0
2 yelts,[9] 2 barrow pigs[10] and 6 suckingpigs		16	0
Eight hens and 2 cocks		3	4
Four sheep		12	0
Ten pounds of yarn		1	8
A malt mill		4	0
His apparel	1	0	0
Sum	24	17	8

[1] Alloy of copper and zinc, similar to fine brass.   [2] A ewer.
[3] Used to keep food hot.   [4] Cooking pot.   [5] Pillow cases.
[6] An open vessel.   [7] A cooling tub.   [8] A soaking vat.
[9] Young female pig.   [10] A castrated boar.

23 Charitable Provision for the Aged, 1588

(*Poor Relief in Elizabethan Ipswich*, ed. J. Webb (Suffolk Records Society, IX, 1966), p. 25)

The 22nd February, 1588

It is ordered and agreed by the wardens of Mr Tooley's Foundation ... that John Wiesman and Agnes his wife, being two old, aged and impotent people of this town who have been inhabitants in the same by the space of 30 years and more and of honest fame and report, shall in respect of their ages and poverty be admitted and placed in one of the houses of Mr Tooley's Foundation, and for that the said Agnes is already of the said Foundation (as a non-resident) and has her admittance to the weekly relief of 12*d* that now the said John Wiesman also shall have for his relief weekly other 12*d* to be paid by the renter-warden out of the revenues of the said Foundation, together with such other ordinary allowances as by the orders and constitutions of the said Foundation is limited and appointed, the first payment to begin on Friday next after the date above written.

Robert Snellinge John Knappe

24 Some Expenses of a Noble Household, 1598–9

(*The Household Papers of Henry Percy, Ninth Earl of Northumberland, 1564–1632*, ed. G. R. Batho (Camden Society, Third Series, XCIII, 1962), pp. 29–33)

24 February 1598 The declaration of the account of Edward Francis, gentleman, officer to the right honourable Henry, Earl of Northumberland, occupying as well the offices of the steward of his lordship's household as the payer and disburser of some foreign payments, as well of all such sums of money by him received and had, as also of the disbursing, paying and laying out of the same, from the 6th of May 1598 in the 40th year of the reign of our sovereign lady, Queen Elizabeth, until the 20th of February [1599] then next following in the 41st year of the reign of our sovereign lady, Queen Elizabeth, as by a book of the particulars thereof with other bills and scripts hereupon examined, cast up and perused briefly appears as follows . . .

The said accountant demands allowance of ready money by him disbursed within the time of this account, viz. in:

Expenses by diet

Acates Paid by the said accountant within the time aforesaid for the diet of his lordship and household kept and held at Petworth as hereafter particularly follows, viz. for beef bought of Christopher Sotcher, the butcher, at several times and rates, 186*l* 16*s* 10½*d*; for 582 carcases of mutton bought and spent within the same time, 274*l* 12*s* 1½*d*; for divers acates, 237*l* 20½*d*; and to Raymant, the poulterer, for wild fowl at the christening of the young lady in August 1598, 52*s*; butter, 63*l* 16*s* 6½*d*; eggs, 22*l* 4*s* 6*d*; to Barnes, the fishmonger, for lings, sturgeon and haberdine[1] the 29th of November 1598, 17*l* 10*s*; the 12th of February, 27*l* 12*d*; and more for small lings as appears in the household book, 111*s* 2*d*; for salt, 37*s* 11*d*; for cheeses, 38*s* 8*d*; and for divers necessaries in diet, 32*l* 18*s* 7½*d*. In all as by the books of this accountant and diverse bills of the particulars examined may appear: 874*l* 13½*d*.

Grocery Paid also by the said accountant to divers persons for spices bought of them within the time of this account, viz. to Mr Ayden, the grocer, the 10th of December upon two bills, 48*l*; more the 22nd of January, 27*s*; to Henry Beach the 17th of December 1598, as by his bill appears, 15*l*; to Mr Agarre, the grocer, the 16th of February [1599], 14*l*; to Mr Helmes for a sugar loaf, 16*s*; for a banquet at the christening of the young lady, 105*s*; and for olives, capers, confects, brunella prunes and cinnamon water at several times, 76*s* 1*d*; and more at several times as in the household book may appear, 34*s* 7*d*. In all as by the books of this said accountant and divers bills may appear: 89*l* 18*s* 8*d*.

Wine Paid likewise by the said accountant to divers persons for wine bought of them within the time of this account, viz. to Mr Jeffreys the 23rd of December, in part payment of 3 ton of claret wine at 30*l* the ton and a butt of sack at 18*l*, as by acquittances appears, 90*l*; to Mr Kynnerston the 6th of December, for a pipe of Canary wine, 20*l*; to Barnes, the fishmonger, the 29th of November for Rhenish wine and the 12th of February, 6*l* 4*s* 10*d*; more paid by the said accountant for claret wine, Canary wine and muscadyne, 115*s* 2*d*; and also for wine at sundry times as in the household book appears, 16*s* 9*d*; and for the carriage of 2½ tons of claret wine from Southampton to Arundel and from thence to Petworth, 63*s*. In all as by the books and bills aforesaid appears: 125*l* 19*s* 9*d*.

Gross provision

Wheat Paid likewise by the said accountant for 104 qtrs. 3 bs. of wheat, spent in his lordship's house and bought at several times of divers persons from the 12th of May 1598 until the 16th of February then next following within the time of this account, viz. of John Mose 28 qtrs., 67*l* 4*s*; of Mris Lukenor 10 qtrs., 21*l* 11*s* 7*d*; of Butcher 3 bs., 16*s* 6*d*; William Ilsley 5 qtrs., 11*l*; bought in the market by John Baker and others 6 qtrs. 5 bs., 8*l* 7*s* 1*d*; of Henry Standon 20 qtrs., 22*l*; of John Ayline 3 qtrs., 4 bs., 4*l* 15*s*; of Christopher Sotcher 12 qtrs. 6 bs., 15*l* 6*s*; of Blundell of Sutton 15 qtrs., 15*l* 10*s*; of Thomas Lybard 6 bs., 18*s*; of Turner of Sutton 2 qtrs. 2 bs., 52*s* 10*d*; and for a bs. of wheat flour, 3*s* 4*d*. In all as by the said books and bills may appear: 170*l* 4*s* 5*d*.

Malt and hops Paid more by the said accountant for 155 qtrs. of malt bought at several times and off several persons as follows, viz. of John Mose 50 qtrs. the 12th of July 1598 at 26*s* 8*d* the qtr., 66*l* 13*s* 4*d*; of Mr Ilsley the 10th of September 10 qtrs., 12*l*; of Mris Lukenor the 19th of December 14 qtrs., 15*l* 8*s*; of Turner of Sutton the 8th of January 20 qtrs., 13*l* 6*s* 8*d*; and of Goble of Chichester, at three several times ending the 12th of February now instant [1599], 61 qtrs.,

50*l* 12*s*. In all for malt, 158*l*. Paid to John Byumble the 18th of December 1598 for 328 lb. of hops, from the 7th of April until the 12th of December aforesaid, at 46*s* 8*d* the 100th, 7*l* 11*s* 8*d*; and for necessaries to the brewer, 20*d*. In all as by the books and bills aforesaid may appear: 165*l* 13*s* 4*d*.

Woodcutting and coals Paid also by the said accountant, at several times to divers workmen for the cutting of 246 cords of wood, 7*l* 5*s* 6*d*; and to Mathew, the collier, in full payment for the making and burning of 82 loads of coals at 4*s* 4*d* the load, 17*l* 15*s* 4*d*; and to Mris Wright for coals at London at several times, 4*l* 4*s*. In all as by the said books and bills may appear: 29*l* 4*s* 10*d*.

Lights Paid likewise by the said accountant to divers chandlers for lights, spent in his lordship's house within the time of this account, 60*l* 12*s*; for torches, 24*s* 8*d*; for soap and starch, 4*l* 13*s* 4*d*; and for vinegar and vergeous[2], 113*s* 5*d*. In all as by the books and bills aforesaid may appear: 72*l* 3*s* 5*d*.

Wages and liveries Paid by the said accountant for the wages of his lordship's servants, viz. to Mr Francis Wycliff for his wage for one whole year at his going away, 10*l*; for the wages of 45 your lordship's servants, gentlemen and yeomen, due at several times as by his book may appear, 163*l* 11*s* 8*d*; for the wages of her ladyship's nurse, and Ellen, her maid, for half a year ended at Christmas last, 6*l* 5*s*; for the wages of Mres Wright, keeper of Barbican House, for one whole year to end at the Lady [Day] 1599 next coming, 53*s* 4*d*; and for the wages of 11 men departed your lordship's service, as by the said book may appear, 19*l* 18*s*. In all as by his book and at large may appear: 202*l* 8*s*.

Paid more by the said accountant to Mr Gibson, draper, the 30th of November 1598 for 106 yards of azure coloured cloth for the liveries of 77 of your lordship's gentlemen and servants, as by the book of the said accountant may appear: 50*l* 7*s* 1*d*.

Stable charges Paid also by the said accountant within the said time for the charges of your lordship's horses, viz. for 143 qtrs. 6 bs. of oats, bought at several times of divers persons from the 16th of May 1598 until the 22nd of January then next following, viz. to Mr Watkins for 1 qtr., 12*s*; bought by John Baker 2 qtrs., 26*s* 8*d*; of John Ayline 5 qtrs. 4 bs., 55*s*; of Prentise of Chidlington 60½ qtrs., 18*l* 3*s* 4*d*; bought by John Duke 4 qtrs., 42*s* 8*d*; of John Mose 6 bs., 6*s*; of Christopher Sotcher 40 qtrs., 13*l* 6*s* 8*d*; Wilford 1 qtr., 5*s*; of Stone of Fittleworthe 20 qtrs., 116*s*; and to one Cooke for 9½ qtrs., 57*s*. In all besides 40 qtrs. received from Mr Kelton for the Little Park, 47*l* 11*s* 4*d*.

For hay, viz. to William Mose for half the Ladypiece of meadow and the haymaking of it, 100s; for 20 loads of hay, 18l 8s; for the making of hay, mowing and leading the same, 7l 4s. For horse charges and pasture for 3 horses in summer last, 26s 6d. For 8 loads of straw, 33s 4d. For mowing of hay at Syon, making, leading and stacking the same, 6l 16s. In all for hay, 40l 7s 10d. In all as by the books aforesaid may appear: 87l 19s 2d.

Foreign payments

Apparel and necessaries for his lordship Paid by the said accountant within the time of this account for divers parcels of cloth and silks for apparel for his lordship as follows. That is to say paid to Mr Gibson, draper, the 30th of November 1598 for divers parcels of cloth for your lordship's use, 17l; to Mr Browne, the mercer, the 9th of December 1598 for velvet, satin, taffeta, and other silks for his lordship's use and apparel, 64l 16s 8d; more to Mr Gibson, draper, the 12th of February for cloth and bays for a gown to your lordship (besides cloth for Mr George Percy), 4l 5s; for a hat and other necessaries, 23s; for tobacco and tobacco pipes, 36s. In all as by his book and bills aforesaid may appear: 89l 8d.

Necessaries for her ladyship and the young lady Paid likewise by the said accountant to Mr Middleton, linen draper, the 24th of May 1598 for divers necessaries for her ladyship against her ladyship's lying in childbed, as by the book of this accountant may appear, besides 9l 6s for holland, lawn and cambric, in the title of linen draper: 42s 10d.

Mr George Percy Paid also by the said accountant for the charges of Mr George Percy, his lordship's brother, as for apparel and necessaries for him, 4l 19s; for the redeeming of his cloak, 28s; and for cloth bought of Mr Gibson, draper, 38s 6d. In all, besides 67s 6d for holland and cambric in the title of linen draper, as may appear: 8l 5s 6d.

Apparel for his lordship's page Paid by the said accountant within the said time, for apparel for Mr Shaftoe, his lordship's page, as for 2 pair of stockings, 9s; a hat and a band, 7s; and for a pair of spurs, 12d. In all as may appear: 17s.

[1] Large codfish.   [2] A household vinegar.

25 The Poor Law Act, 1601

(43 and 44 Elizabeth, c. 2, *Statutes at Large*, II (1763), pp. 702–5)

Be it enacted by the authority of this present parliament, that the churchwardens of every parish, and four, three or two substantial householders there, as shall be thought meet, having respect to the proportion and greatness of the same parish and parishes, to be nominated yearly in Easter week, or within one month after Easter, under the hand and seal of two or more justices of the peace in the same county, whereof one to be of the quorum, dwelling in or near the same parish or division where the same parish does lie, shall be called overseers of the poor of the same parish: And they, or the greater part of them, shall take order from time to time, by and with the consent of two or more such justices of peace as is aforesaid, for setting to work the children of all such whose parents shall not by the said churchwardens and overseers, or the greater part of them, be thought able to keep and maintain their children; and also for setting to work all such persons, married or unmarried, having no means to maintain them, and use no ordinary and daily trade of life to get their living by; And also to raise weekly or otherwise (by taxation of every inhabitant, parson, vicar and other, and of every occupier of lands, houses, tithes impropriate, propriations of tithes, coal mines, or saleable underwoods in the said parish, in such competent sum and sums of money as they shall think fit) a convenient stock of flax, hemp, wool, thread, iron and other necessary ware and stuff, to set the poor on work: And also competent sums of money for and towards the necessary relief of the lame, impotent, old, blind, and such other among them, being poor and not able to work, and also for the putting out of such children to be apprentices, to be gathered out of the same parish, according to the ability of the same parish, and to do and execute all other things, as well for the disposing of the said stock as otherwise concerning the premises, as to them shall seem convenient.

II Which said churchwardens and overseers so to be nominated, or such of them as shall not be let by sickness or other just excuse, to be allowed by two such justices of peace or more as is aforesaid, shall meet together at the least once every month in the church of the said parish, upon the Sunday in the afternoon after divine service, there to consider of some good course to be taken, and of some meet order to be set down in the premises; And shall within four days after the end of their year, and after other overseers nominated as aforesaid, make and yield up to such two justices of peace as is aforesaid, a true and perfect account of all sums of money by them received, or rated and assessed and not received; and also of such stock as shall be in their hands, or in the hands of any of the poor to work, and of all other things concerning their said office; and such sum or sums of money as shall be in their hands, shall pay and deliver over to the said churchwardens and overseers newly nominated and appointed as aforesaid . . .

III And be it also enacted, that if the said justices of peace do perceive, that the inhabitants of any parish are not able to levy among themselves sufficient sums of money for the purposes aforesaid; that then the said two justices shall and may tax, rate and assess as aforesaid, any other of other parishes, or out of any parish, within the hundred where the said parish is, to pay such sum and sums of money to the churchwardens and overseers of the said poor parish for the said purposes, as the said justices shall think fit . . . And if the said hundred shall not be thought . . . able and fit to relieve the said several parishes not able to provide for themselves as aforesaid, then the justices of peace at their general quarter-sessions . . . shall rate and assess as aforesaid, any other of other parishes, or out of any parish, within the said county for the purposes aforesaid, as in their discretion shall seem fit.

IV . . . And the said justices of peace, or any one of them, to send to the house of correction or common gaol, such as shall not employ themselves to work . . .

V And be it further enacted, that it shall be lawful for the said churchwardens and overseers, or the greater part of them, by the assent of any two justices of the peace aforesaid, to bind any such children, as aforesaid, to be apprentices, where they shall see convenient, till such man-child shall come to the age of four and twenty years, and such woman-child to the age of one and twenty years, or the time of her marriage . . . And to the intent that necessary places of habitation may more conveniently be provided for such poor impotent people; Be it enacted . . . that it shall and may be lawful for the said churchwardens and overseers . . . to erect, build, and set up in fit and convenient places of habitation in such waste or common, at the general charges of the parish, or otherwise of the hundred or county . . . convenient houses of dwelling for the said impotent poor . . . which cottages and places for inmates shall not at any time after be used or employed to or for any other habitation, but only for impotent and poor of the same parish, that shall be there placed from time to time.

* * *

VIII And be it further enacted, that the father and grandfather, and the mother and grandmother, and the children of every poor, old, blind, lame and impotent person, or other poor person not able to work, being of a sufficient ability, shall, at their own charges, relieve and maintain every such poor person in that manner, and according to that rate, as by the justices of peace . . . shall be assessed.

26 Draft Regulations of the Orphans' Aid, Plymouth,[1] c.1615

(Plymouth City Records, W 424/2)

1   Of orphans born in the town wherein they first shall be respected, whose parents or father chiefly were of best account for religion and conversation. Next, that they be not sickly of any disease which may hurt the others or be offensive to the house. Amongst equals for other respects that such be first entertained which have least means of themselves or of friends.

2   That they be kept unto prayer both morning, evening, at repasts and upon all other occasions, and besides the good estate of the church of God to be prayed for, to remember and to pray for the realm, the king, and particularly this town. That they be seen to go to the school at the hours for the school, and in the vacant time of their return for breakfast, dinner and supper any of them being able to read shall read by turn some part of the bible or some other virtuous book, the rest in the meantime to be about him knitting and spinning as shall be thought fittest for them. To have liberty for recreation only two days in the week, two hours in the day. In the evenings after supper one of them by turn to be catechized in the principles of religion. That they be enjoined to give attention to sermons and be called to account of what they learn at them. That all swearing, lying, theft, brawling, loitering and idleness be driven from them. That they be mannerly and civil in their carriage, courteous in their conversation, industrious in their employment.

3   By the incorporation the precedent mayor is to be their governor, and divers of the bench and 24 to be his assistants, whereof two of the 24 to be wardens on to change every year. The tutor of the orphans to be deputy or substitute to the governor for governing the orphans in their behaviour and actions. The wardens to be his substitute for keeping the account and supply of necessaries. The governor, assistants and wardens to meet at the house quarterly or oftener if occasion be.

4   The orders to be made for the house, for the orphans, for their tutor or other officers, of occasions to be made by and with the consent of the mayor of Plymouth, the major part of his brethren and of the common council of the said town, or the greater number of them.

5   When any shall accomplish the age of 15 years at the first meeting it shall be taken into consideration how he may be placed away, which placing away should be within 1 year or 2 years following at the most. The incorrigible to be displaced and the supply to be within 6 months of any avoidance.

6   That the wardens for the same be ready to give their account yearly upon the last day of September . . .

7   That no benefactor to the said hospital shall have any monument or memorial set up there of his benefit while he is living.

¹ This charity was a hospital for orphans founded by Thomas and Nicholas Sherwill. These latter were bequeathed £100 by William Lawrence, a Plymouth merchant, in his will dated 3 September, 1612. The sum was to be used within seven years for the erection of an almshouse for poor people or for the education of poor children and orphans.

27 The Personal Estates of Two Bedfordshire Men, 1620

(*Jacobean Household Inventories*, ed. F. G. Emmison (Bedfordshire Historical Record Society, XX, 1938), pp. 55–7)

Andrew Lycet of Milbrooke, labourer. 14 March, 1620

His apparel, 2s 6d; one cupboard, one table, three tubs, 6s; three kettles, four platters, three stools, one bowl, 4s; painted cloths,¹ pot-hangers, one board, 12d; one bedstead, three coffers, one cupboard, painted cloths in the chamber, 6s; two pair of sheets, three blankets, 5s.

The wood in the yard, one ladder, 2s.

The lease, 20s.

Sum: 46s 6d.

The debts that owed—to Mr Saunders, 8s; to Mr Hodkins, 16s; to Green the baker, 3s; to Thomas Kirby, 3s 3d; to Baxter, 20d; to Thomas Beke, 18d; to John Wiley, 4s; to William Maynard, 12d; to Nicholas Sanders, 7d; to Robert Hucle, 2s. Sum: 25s.

Edward Plummer, Rector of Holcot. 14 March, 1620

In the hall and kitchen—a frame table, three forms, a glass cupboard, a dresser board, three chairs, 26s 8d; a pair of andirons, fireshovel and tongs, 3 pot hangers, 4 spits, 2 dripping pans, a gridiron, a mustard quern, and other implements, 13s 4d.

In the parlour—a frame table, a carpet, 6 join² stools, 2 pair of andirons, a fireshovel and tongs, a sidetable, 2 chairs, 3 low stools, a dozen of cushions, a pair of tables, 46s 8d; the wainscote and benches, 53s 4d.

In the buttery—one hogshead, 6 barrels, a safe, a glass cupboard, a poudering trose,³ and other implements, 33s 4d.

In the storehouse—2 brass pans, 4 brass kettles, 3 brass pots, one iron pot, a pestle and brass mortar, and other implements, 3l 6s 8d; 22

pewter dishes and pewter pots and other small dishes, porringers[4] and saucers, a still and warming pan, 46s 8d; 3 tubs, 4 kimnels,[5] 10 milk bowls, a churn, and other lumber, 13s 4d.

In the chamber over the hall—a bedsteddle,[6] a featherbed furnished, a trundle bed[7] furnished, 3 chests, 3 trunks, and other implements, 5l; 11 pair of sheets, 4 board cloths, 3 dozen of napkins, 12 coarse towels, 3l 5s.

In the chamber over the parlour—a bedstead, a trundle bed, a table, a chair, a pair of andirons, fireshovel and tongs, the mats and the hanging in the chamber, 4l.

In the study—a table, a chair and shelves, and all his books, 3l 6s 8d.

In the storehouse chamber—a chest, 2 wheels, 3 coffers, a bolting hutch,[8] and other lumber, 20s.

In the gallery—certain joises and boards, and other lumber, 20s.

In the yards—3 beasts,[9] a stone horse,[10] a gelding, a mare colt, 14l; four shoots,[11] 26s 8d; a pair of wheels unshod, a long cart, a dung cart, a plough, and the horse harness, 30s.

In the garner—7 quarter of malt and barley ready dressed, a boarded garner, a malt mill, and other lumber, 6l.

In the barn—the barley, the pease, the straw and hay, 40s.

A barn of 4 bays upon pattens,[12] a lean-to the barn, a hovel[13] of two bays, 12l.

All the pales about the houses, orchards and gardens and yards, a privy house, a hodge[14] sty, 5l.

A conduit house, a ceston of lead, 4l.

The wood in the yard, 10s.

In fields ready sown, 2 acres of wheat and rye, 6 acres of tilth, and 9 acres of pease ready sown, 12l.

A hive of bees, 5s.

All the poultry in the yard, 4s.

The glass about all the houses, 30s.

His wearing apparel, 6l.

For all other things forgotten, unpriced, 10s.

Sum: 99l 6s 4d.

A note what money the said Edward Plummer to divers men owes upon bond, and to others without any speciality. To John Charnock esquire, upon bond, 21l 3s 6d; to Robert Anstie gentleman, upon bond, 5l; to Thomas Davers, upon bond, 10l; to William Cayno, clerk, upon bond, 50s; to Goodman Nawe, upon bond, 3l 10s; to Henry Geyler upon bond, 20l; to Richard Barrett, 5l; to Edward Hickman, 30s; to John Scott for grain, 6l 13s 4d; to Edward Butterfield, 8l 10s; to John Brown,

4*l*; to Nathaniel Howes of Woburn, 4*l*; to William Venture of Salford, 20*s*.

¹ Cloth or canvas painted in oil, a substitute for tapestry.
² Made by a joiner.   ³ Tub for salting meat.   ⁴ Vessels for porridge.
⁵ Household tubs.   ⁶ Bedstead.   ⁷ Low bed on wheels.   ⁸ A sieve bin.
⁹ Cattle.   ¹⁰ Stallion.   ¹¹ Young weaned pigs.   ¹² Posts or stilts.
¹³ Shed, usually without sides.   ¹⁴ Hog.

28 Plague and its Effects, 1627

(*Records of the County of Wilts.*, being Extracts from the *Quarter Sessions Great Rolls of the Seventeenth Century*, ed. B. H. Cunnington (Devizes, 1932), pp. 85–6)

Civitas Novo Sarum,[1] 30th Sept. 1627

Right Honourable.

May it please your good lordship and the rest of his majesty's justices within the county of Wiltshire to be advertised of the miserable and distressed estate of the poor people in this city. And that you will be pleased to take into your good considerations for the continuance of their relief, without which more people are like to perish by famine than by the infectious sickness which is much more increased very lately than heretofore, as appears by certificate hereunder written.

1   First here are upon relief two thousand nine hundred and odd persons.

2   Whereof there are 88 households shut up of the infectious sickness, of which 27 houses are fallen into that this last week.

3   The relief of these persons at one penny by the day amounts unto 80*l* and upward by the week.

4   The charge of the sick people and their attendants to order them as well by night as by day is very great.

5   We have not received the half part of the contribution agreed upon at the last sessions although we have employed divers of our brethren and good friends to collect the same of the constables. And therefore do humbly desire that some good order may now be taken with the constables and others that are behind in payment thereof.

6   Also, over and beside the loving and charitable benevolence of the cities and towns, and divers right worshipful knights and gentlemen, bestowed and sent unto us, we stand much engaged and indebted for corn and other provisions for the poor and infected.

7   There are not left scarce ten householders within the city that are able to give relief.

8 The number of those that have died for this month now last past viz. from the 31st of August to the 29th September, 73.

John Ivie. Mayor.

Ri. Godfrey, B. Tookie, Henry Pearson.

[1] Salisbury.

29 Cakes and Ale, 1641

(*Rural Economy in Yorkshire in 1641, being the Farming and Account Books of Henry Best*, ed. C. B. Robinson (Surtees Society, XXXIII, 1857), p. 93)

. . . it is usual in most places after they get all peas pulled or the last grain down, to invite all the work-folks and their wives (that helped them that harvest) to supper, and then have they puddings, bacon or boiled beef, flesh or apple pies, and then cream brought in platters, and every one a spoon; then after all they have hot cakes and ale; for they bake cakes and send for ale against that time: some will cut their cake and put into the cream, and this feast is called the cream-pot or cream-kit; for on the morning that they get all done the workfolks will ask their dames if they have good store of cream, and say that they must have the cream kit anon.

30 The Cleansing of a Town, 1648

(*Weymouth and Melcombe Regis, Minute Book, 1625–1660*, ed. M. Weinstock (Dorset Record Society, 1964), pp. 72–3)

25 August 1648 . . . It is also agreed . . . that Thomas Newman shall be the general scavenger of these towns of Weymouth and Melcombe Regis, for the carrying away of all the dirt, rubble and dust from the lands, grounds and gutters, into the void ground newly enclosed at the jutty, and that of Weymouth above the bridge westwards to the void place near the house of Thomas Barnes, and below the bridge against the wall of Mr Denny's brewhouse. And the said scavenger is to carry away the same dirt, rubble and dust . . . twice in every week weekly from henceforth, until Michaelmas[1] next [and] come twelvemonth, on every Wednesday and Saturday, if the weather will permit. And that all the inhabitants of the town shall on every day before those days, rake and cleanse the gutters and grounds before their several houses, walls and lands, and make the same up into heaps that it may be stiff, and put into the scavenger's pot, upon pain for . . . making default herein for every time twelve pence . . . For which pains to be taken the said scavenger is to have the sole benefit of the common belonging to the town, and ten shillings . . . till Michaelmas next, and five pounds more for the other year.

[1] 29 September.

31 Lighting a High Street, 1649

(*The Minute Book of Bedford Corporation*, ed. G. Parsloe (Bedfordshire Historical Record Society, XXVI, 1949), p. 24)

Common Council, 10 October 1649

It is ordained and established by Mr Mayor and the aldermen (his brethren), the burgesses and commonalty in this present council assembled, that every night from henceforth from the feast of St. Luke the Evangelist[1] till Candlemas[2] in every year, the inhabitants of the dwelling houses next adjoining to the High Street of this town, extending in length from the Red Lion in St. Mary's parish on the south unto the county gaol on the north, shall hang out lights in the said street each at the door of his said dwelling house, the lights to be hung out at five o'clock in the evening and to continue there till eight o'clock following; on pain that everyone making default shall forfeit for each his default sixpence. And the town beadle for the time being shall every evening at candle tinding go along in the said street betwixt the limits before appointed, and give public warning in the street for setting forth of the said lights, and shall have for his pains the forfeitures falling upon this ordinance.

[1] 18 October.   [2] 2 February.

32 Working Folk Cause Problems, 1661

(Historical Manuscripts Commission, *Report on Manuscripts in Various Collections*, I (1901), *The Records of the County of Worcester*, pp. 322–3)

Presentments by the Grand Jury. 1661, April 23

We desire that the overseers of parishes may not be hereafter compelled to provide houses for such young persons as will marry before they have provided themselves with a settling. We desire that servants' wages may be rated according to the statute, for we find the unreasonableness of servants' wages a great grievance so that the servants are grown so[1] proud and idle that the master cannot be known from the servant except it be because the servant wears better clothes than his master. We desire that the statute for setting poor men's children to apprenticeship be more duly observed, for we find the usual course is that if any are apprenticed it is to some petty trade, and when they have served their apprenticeship they are not able to live by their trades, whereby not being bred to labour they are not fit for husbandry. We therefore desire that such children may be set to husbandry for the benefit of tillage and the good of the commonwealth.

¹ The word 'so' and the following clause from 'that the master' to 'than his master' are crossed out in the original.

33 The Settlement of the Poor, 1662

(13 and 14 Charles II, c. 12, *Statutes at Large*, III (1763), pp. 243–47)

Whereas the necessity, number, and continual increase of the poor, not only within the cities of London and Westminster, with the liberties of each of them, but also through the whole kingdom of England and dominion of Wales, is very great and exceeding burdensome, being occasioned by reason of some defects in the law concerning the settling of the poor, and for want of a due provision of the regulations of relief and employment in such parishes or places where they are legally settled, which does enforce many to turn incorrigible rogues, and others to perish for want, together with the neglect of the faithful execution of such laws and statutes as have formerly been made for the apprehending of rogues and vagabonds, and for the good of the poor: For remedy whereof, and for the preventing the perishing of any of the poor, whether young or old, for want of such supplies as are necessary, may it please your most excellent majesty, that it may be enacted . . . that whereas by reason of some defects in the law, poor people are not restrained from going from one parish to another, and therefore do endeavour to settle themselves in those parishes where there is the best stock, the largest commons or wastes to build cottages, and the most woods for them to burn and destroy, and when they have consumed it, then to another parish, and at last become rogues and vagabonds, to the great discouragement of parishes to provide stocks, where it is liable to be devoured by strangers . . . that it shall and may be lawful, upon complaint made by the churchwardens or overseers of the poor of any parish, to any justice of peace, within forty days after any such person or persons coming so to settle as aforesaid, in any tenement under the yearly value of ten pounds, for any two justices of the peace, whereof one to be of the quorum, of the division where any person or persons that are likely to be chargeable to the parish shall come to inhabit, by their warrant to remove and convey such person or persons, to such parish where he or they were last legally settled, either as a native, householder, sojourner, apprentice or servant, for the space of forty days at the least, unless he or they give sufficient security for the discharge of the said parish, to be allowed by the said justices.

II   Provided always, that all such persons who think themselves aggrieved by any such judgement of the said two justices, may appeal to the justices of the peace of the said county at their next quarter-sessions . . .

III   Provided also, that (this act notwithstanding) it shall and may be lawful for any person or persons, to go into any county, parish or place, to work in time of harvest, or at any time to work at any other work, so that he or they carry with him or them a certificate from the minister of the parish and one of the churchwardens and one of the overseers for the poor for the said year, that he or they have a dwelling-house or place in which he or they inhabit, and have left wife and children, or some of them there, (or otherwise as the condition of the persons shall require) and is declared an inhabitant or inhabitants there . . .

34 Some Measures for Rogues and Vagabonds, 1676

(Printed in 'Rogues, Vagabonds and Sturdy Beggars', ed. E. H. Vigers (Cambridgeshire and Huntingdonshire Archaeological Society, Transactions, V, 1937), pp. 114–19)

At the general quarter sessions . . . held for the . . . county of Huntingdon . . . the 3rd day of October [1676]

Forasmuch as the grand inquest have informed this court that the daily concourse and great [increase] of rogues, vagabonds and sturdy beggars is a great grievance and annoyance to the inhabitants of this county, and through the negligence or ignorance of those officers who have been entrusted in this concern they are now grown so insolent and presumptuous that they have oft by threats and menaces extorted money and victuals from those who live in houses remote from neighbours, whilst their husbands and servants have been employed abroad in the management of their lawful vocations, and have put the people into a general consternation or fear that they will fire their houses or steal their goods, the consequences whereof may prove very dangerous to this county if not timely prevented. Wherefore this court taking into their serious consideration what remedies may be most [properly applied] to those growing mischiefs do order and command all chief constables, petty constables, headboroughs, tithingmen and all other officers herein concerned that they do forthwith cause all laws and statutes heretofore made against rogues, vagabonds and sturdy beggars, wandering and idle persons to be put in execution, and to that end it is hereby ordered:—

That all high constables . . . and other officers shall within their respective villages, parishes or hamlets within this county according to the number of the people there, appoint two or more sufficient inhabitants to watch and ward both day and night, who shall examine and secure all strangers and suspected persons that shall walk or travel by day or night and cannot give a satisfactory reason for their so doing, that they may be brought before some justice [of the] peace, to be examined and dealt with according to law. And if any such person shall resist or fly away that then such watchmen shall forthwith send hue and cry after them, upon which any person may arrest them. And if any constables . . . or other officers shall neglect to keep such watch and ward in their several [precincts] they shall be severely punished at the quarter sessions for their contempt.

Secondly. That all high constables [and other officers] shall . . . make [proper] search once every week and oftener if need be in ale houses, victualling houses, barns and all other suspected places, in the night time, for the finding out and apprehending of rogues . . . and they shall also apprehend and secure all rogues . . . who travel with forged and counterfeited passes in the daytime, and all such persons which they shall apprehend in any such search or shall take begging, wandering or misordering themselves, the constables [and other officers] being assisted with some other of the parish shall cause to be stripped naked from the middle upwards, and to be openly whipped till their bodies shall be bloody.

Thirdly. That the constables [and other officers] shall strictly examine all and every person and persons, who shall produce any testimonial or pass to travel to any particular place within this realm. And if they shall find [it] be not signed under the hand and seal of some justice of the peace of some county or [the proper officer] of some town corporate or . . . parish from whence the party came . . . or if the party be not in the direct road homewards, or within the time limited by the testimonial or pass, or that the party begs by the way of any person, such person thus offending . . . shall be whipped as aforesaid.

Fourthly. When any rogue . . . [has] been whipped, the minister, constable [or other officer] of the parish where he was so whipped . . . shall give him a pass or testimonial under their hands and seals which may be after this form:—

Hunts,

I.B. a sturdy vagrant beggar of tall or low personage, black haired, and so describe him and his marks, aged about   years, was this 2nd day of   Anno Dom: openly whipped at   in the said county according to law for a wandering rogue, and is assigned to pass forthwith from parish to parish, by the constables thereof the next straight way to   in the county of   where he confesses he was born, or dwelt last by the space of 40 days . . . and the constables of every town where he shall come are required to allow him necessary relief for his passage and to help him with lodging . . . Given at   under our hands and seals. J. B. churchwarden T. B. constable, of the same parish . . .

Fifthly. When such testimonial is thus made every rogue . . . shall be forthwith sent from town to town by the officer of every respective parish through this county the next straight way to the place of his birth, and if that cannot be known then to the parish where he last dwelt for the space of 40 days before the same punishment, there to be set on work, and if that cannot be known then to the parish through which he last passed without punishment, and the officer of that parish shall convey the party to the house of correction or to the common gaol of the county there to be employed in work until he shall be placed some service for the space of one year, or not being able of body he shall be placed in some almshouse in the county.

*   *   *

Eleventh. The constables [and other officers] shall . . . give notice to every householder in person . . . that they take care that neither they nor any of their servants from thenceforth relieve any rogue . . . or any other person unless poor inhabitants of the same parish licensed to beg . . . upon the penalty of 10s for every such offence . . .

Twelfth. That no housekeeper or other person whatever shall [permit] or suffer any rogue . . . to lodge or abide within their house . . . or out houses . . . But upon knowledge thereof they shall forthwith give notice to the constables . . . or other officers . . . to the intent that such offenders may be punished . . . upon pain that every housekeeper or other person so offending shall forfeit 10s for every such offence . . .

Thirteenth. That if any ale housekeeper or victualler shall from henceforth relieve or . . . harbour in their victualling houses any rogues

. . . without special order from the constable . . . their victualling houses shall be suppressed and they shall be further dealt with . . .

Fourteenth. That every person who shall bring any rogue . . . before any justice of the peace shall have 2s allowed him for his pains, to be paid by the constable of the parish through which such rogue last passed unpunished.

*   *   *

Sixteenth. That all chief constables . . . and all other officers . . . shall use their utmost endeavours to execute these laws, and shall give an account upon oath in writing under the hand of the minister of every respective parish . . . at the next general quarter sessions, what rogues . . . they have apprehended and how many they have punished, upon the penalty 40s . . . for every such offence.

And moreover they shall also present at the next general quarter sessions all ale housekeepers or victuallers who have relieved at their door or have lodged or harboured in their houses . . . any such rogues . . . and that in the meanwhile they cause all these laws and directions to be publicly read in their respective parochial churches or at the church door and to be registered in their respective parish churches . . . there to be kept and preserved for the better information and example of those that shall succeed them . . .

By the court.
Robt. Clarke *Clericus Pace Com.*

35 Some Observations on the Population of the City of London, 1676

(John Graunt, *Natural and Political Observations . . . upon the Bills of Mortality*, 5th ed., 1676, printed in *The Economic Writings of Sir William Petty*, ed. C. H. Hull (Cambridge, 1899), II, pp. 369–74, 380–1)

Of the difference between burials and christenings

The next observation is, that in the said bills there are far more burials than christenings. This is plain, depending only upon arithmetical computation; for, in 40 years, from the year 1603, to the year 1644, exclusive of both years, there have been set down (as happening within the same ground, space, or parishes) although differently numbered and divided, 363,935 burials, and but 330,747 christenings within the 97, 16, and 10 out-parishes;[1] those of Westminster, Lambeth, Newington, Redriff, Stepney, Hackney, and Islington, not being included.

From this single observation it will follow, that London should have decreased in its people; the contrary whereof we see by its daily increase of buildings upon new foundations, and by the turning of great palacious houses into small tenements. It is therefore certain, that London is supplied with people from out of the country, whereby not only to supply the overplus differences of burials above-mentioned, but likewise to increase its inhabitants according to the said increase of housing.

*   *   *

We come to show, why although in the country the christenings exceed the burials, yet in London they do not. The general reason of this must be, that in London the proportion of those subject to die, unto those capable of breeding, is greater than in the country; that is, let there be a hundred persons in London, and as many in the country; we say, that, if there be sixty of them breeders in London, there are more than sixty in the country, or else we must say, that London is more unhealthful, or that it inclines men and women more to barrenness, than the country: which by comparing the burials and christenings of Hackney, Newington, and the other country-parishes, with the most smoky and stinking parts of the city, is scarce discernible in any considerable degree.

Now that the breeders in London are proportionably fewer than those in the country, arises from these reasons, viz.

1. All, that have business to the court of the king, or to the courts of justice, and all countrymen coming up to bring provisions to the city, or to buy foreign commodities, manufactures and rarities, do for the most part leave their wives in the country.

2. Persons coming to live in London out of curiosity and pleasure, as also such as would retire and live privately, do the same if they have any.

3. Such as come up to be cured of diseases do scarce use their wives *pro tempore*.

4. That many apprentices of London, who are bound seven or nine years from marriage, do often stay longer voluntarily.

5. That many seamen of London leave their wives behind them, who are more subject to die in the absence of their husbands, than to breed either without men, or with the use of many promiscuously.

As for unhealthiness, it may well be supposed, that although seasoned bodies may, and do live near as long in London, as elsewhere, yet newcomers and children do not: for the smokes, stinks, and close air, are less healthful than that of the country; otherwise why do sickly persons remove into the country air? And why are there more old men in countries than in London, per rata? And although the difference in Hackney and Newington, above-mentioned, be not very notorious, yet the reason may be their vicinity to London, and that the inhabitants are most such, whose bodies have first been impaired with the London air, before they withdraw thither.

As to the causes of barrenness in London, I say, that although there should be none extraordinary in the native air of the place; yet the intemperance in feeding, and especially the adulteries and fornications, supposed more frequent in London than elsewhere, do certainly hinder breeding. For a woman, admitting ten men, is so far from having ten times as many children that she has none at all.

Add to this, that the minds of men in London are more thoughtful, and full of business, than in the country, where their work is corporal labour and exercises; all which promote breeding, whereas anxieties of the mind hinder it.

*   *   *

Having set down the proportions, wherein we find the said three great divisions of the whole pile, called London, to have increased;[2] we come next to show what particular parishes have had the most remarkable share in these augmentations. Viz. of the ninety seven parishes within the walls the increase is not discernible, but where great houses, formerly belonging to noblemen, before they built others near Whitehall, have been turned into tenements; upon which account Allhallows upon the Wall is increased by the conversion of the Marquess of Winchester's house, lately the Spanish ambassador's, into a new street; the like of Alderman Freeman's, and La Motte's near the Exchange; the like of the Earl of Arundel's in Lothbury; the like of the Bishop of London's palace, the Dean of Paul's, and the Lord Rivers's house now in hand; as also of the Duke's place, and others heretofore.

Of the sixteen parishes, next without the walls, Saint Giles's Cripplegate has been most enlarged, next to that Saint Olave's Southwark, then Saint Andrew's Holborn, then Whitechapel, the difference in the rest not being considerable.

Of the out-parishes, now called ten, formerly nine, and before that eight, Saint Giles's and Saint Martin's in the Fields are most increased, notwithstanding Saint Paul's Covent-Garden was taken out of them both.

The general observation, which arises from hence, is, that the City of London gradually removes westward, and did not the Royal Exchange and London Bridge stay the trade, it would remove much faster; for Leadenhall Street, Bishopsgate, and part of Fenchurch Street, have lost their ancient trade; Gracechurch Street indeed keeping itself yet entire, by reason of its conjunction with, and relation to London Bridge.

Again, Canning Street and Watling Street, have lost their trade of woollen drapery to Paul's Churchyard, Ludgate Hill, and Fleet Street: the mercery is gone from out of Lombard Street and Cheapside into Paternoster Row and Fleet Street.

The reasons whereof are, that the king's court (in old times frequently kept in the City) is now always at Westminster. Secondly, the use of coaches, whereunto the narrow streets of the old City are unfit, has caused the building of those broader streets in Covent Garden, &c.

Thirdly, where the consumption of a commodity is, viz. among the gentry, the vendors of the same must seat themselves.

Fourthly, the cramming up of the void spaces and gardens within the walls with houses, to the prejudice of light and air, have made men build new ones, where they less fear those inconveniences.

Conformity in building to other civil nations has disposed us to let our old wooden dark houses fall to decay, and to build new ones, whereby to answer all the ends above-mentioned.

Where note, that when Lud-gate was the only western gate of the City, little building was westward thereof: but, when Holborn began to increase, New-gate was made. But now both these gates are not sufficient for the communication between the walled City, and its enlarged western suburbs, as daily appears by the intolerable stops and embarrasses of coaches near both these gates, especially Lud-gate.

[1] That is, 97 parishes within the walls, 16 parishes within the liberties of the city, but without the walls, and 10 out-parishes adjoining to the city.
[2] Broadly over the period 1600-1660.

36 Removal of a Child, 1685

(*Minutes of Proceedings in Quarter Sessions held for the Parts of Kesteven in the County of Lincoln, 1674–1695*, ed. S. A. Peyton (Lincoln Record Society, XXVI, 1931), II, p. 235)

General Session of the Peace held at Sleaford, 28 April 1685

Ordered, that Gabriel Butler, a male child, who was lately brought from Manthorpe by a travelling woman who left the said child in one John Hammond's barn at Welborne, it is therefore this day ordered that the constable of the parish of Welborne do forthwith carry and convey the said Gabriel Butler to the overseers of the poor of the parish of Manthorpe aforesaid, who are hereby required to receive and provide for the said Gabriel Butler according to law.

37 The Middling Englishman's Table, Mid-1690s

(*M. Misson's Memoirs and Observations in his Travels over England*, trans. by J. Ozell (1719), pp. 313-16)

The English eat a great deal at dinner; they rest a while, and to it again, till they have quite stuffed their paunch. Their supper is moderate: gluttons at noon and abstinent at night. I always heard they were great flesh-eaters, and I found it true. I have known several people in England that never eat any bread, and universally they eat very little: they nibble a few crumbs, while they chew the meat by whole mouthfuls. Generally speaking, the English tables are not delicately served. There are some noblemen that have both French and English cooks, and these eat much after the French manner. But among the middling sort of people . . . they have ten or twelve sorts of common meats, which infallibly take their turns at their tables, and two dishes are their dinners; a pudding, for instance, and a piece of roast beef: another time they will have a piece of boiled beef, and then they salt it some days beforehand, and besiege it with five or six heaps of cabbage, carrots, turnips, or some other herbs or roots, well prepared and salted, and swimming in butter: a leg of roast or boiled mutton, dished up with the same dainties, fowls, pigs, ox-tripes, and tongues, rabbits, pigeons, all well moistened with butter, without larding. Two of these dishes, always served up one after the other, make the usual dinner of a substantial gentleman, or wealthy citizen. When they have boiled meat, there is sometimes one of the company that will have the broth; this is a kind of soup with a little oatmeal in it, and some leaves of thyme or sage, or other such small herbs. They bring up this in as many porringers as there are people that desire it; those that please crumble a little bread into it, and this makes a kind of *potage*. The pudding is a dish very difficult to be described, because of the several sorts there are of it; flour, milk, eggs, butter, sugar, suet, marrow, raisins, &c., &c. are the most common ingredients of a pudding. They bake them in an oven, they boil them with meat, they make them fifty several ways. Blessed be he that invented pudding, for it is a manna that hits the palates of all sorts of people; a manna, better than that of the wilderness, because the people are never weary of it. Ah, what an excellent thing is an English pudding! To come in pudding-time, is as much as to say, to come in the most lucky moment in the world. Give an Englishman a pudding, and he shall think it a noble treat in any part of the world. The dessert they never dream of, unless it be a piece of cheese. Fruit is brought only to the tables of the great, and of a small number even among them. It would be unjust to take, in a rigorous sense, all that I have said of these common dishes; for the English eat everything that is produced naturally, as well as any other nation. I say naturally, in opposition to the infinite multitude of our made dishes; for they dress their meat much plainer than we do.

38 Boys' Dietary in the Bristol Workhouse, 1699

(*Bristol Corporation of the Poor. Selected Records, 1696–1834*, ed. E. E. Butcher (Bristol Record Society, III, 1932), pp. 68–9)

Committee book of Mint Workhouse Committee, 19 July 1699

Ordered that the boys be dieted according to the directions following.
Sunday
Breakfast. Bread four ounces, cheese one ounce, and one horn of beer.
Dinner. Half a pound of beef, four ounces of bread, two horns of beer. Garden stuff threepence for twenty.
Supper. Four ounces of bread, one ounce and half of cheese, and one horn of beer.
Monday
Breakfast. The broth thickened with oatmeal, and six ounces of bread to four.
Dinner. A pint of green beans, one ounce of bacon, two horns of beer.
Supper. A pint and half of milk porridge to be half milk.
Tuesday
Breakfast. Four ounces of bread, one ounce and half of cheese, one horn of beer.
Dinner. One pint and half of peasoup. Each quantity to have half a pint of peas and one spoonful of flour.
Wednesday
Breakfast. One pint and quarter of ditto or milk porridge.
Dinner. Beans, bacon and beer as Monday.
Supper. Bread four ounces, one ounce and half of cheese and one horn of beer.
Thursday
Breakfast. One pint and quarter of milk porridge. Dinner. Beef &c. as Sunday.
Supper. Bread and cheese.

Friday

Breakfast. The broth &c. as Monday.

Dinner. One pint and half of pea soup.

Supper. One pint and quarter of pea soup or milk porridge.

Saturday

Breakfast. One pint and quarter of leek or herb soup.

Dinner. One pint and half of milk soup.

Supper. Bread and cheese as before and one horn of beer.

39 Civic Celebration of Queen Anne's Coronation, 1702

(*Records of the Borough of Nottingham*, VI, 1702–1760 (Nottingham, 1914), pp. 8–9)

Minutes of the Common Council, 14 April 1702

Ordered that Mr Coroner Smith and Mr Chamberlain Collin do search the shops for silk convenient to make two banners on and that Mr Smith do prepare the same against the coronation. And that all the Council and Clothing do attend Mr Mayor and the aldermen upon Thursday seavennight near this hall on horseback to perform the solemnity of the Queen's coronation by nine a clock in the forenoon. And that the cavalcade be made throughout the town in such method and order as Mr Mayor shall direct. And that all the gentlemen in town be invited to accompany the said mayor and aldermen &c. And that against the solemnity is over there be a treat of wine provided at this hall for the better sort of people to drink the Queen's health, and likewise an hogshead of ale for the poor. And that Mr Chamberlain do prepare one dozen and one half bottles of canary, 3 dozen of whitewine and 3 dozen of claret for the purposes aforesaid, and likewise half an hogshead of ale for the town's officers, constables, halberdmen &c., and 5 dozen of French rolls and ten dozen of white bread.

40 Bread for the Poor, 1703

(Plaque in parish church of Bridford, Devon)

In memory of Thomas Hall, third son of Emanuel Hall of this parish, who died the 4th of July 1703, aged 51.

He gave 52*s* yearly to be bestowed in bread for the poor of this parish, 52*s* to the poor of Drewsteignton, and 52*s* to the poor of Cheriton Bishop, and 2*s* apiece to each parish for one that will take care to distribute this charity.

Blessed is he that considereth the poor and needy. Psalm 41: 1.

Q

41 Vagrants Bound for Ireland, 1713

(*Quarter Sessions Records for the County Palatine of Chester, 1559–1760*, eds. J. H. E. Bennett and J. C. Dewhurst (Record Society of Lancashire and Cheshire, 1940), p. 203)

To her majesty's justices at their general sessions of Chester.

The petition of the inhabitants of Great Neston and Leighton, shows that your petitioners do not only provide for their own very numerous and growing poor, and pay their proportion of the yearly charge upon the whole county for relieving of vagrants constantly travelling to Ireland in great numbers, but are also under the greater burden of their passage this way and long stay here before they can get them transported, giving relief to many who by reason of their circumstances could not otherwise be supported by the common allowance, there being many diseased and impotent persons not capable of going to sea. Women that fall into travail and are brought to bed, helpless orphans left with us by parents which happen to die or over run them, and others that die among us and are buried at our charge. Besides the great difficulty and cost of prevailing with masters of ships to carry so many persons who have neither wherewithal to provide for their own sustenance or to pay for their passage; and what is still likely to make it more difficult is that most of our neighbours upon the cessation of arms and prospect of peace having betaken themselves to other employs, we have very few merchant ships left which use the Dublin trade, and of those that do some do not anchor here, and others refuse to carry vagrants upon any terms.

May it therefore please this bench to provide such allowance that this excessive charge may not lie more particularly upon your petitioners, or else the vagrants may be conveyed some other way.

[Signed by sixteen inhabitants.]

[Order:] The Court for the future discharges Neston, Leighton and Little Mollington from receiving vagrants directed to go to Ireland.

42 Fashion and Imitation in Dress, 1719

(*The Just Complaints of the Poor Weavers truly Represented*, 1719, printed in John Smith, *Chronicon Rusticum-Commerciale; or, Memoirs of Wool, &c.*, II (1747), pp. 194–5)

In the next place, he[1] undertakes to prove, that the wearing of calicoes does not hinder the wearing either of woollen or silk; not of the former, because they are much dearer than woollen; nor of the latter, because they are as much below the price of silk. This is only an argument of his own assurance and folly. The very weavers and sellers of calico will acknowledge, that all the mean people, the maid servants, and indifferently poor persons, who would otherwise clothe themselves, and were usually clothed in thin womens' stuffs made at Norwich and London, or in cantaloons and crapes, &c. are now clothed in calico, or printed linen; moved to it, as well for the cheapness, as the lightness of the cloth, and gaiety of the colours. The children universally, whose frocks and coats were all either made of tammies worked at Coventry, or of striped thin stuffs made at Spitalfields, appear now in printed calico, or printed linen; let any one but cast their eyes among the meaner sort playing in the streets, or of the better sort at boarding schools, and in our families; the truth is too plain to be denied.

As to the richer sort of people, ladies, and even persons of quality, the fine chintz and painted calicoes, as well Indian, as English, some of which are even dearer than silk, have so far superseded the wearing of silks, that they prefer them to the finest damasks; and we need do no more, than appeal to the drapers' wives, some of whom would perhaps think themselves affronted, not to be ranked with the best of our gentry. I might take notice here, how the example of our gentry was perhaps the first real occasion of the calicoes being so universally accepted, and worn among the common people; for there is an invincible pride in the ordinary people, of being counted what they are not; they are almost led into all their fashions, in imitation of the gentry; and therefore though it might be true, that some ladies of quality do wear calicoes, more for the sake of variety, than anything else; yet the meaner sort of people were first brought to wear them more, because they saw them worn by the gentry, than for any conveniency or real liking they had to them at first themselves; that is to say, they wear them because it is the fashion to do so. To say then, that nobody wears calicoes, but as superfluities, and that they do not buy the fewer clothes of stuffs or silk, is too gross a fallacy to deserve a reply.

[1] The author of *The Weavers' Pretences Examined* (1719).

43 Obtaining a Settlement in Wimbledon, 1723

(*The Parish Register of Wimbledon, Co. Surrey*, ed. A. W. Hughes Clarke (Surrey Record Society, VIII, 1924), pp. 40–1)

1723, July 2 Susanna, daughter of Moses and Mary Cooper, travellers, born in Martin, and the poor woman being desirous to have it baptised

though she had lain in but a week, carried it in her own arms to Martin
church, to tender it to me to baptise it there on Sunday last, being June
the 30th. But Justice Meriton, being informed by the constable of her
being in the porch with that intention, went out of his seat in time of
service to her, and took hold of her, and led her to the court of his
house, being over against the church, and shut the gate upon her and
her husband, and let them not out 'till sermon and service were over
and I was gone home, and made the man mittimus[1] to send him to the
house of correction if he would not carry his wife and child out of the
parish without being baptised and consequently registered there.
Which being forced to comply with, she brought up her child to me,
to my house on this day, being Tuesday July the 2nd., complaining of
her hard usage and passionately desiring me to baptise it, which I did
by the name above in the presence of her husband, my wife and Dr
Eliz. Pitchford.

[1] Mittimus, a warrant committing a person.

44 A View of the London Poor, 1753

(Henry Fielding, *A Proposal for Making an Effectual Provision for the
Poor* (1753), pp. 9–10)

The sufferings of the poor are, indeed, less observed than their mis
deeds; not from any want of compassion, but because they are less
known; and this is the true reason why we so often hear them men
tioned with abhorrence, and so seldom with pity. But if we were to make
a progress through the outskirts of this town, and look into the habitations of the poor, we should there behold such pictures of human
misery as must move the compassion of every heart that deserves the
name of human. What indeed must be his composition who could see
whole families in want of every necessary of life, oppressed with
hunger, cold, nakedness, and filth, and with diseases, the certain
consequences of all these; what I say must be his composition, who
could look into such a scene as this, and be affected only in his nostrils

That such wretchedness as this is so little lamented, arises therefore
from its being so little known; but, if this be the case with the sufferings
of the poor, it is not so with their misdeeds. They starve, and freeze, and
rot among themselves; but they beg, and steal, and rob among their
betters. There is not a parish in the liberty of Westminster which does
not raise thousands annually for the poor, and there is not a street in
that liberty which does not swarm all day with beggars, and all night

with thieves. Stop your coach at what shop you will, however expeditious the tradesman is to attend you, a beggar is commonly beforehand with him; and if you should not directly face his door the tradesman must often turn his head while you are talking to him, or the same beggar, or some other thief at hand, will pay a visit to his shop! I omit to speak of the more open and violent insults which are everyday committed on his majesty's subjects in the streets and highways. They are enough known and enough spoken of. The depredations on property are less noticed, particularly those in the parishes within ten miles of London. To these every man is not obnoxious, and therefore it is not every man's business to suppress them. These are, however, grown to the most deplorable height; insomuch that the gentleman is daily, or rather nightly, plundered of his pleasure, and the farmer of his livelihood.

45 The Lot of a Weaver's Family, 1758

(*The Check Weavers'* *Apology* (1758), printed in A. P. Wadsworth and J. de L. Mann, *The Cotton Trade and Industrial Lancashire, 1600–1780* (Manchester, 1931), pp. 350–1)

. . . He must be a tolerable good hand that can work half a piece of this sort of check in a week, which when done, comes to six shillings, out of which he must pay one shilling for pinwinding, and sixpence for loomstanding; and I shall reckon threepence per week throughout the year for candlelight, so there remains for him, of neat money, four shillings and threepence, for house rent, provisions and all other necessaries for him, his wife and perhaps four or five small children. Now I will leave anyone to judge how such a family as this must live seven days, upon four shillings and threepence, even supposing it all to go for provisions, and set rent, fire, clothes, and all other necessaries aside, which will make better than two shillings of the money, and must be had somehow or other; and I do affirm that there is not one weaver in six, the whole trade through, that will make half a piece of this sort of work in one week.

I have seen such a family as this I am speaking on (and can bring living witnesses to testify it), that have lived four days out of seven, upon nothing but water gruel without ever a bit of bread to it; and I doubt not but there are hundreds of families who have formerly lived in good repute, have had for some years past not much better commons, and when sickness or any other common accidents of life happens, are with sorrow constrained to fly to the parish for relief, which has at present raised the poor rates to such a height, as in some degree, to affect even the landholders themselves.

Now I would not be thought, from what I have said, to be an enemy to trade and commerce, being very sensible that it is one of the greatest blessings this nation ever enjoyed; and I likewise do acknowledge, that such gentlemen as have, and now do, launch out their money in trade, do not only deserve the thanks of the public, but ought to reap the benefit of their labour, by acquiring moderate fortunes for their descendants. But then it must be allowed on all hands, that the poor mechanic, by whose hard labour and industry, the trade in general is supported and carried on, is, and ought to be entitled by the laws of reason and equity, not only to comfortable maintenance, but to have it in his power to lay up some trifle for the support of his family, either in case of old age, sickness, death, or any other mortality, to which all men are subject to, but I have not only shown above, that it is at present entirely out of their power so to do, but everyone that is acquainted with them can witness, that the greatest part of them cannot get the common necessaries of life, without being beholden to the town they belong to, or to their charitable neighbours.

46 A Christmas Letter, 1759

(*The Williamson Letters, 1748–1765*, ed. F. J. Manning (Bedfordshire Historical Record Society, XXXIV, 1954), pp. 49–50)

Letter of 25 December 1759, from Mrs Christian Russel, wife of a naval captain, to her brother, Edmond Williamson, rector of Millbrook, Bedfordshire

I received yours last night 6 o'clock, on which Mr Russel immediately went to the great fishmonger's in the Strand to bespeak you a fresh cod that were to come in this morning; but to-day being Christmas day it was the worst time in the year to get anything, for turkeys and hares and chines are so much in taste just in this week that they don't buy fish. However, Mr Lamb sent me down the biggest cod that he had of a dozen come in this morning, also 6 whitings and 2 lobsters; shrimps [ ] there was not one that was fresh, so thought a lobster would make [ ] pulled in very small pieces or chopped fine and boiled in some melted butter till it looks red . . . as to the whitings, they are skinned for to fry in hog's lard of a light brown and set up round the cod, which could I have got bigger or a piece of one, I would. The ducks were also fresh and fine, and I hope a barrel of good Purfleet oysters for supper, and some almonds and raisins and barley-sugar, which Mr Russel sends with a kiss to his niece because he hears she is so much improved and holds up her head and turns out her toes. He also begs your acceptance of the oysters, as does Taw and I of the rest of the Christmas fare, and heartily wish you merry with it, and all our compliments to those who share with you, if of our acquaintance. We fully intended to have sent the same next week, as we thought the nights would be lighter. They went this afternoon as you directed and I hope will prove good and to your taste. Teal are at least 2s 9d apiece, so thought ducks would answer better.

I wish I could send you a good account of our tickets, but at one office they are blanks and so are all the rest that Mr Russel had any shares of. I had a mind to try, so I bought an 8th chance, which cost me a guinea; however it came up a 20l prize and so I got 15s 6d back again out of my guinea ...

[No] news stirring at present but the terrible fire in King's Street, Covent Garden, which is not out yet, though not to do any more harm, but the rubbish sometimes flames out so that they keep wetting the sides of those houses which joins to it. There is still a smoke appears from that in Cornhill owing to the great quantity of coals that had been laid in for the winter, and this has destroyed a great many more houses. Whole courts are laid flat, whose houses were chiefly wood, and full of lodgers from top to bottom.

The other street desires their loves and good wishes, and we hope to hear from you soon ...

8

Economic Policy and Thought
1000–1485

Medieval life in all its aspects came under the influence of the teaching of the Church. Economic activity was viewed within a general ethical system which makes it difficult to illustrate concisely thought on economic matters. Christian thought had been framed within the context of an agrarian society and it acted as a brake on those economic forces which eventually were to transform the social order. The Church set great store on maintaining the social order. The expansion of credit facilities, which underpinned the growth of trade and investment, was held back by the scholastic writers' condemnation of interest-taking (*2*). The Church became more flexible as commercial practices and the exchange economy developed in the later Middle Ages, but throughout the period its teaching reinforced prevailing standards of morality (*10*).

The involvement of the monarchy in economic matters was intermittent and was usually the outcome of its concern to establish and maintain strong and secure government (*4, 5*). Royal control over the coinage was important in the Anglo-Saxon period (*6, 1*) as well as later. The standardisation of weights and measures was another area activating government from early medieval times (*1*). The Crown reserved to itself the right of dealing with offences committed during the production and sale of bread and ale, two vital commodities, but the right was often delegated (*5*). The effectiveness of policy was weakened since laws were implemented through local courts (*3*). Much governmental action was clearly directed at the maintenance of the social order (*7, 11*). Such an end motivated attempts to control prices in the fourteenth century (*4*), while the control of wages and labour mobility after the Black Death were attempts to prevent the undermining of the manorial system (*7*). Labour legislation, conservative in nature, was a forerunner to Tudor legislation. Nevertheless from the fourteenth century government action could be motivated by a desire to shape and encourage certain economic developments. One notable case was with the cloth trade (*3, 10*) which the Crown sought to encourage at the expense of the wool trade (*6*). Legislative encouragement was also given to the native mercantile marine (**5**, *10*). Such action was however piecemeal.

Many other institutions were involved in the governing of economic activity (*9*). They included manorial courts, craft gilds and town courts and their effect too was generally conservative, acting as a brake on change.

1485–1760

The impact of governmental economic policy in an age of weak executive ability and a resort to local justices and other possibly interested parties for its implementation, can easily be overstated. Nevertheless governments did affect economic life, while some distinct changes in policy-making occurred over this period. Most striking among these changes was the transition about the mid-seventeenth century from what has been characterised as a policy of provision, a policy that favoured consumers with the end in mind of maintaining good order, to one that favoured producers, by allowing freer rein to their activities. Earlier chapters in this collection illustrate official Tudor and early Stuart concern with agrarian changes that could lead to vagrancy and a reduced corn supply (**2**, *28*, *34–5*), with the rise of a fluctuating textile industry (**3**, *19*), and with the development of policies of poor relief (**7**, *20*, *25*). The disorders of the 1550s gave birth to that most ambitious code of labour regulation and wage fixing, the Statute of Artificers of 1563 (*18*). Anxiety about good order is seen too in attempts to fix London's food prices in the inflationary 1540s (*16*), to check the growth of the capital (**1**, *28*), and to combat trade practices contrary to consumer interests (**4**, *20*). The abiding interest of Tudor and early Stuart government, national and local, with the food supply, can be further documented (*14*, *27*). Policy making pre-1660 can be seen also with regard to communications (**4**, *21–2*, *32–3*), company formation and foreign trade (**3**, *20*, **5**, *17–18*), interest-taking (**6**, *28*) and public finance (**6**, *24*, *29–30*). The Church along with other bodies must be seen too as an arbiter of economic behaviour before 1660, as the 1571 injunctions of the see of York illustrate (*19*).

From about the time of the Restoration government came to look more tolerantly at economic change, as supply conditions improved and in line with the shifting balance of political power. A concern with social order naturally persisted, as seen in the 1662 poor law and its enforcement (**7**, *33–4*, *36*) and in legislation dealing with incipient trade unions (**3**, *38*). Local wage assessments continued (*31*) if more intermittently and anxiety over food supplies still rose when harvests were deficient (**4**, *41*). But the resolve, central and local, to implement the body of Tudor labour and industrial regulation had weakened and did so more as time passed, thus permitting change in domestic production to proceed more freely. A positive tendency was the increasing amount of protection granted both to agriculture and industry (**3**, *32*). Coincidentally commercial policy received more attention, as overseas, especially colonial, trade grew, resulting in a code of nationalist measures (**5**, *26*). Central and local governmental policy-making also dealt with communications (**4**, *34*, *37*) and public finance (**6**, *31*, *36*).

The economic thought of this age was to a high degree problem-oriented. The thinking behind government action can be glimpsed in the preambles to statutes, or more directly, as in William Burghley's letter of 1587 on trade depression (*20*). Parliamentary debates also reveal contemporary attitudes, as in the debate on enclosure in 1601 (*21*), and that in 1621 on the scarcity of money (*23*). Sixteenth-century commentators on leading issues of the age include Thomas More on the 'all-devouring sheep' (*13*), and Thomas Smith on inflation (*17*). Francis Bacon had some trenchant thoughts on riches (*24*). It is difficult to gauge the effect such writers had on attitudes. But the emphasis given by Protestant churchmen such as Richard Baxter in the mid-seventeenth century to the proper trade or calling and the virtue of work (*29*) may have done something to further economic individualism in England. After 1620 economic writing still lacked system, but the forerunners of a modern cast of thought can be seen in Mun on trade (*25*) and Hume on interest (*34*). By the late seventeenth century, apart from a well-regulated trade, the labour of people, not surprisingly in a labour-intensive economy, was regarded as the chief means to prosperity. The relationships between work, poverty and plenty interested a number of writers, among them Houghton (*30*) and Defoe (*32*). Their conceptions were generally static, in their insistence on a labour force content to work no harder than necessary to obtain a subsistence. Another rather despairing, conservative view is that of Mandeville on the disutility of popular education (*33*). By the early eighteenth century more and more writers reveal an awareness of the material progress taking place. In the final document of this collection Dean Tucker in the 1750s notes a growing spirit of mechanical invention, and the stimulating effect this could have on both popular consumption and employment (*35*). Insofar as mechanisation was to be the principal means of ending age-old conditions of low output, laborious work and low living standards, it is a prophetic statement.

1 Assize of Measures, 1197

(Roger of Hoveden, *Chronica*, IV, ed. W. Stubbs, *Rolls Series* (1871), pp. 33–4)

It is established that all measures of the whole of England be of the same amount, as well of corn as of vegetables and of like things, to wit, one good horse load; and that this measure be level as well in cities and boroughs as without. Also the measure of wine and ale and of all liquids shall be of the same amount according to the diversity of liquids. Weights and measures also, great and small, shall be of the same amount in the whole realm, according to the diversity of wares. Measures also of corn and liquids, wine and ale, shall have marks put thereon, lest by guile they can be falsified.

It is established that woollen cloths, wherever they be made, be made of the same width, to wit, of two ells within the lists,[1] and of the same good quality in the middle and at the sides. Also the ell shall be the same in the whole realm and of the same length, and the ell shall be of iron.

It is forbidden to all merchants throughout the whole of the realm that any merchant set in front of his shop red or black cloths or shields or any other thing, whereby the buyers' eyes are often deceived in the choice of good cloth.

It is also forbidden that any dye for sale, save black only, be made anywhere in the realm, except in cities or chief boroughs.

It is also established that in every city or borough four or six lawful men of the same town, according to the size of the town, together with the sheriff, or with the reeves of the city or borough, if the same be not in the hand of the sheriff, be assigned to keep the assize in this form: that they see and be sure that all things are sold and bought by the same measure, and that all measures are of the same size according to the diversity of wares. And if they find any who shall be confessed or convicted of having sold by other than the established measure, his body shall be taken and sent to prison, and all his chattels shall be seized into the hand of the lord the king, nor shall he be delivered save by the lord the king or his chief justice. Touching the keepers themselves it is established that if they perform this keeping so negligently that they be convicted by others than themselves before the justices of the lord the king of transgressing any written assize either of measures of victuals or other measures, or of the width of cloths, the keepers shall remain at the mercy of the lord the king touching their chattels.

It is commanded also that after the feast of the Purification of St.

Mary no man in any county sell anything save by the ordained measure, which shall be [everywhere] of the same size; nor after the fair of mid-Lent at Stamford sell any cloth of smaller width than two ells within the lists.

¹ The selvages. (B, B, T)

2 Thomas Aquinas on Usury, Mid-Thirteenth Century

(St. Thomas Aquinas,[1] *Summa Theologica. Secunda Secundae*, X (1929), pp. 330–1)

Whether it is a sin to take usury for money lent?

I answer that, To take usury for money lent is unjust in itself, because this is to sell what does not exist, and this evidently leads to inequality which is contrary to justice.

In order to make this evident, we must observe that there are certain things the use of which consists in their consumption: thus we consume wine when we use it for drink, and we consume wheat when we use it for food. Wherefore in suchlike things the use of the thing must not be reckoned apart from the thing itself, and whoever is granted the use of the thing, is granted the thing itself; and for this reason, to lend things of this kind is to transfer the ownership. Accordingly if a man wanted to sell wine separately from the use of the wine, he would be selling the same thing twice, or he would be selling what does not exist, wherefore he would evidently commit a sin of injustice. In like manner he commits an injustice who lends wine or wheat, and asks for double payment, viz. one, the return of the thing in equal measure, the other, the price of the use, which is called usury.

On the other hand there are things the use of which does not consist in their consumption: thus to use a house is to dwell in it, not to destroy it. Wherefore in such things both may be granted: for instance, one man may hand over to another the ownership of his house while reserving to himself the use of it for a time, or vice versa, he may grant the use of the house, while retaining the ownership. For this reason a man may lawfully make a charge for the use of his house, and, besides this, revendicate the house from the person to whom he has granted its use, as happens in renting and letting a house.

Now money, according to the Philosopher[2] was invented chiefly for the purpose of exchange: and consequently the proper and principal use of money is its consumption or alienation whereby it is sunk in exchange. Hence it is by its very nature unlawful to take payment for the use of money lent, which payment is known as usury: and just as a man is bound to restore other ill-gotten goods, so is he bound to restore the money which he has taken in usury.

[1] c.1225–74.   [2] Aristotle.

3 Administration of the Aulnage, 1287

(P.R.O. Court Rolls, General Series, S.C. 2/178/93, mm. 2, 3d., printed in *Select Pleas Concerning Law Merchant, Vol. I, 1270–1638*, ed. C. Gross, (Selden Society, XXIII, 1908), pp. 14, 17)

Fair Court of St. Ives, Hunts.
28 April, 1287

Aulnagers of canvas: Richard of Elsdon, Hamon of Bury St. Edmunds, Robert of Shouldham, and Richard of Bromholm. They have made oath that they will be faithful to the lord of the fair[1] in their office and will make honest measurement for both buyers and sellers: and they give the lord 4s in order that no other aulnagers may be associated with them this year.

* * *

6 May, 1287

Robert of St. Leonards and Ralph Pole complain of Richard of Elsdon, for that whereas the said Robert and Ralph were in the vill of St. Ives on Monday last in their booth, which they hired from a bailiff of the abbot in the row where canvas is sold, and had with them a certain Richard of Bromholm, a sworn aulnager, who was measuring the canvas of the said Robert and Ralph, the said Richard of Elsdon came there and impeded the said Richard of Bromholm in his office of measuring, and the said Robert and Ralph in their sale of the said canvas to their damage 40s; and they produce suit. The said Richard is present and denies the words of the court, and craves judgment as to their charge, because the said Robert and Ralph made no mention of any certain amount of canvas, nor designated any certain persons as the buyer of the said canvas. And it is awarded that the said Richard of Elsdon go without a day, and that the said Robert and Ralph recover nothing by their plaint, but that they be in mercy for their false claim. Robert's fine is remitted; Ralph's fine is remitted; each is pledge for the other.

[1] The abbot of Ramsey.

4 Parliament and Price Regulation, 1315

(Thomas Walsingham, *Historia Anglicana*, I, ed. H. T. Riley, *Rolls Series* (1863), p. 144)

In that year, on the day after the Purification[1] nearly all the prelates of the realm assembled together in parliament at London, with the nobles and the commons, to treat about the state of the realm and the lowering of the price of goods on sale, which then had become so dear that the common people were barely able to live, Therefore it was ordained that a better quality fat ox for sale, not fed on grain, should for the rest be sold for sixteen shillings; and if it was fed on grain and is fat, it should be sold for twenty shillings at the most. A better quality cow, live and fat, should be sold for twelve shillings. Every fat two-year old pig should be sold for forty pence; a fat shorn wether should be sold for fourteen pence, a fat woolly wether for twenty. For the rest a fat goose should be sold for twopence halfpenny; a good capon for twopence; a good hen for a penny; four pigeons for a penny; and if anyone selling does otherwise, the goods on sale shall remain forfeited to the king.

[1] i.e. 3 February 1315.

5 An Offence Against the Assize of Bread, 1316

(Guildhall, Letter-Book D, f. 189, printed in *Memorials of London and London Life in the XIIIth, XIVth and XVth Centuries*, ed. H. T. Riley (1868), pp. 119–20)

On the Saturday next before the Feast of the Invention of the Holy Cross, in the ninth year of the reign of King Edward, son of King Edward, Richard of Loughborough was attached to make answer as to a certain false wastel[1] loaf of his. And the same Richard said that he was not a baker, and that he did not have that wastel bread baked; but that, as a regrator, he bought it of a certain baker who lives in Southwark. And upon this he was charged by the mayor and aldermen with being in partnership with the baker aforesaid, in baking such bread, and sharing with him in the gain thereby, or loss, if such should happen: whereupon, being asked how he would acquit himself thereof, he said that he was not the partner of the said baker, nor had he any share with him; and he put himself upon the country as to the same. Therefore the country was summoned for the Tuesday next ensuing, and he was delivered into the custody of the sheriffs . . .

On which day the said Richard came, and the jury came by John of

Eastwood and others in the panel named. Which jurors said upon their oath, that the aforesaid Richard is a partner of the said baker for gain in baking the bread aforesaid. Therefore it was adjudged that he should have the punishment of the hurdle. And he was so punished now for the first time, because his loaf was wanting to the amount of 2s 9d in the proper weight of half a mark for the halfpenny wastel loaf.

Also Alan of Lindsey, baker, was sentenced to the pillory, because he had been convicted of baking *pain demaign*[2] that was found to be of bad dough within, and good dough without. And because such falsity redounds much to the deception of the people who buy such bread, he was committed for punishment . . .

[1] Medium quality.
[2] Fine quality bread impressed with the figure of Our Saviour. (B, B, T)

6 Prohibition of Export of Cloth-Making Materials, 1326

(Guildhall, Letter-Book E, f. 167, printed in *Memorials of London and London Life in the XIIIth, XIVth and XVth Centuries*, ed. H. T. Riley (1868), pp. 149–50)

Edward by the grace of God, king of England . . . to our well-beloved Hamon of Chigwell, mayor of our city of London, greeting. We have read the letters that you have sent us, in the which you have signified unto us that Flemings, Brabanters and other aliens have been suddenly buying throughout our land all the teasels that they can find; and also are buying butter, madder, woad, fullers' earth, and all other things which pertain to the working of cloth, in order that they may disturb the staple and the common profit of our realm; and further, that you have stopped twenty tuns that were shipped and ready for going beyond sea, at the suit of good folks of our said city; upon your doing the which we do congratulate you, and do command and charge you, that you cause the said tuns well and safely to be kept; and if any such things come into our said city from henceforth, to be sent beyond sea by merchants aliens or denizens, cause them also to be stopped and safely kept, until you shall have had other mandate from us thereon; and you are not to allow any such things to pass through your bailiwick, by reason whereof the profit of our staple may be disturbed. We have also commanded our chancellor, that by writs under our Great Seal he shall cause it everywhere to be forbidden that any such things shall pass from henceforth out of our realm, in any way whatsoever. Given under our Privy Seal at Saltwood the 21st day of May, in the 19th year of our reign.

7 The Ordinance of Labourers, 1349

(P.R.O. Close Roll, 23 Edward III, pt. I, m. 8d.)

The King to the sheriff of Kent, greeting. Because a great part of the people and specially of the workmen and servants has now died in this plague, some, seeing the necessity of lords and the scarcity of servants, will not serve unless they receive excessive wages, and others preferring to beg in idleness rather than to seek their livelihood by labour: we, weighing the grave disadvantages which might arise from the dearth specially of tillers and workmen, have had deliberation and treaty hereon with the prelates and nobles and other learned men in session with us, by whose unanimous counsel we have thought fit to ordain that every man and woman of our realm of England, of whatsoever condition, free or servile, able-bodied and under the age of sixty years, not living by trade nor exercising a certain craft, nor having of his own whereof he shall be able to live, or land of his own, in the tilling whereof he shall be able to occupy himself, and not serving another man, shall be bound to serve him who shall require him, if he be required to serve in a suitable service, regard being had to his rank, and shall receive only the wages, liveries, hire or salaries which used to be offered in the places where he should serve in the twentieth year of our reign of England, or in the five or six common years last preceding; provided that lords be preferred to others in the bondmen or tenants of their lands so to be retained in their service; so however that such lords so retain as many as shall be necessary and not more; and if such a man or woman, so required to serve, refuse so to do, the same being proved by two trusty men before the sheriff, bailiff, lord, or constable of the town where this shall come to pass, he shall be taken forthwith by them or any of them and sent to the nearest gaol, there to stay in strait keeping until he find security to serve in the form aforesaid.

And if a reaper, mower or other workman or servant, of whatsoever rank or condition he be, retained in the service of any man, withdraw from the said service without reasonable cause or licence before the end of the term agreed upon, he shall undergo the penalty of imprisonment, and none, under the same penalty, shall presume to receive or retain such an one in his service.

Furthermore no man shall pay or promise to pay to any man more wages, liveries, hire or salaries than is accustomed, as is aforesaid, nor shall any man in any wise demand or receive the same, under penalty of the double of that which shall be so paid, promised, demanded or received, to go to him who shall feel himself aggrieved hereby; and if none such will prosecute, it shall go to any one of the people who shall prosecute; and such prosecution shall be made in the court of the lord of the place where such a case shall befall; and if the lords of towns or manors shall presume in any wise to contravene our present ordinance, by themselves or their ministers, then prosecution shall be made against them in the form aforesaid in counties, wapentakes and ridings, or other such courts of ours, at a penalty of threefold of that so paid or promised by them or their ministers; and if by chance any one shall have covenanted with any man so to serve for a greater salary before the present ordinance, the latter shall in no wise be bound by reason of the said covenant to pay to such a man more than has been customary at other times; nay, rather, he shall not presume to pay more under the penalty aforesaid.

Moreover saddlers, skinners, tawyers, shoemakers, tailors, smiths, carpenters, masons, tilers, boatmen, carters and other artificers and workmen whosoever shall not take for their labour and craft more than used to be paid to such in the twentieth year and other common years preceding in the places in which they chance to be employed, as is aforesaid; and if any shall receive more, he shall be committed to the nearest gaol in the manner aforesaid.

Moreover butchers, fishermen, hostlers, brewers, bakers, poulterers and all other sellers of victuals whatsoever shall be bound to sell such victuals for a reasonable price, regard being had to the price at which such victuals are sold in the neighbouring places; so that such sellers have a moderate profit and not excessive, as shall be reasonably required by the distance of the places wherefrom such victuals are carried; and if any man sell such victuals otherwise and be convicted thereof in the form aforesaid, he shall pay the double of that which he shall receive to him that suffered loss, or, for lack of such, to him who will prosecute in this behalf; and the mayor and bailiffs of cities and boroughs, market and other towns, and ports and places by the sea, shall have power to enquire of all and singular who in any wise transgress against this ordinance, at the penalty aforesaid to be levied to the use of those at whose suit such transgressors shall be convicted: and in case the same mayor and bailiffs shall neglect to execute the premises and shall be convicted hereof before the justices appointed by us, then the same mayor and bailiffs shall be compelled by the same justices to pay to such as suffered loss, or, for lack of him, to any other prosecuting, threefold the value of the thing so sold, and none the less shall incur grievous punishment at our hands.

And because many sturdy beggars, so long as they can live by begging for alms, refuse to labour, living in idleness and sin and sometimes by thefts and other crimes, no man, under the aforesaid penalty of imprisonment, shall presume under colour of pity or alms to give anything to such as shall be able profitably to labour, or to cherish them in their sloth, that so they may be compelled to labour for the necessaries of life.

We order you, straitly enjoining upon you, that you cause all and singular the premises to be publicly proclaimed and kept in the cities, boroughs and market towns, seaports and other places in your bailiwick where you deem expedient, as well within liberties as without, and due execution to be made thereof, as is aforesaid; and that in no wise you omit this, as you love us and the common utility of our realm and will save yourself harmless. Witness the king at Westminster, the eighteenth day of June. By the king himself and the whole council.

The like writs are directed to the several sheriffs throughout England.

The king to the venerable father in Christ, W. by the same grace bishop of Winchester, greeting. Because a great part of the people . . . [as above, as far as 'to labour for the necessaries of life,' and then thus:] and therefore we request you that you cause the premises to be proclaimed in the several churches and other places of your diocese where you shall deem expedient; commanding rectors, vicars of such churches, ministers and other your subjects that by salutary warnings they beseech and persuade their parishioners to labour and to keep the ordinances aforesaid, as instant necessity demands; and that you constrain the wage-earning chaplains of your said diocese, who, as is said, refuse in like manner to serve without excessive salary, and compel them, under penalty of suspension and interdict, to serve for the accustomed salary, as is expedient; and that you in no wise omit this as you love us and the common utility of our said realm. Witness as above.

By the king himself and the whole council.

The like letters of request are directed to the several bishops of England and to the guardian of the archbishopric of Canterbury, the see being vacant, under the same date.

8 Presentments Before the Justices of Labourers, 1351

(P.R.O. Assize Roll, Just. Itin. 1/267, mm. 1, 8)

Hundred of Chelmsford

The twelve [jurors] present that Arnulph le Hierde of Maldon, late servant of John Dodebroke from Michaelmas,[1] 24 Edward III, until

Michaelmas next following, 25 Edward III, for one year and for a quarter of a year next following and for the whole of that time, the said Arnulph took a quarter of wheat for twelve weeks and 5s a year for his stipend. Further, he took from the feast of St. Peter's Chains[2] until Christmas in the same time 10s beyond that which he took above; and hereupon the said Arnulph withdrew from his service before the end of the term, to the damage of the said John of 40s, against the Statute . . .

Trespass.—Further, they present that Robert Grys of Danbury, potter, makes brass pots and sells them at threefold the price which he used [to take], against the Statute, etc., in oppression of the people.

Trespass.—Further, they say that John Sextayn the younger, tailor, John Banestrat, tailor, Roger atte Tye of Great Baddow, take salaries for their labours from divers folks against the Statute . . . and this threefold that which they used to take.

Trespass.—Further, they say that William Denk, servant of Geoffrey the smith, took from the said Geoffrey 20s a year, and is at his table, and was sworn before John of Sutton and his fellows to serve according to the Statute . . . where he should not take but 8s . . .

Trespass.—Further, they present that Richard Smith of Great Baddow commonly takes for his work double that which he used to take, against the Statute.

Trespass.—Further, they present that John Plukkerose, William Smith of Danbury and William Molt, shoemakers, of Great Baddow, make shoes and sell them at almost double the price which they used [to take], against the Statute . . . in oppression of the people.

Trespass.—Further, they say that Alan son of Sayer Banstrat of Great Baddow, sawyer, will not serve unless he take for his salary as much as two others take, against the Statute . . . in oppression of the people. . . .

Grand Inquisition

Trespass.—Further, they present that John Galion, vicar of Nazeing, will not minister to any the sacrament of marriage unless he have from each man 5s or 6s, and in this manner by extortion the said John has taken from John Wakerild 4s 10d, from William Gurteber 5s, from John Mabely 9s, and from many others to the sum of 20s, in oppression of the people by tort and against the peace. . . .

Trespass.—Further, they present that John Hindercle took for stipend from the rector of Parndon for the time of August this year 10s against the Statute.

Further, they present that John Hindercle, William Pourche, are
butchers and forestallers of victuals, against the Statute.

[1] 29 September.   [2] 1 August.

9 The Punishment of a Seller of Unsound Wine, 1364

(*Memorials of London and London Life in the XIIIth, XIVth and XVth
Centuries*, ed. H. T. Riley (1868), pp. 318–19)

Pleas held before Adam of Bury, mayor, and the aldermen,[1] *on Tuesday
the morrow of St. Martin, in the 38th year*[2] *etc.*

John Rightwys and John Penrose, taverners, were attached to make
answer etc., in a plea of contempt and trespass. As to the which, John
Brykelesworthe, who prosecuted for the king and the commonalty of
the city of London, said that the same John Ryghtwys and John Penrose, on the eve of St. Martin . . . in the Parish of St. Leonard Estchepe,
in the tavern of Walter Doget there, sold red wine to all who came
there, unsound and unwholesome for man, in deceit of the common
people, and in contempt of our lord the king, and to the shameful
disgrace of the officers of the city; to the grievous damage of the
commonalty . . . And the four supervisors of the sale of wines in the
city claimed to have cognizance of all defaults therein; and the said
John Ryghtwys and John Penrose were committed to Newgate . . .

And on the Saturday following the said four supervisors appeared
etc. and they said that the said John Ryghtwys was in no way guilty of
the sale of the said wine. Therefore he was to be acquitted thereof. And
they said that the said John Penrose was guilty of the sale of such wine,
and they wished him to be imprisoned for a year and a day.

Afterwards, on the 22nd day of November in the 38th year aforesaid,
the said four supervisors came, and gave another judgment, in form as
follows:— that the said John Penrose shall drink a draught of the same
wine which he sold to the common people; and the remainder of such
wine shall then be poured on the head of the same John; and that he
shall forswear the calling of a vintner in the city of London for ever
unless he can obtain the favour of our lord the king as to the same.

[1] Of London.   [2] i.e. 12 November 1364.

10 The Commons Petition Against Usury, 1376

(*Rotuli Parliamentorum*, II, p. 350)

Further, the Commons of the land pray that whereas the horrible vice of usury is so spread abroad and used throughout the land that the virtue of charity, without which none can be saved, is wellnigh wholly perished, whereby, as is known too well, a great number of good men have been undone and brought to great poverty: Please it, to the honour of God, to establish in this present Parliament that the ordinance[1] made in the city of London for a remedy of the same, well considered and corrected by your wise council and likewise by the bishop of the same city, be speedily put into execution, without doing favour to any, against every person, of whatsoever condition he be, who shall be hereafter attainted as principal or receiver or broker of such false bargains. And that all the mayors and bailiffs of cities and boroughs throughout the realm have the same power to punish all those who shall be attainted of this falsity within their bailiwicks according to the form of the articles comprehended in the same ordinance. And that the same ordinance be kept throughout all the realm, within franchises and without.

Answer.—Let the law of old used run herein.

[1] Of 1363.

11 Opinions on the Balance of Trade, 1381–2

(*Rotuli Parliamentorum*, III, pp. 126–7)

To our lord the king and to all the lords and commons of his realm, make known, as they have often done before these times without being heard, the officers over the moneys of the Tower of London, how for lack of good ordinance no gold or silver comes into England, but of that which is in England a great part has been and from day to day is carried out of the land, and that which remains in England by fault of the deceit of clippers and otherwise is become right feeble, and from day to day such damage increases. Wherefore please it you to take good counsel and remedy hereon, otherwise we, the said officers, warn you, and before God and before you we will be excused, that if you do not apply a speedy remedy thereto in short time to come, where you think to have 5s you will not have 4s.

Richard Leicester.—First, as to this that no gold or silver comes into England, but that which is in England is carried beyond the sea, I maintain that it is because the land spends too much in merchandise, as in grocery, mercery and peltry, or wines, red, white and sweet, and also in exchanges made to the Court of Rome in divers ways. Wherefore the remedy seems to me to be that each merchant bringing merchandise into England take out of the commodities of the land as much as his merchandise aforesaid shall amount to; and that none carry gold or silver beyond the sea, as it is ordained by statute. And let a good ordinance be made hereof, as well by search as otherwise. And so meseems that the money that is in England will remain, and great quantity of money and bullion will come from the parts beyond the sea.

As to this, that the gold is right feeble because of clipping, there seems to me no other remedy than that gold be generally weighed by those who shall take it; and hereon let proclamation be made, and this will be a smaller loss than to change the money, as may be more fully declared.

As to this, that there is a great lack of halfpence and farthings, the master is bound by his indenture to make halfpence according to the quantity of his work of silver. Let the warden of the Mint be charged to survey that the master of the Mint do in all points that which appertains to his office.

As to this, that the gold agrees not with the silver, it cannot be amended unless the money be changed. And to change the money in any manner seems to me universal damage to the lords, commons and all the realm, as may be more fully declared.

As to this, that new money is made in Flanders and in Scotland, let proclamation be made that all manner of moneys, as well of Flanders, Scotland and all other countries beyond the sea whatsoever, be forbidden from having any currency in England, and that none take them in payment except to bring them for bullion to the coinage of our lord the king.

Further, it will be altogether for the better and a very great profit to all the commons, that of the gold money now current, which is so clipped and otherwise impaired, that of this money, when it shall come to the Tower and to the coinage, henceforth our lord the king take for his seigneurage, and the master for the work for him and his other officers, nothing more than 10*d* in the pound.

Further there will be an increase of the money and profit to the whole realm if of all other bullion the king take only 12*d* for his seigneurage and the master of the Mint 12*d* for his work.

Lincoln Goldsmith.—To the noble lords of the council of our lord the king, touching the charge which you have given me, please you to take note of this answer.

Touching the first article, that gold and silver is taken out of the realm, the first remedy against this is that no clerk or purveyor be suffered to take any silver or gold or to make any exchange to be taken to the Court of Rome, and no merchant be suffered to pay any money but only merchandise for merchandise; and also that the money of the noble, at the same weight that it now is, be put at a greater value.

And touching the second article, the remedy is that all the money be of one weight, so that the money that is not of the weight ordained be bought according to the value.

And touching the third article, the remedy is that halfpence and farthings be made in great plenty.

And touching the fourth article, the remedy is that there be one weight and one measure throughout the realm and that no subtle weight be suffered.

And touching the fifth article, the remedy is contained above in the first article.

* * *

Richard Aylesbury.—As to this, that no gold or silver comes into England, but that which is in England is carried beyond the sea, we maintain that if the merchandise which goes out of England be well and rightly governed, the money that is in England will remain and great plenty of money will come from beyond the sea, that is to say, let not more strange merchandise come within the realm than to the value of the denizen merchandise which passes out of the realm.

Further he says that it were good if the Pope's collector were English and the Pope's money were sent to him in merchandise and not in money, and that the passages of pilgrims and clerks be utterly forbidden, upon pain, etc.

And as to this, that the gold is too feeble because of clipping, there seems to us no other remedy than that the gold be generally weighed by those who shall take it, and hereon let proclamation be made.

As to this, that the gold agrees not with the silver, it cannot be amended unless the money be changed, and to this we dare not assent for the common damage that might befall.

As to this, that new money is made in Flanders and in Scotland, let proclamation be made that all manner of money of Scotland be forbidden. Let other moneys also that come from beyond the sea have no currency in England, and let none take them in payment except at the value to bring for bullion and to the coinage of our lord the king. And let none take gold or silver out of the realm beyond the sea, as it is ordained by statute, and hereof let good ordinance be made as well by search as otherwise.

And further he says, if it please by way of information, that [it would be well] if the pound of gold that is now made in the Tower to the sum of 45 nobles (which pound, because the money thereof is so clipped and otherwise impaired, is worth at present, taking one with another, 41½ nobles), were made into 48 nobles, the noble to be current at the present value; and let the king and the master and other officers of the Mint take 20*d* in each pound for the seigneurage and work and every other thing.

12 Action to Ensure London's Grain Supply, 1482

(Guildhall MSS, Letter Book L, ff. 181–2, printed in N. S. B. Gras, *The Evolution of the English Corn Market* (Cambridge, Mass., 1926), p. 447)

21 November 1482 [The king] considering the great scarcity and dearth of corn within his said realm by his open proclamations in all the shires of the same, of late strictly charged and commanded that no manner of man, whatsoever he were, should carry, or make to be carried, any wheat or other grains out of his said realm, upon certain pains in the same proclamations limited and expressed. Nevertheless his highness considering the great scarcity of wheat and other grains within his city of London, where is the concourse and repair of the nobles and other his true liege men and subjects of this his realm of England, and also of strangers of divers other lands, wills and grants that all his subjects whatsoever they be shall, mowe,[1] buy and provide and be at liberty to bring to the city aforesaid wheat, malt, rye, beans, peas and oats, and all other manner grains, for victualling of the same city in all the shires of this his realm of England. And the grains so purveyed and [brought] unto the said city of London, and to none other place, as well by land as by sea and fresh water send, lead, carry or make to be sent, led or carried, without taking of the same grains or any parcel thereof by his purveyors or takers for his most honourable household, or for any other cause whatsoever it be, or any impediment, trouble, arrest, vexation or grief of his subjects, any act restraint, proclamation or commandment to the contrary made notwithstanding. Provided always that every of our said sovereign lord's subjects which shall bring any wheat, rye, malt, or other grains aforerehearsed unto the said city of London by sea out of this his county of Sussex, ship, or do to be shipped, the same wheat or other grains in the ports of Winchelsea and Chichester, and in none other place of this county, finding to the customers there surety by indenture testifying the quantity of the said grains and what they be. And that they shall bring, carry and convey the same grains to the said city of London and to none other place. Of which indenture one part shall remain with the customers in the said ports of Winchelsea and Chichester, and the other part to be delivered and abide with the customers in the port of our said city of London.

[1] May.

13 Thomas More on the 'All-Devouring Sheep', 1516

(Thomas More, *Utopia*, ed. W. H. D. Rouse (1906), pp. 17–18)

. . . But yet this is not only the necessary cause of stealing. There is another, which, as I suppose, is proper and peculiar to you Englishmen alone. What is that, quoth the Cardinal? forsooth, my lord (quoth I), your sheep that were wont to be so meek and tame, and so small eaters, now, as I hear say, be become so great devourers and so wild, that they eat up, and swallow down the very men themselves. They consume, destroy, and devour whole fields, houses, and cities. For look in what parts of the realm does grow the finest and therefore dearest wool, there noblemen and gentlemen, yea, and certain abbots, holy men no doubt, not contenting themselves with the yearly revenues and profits, that were wont to grow to their forefathers and predecessors of their lands, nor being content that they live in rest and pleasure nothing profiting, yea, much annoying the weal public, leave no ground for tillage, they inclose all into pastures; they throw down houses; they pluck down towns, and leave nothing standing, but only the church to be made a sheep-house. And as though you lost no small quantity of ground by forests, chases, lawns, and parks, those good holy men turn all dwelling-places and all glebeland into desolation and wilderness. Therefore that one covetous and insatiable cormorant and very plague of his native country may compass about and inclose many thousand acres of ground together within one pale or hedge, the husbandmen be thrust out of their own, or else either by cunning and fraud, or by violent oppression they be put besides it, or by wrongs and injuries they be so wearied, that they be compelled to sell all: by one means therefore or by other, either by hook or crook they must needs depart away, poor, silly, wretched souls, men, women, husbands, wives, fatherless children, widows, woeful mothers, with their young babes, and their whole household small in substance and much in number, as husbandry requires many hands. Away they trudge, I say, out of their known and accustomed houses, finding no place to rest in. All their household stuff, which is very little worth, though it might well abide the sale; yet, being suddenly thrust out, they be constrained to sell it for a thing of nought. And when they have wandered abroad till that be spent, what can they then else do but steal, and then justly pardy be hanged, or else go about a-begging. And yet then also they be cast in prison as vagabonds, because they go about and work not: whom no man will set a-work, though they never so willingly proffer themselves thereto. For one shepherd or herdsman is enough to eat up that ground with cattle, to the occupying whereof about husbandry many hands were requisite. And this is also the cause why victuals be now in many places dearer.

14 A Municipal Census of Corn Supplies, 1520

(*The Coventry Leet Book: or Mayor's Register, 1420–1555*, ed. M. D. Harris, Early English Text Society, CXXXVIII, Pt. III (1909), pp. 674–5)

October 10, 1520 Memorandum that the 10th day of October and in the [eleventh] year of the reign of King Henry VIII, then Master John Bond being mayor of the city of Coventry, the price of all manner of corn and grain began to rise. Whereupon a view was taken by the said mayor and his brethren what stores of all manner of corn, and what number of people was then within the said city, men, women and children . . .

Summa totalis of the people then being within the city, of men women and children.	Summa totalis 6601 persons.	In malt, 2405 qrs. In rye and mastlin, 100 qrs. 1 strike. In wheat, 47 qrs. In oats, 39 qrs. 2 strike. In pease, 18 qrs. 2 strike.	

Also a view by him taken what substance of malt was then brewed within the city weekly by the common brewers that brewed to sell . . . The number of the common brewers in all the city is—68. Item, they brewed weekly in malt, 146 qrs. 1 bus.

Mem., that there was brought into this said city the Friday before Christmas Day in the year of the said John Bond then being mayor, by his labour and his friends, to help sustain the city with corn, of all manner of grain summa 97 qrs. 6 strike.

Mem., that there was at that time 43 bakers within the city, the which did bake weekly amongst all 120 qrs. of wheat and 12, besides pease and rye.

15 The Municipal Regulation of Wages, 1524

(*The Coventry Leet Book: or Mayor's Register, 1420–1555*, ed. M. D. Harris, Early English Text Society, CXXXVIII, Pt. III (1909), pp. 688–9)

27 September, 1524 [Enacted] that the weavers of this city shall have for the weaving of every cloth, to the making whereof goes and is put 80 and 8 lb of wool or more to the number of 80 lb and 16, 5*s* for the weaving of every such cloth; and if the said cloth contain above the said number then the weaving to be paid for as the parties can agree, and if the cloth contain under the said number, then the owner to pay for weaving but 4*s* 6*d*. And if the cloth be made of rests or green wool, then to pay as the parties can agree; and the payment to be made in ready money and not in wares, as it is wont to be, and who refuses thus to do, and so proved before Master Mayor, to forfeit for every said default 3*s* 4*d*, to be levied by the searchers of the said craft of weavers, with an officer to them appointed by the said mayor, to the use of the common box.

[Enacted] that every clothier within this city shall pay for walking of every cloth of green wool or middle wool, 3*s* 4*d*, and for every cloth of fine wool as the clothier and the walker can agree, and that the clothier do pay therefor in ready money and not in wares . . .

16 The Fixing of Food Prices, 1544

(*Tudor Royal Proclamations*, I, eds. P. L. Hughes and J. F. Larkin (Yale U.P., 1964), pp. 331–3)

Westminster. 21 May 1544

Forasmuch as it is come to the knowledge of our sovereign lord the king that butchers and other victuallers, having more respect to their own private lucre and advantage than the commonwealth of this his highness' realm, have raised the prices of flesh, as of beeves, muttons, veals, and other kind of poultry and victuals, to such excessive and high prices that his loving subjects cannot gain with their labours and salary sufficient to pay for their convenient victuals and sustenance unless that speedy remedy be provided in that behalf.

His highness therefore, by the advice of his most honourable council, and by the authority of the act[1] of parliament made in the 31st year of his majesty's reign, straightly charges and commands that all and every the said butchers and victuallers, selling flesh by retail as well within the city of London and the suburbs of the same as in all other places within this his realm of England, as well within franchises and liberties as without, shall from and after 14 days next ensuing this present proclamation published and proclaimed, according to the said statute, sell the flesh of beef, mutton, veal, pork, and lamb, being good and wholesome for man's body, by retail by weight, not above the prices and rates hereafter ensuing; that is to say, between the 15th day of June and the feast of the birth of our Lord God yearly, every pound of beef to be sold not above the price of $\frac{5}{8}d$ the pound; every pound of mutton not above the price of $1d$ the pound; and every pound of veal not above the price of $1d$ the pound. And that the flesh of beeves, muttons, and veals to be sold between the said feast of the birth of our Lord God and the said 15th day of June not above the prices and rates hereafter following: that is to say, the pound of beef to be sold not above $\frac{3}{4}d$ the pound; the pound of mutton not above $1d$ the pound; and every pound of veal not above $\frac{7}{8}d$ the pound. And furthermore that the flesh of lamb and pork shall be sold at all times in the year not above the prices and rates hereafter following: that is to say, the best lamb to be sold not above the price of $2s$; the second lamb not above the price of $20d$; and the meanest lamb not above the price of $16d$; and the half and quarters of every such lambs to be sold not above the rates of the said prices of lambs. And also the flesh of pork to be sold by retail or otherwise not above the price of $\frac{3}{4}d$ the pound . . .

And furthermore his highness, by the same authority, straightly charges and commands all and singular his subjects, inhabiting within the cities of London and Westminster, and in the suburbs of the same, and in the borough of Southwark, being free men of the said cities and borough, or of any of them, to sell all manner of wild fowl and poultry wares not above the rates and prices hereafter ensuing: that is to say, the best swan, not above the price of $5s$; the best crane, bustard, or stork, not above the price of $4s$; hernshaws,[2] shovelers, and bitterns of the best, not above the price of $18d$ the piece; peacock old, the best, not above the price of $20d$; peachickens the best, not above the price of $14d$ the piece; the capon of Greece of the best, not above the price of $20d$; capon of Kent, otherwise called boiling capon, of the best, not above the price of $8d$; capon good, not above the price of $14d$; hen of Greece the best, not above the price of $7d$; brew and egret of the best, not above the price of $12d$ the piece; bitterns of the best, not above the price of

12d the piece; gulls of the best, not above the price of 12d the piece; green geese fat, sold between Easter and Midsummer, not above the price of 7d the piece; geese great, sold between Midsummer and Shrovetide, of the best, not above the price of 8d the piece; godwits fat, not above the price of 12d the piece; a dozen dotterels of the best, not above the price of 3s 4d the dozen; quails of the best, the dozen, not above 4s; sparrows the dozen, not above 3d the dozen; pigeons of the best, not above 8d the dozen; rabbits, suckers fat, not above 18d the dozen; conies between Easter and Allhallowtide, the best, not above 2s the dozen; winter conies between Allhallowtide and Shrovetide, not above 2s 6d the dozen; mallard, of the best, not above 4d the mallard; teals of the best, not above 2d the teal; widgeons fat, not above 3s the dozen; woodcocks of the best, not above 4d the piece; plovers green, of the best, not above 3s the dozen; bastard plovers, fat, not above 2s 6d the dozen; martlets of the best, not above 18d the dozen; hen snites[3] of the best, not above 18d the dozen; larks of the best, not above 6d the dozen; buntings of the best, not above 4d the dozen; great birds of the best, not above 6d the dozen; eggs from Easter to Michaelmas,[4] not above 16d the hundred; eggs from Michaelmas till Easter, not above 20d the hundred; butter, sweet, between Easter and the feast of All Saints,[5] not above 2d the pound; butter, sweet, from the feast of All Saints till Easter, not above 3d the pound . . .

And furthermore his highness straightly charges and commands by the same authority that no foreign or foreigners sell or cause to be sold within the markets of Leaden Hall, Cheapside, and Newgate market, or any of them, or elsewhere within the said city of London and suburbs of the same, after the time of the open markets finished and ended, any of the poultry, wares, and victuals hereunder mentioned above such rates and prices as be hereafter set, rated, and assessed of and upon the same; that is to say, the mean swan 3s; the best swan 4s; the mean crane 2s 4d; the best crane 3s; the mean bustard 2s; the best bustard 2s 8d; the best hern, bittern, or shoveler 14d; the mean curlew 6d; the best curlew 8d; the mean woodcock 2½d; the best woodcock 3d; the best teal, green plover, or grey 2d; the lapwing 1½d; the best wild mallard 4d; the best wild duck 3d; the best dozen larks 5d; the mean dozen larks 3d; the best dozen snites 16d; the mean dozen snites 12d; the mean dozen great birds 4d; the best dozen great birds 6d; the mean cony 2d; the cony, the kidney half covered with fat 2½d; the best cony 3d; the mean dozen chickens 14d; the best dozen chickens 18d; the dozen lean quails 2s; the dozen best quails 4s; the mean goose 5d; the best goose 7d; the mean dozen pigeons 6d; the best dozen pigeons 8d; the boiling capon

6*d*; the mean roasting capon 10*d*; the best roasting capon of Greece 16*d*; the best pig 6*d*; the mean hen 3*d*; and the best hen 5*d*.

And furthermore the king's most royal majesty . . . ordains . . . that every person . . . the which at any time after the end of 14 days next ensuing the publishing of this present proclamation, shall sell any part or parcel of the flesh or fowl aforesaid above the rates and prices above rated and expressed . . . shall lose and forfeit for every time so doing and offending 10*l* sterling, the one moiety whereof shall be to the king's majesty, and the other moiety to the party that will sue for the same by information, bill, plaint, action of debt, or otherwise in any of the king's courts of his Exchequer, King's Bench, or Common Pleas or else before such of the king's most honourable council, as be appointed to hear and determine the same by authority of the said act . . .

And also the king's most royal majesty straightly charges and commands all mayors, sheriffs, justices of peace, bailiffs, constables, and all other his officers and faithful subjects, that they and every of them, without favour, dread, affection, or corruption, shall put their effectual endeavours for the due execution of this his highness' proclamation, and for the punishment of the offenders thereof, as they will answer to his grace for the same at their uttermost perils, and will avoid the king's most high displeasure and indignation.

¹ 31 Henry VIII, c. 8 (1539).   ² Herons.   ³ Snipes.
⁴ 29 September.   ⁵ 1 November.

17 Thomas Smith on the Rise in Prices, 1549

(*A Discourse of the Common Weal of this Realm of England*, ed. E. Lamond (Cambridge, 1929), pp. 69, 79–82, 104)

Doctor . . . And now I must come to that thing, that you brother merchant touched before; which I take to be the chief cause of all this dearth of things, and of the manifest impoverishment of this realm, and might in brief time be the destruction of the same, if it be not the rather remedied, that is the basing or rather corrupting of our coin and treasure; whereby we have devised a way for the strangers not only to buy our gold and silver for brass, and not only to exhaust this realm of treasure, but also to buy our chief commodities in manner for nothing. It was thought it should have been a mean, not only to bring our treasure home, but to bring much of others; but the experience has so plainly declared the contrary.

*   *   *

Knight I believe well that these be means to exhaust our old treasure from us . . . but how it should make everything so dear among ourselves, as you say it does, I cannot yet perceive the reason.

Doctor Why, do you not perceive that, by reason hereof, you pay dearer for everything that we have from beyond the seas than we were wont to do?

Knight That cannot be denied.

Doctor By how much, trow you?

Knight By the third part well, in all manner of things.

Doctor Must not they that buy dear, sell dear again their wares?

Knight That is true if they intend to thrive; for he that sells good cheap, and buys dear, shall never thrive.

Doctor You have yourself declared the reason, why things within the realm be so dear; for we must buy dear all things brought from beyond the seas, and therefore we must sell again as dear our things, or else we should make ill bargains for ourselves. And though that reason makes it plain, yet experience makes it plainer; for where you say that everything brought beyond the sea is commonly dearer by the third part than it was, do you not see the same proportion raised in our wares, if it be not more, yea in the old coin itself? Is not the angel that was before but 20 groats, now at 30, and so all other old coin after the same rate? But I think there is no more silver given in the 30 groats now than was before in 20, if it be so much. And so I think, setting our coin apart, that we shall have as much silk, wines or oils from beyond the seas, for our tod of wool now as we might have had before the alteration of this coin.

Merchant I would undertake to serve you so.

Knight What loss have we by this, when we sell our commodities as dear as we buy theirs?

Doctor I grant, to one sort of men I count it no loss; yea to some other, gains more than loss; but yet to some other a greater loss than it is profit to the other; yea, generally to the impoverishing of the realm, and the weakening of the king's majesty's power exceedingly.

Knight I pray you, what be these sorts that you mean; and first, of those that you think have no loss thereby?

Doctor I mean all those that live by buying and selling; for as they buy dear, so they sell thereafter.

Knight What is the next sort that you say wins by it?

Doctor Marry, all such as have takings, or farms in their own maintenance, at the old rent; for where they pay after the old rate, they sell after the new; that is, they pay for their land good cheap, and sell all things growing thereof dear.

Knight What sort is that which you said had greater loss thereby than those men had profit?

Doctor It is all noble men, and gentlemen, and all other that live by a stinted rent, or stipend, or do not manner the ground, or do occupy no buying or selling.

Knight I pray you, peruse those sorts as you did the other, one by one, and by course.

Doctor I will gladly. First, the noblemen and gentlemen live for the most on the yearly revenues of the land and fees given them of the king. Then you know, he that may spend 300*l* a year by such revenues and fees may keep no better port than his father, or any other before him, that could spend but 200*l*. And so you may perceive, it is a great abatement of a man's countenance to take away the third part of his living. And, therefore, gentlemen do so much study the increase of their lands, enhancing of their rents, and so take farms and pastures into their own hands, as you see they do; and also to seek to maintain their countenance, as their predecessors did, and yet they come short therein. Others, seeing the charges of household so much as by no provision they can make can be helped, they give over their households, and get them chambers in London, or about the court; and there spend their time, some of them with a servant or two, where he was wont to keep 30 or 40 persons daily in his house, and to do good in the country, in keeping good order and rule among his neighbours. The other sort be, every serving man and men of war, that having but their old stinted wages, cannot find themselves therewith as they might afore time, without ravine or spoil. You know 6*d* a day will not now go so far as 4*d* would afore time; and therefore you have men so unwilling to serve the king nowadays, from that they were wont to be; also where 40*s* a year was good honest wages for a yeoman afore this time, and 20*d* a week's board wages was sufficient, now double as much will scant bear their charges.

*   *   *

Knight Then you think plainly that this alteration of the coin is the chief and principal cause of this universal dearth?

Doctor Yea, no doubt, and of many of the said griefs that we have talked of, by means it being the original of all. And that, beside the reason of the thing . . . experience and proof do make more plain; for even with the alteration of the coin began this dearth; and as the coin appeared, so rose the price of things with all. And this to be true, the few pieces of old coin yet remaining testify; for you shall have, for any of the said coin, as much of any ware either inward or outward as much as ever was wont to be had for the same; and so as the measure is made less, there goes the more sum to make up the tale. And because this rises not together at all men's hands, therefore some have great loss, and some other great gains thereby, and that makes such a general grudge for the thing. And thus, to conclude, I think this alteration of the coin to be the first original cause that strangers first sell their wares dearer to us; and that makes all farmers and tenants, that rear any commodity, again to sell the same dearer; the dearth thereof makes the gentlemen to raise their rents and to take farms into their hands for the better provision, and consequently to enclose more grounds.

18 The Statute of Artificers, Labourers and Apprentices, 1563

(5 Elizabeth, c. 4, *Statutes at Large*, II (1763), pp. 535–43)

Although there remain and stand in force presently a great number of acts and statutes concerning the retaining, departing, wages and orders of apprentices, servants and labourers, as well in husbandry as in divers other arts, mysteries and occupations; yet partly for the imperfection and contrariety that is found, and does appear in sundry of the said laws, and for the variety and number of them, and chiefly for that the wages and allowances limited and rated in many of the said statutes, are in divers places too small and not answerable to this time, respecting the advancement of prices of all things belonging to the said servants and labourers; the said laws cannot conveniently, without the grief and burden of the poor labourer and hired man, be put in good and due execution: and as the said several acts and statutes were, at the time of the making of them, thought to be very good and beneficial for the commonwealth of this realm (as divers of them are:) so if the substance of as many of the said laws as are meet to be continued, shall be digested and reduced into one sole law and statute, and in the same an uniform order prescribed and limited concerning the wages and other orders for apprentices, servants and labourers, there is good hope that it will come to pass, that the same law (being duly executed) should banish idleness, advance husbandry, and yield unto the hired person, both in the time of scarcity and in the time of plenty, a convenient proportion of wages.

II Be it therefore enacted by the authority of this present parliament, that . . . the statutes heretofore made . . . as touch or concern the hiring, keeping, departing, working, wages, or order of servants,

R

workmen, artificers, apprentices and labourers . . . shall be from and after the last day of September next ensuing, repealed . . .

III And be it further enacted . . . that no manner of person . . . after the aforesaid last day of September now next ensuing . . . shall be retained, hired or taken into service, by any means or colour, to work for any less time or term than for one whole year, in any of the sciences, crafts, mysteries or arts of clothiers, woollen cloth weavers, tuckers, fullers, clothworkers, shearmen, dyers, hosiers, tailors, shoe-makers, tanners, pewterers, bakers, brewers, glovers, cutlers, smiths, farriers, curriers, saddlers, spurriers, turners, cappers, hatmakers or feltmakers, bowyers, fletchers, arrow-head-makers, butchers, cooks or millers.

IV . . . every person being unmarried; and every other person being under the age of thirty years, that after the feast of Easter next shall marry, and having been brought up in any of the said arts, crafts or sciences; or that has used or exercised any of them by the space of three years or more; and not having lands, tenements, rents or heredita-ments, copyhold or freehold, of an estate of inheritance, or for term of any life or lives, of the clear yearly value of forty shillings; nor being worth of his own goods the clear value of ten pound . . . nor being retained with any person in husbandry, or in any of the aforesaid arts and sciences, according to this statute; nor lawfully retained in any other art or science; nor being lawfully retained in household, or in any office, with any nobleman, gentleman or others . . . nor have a con-venient farm, or other holding in tillage, whereupon he may employ his labour: shall, during the time that he or they shall be so unmarried, or under the said age of thirty years, upon request made by any person using the art or mystery wherein the said person so required has been exercised (as is aforesaid) be retained; and shall not refuse to serve according to the tenor of this statute, upon the pain and penalty hereafter mentioned.

V . . . no person which shall retain any servant, shall put away his or her said servant, and . . . no person retained according to this statute, shall depart from his master, mistress or dame, before the end of his or her term; upon the pain hereafter mentioned; unless it be for some . . . sufficient cause . . . to be allowed before two justices of peace . . . within the . . . county, or before the mayor or other chief officer of the city, borough or town corporate wherein the said master . . . in-habits . . .

VI And that no such master . . . shall put away any such servant at the end of his term, or that any such servant shall depart from his said master . . . without one quarter's warning given before the end of his said term, either by the said master . . . or servant, the one to the other, upon the pain hereafter ensuing.

VII . . . every person between the age of twelve years and the age of sixty years, not being lawfully retained, nor apprentice with any fisherman or mariner haunting the seas; nor being in service with any kidder or carrier of any corn, grain or meal, for provision of the city of London; nor with any husbandman in husbandry; nor in any city, town corporate or market town, in any of the arts or sciences limited or appointed by this statute to have or take apprentices; nor being retained by the year, or half the year at the least, for the digging, seeking, finding, getting, melting, fining, working, trying, making of any silver, tin, lead, iron, copper, stone, sea-coal, stone-coal, moor-coal or charcoal; nor being occupied in or about the making of any glass; nor being a gentleman born, nor being a student or scholar in any of the universities, or in any school; nor having lands, tenements, rents or hereditaments . . . of the clear yearly value of forty shillings; nor being worth in goods and chattels to the value of ten pound; nor having a father or mother then living, or other ancestor whose heir apparent he is, then having lands, tenements or hereditaments, of the yearly value of ten pound or above, or goods or chattels of the value of forty pound; nor being a necessary or convenient officer or servant lawfully retained, as is aforesaid; nor having a convenient farm or holding, whereupon he may or shall employ his labour; nor being otherwise lawfully retained, according to the true meaning of this statute; shall . . . be compelled to be retained to serve in husbandry by the year, with any person that keeps husbandry, and will require any such person so to serve . . .

VIII . . . if any person after he has retained any servant, shall put away the same servant before the end of his term, unless it be for . . . sufficient cause . . . or if any such master . . . shall put away any such servant at the end of his term, without one quarter's warning . . . that then every such master . . . so offending . . . shall forfeit the sum of forty shillings.

IX And if any servant retained according to the form of this statute, depart from . . . service, before the end of his term, unless it be for . . . sufficient cause . . . or if any servant at the end of his term depart from . . . service without one quarter's warning given before the end of his said term . . . or if any person . . . compellable and bound to be retained, and to serve in husbandry, or in any other the arts, sciences or mysteries above remembered, by the year or otherwise, do (upon request made) refuse to serve for the wages that shall be . . . appointed, according to the form of this statute; or promise or covenant to serve, and do not serve according to the tenor of the same: that then every servant so departing away, and every person so refusing to serve for such wages . . . [shall be committed] to ward, there to remain without bail or mainprise, until the said servant or party so offending shall be bound to the party to whom the offence shall be made, to serve and continue with him for the wages that then shall be . . . appointed . . .

X . . . none of the said retained persons in husbandry, or in any the arts or sciences above remembered, after the time of his retainer expired, shall depart forth of one city, town or parish to another; nor out of the . . . hundred; nor out of the county . . . where he last served, to serve in any other city . . . hundred . . . or county; unless he have a testimonial under the seal of the said city or town corporate, or of the constable or constables, or other head officer . . . and of two other honest householders of the city, town or parish where he last served, declaring his lawful departure . . .

XI . . . no person or persons that shall depart out of a service, shall be . . . accepted into any other service, without showing before his retainer, such testimonial as is above-remembered, to the chief officer of the . . . town and place . . . where he shall be retained to serve; upon the pain that every such servant so departing without such . . . testimonial, shall be imprisoned until he procure a testimonial . . . which if he cannot do within the space of one and twenty days next after the first day of his imprisonment, then the said person to be whipped and used as a vagabond according to the laws in such cases provided; and that every person retaining any such servant, without showing such testimonial . . . shall forfeit for every such offence five pounds . . .

XII . . . all artificers and labourers, being hired for wages by the day or week, shall betwixt the midst of the months of March and September be and continue at their work at or before five of the clock in the morning, and continue at work and not depart until betwixt seven and eight of the clock at night (except it be in the time of breakfast, dinner or drinking, the which times at the most shall not exceed above two hours and a half in a day, that is to say, at every drinking one half hour, for his dinner one hour, and for his sleep when he is allowed to sleep, the which is from the midst of May to the midst of August, half an hour at the most, and at every breakfast one half hour): and all the said artificers and labourers, between the midst of September and the midst of March, shall be and continue at their work from the spring of the day in the morning until the night of the same day, except it be in time afore appointed for breakfast and dinner; upon pain to lose and forfeit one penny for every hour's absence, to be deducted . . . out of his wages that shall so offend.

XIII . . . every artificer and labourer that shall be lawfully retained in and for the building or repairing of any church, house, ship, mill or every other piece of work taken in great, in task or in gross . . . shall continue and not depart from the same, unless it be for not paying of his wages or hire agreed on, or otherwise lawfully taken or appointed to serve the queen's majesty . . . or for other lawful cause, or without licence of the master or owner of the work . . . before the finishing of the said work; upon pain of imprisonment by one month, without bail or mainprise; and the forfeiture of the sum of five pounds to the party from whom he shall so depart.

*   *   *

XV And for the declaration and limitation what wages servants, labourers and artificers, either by the year or day or otherwise, shall have and receive, be it enacted . . . that the justices of peace of every shire . . . or the more part of them . . . and every mayor, bailiff or other head officer within any city or town corporate wherein is any justice of peace . . . shall before the tenth day of June next coming, and afterward shall yearly at every general sessions first to be held and kept after Easter or at some time convenient within six weeks next following every of the said feasts of Easter, assemble themselves together; and . . . calling unto them such discreet and grave persons . . . as they shall think meet, and conferring together, respecting the plenty or scarcity of the time and other circumstances necessarily to be considered, shall have authority . . . within the limits . . . of their several commissions, to limit, rate and appoint the wages, as well of . . . the said artificers, handicraftsmen, husbandmen or any other labourer, servant or workman, whose wages in time past have been by any law or statute rated and appointed, as also the wages of all other labourers, artificers, workmen or apprentices of husbandry, which have not been rated, as they the same justices, mayors or head officers . . . shall think meet by their discretions to be rated . . . by the year or by the day, week, month or otherwise, with meat and drink or without meat and drink, and what wages every workman or labourer shall take by the great, for mowing, reaping or threshing of corn and grain, or for mowing or making of hay, or for ditching, paving, railing or hedging, by the rod, perch, lugg, yard, pole, rope or foot, and for any other kind of reasonable labours or service.

*   *   *

XVIII . . . if any person . . . shall . . . keep any servant, workman or labourer, or shall give any more or greater wages or other commodity, contrary to the true intent . . . of this statute, or contrary to the rates or wages that shall be assessed . . . that then every person that shall so offend, and be therefore lawfully convicted . . . shall suffer imprisonment by the space of ten days, without bail or mainprise, and shall lose and forfeit five pounds of lawful money of England.

XIX And that every person that shall be so retained and take wages contrary to this statute . . . and shall be thereof convicted . . . shall suffer imprisonment by the space of one and twenty days, without bail or mainprise.

*   *   *

XXII Provided always . . . that in the time of hay or corn harvest, the justices of peace . . . and also the constable or other head officer of every township upon request, and for the avoiding of the loss of any corn, grain or hay, shall and may cause all such artificers and persons as be meet to labour . . . to serve by the day for the mowing, reaping, shearing, getting or inning of corn, grain and hay, according to the skill and quality of the person; and that none of the said persons shall refuse so to do, upon pain to suffer imprisonment in the stocks by the space of two days and one night . . .

XXIII Provided also, that all persons of the counties where they have accustomed to go into other shires for harvest-work, and having at that time no harvest-work sufficient in the same town or county where he or they dwelt in the winter then last past, bringing with him or them a testimonial under the hand . . . of one justice of the peace . . . or other head officer . . . testifying the same . . . (other than such persons as shall be retained in service, according to the form of this statute) may repair and resort in harvest of hay or corn, from the counties wherein their dwelling-places are, into any other place or county . . .

XXIV . . . two justices of peace, the mayor or other head officer of any city, borough or town corporate . . . shall and may . . . appoint any such woman as is of the age of twelve years, and under the age of forty years and unmarried, and forth of service, as they shall think meet to serve, to be retained or serve by the year, or by the week or day, for such wages, and in such reasonable sort and manner as they shall think meet; and if any such woman shall refuse so to serve, then it shall be lawful . . . to commit such woman to ward, until she shall be bound to serve . . .

XXV And for the better advancement of husbandry and tillage, and to the intent that such as are fit to be made apprentices to husbandry, may be bound thereunto, be it enacted . . . that every person being an householder, and having and using half a plough-land at the least in tillage, may have and receive as an apprentice any person above the age of ten years, and under the age of eighteen years, to serve in husbandry, until his age of one and twenty years at the least, or until the age of twenty-four years, as the parties can agree . . .

XXVI . . . every person being an householder, and twenty-four years old at the least, dwelling or inhabiting . . . in any city or town corporate, and using and exercising any art, mystery or manual occupation there, shall and may, after the feast of St. John the Baptist[1] next coming . . . have and retain the son of any freeman, not occupying husbandry, nor being a labourer, and inhabiting in the same, or in any other city or town that now is or hereafter shall be and continue incorporate, to serve and be bound as an apprentice after the custom and order of the city of London, for seven years at the least, so as the term and years of such apprentice do not expire or determine afore such apprentice shall be of the age of twenty-four years at the least.

XXVII Provided always . . . that it shall not be lawful to any person dwelling in any city or town corporate, using or exercising any of the mysteries or crafts of a merchant trafficking by traffic or trade into any the parts beyond the sea, mercer, draper, goldsmith, ironmonger, embroiderer or clothier, that does or shall put cloth to making and sale, to take any apprentice or servant . . . except such servant or apprentice be his son; or else that the father and mother of such apprentice or servant shall have, at the time of taking such apprentice or servant, lands, tenements or other hereditaments, of the clear yearly value of forty shillings of one estate of inheritance or freehold at the least . . .

XXVIII . . . from and after [24 June] next, it shall be lawful to every person being an householder, and four and twenty years old at the least, and not occupying husbandry, nor being a labourer, dwelling or inhabiting . . . in any town not being incorporate, that now is or hereafter shall be a market-town . . . and using or exercising any art, mystery or manual occupation . . . to have in like manner to apprentice or apprentices, the child or children of any other artificer or artificers, not occupying husbandry, nor being a labourer, which now do or hereafter shall inhabit or dwell in the same, or in any other such market-town within the same shire . . .

XXIX Provided always . . . that it shall not be lawful to any person, dwelling or inhabiting in any such market-town, using or exercising the feat, mystery or art of a merchant, trafficking or trading into the parts beyond the seas, mercer, draper, goldsmith, ironmonger, embroiderer or clothier, that does or shall put cloth to making and sale, to take any apprentice, or in any wise to teach or instruct any person . . . after [24 June] aforesaid; except such servant or apprentice shall be his son; or else that the father or mother of such apprentice shall have lands, tenements or other hereditaments, at the time of taking such apprentice, of the clear yearly value of three pounds, of one estate of inheritance or freehold at the least . . .

XXX . . . from and after the said feast it shall be lawful to any person using or exercising the art or occupation of a smith, wheel-wright, plough-wright, mill-wright, carpenter, rough mason, plasterer, sawyer, lime-burner, brick-maker, bricklayer, tiler, slater, helier, tile-maker, linen-weaver, turner, cooper, miller, earthen potter, woollen weaver weaving housewives' or household cloth only and none other cloth, fuller, otherwise called tucker or walker, burner of ore and wood-ashes, thatcher or shingler, wheresoever he or they shall dwell or inhabit, to have or receive the son of any person as apprentice . . .

XXXI . . . after the first day of May next coming, it shall not be lawful to any person or persons, other than such as now do lawfully use or exercise any art, mystery or manual occupation, to set up, occupy, use or exercise any craft, mystery or occupation, now used or occupied within the realm of England or Wales; except he shall have been brought up therein seven years at the least as an apprentice . . . nor to set any person on work in such mystery, art or occupation, being not a workman at this day; except he shall have been apprentice . . . or else having served as an apprentice . . . shall or will become a journey-man, or be hired by the year; upon pain that every person . . . doing the contrary, shall forfeit and lose for every default forty shillings for every month.

XXXII Provided always . . . that no person or persons using or exercising the art or mystery of a woollen cloth-weaver, other than such as be inhabiting within the counties of Cumberland, Westmorland, Lancaster and Wales, weaving friezes, cottons or housewives' cloth only, making and weaving woollen cloth commonly sold or to be sold by any clothman or clothier, shall take and have any apprentice or shall teach or in any wise instruct any person . . . in any village, town or place (cities, towns corporate and market-towns only except) unless such person be his son, or else that the father or mother of such apprentice or servant shall at the time of the taking of such person or persons to be an apprentice or servant, or to be so instructed, have lands or tenements or other hereditaments, to the clear yearly value of three pounds at the least, of an estate of inheritance or freehold . . . upon pain of forfeiture of twenty shillings for every month that any person shall [do] contrary to . . . this article . . .

XXXIII . . . all and every person and persons that shall have three apprentices in any of the said crafts, mysteries or occupations of a cloth-maker, fuller, shearman, weaver, tailor or shoemaker, shall retain and keep one journeyman, and for every other apprentice above the number of the said three apprentices, one other journeyman, upon pain for every default therein ten pounds.

XXXIV Provided always, that this act . . . shall not extend to prejudice . . . any liberties heretofore granted by any act of Parliament, to or for the company and occupation of worsted-makers and worsted-weavers within the city of Norwich, and elsewhere within the county of Norfolk . . .

XXXV . . . if any person shall be required by any householder, having and using half a plough-land at the least in tillage, to be an apprentice, and to serve in husbandry, or in any other kind of art, mystery or science before expressed, and shall refuse so to do, that then upon the complaint of such housekeeper made to one justice of the peace of the county wherein the said refusal is . . . made, or of such householder inhabiting in any city, town corporate or market-town, to the mayor, bailiffs or head officer of the said city, town corporate or market-town, if any such refusal shall there be, they shall have full power . . . to send for the same person so refusing: and if the said justice . . . . or head officer shall think the said person meet and convenient to serve as an apprentice [they] shall have power . . . to commit him unto ward, there to remain until he be contented, and will be bound to serve as an apprentice should serve . . .

XXXVI. Provided always . . . that no person shall by force or colour of this statute be bound to enter into any apprenticeship, other than such as be under the age of twenty-one years.

*   *   *

XL Provided always, that this act . . . shall not be prejudicial . . . to the cities of London and Norwich . . . concerning the having or taking of any apprentice . . . but that the citizens and freemen of the same cities shall and may take . . . apprentices there, in such manner and form as they might lawfully have done before the making of this statute.

*   *   *

XLVII ... if any servant or apprentice of husbandry, or of any art, science or occupation aforesaid, unlawfully depart or flee into any other shire ... it shall be lawful to the said justices of peace, and to the said mayors, bailiffs and other head officers of cities and towns corporate, for the time being justices of peace there, to make and grant writs of capias ... to be directed to the sheriffs of the counties, or to other head officers of the places whither such servants or apprentices shall so depart or flee, to take their bodies, returnable before them at what time shall please them ... that they be put in prison till they shall find sufficient surety well and honestly to serve their masters ... from whom they so departed ...

[1] 24 June.

19 An Archbishop's Injunctions for the Province of York, 1571

(*Visitation Articles and Injunctions of the Period of the Reformation, III, 1559–1575*, ed. W. H. Frere (Alcuin Club Collections, XVI, 1910), pp. 276–92)

*Injunctions given by the most reverend father in Christ, Edmund, by the providence of God archbishop of York, primate of England and metropolitan, in his metropolitical visitation of the province of York as well to the clergy as to the laity of the same province, AD 1571
For the clergy.*

6.   Item, you shall not admit to the receiving of the Holy Communion any of your parish which be openly known to live in any notorious sin, as incest, adultery, fornication, drunkenness, much swearing, bawdery, usury, or such like without due penance first done to the satisfaction of the congregation, nor any malicious person that is out of charity, or that has done upon wrong to his neighbour by word or deed, without due reconciliation made first to the party that is wronged or maliced.

*   *   *

21.   Item, you shall from time to time diligently call upon and exhort your parishioners to contribute and give towards the relief of the poor, as they may well spare and specially when you visit them that be sick and make their testaments, and for your own parts also you shall charitably relieve the poor to your ability.

*   *   *

For the laity.

38. Item, that no innkeeper, alehouse keeper, victualler or tippler shall admit or suffer any person or persons in his house or backside to eat, drink, or play at cards, tables, bowls, or other games in time of Common Prayer, preachings, or reading of the homilies on the Sundays or holy days; and that there be no shops set open on Sundays or holy days, nor any butchers or others suffered to sell meat or other things upon the Sundays or holy days in like time of Common Prayer, preaching, or reading of the homilies: and that in any fairs or common markets, falling upon Sundays, there be no showing of any wares before all the morning service and the sermon (if there be any) be done: and if any shall offend in this behalf, the churchwardens and sworn men, after once warning given unto them, shall present them by name unto the ordinary.[1]

* * *

42. Item, that yearly at midsummer, the parson, vicar, or curate and churchwardens shall choose two collectors or more for the relief of the poor of every parish, according to a statute made in that behalf in the fifth year of the queen's majesty's reign, entitled an act for the relief of the poor, and renewed in the last parliament, which collectors shall weekly gather the charitable alms of the parishioners, and distribute the same to the poor where most need shall be, without fraud or partiality; and shall quarterly make unto the parson, vicar, or curate, and churchwardens, a just account thereof in writing: and if any person of ability shall obstinately and frowardly refuse to give reasonably towards the relief of the poor, or shall wilfully discourage others from so charitable a deed, the churchwardens and sworn men shall present to the ordinary every such person so refusing to give, discouraging others, or withdrawing his accustomed alms, that reformation may be had therein.

* * *

47. Item, that the churchwardens and sworn men of every parish shall half yearly from time to time present to the ordinary the names of all such persons of their parish as be either blasphemers of the name of God, great or often swearers, adulterers, fornicators, incestuous persons, or harbourers of women with child which be unmarried, conveying or suffering them to go away before they do any penance or make satisfaction to the congregation, or that be vehemently suspected of such faults, or that be not of good name and fame touching such faults

and crimes, or that be drunkards, or ribalds, or that be malicious, contentious, or uncharitable persons, common slanderers of their neighbours, railers, scolders, or sowers of discord between neighbours: and also all such as be usurers, that is to say, all those that lend money, corn, ware, or other thing, and receive gain therefore over and above that which they lend.

¹ The bishop.

20 Burghley on the State of Trade, 1587

(H. Nicolas, *Memoirs of the Life and Times of Sir Christopher Hatton, K.G.* (1847), pp. 470–2)

To the Lord Chancellor. 12 May 1587
My Lord,
    I am sorry that my pains are such as I cannot attend on you to-day in the Star Chamber, having yesterday, by more zeal of service in the Exchequer Chamber than of regard to my harms, so weakened and pained my leg, as I cannot stir it out of my bed; but this my declaration of my state is to no purpose to occupy your lordship withal. This great matter of the lack of vent, not only of cloths, which presently is the greatest, but of all other English commodities which are restrained from Spain, Portugal, Barbary, France, Flanders, Hamburg, and the States, cannot but in process of time work a great change and dangerous issue to the people of the realm, who, heretofore, in time of outward peace, lived thereby, and without it must either perish for want, or fall into violence to feed and fill their lewd appetites with open spoils of others, which is the fruit of rebellion; but it is in vain to remember this to your lordship, that is so notorious as there need no repetition thereof. The evil being seen and like daily to increase beyond all good remedies, it is our duties that are councillors to think of some remedies in time, before the same become remediless; and briefly the best means of remedy must follow the consideration of the causes of this evil, and so *contrariis contraria curare*. The original cause is apparently the contentions and enmities betwixt the king of Spain and his countries, and her majesty and her countries. The reduction hereof to amity betwixt the princes, and to open traffic according to the ancient treaties of intercourse, would be the sovereign remedy; but this may be wished sooner than speedily effectuated. But yet, seeing there is a signification notified of the good inclination of both the princes, and a great necessity to press them both thereto for the suagement of their people, it were pity any

course should be taken either to hinder this or not to hasten it, which surely in the Low Countries would be done, with whatsoever a reasonable cost may be, to keep the enemy from victuals, and to withstand his enterprises against our friends until this next harvest; and by this proceeding against him, there is no doubt but he will yield to all reasonable conditions meet both for her majesty and her protected friends; otherwise, if the good fortune of our friends do decay, and the enemy recover that which he now lacks, that is store of victuals, he will either underhand make peace with our friends, whom he shall find both weak and timorous, and leave her majesty in danger for recovery of all that she has spent, and in greater charges to maintain her two cautionary towns against the whole Low Countries than two Boulognes were, or else he will, being puffed with pride, make a very Spanish conquest of Holland and Zealand,—a matter terrible to be thought of, but most terrible to be felt. But to insist upon this remedy is as yet in vain, and therefore such other poor helps are to be thought of as may somewhat mitigate the accidents present, and stay the increase thereof, whereof when I do bethink myself, I find no one simple remedy, but rather compounded of divers simples, and to say truly they are but simple remedies, until peace may ensue, which is the sovereign sole medicine of all. To have vent increase, there must be more buyers and shippers than there are, and seeing our merchants say that they cannot have sales sufficient,

1. It were good that the Steelyard men were licensed to trade as they were wont to do, with condition upon good bonds that our merchants adventurers shall have their former liberties in Hamburg.

2. These Steelyard merchants must also have a dispensation to carry a competent number of unwrought cloths that are coarse, which are the cloths whereof the great stay is in the realm.

3. Beside this, the merchant strangers might have a like dispensation for the buying and shipping of a competent number of like white coarse cloths.

4. And if her majesty, for some reasonable time, would abate only 2s upon a cloth, I think there would grow no loss to her majesty, having respect to the multitude of the cloths that should be carried, whereas now the strangers carry few, but upon licences, for which her majesty has no strangers' customs, but English.

5. The strangers also must have liberty to buy in Blackwell Hall, or else there may be a staple set up in Westminster, out of the liberties of the city of London, which, rather than London would suffer, I think they will grant liberty to strangers in respect of the hallage money which they shall lease. Notwithstanding all these shows of remedies, I could

wish that our merchants adventurers were made acquainted herewith, and to be warned, that if they shall not amend the prices to clothiers for their coarse cloths, whereby the clothiers may be reasonably apparent gainers, and that to be put in practice this next week, that then her majesty will give authority to put the former helps in practice. Thus, my good lord, because I understand you are to go to the Court this afternoon, I have thought good to scribble, as I do (lying in pain) these few cogitations, submitting them to a more mature disquisition.

Your lordship's most assured,

W. Burghley.

21 Speeches in the House of Commons on Enclosures, 1601

(*The Journals of all the Parliaments during the Reign of Queen Elizabeth, both of the House of Lords and House of Commons*, collected by Sir Simonds D'Ewes (1682), p. 674)

The points to be considered of in the continuance of statutes were read, and offered still to dispute, whether the Statute of Tillage should be continued.

Mr Johnson said, in the time of dearth, when we made this statute, it was not considered that the hand of God was upon us; and now corn is cheap; if too cheap, the husbandman is undone, whom we must provide for, for he is the staple man of the kingdom. And so after many arguments he concluded the statute to be repealed.

Mr Bacon said, the old commendation of Italy by the poet was, *potens viris atque ubere glebae*,[1] and it stands not with the policy of the state that the wealth of the kingdom should be engrossed into a few graziers' hands. And if you will put in so many provisoes as be desired, you will make it useless. The husbandman is a strong and hardy man, the good footman, which is a chief observation of good warriors, &c. So he concluded the statutes not to be repealed.

Sir Walter Raleigh said, I think this law fit to be repealed; for many poor men are not able to find seed to sow so much as they are bound to plough, which they must do, or incur the penalty of the law. Besides, all nations abound with corn. France offered the queen to serve Ireland with corn for 16 shillings a quarter, which is but two shillings the bushel; if we should sell it so here, the ploughman would be beggared. The Low-Countryman and the Hollander, which never sow corn, has by his industry such plenty that they will serve other nations. The Spaniard, who often wants corn, had we never so much plenty, will not be beholding to the Englishman for it . . . And therefore I think the best course is to set it at liberty, and leave every man free, which is the desire of a true Englishman.

Mr Secretary Cecil said, I do not dwell in the country, I am not acquainted with the plough. But I think that whosoever does not maintain the plough destroys this kingdom . . . My motion therefore shall be, that this law may not be repealed, except former laws may be in force and revived. Say that a glut of corn should be, have we not sufficient remedy by transportation, which is allowable by the policy of all nations? . . . I am sure when warrants go from the Council for levying of men in the countries, and the certificates be returned unto us again, we find the greatest part of them to be ploughmen. And excepting Sir Thomas More's Utopia, or some such feigned commonwealth, you shall never find but the ploughman is chiefly provided for: the neglect whereof will not only bring a general but a particular damage to every man. . . . If we debar tillage, we give scope to the depopulator; and then if the poor being thrust out of their houses go to dwell with others, straight we catch them with the Statute of Inmates; if they wander abroad they are within danger of the Statute of the Poor to be whipped. So by this means undo this statute and you endanger many thousands. *Posterior dies discipulus prioris*.[2] If former times have made us wise to make a law, let these latter times warn us to preserve so good a law.

[1] Mighty in arms and wealth of soil.
[2] The following day is the pupil of the preceding.

22 Administration of the Statute of Artificers, 1605–6

(*Quarter Sessions Records*, ed. J. C. Atkinson (North Riding Record Society, County of York, I, 1884), pp. 1–38)

[*Presented by the jury*][1]
Thirsk. 11 April 1605

Wilfrid Fewster of Byland, for retaining in his service Christopher Black without the licence or certificate of the said Black's late master.

Stokesley. 9 July 1605

John Turner, late servant to John Wells of Heworth, for leaving his service before his term, without cause for it duly assigned before some justice.

Seth Stott, constable of Huntington, for permitting the said John Turner to stay in the said village, notwithstanding the above offence.

Richmond. 11 July 1605

Will. Nelson of Northallerton, indicted for using the art and mystery of a glover, applies for copy &c. [Bound by recognisances in 10*l* to present his traverse].[2]

Richmond. 4 October 1605

Will. Nelson also presents himself, pleads not guilty, and is acquitted by the same jury on the ground that he proves, producing indenture dated 37 Elizabeth, his apprenticeship to Anthony Walker of Northallerton, to whom he served as apprentice for seven years in right of which &c. He is therefore discharged.

Thirsk. 17 January 1606

John Bulmer of West Cottam, husbandman, for hiring servants without recording their names and salaries before the chief constable, *contra formam statuti* &c.; and also Rob. Harrison and Will. Keldell, both of the same, for the like.

Thirsk. 29 April 1606

Tho. Surr and Will. Hunter of Huton-super-Darwent, labourers, *quod usi sunt sive exercuerunt misterium sive artem laniatoris*,[3] Angl. butcher's trade, not having served any apprenticeship to the same.

Tho. Hungate of Bulmer, gentleman, for keeping in his service, without any certificate one Ursula Fitchet, from Martinmas[4] last till now—the said Ursula being a duly contracted and hired servant with Tho. Bamburgh of Cramb, and although she, the said Ursula, being brought on a warrant before Sir Will. Bamburgh, knight, J.P., owned the contract and was ordered to return to her former service.

[Orders made].

Forasmuch as Rob. Hungate, esquire, J.P., did direct his warrant of late to [blank], constable of Clifton, commanding him thereby to bring Tho. Goodrick of Clifton before him to answer . . . for putting away his servant contrary, &c. . . . which warrant the said constable did not execute . . . therefore a warrant be made to bring the said constable, Goodrick, and his servant . . . to be bound to appear at the next six weeks' sessions &c.

[1] All the presentments made at the sessions held between April 1605 and April 1606 are included.
[2] See the next entry.
[3] Because they used or exercised the employment or trade of a butcher.
[4] 11 November.

23 Debate on the Scarcity of Money, 1621

(*Journals of the House of Commons*, I, 1547–1628, pp. 527–8)

26 February 1621

Sir Edw. Sandys remembers his majesty's recommendation to this House, of the scarcity of money. To search both into the causes and remedies.

The necessity of it pressing. The poor man's labour, his inheritance. The clothier's looms laid down, by 200 in town, wherein one loom maintained 40 persons. The want of money the cause of it. A pitiful and fearful case. *Bellum rusticorum*[1] in Germany.

The farmer not able to pay his rent: forfeits his lease, covenants, bonds: has corn and cattle enough, but can get no money at the low prices. Fairs and markets at a stand. The case of the gentleman, and nobleman, tradesmen of cities, &c. How supply to the king, for matters abroad, or distempers at home?

Sir Edw. Mountague, accordant. To have Sir Edw. Sandys now deliver what he knows herein.

Sir Jo. Davis. Of great consequence and difficulty. For a select subcommittee.

Sir Dudley Digges. This already committed to the Committee for Grievances. To have all, out of all parts, give in their reasons of the cause thereof; and so for the remedies. Then a sub-committee.

Mr Secretary, accordant.

Mr Delliverge. Not 200 looms, not now 200. The merchants there brought in heretofore 20,000*l* per annum, in bullion, now, not sufficient to pay the king his impositions, and &c.

Sir Tho. Row. To send for some merchants of the East India, Spanish, and Turkey, Company; who best can inform, how this scarcity of money grows.

Sir Wm. Herricke. Heretofore 2,000,000*l* per annum coined at the mint; since the East India Company up, little. 50 or 60,000*l* per annum carried into Poland.

Patent of leaf gold, and of silver and gold lace. Much making of plate alleged by some to be a cause; but, upon search, found that these last seven years of the king, less made than in the last seven years of the queen.

Thinks well, it is in plate; for, if it were in money, would be transported. The show of the goldsmiths' shops in Cheapside the greatest in Christendom: now above twenty shops set up. Will, at a committee, discover the true causes; and wishes others will answer him there.

Mr Glanvyle. This the principal thing recommended by his majesty. To have this recommended to the grand committee, with some precedency. Moves, where many of the House, of the East India Company, may, in his speech, discover, whether he be of that, or any other of those companies, now questioned.

Robert Gynner, and all that can give intelligence, to be sent for, to inform the grand committee.

Sir Edw. Coke. This the next cause, next God's: commended by his majesty. Has considered, both of the causes and remedies: will only touch some heads. *Duo, quae principatus conservant, et augent; milites, et pecunia.*[2] No life, in peace or war, without money: all beggars without it.

That coined between 1 Eliz. and 16 Jac. in silver, nine million and a half: 161,000*l* and odd, per annum.

Seven heads, as causes. 1. The goldsmiths melting the king's coin into plate. This against law; which against groats, and 2*d.* Now 12*d* which they take to be out of that law.

2. Gilding, &c.

3. Great loss by exchange. Dearer there, than here; which will ever carry away our company.

4. The East India Company. Ever since that up, no silver to the mint. The surer argument from the cause. Never leave before to any to carry out any money. 100,000*l* per annum licence: intercept it, before it comes hither: which they prevent. Is none of the East India Company.

The state in a consumption, must be helped. A leak which must be stopped. The goods imported, more than imported. [sic].

6. The French wines, which brought in in great quantities.

7. The patent of making gold and silver lace of our bullion, and prohibiting the bringing any. Unfit, any such thing should be prohibited, without act of parliament; because, if we prohibit here, others will do beyond seas. Will, at the committee, apply the remedies.

Mr Secretary adds, importation of great store of cattle into England; for which great store of money carried into Ireland from hence.

Sir Jo. Strangeways, shows of the 160*l* [sic] per annum, coined yearly, from 1 Eliz. to 16 Eliz.—100,000*l* per annum by the East India Company; 40,000*l* per annum by the patentees of gold and silver lace.

100,000 cattle per annum brought out of Ireland; for which money only; and will take no commodity for it, but money.

Sir Edw. Sackville. That Sir Edw. Sandys may now speak his knowledge.

Sir Edw. Sandys. That much spoken, which he intended. Adds, the consumption of money here—three heads. 1. Not importing money. 2. Exportation of it; which not possible to observe, till trade balanced. 3. Consuming it, when here. A great mass of silver money heretofore yearly brought into England. West Indies, the fountain; Spain, the receipt and river, from whence flows into all parts.

About 100,000*l* per annum usually brought in; now nothing. 120,000*l* per annum brought in in tobacco; a million lost that way, since the king's reign.

That a policy of all other states, not to suffer any importation of commodities, where they have of their own, till theirs sold. Gascoigne wine in Rochelle:— Spain. That 6,000 quarters of grain now in one port, imported *aliunde*;[3] for which they carry away money, for the most part.

Mr Towerson. That he an East India merchant. To have those merchants warned, of other companies, which are not free of the East India Company.

Mr Crew. Many confluences of causes in this disease. East India Company, which carries out.

The wools of England, the mine of this kingdom: now not half the cloths exported, which heretofore. Pretermitted custom, &c. Will not meddle with the right; but as it hinders the king's profit, and burdens the subject.

We in hand, first to sweep the House of monopolies, and patents, with proclamations, &c.

2. To see how the want of money grows.

3. To beautify the kingdom; as, particularly, with the bills of grace.

Sir H. Poole. That much of our coin transported into Scotland. Not to hinder consolidation of both kingdoms; but to have a care, that our money, being there, may not be transported from thence.

Sir D. Digges. That one of the East India Company. That, for the ceasing of the mint, since the East India Company established; that the reason of it, the want of a true proportion and valuation between the mint here, and beyond sea. In Henry VII a tax of the mint through all countries in Christendom. That this fittest for a committee, where men may go by degrees.

Master of the Wards. Speaks upon knowledge. Offers a way of satisfaction, not by dispute, but by record. A want of money: trade sick. To have one of the day for grievances, particularly for trade. The Customers books will show it. By them to see what the East India—have imported, and exported; for what have not carried out in commodity, must needs be in money. The impost upon the French wines. Three times as much wine now imported, as then; and export not a third of what we did.

For Ireland; will help, a direct note, what has been imported into England out of Ireland, for a year or two last past.

Moves, one special day for the decay of trade.

Sir Edw. Giles. That the East India Company, if carries not out of England, yet meets Spanish money by the way: now no Spanish money brought in. Much corn imported to London, and other parts, and sold there. 100,000*l* per annum, many years, bestowed for corn in Devonshire. That more Irish beef, and other provisions, in the west parts, than of English.

Sir Tho. Row. That one of the East India Company. That the East India Company carries not out of Europe 30,000*l* per annum, money merchandize. A due proportion ought to be between gold and silver. The standard of silver not alike here with other countries. The Dutch raise and fall their money, at their pleasure. Any, that shall bring in money here, shall lose eight per cent.

Sir Wm. Cope. Two causes of emptiness: one a leak, where it may run out. That 12 millions brought in, in the queen's time, by gentlemen of worth: [which] the spring that furnished the kingdom.

That, if we have not some means to fetch in money, doubts, all the rest will not do it.

That ambassadors, bringing in no money hither, peradventure carry out great quantities, both of gold and silver.

Sir Ro. Phillips moves for a set time for this business; and for merchants, and custom books, to be sent for.

Mr Bateman, an East India merchant, moves, the East India books may also be viewed.

Sir Charles Mountague. To have the East India merchants carry out [no] Spanish money, but only English. That one [merchant], viz. . . . . . . carries out yearly 70,000*l* per [annum]—8*s* 6*d* difference in the value of our gold and silver. To have these considered of.

Sir Tho. Lowe. That little corn now imported; but, to restrain it totally, may be dangerous, for a dearth.

Sir Wm. Strowde. That a question about this in the first parliament Jac. 100,000*l* per annum for lawns,[4] and cobweb lawn. Is against the restraint of the importation of corn. England has never two years provision beforehand. The farmers' estate will not suffer it.

Sir Tho. Wentworth moves, this business may be treated of, Tuesday and Thursday; and the committee for privileges, which is particular, in another place.

Mr Brooke, accordant. And the grand committee to appoint a sub-committee, to consider of matter of trade. To see the custom books. Not to have the East India books sent for in. And this to be upon Thursday next.

This consideration, for money, to be referred to the grand committee of the whole House. Every Tuesday to be the day; and to begin to-morrow.

The committee to give some direction for perusing the custom books, and any other books, they shall think fit; and all merchants, and others, to be sent for, which the committee shall think fit may inform them.

¹ Peasants' war.
² Two things which preserve and augment states, soldiers and money.
³ From elsewhere.
⁴ Fine linen.

24 Francis Bacon on Riches, 1625

(*The Essays or Counsels, Civil and Moral, of Francis Lord Verulam, Viscount St. Alban,* 1625 (1971), pp. 205–11)

Of Riches

I cannot call riches better than the baggage of virtue. The Roman word is better, *impedimenta*. For as the baggage is to an army, so is riches to virtue. It cannot be spared nor left behind, but it hinders the march; yea and the care of it sometimes loses or disturbs the victory. Of great riches there is no real use, except it be in the distribution; the rest is but conceit. So says Solomon, 'Where much is, there are many to consume it; and what has the owner but the sight of it with his eyes?' The personal fruition in any man cannot reach to feel great riches: there is a custody of them; or a power of dole and donative of them; or a fame of them; but no solid use to the owner. Do you not see what feigned prices are set upon little stones and rarities? And what works of ostentation are undertaken, because there might seem to be some use of great riches? But then you will say, they may be of use to buy men out of dangers or troubles. As Solomon says, 'Riches are as a strong hold, in the imagination of the rich man.' But this is excellently expressed, that it is in imagination, and not always in fact. For certainly great riches have sold more men than they have bought out. Seek not proud riches, but such as you may get justly, use soberly, distribute cheerfully, and leave contentedly. Yet have no abstract nor friarly contempt of them. But distinguish, as Cicero says well of Rabirius

Posthumus, *In studio rei amplificandae apparebat, non avaritiae praedam, sed instrumentum bonitati quaeri.*[1] Hearken also to Solomon, and beware of hasty gathering of riches; *Qui festinat ad divitias, non erit insons.*[2]

The poets feign, that when Plutus (which is Riches) is sent from Jupiter, he limps and goes slowly; but when he is sent from Pluto, he runs and is swift of foot. Meaning that riches got by good means and just labour pace slowly; but when they come by the death of others (as by the course of inheritance, testaments, and the like), they come tumbling upon a man. But it mought be applied likewise to Pluto, taking him for the devil. For when riches come from the devil (as by fraud and oppression and unjust means), they come upon speed. The ways to enrich are many, and most of them foul. Parsimony is one of the best, and yet is not innocent; for it withholds men from works of liberality and charity. The improvement of the ground is the most natural obtaining of riches; for it is our great mother's blessing, the earth's; but it is slow. And yet where men of great wealth do stoop to husbandry, it multiplies riches exceedingly. I knew a nobleman in England, that had the greatest audits of any man in my time; a great grazier, a great sheep-master, a great timber man, a great collier, a great corn-master, a great lead-man, and so of iron, and a number of the like points of husbandry. So as the earth seemed a sea to him, in respect of the perpetual importation.

It was truly observed by one, that himself came very hardly to a little riches, and very easily to great riches. For when a man's stock is come to that, that he can expect the prime of markets, and overcome those bargains which for their greatness are few men's money, and be partner in the industries of younger men, he cannot but increase mainly.

The gains of ordinary trades and vocations are honest; and furthered by two things chiefly; by diligence, and by a good name for good and fair dealing. But the gains of bargains are of a more doubtful nature; when men shall wait upon others' necessity, broke by servants and instruments to draw them on, put off others cunningly that would be better chapmen, and the like practices, which are crafty and naught. As for the chopping of bargains, when a man buys not to hold but to sell over again, that commonly grinds double, both upon the seller and upon the buyer. Sharings do greatly enrich, if the hands be well chosen that are trusted. Usury is the certainest means of gain, though one of the worst; as that whereby a man does eat his bread *in sudore vultus alieni,*[3] and besides, does plough upon Sundays. But yet certain though it be, it has flaws; for that the scriveners and brokers do value unsound men to serve their own turn. The fortune in being the first in an invention or in a privilege, does cause sometimes a wonderful overgrowth in riches; as it was with the first sugar man in the Canaries. Therefore if a man can play the true logician, to have as well judgment as invention, he may do great matters; especially if the times be fit. He that rests upon gains certain, shall hardly grow to great riches; and he that puts all upon adventures, does oftentimes break and come to poverty: it is good therefore to guard adventures with certainties, that may uphold losses. Monopolies, and coemption of wares for re-sale, where they are not restrained, are great means to enrich; especially if the party have intelligence what things are like to come into request, and so store himself beforehand. Riches got by service, though it be of the best rise, yet when they are got by flattery, feeding humours, and other servile conditions, they may be placed amongst the worst. As for fishing for testaments and executorships (as Tacitus says of Seneca, *testamenta et orbos tamquam indagine capi*),[4] it is yet worse; by how much men submit themselves to meaner persons than in service.

Believe not much them that seem to despise riches; for they despise them that despair of them; and none worse when they come to them. Be not penny-wise; riches have wings, and sometimes they fly away of themselves, sometimes they must be set flying to bring in more. Men leave their riches either to their kindred, or to the public; and moderate portions prosper best in both. A great state left to an heir, is as a lure to all the birds of prey round about to seize on him, if he be not the better stablished in years and judgment. Likewise glorious gifts and foundations are like sacrifices without salt; and but the painted sepulchres of alms, which soon will putrefy and corrupt inwardly. Therefore measure not thine advancements by quantity, but frame them by measure: and defer not charities till death; for, certainly, if a man weigh it rightly, he that does so is rather liberal of another man's than of his own.

[1] In the acquisition of wealth he sought not so much to gratify his avarice, as to find an outlet for the kindness of his heart.
[2] A man in a hurry to riches will not be guiltless.
[3] In the sweat of another's brow.
[4] He entices into his snares the childless and their legacies.

25 Mun on Trade and Treasure, Late 1620s

(Thomas Mun, *England's Treasure by Foreign Trade*, 1664, printed in *Early English Tracts on Commerce*, ed. J. R. McCulloch (1856, 1952), pp. 125–34, 209)

The means to enrich this kingdom, and to increase our treasure

Although a kingdom may be enriched by gifts received, or by purchase taken from some other nations, yet these are things uncertain and of small consideration when they happen. The ordinary means therefore to increase our wealth and treasure is by foreign trade, wherein we must ever observe this rule; to sell more to strangers yearly than we consume of theirs in value. For suppose that when this kingdom is plentifully served with the cloth, lead, tin, iron, fish and other native commodities, we do yearly export the overplus to foreign countries to the value of twenty two hundred thousand pounds; by which means we are enabled beyond the seas to buy and bring in foreign wares for our use and consumption, to the value of twenty hundred thousand pounds; by this order duly kept in our trading, we may rest assured that the kingdom shall be enriched yearly two hundred thousand pounds, which must be brought to us in so much treasure; because that part of our stock which is not returned to us in wares must necessarily be brought home in treasure . . .

The particular ways and means to increase the exportation of our commodities, and to decrease our consumption of foreign wares

The revenue or stock of a kingdom by which it is provided of foreign wares is either natural or artificial. The natural wealth is so much only as can be spared from our own use and necessities to be exported unto strangers. The artificial consists in our manufactures and industrious trading with foreign commodities, concerning which I will set down such particulars as may serve for the cause we have in hand.

First, although this realm be already exceeding rich by nature, yet might it be much increased by laying the waste grounds (which are infinite) into such employments as should no way hinder the present revenues of other manured lands, but hereby to supply ourselves and prevent the importations of hemp, flax, cordage, tobacco, and divers other things which now we fetch from strangers to our great impoverishing.

2 We may likewise diminish our importations, if we would soberly refrain from excessive consumption of foreign wares in our diet and

raiment, with such often change of fashions as is used, so much the more to increase the waste and charge; which vices at this present are more notorious amongst us than in former ages . . .

3 In our exportations we must not only regard our own superfluities, but also we must consider our neighbours' necessities, that so upon the wares which they cannot want, nor yet be furnished thereof elsewhere, we may (besides the vent of the materials) gain so much of the manufacture as we can, and also endeavour to sell them dear, so far forth as the high price cause not a less vent in the quantity. But the superfluity of our commodities which strangers use, and may also have the same from other nations, or may abate their vent by the use of some such like wares from other places, and with little inconvenience; we must in this case strive to sell as cheap as possible we can, rather than to lose the utterance of such wares.

* * *

4 The value of our exportations likewise may be much advanced when we perform it ourselves in our own ships, for then we get only not the price of our wares as they are worth here, but also the merchants' gains, the charges of insurance, and freight to carry them beyond the seas . . .

5 The frugal expending likewise of our own natural wealth might advance much yearly to be exported unto strangers . . .

6 The fishing in his majesty's seas of England, Scotland and Ireland is our natural wealth, and would cost nothing but labour, which the Dutch bestow willingly, and thereby draw yearly a very great profit to themselves by serving many places of Christendom with our fish, for which they return and supply their wants both of foreign wares and money, besides the multitude of mariners and shipping, which hereby are maintained . . .

7 A staple or magazine for foreign corn, indigo, spices, raw-silks, cotton wool or any other commodity whatsoever, to be imported will increase shipping, trade, treasure, and the king's customs, by exporting them again where need shall require, which course of trading has been the chief means to raise Venice, Genoa, the Low Countries, with some others; and for such a purpose England stands most commodiously, wanting nothing to this performance but our own diligence and endeavour.

8 Also we ought to esteem and cherish those trades which we have in remote or far countries, for besides the increase of shipping and mariners thereby, the wares also sent thither and received from thence

are far more profitable unto the kingdom than by our trades near at hand ...

*　　*　　*

9   It would be very beneficial to export money as well as wares, being done in trade only, it would increase our treasure ...

10   It were policy and profit for the state to suffer manufactures made of foreign materials to be exported custom-free, as velvets and all other wrought silks, fustians, thrown silks and the like, it would employ very many poor people, and much increase the value of our stock yearly issued into other countries, and it would (for this purpose) cause the more foreign materials to be brought in, to the improvement of his majesty's customs ...

11   It is needful also not to charge the native commodities with too great customs, lest by endearing them to the strangers' use, it hinder their vent. And especially foreign wares brought in to be transported again should be favoured, for otherwise that manner of trading (so much importing the good of the commonwealth) cannot prosper nor subsist. But the consumption of such foreign wares in the realm may be the more charged, which will turn to the profit of the kingdom in the balance of the trade, and thereby also enable the king to lay up the more treasure out of his yearly incomes ...

12   Lastly, in all things we must endeavour to make the most we can of our own, whether it be natural or artificial. And forasmuch as the people which live by the arts are far more in number than they who are masters of the fruits, we ought the more carefully to maintain those endeavours of the multitude, in whom does consist the greatest strength and riches both of king and kingdom: for where the people are many, and the arts good, there the traffic must be great, and the country rich ... we know that our own natural wares do not yield us so much profit as our industry. For iron ore in the mines is of no great worth, when it is compared with the employment and advantage it yields being digged, tried, transported, bought, sold, cast into ordnance, muskets, and many other instruments of war for offence and defence, wrought into anchors, bolts, spikes, nails and the like, for the use of ships, houses, carts, coaches, ploughs and other instruments for tillage. Compare our fleece-wools with our cloth, which requires shearing, washing, carding, spinning, weaving, fulling, dyeing, dressing and other trimmings, and we shall find these arts more profitable than the natural wealth ...

*　　*　　*

Behold then the true form and worth of foreign trade, which is, the great revenue of the king, the honour of the kingdom, the noble profession of the merchant, the school of our arts, the supply of our wants, the employment of our poor, the improvement of our lands, the nursery of our mariners, the walls of the kingdom, the means of our treasure, the sinews of our wars, the terror of our enemies. For all which great and weighty reasons, do so many well governed states highly countenance the profession, and carefully cherish the action, not only with policy to increase it, but also with power to protect it from all foreign injuries: because they know it is a principal in reason of state to maintain and defend that which does support them and their estates.

26 Derbyshire Justices on their Proceedings, 1631

(P.R.O. State Papers Domestic, Charles I, CCII, 54)

Wirksworth wapentake
To Francis Bradshaw, esq., High Sheriff of the County of Derby. [October ?, 1631]

Sir, In pursuit of the orders and directions given us in command as well by the printed book as also by several letters sent unto us from the right honourable the lords of her majesty's most honourable Privy Council, we, whose names are hereunder written, having within our allotment the wapentake or hundred of Wirksworth, have had monthly meetings within the said hundred and have summoned both the high constable, petty constables, churchwardens, and overseers of the poor within that division and hundred to appear before us.

1. And first we have made diligent inquiry how all the said officers and others have done their duties in execution of the laws mentioned in the commission, and what persons have offended against any of them, and punished such as we have found faulty.

2. We have taken care that the lords and parishioners of every town relieve the poor thereof, and they are not suffered to straggle or beg up and down either in their parishes or elsewhere. But such poor as have transgressed have been punished according to law, and the impotent poor there are carefully relieved. We have also taken especial care that both the stewards of leets and ourselves in particular have taken care for the reformation of abuses in bakers, alehouse-keepers, breaking of assize, forestallers and regrators, against tradesmen of all sorts for selling with underweight, and have made search in market towns and other places and taken away and burned very many false weights

and measures, and taken order for the punishing of the said offenders.

3. We have made special inquiry of such poor children as are fit to be bound apprentices to husbandry and otherwise, and of such as are fit to take apprentices, and therein we have taken such course as by law is required. And we find none refuse to take apprentices, being thereunto required.

4. We do not find upon our inquiry that the statute for labourers and ordering of wages is deluded, and the common fashion of none essoyning of course is restrained.

5. The weekly taxations for relief of the poor in these times of scarcity is raised to higher rates, and we have further observed the course appointed in the fifth article.

6. We have taken order the petty constables within our said division are chosen of the ablest parishioners.

7. Watches in the night and warding by day are appointed in every town for apprehension of rogues and for good order, and we have taken order to punish such as we have found faulty.

8. We have taken care that the high constable does his duty in presenting to us the defaults of the petty constables for not punishing the rogues and in presenting to us the defaulters.

9. We find none presented to us that live out of service and refuse to work for reasonable wages.

10. We have one house of correction at Ashborn within our wapentake, which is near the town prison, where such as are committed are kept to work.

11. We have punished several persons for harbouring rogues in their barns and outhouses, and have observed the further directions of the 11th article.

12. We have had care to see that all defects and defaults in the amending of highways be redressed, and the defaulters have been presented to the next quarter sessions and punished.

And as touching their lordships' letters and orders directed concerning corn and enclosures, we do at our monthly meetings take a strict account that the former orders therein taken by us in pursuit thereof be duly observed and put in execution, and particularly none sell such corn (as they are appointed to sell out of the market) but to the poor of the said parish. And neither the petty constable nor any other officer can (as they inform us) present any engrossers of corn, etc., or forestallers of markets.

The prices of corn (considering the times) are not on our markets in our opinion unreasonable, but are as follow, viz., wheat for the strike 5s, four peck making a strike, rye 4s, barley 3s 4d, malt 5s, peas 4s, oats 2s 6d.

We have made especial inquiry touching enclosures made within these two years, but find very few within our division, for the most of our wapentake has been long since enclosed. Howsoever some few have been presented, which we have commanded to throw down, and have stayed the proceedings of such enclosures as have been lately begun and are not finished.

We have no maltmakers in this wapentake but for their own use.

We have put down a full third part of all the alehouses within this wapentake; yet there are so great a multitude of poor miners within this wapentake that we are enforced to leave more alehousekeepers than otherwise we would.

We have taken order for the binding all cooks, alehousekeepers, victuallers and butchers within this hundred that they neither dress nor suffer to be dressed or eaten any flesh during the time of Lent or other days prohibited, and our recognizances to that purpose do remain with the clerk of the peace, to be by him certified according to the statute.

John Fitzherbert.
Chr. Fulwood.

27 Concern over the Corn Supply and Disorder, 1631

(Privy Council Register, VI, f. 345, printed in E. M. Leonard, *The Early History of English Poor Relief* (Cambridge, 1900), pp. 338–9)

Whereas we have been made acquainted with a letter written by John Wildbore, a minister in and about Tinwell within that county,[1] to a friend of his here, wherein after some mention by him made of the present want and misery sustained by the poorer sort in those parts through the dearth of corn and the want of work, he does advertize in particular some speeches uttered by a shoemaker of Uppingham (whose name we find not) tending to the stirring up of the poor thereabout to a mutiny and insurrection; which information was as follows, *in hæc verba*: "Hearest thou?" said a shoemaker of Uppingham to a poor man of Liddington, "If thou wilt be secret I will make a motion to thee." "What is your motion?" said the other. Then said the shoemaker, "The poor men of Okeham have sent to us poor men of Uppingham, and if you poor men of Liddington will join with us, we will rise, and the poor of Okeham say they can have all the armour of the country in their power within half an hour, and in faith (said he) we will rifle the churls." Upon consideration had thereof, however, this board is not easily credulous of light reports nor apt to take impression from the vain speeches or ejaculations of some mean and contemptible persons; yet because it sorts well with the care and providence of a state to prevent all occasions which ill-affected persons may otherwise lay hold of under pretence and colour of the necessity of the time, we have thought good hereby to will and require you, the deputy lieuts. and justices of peace next adjoining, forthwith to apprehend and take a more particular examination as well of the said shoemaker as of such others as you shall think fit concerning the advertizement aforesaid; and that you take especial care that the arms of that county in and about those parts be safely disposed of; and likewise (which is indeed most considerable and the best means to prevent all disorders in this kind) that you deal effectually in causing the market to be well supplied with corn and the poor to be served at reasonable prices and set on work by those of the richer sort, and by raising of stock to relieve and set them on work according to the laws. All which we recommend to your especial care, and require an account from you of your doings and proceedings herein with all convenient expedition.

¹ Rutland.

28 Complaint over Forestalling, 1648

(*Quarter Sessions Records for the County Palatine of Chester, 1559–1760*, eds. J. H. E. Bennett and J. C. Dewhurst (Record Society of Lancashire and Cheshire, 1940), p. 130)

[*Letter from the Overseers of the market at Middlewich.*]

Brother Yates, the pitiful complaint of the poor in our town for the scarcity and want of bread moves us that are overseers of the market to do our best endeavour to remedy it. Our request is to you and the rest of our neighbours that are now at Nantwich, that you will be pleased to move the gentlemen that some course may be taken that corn may come to the market and not be sold privately at home to breadbakers and none else, and so the poor are forced to have it upon their terms or else starve. Good Brother Yates neglect it not, for yesterday there came 3 load of corn to John Venables and not a corn to the market, in so much that the poor were very harsh with us and thought it to be our fault . . .

John Beckett, Edward Lowe
Middlewich, 12 July 1648

[Endorsed:] To Mr William Yates or in his absence to Mr John Whittingham or any of the rest of our neighbours.

29 The Protestant Ethic, 1673

(Richard Baxter, *A Christian Directory: or a Summ of Practical Theologie and Cases of Conscience*, 1673, printed in M. J. Kitch, *Capitalism and the Reformation* (1967), pp. 156–8)

Every man that is able, must be steadily and ordinarily employed in such work as is serviceable to God, and to the common good. . . . Everyone that is a member of a church or commonwealth must employ their parts to the utmost for the good of the church and commonwealth, public service is God's greatest service. To neglect this, and to say, I will pray and meditate, is as if your servant should refuse your greatest work, and to tie himself to some lesser easy part; and God has commanded you some way or another to labour for your daily bread, and not to live as drones on the sweat of others only. Innocent Adam was put into the Garden of Eden to dress it, and fallen man must eat his bread in the sweat of his brow (Genesis 3: 19). And he that will not work must be forbidden to eat (2 Thes. 3: 6, 10 and 12). And indeed, it is necessary for ourselves, for the health of our bodies, which will grow diseased with idleness. And for the health of our souls, which will fail if the body fail. And man in flesh must have work for his body as well as his soul. And he that will do nothing but pray and meditate, it's like will (by sickness or melancholy) be disabled ere long to pray or meditate, unless he have a body extraordinary strong . . .

It gloryeth God, by showing the excellency of faith, when we contemn the riches and honour of the world, and live above the worldling's life, accounting that a despicable thing, which he accounts his happiness, and loses his soul for . . . When seeming Christians are worldly and ambitious as others, and make as great matter of the gain, and wealth and honour, it shows that they do but cover the base and sordid spirit of worldlings, with the visor of the Christian name . . .

As labour is thus necessary so understand how needful a state a calling is, for the right performance of your labours. A calling is a stated course of labour. This is very needful for these reasons: (1) Out of a calling a man's labours are but occasional or inconstant, so more time is spent in idleness than labour; (2) A man is best skilled in that which he is used to; (3) And he will be best provided for it with instruments and necessaries; (4) Therefore he does it better than he could do any other work, and so wrongs not others, but attains more the ends of his labour; (5) And he does it more easily, when a man unused and unskilled and unfurnished, toils himself much in doing little; (6) And he will do his work more orderly, when another is in continual confusion, and his business knows not its time and place, but one part contradicts another. Therefore some certain calling or trade of life is best for everyman ...

The first and principal thing to be intended in the choice of a trade or calling for yourselves or children is the service of God, and the public good. And, therefore, *ceteris paribus*, that calling which most conduces to the public good is to be preferred. The callings most useful to the public good are the magistrate, the pastor, the teacher of the church, schoolmaster, physician, lawyer, etc., husbandmen (ploughmen, graziers and shepherds); and next to them are mariners, clothiers, booksellers, tailors and such others that are employed about things most necessary to mankind. And some callings are employed about matters of so little use, as tobacco-sellers, lace-sellers, feather-makers, periwig-makers, and many more such, that he that may choose better should be loath to take up with one of these, though possibly in itself it may be lawful. It is a great satisfaction to an honest mind, to spend his life in doing the greatest good he can, and a prison and a constant calamity, to be tied to spend one's life in doing little good at all to others, though he should grow rich by it ...

If thou be called to the poorest laborious calling, do not carnally murmur at it, because it is wearisome to the flesh, nor imagine that God accepts the less of thy work and thee. But cheerfully follow it, and make it the matter of thy pleasure and joy that thou art still in thy heavenly master's services, though it be the lowest thing. And that He who knows what is best for thee, has chosen this for thy good, and tries and values thy obedience to Him the more, by how much the meaner work thou stoopest to at His command. But see that thou do it all in obedience to God, and not merely for thy own necessity. Thus every servant must serve the Lord, in serving their master, and from God expect their chief reward ...

In doing good to others we do good to ourselves: because we are living members of Christ's body, and by love and communion feel their joys, as well as pains.

Good works are a comfortable evidence that faith is sincere, and that the heart dissembles not with God.

Good works are much to the honour of religion, and consequently of God, and much tend to men's conviction, conversion and salvation.

30 Plenty and the Will to Work, 1683

(John Houghton, *A Collection for the Improvement of Husbandry and Trade* (1727 ed.), IV, pp. 382–5)

Tuesday, June 16. 1683. Num. VI

. . . An offer to make it appear that this kingdom will thrive more, and the manufacturers live better when provisions are dear, than cheap . . .
Provisions, by reason of our two last hard winters and our dry summer, being risen to great price which causes much complaint among the generality of people, I do think it a very reasonable thing for me to endeavour to stifle the same, by showing that dearness is so far from being a prejudice to the nation, that it is rather to be wished for . . .

In order to the well understanding of this, I will consider the round or wheel some things are apt to take, and that quickly, if not retarded; for instance, plenty causes laziness, that scarcity, that dearness, that industry, and that plenty.

Now this wheel may be made to move swiftly or slowly, according to the managements of the superior ranks of people.

For example. If there be of food a-plenty, laziness follows it, and this laziness may be prolonged, if so be that the people be compelled to an extraordinary savingness, or by fashion or example, be beaten off or hindered from those things that are wont to make great consumptions: for instance, should they be compelled to eat only brown bread, drink small beer or water, keep near their own homes, so that coach horses and saddle horses, that devour corn, should grow almost useless; should finery, and all superfluous things be beaten out of countenance; for then the generality of people will not work, because they can live without it. This is so plain, that I think it is visible to everybody: but however, that none may have an excuse, I pray consider the gentry, they spend their time in recreations, because they have enough, they say to their souls, Soul, take thy rest, for thou hast much treasure laid up for many years, eat, drink, and be merry. Whereas he that by misfortune, or other ways, through scarcity comes to be pinched, immediately strives for some public office, or other employment; 'tis few that love to starve.

S

The rich merchant or tradesman commonly knocks off, and reckons it his glory to be a gentleman: and the generality of poor manufacturers believe they shall never be worth ten pounds, therefore they seldom strive to get ten shillings beforehand, and if so be they can provide for themselves sufficient to maintain their manner of living by working only three days in the week, they will never work four days; they say, if by sickness they should come to want, the parish is bound to find them: and for the beggar, he cries, it is hard, if I mind my business (especially in London) if I do not get eighteen pence a day by begging (besides having the liberty to see any friend or show, and being but very little at any man's control) it is a hard case; why then should I work hard all day, be tied to one place, and at the checks and chiding, perhaps, of a humoursome taskmaster? I see no reason, I will beg on still, unless the severe execution of a hard law, or the decay of my masters' abilities or charity shall hinder me. And thus they go on.

This I question not but will be granted by all, unless about the manufacturers. But there, that I may not be thought to dream, it will appear, if it be asked of the generality of those men that employ journeymen or day-servants, and if it be put home to them, whether they do not think that their servants one with another, could in cheap times do as much work in three days as ordinarily they do in a week, they would few of them deny it. I am sure several have confessed it to me, particularly when the frame-work knitters, or makers of silk-stockings had a great price for their work, they have been observed seldom to work on Mondays and Tuesdays, but to spend most of that time at the alehouse and nine-pins; nay, almost the whole company entered into a confederacy not to work for a month together, that thereby they might keep up their prices: this was, as I take it, about four or five year ago, and there is hardly any of their company that were then in being, will deny it. The weavers, it is common with them to be drunk on Monday, to have their heads ache on Tuesday, and their tools out of order on Wednesday. As for the shoemakers, they will rather be hanged than not remember St. Crispin on Monday, and it commonly holds as long as they have a penny of money or pennyworth of credit; and very often, especially the good and quick workmen, begin their week's work on Friday morning, or perhaps evening, but then work on till Sunday morning; and when their credit is run so far that it will go no farther, they pack up St. Hugh's bones and march to some other town in England, there to set up afresh. The style the painters give themselves is, honest drunken curs; they often work at heaving of glass, lifting of pewter, emptying of cellars, and such like.

And thus if I would, I could give you such true accounts of most other professions that live by labour; but this, and more than this may anybody know, that will but give themselves a little diversion to look into the public houses of most of the out parts of the City, and the country towns will be found in proportion but little better.

I think, by a consideration of what I have said, it will sufficiently be granted, that plenty causes laziness . . .

31 A Wages Assessment, 1684

(Printed in T. S. Willan, 'A Bedfordshire Wage Assessment of 1684' (Bedfordshire Historical Record Society, XXV, 1947), pp. 135–7)

The rates of wages of all manner of artificers, labourers and servants as well by the day with meat and drink, and without, as also by the whole year, and in gross, made and set forth at the general quarter sessions of the peace held at Bedford for the county of Bedford on Wednesday 9 April, 36 Car. 2d. 1684.

	Day from mid. March to middle of September		Day from mid. September to middle of March	
	with meat and drink	without	with meat and drink	without
	s d	s d	s d	s d
A master freemason	1 4	1 8	1 0	1 4
A master rough mason	9	1 4	6	1 0
Servants and apprentices above 18 and having served 2 years	8	1 0	6	10
Under 18	3	6	2	4
A joiner	1 4	1 8	1 0	1 4
Servants and apprentices above 18 and having served 2 years	1 0	1 4	8	1 0
Under 18	5	9	4 (*sic*)	2 (*sic*)
Master carpenter	10	1 4	8	1 0
Journeyman and servants above 18 having served above 2 years	8	1 0	6	10
Under 18	3	6	2	4
Master bricklayer, tiler and plasterer	1 0	1 4	8	1 0
Servants and apprentices above 18 having served 2 years	5	9	3	6
Under 18	3	6	2	4
Thatcher	11	1 3	8	1 0

	Day from mid. March to middle of September		Day from mid. September to middle of March	
	with meat and drink	without	with meat and drink	without
	s d	s d	s d	s d
Thresher and labourers except harvest . . .	5	9	4	8
Gardeners . . .	1 0	1 6	10	1 0
Men haymakers . .	6	10		
Women haymakers . .	3	6		
Weeders of corn . .	3	6		
Mowers of corn . .	1 2	1 6		
Mowers of grass . .	10	1 2		
Men reapers . .	1 2	1 6		
Women reapers . .	6	10		
A tailor . .	6			
Servants above 18 . .	4			

By the year

	s d
Bailiff of husbandry taking charge to discharge the same . .	5 10 0
A chief hind, best ploughman or carter	5 0 0
Second sort of them	3 10 0
Best woman cook	2 5 0
Second woman servant	2 0 0
Dairy or wash maid	2 0 0
Chamber maid	2 0 0
Servingman, coachman, butler or groom with a livery .	3 10 0
Without a livery	4 10 0

By the great, without meat and drink

	s d
Mowing an acre of upland grass	1 4
In the meadow	1 0
Reaping, binding and shocking an acre of wheat or rye .	3 4
Mowing an acre of barley or oats	9
Mowing, cocking and dragging the same . . .	1 4
Binding and shocking an acre of wheat or rye . . .	6
Dragging and cocking an acre of barley or oats . .	6
Mowing, gleaning, dragging and cocking an acre of beans or pease	1 8
Mowing the same	1 0
Cocking, dragging and gleaning the same . . .	10
Making a new ditch 4 foot wide, 3 foot deep, double sett with quick, and gathering setts for the same at the rate of 16 foot ½ the pole	1 0
Plashing and hedging, every rood of quick . . .	2
Scouring ditches, every pole	2
Every pole of an usual ditch, stuff laid by . . .	2

	s	d
Making faggots by the hundred		9
Broom or furze faggots		4
Sawing board by the hundred	2	0
Plank by the hundred	2	6
Sliving lath by the hundred		3½
Making a new plough, [with] meat and drink	1	0
Making a pair of cart wheels	5	6
Digging of earth, striking and burning every 1000 of bricks, with meat and drink, having straw and other necessaries	4	0

32 Defoe's Causes of Poverty, 1704

(Daniel Defoe, *Giving Alms no Charity, and Employing the Poor a Grievance to the Nation* (1704), pp. 25–8)

... It is plain, the poverty of our people which is so burdensome, and increases upon us so much, does not arise from want of proper employments, and for want of work, or employers; and consequently, work-houses, corporations, parish-stocks, and the like, to set them to work, as they are pernicious to trade, injurious and impoverishing to those already employed, so they are needless, and will come short of the end proposed.

The poverty and exigence of the poor in England, is plainly derived from one of these two particular causes, casualty or crime.

By casualty, I mean sickness of families, loss of limbs or sight, and any, either natural or accidental impotence as to labour. These as infirmities merely providential are not at all concerned in this debate; ever were, will, and ought to be the charge and care of the respective parishes where such unhappy people chance to live, nor is there any want of new laws to make provision for them, our ancestors having been always careful to do it.

The crimes of our people, and from whence their poverty derives, as the visible and direct fountains are,

1. Luxury.   2. Sloth.   3. Pride.

Good husbandry is no English virtue, it may have been brought over, and in some places where it has been planted it has thriven well enough, but it is a foreign species, it neither loves, nor is beloved by an Englishman; and it is observed, nothing is so universally hated, nothing treated with such a general contempt as a rich covetous man, though he does no man any wrong, only saves his own, every man will have an ill word for him, if a misfortune happens to him, hang him a covetous old rogue, 'tis no matter, he's rich enough ...

Though this be a fault, yet I observe from it something of the natural temper and genius of the nation, generally speaking, they cannot save their money.

It is generally said the English get estates, and the Dutch save them; and this observation I have made between foreigners and Englishmen, that where an Englishman earns 20s per week, and but just lives, as we call it, a Dutchman grows rich, and leaves his children in very good condition; where an English labouring man with his 9s per week lives wretchedly and poor, a Dutchman with that wages will live very tolerably well, keep the wolf from the door, and have everything handsome about him. In short, he will be rich with the same gain as makes the Englishman poor, he'll thrive when the other goes in rags, and he'll live when the other starves, or goes a-begging.

The reason is plain, a man with good husbandry, and thought in his head, brings home his earnings honestly to his family, commits it to the management of his wife, or otherwise disposes it for proper subsistence, and this man with mean gains lives comfortably, and brings up a family, when a single man getting the same wages, drinks it away at the ale-house, thinks not of tomorrow, lays up nothing for sickness, age, or disaster, and when any of these happen he's starved, and a beggar . . .

The next article is their sloth.

We are the most lazy diligent nation in the world, vast trade, rich manufactures, mighty wealth, universal correspondence and happy success has been constant companions of England, and given us the title of an industrious people, and so in general we are.

But there is a general taint of slothfulness upon our poor, there's nothing more frequent, than for an Englishman to work till he has got his pocket full of money, and then go and be idle, or perhaps drunk, till it is all gone, and perhaps himself in debt; and ask him in his cups what he intends, he'll tell you honestly, he'll drink as long as it lasts, and then go to work for more.

I humbly suggest this distemper is so general, so epidemic, and so deep rooted in the nature and genius of the English, that I much doubt it is being easily redressed, and question whether it be possible to reach it by an act of parliament.

This is the ruin of our poor, the wife mourns, the children starve, the husband has work before him, but lies at the ale-house, or otherwise idles away his time, and won't work.

It is the men that won't work, not the men that can get no work, which makes the numbers of our poor; all the work-houses in England, all the overseers setting up stocks and manufactures won't reach this case; and I humbly presume to say, if these two articles are removed, there will be no need of the other.

I make no difficulty to promise on a short summons, to produce above a thousand families in England, within my particular knowledge, who go in rags, and their children wanting bread, whose fathers can earn their 15 to 25s per week, but will not work, who may have work enough, but are too idle to seek after it, and hardly vouchsafe to earn any thing more than bare subsistence, and spending money for themselves . . .

From hence comes poverty, parish charges, and beggary, if ever one of these wretches falls sick, all they would ask was a pass to the parish they lived at, and the wife and children to the door a-begging.

If this honourable House can find out a remedy for this part of the mischief; if such acts of Parliament may be made as may effectually cure the sloth and luxury of our poor, that shall make drunkards take care of wife and children, spendthrifts, lay up for a wet day; idle, lazy fellows diligent; and thoughtless sottish men, careful and provident.

If this can be done, I presume to say there will be no need of transposing and confounding our manufactures, and the circulation of our trade; they will soon find work enough, and there will soon be less poverty among us, and if this cannot be done, setting them to work upon woollen manufactures, and thereby encroaching upon those that now work at them, will but ruin our trade, and consequently increase the number of the poor.

33 A Criticism of Popular Schooling, 1732

(B. Mandeville, *The Fable of the Bees, or, Private Vices, Public Benefits*, 1732, ed. F. B. Kaye (Oxford, 1924), I, pp. 287–9)

From what has been said it is manifest, that in a free nation where slaves are not allowed of, the surest wealth consists in a multitude of laborious poor; for besides that they are the never-failing nursery of fleets and armies, without them there could be no enjoyment, and no product of any country could be valuable. To make the society happy and people easy under the meanest circumstances, it is requisite that great numbers of them should be ignorant as well as poor. Knowledge both enlarges and multiplies our desires, and the fewer things a man wishes for, the more easily his necessities may be supplied.

The welfare and felicity therefore of every state and kingdom, require that the knowledge of the working poor should be confined within the verge of their occupations, and never extended (as to things visible) beyond what relates to their calling. The more a shepherd, a plough-man or any other peasant knows of the world, and the things that are foreign to his labour or employment, the less fit he will be to go through the fatigues and hardships of it with cheerfulness and content.

Reading, writing and arithmetic, are very necessary to those, whose business require such qualifications, but where people's livelihood has no dependence on these arts, they are very pernicious to the poor, who are forced to get their daily bread by their daily labour. Few children make any progress at school, but at the same time they are capable of being employed in some business or other, so that every hour those of poor people spend at their book is so much time lost to the society. Going to school in comparison to working is idleness, and the longer boys continue in this easy sort of life, the more unfit they will be when grown up for downright labour, both as to strength and inclination. Men who are to remain and end their days in a laborious, tiresome and painful station of life, the sooner they are put upon it at first, the more patiently they will submit to it for ever after. Hard labour and the coarsest diet are a proper punishment to several kinds of malefactors, but to impose either on those that have not been used and brought up to both is the greatest cruelty, when there is no crime you can charge them with.

Reading and writing are not attained to without some labour of the brain and assiduity, and before people are tolerably versed in either, they esteem themselves infinitely above those who are wholly ignorant of them, often with so little justice and moderation as if they were of another species. As all mortals have naturally an aversion to trouble and painstaking, so we are all fond of, and apt to over-value those qualifications we have purchased at the expense of our ease and quiet for years together. Those who spent a great part of their youth in learning to read, write and cypher, expect and not unjustly to be em-ployed where those qualifications may be of use to them; the generality of them will look upon downright labour with the utmost contempt, I mean labour performed in the service of others in the lowest station of life, and for the meanest consideration. A man who has had some edu-cation, may follow husbandry by choice, and be diligent at the dirtiest and most laborious work; but then the concern must be his own, and avarice, the care of a family, or some other pressing motive must put him upon it; but he won't make a good hireling and serve a farmer for a pitiful reward; at least he is not so fit for it as a day-labourer that has always been employed about the plough and dung cart, and remembers not that ever he has lived otherwise.

34 Hume on Interest, 1752

(*David Hume, Writings on Economics*, ed. E. Rotwein (1955), pp. 47–9)

Of Interest

Nothing is esteemed a more certain sign of the flourishing condition of any nation than the lowness of interest: And with reason; though I believe the cause is somewhat different from what is commonly apprehended. Lowness of interest is generally ascribed to plenty of money. But money, however plentiful, has no other effect, *if fixed*, than to raise the price of labour. Silver is more common than gold; and therefore you receive a greater quantity of it for the same commodities. But do you pay less interest for it? Interest in Batavia and Jamaica is at 10 *per cent*, in Portugal at 6; though these places, as we may learn from the prices of every thing, abound more in gold and silver than either London or Amsterdam.

Were all the gold in England annihilated at once, and one and twenty shillings substituted in the place of every guinea, would money be more plentiful or interest lower? No surely: We should only use silver instead of gold. Were gold rendered as common as silver, and silver as common as copper; would money be more plentiful or interest lower? We may assuredly give the same answer. Our shillings would then be yellow, and our halfpence white; and we should have no guineas. No other difference would ever be observed; no alteration on commerce, manufactures, navigation, or interest; unless we imagine, that the colour of the metal is of any consequence.

Now, what is so visible in these greater variations of scarcity or abundance in the precious metals, must hold in all inferior changes. If the multiplying of gold and silver fifteen times makes no difference, much less can the doubling or tripling them. All augmentation has no other effect than to heighten the price of labour and commodities; and even this variation is little more than that of a name. In the progress towards these changes, the augmentation may have some influence, by exciting industry; but after the prices are settled, suitably to the new abundance of gold and silver, it has no manner of influence.

An effect always holds proportion with its cause. Prices have risen near four times since the discovery of the Indies; and it is probable gold and silver have multiplied much more: But interest has not fallen much above half. The rate of interest, therefore, is not derived from the quantity of the precious metals.

Money having chiefly a fictitious value, the greater or less plenty of it is of no consequence, if we consider a nation within itself; and the quantity of specie, when once fixed, though ever so large, has no other effect, than to oblige every one to tell out a greater number of those shining bits of metal, for clothes, furniture or equipage, without increasing any one convenience of life. If a man borrow money to build a house, he then carries home a greater load; because the stone, timber, lead, glass, &c. with the labour of the masons and carpenters, are represented by a greater quantity of gold and silver. But as these metals are considered chiefly as representations, there can no alteration arise, from their bulk or quantity, their weight or colour, either upon their real value or their interest. The same interest, in all cases, bears the same proportion to the sum. And if you lent me so much labour and so many commodities; by receiving five *per cent*. you always receive proportional labour and commodities, however represented, whether by yellow or white coin, whether by a pound or an ounce. It is in vain, therefore, to look for the cause of the fall or rise of interest in the greater or less quantity of gold and silver, which is fixed in any nation.

High interest arises from *three* circumstances: A great demand for borrowing; little riches to supply that demand; and great profits arising from commerce: And these circumstances are a clear proof of the small advance of commerce and industry, not of the scarcity of gold and silver. Low interest, on the other hand, proceeds from the three opposite circumstances: A small demand for borrowing; great riches to supply that demand; and small profits arising from commerce: And these circumstances are all connected together, and proceed from the increase of industry and commerce, not of gold and silver. We shall endeavour to prove these points; and shall begin with the causes and the effects of a great or small demand for borrowing . . .

35 Machines and their Economic Effects, 1757

(J. Tucker, *Instructions for Travellers* (1757), pp. 20–2)

Q. What machines are used to abridge the process of a manufacture, so that one person can do the work of many? And what is the consequence of this abridgement both regarding the price, and the numbers of persons employed?

A. Few countries are equal, perhaps none excel the English in the numbers and contrivance of their machines to abridge labour. Indeed the Dutch are superior to them in the use and application of windmills for sawing timber, expressing oil, making paper, and the like. But in regard to mines and metals of all sorts, the English are uncommonly dextrous in their contrivance of the mechanic powers; some being calculated for landing the ores out of the pits, such as cranes and horse-engines: others for draining off superfluous water, such as water wheels and steam engines: others again for easing the expense of carriage, such as machines to run on inclined planes, or roads down hill with wooden frames, in order to carry many tons of materials at a time. And to these must be added the various sorts of levers used in different processes: also the brass battery works, the slitting mills, plate and flatting mills, and those for making wire of different fineness. Yet all these, curious as they may seem, are little more than preparations for further operations. Therefore when we still consider, that at Birmingham, Wolverhampton, Sheffield, and other manufacturing places, almost every master manufacturer has a new invention of his own, and is daily improving on those of others; we may aver with some confidence, that those parts of England in which these things are to be seen, exhibit a specimen of practical mechanics scarce to be paralleled in any part of the world. As to machines in the woollen and stuff way, nothing very considerable has been of late attempted; owing in a great measure to the mistaken notions of the infatuated populace, who, not being able to see farther than the first link of the chain, consider all such inventions, as taking the bread out of their mouths; and therefore never fail to break out into riots and insurrections, whenever such things are proposed. In regard to the silk manufacture, the throwing mills, especially the grand one at Derby, are eminent proofs of the abridgement of that species of labour: and some attempts have been lately made towards helping forward the cotton and linen manufactures by means of certain engines.

In regard to the other part of the query, viz. What is the consequence of this abridgement of labour, both regarding the price of the goods, and the number of persons employed? The answer is very short and full, viz. That the price of goods is thereby prodigiously lowered from what otherwise it must have been; and that a much greater number of hands are employed. The first of these is a position universally assented to; but the other, though nothing more than a corollary of the former, is looked upon by the majority of mankind, and even by some persons of great name and character, as a monstrous paradox. We must therefore endeavour to clear away these prejudices step by step. And the first step is, that cheapness, *caeteris paribus*, is an inducement to buy, and that many buyers cause a great demand, and that a great demand brings on a great consumption; which great consumption must necessarily employ a vast variety of hands, whether the original material is considered, or the number and repair of machines, or the materials out of which those machines are made, or the persons necessarily employed in tending upon and conducting them: not to mention those branches of the manufacture, package, porterage, stationery articles, and book keeping, &c. &c. which must inevitably be performed by human labour. But to come to some determinate and striking instance, let us take the plough, the harrow, the cart, the instruments for threshing and winnowing, and the mills for grinding and bolting, as so many machines for abridging labour in the process of making bread; I ask, do these machines prevent, or create employment for the people? And would there have been as many persons occupied in raising of corn, and making of bread, if no such engines had been discovered? The obvious reply to this query is, that probably the wheaten loaf had been confined to one, or two families in a state, who on account of their superior rank, and vast revenues, could have afforded to give an extravagant price for this delicious morsel: but it is impossible, that under such circumstances, it ever could have become the common food of the kingdom. The same remark would hold good, were it to be applied to the art of printing, and to the numbers of people, from first to last, therein employed: for printing is nothing more than a machine to abridge the labour, and reduce the price of writing. But examples are endless; and surely enough has been said to convince any reasonable man, though even the great author of *L'Esprit des Loix* should once be of a different mind, that that system of machines, which so greatly reduces the price of labour, as to enable the generality of a people to become purchasers of the goods, will in the end, though not immediately, employ more hands in the manufacture, than could possibly have found employment, had no such machines been invented. And every manufacturing place, when duly considered, is an evidence in this point.

Index